How You Played the Game

For when the One Great Scorer
comes to mark against your name,
He writes—not that you won or lost—
but how you played the Game.

—*Grantland Rice*

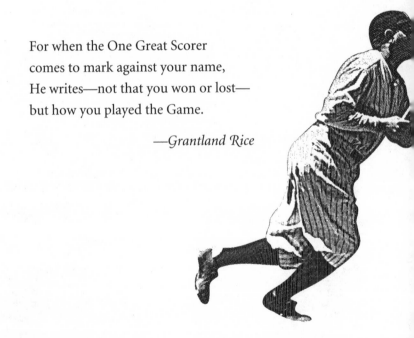

How You Played the Game

The Life of Grantland Rice

William A. Harper

University of Missouri Press
Columbia and London

Library of Congress Cataloging-in-Publication Data

Harper, William A. (William Arthur), 1944–
    How you played the game : the life of Grantland Rice /
William A. Harper.
        p.   cm.
    Includes bibliographical references (p.   ) and index.
    ISBN 0-8262-1204-2 (alk. paper)
        1. Rice, Grantland, 1880–1954.   2. Sportswriters—United
States—Biography.   3. Sports—United States—History—
20th century.   I. Title.
GV7.42.R53H37   1998
070.4'49796'092—dc21
    [B]   98-42218
                                                                      CIP

♾ ™   This paper meets the requirements of the
American National Standard for Permanence of Paper
for Printed Library Materials, Z39.48, 1984.

Designer: Kristie Lee
Typesetter: Crane Composition, Inc.
Printer and binder: Thomson-Shore, Inc.
Typefaces: Minion and Runic Condensed

The University of Missouri Press gratefully acknowledges the
generous contribution of The Community Foundation for
Greater Atlanta, Inc., in the publication of this book.

To my wife, Deborah, with love

Contents

Acknowledgments

A wonderfully competent collection of people helped create this book. For local research efforts, I thank the reference and interlibrary loan librarians at Purdue University, the Tippecanoe County Library, and the Tippecanoe Historical Society. At Vanderbilt University, Maurice Wolfe and her efficient staff in Special Collections (The Jean and Alexander Heard Library) gave considerable time to making possible my study of the collected papers of Grantland Rice. In Atlanta, research was provided by Philip F. Mooney and his staff at the Coca-Cola Corporate Archives. Also at Coca-Cola, Joseph W. Jones and his assistant June Tillery epitomized the meaning of Southern hospitality as they made available the relevant papers of R. W. Woodruff. Additionally, Joseph Jones read parts of this manuscript, and provided helpful comments and interesting anecdotes that clarified the special relationship between Robert Woodruff and Grantland Rice.

Further research contributions were provided by a number of individuals. In Alabama: Roy J. Cochran (Huntsville); Mrs. R. K. Clifford Sharpe Coffee (Jacksonville); Mrs. Franklin Moseley (Eutaw); William H. Tuck (Eutaw); Mr. R. Pruitt (Huntsville); Albert K. Craig, Alabama Department of Archives and History (Montgomery); Glen A. Johnson, Tuscaloosa Public Library (Tuscaloosa); and Marvin Y. Whiting, Birmingham Public Library (Birmingham). In New York: John Terry and Diane Baker, Army, Sports Information (West Point). In Tennessee: Marylin Bell Hughes, Tennessee State Library and Archives (Nashville); Carol Kaplan, Public Library of Nashville and Davidson County (Nashville); and Helen Brown, Linebaugh Public Library (Murfreesboro). In Virginia: Mae D. Taylor, Pamunkey Regional Library (Hanover). At the Library of Congress: Barbara Humphrys, Katherine Loughney, James H. Hutson, and Edwin M. Matthias.

The following people were especially helpful in arranging for the photographs appearing in this book: Strawberry Luck (Vanderbilt University), Dace Taube (University of Southern California), Matthew Boyd Steffens (University of Notre Dame), Andrea Bankoff (The Granger Collection, New York), and Jo Tyler (Corbis-Bettmann, New York).

Fred Russell, the nationally known sportswriter from Nashville, provided profuse and colorful recollections about Grantland Rice, the man, and about both the profession of sportswriting and Grantland Rice's contributions to it.

Had it not been for encouragement from Bil Gilbert, this book might not have been written at all. He patiently read drafts of several early throat-clearing chapters and provided the gentle criticism necessary to help turn those guttural sounds into something resembling a speaking voice. At the other end of the project, a special thanks to my two manuscript readers for their insightful comments and helpful suggestions, Ronald T. Farrar and Randy Roberts.

I have appreciated the support of colleagues, staff, and students at Purdue University over the years in the Department of Health, Kinesiology and Leisure Studies. John Hultsman was personally interested in this book and provided much in the way of energizing conversation about various parts of it. Thomas Templin, my current department head at Purdue, was especially generous with his kind advice and energetic support in the last stages of this project.

Mike Byrnes was the friend who wisely suggested the University of Missouri Press as a potential publisher of this book. The folks at the University of Missouri Press have been absolutely wonderful. There simply couldn't be a better director and editor-in-chief than Beverly Jarrett; it was a joy to work with her. The support staff working on this book was competent, thoughtful, and enthusiastic: Jane Lago (managing editor), John Brenner (copyeditor), Karen D. Caplinger (marketing manager), Dwight Browne (production manager), Nikki Waltz (production assistant), and Kristie Lee (designer). John Brenner's copyediting was remarkably astute in suggesting ways to improve the flow of this story.

Finally, I am deeply grateful to my late mother, Mary Jeanne Storms, for her inspiring example, and to my loving family for the collective interest and support they have given me over the years.

William A. Harper
West Lafayette, Indiana

How You Played the Game

The Literary Revival

(Not boosting our own game, of course—.)
What section now is all the rage?
The Sporting Page.
For clans of every class and age?
The Sporting Page.
Where turneth every eager eye
Early each morn the dope to spy,
Entranced though planets whistle by?
The Sporting Page.

What doth the male and female read?
The Sporting Page.
In fact all of the Human Breed?
The Sporting Page.
The lawyer and the undertaker,
The doctor, merchant, casket-maker,
The grocer, butcher, priest and baker?
The Sporting Page.

Where is the rarest language found?
The Sporting Page.
Where choicest phrases most abound?
The Sporting Page.
Words gathered in a lurid rout
Whose percentage is much in doubt?
Words Webster never knew about?
The Sporting Page.

What makes the summer heat worth while?
The Sporting Page.
That turneth sorrow to a smile?
The Sporting Page.
What makes the "front page" throw a fit,

The "editor" champ on the bit,
The "social section" backward flit?
Of all the paper, which is "IT"?
(What else would you expect the sporting editor
    to say, except)
The Sporting Page.

—Grantland Rice, 1909

1

Where There's Strife, There's Dope

The pioneer American sportswriters were often called shillabers, after the tricksters, hucksters, and barkers of the circus world. As a breed they go back to the days of the early turf journal publishers of the 1820s. Their teachers were the experienced newspaper journalists and sporting magazine editors from England, Scotland, and Ireland who had been popularizing sporting strife and rivalries throughout the British Isles for decades. Writers such as Pierce Egan were the rage in England. Seemingly speaking in tongues, Egan used the idioms of the underworld—the daily speech of bartenders, vagabonds, convicts, soldiers, and actors. A boxer with a black eye, Eganized, became a "milling cove with a touch of the blue bag under the peeper." His coverage of the common recreations—horse racing, cricket, the prize ring, professional foot racing, and tavern sports—was so popular that a convicted murderer who was soon to be hung expressed regret that he could not live a few days longer to enjoy Egan's account of an upcoming fight.[1]

"Sporting intelligence," the name the English and their earliest American imitators gave to the pleasantly addicting but relatively harmless information, gossip, and commentary they fed their readers, eventually came to be called "the dope" by later sportswriters. But the American passion for writing and reading the dope on sports events and spectacles did not exist in any conspicuous way until the new country became decidedly urban rather than rural and frontier. From colonial times and into the days of the early Republic, it

1

would have hardly occurred to anyone that the popular, predominantly folk recreations needed any written discussion or promotion. And even when writers troubled themselves to set down some thoughts about these village and small-town diversions, their words were more often than not aimed at damning idle amusements: the drinking, gambling, loose sex, dancing, and especially the surreptitious but widespread habit of violating the Sabbath by playing games.

By way of example, in 1819 the *Guardian,* a New England periodical subtitled *Youth's Religious Instructor,* published a dialogue between "Sobrietus" and "Levitas" on the lawfulness of dancing assemblies and balls. Sobrietus argues that dancing is an ensnaring exercise because the sensual festivity and vain mirth that it inspires cultivates not easy and gentle behavior, but rusticity and clownishness. Dancing parties and balls, he went on, also enflame excess, spoil good taste, put the final judgment at too great a distance (therefore interfering with preparation for death and eternity), cost too much, waste time, defile and ruin the best interests of the immortal soul, and, finally, dishonor God. Straw man Levitas argues to the contrary but is predictably undone by the weight of Sobrietus's anxieties and scriptural thunderings: "Woe unto you that laugh now, for ye shall mourn and weep."[2]

For the most part, though—and the Sobrietuses of the early Republic aside—the popular forms of diversion and amusement did not provoke much written comment. The first five or six generations of immigrants quietly pursued many of the English versions of play while at the same time modifying and shaping them into more comfortable forms. The result was a mixture of highly individualistic and yet strongly communal agricultural, rural, and frontier pastimes that were distinctively American. Americans in these early years satisfied their playful instincts by hunting and fishing, or by competing informally and more or less spontaneously in physical contests such as shooting, running, wrestling, and rail-splitting, or by gathering together for a play-party, barn dance, or picnic, or maybe just by swapping a few stories over a game of horseshoes, nine-pins, or billiards. Except for those who bet on the local blood sports such as cockfighting or gathered for a village horse race or bare-fisted fight, these first generations were players, not watchers, of sports.[3]

But not for long. Beginning perhaps with a New York horse race in 1823, American sporting interests quietly began turning toward the Big Event watched by all. Horse racing, a sport with an enthusiastic following in the colonies, had been largely illegal in the years following the American Revolution (it was banned by the Continental Congress in 1774). In New York it wasn't actually declared illegal until 1802, when the anti-racing crusade finally gained a foothold in this popular Northern center of racing. But by 1821 New York racing was back in business, complete with a jockey club and a new race-track, the Union Course at Jamaica, Long Island.

On May 27, 1823, a "race of the century" attracted more than fifty thousand race fans to Long Island. New York City virtually emptied for the race, and out-of-towners traveled as far as five hundred miles by stage and steamboat to see a two-horse intersectional race between the North and the South. Eclipse, the Northern champion, and Henry, a Virginian horse representing the South, dueled each other in three four-mile heats with only thirty-minute rests between the heats. In the first heat John Walden, riding Henry, shocked the Northerners by out-jockeying William Crafts on Eclipse in a world record 7:37. In the second heat Samuel Purdy, Eclipse's regular jockey, replaced Crafts. Eclipse responded to the change, taking his jockey home ahead of Henry comfortably in a second heat record, 7:49. It was then the Southerners' turn to scramble, as they sat Walden down and hoisted Arthur Taylor on Henry for the last heat. At the sound of the drum tap, the starting signal for the race, Eclipse took the lead. Taylor was never able to catch Purdy, and Eclipse won the heat and that day's run, the greatest ever witnessed in the young Republic.

Not everyone was impressed with the idea of such a big race. Some were stupefied by the incredible fuss over mere horse speed when presumably it was known in advance that some horses were faster than others. The most outspoken of the critics, however, deplored the amount of money that changed pockets. Besides a twenty-thousand-dollar bet per side, at least another two hundred thousand dollars were staked on the race by the gambling public. One critic, Hezekiah Niles, noted that "the feelings of many were as much excited as when the eyes of the nation were fixed on Washington, during the balloting for Jefferson and Burr!" Niles wildly guessed that one million dollars had been wagered on the race. He couldn't understand how such an utterly useless exercise could justify the expense associated with it. State pride, he thought, ought to be promoted by more praiseworthy objects, for "the money expended or lost, and time wasted . . . is not far short in its value of half the cost of cutting the Erie Canal."[4]

Praiseworthy or not, this first "race of the century" was but the beginning of the modern interest in contrived, rule-bound participatory and spectator sport. Over the next six to seven decades the number of transformed traditional sports and newly created sport forms increased dramatically. Exactly what was behind this sudden revolution in sport is somewhat unclear, but a rough listing of the more important social factors behind it would look something like the following:[5]

- Sports were sponsored by monied society through gaming opportunities and public sporting displays. The rich New York and Virginia sportsmen, for instance, who were largely responsible for the Eclipse-Henry horse race were not exactly patrons, but promoted the race much like the sporting entrepreneurs who would eventually take their place.

- The closing of the frontier enabled sport to serve as a kind of compensation for the lost opportunities for adventure, vigor, physical courage, and heroism.

- Religious objections to sport and games were weakening. Sobrietus-type arguments became less convincing, and by midcentury some Protestants were even promoting sports for youth, calling boldly for a muscular Christianity that could improve not only physical and mental health but also the moral behavior of youth.

- The Industrial Revolution was enormously helpful in multiplying sports-related products and opportunities. Improvements in communication and transportation spread interest in sport from local to regional and eventually national levels. Baseball parks sprang up along railroad lines, allowing teams and their followers to barnstorm from one city to another. Other inventions included standardized manufacturing of equipment and sporting goods; incandescent lighting in indoor arenas and armories for horse shows, pedestrian races, prize fights, and even indoor baseball; popularization of sports through photographs, cheap sporting prints, and calendars; and vulcanized rubber for athletic balls and the pneumatic tire for cycle racing.

- Urbanization, higher standards of living, and increased leisure time allowed greater numbers to become sporting customers. The Victorians, ever so slow to approve of organized sports, gradually defended some sports as healthful or as legitimate diversions from work. Meanwhile, various voluntary sporting associations formed along largely ethnic lines in spite of (and in part because of) the finger-shaking Victorians: English cricket clubs, German Turner societies, Irish baseball clubs, Scottish Caledonian clubs. At first, these groups were distinctively ethnic communities naturally formed in response to the strangeness of a new society. In the face of boring and impersonal jobs and a working day controlled by the tyranny of the clock, these groups could escape in their after-work hours to the comfort and familiarity of the first common American sports promotion sites: the saloons, grog houses, barbershops, hotel lobbies, volunteer fire departments, and gambling halls. There they could find their friends, tell their stories, and measure their spirits—both alcoholic and athletic.

• Educational authorities grudgingly began to support college sports. First crew, then football captured the enthusiasm of students. Since these and other sports were also discovered to attract students and donors, the authorities themselves joined the ardent rooting for Old Home Town U.

Generally speaking, these kinds of social forces all reflect a particularly American bent of mind that came into play about a century and a half after the first colonial settlements were established. Until shortly after the turn of the nineteenth century, most of the American settlements were simply recreated European societies. These transplanted Europeans tried to live much as they had in years past, using European models for their schools, farming systems, fashions, and social customs. But after Independence, and particularly as the frontier moved west, traditional European experience was of less practical use. As the European inheritance became less relevant, Americans began replacing old traditions, myths, customs, allegiances, and habits with new ones of their own.[6]

As the European tradition waned, so too did satisfaction with the recreations of the past. The informal folk games, diversions, and amusements that had served for centuries were now seriously suspect. Faced with the burgeoning American gospel that doing things was eminently preferable to doing nothing, the game-playing tradition was altered by the idea that American games should not be do-nothing in character but should instead be potentially productive preoccupations. The promoters of sport argued that doing sport (or even watching others do it) could result in any number of useful and praiseworthy national by-products: stronger human constitutions, pleasantly diverted and therefore less alienated workers, larger and more spirited student bodies, attractive economic profits, or in general, more "American" Americans with well-honed competitive instincts and better moral alignment.[7]

Doing sport for reasons such as these raised the perception of it: instead of an exercise in slothfulness, sport came to be seen as nearly a patriotic duty. Ironically, the European heritage of informal folk games, which historically had been seen as legitimate, well-deserved, and appropriate leisure-based idleness, was changed in modern America to satisfy the settler's inner needs to produce, to progress, to succeed, and, above all, to avoid being idle (or to appear being so). Consequently, as our idling quotient went down, our sporting intelligence went up.

It fell to the sporting press to help sell young America on the healthiness of modern sport: physical, moral, and psychic. The first genuine American sporting journal was John Stuart Skinner's *American Turf Register and Sporting Magazine* (1829). In the initial issue of this monthly magazine Skinner gave his reasons for publishing the journal: because there was nothing like it; the country needed an authentic register of performances and pedigrees for bred horses; and it needed a purveyor of information on general veterinary subjects, rural sports such as trotting, shooting, hunting, fishing, and natural history. But so too did he give rationale for the existence of the sports themselves. Taking on the Sobrietuses on their own ground by quoting a reverend or two, Skinner wrote that these "innocent amusements" were among the best preservatives of health, constituted a considerable guard against immoral relaxation, and promoted kind feeling and goodwill. Skinner argued further that such sports exhilarated the mind and spirits, invigorating and heightening the "physical capacity to rear our families, and the resolution to peril our lives in defense of political and religious freedom." The true estimate of character and sympathetic and generous dispositions were acquired, improved, and quickened, he thought, by friendly and contentious rivalries.[8]

Skinner's timing was right. Swelling city populations created publishing opportunities that went beyond the typical newspaper interests in politics or mercantile matters. Publishers found markets for churchgoers, for travelers, for women and children, for sportsmen, and for farmers.[9]

The earliest sporting journals did not rely on writers since publishing was still a printer's trade. Like a small house organ, editors relied on their readers to provide much of the content; they also followed the routine practice of republishing news and information from publications in other cities, including those in Europe. Skinner, for example, invited his subscribers to "journalize" their experiences, for there "is not a person at all observant of nature or fond of rural sports of any sort, that may not supply some curious anecdotes and interesting facts, which have happened under his own eye, or which have come to his knowledge." That is what made up a magazine of instruction and amusement, thought Skinner: the concentration of fact and observation.[10]

Consequently, the first gatherers of magazine sporting intelligence were ordinary, if rather well-to-do, subscribers energized by an editor. Club secretaries, enthusiastic fans, participants, proprietors of racing, trotting, or hunting stock, and naturalists combined to produce results of contests, statistics, commentary, letters, how-to instructions, advice on equipment, rule publication and promotion, anecdotes, announcements, challenges, and miscellaneous gossip and trivia. The content of a publication such as the *Turf Register* might include articles from taming ornery horses to hunting wild cats, from hallooing (calling) dogs to breaking them, from the habits of woodcocks to the habitats of snipe, from the digestive power of the gizzards of granivorous birds such as the turkey to the projectile power of rifle wadding, and from comparisons of horse flesh speed and bottom (endurance) with that of the "olden times" to comparisons of human gymnastics such as throwing fifty-six- or twenty-eight-pound weights in the modern times.[11]

Skinner's journal was followed over the years by other even more popular and somewhat less stuffy publications, including, for example, the *Spirit of the Times* (1831), a weekly edited by William Porter. Porter was recognized as about the best of the antebellum sports editors. So successful was the *Spirit* and its editor's "York's Tall Son," a nationally popular sporting oracle, that Porter was able to absorb the *Turf Register* in 1839. Newspapers relied on the *Spirit* regularly, as when, for instance, more than one hundred papers printed *Spirit* extracts from its version of the 1842 Boston versus Fashion horse race, another intersectional race that drew more than seventy thousand spectators to the Union Course.[12]

In the mid–nineteenth century the *Spirit* was without equal as Porter enlarged its scope to include cricket, foot racing, rowing, yachting, and, in the 1850s, baseball. Some baseball buffs have claimed that Porter was the first to publish crude versions of box scores and dope sheets, and that he was the one who announced that baseball was indeed the national game. Porter even coaxed Henry William Herbert, an English expatriate, teacher of the classics, and aspiring writer of historical romances, to contribute field and forest sporting sketches for the then Porter-owned *Turf Register*. Herbert, better known as Frank Forester, was a literary stylist who became nationally famous for his magazine sketches and book-length works on thoroughbred and trotting horses, shooting, and fishing. Forester was America's first prominent sportswriter. Although he took his own life in the 1850s, his pioneering writing remained legendary to the following generations of sports lovers.[13]

Newspapers were reluctant to invest much time or space in sporting news until it became obvious that they could and should. The creation of the penny press dailies after the mid-1830s gave them the means; the success of the numerous sporting periodicals and specialty magazines before and after the Civil War gave them the profit motive. The New York papers had been devoting some space to sport on a casual basis since the 1820s, mostly to trotting, horse racing, and prize fighting, as well as occasionally popularizing the ideological rationale for modern sport by synthesizing the views of the clergy, doctors, and educators. But such New York newspapers as the *Sun, Herald, Transcript, Post, American, Brooklyn Eagle,* and *Statesman* were more the exception than the rule, as smaller cities and towns stuck to partisan politics, mercantile and local news, and editorials. It wasn't until baseball became popular in the 1850s that newspaper editors generally, if often grudgingly, included sports somewhat more regularly in their papers.[14]

By the 1870s and 1880s, however, the New Journalism, led by Joseph Pulitzer's *New York World*, created a natural home for a bona fide sports page. Sport fit the sensational style created by Pulitzer and imitated by Charles Dana of the *New York Sun* and James Gordon Bennett of the *New York Herald*. Pulitzer combined general news and a crusading editorial page with lighter, livelier "human interest" news, including crime, scandals, divorces, gossip, natural disasters, sex—and sport.

Sport fit the requirements of an expanding popular press, for in these later years of the nineteenth century sport was attracting much wider attention. While baseball remained mostly a middle-class diversion, other sports such as billiards and prize fighting were more likely to attract an assorted collection of ruffians, brutes, shysters, and other colorful characters. Furthermore, the various elements of early modern sport—the easy creation of villains and heroes, the relatively concrete resolution of winners and losers, and the drama and romance of physical acts of adventure and riskiness—invited, even justified, the blaring press coverage. Sport was good copy.[15]

The enduring relationship between the press and sport was for all practical purposes set in motion when gathering and writing copy was taken from the hands of subscribers and given to sport-experienced reporters. Except for perhaps the restrained baseball writing of the cricket and baseball expert and promoter Henry Chadwick, who had been writing since the early 1850s, most of the early semi-pro writers wrote pretty boring stuff, at least until the 1880s. Hugh Fullerton, who would be part of the first wave of legitimate baseball writers, remarked in retrospect that most early baseball writing was about as interesting as the market reports; it was less interesting than the obituaries. But a crop of writers emerged in the late 1880s and the 1890s to which baseball in particular and sportswriting in general owes great debt. Fullerton claimed in the 1920s that "regardless of what the present generation of baseball reporters is doing to promote the welfare or add to the box-office receipts of the club owners, the sport owes its popularity and probably its continued existence to earlier generations of scribes who gave their talents and the newspaper space of their bosses to popularize the game and its players."[16]

A few of the early writers were former ballplayers, such as Sam Crane in New York and Tim Murnane in Boston. But most were simply general reporters, some ace reporters, who tried to entertain and amuse their readers. Rather than following Chadwick's knowledgeable but plodding prose style, the new writers—who had a flair for humor, storytelling, and no little exaggeration and foolishness—wrote lively sporting narratives instead.[17]

There were a number of talented and whimsical characters writing sports in Chicago—Leonard Washburn, Peter Finley Dunne (the American humorist who would wear out several apostrophe keys on the satirical Irish dialect of the Mr. Dooley books), and Charles Seymour—who all managed to bring what little they knew about baseball to remarkably popular heights. Their spirited accounts of baseball games drew readers to their respective and traditionally less dignified papers; in turn, their light, almost josh-story articles drew curious fans to the ballpark. Dunne, who worked alongside the baseball-mad American humorist and poet Eugene Field on the *News,* became good friends with Seymour, who was writing for the *Herald.* Dunne, Seymour, and Washburn covered the pride of the Chicago rooters, "Cap" Anson's Chicago White Stockings. The trio introduced a different sort of baseball coverage, which, until then, had been little more than a few lines and a roughed out box score. Their stories included the high points of the game, all the dramatic moments and spectacular and controversial plays, and frequent tributes to the Chicago players who were helping these reporters learn the game, and who at the time included Mike Kelly, Ed Williamson, "Old Silver" Frank Flint, Fred Pfeiffer, Abner Dalrymple, and Billy Sunday (who would later turn evangelist). Seymour once described a grass-cutter hit through the hole by Ned Williamson on an infield that had been carelessly mowed as "Sounding like the hired man eating celery." In 1887 Dunne described Cap Anson at bat: "Capt. Anson marched to the bat to the music of rounds of applause, and found a basket of flowers at home plate. Anson looked a trifle redder than usual, and with his blue suit and white stockings, might have gone to the top of the capitol building as an American flag. He struck out vigorously and the audience laughed him another shade redder."[18]

These Chicago writers and their breezy, humorous style immediately attracted other professional writers to baseball and other sports, whether they knew the games they reported on or not. Maybe sports could not match the sensationalism of the news reporting in this yellow journalism era, but the sporting dope could be a darned sight more interesting than shipping news and market reports, and, if written at the right level, could even be up to the interest generated by the obituaries.[19]

Toward the end of the century, some editors of metropolitan dailies saw the commercial potential of sports pages, sections, and extras. As part of the fight for larger circulations, sports coverage was expanded. In challenging Pulitzer's *World*, William Randolph Hearst's *New York Journal* took the sensational to the super-sensational. Hearst's newspaper is remembered for its lurid and melodramatic character, expressed in its scare-heads, faked interviews, pseudo-science, contrived stories, lavish use of illustrations, and jingoism of the sort that surrounded the Spanish-American War.[20]

This yellow journalism may have set back the cause of legitimate news reporting, but its effect on sports reporting was generally therapeutic. The space allocated to sports events was expanded: the *Journal*'s coverage was two, three, or even four times the typical three to seven columns usually allotted to sports by Hearst's rivals. The multiple-page sports sections, banner heads, sporting supplements, thicker Sunday coverages, pictures, cartoons, and bylines gave the sports pages of the 1890s a surprisingly modern look. Hearst even signed up sports champions, buying their signatures for ghost-written stories; his stable included James Corbett and Bob Fitzsimmons for boxing, Amos Russie and Arthur Irwin for baseball, Eddie Bald for bicycling, and Pudge Heffelfinger for football. He also hired more specialized sportswriters, such as Charlie Dryden for baseball (who once portrayed Ed Walsh, the White Sox pitcher, as the only man in the world who could strut while standing still), Paul Armstrong for boxing, and Ralph Paine for rowing.

Naturally, given the histrionic tendency of the Hearst-like press, sport did not escape occasional exploitation. Typical of the pseudo-news approach to a sporting contest was a headlined announcement of a handicap race between the three fastest boats in the world, the fastest race horse, the fastest bicycle rider, and the fastest train, the Empire Express. But only after plowing through a graph depicting their relative speeds and an illustration showing the six racers in a dead heat, sterns-to-neck-to-wheel-to-cow catcher, does the reader discover that the race wasn't actually held, even though it "would be something to warm the sporting blood of the world"; nor would it be held anywhere but in the reader's mind: "Imagine the three boats lined up on the Hudson. On the shore waiting for the word are . . ."

There were also frequent Ripley-like stories, such as the accounts of wooden-legged track champions who raced each other on cinder paths either by bicycle or by board-foot. Or, finally, there was the occasional editing practice of placing the bizarre next to the ordinary sports story, ostensibly to create sensation by association: next to a promotion for a downhill bicycle coasting match, there is the story of Lizzie Humphrey, fighting for her life after her sweetheart shot her during a nicotine fit, his ten-box-a-day habit causing persecution hallucinations, "and the young man who shot her thinks only of his appetite for paper cigars and raves."[21]

By the end of the nineteenth century, if the newspapers were to be believed, more Americans were doing more sporting activities, and doing them better and with less psychic guilt than any previous generation. The to-do being made over commercial sport, however, made most of the noncommercial recreations seem insignificant in comparison. There wasn't much news value in community camp meetings and field days, or in baseball games between a city's married and single men, or in amateur competition in sack racing or stone gathering, or in homing pigeon speed trials—all of which had been newsworthy in previous decades. Even though it was still possible for a "hill and dale" (cross-country) runner to be arrested for indecent exposure in New York City at the turn of the twentieth century, such quaint throwbacks to the moral standards of the early Republic were rare. The real news was to be found in the twenty-one-round fight between John L. Sullivan and James Corbett, in the *Chicago Times-Herald* automobile race, in the Yale versus Rutgers annual Thanksgiving Day football game, or in the first stirrings of World Series baseball.

Exactly who was demanding the news about these contests isn't entirely clear. There is something of a chicken-or-egg problem in explaining the rapid expansion of the sportswriter's craft at the century's end: was the public demand for sporting news a cause or a consequence of sports coverage? But regardless of which came first, the role of the sportswriter in giving the public what it may or may not have known it wanted should not be minimized. The number of dailies between 1880 and 1900 grew almost 250 percent, from 850 to nearly 2,000. And almost all of these dailies carried sports stories. Greater numbers of writers were drawn to sport as it became increasingly possible to make something resembling a living out of writing up the athletic prowess of others. As more witnesses testified to the potentially inherent excitement of the Big Event, and as the coverage began to include the build-ups and predictions before the Event and analyses and alibis following it, sportswriters created a hot demand for the dope they could conveniently and profusely supply. Sportswriters were no longer semi-pros; they were turning professional.[22]

Early in the afternoon on July 18, 1901, a good-looking, slender, former student athlete out of Vanderbilt University left the downtown Church Street headquarters of the upstart Nashville newspaper, the *Daily News.* He boarded a car on the Sulphur Springs Bottom Special, the five-cent electric streetcar line which motored fans from downtown Nashville to the north-central end of town and to Sulphur Springs Bottom, the site of Athletic Park and home of Nashville's Southern League baseball team. Barring a stall from the frequent interruptions to the electric current or a delay caused by some little devil prankishly Saxon-soaping the tracks, the one-and-a-half-mile trolley ride to Athletic Park took about twenty to thirty minutes. At the end of the line on Cherry (later Fourth Avenue) alongside Athletic Park, the young reporter stepped onto the brick sidewalk to join the crowd of nearly eight hundred spectators leisurely making their way toward the gate to the ball field. Along the way he passed the stream of mule carts going to the city dump, which was directly behind the right field fence and the cause of its unusual closeness to home plate (262 feet). Except for a not-so-portable Remington typewriter, which slightly exaggerated his pigeon-toed walk, nothing in particular distinguished the reporter from the other, mostly male, baseball fans. He was dressed in the custom of the day when men showed no skin below their Adam's apple: a summer suit from the dry-goods store, a white shirt with bow tie, black shoes, and a felt hat.[23]

Union soldiers had brought the game of baseball to Nashville in 1862; professional ball had been played at Sulphur Springs Bottom since 1885, when Athletic Park's construction forced the relocation of buffalo and deer who visited the site for sulfur and salt.[24] The Thursday game was the first of a three-game series between Nashville and a Southern League rival, Chattanooga. Nashville was in first place. Chattanooga was sixth. It was a good day for baseball, hot, but humid from recent rains.

Before the game, after entering the wooden structure through the corner ticket gate—there were no press gates then—the cub reporter chatted informally with some of the Nashville players, many of whom he knew from his own days as a highly regarded Vanderbilt baseball player. Soon he took a seat on top of the roof of the stands directly behind home plate. There he sat precariously above the Nashville rooters in what was called a "press stand"; it was an open structure that looked like a concession stand or a gaming booth on a carnival midway. He opened his typewriter, rolled in a piece of paper, nervously positioned his hands just above the keys, loosely curling his fingers into his palms in a slight fist; then, abruptly he stuck out his two index fingers and pointed them at the machine as if to tell it that since he was ready to go to work it had better be too. He waited for the first pitch as he quietly readied himself for doing his job: writing up the derring-do of others.

The nine-inning game was quickly played, taking about an hour and a half. While the noisy bleacher mates below him were busy cheering, waving, spitting tobacco, stomping their feet, whistling, heckling the umpire, spilling their five-cent bags of "goobers" (peanuts) all over each other, and laughing at the clownish and self-deprecating antics of "Rubber," Nashville's black mascot, the cub reporter knowledgeably watched the game. In spite of the chaos around him, he more or less accurately guided his two index fingers to the sequence of keys that would turn the game into an interesting word picture for the new subscribers to the *Daily News,* which would publish its first issue the next day. It was the reporter's first assignment for the *News.* It was also his first journalism assignment.

Back at the Church Street headquarters after the game, the reporter turned in his copy to the managing editor, Thomas Buford. Then, being one of only seven writers on the reportorial staff, he threw himself into his other responsibilities—for he had other beats than just sports—long into the night.

The paper slowly took form, making its way down through the building, from H. C. Kline's third-floor composing room where the five huge Linotype machines, the Mergenthalers, each driven by its own electric motor, set the type; to the steam table where an impression was taken directly from the type, and the resulting matrix whisked down a special chute to Jesse Johnson's press room on the ground floor where it was put into a casting box for the molding process; to the large perfecting press that rolled the paper off its huge cylinders; and into the mailing room, which opened out into Printer's Alley, the common transportation street used by rival Nashville newspapers, and where the papers were counted, hurriedly bundled, and then either pitched into a wagon and hustled off to the train, or fed through a large window to the gaggle of newsboys waiting outside.[25]

Roughly twenty-four hours after the first Nashville and Chattanooga game, and after yet another ball game had been played between them, the *Nashville Daily News* subscribers received their first copy of the eight-page, one-cent Democratic paper. On page 6, after several pages of editorial puffery and self-congratulation, local and regional news, political analysis, various market reports, and advertisements, there appeared the maiden sports story by the reporter who had watched the game the day before. There was no by-line. But many in Nashville already knew who had taken the sports editor job with the *News;* they knew they were reading the words of the hometown boy turned local sports reporter, Grantland Rice.

After the headline, "Came Strong At The Finish," a sub-headline, "Nashville Wades Through Mud To Victory From Chattanooga," and a sub-sub-head reporting, " 'Whistler's Reubens' an Easy Mark for the Locals And Eight Hundred Fans Were Made Happy," Rice gave his readers an accurate but playfully exaggerated account of the game. His first-ever lead wasn't particularly memorable, but it did grab the reader's attention: "Lew Whistler and his noted aggregation of rag time whistlers arrived yesterday morning preparatory to giving their grand whistling concert and horsehide jubilee at Athletic Park in the afternoon."

In his account of the game, played on a soft, rain-soaked field, the sports editor gave his version of what the fans saw in the sixth inning:

> With two men down Goodeneough secured a single. Then Tom Parrott strolled up with his lengthy ash and he swung at the first ball Barry pitched like he was hitting a free lunch. He landed square, and the ball passed over Swacina's head in center field, landing in the pond. Nothing daunted, Swacina hailed a passing ferry, and went out to drag the lakes for the missing horsehide. Meanwhile, Parrott had borrowed a canoe, and was frantically paddling for home with a couple of bats for oars. As he reached third base the boat was over-turned, and but for the fact that, with usual foresight he had put on Fisher's protector as a life preserver, he would have been drowned. However, he floated across the plate just in time to dive under the catcher's legs and score the tying run.[26]

The fan who happened to be at the Thursday game and who also happened to read Rice's foolery regarding it could have legitimately wondered if he and Rice had seen the same game. And the fan who only read Rice's imaginative account must have thought that the rooters in the ballpark got a lot for their twenty-five cents, what with the added attraction of a ferry and canoe race and the drama of a semi-drowning player to boot. Given the overblown description, it's a wonder that anybody even noticed or cared that Nashville won over Chattanooga that day. For that matter, after the great boat race inning even Rice appeared to think there wasn't much else left. He abruptly ended his account after Nashville tied the score in the sixth with a one sentence summary of the last three innings: "After this Nashville scored two in the seventh, and six in the ninth, winning by a score of 10 to 2."

Thus quietly began the sportswriting career of Grantland Rice, who eventually was to become the most celebrated sportswriter in his day, and possibly the most productive writer in the history of the craft. Beginning with this three-hundred-word story, for six days shy of the next fifty-three years Rice would add another sixty-seven million words to the subject of sport: twenty-two thousand columns, seven thousand sets of verse, and more than one thousand magazine articles. Year in and year out Rice wrote sports, finding the copy for his columns, stories, and articles wherever people played, from the spring training camps to the minor- and major-league ball fields, from the college football stadiums to the often remote sites of heavyweight boxing matches, from the smoky indoor bicycle racing tracks to the fresh outdoor horse racing parks, from the Olympic Games venues to the countless national golf tournaments and tennis championships.[27]

He was forever hopping a Pullman, crisscrossing the country for thousands of miles each year to get his stories. Over the years, in his spare time, he also wrote fourteen books, edited eight others, and for sixteen years also edited the *American Golfer* magazine; he was a regular on various radio programs in the last half of his career; and in twenty-five years he produced some two hundred ten-minute, one-reel sports films on champion athletes, recreational sports, outdoor adventure, and the world of wildlife.

As a group, hustling and nomadic sportswriters played a larger role in the growth and development of modern American sport in the first half of the twentieth century than is customarily thought, for better and for worse. In these days before radio and especially television, their billions of newspaper and magazine words on America's sporting instincts aroused our passions, affected our speech, popularized ideologies and opinions, introduced the bizarre and the miraculous, generated cynicism, exposed and covered up scandals, created myths, legends, and heroes, spread gossip and rumor, entertained and sometimes taught us, and otherwise made the Big Events and the people who were part of them come alive in our minds and hearts. The professional sportswriter was a principle player in the sometimes dramatic, often melodramatic story of a young America struggling with itself for permission to play. When Connie Mack, the legendary owner and manager of the Philadelphia Athletics baseball team, reflected back over his sixty-six years in baseball, he commented on the central role of the sportswriters. He claimed that the massive amount of publicity given to the game moved baseball from the sandlots to the huge stadiums. "When I entered the game (1884) we received only a few lines as news. These few lines expanded into columns and pages. . . . The professional sporting world was created and is being kept alive by the services extended by the press." Ford Frick, newspaperman, ghost writer for Babe Ruth, and later the baseball commissioner, claimed that no other group advanced American sports more than sportswriters, yet "no group has received less public recognition for the job they have done or the contribution they have made." He went on to write that sportswriters remain "a mystical, mysterious group of men avidly read, faithfully followed, generally believed and quoted, yet viewed as impersonally as a Fifth Avenue bus or a Coney Island subway."[28]

Among the many professional sportswriters, it was the personable and gentle Grantland Rice who came the closest to becoming a genuine public personality and a national celebrity in his lifetime—hobnobbing with presidents, radio and movie stars, writers, and larger-than-life sports figures; the subject of Ralph Edward's second-ever *This Is Your Life* radio show; as famous and easy to recognize in person or in voice as those rarefied sports figures whose feats he preserved in words.

He was easy to like. His soft yet husky Southern drawl tipped off his family roots, and his kind yet intelligent face radiated his general good character. From the neck up Rice gave off a certain confidence that was as evident as it was difficult to name. The alert, canny blue eyes, the largish ears tilted slightly forward toward the outer world, and the friendly yet tight-lipped smile, put forward a man who was imminently approachable from the first time you saw him. Sportswriter Tim Cohane called his face "an arresting blend of quiet friendliness and that still unmistakable quality of the lion." Rice had such ease and well-manneredness, said Fred Russell, the Nashville sportswriter from the generation just after Rice's, "that he would not have seemed out of place in the pulpit—or standing in line to make a daily double at the race track."[29]

Rice looked more athlete than writer. His nearly six-foot frame supported about 180 pounds in his prime. Between his vagabondish outdoor travels and his regular rounds of four- to five-handicap golf, Rice managed to stay quite fit and physically strong. Even in his late sixties he won a friendly fall from one of his many friends, the football coach, Earle "Greasy" Neale. Yet his athletic countenance—heavily callused and powerful hands, the pigeon-toed shuffle, and the year-round bronzed face and arms—certainly didn't come from any great effort to create one. He smoked, though not heavily. He drank. He socialized constantly; once in June 1934 Rice averaged three hours' sleep for twenty-two nights. He also swore, and played both cards and the ponies. His habits made him a regular guy in the eyes of his many friends. And if he was a candidate for sainthood, as many thought him to be, he was, in the words of George M. Cohan, "a virile saint." He was the kind of saint, writer John McNulty said, "that a person would love to be around with. The regularly enrolled saints I've read about in books would make me very nervous to have around, I think, but not Granny."[30]

And yet even Rice, with all his fame, friendships, and remarkable productivity, has gone the way of nearly all the sportswriters of his generation. He has passed into relative obscurity. All that popularly remains of him is an assortment of isolated facts and, now and then, a few quotable legendary lines he wrote. It is remembered that it was he who immortalized the 1924 Notre Dame backfield as the Four Horsemen. It is sometimes remembered that he wrote those lines frequently mounted in locker rooms or gymnasiums, "For when the One Great Scorer comes to mark against your name/He writes—not that you won or lost—but how you played the Game." It is usually remembered that he picked the football All-America team after Walter Camp died in 1925. It is remembered, more dimly perhaps, that he also wrote "Casey's Revenge," a sequel to Ernest Thayer's famous poem "Casey at the Bat," in which we learn that "Mudville's hearts are happy now, for Casey hit the ball."[31] Or, and largely within the journalism profession, it is remembered that he was a prominent member of the "Gee Whiz!" school of sportswriting (as opposed to the "Aw Nuts!" variety more popular since his day).[32]

Any number of popular and scholarly biographies and profiles have appeared on the early twentieth century's sports heroes—the Ruths, Dempseys, Tildens, McGraws, Cobbs, Didriksons, Rocknes, Thorpes, and Owenses—but practically nothing wordy on the ever-present watchers and makers of these legends. In Rice's case, only a couple of books have appeared on his life and times in the many decades since his death. And while he lived, since the man wouldn't sit still for many interviews, there were few existing profiles either; when a writer would finally corner him, usually having to play him for some loose change on the local golf course, he always talked about other people and not himself. He simply and sincerely didn't think he was important enough to write about. Sportswriter Red Smith once observed that Rice never suspected that he towered above the tallest of his heroes.[33]

Even in his best-selling autobiography, finished three weeks before his death and published posthumously, Rice steadfastly avoided talking much at all about his own life. "You'll learn most about Grantland Rice," he wrote, "by the memories that I will fetch back about the champions I have known."[34]

But Grantland Rice was a champion too; not a champion *in* any particular sport, but a vocal champion *for* sport and what it did and could mean to the Americans who played and watched it. He conveniently appeared on the sporting scene at the turn of the twentieth century when the nation was just becoming especially fascinated with its sports. His torrent of writing helped bring about and sustain the very idea of the Big Event and the Famous Sports Hero. His five-decade success story was an example to many other would-be sportswriters that there might be something respectable after all about the profession. And yet, ironically, all the while he was running up this nation's sporting intelligence and appetites, and with his journalistic success inspiring other writers to do the same, his was a perpetually restless bellwether voice. Even though he was clearly the major culprit in authorizing the progressively vaudevillian-like direction of twentieth-century American sport, he was by nature a voice alerting his readers to the moral dangers such bigness and fanaticism could engender; he was an indefatigable cheerleader for true sport, but just as vigorously a defender of the fundamental ideals of sportsmanship, which, he thought, when genuinely cultivated could provide the necessary insurance that sport would not be trivialized into show business and its performers into entertainers.

In Grantland Rice's own mind, sport was a separate and significant reality; it stood apart from the ordinary world; fun, naturally, but much more than mere fun and games. The seriousness with which we then did (and still do) take sports and games in this nation, was, to Rice's way of thinking, more than a satisfactory justification for devoting his life to learning sport inside and out. And in spreading its word, especially attentive to the edifying possibilities the sporting world could, from time to time, produce, Rice left us a version of American sport in the first half of the twentieth century that is continuous, interesting, and occasionally edifying in its own right. For when it comes to the legend and lore of what has come to be called the golden age of sport, Grantland Rice was not only there covering it every day, but as much as Cobb, Dempsey, or Ruth, he created it.

2

Up from the South

Henry Grantland Rice was born in Murfreesboro, Tennessee, on November 1, 1880. Tennessean though he was, Rice's deeper family roots were in Alabama, where both of his parents were born. His father, Bolling Rice, was born in 1855 in the small town of Clinton (population then about 250). His mother, Beulah Grantland, was born in 1861 in Huntsville, the Madison County seat, a town that was recognized historically as the social and intellectual capital of the Tennessee Valley. Both the Rice and Grantland families were among the hordes of settlers to catch the disease known as "Alabama fever," which broke out after the Creek War of 1813–1814.[1]

Between 1810 and 1820 some five thousand new settler families arrived in Madison County. William and Susan Draper Grantland, Rice's maternal great-grandparents, left Hanover County, Virginia, in 1816 and struck out for Alabama with four children all under the age of six. The Grantlands had been relatively small tobacco and cotton farmers in Virginia since colonial days. With the invention of the cotton gin, allowing for profitable farming of green-seeded, short staple cotton, the upland cotton culture moved into what was then the "Southwest."[2]

Madison County was prime cotton land. Even before the War of 1812 some 150,000 acres had been sold to the earliest white settlers, many of whom had brought their slaves with them. By 1810 the county was populated by 3,745 whites and 954 blacks. By 1820 the county's white population had more than doubled, to 8,813, and the black population had exploded to 8,668. Rising cotton prices after the war, the richness of the soil, a suitable climate, the convenient, navigable river transportation, and plenty of available land all combined to lure restless American farmers like the Grantlands, to Madison County.[3]

The Rice family arrived in Alabama in 1823. While the Grantland family was clearing their land, planting and harvesting corn and cotton, and rearing children (they added seven Alabama-born children to the four born in Virginia), Hopkins Rice, Grantland Rice's paternal great-grandfather, was farming in Nash County, North Carolina. By 1822 Hopkins had accumulated about nine hundred acres of mediocre land, some of which had been farmed by his father, John Rice, who had served in the Revolutionary War.[4]

Having sold off most of his land during the winter of 1823, Hopkins moved his wife, Jane Williams Rice, and his young family to Alabama. Like most Carolinians, they were drawn to the central part of Alabama, to land that closely resembled the land in their home state. For the rumor was that central Alabama land "would yield cotton in such abundance as to make rich men richer, transform farmers into planters, beget fortunes, and establish dynasties."[5] Their destination was Greene County, about thirty miles southwest of Tuscaloosa. With a few relatives and close friends, the Rices journeyed by wagon and by foot to the town of Clinton, above the confluence of the Tombigbee and Black Warrior Rivers. The trip probably took them about six weeks.[6]

Luck, or good sense, or both, guided Hopkins Rice to occupy a broken, slightly hilly region of Greene County. While the prairie and slough lands at first produced more corn and cotton and contributed to making Greene County the foremost agricultural county in the state until around 1845, in the long run the sort of land that Hopkins worked on the hills and hillsides produced crops more uniformly. The fertility of this soil, improved hillside farming practices, and Hopkins's cleverness for the cotton business all blessed the Rices with extraordinary agricultural success, especially after 1850.[7]

Hopkins slowly built his farming operation beyond merely providing sustenance for his large family. By midcentury he had grown from a farmer to a borderline planter, working about five hundred prime acres. Like most near planters, he grew corn as his main crop and cotton as a subsidiary. But during the next decade, he and his oldest son, John P. Rice, Grantland Rice's grandfather, became bigger cotton planters.[8] Hopkins became the master of a sprawling two-thousand-acre cotton plantation, complete with a house with ten rooms and ceilings fifteen feet high, and the owner of more than one hundred slaves. John, to whom Hopkins had previously deeded some of his land, was so wealthy in 1860 that by the age of forty-two he had retired from the cotton business altogether with personal property valued at more than eighty-five thousand dollars.

At the outbreak of the Civil War, the Rice family holdings clearly placed them in the planter elite of the Deep South. More than six thousand planters in Alabama, Georgia, Louisiana, and Mississippi owned more than fifty slaves and could be called large plantation owners; of these, nearly seventeen hundred were in Alabama. Only 312 of these seventeen hundred, however, held one hundred or more slaves. In Greene County, Hopkins Rice had one of the twenty-five largest plantations. Maybe he was not in the "Gone with the Wind" class—there were at least sixteen super-planters in Alabama with more than three hundred slaves, and some of these owned well over five hundred—but with his $56,000 real property, $110,000 personal property, twenty-four slave dwellings, and $8,000 in livestock, Hopkins Rice was, at the very least, well situated.9

Even so, the Rices were still of the just-common-farmer class. They were not of aristocratic lineage, for most of those who were were not among the westward pioneer stock. Only those who needed to better their situation, mostly the Piedmont farmers, troubled themselves and their families to settle this (or for that matter any) portion of the "Southwest." The Rices may have been among those in Alabama who were called "cotton snobs" and "nouveaux," and they definitely were among those who tried to perpetuate an inhuman form of agricultural production; but behind the image of the blue-blooded Masters leisurely sipping mint juleps on the veranda of the white-pillared Big Houses and gazing at their acres of cotton fields and lanes lined with blooming magnolias stood, in reality, just ordinary dirt farmers who had made good.10

The Grantlands, meanwhile, also persisted in working their northern Alabama land, chiefly in Madison and Morgan Counties, on both banks of the Tennessee River near the Big Bend. But unlike the Rices, they did not grow particularly wealthy doing it. The Grantlands remained mostly farmers, not planters; but they were not "po' white trash." For years the antebellum South was portrayed as having only these two classes of white inhabitants. The two classes did exist, but it is largely myth that they were the only two classes—the very rich and the very poor—and that together they *were* the old South. The truth is that the poor whites existed in about the same proportion to the entire white population as the planter class: about 20 percent. This left a far more numerous class of independent and self-reliant Southerners in between: small slaveholding farmers; nonslaveholding farmers; "one horse" farmers; herdsmen on the frontier, pine barrens, and mountains; and tenant farmers. This massive body of "plain folk" of the old South, as historians have designated them, included the Grantlands.[11]

Most of Grantland Rice's antebellum ancestors were people of the land. One exception was a great-uncle, Thomas B. Grantland. When William and Susan set out for Alabama from Virginia in the spring of 1816, Thomas joined his brother and other Grantland relatives and friends and neighbors on the move west. Perhaps not all that enamored with girdling trees by ax, swinging a grubbing hoe, or living in a hastily built log hut or "Alabama bedstead" (a fifteen-feet-square hut with a dirt floor, one window, and roofed with sage, crabgrass, or corn shucks), Thomas elected to join the townsfolk in Huntsville, almost twenty-five miles northeast of the Grantlands' farming site. By the time Thomas arrived in Huntsville, the town was flourishing (it would become the temporary capital of the new state in 1819). Huntsville contained about 260 brick houses, a courthouse (which doubled as a house of worship), a market-house, about a dozen stores built around a town square, and one newspaper. This newspaper, the *Madison Gazette,* was the first stable journalistic enterprise in the Alabama portion of the Mississippi territory (an earlier paper, the *Mobile Centinel,* lasted less than two years, while the *Gazette* survived until after the Civil War). The *Gazette* was published weekly, and was a typical example of an early, somewhat scrubby frontier newspaper. Thomas bought the *Gazette.*[12]

There is little likelihood that Thomas Grantland's newspaper publishing experiences had any serious impact on his great-nephew's decision to go into the business. Throughout his newspaper career, Thomas remained a printer: even with the last newspaper he published, the *Alabama Sentinel* in Tuscaloosa from 1825 until the 1830s, his reputation was that he "was no writer," and always depended on others for his editorials. When he died in Montgomery in 1835 his occupation was listed as "primer," a term often used to refer to the trade of printing. In fact, it is unlikely that Grantland Rice was even aware that he had a relative who was a significant part of the earliest days of the Alabama newspaper business. Like most people, Rice was not particularly mindful of the doings of his ancestors. And when he took the rare occasion to comment on them he was not terribly accurate.[13]

Rice's sketch, in his autobiography, of his maternal grandfather and namesake, Major Henry W. Grantland, the central figure in the Rice family history, turns out to be a mixture of fact and fancy, a romantic composite of his two grandfathers rather than an accurate picture of Henry. According to Rice, Henry originally came over from England in 1835, settling in Fairfax County, Virginia. Later he worked his way south through Alabama and then up to Tennessee as a cotton farmer. At the outbreak of the Civil War, Henry left his Alabama plantation to serve as a major under General Braxton Bragg.[14]

Henry was in fact the eleventh, and last-born, child of William and Susan, born in 1832 in Madison County, Alabama. Although raised as a farm boy, his activities were confined to the business world. While the secession arguments were warming up in the 1850s, he gradually worked himself off the farm and into a clerk's position with a retail merchant. He married Maria F. Owen in 1857 and shortly thereafter went into partnership with Maria's father, Thomas, in a local sawmill. Maria died unexpectedly that year. By the winter of 1860–1861, Henry had already remarried Lizzie P. Edwards, daughter of a small slaveholding farmer, William Edwards, and was living on the farm with his sixteen-year-old bride; his occupation at the outbreak of the Civil War was once again clerk, this time for his second father-in-law, who along with his farm was running a dry-goods store in the town of Triana. Henry retained his partnership in the sawmill as well.[15]

Alabama left the Union in January 1861, and by March had joined the Confederate States. Eager companies of volunteers were assembled in all parts of the state. Twenty-eight-year-old Henry Grantland was not among the early volunteers. In fact, his actual Confederate service activities are something of a mystery as there is no official record of his ever having served in the Civil War in any capacity, much less as a major under Braxton Bragg. The absence of an official record is disappointing, but not surprising given the destruction of so many records during the Federals' occupation of Southern cities. But even without his veteran record, a plausible sketch of Henry's wartime activities is possible.[16]

According to one of Rice's stories, the incident that drove his grandfather into the Civil War at its outbreak was an attack by a Federal gunboat on the Tennessee River near Triana, his grandfather's residence. Rice wrote, "My grandfather assembled his help, and armed with shovels, spades and one new shotgun, they headed for the river." Presumably the weapons of this local militia were somewhat less than what was needed against the ironclad vessel, as Rice concluded, "The gunboat won that one."[17]

Such a confrontation could have taken place, although not at the outbreak of the war. Federal gunboats did steam up the Tennessee River and in time would have been within shotgun distance of the Edwards's farm on which

Henry and Lizzie lived. By February 1862, two months short of a year after the first shots were fired at Fort Sumter, the Federals were in the process of opening up the Tennessee Valley. General Ulysses S. Grant had been given seventeen thousand men, some transports, and seven gunboats by his superior, General Henry Halleck, and was ordered to take control of the inland waterways, especially the Tennessee and the Cumberland Rivers.

Two forts, Fort Henry on the Tennessee and Fort Donelson on the Cumberland—only twelve miles apart—were all that lay between the Federals and relatively easy land and waterway access to Huntsville and Nashville, both of which were important centers of war production and supply. Fort Henry was third rate and perhaps the "most poorly designed of any Civil War bastion." Its twenty-six hundred men were overwhelmed by Grant's superior forces on February 6, 1862. The better-defended Fort Donelson surrendered to Grant ten days later. Control of the Tennessee River into northern Alabama was in the hands of the Federals.[18]

On the same day that Fort Henry fell, four of the seven Federal gunboats came up the Tennessee River and into Alabama. The gunboats went upriver as far as Florence, just below Muscle Shoals, some miles west of Triana, where they destroyed a partially built Confederate gunboat and burned supplies. The gunboats were the first that Grandfather Grantland could have seen; but if not these, he would have seen the others that soon followed, for this was just the beginning of Union naval and troop movements into northern Alabama. By mid-April, a few days following the Battle of Shiloh, Brigadier-General D. M. Mitchell captured Huntsville. Before and after the fall of Huntsville, Lincoln gunboats were commonplace on the Tennessee River. Raids, forays, and patrols were especially frequent as the Union troops began occupying other nearby river cities in the valley, such as Decatur and Tuscumbia.[19]

Henry may have entered the fighting sometime in the early spring of 1862. He may have been provoked into volunteering by the Federal occupation of most of the land near his home; or possibly he was encouraged to volunteer to escape the odium of being a conscripted soldier, as the Congress of the Confederate States had passed its first conscription act in April. Whichever the case, Henry became a soldier, but not immediately in Alabama. By spring the organization of new regiments of nonexempt volunteers had slowed considerably throughout the state. And the closest site for mustering out, Huntsville, was Union-occupied. So Henry simply went north into Tennessee, about thirty miles from his home, and started up his own company. He was immediately elected captain. This—the practice of the men electing their officers, and usually more on the basis of popularity than military experience or skill—was a common occurrence. Henry's intent was probably to lead his men on repeated skirmishes against the invading armies. With no massed Confederate army remaining in the region, the rebels in the Tennessee Valley were reduced to guerrilla warfare. Leading a small body of irregular "hit and run" troops would have fit Grandfather Grantland's "100-proof individualist" personality, as described by Grantland Rice.[20]

But apparently Henry was not up to the task, as "on account of ill health" he was transferred out of the field. Whatever Henry's health problem was, it was troublesome enough to keep him out of the day-to-day soldiering but not severe enough to keep him from serving the cause. He was transferred to ordnance duty at Blue Mountain, Alabama, where he served out the war. Located at the site of the present-day city of Anniston, about one hundred miles southeast of Huntsville, Blue Mountain was the location of the Oxford iron furnace, built during the war to manufacture iron for cannon shot and shell as well as plates and machinery for the Confederate ironclads. Blue Mountain was also the location of several large limestone caves that were essential to making gunpowder.

Henry was part of the four-hundred-man force working the limestone caves under Captain William Gabbett in the spring of 1862. When the available supply of nitrous earth under plantation buildings and tobacco barns and in old cellars was exhausted, it was necessary to dig it from the floors and crevices of the limestone caves. A good working cave (there were several in Blue Mountain) would contain at least five thousand cubic feet of earth. It would have to be dry, yield at least 1 percent of nitrates, and be within easy access to potash, wood, water, and transportation. The earth in the cave was dug up and put in hoppers. Water was poured over the cave soil to leach out the niter. The lye was caught, boiled down, and then dried in the sun. The niter was then put on trains to Selma for milling into gunpowder.[21]

The work was demanding, and the workforce was composed of persons not able, willing, or expected to fight in the field. The recruits included disabled, ill, or convalescing soldiers, collared deserters, conscripts, refugee women, impressed free blacks, and some assorted malcontents. Even youngsters worked in the niter caves, including Henry's fourteen-year-old nephew, William D. Grantland, a private who entered service in February 1862. As it was customary for office employees to be "exempts" because of physical disability, Henry probably used his clerking experience to good advantage in an office job. Since the niter works were supervised by a captain, it is unlikely Henry ever held the rank of major. The majors—there were only three in the Niter and Mining Bureau—were responsible for large regions, usually several states. There were only a half dozen captains and maybe ten lieutenants in the entire bureau. Most likely Henry simply retained in spirit his elected company captaincy, maybe even awarding himself the majorhood in the years following the war. There were far more majors and colonels after the war than during it anyway.[22]

The niter and mining service was indispensable to the Confederate war efforts. Secretary of War James Snedden boasted proudly to President Jefferson Davis in November 1863 that the service could not have possibly presented "a more decisive exhibition of the resources and exhaustless capacities of endurance possessed by the confederacy . . . than the decided increase (in production) amid unprecedented efforts and sacrifices in the field and numberless impediments in procuring machinery, labor, and supplies of all the great manufactures essential for successful defense." Yet the service naturally suffered from the image of being a safe place for reluctant soldiers to wait out the war. Besides being thought of as an evasion of public duty, it was commonly realized that making bullets provided considerably less ammunition for tales of military courage and valor than did shooting them. But in point of fact, in spite of its Foreign Legion–like makeup, most niter works recruits faced the enemy repeatedly, reluctantly or otherwise.[23]

For instance, in Tennessee, many large and rich caves were captured by the Federals. Work was regularly interrupted by the comings and goings of Union soldiers. The Nickajack and Lookout caves were shelled during a June 5, 1864, attack, but operations continued in spite of the shelling. Workers could be armed for local defense, but any military response was expected to be subordinated to their work, work being "The leading aim and consideration, and second in importance to no other military service." Nonetheless, the popularity of niter works as a Federal target demanded that the cave workmen assemble rapidly when attack was imminent. Major St. John, the chief of the Niter and Mining Bureau, commented on the military preparedness of his workmen in a letter to Secretary of War Snedden: ". . . they go into action on their own ground and with home instincts fresh upon him, and under these influences they have invariably done well." Niter works in Virginia, Georgia, and northern Alabama were repeatedly destroyed and workmen killed or captured. Northern Alabama was particularly hazardous as the caves were perpetually in between the Confederate and Union lines. A particularly productive cave at Blue Mountain, the Santa Cave, was often singled out for Federal attack. Presumably Henry and the others at Blue Mountain handled these interruptions with dispatch, as Major St. John cited these workers in particular to Snedden: "And from Upper Alabama reports equally favorable have been received from the frontier men under Captain William Gabbett, who have been frequently called from their work to resist hostile incursions."[24]

It is still unlikely that Henry faced as many hostile incursions as Grantland Rice's paternal grandfather, the retired planter, John P. Rice, who volunteered for Confederate service in August 1861. For the most part, central Alabama planters were Constitutional Unionists. It is likely that the Rices would have argued against secession, challenging its wisdom but not the right to secede. With the Unionists, they realized that secession would inevitably lead to war. The Rices would have been among the many planters who believed that the national crisis was to a great extent contrived by bad politicians in both the North and the South. The inscription Hopkins had engraved on the tombstone of one of his sons, Alexander Rice, one of John's younger brothers who died in defense of the Confederacy, is telling:

A Youth Full of Hope and Promise Lies Here
A Victim to the Hallucination of Political Demagogues,
Shorn of What Nature Intended He should Be,
An Ornament to Society and a Friend to Agriculture[25]

In spite of their belief that the politicians were foolish and wrongheaded in pushing things toward a violent solution, by the time of the attack on Fort Sumter the Rices, like most of the rich planters, stood solidly behind their Confederate flag. Historian James Roark observed that even though the spirits of Southern politicians and publicists took wing, "planters were conspicuously sober. Rather than tossing their hats in the air, they squared their shoulders in anticipation of the fight of their lives. The stakes were the highest; all agreed that the outcome would be 'rule or ruin.' "[26]

Hopkins Rice was well over fighting age. But his sons weren't. It would have been easy for his four living sons (one son, Neverson, died in 1849) to sidestep military service. Early in the war, slave owners were entitled to one exemption for every twenty slaves owned. The Rice plantation would have been entitled to five exemptions, seven in the war's later stages.[27] But the Rices did not pick up their allotment. Alexander (age twenty-six) and John (forty-four) voluntarily enlisted early in the war's first summer. Alexander, the "youth full of hope and promise," died of battle wounds within a year of his enlistment, on June 20, 1862. John, mustering out of Huntsville, joined the Nineteenth Alabama infantry, Turnip Seed Company. He enlisted as a private. His regiment was badly mauled in the course of the war, at Shiloh,

Stones River (Murfreesboro), Chickamauga, Missionary Ridge, Atlanta, Jonesboro, Franklin, and Bentonville. At the war's outset the regiment was ten companies strong with 650 soldiers; when the regiment surrendered at Salisbury, North Carolina, in the last month of the war there were but 76 men remaining. One of them was John Rice.

It may have been John's Civil War service that Grantland Rice wrongly attributed to Henry, for John's regiment did serve for a time under General Braxton Bragg. Grantland Rice mentioned that Henry didn't think much of Bragg, preferring instead the legendary exploits of the wily Confederate cavalry leader Nathan Bedford Forrest.[28] Bragg earned the reputation for being the most frequently defeated general in the Confederate army. The Nineteenth, John Rice's regiment, served under Bragg at Stones River, Chickamauga, and Missionary Ridge, all in Tennessee. Of these three battles, the first was a draw, the second a victory, and the last an embarrassing defeat. That John Rice survived Bragg's braggadocio engagements had to have been a near miracle. At Stones River, one Federal ordnance officer reported that their artillery fired twenty thousand rounds and their infantry let loose two million rounds of musketry. Figures differ, but in most accounts of this battle, the Confederate casualties included close to eleven thousand killed, wounded, or missing (from an army strength of around thirty-eight thousand); the Federal casualties were more than thirteen thousand (from a strength of forty-three thousand). John Rice's Nineteenth numbered about 150 casualties, one-fourth of its regimental strength. Even at Chickamauga, the one battle Bragg won, John Rice somehow avoided being one of twenty-one thousand casualties, nearly 40 percent of Bragg's field troops.[29]

When the war finally ended, the South's ruin and devastation was unquestionably enormous, whether measured in the quarter of a million dead soldiers, or in the broken spirit and pride of the Southern people themselves as they witnessed the destruction of their rural property and crops, the killing of their animals, or the burning and sacking of their major cities. But popular imagination over the years has exaggerated the degree and effects of the devastation, aided in part by some of the more romantic accounts of the war and its aftermath in novels, and coaxed along by television and motion-picture distortions. For every trampled acre of Tara, there were vast quantities of Southern land that were untouched. And even though the masters of the Big Houses had collectively lost two billions in slave property and were forced to free three and one-half million black laborers, after the war planters persisted as a less wealthy but still powerful class in spite of the changes in the labor system.[30]

The Rice plantation stood after the war as it did before, as Greene County was out of the path of the invading Federal armies; even the notorious Wilson Raiders stayed east of Greene County's plantations on their destructive march from Nashville to the ordnance works at Selma. Hopkins Rice likely would have been among the last of the old master class to surrender to the looming economic hardships of the plantation system had he not died seven months after the war. His death brought an end to the Rice family connection to the plantation system of the Old South.

Both of Rice's grandfathers quickly adapted to the self-help requirements of the New South and the Northern gospel of industrial, commercial, and economic progress. John Rice sold the plantation for about two-thirds of its prewar value. Shortly after the estate was settled, he moved his family—his wife Anna and three children, one of whom was Grantland Rice's father, Bolling, then about age twelve—north into Tennessee and to Murfreesboro. Murfreesboro was in rolling, hilly farmland. From his share of the proceeds from the sale of the plantation, John went on to become one of Murfrees-boro's most successful retail merchants, owning a general store.

Henry Grantland also did not fall in the postwar pecking order. Early in his service in the Mining Bureau he had stashed about a half-dozen bales of cotton in one of the abandoned caves. Over the next few years, while the war raged on, the bales matured nicely in the damp and dripping cave. The bales that before the war would have weighed about four hundred to five hundred pounds apiece weighed about half a ton each by war's end. With the selling price of cotton after the war at one dollar a pound, Henry sold the bales to Butler the Buyer, a Yankee carpetbagger, for one thousand dollars per rotten, waterlogged bale.[31]

By the end of Reconstruction, Henry had turned his cotton stake into a number of investments and businesses. When his father-in-law, William B. Edwards, died in 1874, Henry also inherited the dry-goods store in Triana. The "Brick House," as it was called, was, like John Rice's enterprise, the local general store and makeshift bank. A year later, Henry's second wife, Lizzie, died suddenly at the age of thirty-two, leaving him with four children, the oldest of whom was Beulah, Grantland Rice's mother, then fourteen. Henry was also left with the Edwards's land that Lizzie and her sister, Mary (who would in 1884 become Henry's third wife), had inherited from their father.

While Southern agriculture languished after the war, Henry took advantage of the region's quickly rebounding industry, eventually turning his inheritances and investments into enough money to become a well-healed cotton buyer himself. Henry had packed up his family, including his mother-in-law and sister-in-law, Mary, and moved to Nashville in the spring of 1878. Even without selling his Alabama land, Henry's assets enabled him to start up one of Nashville's first and largest cotton houses. As a cotton factor, his house received cotton from all parts of the South and transported the goods to the Northern markets, in addition to selling the cotton to the three local mills and to exporters.

In the minds of many, the first step toward boosting the South's industrial capabilities after the war was cotton manufacturing, one preacher even claiming that "Next to God, what this town needs most is a cotton mill." Henry Grantland did his best to answer the preacher's prayer.[32]

3

When Morning Ruled the Heart

Business dealings between these well-to-do families, the Rices and the Grantlands, would have been inevitable. John P. Rice's general store in Murfreesboro supplied food, hardware, drugs, sundries, farm implements, clothing, feed, fertilizers, cloth, even whiskey and tobacco. Of all the commodities sold, credit was the most lucrative, as most of the farmers' purchases were advances on their forthcoming crops. The merchant could extend credit until the end of the planting season (crops usually reached market in November or December) because the Northern wholesalers were willing to ship their goods on consignment, often willing to wait for six months to a year for payment. Henry Grantland's cotton house was one of the regional middlemen between the general stores (and by extension, the planters) and the complicated financial network of textile manufacturers, wholesalers, and exporters. Given that he not only was the proprietor of the Grantland Cotton Company but also, simultaneously, was employed as a cashier (equivalent today to a bank manager) at the First National Bank, Henry was naturally in a position to either extend John's store credit or to simply buy the cotton the store had acquired through default on credit liens.[1]

Grantland Rice's parents, Bolling Rice and Beulah Grantland, would have met by way of these routine business dealings between the Nashville house and the Murfreesboro store. Romance led to marriage early in 1880 when Bolling was twenty-five and his bride nineteen. Not much is known about these two, other than that it was clear their first-born son, Grantland, was closer to his mother than to his father. Rice reveals little about them in his memoirs, other than to say that they were "two very gentle people." After their marriage, Bolling brought his young wife to Murfreesboro. They lived with the Rice family in John's large downtown home near the corner of what today are Spring and College Streets. Bolling was a clerk in his father's general store.[2]

In 1882, two years after Bolling and Beulah started their family with the birth of Henry Grantland Rice, John Rice died. With his death, the family business was more than likely sold, as Bolling left Murfreesboro and moved his young family to Nashville at the invitation of Henry Grantland, who hired him as the "office man" for the cotton house. The arrangement gave Bolling even more responsibilities than he had had in his father's store, not to mention more money, and it freed Henry to devote more time to his important bank management duties, for the bank Henry worked for was no small enterprise either. First National was the oldest of Nashville's four national banks, having been established during the Civil War (1863). It was located on North College and Union, in the center of the Nashville banking and finance community; Union was later to be called the "Wall Street of the South."[3]

The young Rice family moved in with Henry, who lived in a huge, high-ceilinged brick mansion on Woodland Street, in Edgefield (East Nashville), a little over a mile from the downtown Public Square just over the Woodland Bridge, which spanned the Cumberland River. The river snaked westerly around the town, and on maps of the day looked like the outline of a ten-gallon hat. Henry's home was near the eastern and suburban brim. Before electrification, railroad companies built mule-pulled streetcar lines that created the possibility of suburban living for the rich merchants and manufacturers who worked in the city. Within a couple of miles of the downtown business center these streetcar lines provided smooth and reliable commuter service to suburbia. Edgefield was one of the first such suburbs in Nashville.[4]

Henry was running up a fortune in the cotton and banking businesses by then and was living quite well. He was a member in good standing of upper Nashville society, where he had been "promoted" once again, as he was now commonly called Colonel Grantland by his many friends and associates. Edgefield attracted the new rich who could afford to escape the expanding business district and the growing threat posed by the teeming slums that almost completely ringed the downtown commercial center. Although the privations were many in the cities of the 1880s—poor sanitation, lack of electricity, polluted industrial air and drinking water, and smallpox and typhoid epidemics—the rich in Edgefield had the best of what there was: indoor plumbing, spacious lots, tree-lined streets, splendid churches, proximity to the country, and the security of the Cumberland River, which served as a moral buffer between them and the saloons, gambling dens, brothels, and slums of the increasingly industrialized city. Edgefield was the most elegant and genteel of the mule-car suburbs.5

Bolling, his family, and Grantland's big Newfoundland dog lived with Henry for five years in Edgefield until they could afford their own place in the country, somewhat farther east of the city, on Vaughn Pike. It was there that Grantland Rice and his two younger brothers, John and Bolling, spent the better part of their childhood. Bolling Sr. continued to work quietly for his father-in-law for some thirty-five years until his death in 1917.

Country living on Vaughn Pike introduced the young Grantland Rice, to, among other things, the hard work of truck farming. Rice's father, a Presbyterian who was strong on the virtues of the work ethic, gave him the responsibility of farming several acres of their land for profit. Rice, his brothers, and Horace, their black hired hand, grew potatoes, tomatoes, asparagus, onions, beets, peas, cabbage, lettuce, and, wrote Rice later, "practically everything else that grows including all kissin' kin of the worm and grub family." When the vegetable crop was ready for market, he would rise at three o'clock in the morning, hitch the horses, load the wagon with crated vegetables, and drive the three miles into town. By six in the morning he would have sold most of his produce, and would then return home to work the rest of the day harvesting, usually not putting down his tools or the plow until about seven in the evening. These sixteen-hour days were the norm during the planting and harvesting seasons.6

Rice's childhood was a happy one, in part because it wasn't wholly given over to work. On his first Christmas on Vaughn Pike, when, as he put it later, "Christmas days were far apart/Back when morning ruled the heart," he was given a football, a baseball, and a bat. The presents, he recalled later, were "the sounding instruments that directed my life." With plenty of space to play, there being a big vacant lot next door, the Rice boys and their many friends played pick-up games hour after hour, football in the fall, baseball in the summer. Football then was mostly a kicking game with the huge teams trying to kick the ball over their opponent's goal line. The popular version of baseball was "One-Eyed Cat," which was played much like the more modern game of "Work-Up." Before the game began, one player would shout "one-two-three-one," which would be the signal for the other boys to shout a position number, "two," "three," "four," and so on. Number one would be "in town," or at bat, two would be the catcher, three the pitcher, and the rest of the numbers would take their place at the bases or in the field. The batter stayed up until put out. Then, when he struck out or popped out, he would go into the outfield. The players would rotate up a numbered position.[7]

In the winter months, when the weather cooperated, skating and sledding kept the Rice children out of doors. At the foot of Shelby Avenue, not far from their home, in a large area called Shelby Bottom, was their favorite ice skating spot. The Bottom was grown up in willow trees and various scrub bushes, much like a canebrake. Shelby Pond was large and deep. After school (which was out around two o'clock) and into the evening hundreds of locals skated. At night there were always a few big bonfires burning on the edge of the pond. On other days, the boys sledded on either Shelby Avenue or the popular Boscobel Street from Tenth down to Fifth. It was common in the evening for the Boscobel hill to have five hundred or more sledders, some with single sleds and others balancing on a "double-decker," a plank ten to fifteen feet long supported on either end by a small sled, the dozen or more riders straddling the plank as the hook-and-ladder creation careened wildly down the slope.

In the spring, the boys played the routine assortment of games and contests that constituted growing up male in Tennessee. Alleys and taws (marbles) was played for keeps, the winner winning the loser's agates. There were various track and field competitions, spinning top wars, and horseshoe pitching contests. Also popular was mumbley-peg, the knife-throwing game, and fox and hounds where one boy, the fox, was given an old newspaper and a fifteen-minute head start. About every fifty feet he was expected to drop a bit of newspaper to leave a trail; it was then up to the rest of the bunch to find him. A good fox could usually furtively roam the many blocks of an entire neighborhood before he was caught.

As the weather warmed up, the boys could be found skinny-dipping in their favorite swimming hole at the foot of Sixth Street, called in those days, for reasons unknown, "Pugley's Gut." Collecting things was also something interesting to do. Some boys collected stamps, others tobacco tags. Since more men chewed than smoked in those days, there were plenty of small stamp-sized, tin tags which had been discarded in the streets and roads. The brightly painted tags with the brand and manufacturer's name printed on them made for a colorful collection.[8]

Grantland Rice was a bird egg collector. The local drugstores sold wooden trays, about twelve by twenty-four inches, in which a youngster could organize and display his finds. Tree climbing was a Rice specialty anyway, and since he so often came across nests while on a climb, he found extra purpose to his vertical forays when he could add a new egg to his tray. The risks of the hunt didn't seem to bother him, either. On one Saturday morning, out with his gang of friends in the woods near what is now known as Shelby Park, Rice spotted a nest high in the limbs of a tree. He climbed up nearly to the top, inched out slowly on the branch holding the nest, and then, just as he reached out for his prize, the branch snapped clear through, dumping him earthward, down through the lower limbs. His friends picked him up and carried him home, gingerly supporting his broken arm. Undismayed, within the week the resilient Rice was out again climbing and collecting even though he had temporarily been reduced by the fall to a one-armed bandit.[9]

Rice's formal education began in Spout Springs Country School, a one-room schoolhouse where the fundamentals of reading, writing, and arithmetic were introduced to the often less-than-willing students. In the first few grades, the classes were without paper and pencils; instead, each child was given a wooden-framed "slate," made from a natural fine-grain rock. The stylus used for writing on the slate, also made out of slate, was almost always dull and the slate itself perpetually dirty. Bricks were used to sharpen the stylus. To clean their slates, Rice and his chums would spit all over the surface and then rub it clean with the heels of their hands; it was their view that only sissies used the damp sponges provided by the teacher.[10]

In the 1890s organized sport in grade schools did not exist. But when Rice went on to military school, he got his first taste of interschool competition. As a young teenager, he played for Tennessee Military Institute, and then, later, for Nashville Military Institute. The institutes were high on sports chiefly because of the self-discipline, courage, mental toughness, and martial instincts athletic contests were believed to encourage. Football, especially, was promoted.

Rice looked nothing like a football player, even by 1890 standards: he was nearly six feet tall and weighed only 120 pounds. As one of the halfbacks, he was rangy, strong, and gutsy, but too light for the sport. In the backfield with him were some pretty strapping youngsters who gave Rice most of his protection. The fullback was Percy Tabler at 6'1" and 195 pounds, who later became one of the many movie actors to play "Tarzan." At the other half was Charlie Moran, who weighed about 185, and who went on to play for Tennessee and later the professional team, the Massillon Tigers. Moran also later coached the Praying Colonels at Centre College and umpired in the National League for more than twenty years. It was in these military schools, and more specifically in this backfield, that Rice learned the rudiments of football.[11]

Worldwide depression in 1893 caught the Rices, like everyone else, off-guard. In Nashville, a couple of banks quickly failed, one of them a national bank, the Commercial National. In spite of the bankers' efforts to stave off a run—the American National piled money in its front window to reassure its customers of its solvency—on the morning of August 10 skeptical depositors began milling outside bank doors to withdraw their money. Most of the remaining banks were forced to suspend or limit payments. All of the banks, including First National, had been speculating on cotton futures, thinking in 1892 that the prices were going up. When the crash came, and when England in particular couldn't handle her cotton assignments, speculators were in deep trouble. Henry's double position as a banking officer and a wheeler-dealer in the cotton business had been an advantage while the cotton market was on the rise, but it was doubly bad when the bottom fell out of the market. Besides the First National cash flow problems, Henry had to deal with the troubling threat to his own company, which was dangerously overstocked with the cotton the growers were overproducing. The price of cotton had been gradually dropping for the previous decade or so, from an average of fifteen cents a pound in the 1870s to around eight cents a pound in 1890. But when the Panic reduced its value to five cents a pound, the Grantland Cotton Company lost more than a million dollars. Nonetheless, Henry, whose scrappy entrepreneuring and individualistic character always seemed to land him on his feet, eventually recovered, and his company continued as a reputable cotton house well into the twentieth century. But the post-Panic recovery was never strong enough to return him to the level of comfortable affluence he and his family had grown accustomed to before the crash. He lived on in relative comfort until he was ninety-four years old, when he died from a bad fall in 1926, "grudgingly," recalled his grandson.[12]

As the effects of the 1893 Panic lingered on, Bolling Rice moved his family off Vaughn Pike and into the city in 1895. The trolley was electrified by then, making the newest refuge for the well-off the western, not the eastern, edge of the city. The Rices bought a large home on the west side on Broad Street (now Tenth Avenue). The depression had affected the Rices too, but it required of them only some healthy belt-tightening rather than any significant change in their comfortable standard of living. Grantland Rice remembered that even during the depression his mother was able to serve up remarkable Southern meals—hog brains, hominy grits, ham and ham gravy, waffles, fried sliced apples, corn pone, fried and scrambled eggs. It appears that the move may even have been a step up for the Rices, for the Broad Street home was quite large, with an enormous backyard more than a block long.[13]

That backyard on Broad Street was the liveliest in the entire neighborhood, as Grantland was forever getting up plays and games. The youngster simply wasn't a follower; much like his spirited grandfather, the Colonel, from early on Grantland had downright entrepreneurial instincts. In his city neighborhood his reputation as the local recreation director quickly spread—by acclamation, not self-appointment. If he wasn't leading his friends in making kites out of red cedar and colored tissue paper, he was advancing the sophistication of lighter-than-air flying by promoting miniature hot-air ballooning. For the ballooning adventures, Rice would dig numerous pits in his backyard and build smoldering leaf fires in them. Then he and his pals would make hand-sewn balloons—complete with small baskets—hold them over the smoking fire, and let them be lifted over the roof-tops. On occasion the group leader was known to have advocated attaching small passengers to the baskets, once giving a neighborhood cat a free ride, figuring that he would follow the balloon and retrieve the cat when the balloon landed. The fire department rescued the crazed cat after it jumped out at the first opportunity onto the closest roof before the balloon sailed out into Nashville's air space.[14]

When he wasn't directing the play in his backyard, Rice could be found with ten or twenty other boys engaged in one pick-up game or another in the vacant neighborhood lots or in the streets. Around the triangle between Broad Street, West End, and Addison Avenue there were plenty of vacant lots to play foot-and-a-half, maybe a leap-frog lot game, or various ball sports or track competitions. Rice and his two brothers regularly hung out at Mr. Robertson's drugstore, next door to the corner of Belmont on the north side of West End. As recreational hangouts, the drugstores were for the kids the equivalent of the saloons and taverns for the adults—both were centers for refreshment, nourishment, fraternizing, and gaming. In the springtime, it was a familiar sight in Nashville to see a tall, slender youngster shouldering a bat, standing in front of the drugstore and knocking out fly balls across the street toward the vacant lot beside the Immanuel Baptist Church long into the evening for the younger boys in the neighborhood to chase and catch. It was great fun for the little ones, as the batsman would shout encouragement and even give a few pointers to the eager boys scrambling for the ball.[15]

Rice's formal education continued in Nashville. The family was doing well enough in 1896 to enroll their eldest son in Wallace University School, a college prep school on South High Street. The school was one of the many Southern prep schools largely modeled after the English public schools of *Tom Brown's School Days*. Plenty of Greek and Latin, to be sure, but such classical studies were to be liberally mixed with athletic sports and games.[16]

The idea at Rugby School in England, according to its famous headmaster, Dr. Thomas Arnold, was to create "true gentlemen of manly conduct and moral thoughtfulness." This goal meant nothing more or less than instilling the very idea of becoming a gentleman, namely, that manliness "was a matter of doing what was right without being told." The role of athletics at Rugby, besides the instrumental usefulness of them in creating healthy bodies and fostering school spirit, was to substitute for the gradual loss of youthful play experiences typically available in the waning pastoral tradition of merry-making associated with the English holidays and village feasts—wrestling, single-sticks and back-swords (stick fighting), blindfolded chase games, sack racing, donkey races, throwing contests. To those who would try to reform the lackluster English public schools without taking into consideration the need to satisfy this deep-running play spirit among youth, one educator warned:

> Don't let reformers of any sort think that they are going really to lay hold of the working boys and young men of England by any educational grapnel whatever, which hasn't some bona fide equivalent for the games of the old country "veast" in it; something to put in the place of the back-swording and wrestling and racing; something to try the muscles of men's bodies, and the endurance of their hearts, and to make them rejoice in their strength. In all the new-fangled comprehensive plans which I see, this is all left out: and the consequence is, that your great Mechanics' Institutes end in intellectual prig-gism, and your Christian Young Men's Societies in religious Pharisaism. . . . Life isn't all beer and skittles,—but beer and skittles, or something better of the same sort, must form a good part of every Englishman's education.[17]

Clarence B. Wallace, the founder and headmaster of Wallace University School, provided for his charges the kind of well-roundedness advocated by English public school headmasters, substituting the conventional late-nineteenth-century Southern substitutes for the once boundless and sponta-neous folk tradition of the Old South: football, baseball, and athletics (track and field). All of which Grantland Rice gratefully played with pluck and gusto. What University School shared in common with most of the prep schools of the day was the belief that books and bookishness were important for the ma-turity of mind, but games were a way by which youths could gain a special kind of moral wisdom that, once fixed in youth, could and should serve them throughout their lives. The mark by which one would know a Rugby product, observed Thomas Hughes, is "their genial and hearty freshness and youthful-ness of character. They lose nothing of the boy that is worth keeping, but build up the man upon it."[18]

Headmaster Wallace was revered by his school's students, most of whom claimed he was the greatest Latin teacher of his generation. It was Wallace who introduced Rice to a language foundation in Greek and Latin that served him well over the years. Wallace believed that studying English was quite unnecessary if these classical languages were mastered. Rice claimed years later that Wallace was the most influential teacher he had ever had, and in a letter to him wrote "that if I have gained any measure of success in writing, I owe it all to you."[19]

During the first sixteen years of Rice's life, the Nashville city fathers (and gradually the mothers) welcomed the modern (meaning Northern) formula for improving Southern culture: that what makes the difference between a civilized and an uncivilized society is the degree to which there is industrial and technological progress. Instead of perpetuating the romanticism of the South's Lost Cause and reverence for the values of the Old South, Nashville increasingly symbolized the rising urbanism of the New South. The city's population was exploding. From an 1860 population of 16,988, Nashville had grown to 43,350 at the time of Rice's birth in 1880; from 1880 to near the turn of the century it almost doubled, swelling to about 80,000. A newer, hotter romance replaced the old, this time between the city leaders and the general idea of commercial and material success.[20]

Even though Tennessee's economy was still largely agricultural and depended heavily on its cotton crop, the Nashville community leaders began to cultivate businesses, charitable organizations, and educational institutions; they began to rely more and more on the newest machinery and technology available in the local manufacturing, production, and trade processes; they aggressively expanded the city's downtown commercial district, merging the old Board of Trade (which Rice's father was a member of) and the city development Commercial Club into the boosterish Chamber of Commerce in 1894; and the banking financiers transformed themselves from entrepreneurial capitalism to finance capitalism.[21]

In the summer between Rice's successful graduation from Wallace and his passing the entrance examinations into Vanderbilt University, there was no better symbol for Nashville's eagerness to promote social reform, interracial peace, and industrial progress—and to thereby attract more Northern investors—than the opening of the Tennessee Centennial Exposition of 1897. The occasion was the one-hundredth anniversary of Tennessee's entrance to the Union (celebrated one year late). The exposition was held at West Side Park, a suburban horse-racing resort near Vanderbilt and within a short walk of Rice's home. Part of his summer was spent roaming the exposition grounds.

The Nashville Exposition, modeled after the Columbian Exposition in Chicago in 1893, was intended, like similar expositions in Atlanta and New Orleans, to convince the North that a New South was under construction. The official opening ceremonies were kicked off by President William McKinley, who pushed a button in Washington, D.C., sending an electric impulse seven hundred miles by wire to set off a cannon and an electric dynamo. The progressive message continued throughout the six-month exposition and was delivered to close to two million patrons. For the admission price of ten cents the local visitors and guests from many other cities, states, and not a few nations could wander in and out of the massive buildings and their displays of the newest innovations in transportation, communication, and agriculture. There were exhibits of the bountiful and unlimited natural forest and mineral resources just waiting for exploitation; there were educational, musical, art, and craft centers; there were even entire buildings devoted to the need to develop untapped human resources: a Woman's Building, and a Negro Building. In the Transportation Building, the entrance of which displayed a statue of the Roman god Mercury, a full-sized Pullman train was parked and open for walk-throughs.[22]

Besides the exhibitions, there were plenty of inspirational speeches, frequent concerts led by Victor Herbert and John Philip Sousa, thousands of electric lights, nightly fireworks displays, occasional baby contests, and a floral parade (Grantland Rice's aunt, Orleen May "Mary" Grantland, rode in this parade in a mule-drawn cart "glowing with red poppies and sheaves of golden wheat"). And, like any good exposition, there was the ubiquitous midway, Vanity Fair, where a visitor could ride the Ferris wheel, shoot-the-chute, teeter on a giant seesaw, or climb the "big tree," a stairway rising about twelve feet to a circular platform where you could look down on a ground-glass surface on which was pictured the entire Exposition grounds and all its bustling activity. Even though the youngsters were barred from seeing the exotic dancing girls in one of the Streets of Cairo booths, they were given a taste of foreign lands with ten-cent camel rides: the camel kneeled down low for the jockeys to climb aboard, and then, as the rear-end of the camel came up first, the attendant would coach the rider to "lean ah-way back" as the camel gathered its front feet under itself before it paraded its happy passenger the entire length of the Streets of Cairo.[23]

The Exposition served to mobilize the Nashvillian spirit to create itself in the image of a new, industrially and socially progressive city. The generally accepted Big Idea behind the show was that this impressive collection of technology and resources, combined with even newer technology and even greater resources obviously coming in the near future, could create the necessary machinery to do most of the human grunt work, thereby freeing up average Americans for pursuing more pleasurable leisure activities. The machine was to be the new slave to humankind, even in the South.[24]

All of this was in the air that summer of 1897 just before Rice entered Vanderbilt University. And even though Nashville aspired to be the "Athens of the South"—symbolized by the Exposition's Parthenon, a scale reproduction of the original in Athens—Vanderbilt was already hurrying along the New South progressivism, emphasizing as it did the practical character of knowledge and the social utility of science, teaching, engineering, and medicine. Vanderbilt—along with many other local institutions such as Fisk, Meharry Medical School, and the University of Nashville (later, Peabody)—was created largely by Northern philanthropy. On March 27, 1873, Cornelius Vanderbilt donated five hundred thousand dollars as start-up money for the school; the donation was subsequently increased to one million dollars, and further donations were chipped in by other Vanderbilt relatives. It was expected that Vanderbilt University would exist primarily to educate a new generation of Southerners who would take leadership roles in politics, business, law, medicine, the various practical professions, and teaching. The teachers among them, it was especially hoped, would in turn pass on these new values and skills to the next generation, who, like the first postwar generation, also could do with a bit of mental reconstruction.[25]

In his four-year program in what was called the Academic Department (the liberal arts curriculum), Rice did well. His major was Greek and Latin. His course of studies did not include English, as Vanderbilt's program mirrored C. B. Wallace's belief that studying Latin would teach English grammar better than studying English grammar itself. Nor was there anything as modern as journalism. In fact, except for a witty paper on the "Class of 1901," Grantland Rice wrote virtually nothing for any reading public prior to his graduation.[26]

Rice's lifelong affair with poetry was given shape at Vanderbilt. His inclination toward the poets had begun a few years before his university enrollment, as he recalled, having "discovered the brilliantly lighted domains" of Keats, Shelly, and Carlyle by the age of fourteen. But Vanderbilt, building on the Wallace tutorials, gave him the classic poets and dramatists; by the time he was twenty he had had full contact too with most of the romantic poets, many nineteenth-century philosophers, and much English literature. Yet his own poetic voice—he referred to the vast quantity of what he wrote over the years simply as "verse"—did not surface at Vanderbilt any more than his journalistic prose interest did. What his friends later recalled, however, was Rice's extraordinary memory for poetry, which made him a walking anthology able to quote at length the words of practically any of the poets he studied. He also had a phenomenal verbal ability to rhyme. "Grant and one other fellow in our class," remembered a college chum, "often carried on conversations in rhyme just for the fun of the thing. . . . That was great practice, of course, making for quick thinking and Grant soon drifted into verse when he started sports writing."[27]

The naturally gregarious Rice was also something of a joiner. He was a member of the chess club, the Wallace School Club (for Wallace alums), and the Dialectic Literary Society. He also pledged the Phi Delta Theta fraternity. The chapter house was a small, frame cottage with three rooms. Two or three times a year the fraternity held a dance. The members and their female guests would occasionally ride to the dance in a horse-drawn carriage, but usually they came by foot, or maybe by streetcar.

The guests were usually students from the local women's schools. The Vandy boys would call on them at the dormitories, either at the Nashville College for Young Ladies, or Mrs. M. E. Clark's Select School for Young Ladies, or perhaps St. Cecilia's Academy for Young Ladies, or the Ward Seminary. At Ward Seminary it was the custom that every afternoon at a certain time Dr. Ward would take his boarders out on an afternoon walk, marching his girls for three or four blocks in a column two by two, with Dr. Ward leading the parade. The boys would make sure they were loafing at the drugstore on the corner of Spruce and Church at the appointed time to watch the girls and flirt. As Dr. Ward was the obvious drake of the procession, the boys playfully called the girls "Ward's ducks."[28]

At the Phi Delta Theta dances, no rowdyism was tolerated. Only punch was served; no alcoholic beverages were allowed. The dances may have been rather short, as one of the chapter rules was that no boy could dance with the same girl more than once. If someone had not cut in on a couple at the end of one dance, the boy would become "stuck." His chapter brothers would then take turns cutting in on the girl for the rest of the evening to make certain that she had a good time. To be sure, Brother Henry Grantland Rice always made sure that everyone had a good time.

Like so many youngsters of the day, however, it wasn't the academic or the social life that especially dominated Grantland Rice's educational experiences. It was sport; that was his passion. Why this was so for him, and why it was the same for so many other middle-class youngsters then, isn't easy to explain. If we listen to the pedagogues, school sport was tolerated, even promoted somewhat, because to them, in the end, it could channel certain wilder and baser instincts into more approved outlets. There was also growing support for the Victorian "it's good for you" philosophy: if not good for your character, then certainly for your good health; if not for these, then at least for a goodly nurturing of your competitive spirit which would be useful later in the business world.[29]

Whatever the rationalization for pursuing these seemingly irrational athletic sports, the common thread running through them all could be reduced to one word: *improvement.* In one such defense, an author was celebrating the marvelous progress in the level of health in Milwaukee in the late 1890s, pointing to the improvements in sanitation, physician care, personal hygiene, and municipal cleanliness. But no less important was the popularity of athletics. Its existence signified the common desire for sturdy bodies and characters, the author went on. This strong preference for an America that was to grow ever more vigorous and lively was even reflected in the naming of children, the author observed: "The day of poetical 'Angelina' and simpering 'Flossie' is past; the 'Theddy' and 'Reggy' dears are no more, but instead we have solid 'Dorothys' and sinewy 'Margarets' and muscular 'Jacks' and 'Wills.' "[30]

Whether or how much of this upbeat medicinal prattle was true is less important in the long run than the fact that many people believed it to be true. Consequently, athletic feats became more valued within education. This growing sentiment in favor of athletics did not go unnoticed by the Milwaukee writer either: he pointed out that the popularity of athletics was largely due to the desire inherent in all classes of people to be well and strong. But while the educational gurus were tying themselves in knots untangling the supposed benefits of athletics, Rice and others like him were happily playing the dickens out of their favorite sports, becoming "well and strong" only incidentally, if at all. Part of their enthusiasm would have naturally come from their times: athletes were growing in public stature on campuses. A little fame did wonders for an athlete's perseverance and self-image. The increasing muscularity of the age did legitimize these athletic doings, prompting more "Theddy dears" to become "Jacks" and one Henry Grantland Rice to become just Grantland or "Grant" Rice.

But there was something else. What the rationales for sport missed, coming as most of them did from hoary minds, was the "doing-it-for-nothing-in-particular-but-doing-it-anyway" youthful exuberance constituting these athletic experiences. No Vanderbilt athletes, least of all Grant Rice, cared one whit at the time about what these experiences were doing for their health, character, or democratic spirit; they cared only about the doing itself. They would have expressed incredulity that such natural, honest, simple, and liberating experiences needed any convoluted justifications. In their minds athletics were self-justifying. Their collective disinterest at the end of the nineteenth century in needing to reason through their sporting inclinations was much like Ben Franklin's view at the end of the eighteenth that inventions such as the hot-air balloon needed any predetermined purpose. When, in 1783, he was in France witnessing Montgolfier's balloon ascension, Franklin was standing next to a skeptic who, when the balloon began to ascend, said, "What's the use of that?" Franklin turned to him and quietly retorted, "What's the use of a newborn baby?"[31]

There was precedence enough in the early days of the Republic for those inclined to give in to such sporting impulses. In the space of that short one hundred years between Franklin's comment and the appearance of the organized sport of the city boys, the frontier had opened and closed and the once-proud Indian had become down and out. But in these years both of these eclectic groups—the frontier pioneers and the Indians—played passionately and more or less spontaneously. It was a time when actions often preceded the reasons later conjured up for them; sometimes the actions themselves became the only reasons. The play reflected the rugged temper of the times. Frontier games and sports—the gouging contests, shooting matches, athletic games, running and jumping events, and bizarre tests of bravery, skill, and strength—were wholly American: individualistic, pugnacious, inventive, contentious, bold, impatient, and pragmatic. Indian sports and games—the ball games such as lacrosse and shinny, foot racing, archery, wagering, and games of chance—were obsessive, competitive, universal, and steeped in folklore, religion, magic, ritual, and ceremony. On the frontier and in Indian villages, sports and games were individually and collectively expressive, and they were central to what constituted being a pioneer or an Indian. There was nothing "extracurricular" about the pursuits. Therefore, cogitating on the whys and wherefores of their play was irrelevant to and unnecessary for justifying their playful acts. They could do it. So they did it, and did it as well as they could. Nothing else needed to be said; doing was saying.[32]

At least among male youths in the new American cities at the end of the nineteenth century, this inclination to be doing athletic things without reason stuck. Their sport experiences didn't improve upon the past in any noticeable way, nor did athletics necessarily improve the sporting bloods who were partaking in them; instead, their play was perpetuating this noticeably American impulse to take game-playing seriously even if there weren't especially good reasons to do so. They were hanging on to a tradition from America's past, not preparing themselves for a future good life.

Grant Rice was a case in point. However good he may have been at doing Greek conjugations and translating Homer for the sake of his future adult development and success, his heart was captured far more deeply by playing sports. When not in classes, he could usually be found on Vanderbilt University's athletic field or in the ninety-by-sixty-foot brick gymnasium. The gym reflected the "therapy-of-it-all" approach to physical education at the time, and was modeled after the European emphasis on gymnastic exercises, but it served Rice and his friends well as a training and conditioning center. It housed all kinds of apparatuses: rowing machines, chest expanders, parallel and horizontal bars, trapezes, inclined and horizontal ladders, springboards, Indian clubs, dumb-bells, and an indoor running track in the gallery. In the basement of the building were not only the dressing and bath rooms, but a barbershop as well.[33]

Rice was a good but not great athlete. Weighing only 134 pounds as a collegian, his effort to continue with football was almost disastrous. In his three years on the subvarsity eleven, he managed to break one arm, tear four ribs from his spinal column, shatter a collar bone, and crack a shoulder blade. His track and field experiences weren't much better, as he also broke a bone in his big toe when he dropped the sixteen-pound hammer on his foot during a training session. He played (and captained) his class basketball team for the first two years of his university life, apparently without serious injury (basketball then was mostly an intramural game). His only four-year sport was baseball, which he played exceptionally well. So damaging, however, were the accumulated injuries from the other sports, especially the injury to his shoulder, that the popular Vanderbilt shortstop was eventually forced to shovel the ball underhanded on his infield throws.[34]

It was customary for Vanderbilt to play early spring tune-up baseball games with leading eastern or western schools. In March one year, the Vandies were up against the University of Chicago, coached by Amos Alonzo Stagg. Stagg had written Vanderbilt a few weeks before the scheduled contest to tell them he would be glad to get down to the land of sunshine and flowers, as he had his team practicing in the snow. Meanwhile, the Vanderbilt team had been working out in warm weather. But the day before Stagg's team arrived, a freak cold spell hit Nashville. On the day of the game it was freezing—and snowing. Naturally, since Chicago had come all that way, they played the game. Rice said the weather was absolutely paralyzing to the Vanderbilt Black and Gold, but just like home to the Maroon bunch from Chicago. A two-hundred-pound football player by the name of Kennedy was playing first base; he could really hammer the ball. Against the Vanderbilt pitcher, who was throwing mostly slow "out-drops," Kennedy hit five consecutive "whizzers" directly at Rice. The shortstop's hands were frozen stiff and blue as indigo. Every time Rice was forced to play Kennedy's whizzers, "the briny tears oozed out in great shape," Rice later recalled. When the game was finally over, the knuckles of his right hand were split in a hundred cross sections and, said Rice, "I was as bloody as a stuck hog."[35]

Rice's Vanderbilt baseball career peaked during his senior year. He was elected captain of the varsity nine. In the course of the season he hit consistently and played his shortstop position nearly flawlessly, even with his unorthodox throwing motion. In one game against Tennessee he had fifteen assists, no errors, and two hits—a double and a home run. Vanderbilt won the game 4 to 3. By the end of the season he had led the Vandies to the Southern Conference championship.[36]

At the end of the spring term in 1901, Grant Rice graduated with a B.A. degree in Greek and Latin. The National Council of the Phi Beta Kappa scholarship society just that year had awarded Vanderbilt its charter; Rice was one of the few students meeting the eligibility requirements of four years of academic study with a grade average of 86 percent or higher. He was graduated in the first Phi Beta Kappa class out of Vanderbilt. With good reason, Rice's voice was one of the thirty-two graduating seniors in his academic class who, during commencement ceremonies, vigorously applauded themselves by repeatedly chanting their self-composed class yell. It was quite spirited and wonderfully unintelligible:

> We! Wi! Wow!
> Ally! Kally! Yi! Yow!
> Rah! Ze! Zi! Zun!
> V.U.! V.U.! 1901[37]

But what Rice did immediately after his formal commencement was a surprise to nearly everyone, and an utter disappointment to some. What his romping childhood, liberal education, and passionate liaison with athletics somehow combined to produce was a real-life, unabashed Romantic. In spite of the progressive forces of his day—the hustling and bustling city, the immediate family business role models, and the professional mission of his university—Grant Rice remained thoroughly unreconstructed. He did not choose a progressive professional career proper to a well-educated son of a highly respected Nashville family; neither did he join up with his father and grandfather in commerce. Instead, and unbelievably as far as most of his family was concerned, he quietly wandered off to play semiprofessional baseball, becoming part of the culture of ragtags, vagabonds, and roustabouts who more or less peopled the sport of baseball at the turn of the century.

4

Pyrotechnic Displays

Semiprofessional baseball at the turn of the twentieth century had about the same shady reputation as its professional counterparts. According to Davy Jones, who played for a variety of major- and minor-league clubs, baseball players were often looked upon as no-account bums. When the parents of a girl he had been dating discovered that he was a baseball player, they refused to let her see him anymore. On the road, baseball teams were never entirely certain they could find rooms to rent, as hotels only reluctantly put up baseball teams for fear that their mere presence would chase away respectable guests. The sport attracted a wild cross section of American males, colorful types mostly. Jones recalled that "we had stupid guys, smart guys, tough guys, mild guys, crazy guys, college men, slickers from the city, and hicks from the country." The hicks were so country that they were usually all called hayseeds or rubes. For many of these men, baseball was an escape from either the farm or the odium of an urban job. One reader wrote *Sporting News* asking why anyone would want to become a baseball player. The editors replied: "It beats hoeing corn or shoveling coal."[1]

The local Nashville semipros were pleased to have picked up their new shortstop, even though the "college boys" were so rare then that they were customarily viewed with suspicion by the regulars. They also couldn't help but notice that his throwing was kind of weird; he looked more like he was trying to skip rocks across a pond than throw a baseball to first base. But

Grant Rice got on with them, and played respectable baseball for about the first six to eight weeks of the summer of 1901. During that time the team was barnstorming throughout West Virginia, Tennessee, and Mississippi. They would get games wherever and whenever they could, playing teams one step above local amateurs and one below the minor-league professionals. Rice, like most of the team members, hoped that the chaotic and scrambling summer would eventually result in a contract with a minor-league team. And from there, who knew?[2]

But Grant Rice would never find out how far he might have gone in the world of professional baseball. During a series in Waterloo, Mississippi, he received a wire from his father. Apparently his family had had about enough of his truancy, as the wire "suggested" that he come home to Nashville at once. Of this event, Rice said much later that he had been riding quite high all summer, from the time of the Vanderbilt conference championship and continuing through his successful semipro debut. Even so, "I didn't question the order and, taking a long last glance over my shoulder, packed my glove and spikes and returned to Nashville."[3]

It is not difficult to imagine what the conversations between Rice and his father might have been like, for choosing to run off and play ball was then on a par with selling your soul to the Devil. When Rube Marquard, the New York Giants pitcher (and a player in the majors from 1908 to 1925), first declared his intentions to play baseball around 1906 at the age of sixteen, he and his father would have go-arounds typical of many families housing young men bitten by the baseball bug:

"I'm going to be a ballplayer."

"A ballplayer?" his father would say, and throw his hands up in the air. "What do you mean? How can you make a living being a ballplayer? I don't understand why a grown man would wear those funny-looking suits in the first place."

"Well," I'd answer, "you see policemen with uniforms on, and other people like that. They change after they're through working. It's the same way with ballplayers."

"Ha! Do ballplayers get paid?"

"Yes, they get paid."

"I don't believe it! . . . Ballplayers are no good," he'd say, "and they never will be any good."[4]

According to Rice's father, what was best for Grant was to get a respectable job doing respectable work and earning respectable money. Which translated into his father using his influence to find him a position with the J. S. Reeves wholesale dry-goods business. Reeves's store was a jobbing firm. Each sales-man from the Nashville store would load up enough dry goods in January to fill seven or eight big trucks. They would take their goods by train to their designated selling territory, transfer the goods onto drummer's wagons, and then travel to all the country stores in their region, selling enough stock to last them through the planting season.[5]

On the first Monday of July, Rice reluctantly joined the merchant class as a stock boy, and was formally referred to as the assistant shipping clerk. His job was to inspect and mark the salesmen's shipments. His "office" was in the basement, which, he remembered, was dark and dank. He also remembered that they treated him fine, but that he just didn't like "marking goods, mark-ing goods, marking goods." His new job lasted exactly six days. At the end of the week he abruptly left the employ of J. S. Reeves, not stopping long enough to pick up his paycheck.[6]

By the second Monday of July, Grant Rice was back hanging around ball-parks. But this time his association with the ball-playing fraternity was justi-fied by his new job as a semipaid sportswriter. He had heard that Jere Baxter, a local real-estate speculator turned railroad investor, was getting up a new city newspaper, the *Nashville Daily News*. Rice somehow talked his way into being hired on as one of their seven staff reporters in spite of the fact that he had no journalistic experience whatsoever. This—the hiring of green re-porters—wasn't an uncommon practice then, especially in the South or the West. In Denver, Otto Floto was hired as sports editor by H. H. Tammen, a former bartender and co-owner of the *Denver Post*, for no other apparent rea-son than that Tammen thought Floto's name was beautiful.[7]

Rice's primary beat was to be sports, but City Editor Edward Martin appar-ently didn't think that there were enough sports to keep him busy, or more probably that they weren't important enough to be too busy about. In any case, Martin also assigned him to cover the city beats at Capitol Hill, the pro-duce market, and the customs house—all this, plus sports, for the whopping salary of five dollars per week, about the salary then of a domestic.

It isn't entirely clear what Rice's father thought about his son's turn toward the newspaper business. According to Rice's own recollections, his dad fig-ured that journalism might be a good fit for his son since at Vanderbilt Grant hadn't taken at all to medicine, law, or engineering, but he had done well in the liberal arts. Nonetheless, Rice's father still must have had grave reserva-tions about his son's newest fling. The ordinary wisdom of the age had it that as a profession, sportswriting was a mere trifling, even slovenly. Being a base-ball player was bad enough, although perhaps forgivable as a short-term youthful lark; but to give up a decent merchant career for the sake of a low-paying, nomadic, and disreputable reporter's job was practically scandalous. Nothing, certainly nothing good, could possibly come of it.[8]

But Rice's father's probable reservations, and the common sense of the age that his reservations reflected, were wrong. Like the fortuitous investor buy-ing an eventual blue-chip stock when it is only a few dollars a share, Rice was in on the ground floor of an enterprise that would eventually make him rich, famous, and influential—ironically all rather revered benchmarks for judging the degree of success in potential New South professions. Grantland Rice started up his career in the very beginning of an era in which sport was to be-come one of the most important and obsessive American mass preoccupa-tions ever.

By the turn of the twentieth century, the psychically addictive power of sports was spreading; it also was beginning to mean business. Any number of sports had begun to reflect the enthusiastic entrepreneurialism typical of any new business venture. Certainly harness and horse racing, boxing, billiards, and crew had, by the 1880s, achieved some degree of commercial popularity. America's gambling instincts ran deep and were usually the excuse for getting up a variety of sporting matches.

Pedestrianism, for instance, started out in the early to mid 1800s as sort of a poor man's horse race, the runners often using the horse and harness racing tracks on off days for two-hundred- to three-hundred-dollar purses, some-times more if the running match was between an English runner and some upstart Americans. Eventually, besides sprint and middle-distance running (ten-mile runs were popular), pedestrianism included jumping matches and long-distance walking events (sometimes six-day marathons) for dollars and were held at amusement parks, some track stadiums, and ethnic and occupa-tional club picnics and athletic meets. A reported fifty thousand fans turned up to watch Edward Payson Weston finish his record walk from Portland, Maine, to Chicago in 1867. Weston was a walker for half a century. In 1910 he claimed to have walked across the entire continent in seventy-seven days at the age of seventy-one. At one of the more notorious gambling cities, Pater-son, New Jersey, a typical running race brought purses of up to two hundred dollars; the side bets often totaled in the thousands. Given that the stakes on the side were always higher than on the main event itself, "throw-offs" (fixed races) were common, with the lowly paid hired athletic hands agreeing to throw a race for the right price; sometimes they would lay down for any price since they were often stiffed by the race backers anyway.[9]

When fans began to tire of one sport, as they gradually did of the pedestrian shows, promoters introduced other, fresher sports that extended the professional sports market's staying power: promoters turned from pedestrianism to roller skating to bicycle racing. August Zimmerman, and later Marshall "Major" Taylor and Frank Kramer, led the turn to professionalizing bicycle racing in the 1890s. Major Taylor, the first black rider of national and international prominence in a largely white game, was an artist at sprint racing. Exhibiting the kind of skill and speed that became the trademark of the early American riders, Taylor, famous for his "gunpowder sprint," took the 1899 world championship premier event, the mile. "I never felt so proud to be an American before," wrote Taylor in his autobiography.[10]

Roller skate racing, a craze in America, gave rise to professional bicycle racing. Roller skating track managers wanted to spice up the skating competition and began looking for a side attraction to the main events. When bicycle riders were added, the cyclists rode on the outside of the track at the same time the skaters raced on the inside. It wasn't long before interest in the speed and distance covered by the cyclists pushed the skaters off the flat rink tracks.[11] Special tracks were then designed for the bicyclists, usually eight laps to the mile and banked to allow full speed on the turns. In the first American six-day night-and-day race in Minneapolis, Albert Shock, Senator Morgan, and Montreal's famous woman cyclist, Louise R. Maindo, went wheel to wheel, covering nearly fifteen hundred miles. Shock won, and the game contestant Morgan, in one twenty-six-hour stretch, was off his bicycle but eighteen seconds, just long enough to relieve himself.[12]

By the 1890s six-day, twenty-four-hour-a-day races were regularly scheduled on the yellow pine track in Madison Square Garden, often in December. The first six-dayer there was in 1891. By Thanksgiving the horse tracks were closed, and since boxing was illegal, bicycle racing was about the only large gambling event in town. These endurance races attracted crowds of "sports" from tin horns to diamond fonts, especially when the matches featured various ethnic or regional riders, or the crack European cyclists. The leisured rich had plenty of spare time and were always looking for something to spend it and their money on; the lower and middle classes had less time and money, but were in need of some kind of nonwork zing to counterbalance the otherwise drab, boring, and often physically exhausting nature of much of their daily urban toil. But no matter the economic class, the racing throngs were there to see or do or be a part of something that was out-of-the-ordinary, inherently interesting, and chancy.

In the earliest versions of the Garden's six-day competitions, the rules allowed each rider to peddle as much of the 144 hours as he wanted to or could. But in the opinion of the health-reformers, such endurance feats were too punishing. Consequently, in 1898 the New York legislature passed a law forbidding any rider from going more than twelve hours a day. Instead of killing off the sport, the restriction increased its popularity. Promoters like the famous Broadway producer Billy Brady thought up an alternative. Brady had been manager of the heavyweight boxer Jim Corbett, but switched to cycling as Major Taylor's manager. Instead of one rider killing himself at the marathon feat, Brady and the other racing promoters simply created two-man teams. More sophisticated strategy was thus introduced, as the two-rider teams could use their own discretion as to when each would ride. The nonrider could then rest up, eat, work on his bike, chat with the fans, and tend to other necessaries. And the sport increased in liveliness.

The two-man-team races quickly took their place alongside other Garden shows: Annie Oakley's gun play, Buffalo Bill's Wild West Show, circuses, and even beauty contests. The galleries at the six-day races were always packed; sometimes as many as fifteen to eighteen thousand fans peered down on the swarming center oval, watching both the dizzying race and the animated gesticulations of the standing, enthusiastic rail birds lined up along the restraining fence.

The big crowds naturally attracted those with keen noses for business, the "fakirs" and the bookies. The entrance hall in the basement of the Garden, which led to the stairs to the racing oval, was jammed with pitchmen and pitchwomen. On the makeshift Midway, a Japanese girl would be running a bagatelle game for china or bric-a-brac prizes; there might be an Egyptian palmist or other various soothsayers and fortune tellers; a cane philanthropist would be selling walking sticks for a nickel; the health-minded could pay to have newfangled machines measure lungs and muscles. For the more competitive, games of skill and chance occupied many booths, located next to tiny amphitheaters behind enticingly pictured curtains intended to catch the curiosity seekers; frankfurters and nickel sandwiches sold famously, along with a perpetual supply of "half-barrels" of beer.

Upstairs in bookie heaven, the forgathering of gamblers, veiled by the thick, curling smoke of cigars and cigarettes, bet on anything from the eventual winner, to the day-to-day leading teams, to even smaller pots of money on momentary and spontaneous sprints between any of the riding teams.

And everybody bet: the fans, the press, the cycling association officers, the police security, the managers and trainers—even the riders themselves.[13]

Two other sports were on the verge of becoming whopping national obsessions at the turn of the twentieth century: college football and professional baseball. The steady growth of both was a telltale sign that the sporting market could and would be extraordinarily bullish for the century to come.

Football had been an early folk pastime before it picked up some of its business trappings in the colleges after the Civil War. Some of the older American universities, such as Harvard, had been playing football-like games as interclass initiation rites as early as the 1820s. They were generally abolished by 1860, however, due to the general impression among the faculty that the game was merely an excuse for a ferocious fight.[14]

Colleges were playing the sport formally by 1869, but the game was mostly organized and controlled by students. When push came to shove between the numerous colleges over enrollments and endowments in the last quarter of the nineteenth century, it was believed that the sport could be useful in building student bodies and school spirit. A good (or better, a winning) football team could give the schools, especially the land-grant institutions and sectarian schools, the exposure and status necessary for growth. In the minds of the administrators, football could put their schools on the map. The competition between the institutions could quite literally take place on the football fields, with students as the designated players.[15]

By way of example, when William Rainey Harper assumed the presidency of the new and Rockefeller-endowed University of Chicago in 1892, he immediately hired well-known Amos Alonzo Stagg to be the football coach, charging him with developing "teams which we can send around the country and knock out all the (other) colleges. We will give them a palace car and a vacation too." According to one story Stagg told later, his team was trailing at halftime to Wisconsin, 12 to 0. Harper gave a locker-room speech, appealing not to routine pep-talk themes of individual pride, courage, honor, and so on, but to what he thought were more basic instincts, or at least to his idea of what their instincts should be: "Boys, Mr. Rockefeller has just announced a gift of $3,000,000 to the University. He believed that the University is to be great. The way you played in the first half leads me to wonder whether we really have the spirit of greatness in ambition. I wish you would make up your minds to win this game and show that we have it." The boys reached deeply into their collective ambitions and won the game 22 to 12, enabling Harper to more easily justify his soon-to-be old grads to reach even deeper into their collective pockets to support their alma mater.[16]

For all of the positive interest the game attracted, especially the admiration heaped on the players for being manly good sports, the sport itself was in fact pretty brutal. The kids who played it got themselves beaten up (witness Grant Rice)—bruised faces, black eyes, scratches, sprains, and broken bones. Harvard's interclass games on the first Monday of the school year weren't called "Bloody Mondays" for nothing.

As the game gradually evolved through its soccer- and rugby-like stages, the devilish fisticuffs hardly lessened, partly because the rule changes tended to bring the players into closer contact rather than to spread them farther apart. The version of the sport that Grant Rice played at Vanderbilt was of this congested kind, where wild goose mass momentum plays dominated the game. First came the V formations, then secondary Vs—a little v inside a big V—and finally flying wedges created to plow through the opposing players, parting them like water in front of a full-speed battleship. John Heisman remembered those days as rough going, even though his players were dressed up to resemble armored medieval warriors: they wore several pounds of horse-hair, padding, mouthpieces, canvass blouses, and nose and ear protectors. The entire outfit reminded one writer of a cross between a baseball catcher and a deep sea diver.[17]

By the end of the nineteenth century, college football was already an impassioned spectator sport. Football fans were beginning to take the game quite seriously, which is to say, personally. On the Vanderbilt football field in November of the year preceding Grant Rice's matriculation, a game between the Vandies and the University of Nashville turned into "the big fight." Tied with five minutes left in the game, it was alleged later that slugging had broken out between the players. The University of Nashville team then left the field without the authorization of the officials. This action precipitated an enormous fight among the highly partisan spectators. Football was temporarily suspended at Vanderbilt, and their next game against Auburn was canceled. A couple of the Vandy players were disqualified from playing out the season, although the last game of the year, against Sewanee, was allowed. In the end, since the officials did not confirm that there was any slugging between the players themselves, the players were reinstated. The Vanderbilt alumni and students adamantly believed that the spectators and not the players were responsible for the unruliness. In Nashville, as elsewhere, the emotional commitment to the sport was not to be taken lightly.[18]

In 1899, Teddy Roosevelt, the just-picked vice-presidential running mate of William McKinley, spoke and wrote in praise of the "strenuous life" and its connection to a strong and healthy America. His view regarding sport in general and football in particular was that they served as a healthy antidote to luxury and effeminacy and therefore should be of national interest. He exhorted the American boy "to bear himself well in manly exercises and to develop his body—and therefore, to a certain extent, his character—in the rough sports which call for pluck, endurance, and physical address." Roosevelt went on to compare football and life. The boy "cannot do good work if he is not strong and does not try with his whole heart and soul to count in any contest. . . . In short, in life, as in a foot-ball game, the principle to follow is: Hit the line hard; don't foul and don't shirk, but hit the line hard!"[19]

Baseball, too, was beginning to capture the nation's heart and soul by the end of the nineteenth century. Organized baseball on a commercial, professional scale had been around since shortly after the Civil War. The rural versions of the sport in America had gradually evolved from the English game of rounders some years before; there are a few accounts of baseball-like games as far back as the Revolutionary War. By the 1840s the basic features of the modern game had been developed, with the credit going to those largely middle-class pioneers from Manhattan and Brooklyn who organized a dozen or so baseball clubs between 1845 and 1855. The man thought by historians to be responsible for calling together the first such club, the Knickerbocker Club playing at the Elysian Fields in Hoboken, New Jersey, was a New York clerk and volunteer fireman by the name of Alexander J. Cartwright, Jr.[20]

The historians also tell us that Abner Doubleday had nothing whatsoever to do with the founding of the game. In spite of the efforts of sporting goods entrepreneur Albert G. Spalding to prove the game American through a fanciful report from a blue-ribbon committee alleging that Doubleday invented the game at Cooperstown, New York, in 1839, the facts show not only that Civil War hero General Abner Doubleday didn't found the game but also that he didn't even like it. As a youth he cared little for ball games, preferring instead to read or spend his outdoor time making topological maps of the countryside.[21]

Uncertainty about whether or not baseball was of bastard origins did not interfere with its growth in America. The sport quickly became the national pastime after the Civil War. In Brooklyn and Manhattan alone, there were more than a hundred clubs; in the nation the same year there were two thousand organized clubs. Even if the game's origins were not wholly American, many felt reassured in saying that given the organization and rule standardization since the 1840s, baseball was unquestionably an American "sport."[22]

The first major league, the National Association of Professional Base Ball Players, was formed in 1871, and for the next thirty years owners and players created one league after another, complete with spirited fighting about territorial rights, player-freedom restrictive reserve clauses, parity, schedules, how to resolve disputes, and salaries. The stakes were considerable, and in the judgment of many, well worth the fight for control and for the profits.

It is therefore mostly myth that professional baseball was simply an indigenous, pastoral American pastime played by backward rural homegrowns. Neither was it a sport graciously underwritten by kindly and generous owners eager to please the public and their players. At bottom, and nearly from the beginning, baseball was an urban business, even if badly run, that sought to be monopolistic. By the end of the nineteenth century it was already beginning to assume a structure that would resemble its modern organized cartel status.

As the fans grew closer to baseball—to its crack players, to its emotional appeal, to the intellectual and aesthetic attractions found in its rhythm, sense of order, and intensification of reality—the game increasingly benefited other businesses: transportation, newspapers, hotels, sporting goods manufacturing, and the myriad other enterprises that tried to link themselves with the growing sport. "To be sure, the baseball business was already being encased in a thick coating of ballyhoo, sentiment, and talk of 'sport' and 'loyalty to the team,'" wrote one observer. "But if one scraped underneath it, he was likely to find the dollar sign."[23]

The Nashville team was in the Southern League. The league was organized in 1884 by the editor of the *Atlanta Constitution*, Henry Grady. Grady was one of the most prominent of the New South ideologists. Much like Henry Grantland, he was of tradesman's stock with a strong family background in cotton manufacturing. After three of his newspapers failed within five months, Cyrus W. Field loaned Grady twenty thousand dollars to buy a quarter interest in the *Constitution*. Victor Newcomb, the young president of the Louisville and Nashville railroad, quickly coached him into some stock speculation to pay off the loan. And within seven years the *Atlanta Constitution* claimed the largest circulation of any paper in the South. In the *Constitution* and in speeches, Grady tirelessly promoted the industrializing of the South. In a speech given at Delmonico's in New York City in 1886, he followed William Tecumseh Sherman to the podium. He described a South on the way to resurrection, gushingly welcoming the wealthy Northern investors: "We have smoothed the path to Southward, wiped out where the Mason Dixon's line used to be, and hung out our latchstring to you and yours."[24]

Grady's Southern League was intended to provide further evidence that the New South was on the rise. Even if the league would not necessarily earn a profit, related businesses such as the railroads, streetcar lines, and newspapers would. And the cities fortunate enough to have a local team would find a healthy sense of community pride (if the team was winning) and a strong feeling of fan identification with the local baseball heroes. All of which could translate into local growth, an up-tempo economy, and a higher standard of living for all, not to mention the creation of personal fortunes for a few.

In the summer of 1901, when Grantland Rice became a scribe, sportswriting had not yet become much of a profession. But Rice had definitely wandered into a field with a future, a vocation which in time he would help certify and legitimize. Yet if there hadn't been a hellish controversy over railroad service in and out of Nashville in 1901, Rice may never have taken that first job with the *Nashville Daily News,* or perhaps even have joined the Fourth Estate at all. Indirectly, it was all Jere Baxter's doing.

The rise of the Louisville and Nashville (L&N) Railroad by 1859 had given Nashville a prominent part in the exchange of agricultural products and manufactured goods between South and North before and after the Civil War. Nashville prospered as the key centers of trade began shifting from the port cities, such as Charleston, Mobile, and New Orleans, to the interior cities, which handled the flow of commerce by rail. Between 1860 and 1880, Nashville's population grew two and one-half times, from 17,000 to 43,350. But what blew the Nashvillians' stacks was that the octopuslike L&N was controlled by nonlocal interests. Worse still, the L&N didn't have any serious competition. Just before Nashville's Centennial Exposition in 1880, the L&N surreptitiously bought out the fledgling, locally controlled Nashville, Chattanooga and St. Louis Railroad.

For twenty years Nashville steamed over L&N's monopolistic practices. All six railroad lines into Nashville were under its control, which was to say under the control of "foreigners" (New York interests). In the opinion of Mayor James Head, the absence of a locally controlled alternative line was stunting the growth and prosperity of the city. Even though Nashville's population had almost doubled (to 80,865) by 1900, there was only a 6 percent growth in the 1890s and the city had fallen from fortieth among U.S. cities in population in 1880 to forty-seventh by 1900.

In the best New South entrepreneurial spirit, Jere Baxter, the son of a prominent Nashville judge and a former lawyer and real-estate speculator turned railroad investor, quietly began organizing an independent railroad. It was to be locally controlled. After seven years of struggle (beginning in 1893), and with the help of a St. Louis syndicate (including the beer brewer Adolphus Busch) and some local Nashville capitalists, Baxter presented Nashville with its own railroad, the Tennessee Central.

But L&N had not been idly sitting by while Baxter put together his line connecting Nashville with Knoxville to the east and Memphis to the west. The L&N had proposed (also in 1893) to construct a Union Station in Nashville, chiefly to win the pouting city over. By the time this elaborate, Romanesque station opened, its two-hundred-foot clock tower would only keep time for L&N trains, as through some years of legislative flimflam at both the state and local levels the L&N had successfully denied "Nashville's own" access to Union Station.

But Baxter was not about to allow the Tennessee Central idea to be side-tracked. He went to the people. He asked the City of Nashville to issue one million dollars in bonds in exchange for stock in a new railroad. The city council called for an election, and the people approved the subscription to the stock of what was to be called the Nashville, Florence and Northern Railroad. L&N fought back, winning an injunction and forcing Baxter to incorporate if his railroad was to cross state lines (his northern terminus was in Kentucky).

To gain popular support for his newest incorporated company, now called the Nashville and Clarksville Railroad, Baxter needed something he did not enjoy: a favorable press. The city's leading newspapers were opposed to Baxter's plans to bring an entirely new set of rails into the city. The *Nashville Banner* and the *American* were both published by men with either existing or former ties to the L&N. Baxter needed his own mouthpiece.

Shortly before the second election for the stock subscription to his newest railroad in the summer of 1901, Jere Baxter started up the *Nashville Daily News* in a building directly across the street from the *Banner* offices. The paper's chief mission was to garner support for his project and to bitterly attack his opponents. Besides that, Baxter had a trust-busting agenda in mind for his Democratic paper, generally going after the Republican party, "the party of selfish and greedy combinations, the party of unjust and unholy protection of one class over another," and pursuing the Democratic principles of "individual liberty and home rule, under which this nation has grown great."[25]

The *Daily News* was convincing. When the second city election took place, slightly more than the necessary three-fourths votes were cast for subscription. Even though the court skirmishes with L&N continued throughout the fall and early spring, Baxter won enough of the battles to complete his dream. On May 27, 1902, Jere Baxter proudly rode the puffing Tennessee Central into Nashville and into its own new depot. The front of the boiler was adorned with a picture of Baxter draped with garlands and evergreens. As he blew the highly polished "Liberty Whistle" loudly enough for those at Union Station to take notice, Nashville's factory whistles answered back, along with the cheers of an estimated ten thousand people waiting at the depot (another five thousand lined the tracks). Wild celebration followed: a procession, complete with fire and militia companies, mounted police, bands, and fancy carriages; a mass meeting convened at the Union Gospel Tabernacle; and a victory banquet with eleven after-dinner speeches, lasting beyond midnight.

In the end, however, Baxter was to lose the war with L&N. He had so alienated the imperious railroad magnates through slanderous newspaper attacks and relentless jockeying for railroad regulation from his newly won seat on the state senate that he was eventually forced to resign as president of the Tennessee Central. With his resignation went the railroad's prosperity. It went into receivership in 1912, was revived in 1922, and hung on until it collapsed in 1968 from bus and truck traffic competition; the L&N was still going strong. Baxter himself died at the age of fifty-four in February 1904, a city hero.

The railroad set-to between L&N and Baxter didn't entirely end with Baxter's death. Three years later a bronze statue was erected to memorialize the Tennessee Central founder. Apparently wanting the last word in the matter, Eugene C. Smith—a director of the L&N, the *Nashville American* publisher, a frequent Baxter target, and a member of the Board of Park Commissioners—arranged for a marker to be erected in Centennial Park to honor the memory of John A. Murrell, the legendary Tennessee horse thief, on the logic that Baxter's acts were on about the same level of thievery as Murrell's, Baxter being "the man who sold the city one million dollars of worthless railroad stock."[26]

To Grantland Rice, Jere Baxter's plucky battles were as spirited as a Hercules taking on Hydra or a Theseus slaying the Minotaur. Rice admired Baxter's spunk when he signed on as a reporter on the *Daily News,* even if his own inclinations were to steer wide of reporting on these controversial political battles. In name Rice was a general reporter, but in his own mind he was going to be a sports reporter. His nonsporting assignments didn't thrill him much.

Rice's attitude toward the "doings of the market," as he sometimes called his produce report, is summed up in one of his brief items: "Country produce shipments continue dull. Market quiet. Eggs and poultry steady at same quotations. No shipments." He just couldn't take the vicissitudes of produce too seriously, once reporting that "butter was strong and there was a flutter in eggs." Not much happened at the customs house in his mind either, or even at

Capitol Hill, although the customs house won out, not for interesting news, but for his happy habit of playing Ping-Pong with one of the employees.27

Rice wasn't above taking shortcuts with nonsporting beats. Once Edward Martin, his city editor, assigned him to cover a fashionable Nashville ball. Reluctantly, Rice went. But since he was utterly incapable of describing the ladies' costumes, he went back to his newspaper's morgue, picked out a Sunday edition of the *New York Tribune,* turned to the society section, and copied. The madams and belles of Nashville's upper crust were flattered the next day by the story, never suspecting that their gowns had been described in the New York paper first and that they had already been worn to one of Mrs. Vanderbilt's parties at the old Waldorf. Only the names were changed.28

Rice was known to go even further to avoid the tedium of general reporting. One of his uptown drugstore hangouts was Demoville's on the corner of Church Street and Fourth Avenue (then called Cherry), across from the famous Maxwell House (the establishment serving "a good cup of coffee" and which later lent its name to the Cheek-Neal Coffee Company; the famous slogan "good to the last drop" was reportedly one of Teddy Roosevelt's sayings when he visited Nashville). Demoville's—which included a wonderful soda-water fountain, a large cigar stand, and a pharmacy in the rear—was one of the most popular Nashville street-corner gossip and conversation spots, with the milling habitués frequently overflowing onto the sidewalk. Louis Brownlow, one of Rice's old friends and a frequenter of Demoville's, was a reporter on the arch-rival *Nashville Banner.* Brownlow's strong suit was political reporting, even though he was sometimes assigned sports, which he detested. For Rice, it was the reverse. Deciding to do something other than grouse about their mutual predicament, and unbeknownst to their bosses, Rice and Brownlow began occasionally swapping their more irritating assignments. Rice would every so often do a sports story for the *Banner* and Brownlow would cover some political meeting or another for the *Daily News.* No one caught on, and presumably their chicanery served to strengthen the coverage of both newspapers, for both reporters were writing what they knew.29

Being the entire *Daily News* sports department in truth gave Rice plenty to do without the additional city-side assignments. For the man was not then, nor would he ever be, lazy. He wrote the entire sports section himself, including a larger Sunday spread. Under the heading "Sports Of All Sorts," Rice focused mostly on local and some regional sporting news, covering horse racing, crew, boxing, athletics, football, and assorted special events. It was difficult for him to do much with national stories because the *News* didn't have a regular wire service. Given Baxter's primary goal of using the paper to bust the L&N, its financial base was shaky. Instead of a wire service, such as the Associated Press subscribed to by the *Banner* across the street, the *News* relied on "pony" reports filed in the office of a Scripps-McRae newspaper, the *Cincinnati Post*. Sometimes, if the *Post* man was either rushed or indolent, only skeletonized dispatches arrived, which had to be fleshed out considerably to compete with what the AP wire provided the *Banner*. Rice had to take these "flimsys," which were delivered by the Postal Telegraph Company, and somehow create a readable story as though it were a bona fide wire story. When the Cincinnati pony failed him, he resorted to the common practice of pirating day-old copy from New York newspapers to fill his page.[30]

Rice mostly covered Southern League baseball in the summer and fall months of his four-month stay with the *News*. By the paper's July start-up, the local Nashville club was halfway into the 1901 season. Interest in the league was heightened because it was the circuit's first year back in business in more than five baseball seasons. The original league Grady sponsored was weak from the very beginning and collapsed in the late 1890s. When Newt Fisher, player/manager for the Nashville club, and Charlie Frank, manager of the Memphis team, put forward the sporting proposition in 1901 that the South should try again to make baseball pay, few were betting that the newly reorganized Southern Association (still popularly called the Southern League) would last out the season.

The skeptics, called "croakers" then, certainly would have outnumbered the fanatics. In Nashville, crowds for the late-afternoon games only averaged from a few hundred to perhaps as many as a couple of thousand. In a tight pennant race, sometimes three to four thousand bleacherites would show up. But in 1901, Nashville baseball wasn't a major draw; other kinds of events did much better. Buffalo Bill's show exhibiting roughriders of the world attracted eight thousand locals on one evening by advertising Cossacks on horseback, Arab tumbling feats, Mexican lassoers, frontier marksmen, and a mock-up of the capture of Pekin by the allied troops. For fifty cents, it was advertised, those witnessing the exhibition would see a "veritable mirror of heroic manhood." Even though New Orleans could boast a paid attendance of nine to ten thousand for many baseball games late in 1901, its population was close to four times the size of Nashville's. On the whole, depending on whether or not the club was a potential contender (and not adjusting for possible statistical exaggeration on the part of the ball club or reporters), Southern League crowds averaged between 1 and 2 percent of the city's population.[31]

Even when everyone behaved themselves, player, manager, and owner turnover during the season made holding the league together exceptionally difficult; when the rowdies began to act up, the league's survival was understandably a toss-up. Not long into the season, the Birmingham manager, Sam Mills, tried to disrupt the league. Owing to some unspecified but clearly unpopular shenanigans in some games against Nashville, Mills quit his team on the spot, went home to Birmingham, dug up home plate, collected the home uniforms and other equipment, even stole the little ten-cent noise bell (rung for good plays and scores) that hung behind the players' bench, and left town.

The league's president was in hot water himself. Only one week after the Mills fiasco, Rice reported that irregularities in the league's accounts were suspected. During the investigation the president was suspended, not for the suspected shortages, but for the fact that he had been living rather gaily, and that such high living had suggested the need for an investigation. Rice simply reported these facts, and in a subhead explained that the president's suspension was due to the "lively gait he was going." Apparently, in the end, his lively gait did have something to do with his being light-fingered, as three days later vice-president W. J. Boles of Birmingham became the new president. Rice included a short, evenhanded notice of the dismissal, writing, "Although [the president] was a fair man in his position and in many respects did the league some good, his exit will not disturb the organization." It didn't, in spite of the fact that he absconded with all the league funds and the statistical records.[32]

The 1901 pennant race was as lively as the president's gait. Nashville opened up in the league lead until their first long road swing throughout the circuit. Extended road trips were customary, and included playing all or most of the clubs in the eight-team league. After Nashville fell back, Shreveport came on with a rush, but they too succumbed to road-play problems. Shreveport had two excellent pitchers, Red Fisher and Guy Sample. But Fisher dropped out on the road trip with typhoid fever, leaving Sample to pitch by himself; once he pitched five games in a row. By the last game, in Nashville, an exhausted Sample gave up eighteen hits. The strain eventually left him with an arm that was curved at the elbow, and, said Rice, "with enough glass in the shoulder to start a window pane factory." Shreveport gradually slid into fourth place, eventually ending the season in fifth.[33]

Little Rock stayed on top for a short while, until Selma won nine straight games in the latter part of June. But Nashville took seven straight from Selma in July, knocking them from first all the way to the league cellar, where they remained, winning only 38 of 115 games. Even in 1901 it was already clear that having a team was one thing, but having a losing team was quite another. By mid-July rumors were spreading that Selma might lose its franchise to Montgomery or Atlanta because the local fans were not willing to support a losing team; so disgusted were the local "cranks" (fans) that in the last two months of the season they refused to patronize the ballpark at all, forcing the management to schedule the remaining games of the season on the road. The owners were understandably miffed and wanted to go to a city where baseball would pay whether the team won or lost. In the end, Selma was the only club to lose money in 1901. Rice observed that the city's populace "became wildly weary of seeing seven assorted varieties of bitumen thumped out of their horse hide representatives six days of the week. . . . The Selma aggregation was about as fast as a slow snail walking sideways when it came to winning games and the same team in Atlanta would not draw a corporal's guard." Selma folded at the end of the season. The franchise was moved to Atlanta; Mr. Peters, the Selma owner and local resident, expressed regret over the move, saying that he hated to take the team away from his own city, "but it is a business enterprise, and the investment at present is not satisfactory."[34]

When Rice took up his writing post for the *Daily News,* Nashville was comfortably in first place. In their three-week July home stand they managed to win 21 of the 24 games played, putting them ahead of second-place Little Rock by 26 percentage points and third-place Memphis by 50 percentage points. Nashville's dominance galled the other clubs, as dominance often does. Many clubs redoubled their efforts to catch the front-runner. On the day Nashville left home for a three-week road trip the *Shreveport Times* tried to reassure its local baseball lovers that they would make a serious run for the pennant (Shreveport was in fifth place): " . . . if money, energy, and ambition to sustain the glory of Shreveport on the diamond can improve the situation in this city, the desired result will be accomplished. . . . Shreveport will have a winner if money and energy can secure the players."[35]

Rice accompanied the Nashville team for most of its road trips, sending by dispatch his narrative descriptions of the games, the "pyrotechnic displays" that the confrontation between Nashville and the other clubs generated. But the Nashville fans did not always have to rely exclusively on Rice's coverage. His afternoon newspaper accounts were always, of necessity, one day old. In the interests of getting more immediate results to his readers, and with the backing of the *Daily News* management, Rice helped arrange for some of the more important games to be "detailed." Using telegraph wire hook-ups at the road ballparks, the *Daily News* sponsored bulletinlike accounts of the games while they were progressing. Crowds gathered at the Masonic Theater or at one of the two bowling alleys, both on North Cherry Street, or at the old Fish and Weil building on Summer Street. There, for a small fee, the fans were distant but seemingly firsthand witnesses to the fiery contests. Telegraph operators with a bit of a theatrical knack were recruited to relay the dot-by-dash accounts of the games, enabling the fans to imaginatively play them out. Perhaps to assist those with less imaginative skill, an artist was sometimes recruited to graphically and instantly depict various game-turning plays, rank umpire calls, and heroic actions. Occasionally youngsters were recruited to dramatically act out the play-by-play on a stage. Given the summer heat and humidity, electric fans were provided, along with plenty of ice water. Ladies were often admitted free. Even Sunday games were detailed for the locals.[36]

Sometimes, when Rice wasn't able to be with the team on the road, he would cover the game from one of the detailing sites. This made for an interesting narrative account in the next day's paper, as he was not only reporting the outcome of the game but also the animation of the operator and crowd—all in the absence of a real, live game before any of their eyes. In a game against New Orleans, "the stuff was on"—which meant the game would be detailed to a local crowd, on this occasion at the Masonic Theater. It was the Wanderers—as Rice called the Nashville team when on the road (they didn't have a nickname then)—versus the Pelicans of the city of dikes (New Orleans). More than three hundred people assembled to hear the contest detailed by Operator Atkinson. For eight innings the two teams traded scores. It was 3 to 3 in the ninth. Then the fireworks.

Nashville went down one, two, three in the top of the ninth. With the heavy part of the New Orleans line-up due to bat in the bottom of the ninth, Rice reported that the Masonic crowd grew restless. The first man up singled hard to left. A community groan could be heard; "The stuff's off now, boys," someone called out. The next hitter nailed one to Abbaticchio (the second baseman), said Atkinson. Before he could continue, the crowd in anticipation cheered variously, "He's out," "Double play," "Take him down." When the crowd quieted, Atkinson bent closely over his instrument, and "in a voice," says Rice, "as pathetic as if he were bidding his wife and children a last farewell," announced: "Abby fumbles." Groans from the crowd.

Part of the crowd got up to go; even though the next willow wielder (batter) sacrificed, men were on second and third with only one out. "Mullin up," ticked the instrument. "He hits a liner to right." Louder groans. Then, silence. Everyone waited for the instrument to continue its frantic ticking. After what seemed like an eternity, knowing in their hearts there was only one chance in a hundred of holding the man on third, the instrument started up again. "Holland makes a sensational catch . . . and the man on third stays there!"

shouted Atkinson. The fans went wild: "We'll win the game yet," some fan called out, and then he yelled again. Nashville got the last out. Three down. Extra innings.

The excitement built. Says Rice, "every play was listened to with breathless interest. Every tick meant a hit and a hit meant a run, and a run meant the game." No change in the tenth or eleventh. But in the twelfth, "Smiling George" Blackburn came to the bat. He had already tripled. And the crowd figured out, Rice reported, "that what a man has done a man can do." But he beat that by a block, as Rice went on, for Blackburn had figured that what a man can do he can do better. When the ticking stopped, Atkinson jumped clean over his table on the theater stage where he was sitting, screaming: "He hits it over the sewer for a home run!" What the crowd did then was "a plenty," according to Rice. The rooters turned loose in a wild celebration lasting more than five minutes. In the meantime, with few then paying attention to the caller, Nashville scored another run.

But the instrument kept ticking into the bottom of the twelfth. New Orleans tied it up while making "a desperate effort to win out," 5 to 5 in inning thirteen. Nashville at the bat. Fisher doubled deep to left. Holland bunted to Freeland who overthrew first, scoring Fisher, with Holland strolling to second. The fans were screaming. The ticking was barely audible with all the noise. Atkinson listened carefully, as the fans began to quiet down. Another hit! And another! And another wild throw! Nashville led 8 to 5. In their half of the thirteenth, the Pelicans rallied gamely, but to no avail, as "Smiling George" struck out the last batter with two men on base. When the ticking stopped, Bacchus-like celebrating began. The Nashvillians were the winners. Everybody at the Masonic went home happy.[37]

Losing none of his early-youth enthusiasm for fostering the cause of spirited play, Rice not only reported on baseball but also used his newspaper position to promote a larger scope for local and national sporting contests. At one point in the 1901 baseball season he stumped for a challenge championship series between the Western and the Southern Leagues, modeled after the proposed National and American League series. He thought the match-up would meet with local fan enthusiasm and would be a financial lift to the baseball managements. The idea didn't catch on. On another occasion, while the Nashville team was on the road and Athletic Park was vacant, Rice proposed that the local firemen meet the police in a rematch of a game played a year earlier that had been well attended in spite of there being no Nashville professional team and consequently little interest in baseball at the time. It too died for lack of a significant second. Failing these, he then suggested a baseball match between the married men and the single men on the green diamond, which Rice thought to be an interesting parody on the national game. This game was played, but there was some confusion as to who had won out, so at the conclusion of the game Umpire Robinson said that somebody ought to have won the game and therefore he gave it to both sides.[38]

Rice also tried to promote ceremonies around local baseball. After one of Nashville's successful road trips, Rice and the *Daily News* proposed to give the team a hero's welcome when they came home. Rice requested that his readers make financial contributions to put on a parade and a banquet to celebrate the team's winning ways. He asked for $150, half of which was to be donated by the time the team arrived home. The parade was to be led by the mayor and the board of public works, and was to include mounted police, plenty of prominent clergymen, a brass band, and two baseball teams, Nashville and its first home-game-in-awhile foes, Selma. After the ball game between these first- and last-place teams, an invitation-only banquet was to be held on the players' behalf at Glendale Park. The local ball club's athletic feat was clearly big news in his mind and called for some harmless hoopla.

Even though it rained on the planned morning parade, the game against Selma was played in the afternoon. Rice's first-ever front-page story appeared the next day. He covered the game and the banquet that did in fact follow the Nashville win. The story was headed "Baker Was An Easy Mark/Pounded Hard Over Park." The Rice-composed head was followed by Rice subheads, "Selma's Infield Is A Peach, but Nashville Now Is Out Of Reach—All of the Boys Go Out To Dine, and Some of Them Get Full of Wine." Without ever giving the final score of the game (it could be found in the box score—the first one to appear in the *Daily News*), Rice happily narrated Nashville's come-from-behind win, mostly from the fourth inning on.

About fifty people attended the banquet that evening: players from both teams, a number of prominent fans, businessmen, and politicians. The feasting table was decorated at first with flowers and ferns, and later with several potted players and guests, as the drink flowed as effusively as the toasts. Various speakers took their turns, giving short lectures ranging from the inane to the unintelligible. The first speaker, a superfan by the name of Alex Fite who was clad in a Spaulding's patent bust developer and a Tam O'Shanter, held forth on the subject of "the man with the bat." The core of his short treatise was that "The rising sun had bathed the west in purple, while Goodenough (Nashville's center fielder) leaned upon the bat." Bats, he went on, are very useful articles, especially in baseball. His rousing finish cited the well-known, but often overlooked fact that bats have saved many people's lives by not being swallowed. At this point Mr. Fite was overcome by emotion, and sat down amid plaudits.

Not to be outdone, and sensing that Fite had not given the whole truth in regard to the significance of baseball, a Mr. Garrabrandt rose to explain as best he could the meaning of the game itself. He asked his audience to put themselves in the place of the poor baseball that is hammered and beaten all over the lot. "Yes," he said, "mumble peg has slain its thousands, croquet its ten of thousands, but baseball"—here the speaker's voice sank trembling in his boots—"but baseball swept the land of its inhabitants and gathered them together each day at the confines of one park." Sensing perhaps that this explanation was not entirely convincing or even clear, Mr. Garrabrandt elected to close with a clarifying quotation he alleged was from Tennyson: "The boy stood on the umpire's neck, doing a song and dance; the crowd swarmed out upon the field, and tanned his baseball pants."

And so it went into the fun-filled evening. When the self-styled speechmakers finally exhausted themselves, Mr. Peters, the Selma manager, jumped on the banquet table and yelled, "Three whoops and a pretzel for Fisher" (the Nashville manager), which, Rice noted, were given with a will. At this point the lights went out.[39]

Nashville continued its winning ways throughout the season. As Rice became more comfortable in his role of baseball reporter, he began informally stretching his stories. He lengthened his accounts of the games and added additional commentary and notes about the regional pennant race, other team information, and generally interesting dope about the high quality of ball being played in the league. In this very first season as a sportswriter, Rice began comparing sports contests, such as baseball, to various historical, often warlike, heroic human struggles. The day after the homecoming banquet at Glendale Park, he reported on the next game between Selma and Nashville. Perhaps buoyed by the spirits of the previous evening, Rice tried to give his readers an idea of what this game was like (it was not settled until the top of the ninth when Selma got the only run of the game): "Did you ever hear of the battle of Gettysburg, Bull Run or Waterloo? Of how Napoleon crossed the Alps on a mule and Washington the Delaware on a piece of floating ice? Well, all these were mere skirmishes compared with the struggle that took place yesterday at Athletic Park."

Nothing of the sort took place at Sulphur Springs Bottom. What did take place was a good, tight ball game made low-scoring no doubt by the two clubs' collective hangovers: Bailey, the Selma pitcher, "handed up all sorts and his fast ones, slow ones and his gravity drop made Nashville's heavy hitters resemble a kindergarten with cramp colic." Only one player was thrown out of the game for arguing—low by the day's standards. All in all, and Rice's exaggeration notwithstanding, the game was rather ordinary, not a battle royal, and was over in one hour and fifteen minutes, witnessed by a mere five hundred fans. Hardly Napoleonic.[40]

By the last home stand of the season, Nashville was still in first place, but was being pushed hard by Little Rock. As a token of appreciation for the Nashville ball club's season-long work, at their last home appearance of the year all the members of the local team, including the highly thought of Umpire Johnstone who had fairly umpired a number of their games, were given camp stools that rolled up into small balls by Rev. Purdy, who, Rice noted, was colored.

Colored or otherwise, the local clergy were prominent, visible, and vocal supporters of the Nashville baseball organization. Gone were the days when baseball was one of the favorite targets of religious leaders for its tendency toward idleness and degeneracy; seemingly, the sport was now thought to be a potential source of civic pride and perhaps even a useful vehicle for improving the social substance, virtuous behavior, and moral character of spectator and player alike. A few days before the final home game at Athletic Park, six leading Nashville clergymen gathered at the field to publicly present Manager Fisher with a Bible. Although certainly not a ringing statement of overwhelming evangelical support, the Bible's inscription was indicative of the local religious community warming to the sport: "In recognition of the fact that your management of baseball this season in Nashville has been such that we could without hesitation attend and enjoy the games, we ask you to accept this present as a token of our appreciation of your service to the many who enjoy this interesting sport."[41]

With Nashville on the road for the last few weeks of the season, the pennant was suddenly in danger. In a crucial series in Little Rock, whose team was then only three games behind Nashville, passions rose and tempers flared. On September 16, without playing a single complete game, both Nashville and Little Rock each won and lost a game. In fact, only three pitches were thrown, but to a hitter-less plate. It seems that the two managers couldn't agree on who should umpire the game. Nashville's Manager Fisher claimed that Umpire Murray, Little Rock's choice of umpire, had been robbing the visiting teams at the Travelers' home park. Fisher requested that the Southern League president send Umpire Johnstone from Memphis, whom he (and Rice) thought to be the fairest in the league. Little Rock's Manager Finn wasn't happy with that alternative, as Johnstone had umpired an earlier series in Nashville; he, too, thought that their team had been robbed a time or two. Furthermore, Finn had heard (correctly) that in a recent game against the New Orleans Pelicans, the Nashville crowd was so taken by Johnstone's work on the field that they took up a collection for the umpire; Johnstone gratefully accepted the thirty-six dollars from the hat passing.

When the Nashville and Little Rock game was finally called, both umpires were on the field. Neither would give way to the other, and neither Fisher nor Finn would play without their man in charge. When a compromise was reached suggesting that both umpire, Johnstone, knowing he and he alone had been assigned the game from the league office, walked off the field, giving the game to Nashville, 9 to 0. Murray then called the game anyway, threw the ball to the Little Rock pitcher and instructed him to start pitching. After throwing three balls to his catcher, and since Nashville had not taken the field, Murray gave the game to Little Rock, 9 to 0.

The next day didn't help change the standings either. Umpire Johnstone was finally authorized again to call the game, which was played. Five thousand fans saw Little Rock go up by four in the fourth, but Nashville scored six in the fifth. Being a weekday, the game began around 3:30, a common starting time to help attract the middle-class audiences who often were able to finish their white-collar workday by 3:30 or 4:00. There was then ample time to get to the park, see a game, and still get home for supper. By the end of the ninth inning in this game, however, the two-hour-and-thirty-five-minute game produced a 7 to 7 tie. Umpire Johnstone was forced to end the game.

Grantland Rice didn't mind spunky baseball. He knew that each team was trying hard to play well and win, and that sometimes such single-minded efforts created hard feelings, disagreements, and emotional outbursts. But he seemed to instinctively know where to draw the line between acceptable and destructive behavior. Throughout the 1901 season, Rice would every so often gently remind his readers that playing and watching baseball should be reasonably civilized, for the sport—sport in general—was inherently capable of being a civilizing agent. He especially tried to soften the irresponsible knocking fans sometimes gave the ballplayers. All players have their bad days, he would say, and just because a player who in trying hard fumbles or strikes out is not justification enough to open up on him. Some of the balls that players muff and that are the rankest errors to the bleacherites, he would subtly instruct his audience, are often the hardest to handle safely. "Let a man come up and knock an easy, twisting grounder to a fielder that he has to handle quick for a fast man, and the crowd gets disgusted if he fumbles it." Rice, who could speak confidently from the standpoint of having been a player, cautioned his readers that those plays are twice as difficult to handle as a hard ball hit to one side or another. "This habit of knocking a man that is doing his best never did and never will do any good."[42] He gave some polite suggestions to the baseball fan:

> When you're sitting on the bleachers
>   and your yelpings rend the sky,
> As you watch the lissome base hit or the
>   long and twisting fly,
> Don't forget your parlor manners, do not
>   raise particular Ned,
> And don't saturate your neighbor with
>   the pop when it is red!
>
> If you see a head below you, pool-ball
>   like, devoid of hair,
> Don't hit it with your cushion—let it
>   roost in calmness there—
> And when evening comes in silence, and
>   the sun sinks in the West,
> Shake the peanut shells from off you, and
>   go home to well-earned rest.[43]

Given his steady ethical homilies, it is not surprising that Rice would get beside himself at the less-civilized baseball pyrotechnics when they occurred. Such happened in this last meeting with Little Rock, a scheduled doubleheader. Umpire Johnstone, in the previous day's game, had allowed Abbaticchio, the Nashville second baseman, to score late in the game to create, in the minds of the Little Rock fans, the tie. It was not forgotten the next day. When the umpire appeared on the field, an angry crowd murmur could be heard. Even at the outset of the first game it was clear that trouble was brewing: "The crowd was for Little Rock to win, no matter how," observed Rice. First, there was an argument over whether or not Bailey, a new left-hander acquired recently from Selma, could start the first game for Nashville. But Johnstone was able to produce a telegram from the latest league president, J. B. Nicklin, saying that the Blackburn-Bailey trade was within the Southern League rules. Bailey started.

Nashville scored two in their half of the first. Bailey was ushered to the mound in the bottom of the first with a loud chorus of boos and jeers. Crozier, Little Rock's left fielder, singled and stole second. Second baseman Martin singled. Crozier rounded third and started for home. According to

Rice, the throw was perfect, and Crozier was called out at home, clearly two feet short of the plate. Upset at being called out, Crozier then laid his hand on Johnstone's arm to get his attention. At the same moment, Wright, a Little Rock bench player, rushed onto the field, intoxicated somewhat with anger but mostly with liquor, and ran directly into Johnstone, knocking him down. The crowd then swarmed onto the field, as did the remaining Nashville players. Then the police joined in the fracas, there having been about thirty officers assigned to the game in anticipation of this kind of rowdiness. It took the combined efforts of the entire police deployment to save Johnstone from being mobbed and mauled.

When some degree of order had been restored, Umpire Johnstone was immediately arrested, but not before one of the policemen tried to kick him in the head; as Johnstone blocked the blow, the heavy boot landed directly on his wrist, creating instant swelling and temporary loss of the use of his fingers. Since Johnstone had been taken into custody, Fisher demanded that Wright should also be arrested. Done. Both men were taken directly to the calaboose. Johnstone was officially charged with inciting to riot.

Back at the park, Manager Finn of Little Rock promised to control the situation and said he could get Johnstone released if Nashville would continue to play out the game. Fisher was willing, but just then Little Rock's Mayor Duley stepped in, telling the scowling managers and the howling crowd that he could not in good conscience permit either Wright or Johnstone back on the field because of the temperament of the crowd and the possibility of further riotous behavior. The game was off.[44]

Preparations were made for Johnstone's bond. But when the bondsmen learned that a local mob was making plans to "get" Johnstone while on the train to Memphis that night, they backed out. And as the angry crowd had since then regrouped outside the jail and was threatening to lynch Johnstone, the hapless umpire was rearrested. Wright, meanwhile, had been pardoned by the governor, who also happened to be on hand that day along with the city's mayor to watch the important game. Johnstone later said that he had been warned not to come to Little Rock to umpire the series under the threat of being shot or killed—and this by the directors of the Little Rock club itself! "I have worked hard and conscientiously all season and given satisfaction to every club in the league," said Johnstone. There had not been one protest against his work, and in the course of the season he only had to fine one ballplayer and put only four out of games. "I try to do my work honestly and fairly," Johnstone continued, "and consider my treatment at Little Rock contemptible. I was submitted to almost every indignity possible while in that city, as everyone seemed to be in league to get me into trouble and jail at the earliest possible moment." In the end, Wright admitted to Johnstone that the entire affair and his own attack on the umpire was a put-up job by the Little Rock management to get Johnstone off the grounds.

Manager Fisher stayed over with Johnstone to help him get out of jail and on his way home to Memphis. He was eventually fined twenty-five dollars and released. Rice went on to Shreveport, their next foe, with the rest of the team. They left quickly, but not before the angry crowd hurled stones and other kinds of missiles at them as they tried to make it safely back to their hotel. Some of the rabid Little Rock fans got close enough to leave bite marks on the exposed flesh of a few of the Nashville players.

On the day of President McKinley's funeral, and while the entire nation bowed their heads in sorrow for their fallen chief, all baseball parks were deserted. In Shreveport, the Nashville players took the opportunity to rest up from the nightmare in Little Rock, glad, Rice reported, to once again be among human beings. They tended to their jagged bite wounds, and to their accumulated abrasions and cuts and, as Rice called their injuries, "battered pulses and punched slats." Not a man was without some physical badge of courage.[45]

Besides the wounds, the Nashville team had little else to show for their series with the Travelers. Of the four scheduled games, the first was never played, the second didn't count as it was tied when it was called off on account of darkness, and the double-header ended in the riot. The only game Nashville believed they won for sure was the first, as President Nicklin sustained Johnstone's decision to have Little Rock forfeit the game to Nashville 9 to 0 since Johnstone was the officially scheduled umpire for the game (this decision was later reversed). Nashville was still four games ahead of Little Rock with eight games to go. The issue of the most recent events in Little Rock and how the double-header would be scored was sent to the league office for deliberation. Rice thought the whole affair was the most disgraceful scene that had ever occurred on a Southern League field. Given such behavior, and from so many of the Little Rock citizens, the incensed Rice called for the team to be thrown out of the Southern League and the city blacklisted from all future participation in Southern sport. It wasn't.

After taking the first game from Shreveport, and staying four games ahead of Little Rock (who also won, beating Chattanooga), Nashville gave up a five-run lead in the ninth inning of the next game to lose. Little Rock took a double-header from Chattanooga, and closed in on Nashville, down only two games and 23 percentage points. Nashville won their next game, 13 to 1;

Little Rock was idle. Nashville finished the season at New Orleans, who they had embarrassed in their last meeting, winning three from the Pelicans at Nashville.

Nashville won their first game in New Orleans, but Little Rock also won, beating Birmingham. The next day, Nashville gave up a three-run lead, again in the ninth inning, as pennant pressure apparently began to get to Manager Fisher's team. A double-header was scheduled the next day, coincident with Little Rock playing two at Birmingham. The pennant was still in doubt, since if Little Rock won both of their games and Nashville lost both, the pennant race would end in a dead heat.

"Oh, what a bitter pill," wrote Rice the next day, September 26. The worst happened, at least as far as Nashville was concerned; Nashville lost two and Little Rock won two. President Nicklin announced that the 1901 Southern League pennant race, which had gone down to the last day of the season, had ended in a tie. He also said that the final determination of the league champion would be made by the board of arbitration when the resolution of the issue of that last series between Nashville and Little Rock would be settled—which he predicted would be mid-October!

Rice's response was predictable: play-off! "From every standpoint it is not only feasible but the most fitting end of a great race. Public opinion is evenly divided as to which has the stronger team. This would settle the matter once and for all." Rice's plan would have put the two teams in a neutral city, such as Memphis (certainly not a neutral state), to play the best of three games; or maybe a best-of-seven series, with three each in home parks, with the last game, if necessary, in Memphis. He argued that such a play-off, which would certainly be the greatest event that had ever occurred in Southern baseball, would not only settle the matter fairly, but would bring in large chunks of money to the managers. He reasoned that a similar experiment was successfully conducted a few years back to settle the National League title between Baltimore and Cleveland. Rice predicted that a Southern League play-off could draw upwards of twenty thousand to twenty-five thousand spectators. Best of all, the championship would not be decided in a council chamber weeks after the season was over on the basis of a forfeited game, but in the spirit of true sport, on the playing fields where such matters should be decided.

Even though the fans, Rice claimed, were screaming for a play-off, and Manager Fisher said in a telegram to Rice that he was willing to play Little Rock for the championship and for a side bet of one thousand dollars, Rice was unable to squeeze the baseball higher-ups into arranging a series between the two teams. The Little Rock team had already disbanded, Manager Finn explained. If President Nicklin ordered a series, Finn would find his team; but until that happened, he was bound to let his team go. No order to play ever arrived.

Instead, time passed. Two weeks, then three. About the pennant, Rice versified, "If we get it, it is tattered/Won by forfeit, leaves it shattered." While the college football season got underway, the Southern League fans more or less patiently awaited the outcome of their pennant race. Finally, on October 19, the board of directors met (this was also the arbitration board, and included managers Charlie Frank of Memphis, Will Hardin of Chattanooga, and Abner Powell of New Orleans, along with President Nicklin). Lobbyists and wire-pullers for each team crowded into the Stanton House in Chattanooga. All day long the board collected evidence, listened to arguments, and tried to make up their minds—all behind closed doors, and with the participants sworn to secrecy, behaviors not particularly endearing to newspaper reporters.

To make matters worse insofar as press relations were concerned, when Mr. Peters of Selma, and secretary to the board, released the official statistics (batting and fielding averages) to the press, he sold the right to publish these stats exclusively to a combine of several papers for ten dollars each, rather than giving them out to all of the papers simultaneously and for free. Allegedly the money was needed to defray the costs of putting the statistics together. Rice's paper had been excluded, presumably because they (he) refused to pay the fee. Rice was irked. Somehow, and without paying, he got the privileged information. He published the summaries on page one of the *Daily News* the next day, chastising Peters in the process.

As the press breathed down the board members' necks, and after much rag chewing, the arbitration body voted to give the 1901 Southern League baseball pennant to Nashville. The gist of their reasoning was that Nashville was to be given two forfeits for the riot game because Little Rock failed to provide Umpire Johnstone with proper police protection to enable him to umpire the double-header. The actual evidence and arguments were not to be made a matter of public record.

It was Rice's opinion that the two-day board meetings themselves were almost as riotous as the forfeited games they were awarding to Nashville. The meetings were so blatantly unresponsive to the interests of the public, Rice said, that if this was the best the Southern League administrative "hot air generators" could do, then baseball should take its departure from the South altogether. And if the Association was too financially strapped to pay for its own record compilation, then its financial base was too shaky to warrant further investment in it.

Rice knew full well that the Southern League was financially stronger than it had ever been, with every team save one making a sizable profit. New Orleans had a net profit of more than twenty thousand dollars; Little Rock, Nashville, and Memphis raked in ten thousand dollars over expenses. In his view, the baseball magnates were getting greedy. Rice lectured that "there is room for a baseball league in the South, so long as it is conducted on a fair plane, and with some regard to the patrons of the sport. But when managers who have grown fat on public patronage contemptuously ignore the right of the public to have the decisions vitally affecting the various teams, it lessens the enthusiasm and jeopardizes the very life of the league itself." It was a case of "everybody grab," according to Rice, with the baseball magnates becoming ludicrously "chesty and peevish" out of all proportion to the general significance of the game they are managing.

The agony of waiting was finally over, and at least the Nashville club came away with the pennant even if it was delayed by red tape. Hoarse cheers arose from the Nashville citizens, as Rice concluded his baseball season commentary, perhaps cynically: "We are the best . . . for the board has said so, and the board ought to know."[46]

5

Friends, Scoops, and Sputtering Death Boxes

One of the many people crossing Rice's wide and welcoming path before his short stint on the *Nashville Daily News* was the Sewanee (University of the South) football coach, Herman Suter. Rice had played against Suter's Tigers while at Vanderbilt during the seasons that Sewanee was dominating the Southern gridiron; for the three seasons prior to 1901, the Sewanee goal line was crossed only once. But Suter had since gone into journalism. He was editing a publication in Washington, D.C., called *Forestry and Irrigation Magazine*. Rice covered the Suter-less game in 1901 between the Vandies and the Tigers when the two schools struggled to a 0 to 0 tie, a moral victory for Sewanee, who had weakened considerably since Suter's departure. "Rah-Rah-Ree, Varsitee, Hey Hip, Hey-Hip, Sewanee," the Tiger students hurrahed later that night on the local mountaintop where their jolly bonfire flashed flames on the tall trunks of the aged trees.[1]

Suter had stayed in touch with Rice after his departure for Washington and had followed much of Rice's copy in the *Daily News* during the late summer and early fall months. Shortly after the game between the two Tennessee teams, Suter invited Rice to join his magazine staff. Since sports were winding down for the season, Rice once again surprised his friends and family by accepting the position. But in truth, the *Daily News* wasn't doing particularly well and Rice probably figured that his future there was bleak. He gave up his *News* position and followed Suter up north to write not about such things as the occasions for bonfire celebrations like Sewanee's, but about the kind of stuff such bonfires were made of—even though in Rice's own words he "didn't know a Christmas tree from a Northern Blue Horned Spruce."[2] But fate intervened: Rice's plans were rudely rearranged when an appendicitis attack struck the errant sportswriter down practically upon his arrival in Washington. He spent five weeks in the hospital before his mother came up from Nashville to take him back home. He never wrote a word on the subject of trees for *Forestry and Irrigation.*

After healing up in Nashville and returning briefly to the failing *Daily News,* Rice again took to the road for the sake of sports journalism. He landed his second sportswriting job in 1902 in the city of Atlanta. His salary was $12.50 a week; sober bakers could earn $18 to $20 a week. For his salary he was expected to get out the entire sports section for the daily *Atlanta Journal* and also to be the theater critic. The paper's circulation of thirty-eight thousand was more than twice that of the *Daily News,* although Atlanta's population was only slightly larger than Nashville's. But Atlanta was growing faster than the Tennessee city. Between 1890 and 1900 Nashville's population increased only 6 percent, while Atlanta grew by 75 percent, from a bit over sixty-five thousand to nearly ninety thousand.

Rice covered the entire range of Atlanta sports: baseball and football, as well as trotting, horse racing, golf, tennis, rifle shoots, bowling, indoor baseball, the field sports, cycling, handball, and even gymnasium demonstrations that included the "ground and lofty" tumbling, Indian club swinging, horizontal bar work, dumbbell exercises, and other gymnastic stunts. He also covered YMCA basketball and occasionally some college basketball for women.

These were still the days in which men were often discouraged from watching the women's basketball games; men would sometimes bring augers and bore small peepholes through the outside wall to catch a glimpse of their play; or even dress up as women and try to gain entrance to the gymnasium for a closer look-see. Nonetheless, whenever there was an invitation, Rice would check up on the girls' version of the sport, which, he noted, was sometimes as rambunctious as men's football. In one women's game, "the girls struck each other in the face, pulled hair, tripped and threw one another to the floor and lost all control of themselves . . . the girls were oblivious to all else and they reached at each other with true ferocity."[3]

Another young journalist, two years older than Rice, arrived in Atlanta at about the same time. His name was Don Marquis. Marquis was later to become the highly regarded humorist and columnist for the *New York Sun* and later for the *New York Tribune,* and a successful playwright. He was also to become one of the first of Rice's lifelong journalism cronies. The Rice-Marquis friendship was typical of the way in which Rice's natural gregariousness and unpretentious manner attracted and held companions, whether writers, athletes, coaches, or people from worlds other than Rice's own. "For friends are all that a little earth/Has yet to give that has any worth," Rice observed.4

Marquis's route to the hospitable and entertaining town of Atlanta and to a journalism career was a good deal more circuitous than Rice's: born in Walnut, Illinois; grocery wagon driver in Chicago; drug clerk, clothing store helper, chicken plucker, cook in a bakery, sewing-machine agent—all in Walnut; railroad track straightener west of Chicago; near-hobo; country schoolteacher—with no advanced education, but with self-styled book learning causing the man who hired him to decide that he had been born educated; a stab at formal education, a few months, at what he later called his "alma stepmater," Knox College at Galesburg, Illinois; printer for a country weekly; Census Bureau clerk in Washington, D.C.; art student at the Cocoran Art School; and copy desk work for newspapers in Washington and Philadelphia.5

But in Atlanta Marquis landed a real newspaper job, first with the *Atlanta News*, then sometime later as an editorial writer for the *Atlanta Journal*. It was still short of his goal of eventually becoming a daily columnist, but the Atlanta job was certainly a step up. Marquis was introduced to Rice almost immediately after his arrival in the city and the two became instant friends, according to Marquis's biographer, gravitating toward each other as if they were obeying a natural law; and, quite naturally, they roomed together. Even though Rice had only arrived in Atlanta a short while before Marquis, it seemed to Marquis that Rice had been there for years as he knew almost everybody in town.

Rice took it upon himself to introduce Marquis around, including arranging meetings between Marquis and local journalistic legends whom Rice had already met, such as Joel Chandler Harris ("Uncle Remus") and the poet and columnist Frank Stanton, two cornerstones for the *Atlanta Constitution*. Like Marquis, Stanton, who was considered by many to be the James Whitcomb Riley of the South, had been at one time a printer on a country weekly. The two got on well, swapping poet stories, both remembering days when, as printers and practicing poets, they would set the type for their poems directly and without putting them on paper first. Marquis called this bit of tricky typography the "Tripe-to-Type-in-One-Operation School of Poetry."6

These three—Stanton, Marquis, and Rice—were quite an institution in early Atlanta journalism. Rice and Marquis were both still single. Stanton, older and more settled than the other two, was married. For three dollars a week, the "two demon reporters," as Rice referred to himself and Marquis, shared a flat at the Aragon Hotel. Once they tried to live on ten cents a day, which was the exact price of a sizable piece of mince pie they shared for breakfast. Rice remarked that it was guaranteed to cause an acute case of twenty-four-hour indigestion for two.[7]

The three hung out at the bar of the Aragon. Stanton would often have to be extricated from his home, occasionally by some clever trick devised by the other two. Once gathered, and from their first swallow, their poetic juices flowed together profusely and just about in proportion to the amount of Randolph Rose's corn whiskey they were throwing down. None of them had much money, and when it would run out, Stanton would sometimes offer to "write a poem for thee" in exchange for three fingers. Stanton, Rice remembered, turned out more classic lines for bartenders—usually written on wrapping or butcher's paper—than most mortals have set down for publishers.

The poets would kid each other unmercifully. Rice knew that Marquis had no formal schooling beyond the age of fifteen (except for the few months at Knox) and that Stanton was largely self-educated. Stanton was born in 1857 and his formal education was interrupted by the Civil War; after the war his learning was in private and without a teacher. In a mock grave tone that was so natural for Rice to take up, he would not-so-subtly remind them both of his highfalutin Vanderbilt degree and offer to tutor them for a fee. If not that, then he certainly thought they should attend night school on the side until they earned a proper degree. He invited them to hereafter refer to him as Professor Rice, urging them to tend to their degree-getting as soon as possible because he wasn't sure what was happening to his Atlanta social standing when he was found so frequently in the company of such an unlettered pair. It didn't take much to counter Rice's low blows. The two would quietly remind him of the remarkably low social status and income level he had so deservedly achieved by way of the sportswriting career his formal education had prepared him for.

Rice respected both men and their talents greatly. His two friends were widely read and had voluntarily learned well beyond what formal institutions could ever have induced by way of requirements or examinations. Marquis, for example, read out of the library of his father, a doctor, hundreds to maybe even thousands of books—Darwin, Shakespeare, Herbert Spenser, and most all of the poets. Then and later, Marquis often commented on the generally low level of literacy among college people: "They seem to have read so very little, except along a few special lines, and this is true of a good many of them who have degrees of one sort or another. They are not really educated, in any broad sense, many of them."[8]

Often the perpetual kidding between the three resulted in poetic comment. Marquis got into a name war with Rice. He knew that Rice wasn't too pleased with his first name, Henry, and that he was trying to avoid using it, going so far as to drop the initial, H. Naturally, Marquis called him Henry, or Old Aitch. Rice retaliated by calling his friend Donald, one of Marquis's nonpreferred names (his full name was Donald Robert Perry Marquis). Eventually the two of them agreed to stop taunting each other, but Stanton would have nothing of it. He urged Marquis to reconsider his decision to drop the "H." in Rice's name, claiming that "the crash of a dropping 'aitch' always got on his nerves." He then let a whiskey glass in his hand tumble to the floor to illustrate his concern, saying "See what I mean?" Stanton then took up pen and some nearby wrapping paper and wrote a ballad on the subject, including the following couplet:

> The jarring sound of a falling "aitch" as it hits the
>   barroom floor
> Is worse on the nerves than a thunderous belch or a
>   shrill falsetto snore.9

When Rice wasn't on the road covering the Atlanta Southern League baseball club or the fortunes of Georgia football, he and Marquis kept regular company. Rice was forever getting people into things; sometimes, he thought, for their own good, sometimes, always in a good-natured way, for his. Marquis learned this quickly. As the designated theater critic for the *Atlanta Journal*—his enthusiasm for the assignment was about as high as it had been for covering the produce market in Nashville—Rice would drag Marquis to opening night after opening night. The Northerners were sending the best of New York's Broadway on tour for one-night stands throughout the South. The likes of such actors as John Drew, Richard Mansfield, and the Barrymores were all doing their bit to improve the culture of the South. Even though Marquis was then writing for the rival *News*, Rice convinced Marquis to be an apprentice (and ghost) theater critic for the *Journal*, probably joshing him into doing it on the grounds that he should be seen publicly at some kind of culture-producing event to show that he was sincerely striving to join the world of the lettered.

They shared many of the theater experiences, but only one of them would write the review, often Marquis. In his autobiography Rice wrote later that "I can't tell you how many nights a young writer from Indiana—a squat, heavyset former athlete from DePauw University named Don Marquis—and I had two-on-the-aisle as theater critics for the old *Journal*." Rice got his states and his universities a bit mixed up; he also forgot to mention that he was the only paid *Journal* theater critic of the two.[10]

Later, in 1922 when Marquis's "The Old Soak" turned out to be a successful comedy hit on Broadway, in a newspaper interview he gave credit to Grantland Rice for getting him interested in the theater. The offhanded comment implied that Rice was a voluntary theatergoer and, since he invited Marquis to join him regularly, that Rice's enthusiasm for the stage rubbed off on this successful journalist-turned-playwright. No doubt Marquis was having fun with the interviewer, for Professor Rice was giving little in the way of learned theater tutorials, and instead a good lesson in how to creatively dodge an assignment. The irony is that while Rice was earning part of his $12.50 a week with Marquis's free help, Marquis was eventually paid in full for whatever he learned in the company of Rice. The Prohibition-inspired character "The Old Soak" netted Marquis $85,000 (some say more than $100,000 for the 423 performances) even before it was later turned into a book and made into both a silent and a sound film.[11]

Each fall the pair would give up some of their afternoons to help coach football at Georgia Military Academy, about twenty miles south of Atlanta. No doubt Rice got Marquis into this one too, for even though Rice characterized Marquis as a squat, heavyset former athlete, he was only squat and heavyset. Or, at the most, Marquis did not make much of an impact on the sporting world in his three-month stay at Knox College. "I never got any farther than an assistant substitute tackle on the second team," wrote Marquis. He explained that his insatiable appetite for food and his being frequently massacred on the football field led to his downfall at Knox. He used to go to the three-cent restaurant, he said, and consume twenty-seven cents' worth of food at one meal. And on the scrub team he was tackled in practice by two real athletes at the same time, doing something to his leg that produced both a permanent ridge across the leg and the end of his short football career.[12]

As a friend, Rice's personality was perpetually upbeat even and especially when those near him were down. When Marquis first arrived in Atlanta, he was disappointed that he was not given the chance to write a humorous column, and instead was expected to write mostly editorials. With his friend weighted down with self-doubt, Rice urged Marquis to stick to his original objective and keep writing the humor pieces even if they were not then to be published. Rice also told him that Atlanta was probably not the place to create such a column since everybody was in the habit of reading the sentiments of Stanton in the *Constitution*. And given Marquis's tongue-in-cheek, even ribald style, some readers might get the idea that this upstart columnist was mocking the revered Stanton. Marquis took this advice, kept writing, and when his big break came in 1910 in New York, he was ready. He finally landed his own column, "The Sun Dial," giving him the opportunity to use his creative wit to produce much Atlanta-born commentary, satire, fable, and sketches; and he quickly developed the amusing characters he became famous for, such as archy the cockroach and mehitabel the alley cat whose names began with lower case letters because neither of the two could hold down the shift key on the typewriter at the same time they struck the letter keys, especially archie who wrote at night, while his boss was gone, by jumping from key to key.[13]

Marquis said he needed someone like Rice then to tell him he had the goods to make it. "To know Grant Rice," Marquis often said, "is to like him." So much so that while Marquis was with Rice in Atlanta, in mock-seriousness he tried to persuade Rice to run for political office, figuring that with his essential likability and sincere manner he couldn't miss. Marquis offered to be his campaign manager and promised to see to it that Georgia politics send the sportswriter to the governor's mansion. Since the state newspapermen regularly whined that there weren't enough good political stories in the town, Marquis thought the campaign could be spiced up if Rice ran on the platform that he would, if elected, disqualify for state jobs all who were neither athletes or former athletes. That, Marquis theorized, would give both the political and the sports reporters something interesting to write about. Rice told him he would think it over.[14]

Without question baseball was big news during the years Rice spent in Atlanta, during the season and also through the popular "hot-stove" league played in the newspapers throughout the winter months, where spring prospects, trades, and other related dope was tossed around. Baseball salaries were beginning to take the major league ballplayers out of the ranks of the indigent, and this was a frequent hot-stove subject.

Outfielder Willie Keeler, for instance, jumped from the Brooklyn National League team to the New York American League club in 1903, improving his salary to ten thousand dollars. His six-month season figure was only six hundred dollars short of the combined seasonal salaries for the entire ten-man roster of the old Cincinnati Reds who played through the 1869 season without a loss. The Reds, the first professional team, paid their three stars—Harry Wright, George Wright, and Asa Brainerd—fifteen hundred dollars each. In the 1903 season the highest paid players (including John McGraw, Napoleon

Lajoie, Ed Delehanty, Cy Young, and Rube Waddell) had salaries that were nearly ten times the combined total of the ten Cincinnati players thirty-four years earlier. These richer baseball salaries exceeded the earnings of most state governors and legislators, causing Rice to comment prophetically that the way things were going, "the time will come soon when the more select of the diamond circle will receive stipends for a season's work that will rival the salaries of railroad presidents or even the president of this great commonwealth."[15]

Rice was designated as the official scorer for the Atlanta Southern League ball club, the former Selma team, now coached by Abner Powell. He was also an unofficial scout for the club—there were no official scouts. Given that he was one of the most knowledgeable and best-known of the local sportswriting cheerleaders, he was often a conduit for tips passed Atlanta's way. On one occasion, on the basis of one such tip, Rice got Powell to sign a fast-baller by the name of Harry Hale, a giant right-hander (by the standards of the day) built like a tuning fork at six foot six and about 150 pounds. On March 27, 1903, Rice announced in a captioned picture of the new recruit that Harry Hale "will be given a thorough trial by Manager Ab." Hale's spring training debut a couple of days later was against Manager Griffith's New York Americans (later, the Yankees). Hale went six innings, giving up six runs. Rice went wild about Harry: "It wasn't Harry's fault that 6 runs were scored. Outside of a few raspy bingles in the first three innings . . . the heavy hitters from Gotham were powerless before the fuzzy foolers of the bean pole twirler. Hale put in a busy day on the slab and won the plaudits of the multitude. Fanatics who wish to cheer Mr. Hale for his deeds of valor should write their remarks on a card and ship it out to the twirler by a bell boy."[16]

On April 5, the day after Harry's next appearance against New York, another photograph of him appeared, this time nicknaming him "Happy Harry" Hale. He did poorly, as one of five pitchers necessary to survive Griffith's team and slugger Willie Keeler's lively bat. In his next appearances, he allowed the Cincinnati Reds no hits in two innings, then two hits in three innings, then, against the Milwaukee Brewers, after Atlanta was already down 7 to 0, he finished the last three innings without giving up a hit. This made Hale's one-week exhibition totals eight innings pitched, only two hits given up. Rice crowed: "The Happy Hollow phenom is fast developing into something of a wonder. . . . This is making good with a vengeance. If Happy can only retain this stride Rube Waddell (the famous Philadelphia pitcher) will be jarred from his pedestal."[17]

When Harry, or for that matter any of the other Atlanta pitchers, weren't on the mound, they were usually assigned to man the turnstiles at Piedmont Park. The wooden park had been refurbished that year, increasing the turnstiles from one to three. The fans entered the park first through two gates, one for the grandstand cranks and one for the sun-kissed bleacher bums. The grandstand extended from beyond first base all the way around to within twenty feet of third. The bleachers extended from there out and beyond third base. The grandstand seats were widened and improved. Box seats were added, built in a second-level tier under the roof of the park. The bleacher seats were smoothed out with chisels and sandpaper. The bleacherites entered at the first gate, and wound their way down a grassy pathway to the box office, located just within the grounds, then through one of the turnstiles. The grandstand people entered about forty feet farther down.

Just within the tall wall that separated the outer world from the park below was an up-to-date "refreshment laboratory." Cooling pop and tinted lemonade was dispensed there, an addition to the routine of using youngsters who wended their way in and out of the stands and bleachers and in shrill-voiced yells peddled the refreshments. The most popular soda was Coca-Cola; Atlanta was (and still is) the headquarters for the popular and by then already famous drink. Just beyond the soda stand was a private sanctum where the gate money was stored in two strongboxes made of pure Carnegie steel. Next to this, and to the right of the stairway leading to the grandstands, Abner Powell built a "ladies waiting room." Lace curtains covered the windows, and besides two mahogany tables and a dresser, there were placed a dozen assorted mirrors. To the right of the grandstand, a players' dressing room was erected, complete with stalls.

The inside walls of the park were repainted, sprayed a beautiful blue-bottle green, while gallons of white lime soused the outside of the fences. Against the inside of the right field fence a large scoreboard was painted directly on the fence. Dazzling white numbers and letters were hung up to display the runs and outs, and the line-ups and batteries for each game. The new Piedmont Park also added another new feature: a press box. It was located on ground level, directly behind home plate, under the eight-sectioned double-decked grandstand. It looked like a World War II machine-gun bunker set into a hillside, with two side-by-side windowless openings maybe three feet high by five to six feet wide and a dirt floor. The box measured about twelve feet wide and six feet deep, enough room for two to four reporters. This was a significant step up for Rice and the other sportswriters who had until now covered the Atlanta games from a press stand. The press stand had been merely a designated area in the grandstand where the press was allowed to sit together, yet in the open and adjacent to the grandstand rooters who completely surrounded them.[18]

It was from this new press box at Piedmont Park that Rice watched Happy Harry's fall. On a chilly April 15 day, Harry Hale faced St. Paul from the American Association. As the starter, he gave up seven hits and seven runs in two innings. Rice alibied: "When the sad news hit Happy Hollow [Hale's home, in Tennessee] the citizens crept into hiding and the town put on a mourning aspect. No one can blame Harry for his work. The weather was cold enough to freeze a gangplank to a Boston wharf, and the high rate of speed which usually characterizes Happy's delivery was missing."[19]

The next mention of Harry was that he gave up seven hits in an intrasquad game a few days before the opening of the regular season. Then, and finally, he appeared in the second game of the regular season against Montgomery. He pitched four innings, gave up three hits, walked five, and committed a couple of errors to boot. It turned out that opposing teams eventually discovered that the lanky fireballer was so slow and awkward coming off the mound to field his position that all they had to do was bunt for base hits. Even if he got to the ball in time, he couldn't make the play because, lanky arms over spindly legs, he would crash to the ground trying to pick up the ball. Against Montgomery he finally spiked his own hand. That was the end of Happy Harry Hale and sportswriter Rice's first big discovery.

In his story of Happy Harry's release, Rice gingerly noted that Hale was "sufficient pumpkins in the box so far as throwing the ball was concerned, but the lengthy twirler was unable to field his position with the ease and grace required in these latter days and times when the bunt is so in vogue." Rice reluctantly reported Abner Powell's more extended critique of Hale's baseball skills: Harry couldn't handle a bunt or scoop a grounder without hurting himself; neither could he hit or run the bases. "Why, he would have to pitch a no hit game in order to win, as he don't know how to watch the bases." Sadly, Rice reported that Harry was leaving Tennessee forthwith, and that his little Tennessee village, "once standing a fair chance to loom up and get on the map, will now drop back into the dim obscurity from which Happy rescued it for three short, but delicious weeks." He gave Harry one final boost, noting that he made a lot of friends in Atlanta and that he was one of the hardest workers and most conscientious of pitchers. "As soon as he gets to the knack of fielding his position he will make somebody a valuable slab man." That was the last anybody in baseball ever heard of Happy Harry Hale.[20]

Although it probably should have, Harry's fate didn't discourage Rice from scouting other ballplayers. During the winter months before the next season Rice ran across a story from Shreveport about an eccentric pitcher who had made a bet that he could win a double-header after downing two bottles of whiskey and devouring a whole turkey. Rice didn't believe the story, but thought that the pitcher had color and spunk and persuaded Powell to buy him up. His name was "Bugs" Raymond.

"Bugs" reported to Atlanta that spring. Before going to Piedmont Park to cover and score an early exhibition game, Rice happened to be standing at the Aragon Hotel bar having a drink and a free lunch (sandwiches were often served free to those who bought drinks). Raymond came up behind him, slapped him on the back and said, "What about a drink?" Rice recognized the twenty-two-year-old, welcomed him to Atlanta, and bought him a drink. Bugs asked for another.

"I thought you were pitching today," Rice gently reminded him, beginning now to believe that the Shreveport story might actually have been true.

"I am," he retorted. "What of it?"

"Do you know what team you are pitching against? Rice asked him.

"No," he replied, "and I don't care."

"It's only the Red Sox . . . from Boston," Rice said. "Champions of the world. You recall, perhaps, they beat Pittsburgh last fall. It's an important exhibition game—for Atlanta."

Bugs wasn't interested in Rice's friendly warnings, and instead asked him how to get to the ball park. Rice was walking. "It's only two miles," he told Bugs. They walked to the park together, neither Rice nor Bugs having the nickel trolley fare at the time. All the way to the park Bugs threw rocks: at birds, at telegraph poles, at stray animals. Rice said Bugs must have pitched practically a complete game before he got to the ball park.[21]

Once in his new Atlanta uniform and on the mound—no telling how many drinks under his belt from visits to bars before he found Rice at the Aragon—Raymond began taunting the Boston club, especially their star third baseman and manager Jimmy Collins. By the third inning he had the Red Sox raving mad. Combining a marvelous spitball with his constant needling, he managed to beat the angry Boston club 3 to 0, striking out 12 men, and giving up only three scattered hits. Bugs went on to create quite a zany major league reputation for himself as one of McGraw's Giants. It almost seemed that the more he drank the better he pitched; about his famous spitter it was said that he didn't actually spit on it: he just exhaled all over it and the ball would come up drunk. In time, however, the New York manager finally got fed up with his mostly alcohol-produced antics and kicked him off the team in 1911. He died a year later.[22]

The same year that Bugs Raymond came to Atlanta, Rice got a fortuitous tip about yet another ballplayer. About mid-March Rice and his fellow reporters were in the middle of their regular poker game in the "local room" of the *Atlanta Journal*, waiting for the signal for quitting time, the rolling of the presses. At about 2 P.M. a messenger boy raced in with a late telegram for the sporting page, which had been put to bed about two hours earlier. The hundred-word special—sent by wire at the usual rates—announced that a young phenom who had played the previous year in Royston, Georgia, named Tyrus Cobb, was practicing daily at the bat, preparing himself to take his place as a member of the Augusta Club of the South Atlantic League for the 1904 season.

After the local room shook with belly-laughter at the idea that any correspondent would pay telegraph rates to send such a silly piece of non-news, the telegram was crumpled up and tossed in the waste basket. Rice did, however, briefly respond to the telegram-sender, saying that in the future the ordinary mails would be fast enough to relay information about Cobb or any other farmer making a debut in the Grass Cutter's Circuit.

But for the duration of the spring, Rice was deluged with letters and postcards about Cobb's remarkable hitting, his base stealing, and his overall baseball savvy and skill. Cobb started with Augusta, then was shipped off to Anniston, Alabama (Southeastern League), and finally called back to Augusta when that club came under new management. From all points of both baseball circuits, Rice received the enthusiastic pronouncements: "Keep your eye on Tyrus Cobb." "Watch Cobb of Anniston. He's sure to be a sensation." "Have you seen Cobb play ball yet? He is the fastest mover I've seen in baseball." These messages and many more like them were signed variously, Brown, Jackson, Holmes, Smith.

Eventually curiosity got the better of Rice. He wrote the kid up sight unseen, but then went over to Augusta to see firsthand what he had been hearing so much about. The five-foot-eleven, 155-pound eighteen-year-old met Rice in the dugout.

"I've been hearing about you," Rice said. "My name is Rice. I write baseball for the *Journal*."

"Is that so?" Cobb replied. "I've heard of you too." The only paper around the Cobb home had been the *Atlanta Journal* and Tyrus had taken to reading Rice's copy regularly.[23]

A little more than a year later, Rice's discovery was playing in the majors for Detroit in the American League. A few years after that, Rice recalled the first telegram he had received about the youngster who would eventually hit safely 4,191 times, steal 892 bases—including 96 during the 1915 season—lead the American League in batting for twelve out of thirteen consecutive seasons, and have a batting average of .367 for his twenty-four major-league seasons. "If we remembered that correspondent's name today," he wrote, "we would offer him a deep and abject apology for the call-down." Rice added—this was in 1910—that whether the correspondent had a psychological hunch or whatever it was, that telegram would have been the prize souvenir of the era for it marked the first public announcement of the opening appearance of one of baseball's all-time legends. The Royston Special was definitely a joke at the time, admitted Rice, but it certainly wasn't a joke on the correspondent who sent the telegram.[24]

In the end, however, the joke happened to be on Rice himself. More than forty years after the date of that telegram, Ty Cobb drove out to the San Francisco airport to pick up Rice, along with Rice's writer-friends Gene Fowler and Henry McLemore, who were paying the retired ballplayer a visit at his home in Menlo Park. On the way to the Cobb home, Ty chatted with Rice and friends about the old days. Eventually, Ty asked Rice if he remembered the telegram from 1904 about the Royston standout.

"I sure do, Ty," replied Rice.

"And do you remember a flock of postcards from all over Alabama and Georgia, telling you what a hot shot I was . . . all with different names?"

"I certainly do . . . why?"

"Well, I sent you the wire and all those notices," laughed Cobb. Rice, who was stunned, took the joke pretty well.

"It's taken you a few years to get around to telling me," Rice finally said. "Why did you do it?"

"Because I was in a hurry," replied Cobb. "We were both youngsters on the way up. I didn't know it then but I was trying to put you onto your first big scoop!"[25]

Which it was.

But there was another sport in Atlanta during Rice's stay there that attracted much local attention and quite a bit of Rice's time and copy. It was cycling. Amateur and professional bicycle racing was big in Atlanta. Chiefly because of the fame of one local rider, professional bicycle racing regularly outdrew professional baseball. Even the amateur races, which usually preceded the pros on the same evening card, were enthusiastically followed by the Atlantans. Rice was up to his hip sprockets in promoting and covering these cycling contests.

As major improvements were made in the quality of bicycles, recreational riding made a strong comeback from the more popular days of wheeling in the 1890s (in 1890 there were about 150,000 bicycling enthusiasts, and by 1893 some estimates put the number of recreational riders at close to a million). In Atlanta, in 1898 when recreational bicycling was still the vogue, there was only one place to take a good ride. This was College Park. But to reach it the riders had to bounce, jiggle, and vibrate their way over rough cobblestones through the West End. By 1903 in Atlanta there were many miles of good riding courses available, including one twenty-mile straight-away ride over asphalt and chert roads. Smoother roads, combined with such bicycle-comfort improvements as the cushion-framed "Pullman Palace," complete with coaster brakes, took most of the legendary jolts and jars out of everyday cycling and helped its popularity soar.[26]

Rice's newspaper was instrumental in promoting amateur competition throughout Atlanta and the surrounding, smaller towns by not only covering the amateur contests but also arranging for regular newspaper-sponsored road races. The year before Rice joined the *Journal* staff, the newspaper successfully staged its first Fourth of July sixteen-mile race. It was an unqualified success, which encouraged the paper to make the amateur competition an annual affair.

The "great second annual road race" for amateurs only—this time a handicapped race of twelve miles—was promoted for weeks prior to the event in 1902. Much hype preceded the race, planned again for the Fourth of July and scheduled to fit in with other Atlanta celebrations, including a sham Revolutionary War battle, a parade, and a ball game. The paper had originally predicted that more than fifty riders would enter the race, both local and statewide, including two well-known riders from Florida. The big amateur race would be preceded by a messengers' race between the Postal and the Western Union boys. For the amateur race a gold medal was to be awarded, along with a new "bicycle wheel of the best make" (meaning a new bike, not just a wheel), and other valuable prizes.[27]

By two days before the race, a number of hopefuls had dropped out because of the fast times recorded in practice runs over the course; most of the accomplished riders peddled the six-mile-up and six-mile-back course in around thirty-four minutes. The field was eventually reduced to sixteen racers, including the best amateurs that Atlanta and the neighboring towns could put up. No Floridians entered. Each rider was handicapped on the basis of previous times, ranging from Gaston Matthews, the slowest of the bunch who was given a five-minute head start, to several other local riders who rode from scratch with no handicap time.

At exactly five minutes past three, the first rider, Gaston Matthews, was sent on his way. As he left the starting tape, the four thousand spectators who had gathered to see the exciting race roared out in unison, "After you, my dear Gaston!" After five minutes had elapsed, the other fifteen riders had been given their starts, all in hot pursuit of their dear Gaston. The race was close, highlighted by a couple of rough tumbles; one rider, Ralph Magruder, who had won the race the previous year, fell in a heap and badly bruised his arm and somehow or other tore most of his clothes off, but delighted the crowd as he gamely remounted his silent steed and peddled half-naked to the finish line, taking eighth place. Although several riders pushed themselves faster than Gaston that day, no one caught up to his five-minute head start, and Gaston Matthews crossed the finish line first, winning a Dayton special bicycle for his front-running ride. The booby prize given to the last placed rider, Ike Hirschfield, was offered by Fred Lang of the Royal Barber Shop: a singe (shave), haircut, shine, shampoo, bath, and massage.[28]

Atlanta was a Southern hot spot for the professional versions of the two-wheeled sport. Much like the Madison Square Garden variety, six-day races were especially popular in Atlanta. In one of these races, a two-hour-per-night contest, eight teams, each composed of a sprinter and a plugger (endurance rider), faced off in front of several thousand spectators in the local, lighted indoor coliseum for a prize of about four thousand dollars (not including private purses of about one hundred dollars offered each night if one team could lap another). Rice showed up at the races each night. After five nights the teams were all on mile 244. The sixth night was memorable. "Of all the wild, woozy, weird and wonderful scenes ever enacted within the four walls of the coliseum," wrote Rice the next day, "the finish of the six-day race last night was the most remarkable on record." After dragging into his account of the festivities his stock references comparing the cycling contest to the various historic battles such as Bull Run, Bunker Hill, and Gettysburg (which, as it turned out, wasn't so far-fetched), Rice described the sporting evening.

Going into the final dash, and with all of the teams in close contention for the win, the leader, Jimmy Moran, was being chased from behind by John Bedell, who in turn was closely followed by the rest of the riders. With just three laps to go, and as Bedell started his sprint, he approached "accident corner" on the banked track (the site of many previous crashes) when his wheel suddenly veered to the right. The rider directly behind Bedell, Billy Fenn, hit Bedell broadside, whirling both riders into the air. Together they landed with a sickening crash on the middle of the track. All of the trailing riders plowed into the prostrate forms, while Moran, still ahead of the pack, rode around the pile-up on the last two laps and on to victory, the only cyclist of the bunch still upright.

All the riders were badly banged up, with Bedell and Fenn getting the worst of it. Bedell had a three-inch gash in his head and bicycle spoke plunged three inches through his thigh. Fenn found a six-inch splinter from the wooden track stuck in his thigh, just above the knee. But besides the injuries, there were a number of unhappy cyclists, at least four teams crying "foul" to the judges. Amid the groaning and whining, George Leander, who was in third place at the time of the crash, went after Bedell, claiming that "John Bedell did it. Yes, Bedell was the one that threw us!" The crowd hissed the bad sport, Leander. Leander then threw a punch at Bedell, which John gamely side-stepped, even with the spoke in his leg. John then turned and limped directly toward his tent. (A resting tent was given to each rider, with a cot and often the services of a "rubber" who gave massages in between their tours on the track.) And, as the Bedell cycle team had done the previous five evenings, John stepped into the tent, and tagged his big brother, Amos. Amos Bedell calmly strode out of the tent and flattened Leander in a two-round go, with a right to the jaw followed by two body blows.

Both Amos Bedell and Leander (when he came to) were arrested by Officer Martin, the on-duty police officer at the races. But by then the other riders were all taking funny punches at each other. The spectators, meanwhile, began to get into the spirit of the thing, and quickly swarmed over the railings, yelling, shouting, and throwing up clouds of dust, as they romped up and down trying to observe the melee up close. It was at this point, noted Rice, who was at rink side in the middle of the fracas, that a remarkable, inspiring scene took place. While the noise and rioting was at its peak, the local band, which was always on hand at such events, struck up "Dixie." Over the "tumult and the shouting, the wild confusion and racket," wrote Rice, "the strains of the old southern war song swelled and reverberated throughout the building. As the magnetic and well beloved strains of the martial air swelled out upon the scene for one brief instant the shouting was hushed and then followed such a wild cheering and enthusiasm as was never heard." And then all the people left.[29]

In police court a couple of days later, charges of disorderly conduct were brought against George Leander and Amos Bedell. Judge Broyles fined Leander $15.75 and Bedell $5.75. Leander's defense for his behavior was that he was so full of dope—real dope, not the journalistic variety—that he was not responsible for his actions, either on the track or in the arena after the race. He claimed he had no idea what he had done. But what irked the judge and caused Leander's heavier fine wasn't what went into Leander's mouth before the race, but what came out of it afterward: "If I had thought the language which Leander used," said the stern judge, "could have been heard by the ladies in the audience, I would assuredly have sent him to the stockade without the privilege of paying a fine. Such outbursts of rowdyism will not be tolerated in Atlanta for an instant, and races shall not break up into free-for-all fights."[30]

Speed dazzles. Such inventions as the typewriter and high-speed printing presses, for instance, dazzled everyone because they increased the rate at which words and ideas could be passed on. Similarly, race promoters were able to dazzle spectators by offering progressively faster races, as technological inventions made them possible: the foot gave way to the skate, the skate to the bicycle wheel, the wheel to the motorized bicycle, the motorcycle to the automobile—all in the space of about twenty years. When the motorized bicycle appeared, some of the crack professional bicyclists took up the new sport. Others, however, stuck to bicycle racing, but with a motorized twist. These daring young men (and a few women) put motors and bicycles on the *same* track and at the *same* time; it was still bicycle racing, but the cyclists used motorcycles to set an exact pace and to create a wind draft to enable them to ride at self-propelled speeds before then not even imagined.

The motorcycles, which Grantland Rice called "sputtering death boxes," were either singles (handled by one pace setter) or tandems (ridden by two pace setters, and looking like motorized bicycles built-for-two). They ranged in weight from one hundred pounds for the singles to five hundred pounds for the tandems. The engine size went from four horsepower to sometimes ten, twelve, and later even fourteen. The races were held on small, specially built ovals, outdoor and indoor, anywhere from six to eight laps per mile to as many as ten to twelve laps per mile. The tracks were composed of dirt, cement, or wooden slats, and were usually about sixteen feet wide. The general idea of the bicycle/motorcycle combination was for the bicyclist to tailgate one to three inches directly behind his pace motor. It wasn't unusual for the races to go distances from the best of three five-mile races to longer races of twenty-five miles and sometimes more. The pace motorcycle was capable of creating a draft for the cyclist at speeds of forty to fifty miles per hour. Sometimes in a challenge match there were only two cyclists plus their motors on the track; but at other times there might be as many as four to six cycle-motor combinations on the same small tracks racing for the substantial cash prizes.

Motor-paced racing (as it was called) was even more popular than conventional bicycle racing, especially in the Northeast and the South. For fifty-cent grandstand or one-dollar box seats, Atlanta locals could sit in on weekly motor-paced racing for two seasons per year, spring and fall. Jack Prince, a former world champion rider, and a cycling promoter and race track manager from Philadelphia, regularly arranged for the Atlanta matches, and built a number of racing ovals in the South (there were any number of tracks in the North in such cities as Pittsburgh, Norfolk, Trenton, New York, Boston, Chicago, and Philadelphia). In addition to the track in Atlanta, Prince also brought race tracks to Savannah and Jacksonville.

Tom Eck, who was out of the Woodside track in Philadelphia, was one of the foremost trainers in the world. Eck, known commonly then as "the silver haired veteran," was a prematurely graying entrepreneur who had discovered some of the motor-paced bicycling greats: Archie M'Eachern, Jimmy Michael, Harry Elkes, Earl Kiser, Bennie Munroe, and, one of his greatest finds, Atlantan Bobby Walthour. Walthour had been riding sprints in Jacksonville in 1901 when Eck picked him out as a comer. He encouraged Walthour to try middle distance and to follow pace, a heady decision that turned a good rider into a great one.

Eck was a former horse trainer, but switched to developing bicycle racers in the 1880s. He made his international reputation around 1886 when he brought John Shillington Prince over from England and entered him in a great open race in Boston under the name of John Shillington. Whittaker was then the American champion, and he and many other outstanding American riders were not in the least bit concerned that one John Shillington from England was entered in the Boston race. Whoever he was, he was expected to finish somewhere toward the end of the fast pack of riders. This was before the National Cycling Association had rules prohibiting what Eck had pulled off; for John Shillington was none other than Jack Prince, the famous English rider and world champion, who had never before been in America. Shillington (Prince) rode circles around the American riders. Eck and those of his friends who bet the farm on Shillington made several hundred thousand dollars on the race. Fifteen years later it was Prince who invested so prominently in Southern racing after he retired from the sport, having personally won nineteen six-day races along the way.[31]

Eck became widely known for his talent for training racers. He took the first team of American riders (Knapp, Whittaker, Crocker, Christ, and Barber) to Europe for a tour; this team defeated nearly all the European riders. He also brought over the first European team to ever compete in a six-day race in the Garden. Eck's manner of training "was greatly commended by the racing men." Eck even included at least one woman in his stable of thirty-five to forty racers. He managed Lottie Brandon, the world's champion female rider. In 1903 Brandon held every record for a woman from a quarter mile to one hundred miles; she was the first woman to ride a mile in less than two minutes when she rode a 1:36 behind motors at the famous Vailsburg track at Newark, a faster time then than most men were capable of turning in. Eck even took Lottie out on a vaudeville circuit where she performed a tricky and popular bicycle stunt, the loop-the-loop specialty.[32]

One of the cities on Lottie's vaudeville tour was Atlanta, where the *Journal*'s theater critic, Grantland Rice, covered her trick—at least it is assumed the reporter this night was Rice and not Marquis since the evening bill included athletes. Lottie would ride her bike furiously on a home trainer which was elevated slightly above the stage. The trainer was a device that had two fast-spinning rollers spaced the same distance apart as her bicycle wheels. After getting up to top speed, she would be lowered to the stage, and her already racing bicycle would take her upside down and full circle, three times around the constructed loop-the-loop. But Lottie's performance at the Atlanta Bijou apparently didn't measure up to Rice's own promotions of her gravity-defying act. He found that her act "did not loom up quite as thrilling as one expected to see," especially when her performance was compared to other loop-the-loop performers. Her performance, in Rice's mind, was less sensational than that of the marvelous daredevil Diavolo, the Human Barrel Hoop, who dressed up daintily in pink pajamas, rode down a steep incline, and whirled around the loop many times. "But she was very clever," said the ever-courteous Rice about Lottie, "and was received with applause." Actually, Rice thought her act was outdone by Crawford and Stanley's Mexican cowboy and piano act.[33]

Bobby Walthour was the first national sporting hero that Grantland Rice had a direct hand in promoting. The blond, genial, and confident 150-pound champion cyclist was good copy. His riding pluck and ability were next to none at motor-paced racing's peak. Years later, when the motors began getting too big and dangerous for the riders and when the sport was beginning to die out, Walthour had earned the reputation of being to bicycle racing what Babe Ruth was to baseball.[34]

In one fifteen-mile race late in 1903 against George Leander and Deguichard, a Frenchman, Walthour set world records for oval tracks for every mile from one to fifteen. When only one year earlier it was not thought possible to ride repeat miles at a 1:10 clip, Walthour nearly put fifteen of them together, averaging less than the 1:10 for the entire race on a five-lap-per-mile track. Bobby's remarkable ride was even more astonishing because the fastest motorcycle mile ever run up to that time (without a cyclist on a bicycle behind the motor) was Albert Champion's 1:04.4 on the Empire automobile mile racetrack, riding a specially built motorcycle. In Walthour's record-breaking ride he rode his last mile in 1:07 flat. He almost proved, at least then, that the human could be nearly the equal of the newfangled self-propelled machines.[35]

Rice and Walthour became good friends. Bobby got into the practice of telegraphing Rice directly with news about his out-of-state competitions. When he was in Paris in 1904, Bobby cabled his friend often enough to allow Rice to scoop the other Atlanta papers with inside information. Rice would often publish the wire or cable verbatim, as he did with this Paris cable: "We are whooping things up for old Atlanta over here. . . . I won from Contenet, the national French champion, yesterday in easy style, taking both straight heats. I could have lapped him but am taking no chances. Nearly 15,000 people were present and the American colony tore things up for a few minutes after the race. I am in fine shape and expect to win every race and establish new records from one to fifty. The tracks here are lightning fast. . . . There is big money in the game over here."[36]

As Bobby's fame spread worldwide, he became a genuine sports hero. Zermo Cruselle came all the way from Galveston, Texas—a distance of more than one thousand miles—to watch Walthour ride in Atlanta. Alone and unattended, Zermo, who was only five years old, took the train to see his hero perform. His grandmother, who lived in Atlanta, took him to see the speedy man he had heard so much about, Bobby Walthour, who could ride like the wind. Every time Walthour would shoot away on a sprint, the little Texan would jump up in his seat and, in his shrill voice, yell wildly "Bobby—Bobby—Bobby." When other riders were out on the track, the small, chubby lad would sit way back in his seat, taking little interest in the race. But when Bobby hit the boards again, the youngster would be up and shouting immediately. Mrs. Williams, his grandmother, had a difficult time restraining the wild impetuosity of her visiting charge. When Bobby went down in a crash late in the race, taking his team out of the race, Zermo was bitterly disappointed. He had been certain ever since he left the Lone Star State that Bobby would be the winner of the race.[37]

Jack Prince capitalized on the popularity of the local Atlanta hero and middle-distance world champion Walthour, the "Dixie Flyer." Prince would sponsor matches featuring Walthour against such nationally and internationally famous riders as Albert Champion, Johnny Lake, Gus Lawson, Will Stinson, Archie M'Eachern, Harry Elkes, George Leander, Eddie (the Cannon) Bald, "Plunger Bill" Rutz, and Hugh Caldwell. Many of these riders, including Walthour, would travel wherever there was contract money; they all took their careers seriously enough to train regularly. Most in-season workouts depended on just riding ten to twenty miles at a time with frequent pace changing, maybe averaging each mile at a 1:45 to 1:50 pace (race pace was in the 1:30s and 1:20s). Occasionally, they would also walk or jog three to five miles as well. It wasn't unusual for the cyclists to change their daily diet to a training diet before a big race, often consuming healthy quantities of raw food (which they thought was muscle-making): raw toast, raw eggs, raw meat. In the off season (winter), the cyclists would sometimes go to Hot Springs "to take baths" for weeks on end; others would ice skate competitively; still others would stay fit by cutting firewood, usually averaging two cords per day; a few would keep their general conditioning through playing handball, or through the use of punching bags, ring work, Indian club swinging, and light dumbbell lifting.[38]

It was also a common practice for some riders to resort to various stimulating concoctions to get them through their exhausting racing schedules (which were longer than the baseball season). As Amos Leander argued in police court, riders regularly used "the stuff," as they called it. Will Stinson, another highly skilled motor-paced racer, was forced to return home from competition in Paris when his eyes began failing him. It was reported that he was suffering a general breakdown due to regular use of a mixture of cocaine, strychnine, and other sundry ingredients, including a dash of opium. Most believed he would become completely blind, but within a few months he was back racing and with more "stuff" than ever. For the most part, such drug use was unexceptional and an accepted part of the sport, and was rarely mentioned by the press. When "the stuff" got the best of the cyclist, "on account of ill health" was the standard public explanation for an athlete's overzealous forays into the world of stimulants and medicinal nostrums.[39]

A greater source of ill health for the riders was the inherent danger in the motor-paced competition itself—which accounted for much of its popularity. It was bad enough falling from an unpaced racing bicycle. But putting a rider on a bicycle, strapping his feet to the pedals, and inviting him to tailgate an inch or three behind a ten-horsepower motorcycle on a small oval with other rider/pacers, and at speeds of forty-five to fifty miles per hour for five or ten miles, made for a sport that would have satisfied the conditions for daredeviltry the Roman citizens came to expect in their gladiatorial contests. The spectator could almost always count on some kind of mechanical failure figuring into the evening's racing. Often the failure was with the bicycle itself, either throwing a chain or popping a tire, both mishaps usually causing a spectacular tumble. The rider, usually in a gimpy rush to the sidelines, then grabbed a spare bike, caught his pace motor, and got on with the contest.

But even more often, it was the clunky motorcycle that caused danger to life and limb. Motorized know-how around 1903 and 1904 wasn't exactly practiced. Sometimes the mechanical heart of the machine, without warning, would begin palpitating; as it continued to fibrillate, the motor, and consequently the rider behind it, would gradually "lose pace." The rider was then forced to pass his own racing machine and ride on along until the motor could be fixed, or until some other pacer-with-motor on the sidelines would voluntarily help out. Just as frequently, something on the motor would suddenly snap, such as the chain or, in the more sophisticated motors, the belt drive, and the motor would instantly lose power. Explosions were also possible, sometimes only in the tires (usually from the friction produced from the speeds and the sharp banked turns), but on other occasions the entire flaming machine would simply blow up.

Most of the major accidents on the tracks were a direct result of the unpredictable behavior of the heavy vehicular traffic. When the pacing motor stopped dead, the bicycle rider was catapulted forward, up and over the machine; usually the bike went right with him since his feet were tied to the pedals. If that weren't enough of a risk, the thrown rider was next vulnerable to the speeding motors directly behind him. It was the lucky rider who wasn't directly run over by a competitor's snorting, bullish machine.

For good reason, the cyclists sometimes called their pace vehicles by disquieting names: White Ghost, or Black Murderer. Although Bobby Walthour named his pacing motor Candy Jr., even his own children knew of the potential danger of following pace. When his small daughter, Veva, watched him at practice one day, Bobby's steersman, standing on the edge of the practice track, held the little girl in his arms while her father whirled around and around like an out-of-control merry-go-round ride, peddling faster and faster. She begged that "Papa would not go back of that motor." The youngster had obviously seen her papa fall before, and perhaps had witnessed something like the fall he took later that season in 1902.[40]

At the Charles River track in Boston, Walthour was following closely behind a nine-horsepower tandem motor at a forty-five-mile-per-hour clip when the chain on the motor suddenly broke. One end of the chain dragged behind the tandem, sparking on the cement, the length of it just long enough for Walthour's front wheel to ride over it. The whipping chain pulled the bike out from under Walthour with enough force to entirely separate Bobby from his wheel. The bike was thrown in the air and over the retaining fence, between some posts and the many boys and young men hanging on the fence for an up-close look at the race. The bike missed hitting anything or anyone. Walthour did a complete somersault over the dead-on-the-track motor, six feet in the air, landing on his hands and knees on the concrete track, near the grassy-edged fence line. He then skidded through the grass for another forty feet, in head-first baseball slide fashion, where he rolled over, unconscious. A sobbing Mrs. Walthour, along with many in the crowd, rushed to the fallen rider. Hearing her voice apparently helped young Bobby regain his senses, it was reported. Luckily, after he was examined by the track physician, Dr. Dwyer, it was discovered that the Atlanta champion rider only suffered superficial injuries, cuts, scrapes, and scratches. He raced a few evenings later, on the eve of the Jim Jeffries and Bob Fitzsimmons heavyweight championship fight, beating three other riders in record-setting style. Behind his motor he rode the twenty-five-mile race in 35:00.4, averaging 1:24 to the mile.[41]

Walthour had repeatedly told reporters that motor-paced racing was a risky proposition. "Every time a man goes out behind the motors he takes his life in his hands," Walthour said. Even though some people derided the statement, Walthour insisted that "it is a dangerous game, and every man who has ever followed a motor knows it." Severe accidents increased, especially as the horsepower on the big machines was gradually boosted. And there were deaths.[42]

Harry Elkes, a good friend of Walthour, was riding in a paced, twenty-mile race in Boston in 1903 against a number of riders, including Walthour. Just before the race, Walthour wished Elkes success and said he hoped that he would not meet with any accident. "Thanks, Bobby," Elkes said, "but you know Decoration Day (Memorial Day) races are my hoodoos, and I will be glad when the race is over." In each of the previous three Decoration Day races Elkes had met with severe falls, breaking his arm on one occasion and his collar bone on another.

Eighteen thousand spectators witnessed the highly touted race, which featured the massive fourteen-horsepower motors, nicknamed "freight cars," on the New Charles River track, five laps to the mile. Walthour won the twenty-mile race in twenty-six minutes and fifty seconds, breaking the world's record—and this with more than half of the race paced behind his small four-horsepower motor (Candy Jr.), without a wind screen, as his big machine (which he had named Ben Hur) quit on him in the seventh mile. Elkes was the only rider in the race equal to Walthour. But while chasing Bobby, Elkes's small French rear tire on his bicycle exploded (the thinner French tires were preferred by the riders to the American tires for their speed, but being only one-sixteenth of an inch thick, the heat from the friction at high speeds increased the risk of explosion). Elkes fell to the track, directly in front of the fast-closing Will Stinson, whose motor ran over Elkes's head, crushing his skull. Elkes died of the injuries sustained in the accident.[43]

Even though Elkes and Walthour were among the first of the professional riders to use the big motors (they jumped from the four-horse to the nine and ten about a year earlier), Walthour never did see the sense in them. After Bobby got his first big tandem in 1902 he commented that a baby could ride more than forty miles per hour behind one of those wind-shielded machines: "It's a case now of not how fast you are, but how big a motor you have got." And after Elkes's death, he said, "Poor Harry. I regret his death very much. . . . I am sick and tired of the game with the new motors. They weigh 500 pounds, and there is not a man capable of handling them at a 48 mile an hour clip."[44]

As a family man, and as a rider who would not compete or even train on Sundays, Walthour was principled. After Elkes's death, Walthour became almost unbeatable. There was concern among the riders and promoters in the riding circuit as to whether spectator interest could be maintained, given Walthour's superiority. Almost predictably, Bobby began to have unexplained mechanical trouble. He confided in Rice that he thought he was being sabotaged. In a race in Atlanta, where Bobby owned the track record of 7:20 for five miles, he was beaten by Nat Butler in a surprisingly slow time of 7:50. Earlier that day Bobby had worked out at a 1:22 pace per mile; in the race that evening, Walthour's fastest mile was 1:34. Rice and Walthour talked after the race. After some inspecting it was discovered that Bobby's pacing motor speed lever was broken loose and a nut on the carburetor was also loosened. Bobby cried foul; Rice went to press, charging that somebody had tampered with Bobby's "corbrutter" (about as close as the nonmechanical Rice could get to the Southern rider's reference to his motorcycle's carburetor).[45]

But these indirect tactics failed to slow Bobby's winning ways, especially as he began watching over his equipment far more carefully. Colonel Wendelshafer of Providence, Rhode Island, Walthour's manager, decided to take the direct approach. Even by 1903 the motor-paced circuit was beginning to weaken in both the North and the South. Although Wendelshafer had signed

Bobby to a contract a year earlier because he wanted to have the best racer, he certainly didn't want anyone to be so good as to kill interest in the sport. So the manager told Bobby before a race that he must let the other rider win—for the sake of the sport. Walthour told the Colonel, in effect, to mind his business and let the riders worry about the sport. But as the sport and the business were, in Wendelshafer's mind—and in the minds of promoters in general—one and the same, he fixed Bobby's motor so it would not give proper pace. Walthour lost. Immediately after the race Walthour told the Colonel that he was through with him.

This was not the first time Walthour had been approached, for he was repeatedly offered money to lay down in order to help the gate. He always refused. Rice was well aware of the seedier side of the sport, as Walthour shared such information freely with him. He told Rice that he would rather win a race and get ten dollars than lose and get two hundred. "Time and time again," Rice told the local Atlantans, "he has been offered big sums of money to lose a race here, but the donors of such offers generally caught a good roasting from Bobby." Rice went on to say that "his many friends have learned to know that to bet on Walthour is to get a run for their money, and that he rides all races on the square."[46]

But the circuit was slowly collapsing in America. Not only did the predictability of the races hurt the sport, but the power and noise of the motorcycles themselves became of much greater interest to the speed-loving spectators than the human feats of the trailing riders. More and more, exhibitions of the motorcycles themselves were put on the evening cards. Albert Champion, also called the "Demon Devil," frequently rode for track records on his new sixteen-horsepower motor, "Man Killer." Even though Rice reported that Bobby considered switching over to motorcycle racing when the motor-paced circuit began to die, his real specialty was riding, not motoring.

The National Cycling Association soon passed a resolution restricting the motor-paced races to only a few tracks, one of which was in Atlanta, on the grounds that the sport was not a true test of a rider's skill since mechanical fallibility often determined the outcome of the races. They pushed sprint and endurance racing instead, both unpaced and both cheaper to promote. In 1902 there were twenty-six motor-paced cyclists; in 1903, twenty-one; and by 1904, only twelve.

In spite of the fact that motor-paced racing was losing speed with the riders and spectators alike, Jack Prince continued to build tracks in the South. In Atlanta, maybe to make more concrete the connection between modern ways and the days of glorious Rome—which the circuslike world of motor-paced racing sometimes suggested—Prince put up an actual coliseum that was to be a perfect copy of a Roman stadium. But such desperate ideas could not save motor-paced racing. Even the motorcycle racers were soon to be eclipsed by the newest pioneers of speed and daring, automobile-racing juggernauts such as Barney Oldfield and his "Green Dragon," Paul Sartori, Henri Fournier, H. L. Bowden, and Tommy Cooper, some of whom were cyclists turned "chauffeurs."[47]

Unwittingly, Walthour and one of his early riding partners, Bennie Munroe, had actually, if only symbolically, signaled the end of the American motor-paced racing in one of those big, twenty-four-hour, six-day Madison Square Garden races in 1903 (the racing continued in Europe for a while longer, where Walthour raced, earning as much as five thousand dollars for a three-month tour). George Leander, one of Walthour's strongest competitors—the rider who was the "bad sport" of that earlier free-for-all fight in Atlanta, and who would tragically die in a cycling accident in 1904—was the sprint man for a tandem riding in this race against Walthour and Munroe. Walthour and Munroe were particularly interested in winning the race, but they especially wanted to beat Leander because the New York papers had quoted George, a Northerner, as saying that he did not care where he finished the race just so long as it was ahead of "that rebel." Somehow or other, Walthour convinced the officials that his partner, Munroe, had gone "bug house" (slightly crazy or sick, or both) and that to satisfy him so he could race, he had to have an automobile squawk horn mounted on his bike. "Now I have heard those auto horns," said Leander, "but this one that Munroe had was the loudest I ever heard and Bennie seemed to take a delight in getting right up close to me with the big end of that horn close to my ear and for miles and miles would get very busy with it." Leander was so rattled after several days of this that no matter whether he ate, slept, or rode, all he could hear was that blasted, squawking horn. It so jangled his nerves that after riding four or five hours with the horn serenade, he often forgot he was racing and believed that he was on Broadway dodging automobiles.[48]

In the end, even though Bobby Walthour wasn't above tooting his own horn, the champion cyclist was the kind of competitor, in character and in deed, that Grantland Rice came to enjoy promoting. The flamboyance of the rider and the romanticism of the writer enlivened the Atlanta sports pages. Typical was the March 1903 challenge motor-paced race in Atlanta between Walthour and the "Terrible Swede" Gussie Lawson. The day of the race Rice featured Walthour, in an action photograph and in an accompanying story, who claimed that "I'll break records tonight . . . I feel fit to ride that track, if the motor can go, at a 1:20 clip." After a promotion of the upcoming race, Rice, the barker, teased his readers by announcing that the races would commence at 8:10 and end at 10:15, and that "tickets are selling fast, but quite a number of good seats are still to be had at Folger Bros., 41 North Pryor Street."

Walthour didn't ride at 1:20, but he did win. He also, as promised, broke his own track record. Rice's typically overwritten account of the ride made it quite clear that those seeing Bobby Walthour following pace were witnessing history in the making; he also made it clear that those who were not there in the flesh to see the man ride had really missed something special. After noting that Walthour won, and that young Lawson was defeated but not disgraced, Rice careened through his thousand-word story:

> For Walthour rode. And such a race as that wild dash in the last two miles of the final heat was never seen before in the local arena. Like an angel of death who had slipped the leash from the land beyond the skies in search of mortal life, Atlanta's speedy champion of the world set sail for glory in the wildest dash on record and lapped his opponent three time [sic] before the pistol shot sounded the end of the conflict. It was a dash such as thrills one to the very marrow, one that should live in the history of cycling annals, for track records were smashed to smithereens and the big crowd lifted from its feet in the wildest outburst of enthusiasm that has ever echoed and re-echoed throughout the walls of the coliseum. Not even in the days of old when Roman thousands watched the struggles of life and death in the arena below could there have been more thrilling interest shown.

Rice went on to describe the details of this final, record-breaking five-mile heat. For the first three miles Lawson and Walthour were scarcely a wheel's length apart. But then, "Like a streak of jagged lightning out of a sky of summer blue, the streak that always betokens the approach of a coming storm, Walthour leaped forward at a terrific gait. On and on sped motor and rider, whirling by the shouting thousands like some spectre of light that gleamed from curve to curve until with scarce a moment's notice the local boy rode directly above his struggling opponent.... The crowd were watching with bated breath the daring cyclist who wore beneath his belt the shamrock of Ireland twined around the stars and stripes."

The evening of racing didn't end until around midnight. Rice's account continued to celebrate Walthour's ride; by comparison, the rest of the evening card was "as tame as a Ping-Pong festival in Kokomo." It was Walthour's show, as he had "proven conclusively that to beat him men must ride as never mortal rode before." The praise-singing ended in verse, Rice leaving no doubt in his reader's mind that the cycle-riding feats of Atlanta-born Bobby Walthour were of heroic proportion. For in Rice's mind, especially given the patriotic gesture of Bobby riding with the stars and stripes laced in his belt—and given Rice's natural bent toward hyperbole—we find the Atlantan's midnight ride unabashedly compared to a certain Bostonian's:

> Paul Revere was a rider bold—
> Oft has his dashing sprint been told . . .
> But listen now while we recite
> The ride that Walthour made last night.
>
> He rode like a flash from the star-lit sky—
> Like the gleam of a meteor flashing by.
> With never a look to the left or right,
> On, on, he sped like the spirit of night.
> No wonder young Lawson lost out in the race,
> For no living man could have held that pace.
>
> There may be riders living today
> Who can beat Walthour. Hidden away
> There may be others who even now
> Might snatch the wreath from the victor's brow.
> But none can rival the rider who
> Wears the Shamrock twined with the red, white and blue.[49]

6

Mudville Hearts Are Happy Now

Until late in 1905, Rice's sports-related travels were mainly limited to road trips throughout the South, accompanying either John Heisman's Georgia Tech college football team or Atlanta's Southern League baseball club. A spring preseason baseball tune-up, for instance, would find him covering exhibition games between Atlanta and minor-league baseball clubs in the South Atlantic League, at Macon, or Charleston, or perhaps Jacksonville. He did double duty on these trips. He was a baseball reporter primarily, but Judge James Kavanaugh, the president of the Southern League, had also reappointed him the official scorer for the Atlanta baseball team (his first appointment was in 1903). These trips would last a week, maybe ten days, with the distances between the baseball camps short enough for day train travel. Rice would send a number of daily special dispatches to the *Journal* while on the road; there might be as many as six or seven stories published under the Grantland Rice byline in each edition. In these dispatches he covered the games and gossip; he sometimes also reported what the sixteen players did when they weren't representing Atlanta on the ball field.[1]

To kill ennui on one such baseball spring training jaunt, the players, besides partaking in plenty of eating and sleeping, sought out a variety of day and evening amusements. Rice joined right in, and probably at times was their self-appointed group leader. In Macon, on a rain-out, it was a friendly small-limit poker game; or at least it was friendly until one of the players, who had taken off his shoes and socks for comfort, was caught passing an ace to a fellow player under the table, between his toes. At their Macon hotel, the Plaza, a pool and billiards emporium adjoined the hotel's office. The players and their chronicler could sometimes be found there during their free time in the mornings before the afternoon games. One Atlantan, pitcher Charles Smith, explained that his pool sharking was actually part of his baseball training regimen: "Any fellow able to put up a stiff game of pool would soon make an ideal bunter, using reverse English on each occasion."[2]

A few days later in Jacksonville on a Sunday morning, a fishing excursion served as the boredom chaser. Along the St. Johns riverfront wharf, they vied with the local fishermen among the palmettos for the biggest catch, using crawfish and mangled crabs as bait. Lunches were provided for the players by the locals for ten cents, for which they received one thin slice of ham buried between two thick pieces of spongy bread and a soft shell pudding neatly wrapped in tissue and tin foil on the side. "And where is the best place to catch fish?" Charlie Smith asked a veteran fisherman. "Under the water," was the curt rejoinder. The advice did no good, as the ball club, collectively, caught nothing.[3]

Having lost the wharf fishing contest, the squad plus Rice took directly to the river itself by way of a gasoline-powered, fly-paddled launch. For the rest of the day's work, the team's river fishing average was just about as dismal as the wharf fishing had been: one fished-out baseball cap (which had blown off ballplayer Smith's head), a couple of missed nibbles, and one swimming turtle snagged and pulled into the launch by third baseman Krug, who swore during the struggle he was certain it was a small whale. Otherwise, except for a cold that shortstop Morse caught, the Atlantans had nothing else to show for their fishing trip in St. Johns River.

Adding to what Rice called their "gay butterfly existence outside of working hours" in Jacksonville, later in the day the athletes lounged around their hotel, the Aragon, either on the broad verandah or in the lobby. Before and after each meal at the Aragon, a soprano played piano and sang popular melodies to the guests and to those just loitering about the hotel. This particular Sunday evening two Atlanta players, McCay and Krug, beat the singing soprano to the piano and banged out a few songs, much to the delight and generous applause of the audience. About Krug's musical ability, Rice said that "any one who thinks the Dutchman can't fight a music box of any sort should hear him tackle a piano once. He plays it as well as he does third, anything from grand opera down."[4]

But in 1905 Rice's travels weren't wholly restricted to regional sports coverage. On October 7 his paper announced to all "lovers of baseball" that Grant-land Rice, the *Journal*'s "incomparable sporting editor," would be leaving that evening to cover the world's championship baseball series between the Philadelphia Americans and the New York Nationals. Rice had talked the management into sending him north on the grounds that the *Journal* would be able not only to use its exclusive Associated Press coverage but also to double readers' pleasure and scoop the other Atlanta newspapers with a firsthand account of the biggest national sports event to date. It would be a circulation builder, for sure. Excited at the prospect of covering his first World Series—practically the first-ever such series—Rice boarded the Pullman at midnight for the trip to Philadelphia, the site of the first game of the best-of-seven championship. He intended to bring to his Atlanta readers the color and excitement of what Henry Chadwick called in *Spalding's Guide* that year "the greatest Base Ball tournament known in the annals of our National game."[5]

Baseball by then was already well on its way to becoming grafted permanently into the American psyche. Even though its critics would try to reduce its importance by complaining that the sport appealed to the lowest human instincts for mere excitement and sensation, and that it gave youngsters the wrongheaded idea that personal and national greatness depended largely upon muscular development, the sport had already become the preeminent national commercial spectator amusement.[6] In fact, in the *Washington Post*'s build-up to the championship series between John McGraw's New York Giants and Connie Mack's Philadelphia Athletics, an editorial writer noted that the season just finished had brought more people than ever to the nation's ballparks. It was entirely safe to say, the writer went on, that the "great sport has reached the point where it may be called the great national game in fact." The writer even speculated that the main reason for its popularity, in addition to the elements of the game that appeal to the American character, was its cleanliness. While other professional sports of the day were sometimes dishonest, professional baseball games "go on without dishonesty or manipulation, furnishing a confiding public with a genuine article upon which they can rely." Chadwick added that baseball fans were drawn to the ballparks by the inherent beauties of the game, and not, as with horse racing, by the extrinsic aid of betting.[7]

Despite its reputed cleanliness and elemental appeal, baseball was business as usual for most team owners, who often gladly referred to themselves as "magnates" after the industrial captains of the day. Many trade wars and a few player rebellions finally produced two major leagues, the old National League (founded in 1876) and the upstart American League (underway in

1899, as Ban Johnson led the minor Western League into major-league status to challenge the National League monopoly). When the dust settled, territorial and reserve clause agreements produced an even larger monopoly, loosely overseen by the three-member National Commission. One National League owner, Charles Murphy of the Chicago club, put the matter quite clearly when he said that the "baseball business is not one that should be conducted on a sentimental basis, but it is purely a business proposition."[8]

There was no provision in the new agreements for any interleague contests or postseason play, leaving such games up to the discretion of the teams themselves. In 1903, Boston of the American League agreed to play Pittsburgh for a "world" championship. Boston won the first World Series with the able pitching of Cy Young, who won two games. When Boston again won the American League pennant in 1904, John T. Brush, the New York Giants owner, refused to allow his pennant-winning team to play what he thought was still a minor-league outfit. Both Brush—who some sportswriters nicknamed "Tooth"—and his manager, John J. McGraw, were crucified in the papers for being so small as to not comply with the spirit of the fledgling World Series. The crux of the criticism was that the Giants were afraid to play Boston. "Tooth" Brush's justification was that there was no agreed-upon provision for such a contest and no governing body. "He did not see why we should jeopardize the fruits of our victory," McGraw wrote later about Brush's position, "by recognizing and playing against the champions of an organization that had been formed to put us out of business." The stinging attacks eventually got to Brush, that or the realization that there was money to be made in the proposition, or maybe even face to be saved. During the next season he offered Harry Pulliam (the National League president, a former newspaperman) a set of recommendations for organizing a best-of-seven series. These "Brush rules," which were refined by the National Commission, became the heart of the World Series institution from then on.[9]

Rice composed his first special report on the 1905 World Series for the *Journal* somewhere between the Carolinas and Virginia, as he rode north through the cool and clear late October night in his Pullman car. The only object visible outside his window seat, a hunter's moon, caught his bloodshot eyes and gave him this somewhat tortuous lead: "From the way it looks at this distant angle there will be a large, pink clot of blood on Philadelphia's moon tomorrow night. Whether the gore will ooze from the ball playing systems of McGraw or Mack will not be known until Monday's moon skims out into the misty Quaker sky as the mottled gloam bulges over the landscape but we'll do our best to explain the details of this great blood-letting event from a closer point of view. Any way you take it this scrap is pretty sure to be the most kazippa ever known in balldom."[10]

Rice wasn't an entirely unknown quantity among the big-league baseball crowd. He had occasionally provided copy as a Southern correspondent for the *Sporting News,* which had given him some name recognition in national baseball circles. And, too, the major-league clubs had begun the practice of taking spring training in parts south since 1902. Atlanta was one of the more popular host cities for clubs from the two major leagues during March and early April. The New York Americans set up camp for a couple of weeks in 1903 and 1904 at Atlanta's Piedmont Park. In 1905, Napoleon Lajoie's Cleveland club stayed in Atlanta for twenty-three days. In addition, several teams barnstormed through the city during these years to play the Atlanta club in preseason series, including Boston, Milwaukee, Cincinnati, St. Paul, Detroit, and Philadelphia.[11]

When Philadelphia played in Atlanta for a couple of days in late March of 1905, Rice met Connie Mack and the Athletics, and also the baseball reporters from Philadelphia who were traveling with the club. Subsequently, and given these connections, when he arrived in Philadelphia for the series, he had little difficulty getting himself reintroduced around. One of Philadelphia's pitchers, Weldon Henley, was especially helpful in extending Rice's contacts. Henley and Rice went back a few years. When Nashville was making the run for that Southern League pennant in 1901, Weldon Henley joined the club in mid-September. Henley was the son of a prominent Atlanta family and a college boy out of Georgia Tech. He had originally signed a contract to play for Nashville at the beginning of the 1901 season, but, like Rice's own history, his family summoned him home. Henley's "people" did not look kindly on his professional debut with Nashville and objected strongly to his becoming a professional. Somehow or other the college boy continued to play ball in lesser leagues anyway throughout the summer. When, with the Memphis Chickasaws, he threw a no-hitter against a St. Louis club, a shutout against a Chicago team, and struck out fifteen in a game with a Western League team, Nashville insisted he return to their roster. His parents gave in, but they made it clear that upon the completion of the season Weldon would take up engineering work on the Mexican Central Railroad.[12]

But Henley, with Rice's sympathetic help, continued his pitching in 1902, this time in Atlanta where Rice's journalistic career had taken him. The following year Connie Mack picked the youngster up, gave him a try in spring training, and kept him. In 1905, Weldon Henley was still with the Philadelphia pitching staff, which included "Big Chief" Bender, Rube Waddell, Andy

Coakley, and Eddie Plank. "Hen" was now twenty-four, married (more than half the players on these World Series teams were married men), and still playing over his family's objections. Henley was the weakest of the five Philadelphia pitchers, and although he did throw a no-hitter in July against St. Louis of the American League, he only won four games against twelve losses. He did not figure prominently in Mack's plans for the games against McGraw's New York club.[13]

At the end of his career in 1923, "Mugsy" McGraw, as he was sometimes called by the baseball writers—a name he hated—regarded the 1905 Giants as the greatest ball club he had ever managed. Before McGraw's arrival as manager in 1902, the Giants had been milling around in the cellar for the previous six or so years. But under his leadership, the Giants finished second to Pittsburgh in 1903, then won pennants the next two years. The 1905 club wasn't particularly fast, but they were a thinking team led by such outstanding players as "Iron Man" Joe McGinnity, the deaf-mute Luther "Dummy" Taylor, "Turkey" Mike Donlin, Sam Mertes, Dan McGann, William F. Dahlen, Roger Bresnahan, and Christy Mathewson. When McGraw took over the club, Mathewson had been stationed at first base: no one had seen his potential as a pitcher. It wasn't long before Mathewson, as a pitcher, became one of the most popular of the early baseball immortals. A Bucknell graduate, the husky and handsome young man became known for his religious scruples, sportsmanship, keen memory, and outstanding talent. With his speed, fine control, and famous "fadeaway" curve (screwball) he won 373 games in his career. In his spare time he played checkers, poker, and later chess with anyone who would sit down with him. He became so masterful at checkers that he could play as many as eight experts at the same time and beat them all. McGraw remembered that he could even play blindfolded, so picture-perfect was his memory for the previous checkerboard moves.[14]

The 1905 World Series was expected to produce a championship showdown between Mathewson and another outstanding pitcher, Philadelphia's George "Rube" Waddell. In answer to Mathewson's talent, character, and checker-playing ability, Waddell countered with great but not completely realized talent and a checkered career. For the most part, Mathewson was a hero loved by the baseball masses; the illiterate Waddell was an antihero alternately cheered and booed by the fans and even by his own teammates. Waddell, the zany southpaw, is still regarded as one of the best-ever hurlers, this in spite of his only being about half-interested in big-league baseball.

In 1903, National League President Harry Pulliam was beginning to collect for posterity some pictures and memorabilia of the league's outstanding players and teams. This embryonic version of a baseball hall of fame was housed in his office. In an interview, he said there was only one American Leaguer who would ever be added to his walls: Rube Waddell. Even though Rube was clearly a backslider, Pulliam said, he was also the best and truest man he ever found among ballplayers. "True, he has not the stability of some others, but as far as I am concerned, he proved all that a man should be. When I say stability I have no reference to character. I mean he simply was irresponsible, and could not and would not bring himself down to routine and discipline."15

Pulliam recalled one Saturday when the Rube was scheduled to pitch in an important game against Pittsburgh. A large crowd had come to see him play. But Rube never showed up. While walking to the grounds for the game, he happened upon a vacant lot where two teams were playing for the championship of the Thirteenth and Fourteenth wards. He became interested in their game, and before long he was in the middle of it with all his heart and soul, pitching for the eventual winners, the Fourteenth ward.

It was Henry J. Spuhler, a Pittsburgh millionaire stockbroker, who first spotted Rube's talent. In his early years, Spuhler was a western Pennsylvania hotel proprietor; Waddell, at the same time, was working on his family's farm in Butler, zapping birds on the wing with rocks as he paused between plow rows. He pitched for his local town team until it was clear to all of the neighboring villages that no one could hit him; he was finally barred from pitching. Other Pennsylvania towns tried to get Rube to leave Butler and pitch for them, but he was supposedly fully domesticated, happy just plowing. One day a traveling minstrel troupe found its way to Butler, where they gave the small town a street parade that the young plowboy witnessed. When the troupe left town the next day, Rube wasn't to be found. A few weeks later he turned up about fifty miles northeast in DuBois, as a member of the troupe. The black barnstorming entertainers had acquired a proud, high-stepping white drum major. Waddell led the instrumentalists down the DuBois main street, bedecked in a uniform and a high fur hat. His strut was accentuated with the rhythmic sweeps of his gold-headed mace.

On the day of the parade, DuBois was scheduled to play a baseball game against their nearby rivals from Punxsutawney. Spuhler was part-owner of the DuBois team, the decided underdogs that day due to weak pitching. He stood to lose a good deal of money in some bets he had placed on his own team, but he had heard of the "phenom" Waddell and recognized him instantly as the leader of the band. Rube accepted Spuhler's offer of twenty dollars to pitch that day for DuBois. On one condition. As the story goes, Rube was so proud of his marching band regalia that he insisted on taking the mound in full dress, fuzzy hat and all. In the eight-inning game that followed, the drum major struck out nineteen Punxsutawney batters; the other five grounded out to infielders. A no-hitter. The band left town the next day without Rube, as the much richer DuBois hero-worshipping revelers had kidnapped him, costume and all. He continued to pitch for DuBois until no one would play them. One day Spuhler managed to get Rube a tryout with the Pirates, then managed by catcher Connie Mack. Mack apparently liked what he saw, as Waddell pitched the same afternoon against Boston.[16]

Largely because of Rube's frolicking nature, the anticipated World Series showdown with Mathewson did not come off. Waddell came up with a lame arm a few weeks before the series, losing the steam off his smoke-ball and the control from his snap-ball. After a heroic season—he had pitched forty-four consecutive shutout innings, and established the season's strikeout mark and the league's highest won-lost percentage, 27 wins, 10 losses for a .730 percentage—his pitching hadn't been able since September 9. He did try to throw on September 28 against Detroit, but could only manage seven pitches, most of them hurled into the dirt in front of the plate, three of them rasping the catcher on his bunions.[17]

Rube claimed he had a sore shoulder. He explained that he had gotten it either from falling over some baggage left in the aisle of a Pullman, or, more probably, from bumping into the train while boarding it, or else by being hit with a hand satchel when he was skylarking on the loading platform with teammate Andy Coakley. Rube said he was trying to snatch Coakley's straw hat as the team was climbing aboard the train in New London, Connecticut. Being September, Rube joshed Coakley that the lid he was wearing was out of season. If it wasn't by these accidents, then he supposed it could even be some kind of rheumatism.[18]

Another version of how Waddell missed the series had nothing to do with a sore or rheumatoid anything. Charlie Dryden and Horace Fogel, both Philadelphia sport reporters (Fogel was later the president of the Philadelphia National League club from 1909 until 1912), gave air to the theory that old Rube had simply laid down on his team for money. They believed that Rube had been "interviewed" by the New York gamblers and bought off for seventeen thousand dollars. Even though baseball's bleakest—and some say the only scandalous—experience, the thrown 1919 World Series, was half a generation away, rumors of attempted bribes were common in the earliest days of World Series play. Lou Criger, the catcher with the Boston club in 1903, in an affidavit given to McGraw in 1923, disclosed an attempt to get him to influence the outcome of the 1903 series, for which he would receive twelve thousand dollars. He turned the payoff down, at the time confiding only to his team and battery mate Cy Young.[19]

According to McGraw, and contrary to Chadwick's belief that gambling wasn't an attractive feature of the game, betting then was extremely popular. In the hotel lobbies during the 1905 series, especially the team hotels, the Bellevue-Stratford in Philadelphia and the Marlborough in New York, the scenes were "lively" with Giants and Athletics rooters climbing all over themselves to get bets down.

In fact, Grantland Rice, in milling among the collection of players and fans in the Philadelphia hotel lobbies the day he arrived in town before the first game of the series, was able to relay the betting line back to Atlanta. "The general opinion among New York sporting men is that the betting on the series ought to be at even money and that the odds of $10,000 to $9,000 obtained by Frank Farrell in his big wager were unwarranted." Rice went on to report that the word was put out that the actor Louis Mann was looking for a bet of thirty-five hundred on the Giants and that he would be satisfied with an even-money bet when he arrived for the game the next day. The *New York Times* reported that McGraw himself had placed a bet of four hundred dollars on his own team, and other Giants players—Clark, Donlin, and Dahlen—had succeeded in getting a few bets down too.[20]

In the weeks prior to the opening of the World Series, Waddell claimed that he was trying everything he could to get his arm back in shape, hurried along no doubt by once-loyal fans resentfully calling him a traitor to the club. Even though he couldn't find anything on the outside to indicate an injury, the team's trainer, "Professor" Newhouse, applied liberal doses of lineament to heal anything that might be wrong on the inside. The concoction was composed of witch hazel, ammonia, alcohol, and a dash of arnica. It didn't work. Two days before the series, the Rube almost healed himself as his "smoke-ball ligament" suddenly jolted back into place while he was beating the barber out of a dime, shaving himself. Mrs. Waddell heard the welcome snap and even went to the ballpark to bear out Rube's statement. The jolt quickly inspired a company to offer Waddell a large sum of money to write a testimonial for their new safety razors, which they thought were unexcelled, and which now seemingly had mysterious healing powers.[21]

With the series only two days away, Rube tried to pitch against the Washington Nationals, relieving Coakley in the third inning. His unconvincing appearance in the 10 to 4 loss was met with some applause "sprinkled with some hisses of the peevish." The next day he started the first game of a double-header, also against Washington (the pennant had been clinched two days earlier), but was relieved after one inning. He seemed to have all the motions, but, reporters said, not the goods. The shaving-induced jolt apparently wasn't enough to bring back a sufficient amount of Waddell's smoke or Connie Mack's continued indulgence of his antics in time for the World Series, as Rube sat the entire shindig out.[22]

The Giants had planned to take the ninety-mile train ride from New York to Philadelphia on Sunday, giving them a short rest before Monday's game. But their thousands of supporters arranged for a special vaudeville bill to be played at the Majestic Theater in their honor on Sunday evening in New York. McGraw and Brush held the club over and attended the jollification, which featured headliners such as Nat Willis, Jim Corbett (the boxer), Louis Mann, Nella Bergen, Emma Carus, the Empire City Quartet, and many others. The general master of ceremonies was comedic actor and bass singer De Wolf Hopper, who recited Ernest Thayer's famous "Casey at the Bat." Hopper had been doing Casey regularly since around 1889 when he first performed it as a special gesture for the New York Giants and Cap Anson's Chicago White Stockings, who had been invited as guests of the management at the Wallack Theatre on Broadway where Hopper was appearing in a comic opera, Prince Methusalem.[23]

The next day about five hundred New York fans arrived with their team at about 2:15 at Columbia Park, the Athletics' ball field at Twenty-ninth and Columbia Avenue, for the first game of the championship, set to start at 3:00. Columbia was a rustic little wooden ballpark about three miles from the center of town in the part of the city known as Brewerytown. In the air floated the aroma of yeast, hops, and freshly brewed beer. The park's capacity was only about ninety-five hundred. Even though the commission had increased ticket prices to limit the size of the throngs throughout the series, this day the Columbia Park grounds somehow found room for nearly eighteen thousand fans; grandstand and bleachers were packed tight, and the outer fields surrounding the players were twenty deep, with a cordon of police holding the rooters back off the field of play. There was no fence (a ground rule double was given for balls hit into the crowd). A reported ten thousand spectators were turned away at the gate.[24]

The five hundred Giants fans, who were parceled off in one corner of the grandstand, were like "a peanut in a bushel basket when compared with Philadelphia's representation," wrote one reporter. But they were noisy out of proportion to their numbers, and didn't spare the Philadelphians their comments. One Giants fan appeared with a six-by-four-foot manila paper pad. When he wanted to express his partisan opinions, he wrote them out on the huge pad with a chunk of charcoal, then displayed them for all to read. Another New Yorker led a cheer: "Johnny get cher gun, my son, we've won. Johnny get cher gun, it's 10 to 1." To which McGraw, who had taken the field by then and who waved his hand in reply, said, "The odds are too big boys. Take even money!" The New York band was playing "Tammany."[25]

McGraw had outfitted his club in uniforms made especially for the series: baggy black flannel blouses and trousers, trimmed with white; the letters across the chest were in white, as were the caps, belts, and stockings. McGraw had heard some army men claim that the snappiest-dressed outfit is usually the best fighting unit, so he thought he'd try the idea out. If nothing else, the psychological uplift it would give his team, as against the dullness of the regular-season uniforms of the Athletics, might be the difference in the contest. Dryden thought the sassy Giants looked like a flock of blackbirds that had waded in lime. Their gaudy uniforms contrasted with Philadelphia's, which Rice described as dingy, dirty, ragged, sweaty, and torn: "cross-patched here and sewn up there with the stain of soil from a hundred battlefields upon them."[26]

When the Philadelphia club arrived, a standing ovation greeted them. Connie Mack was especially singled out, with the fans shouting over and over, "Connie Mack, the crack-a-jack!" As was his custom, the tall and angular Mack, solemn and sedate as compared to the pert and lively McGraw, was dressed in street clothes, and proceeded to take his seat on the team bench. McGraw, meanwhile, stayed on the field to meet with Lave Cross, the Athletics' captain, and the two umpires, Sheridan and O'Day. Just before the beginning of the game, McGraw was presented with a special token of esteem from Philadelphia's management, Benjamin Shibe. He was handed a toy white elephant mounted on a green stand. Grantland Rice was standing near home plate with the other reporters, just in front of their designated bleacher location. He was close enough to see the little elephant, and later explained the joke to his Atlanta readers, reminding them that it was McGraw who prophesied in the spring of 1902 that the American League club in Philadelphia would prove to be a white elephant (instead, they came in first that year). The scorecards sold for the 1905 series in Philadelphia and given to the sportswriters bore the twin-pennanted white elephant on the front cover page. Dryden reported that McGraw wiggled and blushed some, but did the proper thing by snatching off his cap, and, facing the crowd, placed the beast on his head, bowing in mock courtesy.[27]

Rice's prediction before the series started was that with Waddell out, even though he favored Mack's club, he thought that the odds were with the Giants, "from a professional standpoint." Rice seemed to like the plugging and plodding nature of the Athletics to the haughty show and dash of the Giants. But he knew that the Giants had what he called "a potent factor": Christy Mathewson. He claimed that Mathewson would win two of his three starts. Rice had met the pitcher for the first time during the preliminaries of game one. Rice described him as a tall, willowy youth, "with a blond wig, pink epidermis and buoyant stride, cheerful smile and sinewy frame." He found him then to be a gentleman, upbeat athlete; he also turned out to be, in Rice's judgment years later, the greatest pitcher he ever saw, over the likes of Cy Young, Grover Alexander, and Walter Johnson.[28]

Rice's expectations started to come true in game one. Matty's first game was a four-hit shutout over Eddie Plank and the Athletics; the Giants won 3 to 0. In his account, Rice ordered his constituency, "Kindly remove your fall bonnets, my fellow-settlers in Dixie, when you hear the name Christy Mathewson pronounced. All Philadelphia and New York are doing the same today, so don't drop behind the times. Get busy. Kowtow to Christy and you won't get wrong." In Rice's eyes, the bearing of the two opposing pitchers told all about the outcome of game one. Plank was somber, nervous, careworn, and as gaunt as a shadow before the game; Mathewson "was buoyant, cheerful and as peppery as a two-year-old bred in the purple upon a frosty morning." Besides Mathewson's outstanding pitching performance (and able fielding and hitting), however, the first affair didn't seem to measure up to Rice's pregame enthusiasms. He even noted that the game didn't get the eighteen thousand fans going in the way he was expecting. In an interesting postgame comment, he even remarked on the lack of cheering and tumultuous applause—which in his bailiwick was customary, whether the crowd's favorite was winning or losing. The folks, he said, were all keyed up to such a high tension that they were breathing heavily instead of letting loose the kind of lusty roars typical in the Southern parks: "Everyone seems too deeply involved in the final outcome to whoop things up to any feverish extent."[29]

After seeing Mathewson in action, Rice changed his prediction: Mathewson would pitch three of the games and shut out the Athletics in each game. The series moved the next day to New York, to the old Polo Grounds at Coogan's Hollow. It sat about sixteen thousand. But like Columbia Park, during the regular season the Polo Grounds catered to the carriage trade. The horse and buggy crowd would pull up and park in the outfield, just behind a retaining rope attached to white posts set fifteen to twenty feet apart around the entire perimeter of the field. For the 1905 World Series, Polo Grounds fans were allowed to stand in the outfield as they had in Philadelphia. Game two brought in around twenty-five thousand paying customers, with another fifteen thousand nonpayers sitting among the rocks and scruffy brush on the hillsides that rose up well above and behind the wooden park.

The reporters at the Polo Grounds were given special accommodations: they were seated together in a press stand, in the balcony of the grandstands, directly behind home plate. The old parks built before the turn of the century did not yet include actual press boxes. Still, even press stands were progress for the reporters, for it wasn't uncommon for the typical baseball writer then to have to find writing space catch-as-catch-can. This was still a few years before the Baseball Writers Association was formed (1908), and writers were able to demand not only more press boxes but also that such spaces be reserved exclusively for association members. "It's pretty difficult to turn out deathless prose," wrote newspaperman and later baseball commissioner Ford Frick, "with a typewriter perched precariously on your knee, and your posterior balanced on an upturned beer case borrowed from a sympathetic concessionaire; it is doubly difficult when you face the added obstacle of the free-loading spectators yelling in your ear, stomping their feet, and waving madly to friends while you try to write." Surrounded by fans, and inevitably joined by a few nonreporter freeloaders, it was from this Polo Ground press stand that Rice watched Chief Bender nearly duplicate Mathewson's performance the previous day, beating New York 3 to 0: "Right on the heels of Mr. Mathewson's awful jolt on Monday, Mr. C. Bender, Indian by trade, turned without any warning and beat those blood-eating Giants on their own hillside to a soft pulp. . . . It was a great day for the wily redskin, and don't you forget it."[30]

With a rainout on Wednesday, the series resumed on Thursday back in Philadelphia. Again, Mathewson made "dreadful carnage" of the Athletics, pitching his second shutout. The Giants won 9 to 0. Large sums of money were changing hands daily, as Rice reported regularly on the outcomes of some of the more notorious bets. A Mr. F. S. Kenfield from Denver, a former minor-league ballplayer who had run up a fortune in Colorado mines, was claiming to be willing to wager seventy-five thousand dollars on the Athletics (that was before they lost the third game); another Athletics supporter, Felix Isman, wagered five thousand; Casey's singer, De Wolf Hopper, went with the Giants for one thousand; Patrick Leedom, of Pittsburgh, put out fifteen hundred dollars on the Athletics. After Mathewson's second shutout, Rice reported that Mr. Guggenheimer of Baltimore dropped twenty-three thousand dollars to the New York syndicate. "Bad business this gambling," wrote Rice, "for the loser." About Thursday's winning pitcher, Rice exploded: "Those who have never observed a volcano in action missed the treat of their lives in Philadelphia Thursday. For the second time this week Mr. Mathewson erupted and the result was all to the Mount Pelee for Mr. Mack and his people. Looks now as if they were buried for keeps unless the Messrs. Plank and Bender can dig them to life again."[31]

The *Atlanta Journal* virtually gave over its sporting page to Rice's firsthand accounts of the championship games. This was an era in which newspaper sportswriting lead or story space was rarely restricted in advance; it was also a time when subscribers seemed to read every word of what the sportswriter wrote. The *Journal's* Associated Press wire stories were featured on page one of the paper as they were same-day reports, though since the games were played in the late afternoon, the evening *Journal* couldn't use more than brief accounts of the first few innings. Rice's copy, always about the game played the day before, was featured under anywhere from a five- to seven-column, bold and black three-line or double-decker headline. The three-line head covering his accounts of the Friday game in which Iron Man McGinnity of New York shut out Plank and the Athletics, 1 to 0, read: "Perfect Pitching and Perfect Fielding Beats Perfect Pitching and One Error; Grantland Rice Tells How Giants Won." Six descriptive Rice stories and a few short Rice-authored fillers, some of which were in tiny agate type, tallied up to nearly four thousand words of copy. There was also a bit of tongue-in-cheek verse, pointing out how one-sided the contests had become:

> Sometime in the distant future,
> Ere this century is done,
> You will hear the sentence murmured:
> "Mack's brigade have scored a run."[32]

Game four had been played in New York. The night before game five, also to be played at the Polo Grounds, Rice caught up with Rube Waddell in the lobby of the Marlborough Hotel. Waddell had been present during all the previous games, but except for a little base-runner coaching, he mostly sat alone, largely shunned by his teammates and the fans. The only conversation Rice had seen him having during any of the games was a finger-to-finger chat with the Giants pitcher Dummy Taylor, to whom he was explaining his troubles. McGraw had required all of his Giants players to learn sign language for Dummy's sake, though he also found that the signing was useful in relaying his coaching signals to his team in the course of their games. But somewhere or other Waddell had also picked up the language, much to Dummy's admiration and McGraw's consternation. Rice asked Waddell for the gist of those quiet conversations between the two of them.

Waddell elaborated on his original conversation with Taylor, probably stretching it a good deal. "I'd give a thousand dollars if my arm was right and I could go against Mathewson," said Waddell. "He (Mathewson) has a streak of yellow up his back as wide as Broadway. Make three runs off him and he'll blow up like a powder magazine set on fire." Rube went on, complaining that Mathewson was the worst swell-head in the business (which there was some truth to, as some players and fans did find him arrogant and less the ideal human he was often portrayed to be, a criticism no doubt reinforced by his way of walking, often called his "turkey-gobbler strut"). Rice wrote that the Rube was disconsolate and tearful that he could not play. Even though the Atlanta reporter was skeptical, knowing full well that Waddell was sore at being replaced as the leader of the Athletics' parade and angry about the ugly rumors that he was on the take, Rice softened his earlier gentile snobbery that the no-account Rube had "deserted" his club. Henley had told Rice that the reason Waddell jumped into those Washington games two days before the series was because he really had been hurt, and that he was desperately trying to get his arm in shape before the championship. But the outing did him no good, said Henley, and maybe more harm. "Few believe here," Rice generously concluded, "that the southpaw has been tampered with. That great left salary whip of his is simply a useless mass of flesh and mangled muscle."[33]

Hats and cushions were thrown in the air the next afternoon, and the small field overrun entirely, as about thirty thousand fans (twenty-four thousand in the park, six thousand outside on the bluffs) witnessed Christy Mathewson pitch his third World Series shutout. New York beat Philadelphia 2 to 0, winning the series four games to one. More than ninety thousand paid fans had assembled over the six days for the series, creating unprecedented receipts of nearly seventy thousand dollars: winner's shares of $1,142 per player, and loser's shares of $832. To Rice's mind, it was Mathewson's performance that ensured the success of the series. He said as much on page one of the *Journal* on Sunday morning, October 15. "There is a new champion ball team on this globe tonight and its name is Christy Mathewson, sometimes called the New York Giants." Rice concluded that Philadelphia, even with Waddell, was no match for Mathewson, for to win a team has to score. "Mathewson is the monarch of the firing line tonight and all Broadway is illuminated in his honor . . . and [the] incomparable Christy achieved the greatest feat ever accomplished in the annals of the game." In his twenty-seven innings, only two base runners reached third, only five got to second, and he walked but one.

He gave up only fourteen hits, and no runs. About the spirited ovation following Mathewson's accomplishment, Rice told his readers in his typically ornate way that it was "no wonder when the final plunk of the swat boomed out, as the gray shadows of approaching night fell athwart that field that 30,000 frenzied fans did homage to his prowess with [the] wildest vocal cataclysmic outburst that ever echoed under Coogan's bluff."[34]

On his train ride home on Sunday, Rice had some time to reflect on the week-long baseball finale. In his thousand-word analysis, "after the tumult and the shouting" had died away, he still found Mathewson to be what made the series what it was. "You should have seen him as he strode to the slab with flashing eye and distended nostrils," Rice wrote. He marveled at Matty's tantalizing assortment of pitches—his high, darting fast one, his ambling slow one, and his mystical drop ball "starting about neck high on the inside corner, this weird shoot sailed up and then snapped below the waist on the opposite side of the pan." And through it all, noted Rice, Mathewson was calm, relaxed, and smiling throughout each nerve-wracked inning as he made Mack's Quakers look simple and foolish. His consummate coolness provoked an Englishman sitting near Rice in the press stands at the Polo Grounds to say: "He's the most ripping calm and cheerful chap I ever saw. I should be in a bloody funk, and all that sort of thing, by Jawve. I should, y'know." That summed it up for Rice, who summed it all up for his readers: "That about hit the premier slabman off. He was calm and cheerful and did just a bit of 'ripping' to boot."[35]

Waiting for Rice when he arrived home from New York was a letter from the offices of the *Cleveland News,* an upstart newspaper within the fast-growing chain owned by Edward Wyllis Scripps. By letter Rice was offered the staggering sum of fifty dollars a week to move north and become the sporting editor for the new Cleveland paper. The letter and the offer may not have been entirely a surprise to Rice, for there is some evidence that he may have briefly detoured through Cleveland on his return from New York; it wouldn't have been a surprise for him to show up in Cleveland for a social visit either, for he was friends with the Northern sportswriters there (and, increasingly, everywhere). If polled, his Cleveland cronies would have remarked on Rice's work habits, creative bent, and imaginative writing firsthand, for they had spent a good deal of time with him during their ball club's three-week spring camp in Atlanta earlier that year. Rice had also endeared himself to Larry "Napoleon" Lajoie's players and to the Cleveland baseball writers with his unfailing courtesy and his unselfish efforts to see to it that the Northerners were pleasantly treated during their extended visit to Atlanta. Besides Duke Wellington of the *New York World*, Rice was host to Elmer Bates of the *Cleveland Press*, Harry P. Edwards of the *Plain Dealer*, Will McKay of the *Leader*, and L. Van Oeyen, staff photographer of the Newspaper Enterprise Association.[36]

As sportswriters will, the visitors studied the *Journal*'s sports page. They couldn't help but notice its fresh, readable, and lighthearted appearance. Rice was forever experimenting with his page layout. That spring he had regularly used a seven-column, bordered headline-like title (with his name underneath as editor) for the sports page. The title-phrases changed every day. One day it was "Sport Melodies Which Herald the Advent of Spring," Soloist—Grantland Rice; the next it was "First Beneath the Sporting Wire Under Whip and Spur," Piloted by Grantland Rice; a few days later, "Sport's Gardens Fresh and Fragrant With Flower Plats of News and Dope," Tended by Grantland Rice; and later in March, "Today's Sporting Jack-Pot Opened With a Pat-Full House," Dealt by Grantland Rice. His stories and sidebars focused on local, regional, and national sports news. Some of the stories were AP dispatches, some were rewritten (or pirated) from other papers, but most of the copy was pure, unadulterated and youthful Rice. Peppering the pages were short anecdotes, letters from readers, interviews, announcements, predictions, features on amateurs and youth sports, humorous stories, photographs and drawings, occasional serious-minded discussion of excesses in crowd behavior, ghosted stories (by Rice) under sport hero's bylines, box scores, human-interest news, speculative analyses of various athletic talents, and routine sports gossip—sometimes called "chaff from the fan mill," or "sports gossip caught on the fly."

There was also an ever-so-slight increase of verse, what Rice called "near-poetry." It certainly had not become a trademark yet, but local and visiting readers of the *Journal* couldn't miss the sporting editor's inclination to occasionally mix rhyme with his reason. In jest he explained what a near-poet was. He considered such people "the only real thoroughbred brand." The genuine poet who can grind out the real article, he joshed, should get no credit at all for his or her poetical labors. They don't have to work hard enough. "Whereas the blighted being who is hurled astride Pegasus, *nolens volens*, and continues riding even when thrown day in and day out; who courts the muse while she spurns his attentions and hands him a lemon when he asks for meat and bread—verily there should be a rich reward for him." More seriously, and quite personally, he went on that there was in truth no happier class than the near-poets: "They sing the songs that are in their hearts—take life as it comes and write as they run, unmindful of the taunts and jeers of the outside world."[37]

Besides being an acknowledgment of his talents, the Cleveland offer also added a kind of national credibility to Rice's approach to sports reporting. During the Cleveland club's stay in Atlanta, Rice and Elmer Bates chatted at length about sportswriting in general and being a baseball writer in particular. The veteran Bates had been covering Cleveland baseball for fourteen seasons. The secret of his staying power, Bates theorized, was that he had somehow managed to win the confidence of the players and the magnates both. This was extraordinary in the early days of the game because side-taking in the baseball wars between owners and players was just about impossible to avoid. Then there was the difficulty that was posed while traveling with the ball club itself. The wild and hilarious life on the road could create ill feeling between the players and the writers covering them, especially if the writers did not have much firsthand acquaintance with baseball culture. And too, Bates said that the sportswriter often had to become a general reporter, as sometimes the game itself was only one small incident in a story wired back to his paper at night on the road because "frequently the account began with the details of a riot and ended with a prophesy of a killing the next day." Bates's rule was this: If you can't boost, don't knock.[38]

For the most part, Rice was already taking this rule to heart. But his version of it, which explained to a great extent his reputation for fair-mindedness in the South, was simply this: good sportsmanship should apply not only to playing sport but to writing about it as well. No cheap shots. When it comes to the negatives, state the facts, not warped prejudices. Much to the annoyance of some fans, judging by a few of the letters he printed, Rice even expected his readers in the bleachers to show the same sporting behavior he demanded of himself when he sat in front of his typewriter in the press stand.

In the short series against Philadelphia the past spring, a second-string Atlanta third baseman by the name of Norblett, who had a sore arm, cheerfully substituted for the more seriously injured regular third baseman, Krug. Norblett tried gamely, but had a bad day. Apparently the fans roasted the youngster unmercifully, for the next day Rice lectured them all. He told his readers that nobody regretted Norblett's bad day more than Norblett, and that under the circumstances he was doing as well as he could. "Those fans in the stands who were wielding the battle ax would make ideal tin-horn sports, but nothing else," Rice wrote. "The word 'sportsmanship' isn't in their vocabulary." His criticism of the crowd brought responses to the paper, many agreeing with the sportswriter, but some not. "Knocking booms the game," said one fan. There are a lot of fans who wouldn't go to the games, the fan continued, if they couldn't express themselves and whoop things up a bit. "If a player makes an error, he should be roasted for it anyhow. No more than he deserves."

To which Rice replied that such knocking has as little place in the sporting world as it would in any other world. A bank clerk, for instance, who made an adding error would hardly do well on another column of figures if the customers let loose a whirlpool of jeers and catcalls during his efforts to continue his mental figuring. Take the case of any one in any job or calling in life, he went on, and if they knew that "2,000 wild-eyed citizens were only waiting for the slightest bobble to crack open the Anvil Chorus . . . the chances are that few would deliver enough goods to clothe a chorus girl." About his own sportswriting role in this situation, Rice said that should an athlete lose a game through some mistake, it is the duty of the critic "to tell the public just how and why the battle went glimmering down the wrong channel as much so as to burst into bravos over some deed of valor." But reporting the facts and knocking are two different propositions, he lectured. Knocking in any walk of life, much less in sport or sportswriting, never did any good and it never would (except perhaps when it came to knocking the knockers).39

Rice accepted the Cleveland offer. But he didn't take the position just because of the professional advancement of going to a city with a major-league ball club. It was also for the money. But to say it was the money wasn't to say it was greed, or that he had suddenly become dissatisfied with his diet of corn whiskey and the contents of tin cans. It was simpler than that. It was a matter of the heart. A special woman had recently entered his life. "That was real money," Rice wrote later, "and for a fellow with marriage on his mind— money never hurt."40

Katherine Hollis, one of eight Hollis children from Americus, Georgia— about 175 miles south of Atlanta—would six months later become Grantland Rice's wife. Much earlier in the year, well before the World Series, Kate (or Kit, as Rice called her) had gone up to Atlanta to visit with a girlfriend for a while; Kate was a frequent visitor to Atlanta. On one Saturday, Kate and her friend accompanied a small group to a local amusement park. While she was riding sidesaddle on a merry-go-round, "having a gay time," she noticed a tall, blond young man watching her and smiling. "He looked awfully nice," she wrote later. They were introduced. When in a few days Grantland called on the object of his gaze, a very pretty, brown-haired Southern belle, he arrived with a rented horse and buggy. He took Kate for a romantic ride. All was proceeding well enough until a quick-forming thunderstorm rolled into Atlanta. Rice wasn't very sure of himself with a horse and buggy, or for that matter with anything with moving parts, or even with anything moving. With the first, loud clap of thunder the horse bolted and started to run away. The brave but inexperienced Rice couldn't control the terrified steed as it took off for the next county. Both he and Kate were thrown from the buggy as the horse galloped out of sight. Neither of them were hurt. They hitched a ride back to Atlanta on a milk wagon.[41]

The two continued to see each other whenever they could. Over the previous couple of years, Rice had been playing a little amateur baseball for Atlanta when his schedule would permit it; he was even selected to become the first president of the Amateur City League (he was a prime mover behind reinstituting this league, which had died from lack of interest years earlier). Consequently, he was able to wrangle games with the local Americus team from time to time. He also was a popular amateur-league umpire who quickly accepted "wielding the indicator" for games in or near Americus. Rice found enough time to keep the romance going, even though by the end of the year the distances would be practically insurmountable. He was on his way to Cleveland, but not with any particular enthusiasm, for he was leaving both his roots and his gal.

Shortly before Rice packed up for his relocation north, Don Marquis and Frank Stanton threw their good friend a farewell party. It was said to have been "one of the most hilarious in Atlanta journalistic history." The main event was a contest between the three over who could produce the most barroom poetry, timed. The line count afterwards showed Stanton to be the winner by the close margin of the first six lines of a sonnet. But Rice and Marquis were thinking of protesting the decision because Stanton's practiced habit of writing his saloon poetry on one big sheet of paper gave him the advantage over the other two, who had to keep reaching for fresh sheets.[42]

When Rice set off for Cleveland in the late fall of 1905, a rival newspaper, the *Atlanta News*, published a 250-word tribute to the *Journal* sportswriter. In it Frank Buxton acknowledged that Rice's full measure of professional talents had earned him the premier honors among sportswriters. The farewell referred to the unique and original turns his stuff took, and to his poetic vein, just enough to get the touch of nature that is inherent in all sports. It claimed that there was no sportswriter who had so many friends and well-wishers. Buxton ended the tribute with the generous statement that it had been a pleasure for the *News* to work either with or against him, and that Cleveland's fourth estate would be getting a gentle-hearted, well-qualified, and fair-minded gentleman.[43]

After arriving in Cleveland, Rice discovered much to his disappointment that he was in the middle of a controversy. The offer extended to Rice wasn't close to being unanimous. There was another writer by the name of Bill Phelon, a Midwesterner, who had the support of about half of the staff. Someone made the final decision to offer the job to Rice, but the fight between the Phelon and Rice supporters was bitter enough to create some residual hostility toward Rice. Phelon wasn't too happy either, Rice learned.

Rice and Phelon did not know each other at the time, other than that they were competitors for the same job. The *News* staff must have had radically different perceptions of the kind of sportswriter they wanted on their paper, for the two were as different as they could be. Phelon, who already had a somewhat screwballish reputation, went to Chicago instead, and later to Cincinnati. Eventually the two sportswriters did become friends, but not close ones. Rice, commenting somewhat later on the individuality of the great sportswriters of his day, thought Phelon was "as odd as a Chinese puzzle." Like the New York columnist Heywood Broun, Phelon dressed and looked like a great shaggy dog. He could write almost anything besides sports, and did: anthropology, burlesque sketches, vaudeville acts, and stories. He was a student of the American Indian. He also spent years studying and making pets of such animals as scorpions, snakes, and Gila monsters. Hugh Fullerton thought of him as the Rube Waddell of the sportswriters. Even though he stayed clear of drinking and smoking (with women it was different), he was a notorious, almost juvenile practical joker. Once Rice was with Phelon and fellow sportswriter Harry Salsinger in the press box of the Polo Grounds. Directly in front of Rice there was a cigar box—punctured with many holes. He was leaning on it. "By the way," Phelon said, "I was down at the wharf this morning and I bought a young fer-de-lance. Most poisonous snake in South America—a slender snake who strikes quick. I got him cheap."

"Where is he?" Rice asked.

"In that box you are leaning on," Bill said. Had Rice's exit been timed he would have rivaled the speed of a shooting star; and Salsinger beat that. The holes in the cigar box were bigger than the deadly snake.[44]

Rice wintered in Cleveland, mostly trying to get his bearings. His main beat beginning in the spring was to cover the 1906 Cleveland ball club. On its spring training swing through Georgia, practically between games and shortly before the opening day of the baseball season, Grantland Rice and Katherine Hollis were married. They exchanged vows on April 11, 1906, at the Americus Methodist Church (Rice was Presbyterian). Rice, who was not particularly time-conscious, did manage to make it to the church on time in his rented cutaway, but did create some suspense by being late to the ceremony itself. He got so caught up in the reunion with his younger brother and best man, John, that he hadn't noticed that his bride-to-be was walking down the aisle, slower and slower, since her young knight wasn't within eye- or apparently even earshot. "After an eternity," said Kate, "the door swung open and out flew the groom—coat tails flapping, with brother John in his wake." Their honeymoon was spent chasing the American League Cleveland club, which had already started north for the opening game of the season. Grant and Kate caught up with the team in Louisville.[45]

For the remainder of the year, besides setting up house with Kate in a Cleveland flat and giving some thought and action to becoming a prospective father, Rice wrote baseball. As usual, he got on with everyone, especially the players. Napoleon Lajoie, Cleveland's slugging second baseman and player-manager, had been good friends with Rice since the spring training days in Atlanta. Upon Rice's marriage, Nap gave Kate a huge barrel of china, which the newlyweds lugged to Cleveland.

Lajoie was an exceptional ballplayer. He led the American League in hitting in 1901, 1903, 1904, and, according to the *Spaldings Guide,* in 1905. While Rice was on the staff of the *Atlanta Journal,* he featured the "champion batter of the world" in a couple of stories. According to Rice, Lajoie was the mightiest swatter since the immortal Casey—Lajoie did end up his career as one of only eight ballplayers during Rice's lifetime to get three thousand hits, and starred in the majors for more than twenty years. Lajoie was bringing down a salary of ten thousand dollars a year then, and he was worth every dollar of it to Cleveland. Before his arrival, Cleveland's Saturday contests drew around four thousand to five thousand fans; after his debut, having jumped from Philadelphia in 1902, the Saturday fan count rose to fourteen thousand. Ban Johnson, the American League president, said that Lajoie's presence alone in the American League added about twenty thousand dollars to its seasonal revenues, for the graceful and excellent-fielding second baseman attracted fans in every ballpark Cleveland visited.[46]

The comparison of Lajoie and Casey was somewhat fortuitous for Rice's poetic legacy, for it got him to thinking about doing a comic sequel to Casey. After only having seen Lajoie hit for a couple of weeks in Atlanta, Rice told his readers that had he been at the bat, the ending of the famous Thayer poem wouldn't have been the same:

> "There will never be another Casey," hear old timers say.
> They are talking futile piffle through the hat.
> 'Twould have been a different ending—and the poem would need mending
> If written about "Larry at the Bat."[47]

In the 1906 season Cleveland started out hot, but eventually the club slumped. Lajoie was spiked badly, but still managed to hit .329. Cleveland finished third, behind New York and Chicago. Perhaps to console the disappointed Cleveland fans and give them a light-hearted reason for renewed hope for 1907, Rice, with Thayer's poem not far from his mind, let his near-poet juices flow and composed "Casey's Revenge." In Rice's famous sequel to "Casey at the Bat," the mighty Casey is given a second chance.

The gist of the much-reprinted sequel was to describe what happened to Casey after his "great and glorious poop out." Rice's verses depicted the saddened hearts in Mudville who soon forgot Casey's fame, as "he was now a hopeless 'shine' " (a bum). They called him "Strike-Out Casey," and when he heard them hoot, he either fanned or popped out. As his nerve and batting eye vanished, and Mudville began to slump, rooter's row began to crow, "Get some one who can hit the ball, and let that big dub go!" But just before Casey and the team hit bottom, the pitcher who started all the trouble came to town. "He doffed his cap in proud disdain, but Casey only smiled."

Mudville had no chance to win, although ten thousand fans crowded in to see the rematch, twice the number who had seen him fan. In the ninth Mudville was down four to one. In their last turn at bat, the first hitter singles, the second is hit, and the third walks. Three on, no out. But the fourth fouled to the catcher, and the fifth flew out to right. "A dismal groan in chorus came; a scowl was on each face/When Casey walked up, bat in hand, and slowly took his place." The crowd hissed and hooted: "Strike him out!" But Casey gave no visible sign that he heard this shout, and dug in. The grinning pitcher cut one loose across the plate—Strike one! Zip, a second curve broke just above the knee—Strike two! the umpire roared. And then, the pitcher whirled again. A whack, a crack:

> Above the fence in center field in rapid whirling flight
> The sphere sailed on—the blot grew dim and then was lost to sight.
> Ten thousand hats were thrown in air, ten thousand threw a fit,
> But no one ever found the ball that mighty Casey hit.
>
> O, somewhere in this favored land dark clouds may hide the sun,
> And somewhere bands no longer play and children have no fun!
> And somewhere over blighted lives there hangs a heavy pall,
> But Mudville hearts are happy now, *for Casey hit the ball.*[48]

Rice didn't work long on "Revenge." He never spent much time with his verse. He said about his verse-writing that it came more easily than prose.

"Sometimes I can write one in twenty minutes," he said; other times, a verse might take a couple of hours or, rarely, a day or two. The existing original copy of some of his verse—little of it exists—shows that he usually composed his poems straight-away on a typewriter in one sitting and, except for correcting typing errors typical of a two-fingered typist and occasionally changing a word here and there, his poems were published without further editing. "You know how it is," he once told an interviewer, "It all depends on how I get started. . . . Once I'm started, it's easy." About how his poetry flows, he commented that "the thought and the song began to hum together in my head. I didn't know it was in me," but he added much later in his career, "I now know it is in everybody. Everybody has a song in his heart, I don't care what his business is."49

"Revenge" plays on a theme Rice voiced frequently over the years. Since much—but not all—of his daily verse-making was space-filling doggerel destined to wrap yesterday's garbage, and since he couldn't remember a single line of his own verse from day to day or year to year, he inevitably repeated himself over the years. Rice thought that Casey was a wonderful poem and that its simple and realistic truth that striking out happens in baseball and in life was what accounted for its popularity. The dramatically staged strikeout makes the poem, gives the lesson, and seals off our sentimentality. All Rice does in his romantic sequel, clumsy in parts given its parodic style, is to say, after we strike out, "then what?" It is what we do next that in large measure determines what we, all of us, are to become. As Rice tutored in "Revenge," "The lane is long, some one has said, that never turns again,/And Fate, though fickle, often gives another chance to men."50

7

Back Home

Rice struck out up north. Cleveland was a good baseball town, and Rice was certainly a good enough baseball writer. The *News* even offered him a ten-dollar-a-week raise late in 1906. But the situation simply wasn't right for him. Even his ubiquitous sunny disposition couldn't overcome the professional and personal complications presented by remaining in Cleveland. Inevitably, there was still some newsroom resentment that Rice was chosen for the job. Kate had been with child since sometime in May of the 1906 baseball season; she was also usually without Grantland, who was on the road a great deal with the major-league team. Neither of them had many Northern friends or any Northern relatives, which left the gregarious couple without a rooted circle of companionship of the kind both were accustomed to. Then there were the frigid winter blasts off of Lake Erie. And so on and so on. It added up to a good case of loneliness and homesickness for both of them, but especially for the otherwise stalwart Kate Rice. The Rices wanted to go elsewhere—Grantland's reputation by then could have taken him practically anywhere—Chicago, Detroit, Philadelphia; but they wanted to go back home. Fate stepped in.

About this time, Luke Lea, a twenty-seven-year-old Nashville entrepreneur and later U.S. senator, was preparing to enter the newspaper business in Nashville. He was starting up a new paper, the *Nashville Tennessean*. As editor, Lea had hired Herman Suter, Rice's Sewanee friend and the *Forestry and*

Irrigation editor who had earlier coaxed Rice to Washington, D.C. Now Suter wanted Rice to be his sports editor. The timing was perfect, for by early in 1907 the Rices were quite willing to move out of the major-league city. Suter added another ten dollars a week to Rice's new *News* salary, and brought him home to Nashville as the *Tennessean*'s first sports editor for a healthy seventy dollars a week.[1]

While the offer was being discussed and the Rices were still in Cleveland, on Valentine's day Kate gave birth to the Rices' only child, a daughter, whom they named Florence Davenport Rice (after her maternal grandmother). They nicknamed her Floncy.

One month later, the young Rice family was home in Nashville. The Rices were thrilled with the move, even though for Grantland it was a step backward professionally; but it was nonetheless good to be back among his kin even if psychically he most likely felt like a ballplayer who had been sent back down to the minors after a one-year debut in the majors. About the only recollection Rice had of his first few days home, while he and Kit were temporarily moving into his mother's home, was of Kit getting after him for carrying Floncy up the porch steps under one arm like a football.[2]

The *Tennessean* was the second upstart paper Rice had worked for in Nashville. On May 12, 1907, Luke Lea officially entered the newspaper publishing business with a nearly fifty-page Sunday edition. The morning paper was promoted as broadly and independently Democratic; it was intended to compete with the only other morning paper in the city, the *Nashville American*. During the previous ten years no other paper had successfully challenged the *American*, which was subsidized to a certain extent by corporate interests. Lea picked up the Hearst service, not only for national and international news but also for literary and art features, human-interest stories, cartoons, and sports.[3]

Suter, whose Washington experiences were with not only *Forestry and Irrigation* but also the *American Spectator* and the Washington edition of *Ridgeway's Magazine*, assembled a young but experienced newspaper team. Besides the well-known Rice, he brought in writers and editors from as far away as Los Angeles, several from Washington, a few Associated Press reporters, and a number of staffers from other papers in the South, including a couple from the *Nashville American*. Besides hiring two women as society editors, Suter recruited a third woman, Ganelia Fitzgerald Nye, the daughter of Bishop Fitzgerald of the Methodist Episcopal Church, as an editorial writer and exchange editor. Nye had been on the staff of the *Nashville Daily News,* Jere Baxter's old paper, until it suspended publication in February 1905.[4]

Besides the *American,* the other Nashville papers were the *Banner* and two black newspapers, the *Clarion* and the *Globe*. With financial strength and liberal advertising support, the *Tennesseean* seemed to reflect the vigorous youthfulness of its staff. The secretary of the Board of Trade commented that the paper was ensured success because the young people of the day, he thought, were "displaying ambition, push, patience, and perseverance, which, with the spirit of 'hands all around and pull together'" meant much for the growing city. The *Tennessean*, in talking about itself, claimed that it would serve no factional interests, that it had no specious policies to advocate, and that it had no axes to grind. In his inaugural statement of editorial philosophy, Lea was proud enough of his new sporting editor's personal philosophy to include specific reference to Grantland Rice's special and growing interest in the subject of sportsmanship: "We start with a clean slate; amply equipped; without prejudices; with a love of fair play; with positive and independent opinions; in a spirit of helpfulness and progressiveness; and withal, in the buoyancy and hopefulness of youth."[5]

The *Tennessean* was published in a building on the northwest corner of Church Street and Eighth Avenue in downtown Nashville. Rice sat near the window on the Eighth Avenue side, across the street from the Tulane Hotel, at a small typewriter desk. The Tulane often housed visiting baseball teams, and in years past, while Rice was growing up in Nashville, the hotel had always been a leisurely, peaceful sort of place, like a resort where soup was served on Wednesdays and Sundays. But the recent increase in industrial activity in Nashville had considerably altered the restfulness of the Tulane, as the city's decibel level had increased dramatically during the time Rice had been away.[6]

Rice noticed the difference. Outside his window was possibly the noisiest intersection in the city. Streetcars turned onto Eighth Avenue, while others clanged up and down Church Street. To make matters worse, the street was paved with granite stones called Belgium blocks, which tended to amplify the racket. The noise of horses' hoofs and steel-tired wagons, added to the trolley traffic, was practically intolerable. Rice said as much by the middle of the first week on his new job, comparing a walk down Church Street with the Wreck of the Hesperus. In verse he imagined a father and son walking by the tin organ music advertising the new five-cent picture show, and the maudlin shouts of its customers after it had begun. The general din registered with the son: "Look, father—I saw a man rush by with cotton in each ear./'He works upon the street, I guess,' said father with a leer." His son's preoccupation continued: "Oh father, what is that jangling noise that gives my head a jar?" while the "father answered never a word—but caught a depot car."[7]

Rice's four-year stint on the *Tennessean* was rugged. This was well before the American Newspaper Guild—the newspaper workers' trade union, established in 1933—would begin to collectively bargain for improved working conditions and salaries. Rice's daily assignments included getting out two pages of sports (four on Sunday), with no regular assistant; writing a witty commentary column on the editorial page similar to the well-known verse-and-paragraphers of the day such as Franklin P. Adams (*New York Evening Mail*), Bert Leston Taylor (*Chicago Tribune*), and Judd Mortimer Lewis (*Houston Post*); and covering the theater beat, as Nashville, like Atlanta, was a prime town on the one-night-stand theater entertainment circuit.[8]

Rice's typical working day on the *Tennessean* was sixteen hours, often eighteen. A "short day" was twelve. He would arrive at the newspaper offices at eight in the morning. His most difficult duty was tackled first, his editorial column. Since this column, which he called "Tennessee 'Uns," required fresh and jaunty commentary or verse on local or national happenings, he would first scan a variety of papers, especially those out of New York, to get a feel for what was in the news. These papers he would scatter all over the place, literally surrounding himself with newsprint. His small desk was always cluttered besides. It was apparently quite a sight, as when seated Rice would practically disappear under these newsy mountains. Verner M. Jones, one of Rice's coworkers, recalled that even without the ten or twelve open newspapers cushioning Rice as he hunched over his typewriter, he maintained the most disorderly and disreputable desk Jones had ever seen. Once when Rice was out of town, a mob of his well-meaning colleagues decided to beat the health department to cleaning up and out his desk for him, since it was obvious he had no intention of ever doing it himself. At the time the desk was piled high with its usual collection of miscellaneous papers, news copy, and various foreign articles. Like rescue workers unpiling debris from a collapsed mine and handing it down the line, they gradually approached the bottom of Rice's personal dump. There, underneath it all and much to their surprise, they found a perfectly good, but unused, typewriter.[9]

When working on his "Tennessee 'Uns," Rice would emerge out from under his paper mountain within a couple of hours, having read and written enough on current affairs and current complaints to create his lighthearted look at the news of the day. The habitual process never failed to amaze his colleagues, for once he set to typing his rondeaux, ballades, short sentiment items, and fictitious letters, his two fingers rarely paused. As usual, his verse came quicker than his prose: "Grantland could write a poem on any subject almost as quick as you could write it down," recalled one of his Nashville newsroom friends.[10]

When he was finished with the day's "Tennessean 'Un," Rice would then take an early lunch, usually with reporter friends or sometimes with local sports people; as he could, he also tried to eat at home with Kate and their young daughter. Returning to his office, he would take up his sports editor duties and begin to put together the next day's layout. He pieced the page together using various wire stories and special dispatches, with the general adhesive being his own writing on local or regional sports. He almost always had a columnlike collection of commentary, usually around six hundred to seven hundred words and introduced by some verse. Typically he rooted for the inclusion of more and larger graphics because their use cut down on the amount of copy he was forced to produce. And, too, what helped reduce his personal output somewhat was his decision to recruit special correspondents. During the football season, for instance, Rice obtained the services of John Heisman, then an already celebrated football coach at Georgia Tech. Heisman contributed a weekly column of "masterly and readable" (said Rice) gossip, analysis, and predictions. When Rice engineered the first and only colored-ink sporting Sunday supplement in the South in 1907, he featured a variety of football correspondents, including Dr. Joe Selden who covered Sewanee, Joe Pritchard at Alabama, Percy Whiting at Tech and Georgia, "Manhattan" and W. S. Farnsworth who covered the East in special reports to the *Tennessean,* and Clarence Eldridge, a Southern League umpire, who covered activities at Michigan—a regular Vanderbilt opponent.[11]

By early afternoon he was out of the office and on his way to one or another of the sporting sites, usually, depending on the season, a baseball or football game, or occasionally to the horse races at Cumberland Park. Then, back to the office to finish writing up the action he had just witnessed—this took another hour or so. A quick dinner at home followed, downed just before he set off to the theater to cover whatever show had hit town. After the performance, and almost before the curtain calls were over, Rice was back at his desk, thinking up something nice to say. Now without Marquis's help, Rice's theater reviews detained him late into the evening, usually until somewhere around ten or eleven o'clock, sometimes much later. Except when he was on the road, this schedule was maintained seven days a week. His duties usually demanded close to thirty thousand words and twenty sets of verse in any given week.

Kate Rice managed well enough in spite of her husband's second marriage to the *Tennessean.* Kate, Floncy, and Grantland lived with Rice's parents on

Broad Street until October of their first year back in Nashville. At least Kate and her young daughter were among family now and close enough to the Hollis home in Americus for visits. Kate and Rice's mother tended to Floncy's needs and otherwise kept the Grantland family household running smoothly while the reporter was busy earning their living expenses. The help Beulah Rice gave also enabled Kate to join Grantland from time to time on some of his beats, especially his theater duty.

Sometimes, but surprisingly rarely, when Rice desperately needed material for his "Tennessee 'Un," he would personalize his copy. On the occasion of moving his family out of the large Grantland home into a small downtown flat in the fall of 1907, he sung:

> I'm being moved to write today
>   An opening ode about October;
> I feel the spirit now at play
>   To speak of gaudy things that robe her.
> (Say, what's that smashing on the stairs
> That makes a noise like breaking chairs?)

A couple of stanzas followed, with his ode to October and its festive falling leaves interrupted repeatedly just as he would get into the swing of the thing by various crashes and bumps, until he finally gave up:

> There's no use, Bo; I can't go to it;
>   They say I'm in the way, and so,
> While I would dearly love to do it,
>   I guess I'll have to quit and go.
> (I cannot write, though it behooved—
> Because today—I'M BEING MOVED.)[12]

About the cost of the flat and the inflationary increases of prices of things in general, he lamented later in the month:

> There's a big advance in the rent of flats;
>   It costs us more to exist each day.
> The price grows greater on clothes and hats;
>   Wherever we wander we've got to pay.
> Everything's booming, from pie to hay—
>   A general advance in the law of the game;
>
> But tell me now—on the level—say,
>   Why do our salaries stay the same?[13]

Even later in the same month, after Rice had gotten his family settled in, the sounds of his own daughter's laughter prompted some reflection on another side of the cost of living:

> Clearer than any mock-bird's note, or the song of a woodland stream;
> Softer than any dove's lone call, or the sigh of a twilight dream;
> As sweet and soft as the southern breeze, or the winds of the dawn at play;
> Too soft and low to be heard, you know, ten baby-steps away.
>
> And yet it echoes around the world, over lands afar.
> And it wings its way through the realms of day to the rim of a hidden star;
> And to him who must, when the laughter stops, bow down to the Master's will,
> There falls a hush that will last for aye—and the Voice of the World is still.[14]

Rice's sentimentality and romantic drift were well suited to producing, almost daily, some kind of poetic reflection on life. For the most part his homilies tended toward the inspirational or the philosophical; although he had no ready-made formula for living a good life, he didn't stray too far from the general theme that modern life could be frightful and that getting through it successfully depended upon honing certain essential character traits. In other words, he was no escapist when it came to recognizing the basic character of the human predicament. What made his poetic exhortations useful—the kind of verse that the reader might tear out of the paper and tack up on a wall—was this realistic expression of the problem of being human combined with his thoughtful, if romantic, suggestions regarding a reasonable life-stance in the face of such perplexities. To him it was a given that whether life was a stage play, a race, or a game (he variously looked at the mystery of life all three ways), the doing of it was unrehearsed and unrehearsable, a constant struggle, and that the end, for all of us, was a this-worldly tragedy.

For Rice, the modern habit of merely getting and spending wasn't much of an approach to life. He was in complete disagreement with the growing tendency, even then, to measure success by acquisitions and possessions. In the "Tennessee 'Un" Rice commented facetiously, " 'It isn't what you used to be—it's what you are today,' is the chorus of an old song. Which properly amended to the ways of the present era runs—'It isn't what you used to be—it's what you've got today."[15]

His prescription was to cultivate a sturdy and steady *uphill* personal attitude. For even if life's problems at times seem insurmountable, what is always within a person's control, even if the surrounding circumstances are out of control, is one's general attitude toward this problem or that. Rice urged upon his readers an attitude that displayed a particularly fibrous, yet tender-hearted, inner constitution. The measure of a successful life was the extent to which a person could develop and habitually exhibit a self-reliant yet para-doxically interdependent virtuous behavior; he was stumping for his fellow humans to be essentially and collectively resolute beings who lived with courage, honor, and a sense of fair play. In "The Measure of a Man," he prodded:

> This is the measure of a man—I hold—
>   To love with honor and to lose with grace;
> To fight with courage, stalwart, strong and bold,
>   And, smiling, look misfortune in the face.
>
> To fear no man, nor shrink from any right.
>   Nor care an atom what the world may say,
> So long as deep within his inmost sight,
>   The ground looks clean whereon he makes his way.
>
> To live with faith where no doubt shall avail,
>   Refuse no friend or brother ready aid—
> And when, at last, he meets the endless Trail,
>   To go with Death, unbowed and unafraid.[16]

From his childhood days on, Grant Rice was known as a dreamer. Dreams had a particular function in the young sportswriter's understanding of the scheme of things. However fateful life seems to be, however often angst seems to close off our own possibilities, it is the capacity to dream that keeps us going day after day, year after year. Dreams energize; they give life meaning and direction. According to Rice, the measure of humanity is the measure of dreams:

> He, who has held his dreams, has met success—
>   The rest have failed—at least in greater part.
> For in the darkness and the deep duress
>   Dreams are the beacon lights of soul and heart—
> That gleam through sunless day and moonless night,
>   And glint with golden radiance the gloom,
> That sweep the shadows from the realm of light
>   And leave the star of hope beyond the tomb.
>
> But he who holds no dream—though he has won
>   The laurel wreath—what is there to attain?

> What is there left him when the race is run
>   And no dream beckons to a greater gain?
> Ambition's lure—fond hopes and endless faiths,
>   Dear memories—love's glowing fire that gleams—
> Without our dreams would be but pallid wraiths,
>   But he has all, who has still kept his dreams.[17]

In addition to his lessons in philosophy, Rice tried ably to entertain and humor his readers, usually in jesting fashion. After the especially rotund William Howard Taft defeated William Jennings Bryan for the presidency in 1908, Rice commented on what was inevitably going on at the White House:

> The carpenters are flocking with their hammers and their saws;
> They're crowding out the makers of the nations creeds and laws;
> The crowbar rattles merrily, the mortar and the wood
> Are flying hither, thither as they really oughter should;
> The front wall's on the topple—O hear the mighty din—
> They're
> Opening
> Up a
> Doorway.[18]

The writers across the country regularly read each other's stuff. This sometimes produced public exchanges between them. Rice got himself into a good-natured and long-running bashing match with the *Houston Post*'s George Bailey over the virtues of their respective home states. When the first edition of the *Tennessean* appeared, a Rice-authored poem appeared on page one entitled, "God's Country." The gist of the three-stanza verse was that when God mapped out the world, of all the lands, it was Tennessee that was given special attention: its sky a deeper, richer blue; each bird a sweeter and clearer call; the blades of grass a deeper green; more gold in sunlight's sheer. Bailey remarked in the *Post* that even if that were true, the Garden of Eden was located in Texas. Rice returned the volley. Texas was all right, Rice admitted, for Tennessee had a big hand in making it; but until the likes of Sam Houston and Davy Crockett dragged it on the map, who had ever heard of it? Rice argued that Eden was in Middle Tennessee, along the banks of the Cumberland. About twenty miles up this river, there could be found the footprints of Adam and Eve turned in the direction of Texas. "Why then," might ask the Houston writer, "if Tennessee is the Garden of Eden, did so many Tennesseans glide into Texas?" To which Rice replied, "For the same reason so many missionaries have left and are leaving for China, the Congo, and the Fiji

Islands." Given that Tennessee was "absolutely perfected," it was only natural that the pioneering Tennesseans with a missionary hunch turned to the place needing the most redemption.[19]

Later, while ringing in the 1908 New Year, Rice extended his playful attack on his fellow writers, this time going after Franklin P. Adams and New York. He referred to the "singing streams of Tuneful, Tintinabulating Tennessee" as the welcome place to start the new year; glad was he not to be eking out an existence along the "murky, misty, mournful and mischievous moors of Miserable Manhattan, where the facetious, flossy, foxy, festive and frapped Franklin P. Adams finds a home." On and on the exchanges went, each extolling the virtues of their own city and slinging mud at the others. Adams even found something good to brag about during March in New York, for at least in New York the month was distinctively March and not some weak facsimile: "March in Marvelous Manhattan is an infinite number of times as foggy, chilly, damp and utterly Marchish as the insipid, tepid variety in vogue in Cheerless Charleston, Nebulous Nashville and grandold Texas combined."[20]

Sometimes, when the writers weren't pounding on each other, they would get a verse/story chain going amongst themselves. One paper would print a little ditty, another would add to it, then another, each resident poet extending the original doggerel with some clever verse of his own. The *Pittsburgh Post* started one out:

> The girl proposed,
> Her luck was bad,
> The chap referred
> Her to his dad.

The *Chicago Tribune* then took it up:

> But dad said yes—
> He sort o' thunk
> He liked the gal
> What had some spunk.

Next, the *Columbus Press-Post*:

> You see he thought
> She had some scads,
> But their address
> Is same as dad's.

George Bailey, of Houston's *Post,* then added:

> But dad's pleased with
> The chance he took.
> She's teaching mother
> How to cook.

Finally, Rice took a turn and another playful swing at Bailey:

> Some one is talking
> Through his hat.
> What mother-in-law would
> Stand for that?[21]

In the spring of 1908, Rice had added to his newspaper and family activities a tour of duty as the Vanderbilt University baseball coach. Lifelong it was always difficult for Rice to say no when people or institutions asked for his help. He hated to hurt other people's feelings. When an emergency came up at Vanderbilt that left the baseball team without a coach, Rice stepped in and somehow found the time to rescue the team. They played twenty-two games against such teams as Tennessee, Milligan, Michigan, and Cumberland; it was a .500 season, what is now called "a building year." The yearbook description of the team's season was brutally honest: "The outfield was all right as long as the balls were batted into the air, but were out of the game when it came to stopping them on the ground." With an inexperienced squad to work with, Rice was mostly teaching fundamentals: "The nine, as it played in the final series (where they beat rival Sewanee three out of four games) might well have been called a representative college team—but it had taken a whole season to reach that stage." The yearbook editor summarized the overall impact of the season by saying that it would "hardly go down as a bright era in Vanderbilt Athletic history."[22]

With his coaching duties over by mid-June, Rice threw himself into covering the remaining months of the Southern League baseball season. By mid-September, the Nashville citizens were riding high as their local ball club, now called the Nashville Vols, was in the midst of a tight three-way pennant race. The club was still playing its games at what had been called Sulphur Spring Bottom. Rice had always been frustrated with the clumsy name of the park, mostly because it was hard to find any words that would rhyme with "bottom." On his return to Nashville, he prankishly suggested that the park should be renamed Sulphur Dell because it was a more aesthetic name, in spite of the fact that the route to the park and the park itself weren't especially picturesque. Surprisingly, the rhythm of the new name caught on as he used it more and more frequently. It wasn't long before the city fathers officially changed the name of the ballpark from Sulphur Springs Bottom to Sulphur Springs Dell.[23]

The 1908 pennant race was a nail-biter. The season came down to the last three games with the New Orleans Pelicans, managed by Charlie Frank. The Vols, with manager Bill Bernhard, had to win two of the three games to take the pennant away from the front-running Pelicans. Nashville lost the first game 5 to 1, a clean-cut, undebatable victory for New Orleans. Where most other writers figured that New Orleans would now easily take the series and the flag, Rice hung with the Vols, knowing they still had a fighting chance. Nashville took the second game, although nowhere in the text of Rice's excited account does the score of the game appear (it could be figured up from his narrative). Rice's account of the third and deciding game opened with the following lines, with his apologies to Rudyard Kipling:

> When the earth's last ball game is finished
> And the bats are twisted and dried;
> When the oldest player has vanished
> And the final Rooter has died;
> From the gold-covered gateway of Heaven
> To the red-cindered pathway of Hell,
>
> We shall dream for aeon and aeon
> Of a battle in Sulphur Dell.

Rice went on for three more stanzas, finally ending with the results of the contest: "Ay the soul of the Nashville rooter/Shouts 'Skoal to the Volunteers.'" In a pitcher's duel witnessed by 10,711 paying fans (another fifteen hundred got in when the gate was rushed), Nashville beat New Orleans 1 to 0. Holding back nothing, Rice led off: "By one game—by one run—by one point—the legions of Bernhard Saturday afternoon won the greatest race in the annals of all baseball history—a race that must go down in the archives of balldom as an epoch maker, figured in the glare of spectacular battle, capping the climax of the most spectacular pennant fight the great American pastime has ever known." As to its history-making, Rice reported that it was the first time in organized baseball that a league championship hinged on one game played between two leading teams, and the first time a championship was won by one point and by one run, the only run in the game. Nashville's winning percentage was .572, just edging New Orleans's .571. Besides the history, Rice also marveled at the well-played game, the absence of disputed umpire calls, and the remarkably well-behaved crowd.[24]

There was even a heroic performance, that of the Vols pitcher, Vedder Sitton. In the seventh, Nashville loaded the bases. A single drove in what turned out to be the winning run, but on the play Sitton tried to score from second. As he slid head-first into home, his head smashed into the Pelican catcher's knee cap. Just before Nashville was to take the field in the eighth, Sitton, with the help of two doctors, regained consciousness. Staggering to his feet, he insisted on continuing to pitch. With bandaged head and drawn face, he electrified the crowd by striking out three of the last six batters he faced, preserving the win for the Vols. To Rice's mind, the final series demonstrated what sport could be when taken to its highest, most honorable levels: "It was a grand victory, nobly fought for and honestly, fairly, squarely, and worthily won." For his heroic and masterly achievement, the appreciative Nashville fans gave Sitton three hundred dollars in cash.[25]

All Southern League attendance records were broken in the series with New Orleans: more than twenty thousand spectators paid, netting about seven thousand dollars, of which close to five thousand went to the home club. At the final game's end, the fans hurled balls into the air for fifteen minutes, and carried many of their heroes around on their shoulders. The celebrating continued late into Saturday evening, players and fans parading in the streets.

But fifty-one days after the pennant-winning game, Nashville would fall from grace. During Rice's four-year stay with the *Tennessean,* his editorial-related assignment was expressly to have fun with the news and to comment on the nature of the human comedy. His city-side duties did not include doing any actual news reporting. Except once. During a couple of Nashville's darkest weeks, Grantland Rice voluntarily became a temporary regular reporter. The tragedy took most of its citizenry's minds far away from the Big Event that came out of the idyllic world of Sulphur Dell. And Rice's newspaper, the *Tennessean,* figured directly into the headline-grabbing story.

About three weeks before the final games with New Orleans, Luke Lea announced the hiring of Edward Ward Carmack as the new editor of the *Tennessean.* Suter, who was being replaced, was invited to remain on as general manager but elected instead to go back to New York. Carmack, then almost fifty, had been a country lawyer, but in 1886 became a journalist at the invitation of the politically powerful owner of the *Nashville American,* Colonel Duncan B. Cooper. Six years later he was offered the job as editor of the popular

Commercial Appeal in Memphis. His outstanding newspaper work took him into politics, where he won a congressional seat in 1896 from the elderly Josiah Patterson, the father of Malcolm R. Patterson, who in 1906 was elected governor of Tennessee. Four years later Carmack was elected to the U.S. Senate, where he gained a national reputation for gifted but often intimidating oratory and sometimes peacockish behavior. Among Southern political statesmen of the day, he may not have had a peer, even though he lost his seat in 1906 to a former governor, Robert Love Taylor. Duncan Cooper supported Taylor, and helped him defeat his one-time employee Carmack. In 1908 Carmack decided to challenge incumbent Governor Patterson, who still had his powerful friend, Cooper, behind him.

Carmack was supported in his gubernatorial bid by the Anti-Saloon League, although it could be wondered why since he wasn't a complete stranger to tippling. Some even claimed that Carmack was an alcoholic; if not, he was still an unlikely temperance leader, since while he was on the Nashville newspapers in the 1880s he opposed prohibition and ridiculed those who wanted the "whiskey devil" thrown out of the city. Now, on the other side, Carmack welcomed the support of the Protestants who had been trying for years to curtail the city's interests in booze, faro (baccarat), and other nasty habits. (Nashville had 170 saloons—one saloon for every 476 inhabitants—and plenty of gaming dens, such as the Southern Turf, the Climax, and the Utopia, strung out along Cherry Street.) When religious sermons, revivals, and good examples all failed to bring reform to Nashville, the battle against loose morals was taken into the political arena; the "drys" hoped to elect sympathetic officials who would strictly enforce existing state laws and local ordinances banning such low-life pursuits and diversions as gambling and Sunday drinking. Carmack was the prohibition candidate of choice.[26]

But Patterson had built a powerful machine while in office and had the support of the whiskey interests—the whiskey wholesalers, retailers, and their grateful customers. With "Dunc" Cooper's behind-the-scenes help, Patterson was reelected. During the campaign, Carmack attacked Cooper as much as he did Patterson. Cooper, at age sixty-five, was bald; Carmack called him a "baldheaded angel," but wondered if he was an angel of darkness or of light, "or if there is not the smell of sulphur in his feathers."[27]

Two months after he lost the election, Carmack took up his new post as editor of the *Tennessean*. Now without public office, he returned to using the pen to right what he thought were wrongs; conveniently, he also thereby was able to keep his name in front of the state's voters. From the start, Carmack's editorials continued his campaign platform against Patterson's machinery and for the cause of prohibition. Especially interesting to Carmack was Cooper's political string-pulling, which he frequently pointed out. These attacks, which Cooper thought were unwarranted, did considerable damage to both Patterson and Cooper.

The *Tennessean* had grown remarkably in its first sixteen months; by late 1908 it was only exceeded in state circulation by the *Banner* and the *Memphis Commercial Appeal.* Carmack's state, Southern, and national popularity would help the paper's circulation even more. The *Tennessean* was gaining a reputation for leading the fight, in the paper's words, to arouse public sentiment to "enforce measures to overthrow the rule of the machine and restore the rule of the people." More generally, the paper claimed to be a fearless truth-teller, unwilling to betray its journalistic responsibility to "win fickle favors or feed tainted coffers."[28]

By November, Cooper had had about enough of Carmack's attacks. On the evening of November 8, after what he considered another unjustified Carmackian vitriolic editorial on his character, Cooper met informally at the Tulane Hotel with a friend, E. B. Craig, who was also friendly toward Carmack. Cooper asked him to go over to the *Tennessean* offices across the street, reportedly to tell Carmack to lay off: "If my name appears again, one of us must die," Cooper told Craig to tell Carmack. Carmack must not have feared the threat, for the next day he went after Cooper again in print; but he must have believed the threat, for he promptly armed himself with a borrowed pistol. Cooper must have intended to press the threat, for he, too, carried a pistol on Monday, November 9. What happened next depends on which version, the *Tennessean*'s or Cooper's (as given in the *American*), is believed.

Grantland Rice had spent the weekend covering the hoopla surrounding a big game between two undefeated football teams, Tennessee and Vanderbilt. Rice portrayed the game, which Vanderbilt won, as a mixture of drama, vaudeville (the game was error-prone; Vanderbilt alone was called for nearly three hundred yards' worth of penalties), and tragedy (in the Tennessee players' heartache over their loss). Ironically, Rice's account of the game almost exactly portended the next day's events and their aftermath, as the feud between Carmack and Cooper took on all the elements of romantic drama, vaudeville, and tragedy. Dunc Cooper, his young Nashville lawyer-son Robin, and the former sheriff of Davidson County, John Sharp, were walking to the governor's mansion for a meeting. Robin had also armed himself because he knew the two crippled fingers of his father's right hand would put him at a disadvantage should any trouble arise.

Colonel Cooper happened to see Carmack, who was about to enter his boardinghouse on Seventh Avenue, pausing briefly to tip his hat and speak to a woman, Mrs. Charles H. Eastman. Cooper approached Carmack from the corner of Union and Seventh, his son trailing behind. One thing led to another. There was a shoot-out. Carmack was hit three times at close range, and killed, by the Colonel's son. Carmack may have gotten off a couple of shots, one of which caught Robin in the right shoulder. Both Coopers and Sharp were arrested and charged with murder.[29]

These were the days when the word "alleged" was not customarily used in newspaper accounts of murders and other crimes. The *Tennessean* immediately put all of its staff on the story, including Rice. On Tuesday morning, in black-boarded headlines and columns, the entire spread on page one was covered with stories about the shooting. The paper called the killing a heinous act, a cold-blooded murder, a conspiracy, and an obvious assassination:

> Because he dared to oppose the might of the saloons in Tennessee, Edward Ward Carmack lies in cold death, and three gaping wounds cry out for vengeance on his murderers, Col. Duncan B. Cooper, and his son, Robin Cooper. The killing was murder—cold-blooded, deliberate, premeditated, with every detail planned out before hand; murder without justification; a dastardly crime without a parallel in the annals of the state. . . . Senator Carmack had been warned that Col. Cooper and his son had announced their intention to shoot him on sight. . . . Although the first shot that struck him was a mortal wound, he was able to draw his revolver and fire one shot, it taking effect on young Cooper's right shoulder and inflicting a slight wound.[30]

The Coopers' version, laid out in a low-key format in the *American*, claimed self-defense, not murder or an execution. All he was going to do in approaching Carmack, Cooper claimed, was to try to talk with him. Cooper said he raised his hand in greeting, but Carmack was surprised and reached for his pistol, shielding himself behind Mrs. Eastman. Cooper called Carmack a coward for hiding behind a woman. Mrs. Eastman, at the sight of the pistol, fled through an open gate. Carmack then ran behind two telephone poles standing only two feet apart at gutter's edge, thrust his shooting arm between them, and opened fire. Robin jumped between the two men, taking the bullet meant for his father. Then Robin ran around the phone poles, while Carmack fired again, this time directly at Robin, the bullet passing through an overcoat sleeve. Before Carmack could get his arm out from between the poles, Robin shot him from behind, felling him with three deadly steel-jacketed bullets.

By the time the murder had taken place, Rice had already put together the sporting page. His regular "Tennessean 'Uns" copy was killed and in its place the paper ran lengthy commentary on the tragedy clipped from other papers, both regional and national—a kind of opinion poll on the crime. This went on for days after the killing; in the accounts, there was substantial agreement with the *Tennessean* version that it was a wanton and premeditated killing. Rice helped collect the copy from the Southern newspapers and otherwise served duty as an editorial-page assistant while continuing his duties as sports editor. Although his sports pages for the next several days were somewhat skimpier, they were still there, and there was no indication from them that the newspaper, the city, or the South in general was in mourning.

Privately, Grantland Rice would not have been especially enthusiastic about his paper's eagerness to shut down the neighboring watering holes, but he was a staunch proponent of a free press. He may not have agreed with the single-mindedness of Carmack's cause or his ad hominem editorializing style, but he certainly defended his right to have a cause, to speak in favor of it, and to be protected by the law while doing so. Rice also seemed to admire his new editor's basic character, even though he probably didn't know him too well.

There were no bylines on the Carmack shooting stories in the *Tennessean*, so it is impossible to say exactly how much actual reporting or editing Rice contributed. However, three days after the murder, in place of his usual "Tennessee 'Un" column, Rice published a poetic tribute to Carmack, called simply "The Chief." Rice spoke for many, so well in fact that requests for reprinting the poem were immediate, and it appeared again only a few weeks after the killing, and then again one year later. Dealing now with actual drama and death rather than the fictive sort he could so easily conjure up on the sports page, he eulogized:

> The Chief is fallen! So the Troop
>   Today rides slowly;
> Sad heads bend low—broad shoulders droop
>   Where Death lies holy;
> And there are tears in watery eyes
> As rain from winter's weeping skies
> Where every sobbing southwind sighs
>   A requiem lowly.

Besides the appropriate amount of wailing and despairing, Rice also condemned the murderous act. It was not self-defense, but done by "coward heart and hand, 'shot in the back.'" And all Carmack did to deserve such a death was that "He dared through Faith and Pride to stand for Right!" Rice advised the outraged citizens, who sensed that "Shame crowns the State where, thrown away/sad Honor weeps," to fight back, but cautioned them not to go for Cooper's eye: "But blood shall call for blood the day/Justice sleeps." Instead, in an emotional appeal, he presumably urged Carmack's followers to take up his cause against the Patterson political machinery and, indirectly, for temperance:

> The Chief is fallen! But the flag
>   In rippling roll
> Waves proudly. Let no Trooper lag
>   Of stalwart soul;
> Up! Boot and saddle! To the fray!
> And in the mad, wild charge today
> God pity him who blocks the way
>   Or bars the goal![31]

If closing the bars was the goal, Carmack's martyrdom, as permanently fixed in Rice's fervent eulogy, provided the necessary energy for the statewide prohibition forces to successfully legislate a bone-dry state. On January 21, 1909, the Tennessee legislature passed over Governor Patterson's veto of the law to ban saloons. On July 1, the day the dry law would take effect, the temperance forces held a thanksgiving service at McKendree Methodist Church, while the losers held their own services at the saloons on Cherry Street to throw down their last legal beverages of choice for about the next thirty years.[32]

The Cooper-Sharp trial lasted two months. Sharp, an accessory before the fact, was acquitted. The jury found both Coopers guilty of second-degree murder and sentenced them to twenty years in prison. But in an appeal before the state supreme court, Robin's conviction was reversed on the grounds that the jury wasn't instructed properly with regard to the possibility that he could have had the right to shoot Carmack if he thought his or his father's life was in danger. In the end, Governor Patterson pardoned his friend, "Dunc" Cooper: "In my opinion, neither of the defendants is guilty and they have not had a fair and impartial trial, but were convicted contrary to the law of evidence." Beneath the pardon announcement, the *Tennessean* ran a clipped version of Rudyard Kipling's 1890 poem "Cleared," italicizing its last line: "*We are not ruled by murderers, but only—by/Their friends.*" There is little doubt that the selection of the poem was by the newspaper's resident Kipling expert, Grantland Rice.[33]

When the state went dry, Rice was none too happy, in spite of the fact that the prohibition band wagon was energized, in part, by the kind of emotionalism his "fallen Chief" poem whipped up. In a booze-bottle-shaped essay, called "In Memoriam," published the day the law was passed, Rice tells of his weeping eye and dusty mouth, no more able to call upon the Booze to help him find inspiration out of deep stagnation; no more would the juice assist him in groping for a theme for a verse; no more would his Muse carry him up in airy flight or thaw the frozen matter in his brain. Of course, he also pointed out that no more would he have to hide beneath the sheets after seeing purple rabbits crawling on the wall, or skeletons with bony treads doing a clog around his bed, or wake up "blear-eyed, disgusted, and forlorn, with fuzz upon my tongue, O Love, that feels like a conductor's glove."[34]

In Nashville, however, Rice needn't have worried too much about the law, for Hilary E. House, a gregarious furniture merchant, was soon elected mayor on a more liberal urban political philosophy: "As for whiskey, I am not a drinking man, but as long as I stay in a free country I will eat and drink as I please." The saloons and gambling houses on Cherry Street were soon quietly operating again, even though their patrons had to enter by way of back entrances on Printer's Alley, which were especially convenient for Rice and his newspaper cohorts. The locals could also still import liquor for their own consumption and policemen usually could be counted on to look the other way when soft-drink stands supplied some harder stuff to their customers, who included a weary sportswriter needing a lift "unto some tall poetic height."[35]

In his years at the *Tennesseean,* there were any number of local and national sports controversies demanding Rice's attention and requiring him to take some kind of position. Horse racing was about to be outlawed in New York with the reelection of Governor Hughes. Even though the racing game would go on elsewhere, with New York out of the picture, Rice thought that the sport would be dulled. He didn't fault the game itself, or even the laws against horse racing—or boxing either—for the setback. Instead, he thought, the American people themselves were ultimately responsible for such problems. He thought that their plunging (gambling) on the sport was so unreasonably heavy that it was inevitable that contestants would be bought off. There were sensational stories around about turf plungers who would bet as much as forty thousand dollars on a single race. When the evidence of a scandal surfaces, Rice observed, then the public becomes indignant and turns around and howls at the crookedness in the sport. "In other words," he wrote, "there seems to be too many crooks wandering broadcast in these goodly United States for a fair, clean game to linger long without a blot against it."[36]

Closer to home, in the South, another sport had grown so popular that it too was beginning to become a victim of its own success. College football was supposedly an up-and-up amateur game without the longer and shadier history of professional boxing and racing. But during his first football season back home, Rice had caught wind of a potential scandal regarding the playing of "ringers" (illegal players) during an intrastate game between John Heisman's Georgia Tech team and the University of Georgia. It isn't known who Rice's snitch was. However reluctant he may have been to go to press with the story, he was the first of the Southern sports editors to drag Georgia up and down the field: "Of all the bare-faced and flagrant violations of collegiate sport, the stunt perpetrated by the University of Georgia in her game against Tech sets a new limit."[37]

Georgia, ten days before the game with Tech, held a secret, closed practice (which was extraordinarily unusual then). On the same day, a number of men matriculated into the University's agricultural department and were put into courses. Then they practiced with the bona fide team until the game with Tech. When they arrived in Atlanta for the game, Georgia's coach, Whitney, refused to give out any game-day lineup and hustled his team into the hotel without even registering them. Signing in the team's players would have been difficult, for as it turned out, there were at least six of them who, by hotel check-in time, may have had game faces, but had not yet been given their game names.

In these days before platooning and free substitution, the football squads were rather small in number, often only fifteen to eighteen men; six was a goodly percentage of the team. At game time, the Georgia "team" was hardly recognizable; besides confusing the press, even the student body contingent from Georgia found themselves cheering for complete strangers: "Go, whozits, go!" Tech lost, 10 to 6, although when the game was called on account of darkness, Tech was on the Georgia goal line.[38]

From his informed source, Rice learned that Georgia had gathered quite a collection of players for the Tech game, including a fellow by the name of Edmondson, who had played football seasons ago for Georgetown and more recently had become the right fielder for a professional baseball team. His Georgia game-name was McDuffle. The team also included two other former Georgetown players and two former Syracuse athletes, one of whom was captain of Savannah's two famous Blue and White professional football teams.

Apparently, the players confessed to the stunt when they were safely out of Atlanta on a train north. They claimed they had received $150 and all expenses from the Georgia management.

About the scandal, Georgia's Coach Whitney said, "Mr. Rice has made his charges. Now he should prove them." Which Rice apparently did. His charges and proof of professionalism must have been compelling, as Whitney was himself on a train north the next day, having been forced to hand in his resignation to the University officials. Rice even suggested that Chancellor Barrow of Georgia continue to clean the entire house and remove the entire Georgia Athletic Board.39

While such cheating wasn't the norm in the South, it wasn't particularly exceptional either. One year later, Rice came across another example. LSU was claiming to be the strongest team in Dixie, having beaten almost everybody in fairly convincing fashion. Rice questioned whether or not the wins were fairly earned. He publicly challenged LSU to show that they were an amateur team composed entirely of eligible, nonsubsidized students.

Rice learned about the probable LSU cheating through some informal conversations with an out-of-state pigskin coach. In October, Vanderbilt had beaten Rose Poly (in Terre Haute, Indiana) 32 to 0. After the game, Hozey Clarke, the Rose Poly coach, was in Rice's newspaper office, along with the Vandy coach, Dan McGugin, and the officials who refereed the game that day. (This was a common habit following the contests, the competitor-coaches and the officials and a newsman or two meeting together to rehash the game and otherwise talk sports.) As the conversation expanded from reliving that day's game to football in general, the LSU team came up. Clarke mentioned that he knew a couple of players on the team. He recalled that one of the LSU players, going under the name of Charles C. Bauer, was an Indianapolis football player by the name of Charles Ora Buser who had played for a while for Wabash College in Crawfordsville, Indiana. Clarke explained that he had played high school football with Buser (alias Bauer). Coach Clarke also said that at about the same time Buser and several other Indianapolis athletes went south for the fall, a businessman approached him and said that if he would also go to LSU he would get the same inducements given the other players.

It turned out that the LSU coach, a Mr. Wingard, who was new to the school in 1907, had coached previously at Butler University in Indianapolis, and had played his football in Pennsylvania. His 1907 and 1908 LSU football squads were composed almost entirely of athletes without Southern accents, gathered up from the West (Indiana was considered part of the West) and from Northern schools familiar to him. All students entering Southern universities and intending to play football (or any other sport) were expected to sign an affidavit swearing that they were amateurs and that they had not the year previously played football anywhere else; on their honor, if they couldn't so swear, they were ineligible.

Wingard's entire team so swore, but the snail's pace investigation (demanded by Rice) carried out by the Southern Intercollegiate Athletic Association executive committee—completed one year later—eventually verified Rice's claims of ineligibility. Players were being paid to play; Buser, for sure, was playing under an assumed name and received liberal and regular subsidies; there were "grounds for suspicion" regarding the eligibility of the entire team, even though concrete evidence was lacking; and Coach Wingard was found to be the primary culprit who had either arranged for or consented to bringing the ringers to Baton Rouge. The University faculty and authorities were exonerated from "knowledge, connivance or suspicion" as to the irregularities involved. About which Rice said that no committee on earth could clear the LSU officials from an astounding laxity of guardianship and control of their athletic affairs.[40]

Rice's whistle-blowing was appreciated on the whole, but it did make him unpopular in some quarters. In particular, some Georgians were especially unhappy about Rice's nose being too far up their business regarding the University of Georgia affair. One message arrived from Quitman, Georgia, a few days after the Southern Intercollegiate Athletic Association found the athletic conditions at State University disgraceful and scandalous, and after the SIAA called for the Georgia faculty and administrators to root out any further source of corruption that they could find: "Dear Grantland Rice, Nashville, Tenn. In behalf of the University of Georgia and the state at large, we wish to say that Georgia is 50 percent better in the way of clean ball playing than Tennessee. Tennessee is the worst state in the union for rotten sports. There are many professionals there and others who are rotten in Tennessee, including yourself. So brace up, you d____ butter-in." The message ended with the severe admonition that Rice ought to "go way back and eat chestnuts."

The letter, which went on to brag about Georgia's success over Tennessee in sports, added a name-calling postscript: "You are a vagabond." Rice politely responded to the letter, simply pointing out the facts, passing up most of the letter-writer's charges, except for the postscript: "From that crushing rejoinder we have no recourse. We take the count with visions of a stellar constellation dancing before our eyes. Alas, it is true."[41]

College football was also suspect for its continued reputation for violence and brutality. Things hadn't changed much from the 1890s. John Heisman remembered his Oberlin team beating Stagg's Chicago team 33 to 12 on a Saturday, then taking the train over to Champaign to carry out more mutual manslaughter with Coach Hall's University of Illinois team on Monday. The victories were costly, as the two-in-one-week games reduced his team to "crutches, canes, splints, and yards of plaster thereby." The team took day-train coaches that evening to Toledo in order to transfer to another train about midnight. Eight of Heisman's players were under a doctor's care, and three others had to have their cauliflower ears lanced; many had bandaged heads or arm slings, and a few faces were court-plastered. When they helped each other off the train at the Toledo station, they even had one man on a stretcher—the manager, who boarded the train healthy but ate himself into a painful attack of indigestion. A solicitous mob closed in on them, clucking and murmuring.

"Good heavens," cried a woman standing near one of the total wrecks, "look at this one. He must have been underneath."

"I was, madam," he groaned. "Every time, it seems." An ambulance driver ran over to Coach Heisman.

"All right sir, all right," he cried. "The ambulances are over this way."

"See here," Heisman said a bit peevishly, "we did get bounced around a little but you people are overdoing this. We can make it on our own steam."

Just then a newsboy arrived carrying wet-inked papers, just off the press. "Hee yah, hee yah. Yextraaaa . . . All abouta wreck ona Clover Leaf . . . Yaaaaaaah." It seems that the ambulances and interns had arrived at the station to take care of the survivors of the Clover Leaf train wreck who arrived a few minutes later.[42]

Throughout the first decade of the twentieth century, the newspapers were principal players in the ongoing debate about the violent nature of football: reports of crippling injuries and deaths were growing in number; twenty-one deaths and more than two hundred injuries were reported in 1904 alone. As the game attracted more attention and drew more protests, reported casualties increased. Some schools dropped the sport altogether. The dean of the Divinity School at the University of Chicago, Shailer Mathews, was quoted in 1905 as saying that football "is a social obsession—a boy-killing, education-prostituting, gladiatorial sport. It teaches virility and courage, but so does war. I do not know what should take its place, but the new game should not require the services of a physician, the maintenance of a hospital, and celebration of funerals."[43]

Even with the involvement of President Teddy Roosevelt, who was dragged into the fray at one point, not much progress was made in reducing the violence of the sport. Although he was sincere in his concern that intentional maiming of players must cease, and even though the *New York Times* claimed that Roosevelt's efforts to reform college football were on a par with his 1906 Nobel Peace Prize–winning efforts to help settle the Russo-Japanese War, absolutely nothing happened except that a statement was released by the president that the representatives from the Big Three (Harvard, Yale, and Princeton) had promised to stop their mucking play. Some rules were changed and the football world slowly began adopting Heisman's solution, the forward pass. But the game went on as before. Gaining ten yards (up from five) with mostly mass-formation plays and an occasional willowy pass (a fifteen-yard penalty was imposed for an incomplete pass—hardly an incentive for spread formations and long bombs) was so discouraging from the outset, especially when a team was deep in its own territory, that the kicking game was revived. Drop-kicking the ball on early downs became routine strategy. When a team was inside its own ten-yard line, a standard rule was to drop-kick on first down, inside the twenty, kick or punt on second down, and so on. Forty to fifty yards a kick were commonplace; Heisman remembered the Wisconsin kicker, Pat O'Day, who once drop-kicked the ball sixty-two yards for a score, and Pop Thayer of Pennsylvania who, he claimed, could punt the ball seventy to seventy-five yards in a tight spiral. With the focus on kicking, typical football contests would have looked much like one of Rice's hardly gripping play-by-play accounts of the opening of the second half of the Vanderbilt vs. Ohio State game in November of 1908:

> Blake kicked off to Harrington 40 yards, and Harrington made a return of 20. Wells failed to gain, and Gibbon kicked 40 to Morrison, who ran back 10. Metzger made 2 and Morton failed to gain. Blake punted 40 to Barrington, who came back 8. Gibson punted 35 to Morrison, who was unable to make any return. Metzger made 4 and Morrison 3. Blake punted 15 yards out of bounds, and the ball was in Ohio's possession on her own 45 yard line. Wells made 5 and Barrington failed to gain on a fake kick.[44]

With the typical loyalty of a former player, Rice contended that most of the debate on the violence in football was blathering. The facts in the matter, he claimed, did not show football to be especially dangerous, even though it could be rough. He researched the matter, and reported that after eighteen seasons of Southern football among the twenty-odd colleges playing it, in the literally thousands of contests that had been played, only two deaths were reported. In Tennessee alone, in 1909, there were four deaths from baseball.

Such schools as Vanderbilt, Auburn, Sewanee, Georgia Tech, Alabama, Clemson, and LSU had to that date yet to face their first serious life-maiming injury. Yet at Vanderbilt there were two athletes who had had such crippling injuries—one was in track athletics, the other in basketball. He noted that there had not been one death or over-serious injury reported at Chicago, Michigan, Wisconsin, Illinois, or Minnesota in the West; nor at Yale, Harvard, Princeton, Pennsylvania, Cornell, or Dartmouth in the East. "Yet to hear a good many speak, one would think football was leaving a general harvest of death," wrote Rice, "where war, pestilence, flood, fire, and famine combined was nothing in comparison."[45]

Rice offered his readers a fable about a nation that decided to abolish all games where statistics showed that anyone had ever been killed or wounded. A committee appointed for the purpose of overseeing the job listed the sports to be dropped: football, baseball, motoring, hunting, airshipping, basketball, hammer throwing, high jumping, pole vaulting, prizefighting, bicycling, horse racing, wrestling, horseback riding, politics, and a few others. The only two sports left were Ping-Pong and pink teas (drinking). In time, however, two competitors in pink teas were reported to have overtrained, and another in Ping-Pong slipped while swiping at a ball and broke a shoelace. In view of the horrifying statistics, the committee could do nothing but ban sports altogether. By then the only real men left in the nation were the suffragettes, who, he thought, still "played the game with enough vim to keep their lungs open." The suffragettes took over the husky jobs in government through force of arms, and restored the old sporting schedule. The moral: If a man can't be a man let him step down and give the women a chance.[46]

Clearly, even by the time Rice was covering the Vandies, college football was well on its way toward its eventual gigantic status among sports. The creation of professional coaches, and in turn their devising of elaborate systems, techniques, strategies, logistics, and organizational and psychological battle plans, had rather quickly turned the sport into a fairly heady, time-consuming, and serious undertaking. The increasing numbers of old grads swelled alumni contributions, both spiritually and monetarily, helping create a more commercial, winning-oriented and big-business approach to the sport.

Yet, in spite of these trends, there were still features of the sport then that could be almost quaint. One fall, Vanderbilt was scheduled to play "Hurry Up" Yost's Michigan team. Between 1901 and 1905 Michigan had lost only one game, partly due to Yost's creative interpretation of rules of recruiting and eligibility. In his playing days, well before there were conferences and eligibility rules, Yost had once been hired by Lafayette College to play in a crucial game against the University of Pennsylvania. At the time he was a student at West Virginia. He transferred to Lafayette, played in the game, and transferred back to West Virginia. As a coach at Michigan, Yost routinely played graduate students, believing that a student is a student. But in 1906 the Western Conference tightened up its eligibility rules, restricting retroactively player eligibility to three years, insisting that all players be undergraduates, and requiring that all coaches be regular faculty members with professorial rank. Michigan alumni and students protested the new rules, which would have hurt Michigan severely given Yost's system. Michigan refused to play under the new rules and eventually withdrew from the conference in 1908, not to rejoin what later became the Big Ten until 1917. In the years between, Michigan had difficulty scheduling major opponents, but gladly continued to play Vanderbilt as they had since 1904.

Besides the relatively competitive strengths of the two schools, there was another good reason for Vanderbilt and Michigan to play each other. The two coaches were teacher and pupil, and brothers-in-law as well. Dan McGugin, the Vanderbilt coach since 1904, had played for Yost on the crushing Michigan teams of 1901 and 1902. McGugin would have been one of the types of players Yost relied on, but whom the new conference rules prohibited from play. With a B.A. degree in hand from Drake University, McGugin joined the Yost recruits upon entering the University of Michigan Law School. The graduate student was on the team that defeated Stanford on New Year's Day 1902 in the first Rose Bowl game. When McGugin's eligibility finally ended in his third year of law school, he stayed on with Yost as an assistant coach. Vanderbilt hired him in 1904. At the time he was a practicing lawyer in Detroit. After a couple of coaching seasons, he moved permanently to Nashville, where he coached and practiced law until his death in 1936. Yost and McGugin married Nashville sisters, McGugin marrying Eunice Fite in 1905 and Yost wedding Virginia Fite in 1906.

The 1908 contest between the Vandies and the Wolverines exhibited much in the way of the friendliness that existed between the coaching brothers-in-law. Even though they were exact opposites—Yost ever-serious (Rice later said that Yost was the most serious man he had ever met) and McGugin owning a keen sense of humor—they respected each other. Michigan had beaten Vanderbilt, which they usually did, 8 to 0 the previous year before seventy-five hundred spectators at Vanderbilt's Dudley Field. The 1908 Vanderbilt Commodores had been winning lustily over such schools as Rose Poly, Clemson, and Mississippi, but had to meet Michigan, their first major test, on the Wolverines' home field. Michigan had been winning too, against Case, Notre

Dame, and Ohio State, mostly on the uncanny kicking skills of their outstanding right halfback, Allerdice. Rice commented before the game that the Commodores would have to spend most of the afternoon sitting or standing on Allerdice's right toe, "for he has shown that within striking distance of the bar" (wooden, not alcoholic, Rice added), "he is a thing of beauty and a pain forever."[47]

Oddly enough, Rice did not comment on the composition of the Michigan team or upon Yost's recruiting practices. If there were "tramp" athletes on Yost's roster then, Rice either had no firsthand evidence for it, or, if he did, he declined to publish the information, perhaps out of courtesy and friendship for McGugin. It is even possible that Rice may have held a double standard of sorts, for the Michigan games enhanced Vanderbilt's football reputation (as did their contests with Yale). Perhaps the glitter of playing a Northern national powerhouse blinded Rice to Yost's well-known shortcuts. Whatever the reason, Rice's role in this particular series was that of an unabashed rooter—and then some.

Before the team left for Ann Arbor, Rice and the Vanderbilt Alumni Association arranged for the game to be detailed to the local fans at Ryman Auditorium. The Postal Telegraph Company arranged for a special wire directly from Ferry Field in Ann Arbor to the auditorium some five hundred miles away. On the auditorium stage, besides the telegraph caller, the stage sported a large diagram of a football field, complete with a ball that could be moved up and down the field at the direction of the caller. A modest price was charged to cover expenses, with a special rate for students.

On the night before the team left for Michigan, the Vanderbilt student body and their Nashville supporters gave the team a "hullabaloo." The next morning at 7:50 the Commodore Special pulled out of Union Station. Besides the team (sixteen players: the starting eleven and five reserves "for emergencies"), the coach's family, including his two-year-old daughter, Lucy Ann, and some Nashville groupies, Grantland Rice also made the trip. The journey through Kentucky and on toward Ohio was uneventful, except for the day-long view of a badly scorched landscape, the result of a terrible summer and fall drought. Arriving in Cincinnati around 5:30 P.M. and facing a four-hour stopover, the team dashed over to Cincinnati University's gridiron for "a lively signal practice" in the twilight to work out the kinks from the day-long confinement in the train compartments. By 9:30, the train pulled out for Michigan, and arrived early Friday morning. Rice was sending back telegraph copy to his paper all the while.

That evening, the night before the big game and after another signal practice and some fidgety rest, the Commodores were given another rally. This time, however, it wasn't at the hands of Nashville's rooters, but Michigan's. About five thousand Michigan fans crowded into the university's big chapel to treat the Vanderbilt team to their own hometown welcome. The McGugin men were cheered again and again in what the head orator called the greatest demonstration ever seen in the Wolverine lair. "The vocal cataclysm reached a dizzying height," wrote Rice, following the speeches of the various parties to the contest. Even the Vandies' team mascot, Miss Lucy Ann, was said to have thoroughly enjoyed the lively welcoming celebration.[48]

The contest on Ferry Field that next afternoon featured size against speed. Michigan was big (for those days), especially their 232-pound center, "Germany" Schulz. The lightest man in the Wolverine interior line weighed 190. The much lighter Commodore team, which averaged about 170 pounds, was quick, but young; seven of the sixteen players had yet to play in a big, intersectional game such as this one.

Rice had an interesting perspective on the game. Besides being expected to write up the Vanderbilt game in stirring fashion, he also happened to be the designated head linesman for the game. This—his practice of refereeing a game he was reporting on—wasn't unusual, or even suspect, for Rice was highly sought after as an official. His reputation for fair-mindedness had spread even beyond the South. No one thought twice about having him officiate in a game featuring a Nashville team; he nicely balanced the crew, as besides the referee from Virginia, the umpire and the field judge were from Michigan. Armed only with a keen memory for the sequence of plays and the various highlights, the reporter/head linesman successfully pulled off his double duty. The only adjustment he seemed to make in his written accounts of the game was to be less windy than usual; his report was shortened from his typical three or four thousand words to about two thousand; that and he didn't say much about the quality of the officiating. One day later, this low word count account was supplemented with a second and wordier summary of the entire game's action.

From his privileged vantage point, the game was a good but losing fight for the Commodores: the final score was 24 to 6. Once again, Yost's machine overran and outkicked McGugin's courageous players. Allerdice won the kicking duel with the Commodore kicker and captain, Blake. Allerdice's kicks soared fifty to fifty-five yards, while Blake, often kicking under a swirling onslaught from the maize and blue, had two kicks blocked, and several that traveled out of bounds hardly beyond the line of scrimmage. In the win, Allerdice's kicking, Rice reported, was as "true as a bullet from a Kentucky rifle." His three field goals (four points then), combined with two Michigan touchdown runs (five points, plus the one extra point for each), gave the Wolverines the lopsided victory. Both teams used the forward pass, Vanderbilt on one occasion even using a triple-forward pass.[49]

Meanwhile, the folks back home in Nashville didn't seem to be bothered much about their representatives coming out on the losing end of the game. Three thousand rooters gathered at the auditorium for the detailing—which wasn't bad, considering that the game played in Ann Arbor was in front of about ten thousand fans. The crowd at the Ryman didn't mill and mull around waiting for Vanderbilt to do something especially heroic before it began its hurrahing; bunches and knots of yelling would burst out any time Vanderbilt did anything, anything at all. Even when the fans knew Vanderbilt had lost, they yelled with the same fighting spirit and gusto they demonstrated at the beginning of the contest.

And even when there was some confusion as to exactly what was happening up north, the fans roared on anyway. The telegrapher in Ann Arbor had all he could do to keep his instrument ticking and clicking accurately, as the game was played on a very cold and gray October afternoon. Without any kind of protective press stand accommodations, the operator was prone to frequent telegraphic stuttering, as the frigid weather occasionally got his hand to shaking uncontrollably. But the crowd didn't care. At halftime, when the Commodores were down 14 to 0, the auditorium rooters sent the team a telegram to tell them that Vanderbilt was still game, and that the local fans were "still pulling with might and main."

The operator added to the excitement with his animated calls. When Vanderbilt made its lone touchdown, he intimated to the crowd what was happening by running into center stage waving his arms wildly. Before he even announced the touchdown, he cried ecstatically, "Vanderbilt, rah, rah!" When he finally told them what was happening, all the other rooters yelled likewise, making all kinds of uncommon noises.[50]

The sport of football furthered Rice's preoccupation with the special virtue of the well-played game. These days in Nashville reinforced in him the conviction that the ends do not justify the means; and more, that how something is striven for is often a good deal more important in the long run than whether or not the goal is achieved. When the Vanderbilt Alumni Association asked Rice to write an inspirational poem to serve present and future alumni, he quickly put together a twelve-stanza verse called "Alumnus Football." Although over the years he tinkered with different versions of the poem—not noticeably improving it—the final two lines of the last stanza remained largely the same; these lines made sport and sportswriting history, for as part of America's sporting lore they have been quoted and misquoted, praised and ridiculed ever since:

> For when the One Great Scorer comes to mark against your name,
> He writes—not that you won or lost—but how you played the Game.

The original version told the romantic story of one Bill Jones, once a shining star on his football team, who later, when facing life's trials, met with unfair competition, disappointment, and failure after failure. Old coach Experience finds him low, about to give up, and lectures him: "Don't lie there whining—hustle up—and keep on coming back . . . and though the world may romp across your spine—let every game's end find you still upon the battling line." In the original published version Rice added a thirteenth stanza, slightly set apart from the body of the poem. In it he reiterated the life-as-a-football-game theme, then added:

> Such is Alumnus Football on the white-chalked field of Life—
> You find the bread-line hard to buck, while sorrow crowns the strife.
> But in the fight for name and fame among the world-wide clan,
> "There goes the victor," sinks to naught before "There goes a man."[51]

Had Rice actually expected these inspirational words and the virtues they extolled to be the standard for moral conduct, he would have been a remarkable exception to the norm in Nashville then. But however lofty the sentiment about playing the game well and fairly versus merely winning it, and no matter how much never-say-die behavior the words might have inspired, Rice shared a common prejudice then which made this philosophical sermonette somewhat hypocritical. It was an exhortation apparently limited to the white players and to the games played on their white-chalked fields.

A promotional blurb for Thomas Dixon's play "The Clansman" put things just about the way they were, racially speaking, in Nashville and throughout the South at the end of the first decade of the twentieth century. The play, which was a retelling of the Reconstruction struggle and which was originally the second part of a trilogy before it was dramatized on the stage, had been touring for three years. It was to have a two-day run in Nashville in the spring of 1909. According to the blurb, predictions that the performances would stir up sectional animosity and inflame race hatred had not proved to be true; instead, the announcement happily went on, the effect of the play had been generally therapeutic. "It has indeed drawn racial lines more closely," the writer explained, "but in a manner beneficial instead of evil."

In cities where the play was performed, someone gathered statistics to show that violent crimes between the races dropped, and that assaults by blacks on white women were much fewer. "The status of the Negro has improved, as the white man has learned how to handle him," claimed the promotion. The play was even beneficial to the prohibition movement, so went the argument, in that justification for the new liquor laws could be found in the improvement in race relations by keeping liquor from the "brutish and ignorant, for the drink-crazed Negro is the chief menace of the white homes." The lesson that the play apparently tried to teach was what Dixon believed four thousand years of Aryan civilization had taught: the white must cling to the white, the black to the black, and the yellow to the yellow.[52]

This promotion appeared on Rice's sporting page, just below his sports column, "Sportograms." It isn't clear who wrote the blurb; but as the theater critic, Rice would at least have had to approve of running the promotion, even if he hadn't written it. In a short review of the play published a few days later, Rice noted that "The Clansman" could not exactly be called an artistic drama, but that "it has certain powerful elemental features that make a strong appeal and these elements of the play won their usual applause last night at the Vendome." In his low-key and fairly objective account, Rice thought the play mostly just "lumped along."[53]

Nashville was a segmented city. As the electrified, semirapid transportation system made the suburbs more attractive for commuters, and as the wealthier whites moved out of the central business district, the downtown and the slums surrounding it were left to less well-off whites and the ethnic subcommunities. There was the "Green" community, the Catholic Irish, first near the riverfront in squalid shanties and tenements, and later toward the western end of the city, closer to railroad work, which was a step up from the unskilled riverboat dock work. The religiously diverse German immigrants—arriving about the same time as the Irish but with a head start on skills, capital, and experience—settled mostly in the northern end of Nashville, and into middle-class cottages. German Jews were joined by Jews from eastern Europe, who, being on the run from the Russian and Hungarian pogroms, were often desperately poor and started out near the docks, sharing the former homes of the Irish poor with yet another subcommunity—the largest—the blacks. This low-lying and grimy slum area quickly became known as "Black Bottom."[54]

More than a third of Nashville's population was black at the turn of the century. For the preceding thirty years, black freedmen had steadily come to the prosperous city in search of independence, economic security, and personal dignity. First they were simply a low-wage-earning class—the men worked in lumber mills, fertilizer plants, and iron foundries; the women in domestics or nursing. But soon a middle-class black bourgeoisie emerged to serve the laborers: lawyers, doctors, clergy, businessmen, newspaper publishers, undertakers. With the creation of a number of black colleges in the city (Central Tennessee College, Roger Williams University, Fisk University, and Meharry Medical College), the black community began to produce educated, professional, and prosperous citizens.

White citizens grew increasingly irritated by this development: the migration continued to increase the numbers of blacks in the city; blacks were not as easily satisfied with "Negro jobs"; the concentration of the poorest blacks in slums such as Black Bottom and Hell's Half Acre were perceived to be threats to public health; and the black vote became a powerful challenge to white political control of the city.[55]

The growing hostility of the whites, combined with a curious white paternalism, was met by the blacks not with confrontation, but with accommodation mixed with low-level militancy. The Nashville black community sided more with Booker T. Washington's self-help ideology (symbolized by Washington's organization, the National Negro Business League) than with Fisk-educated W. E. B. DuBois's program of equality and full civil rights (the goal of DuBois's organization, the National Association for the Advancement of Colored People). The result was that as the black community promoted and patronized private black ventures, it was only natural, in the minds of the whites, to assign the black community separate, but hardly equal, accommodations in the public sector as well: schools, hospitals, transportation. Housing and public facilities were also divided up, each group served by their own: separate fairgrounds, separate grandstands, separate railroad waiting rooms, separate saloons, separate areas within the parks, even separate cemeteries, presumably to ensure that there would be no mixing even in death.[56]

Things weren't much different in sport. The legendary claims for the virtue of sport had been that besides its character-building and morally uplifting nature, it was a reasonably just world sensibly separated from the often harsh and unfair ordinary world. In sport, so the claim implied, performance, not social background or special privilege or race, mattered most. But when this rhetoric was stripped away, the actual conduct of sport wasn't particularly exceptional at all—at least when equal opportunity was the issue. Sport was just as real-world as the real world: it was segregated as well.

In this regard, Grantland Rice was typically Southern and typically white.

Rice's views on the Jack Johnson vs. Jim Jeffries fight in 1910 is illustrative of his racial insensitivity in his early years and indicative of the views of most of the white sportswriters of the day.

Before the 1880s, black boxers—many of whom were slaves—were often among the best representatives of young America when it tested itself against the British counterpunchers. Bill Richmond ("The Black Terror") and Tom Molineaux were among the best-known early black pugilists, willing to take on any opponent, regardless of color. For instance, West Indian–born Peter Jackson battled Jim Corbett to a sixty-one-round draw in 1891. But like horse racing, baseball, golf, even football to some extent, after the 1880s boxing became decidedly segregated; this segregation was given legal status when the U.S. Supreme Court in 1896 authorized and therefore institutionalized the concept of "separate but equal" in *Plessy v. Ferguson*.[57]

Boxing was somewhat less definitive in drawing the color line than its other sporting counterparts. In the lighter weight classifications, the exclusionary practices were less severe, ostensibly because the smaller physiques symbolized no serious threats to white domination. Furthermore, the interracial battles could be profitable for the promoters. Canadian bantamweight George Dixon, nicknamed "Little Chocolate," held his title from 1890 to 1892, then the featherweight title until 1900; Joe Gans defended his lightweight title from 1901 to 1908. And Joe Walcott won the welterweight title in 1901 and defeated all challengers, regardless of race, for the next five years.

For the most part, the white press—and not only in the South—simply ignored the black fighters, choosing instead to celebrate the strength and courage of heavyweights, men such as John L. Sullivan, Jake Kilrain, James Corbett, and Robert Fitzsimmons. Sullivan had drawn the color line in his 1892 challenge to the world's best: "In this challenge I include all fighters—first come, first served—who are white. I will not fight a Negro. I never have and I never shall."[58]

After Jeffries retired undefeated in 1905, the title eventually went to little-known Tommy Burns, who defended his title successfully against whites in California, and then overseas in Europe and Australia. Jack Johnson, a competent black boxer and a veteran of nearly eighty fights, eventually landed a fight with Burns. In a wooden amphitheater in Rushcutter's Bay, near Sydney, Australia, twenty-five to thirty thousand spectators from all over the world paid anywhere from five to twenty-five dollars to watch Johnson get a fourteen-round decision over Burns. The new heavyweight champion of the world was black.

The American press had figured going into the Burns-Johnson bout that one of two things would happen. Either Johnson would lose, as they theorized that white supremacy in matters physical and intellectual would naturally prevail. Or, if Johnson won, since Burns was uncharismatic anyway, boxing would be better off because a white boxer would quickly come forward and beat the new champion, thereby symbolically sustaining their theory of white superiority and, at the same time, reinvigorating the sport.[59]

Grantland Rice was in the middle of a two-week vacation when Johnson fought Burns the day after Christmas in 1908. During the weeks preceding the fight, Rice covered and commented upon all kinds of sporting interests in his column: indoor baseball, bowling, six-day bicycle races, YMCA basketball, the novelty of women at Parisian prizefights, and the show-business cheapening of Johnny Hayes's marathon victory over Dorando in the 1908 Olympics when the two amateurs capitalized on their fame, rerunning the famous marathon for cash in vaudeville—"this seems to be an age in which money has the call over the field."[60]

With a somewhat dead preholiday sporting calendar, Rice even filled up space the day before his vacation with an explanation of the origin of the newest slang phrase, "On your chin, Irene!" A University of Michigan yell leader was urging his team on against Pennsy (Pennsylvania). On a Michigan goal line stand, "Sully" Sullivan, the peppery yell leader, burst forth with: "Hold 'em Stubb! [nickname for Crumpacker, a Michigan lineman]. On your chin, Irene! Oh, you kid! Hold 'em!" The phrase swept the Michigan campus. Nobody had any idea what it meant, but it didn't seem to matter. Rice thought it was a worthy successor to "Twenty-three, skidoo." This was one week before the Burns vs. Johnson fight, which he did not even mention.[61]

In early January, after his vacation, Rice finally commented, not on the Burns fight, but on the possibility of Jeffries taking on the "Smoke champ." Promoters were waving fifty thousand dollars under Jeffries's nose. "At the opening call the Big Fellow pooh-poohed the idea of re-entering the ring," wrote Rice, "but the chance to make in less than an hour as much as the President cleans up in a year has started the Californian into thinking it over again." A couple of weeks later Rice told his readers that it looked more than ever that in the end Jeffries "will take up the 'White Man's' burden and go out after the scalp of the Demon Dinge."[62]

Even though the out-of-shape Jeffries—weighing then well over three hundred pounds—looked to W. W. Naughton, the San Francisco sportswriter, like a middle-aged fat man (he was thirty-five when he finally fought the thirty-two-year-old Johnson), the press continued to call for a battle of the races. In the meantime, Jeffries had signed a three-thousand-per-week vaudeville contract to begin preliminary conditioning. Rice wrote: "It's all mapped out. If there is any chance for him to get into condition again, he'll be out after the ebony Texan's kinky scalp." And again, in late January: "A general proposition to the Fight Fan of Dixie rebels at the idea of a White Man mixing it with a Smoke, but even this feeling of inherent prejudice has partially passed with an African on top of the pugilistic ladder at last." Rice then explained what he thought the Dixie fight fans would love to see: "They would deem it the height of piercing bliss for Big Jim to waltz in and knock a few bushels of splinters out of Mr. Johnson's block and thus remove the Dark Blot from the landscape."[63]

In stating the inherent prejudice of the Dixie fight fan, the ordinarily fair-minded Grantland Rice revealed his own bigotry. Part of his insensitivity came from his skepticism about the questionable sporting spirit surrounding the fight. Tex Rickard, who later became known as the "King of Ballyhoo," was promoting the circus. The biggest hoopla in the young history of the American sporting press bothered Rice greatly. As an athletic event, he thought, the physical contest, pure and simple, would stand out as probably the greatest human-interest feature in the history of the game. But in all other respects, he said, the affair was enough to turn the stomach of an ostrich or to drive a buzzard to take up a diet of expurgated cream. He didn't think too much of the commercial motive behind the match, or, for that matter, the extent to which all of the principals were queering themselves for the sake of money.[64]

Nor did Rice care much for Jack Johnson, even though he didn't know him. Just of him: his high-living, flashy-dressing, white-womanizing, and otherwise swaggering nature. To Rice and the other white sportswriters, it wasn't merely that Johnson was black, but that he was the epitome of the bad black. When the black boxer Joe Gans died the same year of tuberculosis, only two years after having lost his lightweight title to Battling Nelson, Rice praised Gans as one of the greatest champions of the ring in that day. But, he added, even though Gans was black, he "was the whitest black man that ever entered the ring, and a good bit whiter than some of the whites in that profession." Gans, he eulogized, was always respectful. "He knew his place," wrote Rice, "and made no attempt to overstep it." There was nothing of Johnson in him, he added, as the only time Joe Gans entered the limelight was when he entered the fire of battle.[65]

To Rice's mind, which he freely spoke, Johnson had both counts against him: he was disrespectfully black. Only a couple of months before the fight was to take place, and many years before newspapermen could be sued for libel, Rice sputtered that inserting a man like Jack Johnson into any program of sport was a crime against the standards of the game itself. "The Smoke is of the lowest possible type of humanity—ignorant and vicious. The ethics of the sport," he railed on, "mean about as much to him as they would to a piebald gorilla, two days out of the jungle." Like most of the newspapermen, above and below the Mason-Dixon line, Rice didn't hesitate to focus on the racial aspects of the fight. Jeffries was "answering the call of his clan to wrest the laurel from the champion of another and widely distinct race who has come through the fire and smoke of battle with the laurel twisted around his dusky brow." To Rice, Johnson was representing the "Dark Continent," coming out of the mist with the black flag on his spearpoint, challenging the nation.[66]

The day before the two representatives faced each other under the parching sun in Reno on July 4, Rice, now more or less resigned to the fight, did his best to put the contest into perspective—the white perspective. Call it what you will—uncivilized, degrading, brutal, savage—the meeting of these two fighters, he wrote, had become such a massive spectacle that it was hard not to give in to the thrill of it all, especially given the worldwide attention focused on the outcome. Disgusted as he was that a white man should enter the ring with a black, Rice still managed to be somewhat philosophical about its inevitability: "It may or may not be better than it should be otherwise. The most of us know only that it is so and wait with badly restrained eagerness for the flash that shall furnish us the answer at tomorrow's twilight."

There should be no surprise at Rice's pick. Mostly based on sentimentality and an assumed white superiority rather than on an objective study of the two boxers' relative skills and training strategy, he believed Jeffries would win. Even if the two were evenly matched physically, lectured Rice, "a good white man can beat a good black man seven days in the week and have something left on the side." This fact, he claimed, had been the proven law of the two races, "whether the law of civilization or the law of the wild." If Johnson were to beat Jeffries, he theorized further, Johnson would only be one of the few exceptions that proves the rule. As to his prediction, even though it was a close call, Rice in the end simply could not figure that Jeffries could be beaten to the ground, an inanimate mass of flesh, "where anything in human form stands above him big enough and mighty enough to put him there." Rice went with the odds: 10 to 7 on Jeffries.[67]

Except perhaps during the gold rush, never before in Nevada history had such a wild assortment of humans collected themselves in the shadows of the Sierras: politicians, crooks, whores, sharps, businessmen, celebrities, former fighters, cowboys, red-shirted miners, members of the sporting fraternity, and various and sundry sensation-mongers. Jack London, who had been commissioned by the *New York Herald* to cover the fight, was himself caught up in the enthusiasm that attracted the weird assembly. He, too, "wanted to see the fight so bad that it hurts." This fighting contest between two men with padded gloves, he thought, was no superficial thing. No philosopher thought it up and persuaded the masses to adopt it as their sport of sports. "It is as deep as our consciousness," he went on, "and is woven into the fibres of our being."[68]

"Hardly had a blow been struck when I knew that I was Jeff's master," recounted Johnson later, reflecting on the fight. By the end of the sixth round Jeffries and the twenty thousand fans sweltering in Reno knew it too. Jim Corbett had devised a scheme to distract Johnson by standing near one of the neutral corners and throwing cutting comments at the Galveston fighter as fast as he expected Jeffries to throw punches at him. But Johnson handled this second fight simultaneously with and as well as the first: while he toyed with Jeffries, he debated Corbett over such topics as family ancestry and the relative strength of various knock-down arguments for fair play in sports. At ringside, Jack London marveled at Johnson's witty and laughter-provoking—but never vile or harsh—wordplay, even going so far as to call him a "master at mouth fighting when in the ring."[69]

Jeffries gamely hung on through the fourteenth, as Johnson systematically punished the not-so-great White Hope. Corbett's jeering slowed considerably in these later rounds, as it was obvious to everyone that it was just a matter of time before Jeffries hit the canvas for good. In the fifteenth, all the Californian could do was stumble around, clinch, fumble, and duck. His right eye was closed, his left swollen; his nose was split, and blood was trickling from his mouth. A jarring right to the body followed by a left to the chin, and Jeffries fell over backward, half in and half out of the ring. "Get up, Jim, for God's sake, get up!" Corbett yelled, "Hurry up, get up!" Jeffries righted himself just before the count expired, but was staggering, punch drunk. Johnson quickly moved in again. "Package being delivered, Mistah Jeff," taunted Johnson, as he dropped the boilermaker with another left hook to the chin. Jeffries didn't move for four seconds, then rolled over, and crawled to his hands and knees. From the west side of the arena the crowd was yelling, in pity, "Stop it Tex, stop it! Don't let him be knocked out" (Tex Rickard was the referee as well as the promoter). Jeffries lurched up for the third and last time, spitting out a great mouthful of blood as he did so. "Put up your hands, Jim, my old pal," Corbett said, now mostly to himself; "Don't let him land another one—there he goes. I don't want to look at it. Jim! Jim!" Johnson hit him with a left, a right, and another left. The short, snappy blows dropped Jeffries down and out. His seconds interrupted the counting by entering the ring at the count of seven, and even though Rickard did not finish the count, he knew it was over too, and placed his hand on Johnson's shoulder, declaring him the winner.[70]

Like almost every other sporting editor in the country, Rice gave generous space to the fight in the *Tennessean*. Whatever the Hearst service provided him, he used: cartoons by TAD, Jeffries bylines, coverage of the training camps and the fight itself by writers such as W. W. Naughton, C. E. Van Loan, and Ed W. Smith, and predictions and commentary by various former fighters, trainers, and sporting celebrities—even "Hurry Up" Yost's observation that Jeffries had been mollycoddled in camp.

Rice was not among the corps of sportswriters who could later say, "I was at Reno." Instead, he arranged with the International News Service to detail the big fight for his Nashville constituency, and for free. At the Eighth Avenue side of the *Tennessean* offices, by megaphone and bulletin, the large crowd heard the round-by-round description of the battle. One can only imagine how the Nashville crowd reacted to the beating Jeffries was taking. Rice did not cover the detailing crowd or the telegraphic fight; it is not known why he skipped this Big Event. The day after the fight, Rice ran a lengthy and depressing interview with Jeffries as told to William Muldoon, the famous heavyweight Greco-Roman wrestler and strong man who later would become chairman of the New York State Athletic Commission. In the rambling story, Jeffries, practically catatonic, said he was beaten fairly, but that he simply couldn't fight.

"Why didn't you mix it, Jeffries, and whale away and take chances?" asked Muldoon. "If you had happened to land a good swing, or hook, or punch early, you might have turned things in your favor."

"I don't know," answered Jeff, "I didn't feel able."

"You were able in the first round or two," pressed Muldoon. "Any man that has trained at all can fight one or two rounds. Surely you, who have trained a year and a half could have fought two fast rounds?"

"I was weak and simply played out from the very moment I entered the ring," said Jeff. "My head seemed queer . . . I could not tell whether Johnson was a block away or a foot away."[71]

As far as Rice was now concerned, in his own commentary a couple of days after the fight, it would have been best if the two fighters had been kept several states away. It was now clear to him that Jeffries couldn't have possibly come back—"they never do," he said. The tone of his text was that Jeffries lost, not that Johnson won. In hindsight, Rice admitted, it was Jeffries's stub-

bornness that finally did him in, for he refused to take the advice of his trainers. They begged him to box his way into shape. Instead, he ran eight miles a
day, played pinochle, watched newspapermen play baseball, jumped the rope,
and enjoyed frequent rubdowns. And all this in spite of the fact that he hadn't
faced a real fight in nearly seven years. Except for an occasional spar, in a halfhearted and listless sort of way, Jeffries really never took on the roughhouse
kind of training that could have given him the chance to come back. He could
have won a four-mile race, or maybe a fishing contest, said Rice, but he certainly wasn't preparing himself to fight for the championship of the world. As
far as he could tell, Jeffries was a joke from beginning to end, for at the very
least he might have "made it interesting and given Johnson a chance to warm-
up and show the extent of the Smoke's gameness. It may take some skill, but
not much gameness to beat a drum."[72]

Rice even took the joke-of-a-fight tack one better a few days later, this time
referring to all those who picked Jeff to win, including himself. Again commenting on the foolishness of Jeffries's shotgun approach to training, Rice
wrote: "Now that it is all over, just how anyone could have figured him the favorite looms up as the prize joke of the age."[73]

Ten days after the bout Johnson's former manager, George Little, gave the
papers the story that the fight had originally been fixed in order to improve
the motion picture profits. "Dishonesty is a very mild term to connect with the
fights and promoters on the [west] coast," charged Little. Nearly all the matches
out west were fixed, he claimed, including the Johnson and Ketchel bout in
Coloma, California, in October 1909. After the gutsy, 160-pound middleweight
floored Johnson with a haymaker in the twelfth round, Johnson got up on the
count of eight, waited for Ketchel to advance, and plastered him to the canvas
with a wicked left to the jaw, followed by his famous right uppercut. Little said
that Johnson and Ketchel went so far before the fight as to pile pillows on the
floor of the hotel room of Ketchel's manager, Willis Britt, where they actually
rehearsed the knockout three or four times.[74]

The last lengthy commentary Rice made on the historic Johnson vs. Jeffries
fight appeared about a week later. With the news of a possible fix, all of a sudden Jeffries's loss made more rational sense to him. Rice wrote that Johnson
simply double-crossed Jeffries. And the reason Jeffries refused to train properly was that he still believed the fix was in until a couple of days before the
fight; all he had to do was to be in shape to go a good number of rounds and
look good, but that he wouldn't have to do much mixing it up with Johnson.
That would explain Jeffries's mental collapse and, in his doctor's words, his
"suffering from a severe case of nervous prostration," just before the fight, for

he must have realized then that he was not in shape for a real fight and only in store for a real beating.

But even with his rationalizing, Rice still maintained that the whole thing was just a big "flunking." Any brief chance that the pastime of boxing might have had to come back to respectability, he noted, was deader than Hector, who Achilles had killed and then for good measure dragged behind his chariot around the walls of Troy. Those connected with the sport, he continued, had no one but themselves to blame. In his mind, the shenanigans of Rickard and company had dragged prizefighting to the low-life level of professional wrestling, "and that place is jam up against the limit" of anyone's tolerance of a true sporting proposition.75

But the blame could be shared by the sportswriters. For Rice, as an example of a reporter and sporting editor who wouldn't or couldn't hide his racial insensitivity, was directly responsible for helping create the worldwide interest in the fight and exacerbating its overtones as a war of the races. Had Rice more closely followed his own tutorials on the nature of the well-played game and fair play as such rules applied to sportswriting, he might have helped foster a different atmosphere for the Jeffries-Johnson bout. Failing that, Rice did nothing to bring acceptance to interracial sporting events; he was little more than a typical and bigoted American sportswriter.

8

The Big Show

When Grantland Rice took his annual two-week vacation in 1910 during the slowest of the sporting months, December, he told his readers that if they wanted to reach him they could write to Takeiteasy Tavern, Helvatime, Somewhere U.S.A, where the legend inscribed above the door would read: "We sleep while you work." But when Henry L. Stoddard offered Rice fifty dollars a week to be a sportswriter and columnist for the *New York Evening Mail,* his vacation address abruptly changed. So did his permanent address.[1]

Although Rice recalled that he did briefly hesitate to take the offer because the salary was a comedown, Kate said, "Go ahead!" When the thirty-year-old did finally accept the job, he appeared to reason this way: he didn't know for certain that he had what it took to be successful in the big time, but he did believe that this was the right time to find out. His four-year stint on the *Nashville Tennessean* had been exhausting. By narrowing his responsibilities in joining the staff of a larger metropolitan newspaper, he theorized, not only was he crashing the big time, but the move would give him the opportunity to concentrate his talents exclusively on covering the sporting world. No more "Tennessee 'Uns." No more theater reviews. No more responsibilities for sports page layouts and headline writing. Just sportswriting. Looking back on his move years later, Rice said, "Kit, Floncy and I had made the big step, a step destined to take me to the press boxes and behind-the-scenes rooms of the nation and the world."[2]

The *Tennessean* editors knew what they were losing. In their good-bye tribute to Rice, the editors acknowledged what most Southerners already knew:
Rice was revered in the region. Their tribute also sketched out most of the
personal characteristics that were to eventually and collectively set him apart
from the vast majority of other successful sportswriters of his day in New
York. Clever paragrapher. Serious verse writer. Poet laureate of athletics and
the sporting world. Rollicking humor mixed with sweet sentiment. Cheerful
disposition and view of the world. Friend of everyone. Unusual capacity for
work. Uncanny knowledge of the ins and outs of all sports. Above all, a natural ability as a newspaper writer. Grantland Rice was just about the best—
writer and person—that the South then had to offer the North in the sporting
department.

After his departure, imitation being the sincerest form of flattery, all the
Nashville newspaper editors scrambled to find another Grantland Rice. After
all, this was business. Rice was popular. Popularity meant readers. Readers
meant money. For instance, shortly after Rice had left Nashville, Marmaduke
B. Morton, the editor of the *Nashville Banner*, a *Tennessean* rival, was out to
hire a new sportswriter for his paper. Morton was tall and gaunt, and known
especially for his love of corn-cob-pipe smoking. When a prospective sportswriter he was interviewing dutifully began to recite his job qualifications,
Morton rudely interrupted the young man, thrust the cane of his pipe stem
directly in the face of the startled hopeful, and said: "Listen, young man, I
don't really care whether you can tell a baseball bat from a bull fiddle. This
goddamned Grantland Rice has changed sports writing. What I want to know
is can you write rhymes? If you can, you're hired. If you can't, you aren't!"[3]

Rice's reputation by then was as much for his verse as it was for his lively
yet studied sportswriting. Locally, some of Rice's "rhymes" had even been
collected for publication in something more permanent than the daily newspaper. The *Nashville Tennessean* had published a small collection of Rice's
baseball poetry in a paperback work called *Base-Ball Ballads* (1910). This
would be the first of four collected verse publications by Rice. *Base-Ball Ballads*, a somewhat rare 128-page book, includes fifty-seven of Rice's playful re-
flections on the game of baseball and life. He dedicated the volume to "The
Fan." The collection opens with verse celebrating the eternal slogan of the
game and the bugle call to play again: "Play Ball." He reminded his readers
that in life too "The player plays the game of life/Until the final shadows fall."
The collection closes with the dying down of the tumult when the final jeer
and cheer have passed and the fight is done, won or lost: "Game Called,"
where no victory, nor yet defeat is chalked against any player's name, "But

down the roll the final scroll/Shows only 'How he played the game.'" The collection includes "Casey's Revenge," a few other Casey-centered poems, some parodies of other poets such as Rudyard Kipling, Edgar Allen Poe, and Henry Wadsworth Longfellow, and various songs and tributes to the "bugs" (the rooters), the players, the game itself, the "bushers" (the rookies), the Fates, Luck, the "moguls" (the owners), and the player-coaches. In a poem written when Teddy Roosevelt was still president, Rice invited Teddy to consider what he was going to do when he retired from the presidency. Rice took it upon himself to look around on Roosevelt's behalf for something challenging to do with his time. After all, Rice noted, the president needed a husky job, something that could match or even exceed his previous life-challenges: chasing African lions, choking hungry wolves to death, charging up San Juan Hill, fighting the predatory wealth of the kings of high finance, battling against the trusts, and calling down the railroad moguls. Well, Rice found a possible job for Teddy when he was ready. In baseball. Something rough-and-tumble, something requiring a big stick everyday, something to make the pulse leap, something full of smoke and fire, a real job:

> Though I've hunted far and near, there's nothing else to do
> Where you'll get what's coming, Ted, all that's coming unto you.
> You should be an umpire, Ted; and I'll bet two weeks would be
> Quite enough to curb your rash, headlong stren-u-os-i-tee.4

Naturally, when Rice left Nashville for New York, the *Tennessean* also tried to find a Rice-imitator replacement, hoping to hold Rice's devoted readers and thereby maintain the sturdy circulation that the sportswriter was in part responsible for. Spick Hall was the heir apparent. Hall's new column was called "Sports A La Carte." In his debut, Hall tried in vain to get into the Rice-rhythms with this preachy, sophomoric, and clumsy little ditty about the common practice of boozing it up in big league baseball:

> Big-league-wide prohibition is
> The thing to boost the baseball biz.
> Base hits and high balls do not mix.
> If tried, you'll go back to the sticks.5

But there was only one Rice. Even if others could have approached Rice's intimate knowledge of sport, giving rhythmic expression to it belonged in the South to Rice alone. Hall's ditty-writing, for example, just couldn't compete with the Ricean verse-writing. For the sake of poetic comparison—Hall's first column with Rice's last "Sportograms" column for the *Tennessean*—Rice gave his Nashville readers a rousing, if typically gushing and sentimental, ballad on bravery, the first verse going this way.

> We have fought, but we have lost;
> We have striven but we have failed;
> We have paid the bitter cost,
> Yet our hearts have never quailed;
> We have fallen in the fray,
> Through the sweep of countless suns.
> Yet we've risen and today
> We're standing to the guns.[6]

It has been said by some of Rice's friends at the time that there was something of this stout-of-heart business figuring into the biggest step in his professional career. Irvin S. Cobb, the Paducah, Kentucky, humorist and New York journalist, heard it from some of Rice's closest friends that when he accepted the offer from the *Mail*, he was scared stiff. Rice was genuinely fearful that he would fail this test, that when he did make it to the Big Show he wouldn't be able to deliver.[7]

Stoddard, the *Mail* publisher, didn't help matters much when he first met and spoke to Rice personally. Kate and Floncy stayed behind in Nashville while Grantland took the train to New York to find a place to live. On his arrival, Rice went immediately to the *Mail* offices at Broadway and Fulton Street on Park Row to introduce himself to the man who had hired him.

"Rice," Mr. Stoddard blurted out, "I've been reading your verse. I never knew a sports writer worth fifty dollars a week, but in your case I'll risk it!" Rice recalled later that he left the *Mail* offices reeling. It was clear then that even if the South generally knew quite well what they had lost in losing Rice, New York wasn't at all clear about what they had gained in hiring him. In his own mind, Rice must have realized that he was, himself, "standing to the guns."[8]

The *New York Evening Mail* was one of the city's seven evening papers; there were another seven morning New York dailies at the time. In the New York newspaper pecking order, the *Mail* was in the second of two tiers. The early-twentieth-century circulation wars produced such renowned, first-tier papers as Pulitzer's *World*, Hearst's *Journal*, Ochs's *Times*, Bennett's *Herald*, and Ogden Reid's *Tribune*. Of less stature, along with the *Evening Mail*, were such papers as the *Globe*, the *Telegraph*, and the *Post*.[9]

The *Mail* was not the kind of upstart paper with which Rice had customarily thrown in his lot. It had been around in one form or another since just after the Civil War. With the increasing use of telegraphic news during the Civil War, so-called late editions of morning papers became quite popular. Separate—and often separately owned—afternoon or evening papers were attractive because of street sales to homebound workers or shoppers. Same-day news was also frequently fresher than the morning-after versions.[10]

All but two of these fourteen papers, including the *Mail*, were located in a romantic little place on a short street in lower Manhattan called Park Row. Directly across from City Hall Park and the City Hall itself, the newspaper section of Park Row ran northeast from Broadway and Ann to Printing House Square, a tiny triangle at Nassau Street, just south of the entrance to Brooklyn Bridge. The *Herald*'s white marble building at Broadway anchored the south end of Park Row; the *Sun* and the *Tribune* buildings anchored the north end. The *Times* had built there in 1889, the *World* one year later, and at the cost of two and one-half million dollars. The clatter of the Linotypes and rumble of the cellar-housed Hoe printing presses echoed interminably up and down the row within and without the building walls.[11]

By far the most visible, nostalgic landmark of Park Row was the nine-story red-bricked New York Tribune Building at 154 Nassau Street, with its clock tower rising 260 feet above City Hall Park. Built in the 1870s for about one million dollars, the building dwarfed the other newspaper buildings, most of which were three stories or less. Besides housing the *Tribune*'s city room, composing room, and the foundry and cellar presses, it was large enough to accommodate rental space for other commercial enterprises, even to rival newspapers such as Pulitzer's *Journal*.[12]

Newspaperman and writer Gene Fowler recalled that when he first came to New York in the same decade as Rice and was escorted through Park Row by newspaperman Damon Runyon, he was quite taken by the imposing Tribune Building. Besides being huge, in spirit it even reminded Fowler of his frontier upbringing. High up on its northern face Fowler noticed a large painted sign—a black-bordered drawing of a fearsome serpent, ready to strike, was just above the legend: "Coiled in the Flag! Hears-s-s-ss-sss-t!" In the West, Fowler told Runyon, to so blatantly insult a rival editor—in the manner that the *Tribune* editors were publicly insulting the Hearst papers—would bring out the horsewhips and the six-shooters. Runyon admonished Fowler that this was New York, a more civilized place, and that he should not come to expect Wild West displays over such insults. This, implied Runyon, was just business-as-usual in the New York newspaper wars.[13]

In the North, industrial changes had begun to speed up the pace of life. The cities grew and became more congested. A more standardized and clock-governed way of life was evolving; the transition seemed to be creating more rather than less work for the average American. Correlatively, it appeared that Americans, as hell bent as they were on harnessing themselves to making the machines that were ostensibly designed to save time, actually were losing much of their leisure time in the bargain.

Consequently, in the newspaper business, publishers responded to this time shortage by helping the reader speed through their papers. Whereas an earlier generation might have had a few lazy hours to read the daily newspaper, the early-twentieth-century reader only spent from twenty minutes to an hour reading the daily news. Headlines grew bigger, brief news summaries of yesterday's events were included, stories were condensed, press associations were formed to more efficiently gather and centralize the news, and greater emphasis was placed on entertaining the reader.[14]

Although information was generally and gradually restricted in space, newspapers actually grew in size as business trends created enlarged advertising needs. In the twenty-two years between 1892 and 1914, newspaper advertising reached about $250 million; ads multiplied three and one-half times; advertising increased at a ratio of ten times the increase in number of daily papers. In the race to out-entertain each other, newspaper publishers strove to catch the reader's eye, even at the risk that they might miss their reader's mind's eye: they resorted to more illustrations and photographs, special features, more columnists (especially humorists), fiction, society accounts, comics and cartoons, profiles of celebrities, special departments—many aimed at attracting more women readers—sensational and bizarre stories, competitions sponsored by newspapers for the best limericks or cutest baby faces, and, naturally, expanding coverage of sports and athletics.[15]

The *Mail* may not have been among the most prestigious of the New York papers then, but Rice was joining up with first-rate newspaper people; there were more first-rate people than first-rate newspapers could accommodate. This one-cent, sixteen-or-so-page paper was staffed by such journalists as Jimmy Sinnott, O. O. McIntyre, Homer Davenport, Franklin P. Adams, and Rube Goldberg. When Rice stumbled out of Stoddard's office that day in New York, the first man he bumped into was Goldberg, the cartoonist and sportswriter. Goldberg, like many young reporters who had not been invited to New York as Rice had been, left on his own initiative from his job in the San Francisco newspaper world in hopes of getting work in New York. Brisbane of the *Journal* turned him down. Stoddard of the *Mail* wisely put him on salary. Goldberg quickly introduced Rice to Adams, the man Rice had play-fully dueled with during his years on the *Tennessean* editorial page. This was the irascible Adams who, in his "Always in Good Humor" column in the *Mail,* would let go with such memorable one-liners as this one, uttered, he said, by a widow who was stepping out with another man the day after the death of her husband: "Dance slower dearie, I'm in mourning!"

"Hello, Rice," Adams said. "Where are you going?"

"Nowhere's, yet," Rice replied, not having any place to stay in New York.

"Come with me," Adams said. "I'll dig you up a room in the flat I'm in."[16]

An hour later, Rice had a roof over his head and a place to stash his few be-longings at 616 West 116th Street. He wrote Kate that he had arrived safely and was about to find his way around the big city. Kate and Floncy wouldn't arrive until February.

Diagonally across from the Tribune Building, situated in the triangle where Nassau Street and Park Row converged, was Lipton's, a bar. Newspapermen hung out there. You could enter the bar by way of swinging doors from either the Nassau Street side or the Park Row side. For newcomer Rice, regularly passing through Lipton's was a natural way to make new friends, which he did, easily. He also renewed a friendship or two.

Don Marquis had arrived in New York two years earlier, uninvited, like Rube Goldberg. Marquis had left the *Atlanta Journal* in 1907 at the invitation of Joel Chandler Harris to be the associate editor of Chandler's Atlanta-based new monthly, *Uncle Remus's Magazine.* Marquis left *Uncle Remus* not long after Harris's death a year later, and headed for New York to look for a news-paper editor who would allow him to write a daily column. He was still bouncing around without a steady job when Rice landed in New York. As they promised each other in Atlanta in 1905, they renewed their friendship. In Lipton's Bar. Sitting in high-backed booths under the large, stained-glass windows, Rice and Marquis found themselves in roughly the same predica-ment as far as their careers were concerned. They were both starting over again. They knew perfectly well that it didn't really matter what either of them had been, done, or written previously. So far as New York was concerned, their histories were of no particular interest. It was what they were yet to do that would determine what New York would do with them.[17]

Lipton's, and taverns like it, helped journalistic newcomers overcome New York's dizzying round. On that first Gene Fowler excursion to New York, after taking in a ball game at the Polo Grounds, Damon Runyon and Fowler were taking a cab to Park Row. "Just listen to it roar!" Runyon said, not talking of the baseball crowd, but of the never-ending noise of the city. Rice called the city a maelstrom. The journalists could escape the fury of the city at the taverns, where they could lick their wounds, tell a good story, laugh and argue, and otherwise get much-needed perspective on their lives—or sometimes drink themselves silly to forget those lives.[18]

Occasionally, the place even inspired. After Marquis finally got on with a paper, the *New York Sun,* in 1912, and over a drink with fellow *Sun* staffer Frink Dana Burnet at Lipton's, Marquis gave birth to archy, the lower-case cockroach. "Frink," said Marquis, "this morning there scampered across my desk the goddam biggest cockroach you ever saw. I believe he could damn near play my typewriter."[19]

Burrowing in Lipton's Bar from time to time with Marquis and other journalism confederates helped Rice overcome his initial self-doubts and homesickness for the more sedate ways of Nashville. This he did in part by convincing himself that he would eventually go back home:

> I'm going home some day—
>   If I can only find the pathway back—
> For I have come too far, too far away,
>   A wanderer on a strange and alien track;
> I saw the world go ahead and only meant
>   To go a little way beyond—and then
> To seek the old-time highways of content
>   And live back home among my clan again.[20]

When Kate and Floncy (now four years old) arrived with baggage and Napoleon Lajoie's china in tow, the Rice family found a comfortable apartment at 450 Riverside Drive. There they lived for almost the next twenty years. At the time they took up this residence, they found themselves in the middle of a remarkably creative neighborhood, sharing space with a variety of talents, including editor Walter Trumbull, actor Milton Sills, writer Irvin Cobb, Dick Tully and his novelist wife, Eleanor Gates, and journalist Herbert Swope. Not far away lived the illustrator Arthur William Brown, and then-sportswriter Heywood Broun, who had been working on the *Telegraph*—which mostly specialized in horse racing and vaudeville news—for sports editor Bat Masterson, the legendary Dodge City sheriff. Almost from the start, the Rice apartment became a congregating place for many of these friends. Damon Runyon, who also lived nearby, would "'wander by' our place around midnight to drink coffee and talk by the hour," recalled Rice. In spite of his occasional sad-voiced verses about missing the rose-rimmed gates of Nashville and family, the Rices were settling in.[21]

The *New York Evening Mail* claimed in 1912 that their daily circulation was 145,000 readers. This was no doubt greatly exaggerated. At the time the *Tribune*'s circulation was less than 50,000; the *Sun* around 75,000; and the *Herald* came in with around 90,000. All three of these more prestigious papers clearly were experiencing first-decade circulation slides, but it is unlikely that the *Mail* was outdistancing them as convincingly as it claimed. If the *Mail*'s figures were believed, it would have been about the fourth-biggest New York daily. The staid *Times,* published by Adolph Ochs and run by Managing Editor Carr Van Anda, was pushing 200,000 in circulation. And the spectacular circulations went to the sensationalistic papers, the *World* and the *Journal.* Even after Pulitzer's death in the fall of 1911, the *World* attracted nearly twice the circulation of the *Times;* Hearst's morning and evening editions of the *Journal* peddled hyperbole and the bizarre to one million New York readers on a daily basis.[22]

Baseball news, in particular, generated nearly year-round sports-page copy—including the hot-stove league (also called the "typewriter league") winter gossip—for all of the New York papers. Big-league baseball was getting respectable, or at least it was becoming ever more businesslike. The biggest change, according to sportswriter C. E. Van Loan, was in the attitude of the management. There was far less tolerance for player dipsomania and other sinning ways. Fading were the days when a player was doing well if he stayed out of jail. "The world do move," Van Loan explained, as he cited the increasing number of "college boys" attracted to baseball as a career. If you pay enough money you will attract the higher-class player: sober, clear-eyed, big-brained, so the argument went. Of course, not all college men had class, explained Van Loan—some of them have been hanged for horse stealing.[23]

Harry Hooper, who joined the Boston Red Sox in 1909, shortly after graduating as a civil engineer from St. Mary's, guessed that in his day about one out of five or six big leaguers had attended or graduated from college. Which didn't mean that only college men were gentlemen or remarkably intelligent; only that the players were not the entirely uneducated or illiterate bunch of "rowdies" that many believed them to be. On the Red Sox team there was catcher Bill Carrigan, who had gone to Holy Cross; first baseman Jake Stahl, University of Illinois; Larry Gardner, the third baseman from the University of Vermont; outfielder Duffy Lewis, of St. Mary's; and pitchers Marty McHale from the University of Maine, Chris Mahoney from Fordham, and Ray Collins from Vermont. And from the other teams, recalled Hooper, there was Mathewson from Bucknell; Frank Chance, Washington University; Hal Chase, Santa Clara; Buck Herzog, University of Maryland; Chief Bender, Dickenson College; Art Devlin, Georgetown; Eddie Collins, Columbia. John McGraw went to St. Bonaventure for a short time; Miller Huggins and Hugh Jennings both became lawyers; and on and on.[24]

So on the whole, and in comparison to the previous generation, baseball was being elevated by a gradual influx of educated men who saw baseball not as a sport or a trade, but as a business profession. Correlatively, baseball management was beginning to see these players as an investment with potential high-yield payoffs. Because of this, the owners expected classier, more upright moral behavior. Van Loan wrote, "The national game, being one of the greatest money makers in the country, has fallen for the most part into the hands of shrewd business men, and these men want value received from their hired hands. . . . Baseball has been put on a business footing. If a man's name is on the pay roll, it is there not out of any sentiment but because he is worth something to the club management."[25]

World Series box office receipts and attendance figures bear out Van Loan's observation that baseball's popularity was still growing at the start of the second decade of the twentieth century. In 1884, the first so-called world's championship, between the Providence and the Metropolitan clubs, was so lightly taken that the gate wasn't even reported. But it couldn't have been any larger than the mere two thousand in receipts reported for the next year's seven-game contest (played in four different cities) between the Chicago club of the National League and St. Louis of the American Association. When the Temple Cup was contested, almost ten years later, in only four games between Baltimore and New York, receipts were eighteen thousand dollars.

When the National League and American League pennant winners played in the World Series in 1903, attendance for the eight games topped one hundred thousand, and fifty thousand dollars were collected at the gate. But in the 1912 World Series, more than a quarter of a million fans saw the New York Giants and the Boston Red Sox play, and nearly a half a million dollars—$490,449—were taken in at the box office. The price of World Series seats had gone from a quarter for bleachers and fifty cents for the grandstand to a dollar for the bleachers and twenty-five dollars for a box seat; the fan could no longer saunter leisurely through the runways to the field and pick out the best seat he could find at game time, but now had to wait in line overnight and surge into the park hours before the game to find a place to sit or stand.[26]

Besides the pennant races, off-the-field relationships between players and owners were heating up as well. Baseball players have never been especially excited about unionization for a variety of reasons. Still, in 1885 and then again ten years later, the ballplayers found themselves in need of "brotherhoods" or "protective associations." Both fizzled within a few years.[27] A third try was underway during the 1912 season. There was no shortage of grievances: salary disputes, reserve clause problems, owner collusion, blacklisting, bogus transactions, loopholes in the draft, farming practices in the minor leagues, injury compensation, accident insurance, pensions, and the general paternalism of the owners in regard to controlling off-the-field player-life choices regarding drinking, rowdyism, card playing, endorsements, ghost-written publishing, barnstorming exhibition games, playing baseball with or against the "coloreds," and limitations imposed on postseason recreations, such as playing football or winter skiing, that might cause injuries.

Dave Fultz, a former major leaguer for the Athletics and the Yankees and a Brown University graduate and practicing lawyer, was a leader in the formation of the Mutual Protective Association of Baseball Players in August. By September it was chartered in New York as the Base Ball Player's Fraternity. The idea was to create an association that could represent the players at all hearings before the National Commission—the so-called three-member Supreme Court of Baseball (the two major-league presidents and a third member chosen by them to serve as chairman; the original membership included Harry Pulliam, Ban Johnson, and August "Garry" Herrmann, its first and only chairman). By November membership in the players' association was around three hundred; it peaked in late 1916 with a membership of more than twelve hundred ballplayers, not long after the ending of the trade war with the upstart Federal League.[28]

By the fall of 1912 Rice was into his second year on the *Mail*. His major responsibility was his daily column, variously titled, until in October 1911 Adams suggested it be called "The Sportlight." Rice liked it, so much so that "The Sportlight" was the name Rice used for his column for the rest of his newspaper writing career; the title was almost always accompanied by a small year-book-like photograph of him. For the inaugural column-naming on October 31, 1911, Rice—pictured unsmiling but not stern, scholarly and gentlemanly with suit coat and bow tie—decided to reprint a version of his famous poem "Alumnus Football" from the *Nashville Tennessean*. What had been regionally known and memorized until then, soon became national property, forever identified with Grantland Rice's philosophy, for better and for worse.

Rice's baseball writing for the *Mail* was largely devoted to covering the New

York Giants. He shared the travel to road games with fellow sportswriter Harry Schumacher; always, however, Rice was in the press box at the Polo Grounds for the home games. His writing was also, and remarkably, strictly devoted to the *playing* of the game—the congenial versifying, chatting, and occasional moralizing about the hows, wherefores, and whatnots of the on-the-field sporting life that was and continued to be his personal trademark.

The off-the-field power struggles between management and the players during the 1912 season, reflected by the newly formed Base Ball Fraternity, were certainly news. They no doubt provided juicy stuff, too, since Rice couldn't help but be privy to player and owner gripes as he grew closer and closer to the inner workings of the Big Show. After all, during the baseball season he traveled and roomed with the Giants, played cards with them, shared their meals, interviewed them, and otherwise spent the major part of his working day in their company. Still, during the several months the union was getting underway during the winding down of the 1912 season (in fact, union talk had been in the winds since 1910), Rice gave practically no attention to the subject of unionization, player morale, owner politics, or any of the disputes then troubling baseball.

In one instance, he did mention the "Ball Player's Association," but it was only to urge the new group, along with the owners, to try to curb the popularity of brow-beating umpires, for the sake not only of the well-played game but also of discouraging the spectators from "mucking around." Scrappy play was one thing; abuse, assault, and excessive profanity was quite another. Even though Rice didn't report much on the disputes, it is clear that if he was asked what he thought, he would have sided with the players. Someone must have asked him as much in a letter, for in November of 1912 he said that on the whole, the players had been of much greater credit to the game than the average club owner. If any ballplayer had pulled some of the stunts that some of the owners had pulled over the years, they would have been driven from the game. He remarked that the efforts of the Player's Association to uplift the game would appeal to the public. "Why should those with power who are in more responsible places," Rice asked rhetorically, "be allowed to wreck a game in which their only interest is the gate receipt?"[29]

But instead of covering the politics of the baseball season, Rice stuck to doping out the ins and outs of the pennant race itself; always, it seemed, with an innate sense of balance and proportion. Consider these two letters Rice received from his 1912 readers about the time the hometown Giants were stumbling in their drive to repeat as pennant winners: "Allow me to suggest that you stop boosting the Giants and give them proper criticism, as they surely deserve. Of course, you know, they are to-day the most overrated team in the game and will be lucky to win even with their present lead. And in case they do win, what a joke they will be against the Red Sox. Come out and be square and admit the truth. Are you paid by the club to boost this team, or is it necessary to hold your job?" The next day Rice received this letter from another reader: "Why all this stuff about the Giants having a hard fight ahead to win out? Why don't you show more loyalty and stand back of them in better style? They have been in a slump, but have shown that they have the league outclassed, and will win easy. I can't figure out where knocking the home club will get you anything when everyone else admits they are the class of the race."[30]

By the third week of August, Boston was up eight games over Washington in the American League; in the National League, New York led Chicago by four. Rice had a hunch that "the Giants are about to suffer grievous trouble in Pittsburgh the rest of the week"; he whipped up the drama further, speculating that the Red Sox may be due for a "tall slump." This in spite of Boston pitcher Smoky Joe Wood's growing string of consecutive winning performances, which would eventually reach sixteen (stopped by Detroit in late September), tying Washington's Walter Johnson's American League record earlier the same year (each won more than thirty games in 1912). This was the same year, ironically, that New York's Rube Marquard won nineteen straight in the National League.[31]

In the meantime, the city was paying tribute to the Olympic athletes returning from the 1912 Games in Stockholm. A massive parade from Forty-second Street to City Hall Park was planned. On the day of the celebration, Rice could easily see the marchers from the offices of the *Mail*; but for this affair he was a spectator, not a reporter.

"Look, there's Jim Thorpe," fairly screamed a pretty girl at the parade. "I want to hug him. Didn't he do well?"

Thorpe rode in one car; in a separate automobile, directly in front of the hero-of-the-day, were the two big gifts he had received for winning the pentathlon and the decathlon. There was the bronze statue of Gustavus Adolphus, presented by the King of Sweden, and the silver Viking ship, given by the czar of Russia. In the presentation ceremony, in Stockholm, the king had said to Thorpe, "Sir, you are the greatest athlete in the world."[32]

In time, Rice would come to roughly the same opinion. And it was the memory of this parade, and what it meant to the Indian from Carlisle, that would later move Rice to support Thorpe when he needed it most. But for now, it was *Evening Mail* sportswriter Francis Albertanti, whose byline was simply "Francis," who was covering metropolitan athletics (what was later called "track and field") and the welcome home parade. Rice was busy digging in for the last few innings of the pennant race.

In spite of Rice's intuitions that the Red Sox and the Giants might be seriously challenged in their league races, by early September Boston had easily taken the American League flag, and the Giants were still six games up on Chicago and holding their own. Rice commented: "With all the deftness and celerity of a fat, short-legged poodle pursuing a meat wagon, the puffing Cubs to-day are still wobbling about the highway back of the Giants. To switch the simile, the hair-raising pennant sprint in the National League to-day reminds us of a hundred-yard dash between two marble statues clamped to the ground with thongs of steel." Three weeks later the Giants clinched the pennant, up ten games with only nine games to go. Rice wrote, "Hip! hip! hooray! and likewise whee! Oh bliss! Oh joy! O, wild elation! We've won the pennant! Hully gee! Let's go and have a celebration!" It was now certain: the 1912 World Series would be between Boston and New York, and would feature the pitching of Smoky Joe Wood for Boston, and Rube Marquard and thirteen-year veteran Christy Mathewson for New York.[33]

The National Commission's preoccupation during the World Series preparations was the problem of ticket sales. In 1911 the "speculators" had somehow gotten hold of a considerable number of tickets and gleefully scalped them throughout the series. For the present series, the approach in New York, for example, was to deny mail-order applications, to restrict ticket purchases to two per person, and to open the gates for each Polo Grounds game at 10 A.M., compelling each ticket purchaser to then pass directly into the park. Box seats went for twenty-five dollars, the eighty-five hundred reserved upper grandstand seats cost three dollars, the seventeen thousand lower grandstand seats were two dollars, and the thirteen thousand bleachers went for a dollar. About forty-five hundred of the reserved seats were set aside for the National Commissions "preferred list": club stockholders, season box holders, players, Commission "friends," and the newspapers.

The *New York Evening Mail* sports department assigned Rice, Schumacher, and Goldberg to cover the series, but the word count went undeniably to Rice. Goldberg provided some color, and Schumacher had to split his time between the series and college football. In addition, the *Mail* hired on Charley "Buck" Herzog, the Giants third baseman, to provide the player's perspective. Through conversations with Schumacher, Herzog, "one of the brainiest, one of the most mentally and physically alert ball players of the game," was asked to give the "inside story" of each game, "not a so-called Expert Account, but a plain, simple story of each battle from a wise ball player's viewpoint."[34]

Rice didn't take sides in the World Series even though a hometown team was involved for the second year in a row. In a short note to his readers (or, reader, as the case may be, he added), he pointed out that for a sportswriter, a baseball contest of the magnitude of the World Series should be above home-grown prejudice. Both teams, he said, were composed of fine ballplayers and clean sportsmen. The game, he argued, is big enough to be above the partisanship of anyone playing it, or any noncombatant who may trail along from the sidelines. He warned his reader(s) that he would "view the contest in the desire that the team playing the best ball shall win."[35]

Neither did he predict which team would win. If he had a gut instinct, he kept it to himself. And insofar as predicting a winner on the basis of figures and statistics, he typically avoided this too—even though he commonly studied figures, was familiar with all the favorite statistical angles, and used them freely to analyze tendencies, strengths, and weaknesses. Statistics, he thought, were often overrated; baseball had too many angles to consider, and statistics, when flashed and whirled from the many possible directions and with such dizzying revolutions, inevitably left the figure-minded as confused as the newly arrived Dutchman who saw his first electric fan and exclaimed, "Py golly, dat's a tam busy squirrel."

Rice did note, however, that when the two ball clubs were compared over the last three months of the regular season, Boston got the edge. New York was a Jekyll-and-Hyde club. The Giants' team batting average had dropped from .302 in early July to .252 at season's end, whereas the Boston team steadily hit .273 in July, and .275 through September. As to what might happen, Rice stated the obvious: if things continued as they had, Boston would win; if Boston slumped and New York played as they had earlier in the season, New York would win. What was more likely, he thought, was that the series would go the distance and the winner wouldn't be determined until the ninth round of the last game, since statistics give us only the past, not the future.[36]

> The dusk comes soon whatever the game,
> The day is brief on the trail of Fame;
> But we loaf along and we look ahead,
> Till the race is run and the dream is dead;
> Until, far back of the winning score,
> We find that we come to bat no more;
>
> We curse the luck and we call it Fate,
> The season ends—but the Record's Wait.[37]

In addition to its sporting staff, the managing editor of the *Evening Mail* also sent Franklin P. Adams to the World Series. Adams wasn't a stranger to covering baseball. About four years earlier, he had been in the Polo Grounds watching a regular-season series between the Giants and the Cubs. Rally after Giant rally was dashed by the lightning-quick double plays of Cubs infielders Tinker, Evers, and Chance. Adams's typewriter gave the trio immortality with these lyrics:

> These are the saddest of possible words—
>   Tinker to Evers to Chance—
> Trio of Bear-cubs and fleeter than birds,
> Tinker to Evers to Chance;
> Making a Giant hit into a double,
> Pricking forever our gonfalon bubble—
> Words that are heady with nothing but trouble—
>   Tinker to Evers to Chance.[38]

But for the 1912 series, Adams's assignment for the *Mail* was to catch the spirit of the crowd, not the skilled actions of the players. His beat was to mill around with the World Series crowds before the games and see what he could see. Before the start of game one in New York, his milling produced the following observations:

• "This here world's serious. . . . The same variety of fans, who mightn't walk two blocks out of their way to get a job, stood in line here all night."

• By 10:27 A.M. there were 9,128 persons in the Polo Grounds—gathered from the arts, businesses, and professions, and from the various sexes. None of them were too excited, yet.

• The folks looked slumberous and bored, he thought. He saw games of auction pinochle, one man reading "Foreign Short Stories," and several men pitching pennies.

• Traffic was picking up about 11 A.M. as streetcars began dropping off their passengers in droves. The new double-deck omnibus streetcar, complete with a glassed-in, roofed hurricane deck, could carry almost twice the number of riders as the ordinary car. The conductor, who sat at his cashier's wicket, sounded the loud car whistle, and bellowed the stop through a megaphone, "Coogan's Bluff! Polo Grounds!"

• The crowd grew a bit nervous a couple of hours before the 2 P.M. start. "It is about to see something that perhaps fifty million people are thinking about at once. It knows that it is a great thing to be here. That undoubtedly is one reason why men who don't see a game all during the regular season, will pay $50 for a seat." Seats in the shade were selling for eighty-five dollars at noon, which was the price the ubiquitous speculators were getting for a grandstand seat.

• The crowd grew to twenty-five thousand an hour and a half before the first pitch. That's when Adams began pondering (the important business one is supposed to do before a big game): "Are the shaggy behemoths to triumph over the abysmal vermilion-socked Bostonians?" Or, "Are the Brobdignagians, champions of the National League, to defeat the carmine-hosed victors of the American League?" "Are the Titans to overcome the scarlet buskins of St. Botolph's town?" "Or are the crimson-legged Hubbers to defeat the gargantuan Manhattanites?" Who will win? Who will lose? "We are curious to know."

• With his obligatory and heavy-headed pondering over, Adams eased out of his pregame ruminations: "And that concludes our part of the afternoon entertainment. On with the game! Let Rice be unconfined!"[39]

Rice, meanwhile, took up his post in the new Polo Grounds press box. In April 1911 an early morning fire had burned the then wooden Polo Grounds to the ground, all except for the "cigar boxes," the bleachers in deep center field. The Giant owner, John T. Brush, rebuilt the entire park, this time in steel and concrete. He decorated the summit of the grandstand with the coat of arms of every National League ball club. These new grounds were expanded to seat slightly more than thirty-eight thousand fans, surrounding but not fully encircling its horseshoe-shaped configuration. The clubhouse was in right center field.

Even though Brush created more space for the fans, the sportswriters didn't benefit much from the rebuilding. The new press box facilities in the grandstands weren't much larger than the old bleacher/wire mesh press coop that had been directly behind and above home plate in the upper deck. In place of the old coop, and in about the same general location, was a press area that Rice once said was fit only for the training of a small shoal of sardines preparing to meet their tin maker. Since the telegraphers occupied the press box too, Rice said that the only way he could cover any game, much less the World Series, was to place his telegrapher in his lap while he wrote.[40]

Cramped, yes, and malodorous. One can only imagine these press box smells. Ordinary body odors would have been particularly noticeable, especially since the mostly unathletic and out-of-shape sportswriters typically worked up a lather just lugging their huge typewriters around with them, as they puffed their way up the steps of the ballpark to the press box. Even though it wasn't hot—game time temperature was 59 degrees—the sportswriters were still dressed to perspire: three-pieced broadcloth or velveteen suits, long-sleeved shirts, high collars, ties, overcoats, and hats.

Their habits reeked too. There were the park beverages they often spiked with Old Crow flasks, and plenty of bottled beer; there were the opened tobacco quids and the stale odors from the contents of the spittoons; smelly smoke was courtesy of the popular Turkish blended Fatima cigarette or the Corona cigar. The cigarette butts and cigar stubs littered the slabbed floor. Neither the delicate aroma of concessionaire Harry Stevens's ham sandwiches nor the unmistakable smell of his frankfurters and mustard could even begin to deodorize the lingering scent of perspiration, juiced-up expectorant, and spirited fortifications.[41]

Rice sat shoulder-to-shoulder-to-shoulder-to-shoulder with the likes of Hugh Fullerton, Sid Mercer, Irwin Shaw, Damon Runyon, Heywood Broun, Harry Salsinger, William B. Hanna, and other sportswriter veterans. Before the first game of the series even started, Rice had already dashed off fifteen hundred words on the pregame warm-ups from his crowded perch, marveling at the batting practice wallops of Red Sox center fielder Tris Speaker. Speaker had crashed the first pitch of batting practice not just into the right field stands, but clean over them, and by Rice's judgment some ninety feet high. The three-hundred-strong Boston fan contingent waved their red flags. Giants fans groaned. Impending Giants danger, Rice noted. Mathewson began warming up at about 1:40, New York's expected starting pitcher.[42]

Red Sox manager Jake Stahl started thirty-four-game winner Smoky Joe Wood. But with exactly one minute until game time, McGraw, in a move that surprised everyone, including Rice, countered not with Mathewson or Rube Marquard, but with the 235-pound, Ozark-born, lefthanded rookie spitballer and seventeen-game winner, Jeff Tesreau, who had one month earlier thrown a no-hitter against Philadelphia. Ironically, one month before that game, Red Dooin, the Philadelphia manager, had petitioned President Lynch of the National League for permission for his pitchers to use a disinfectant on the ball when they were opposing a spitball artist. It seems that Philadelphia pitcher Al Brennan got sick, was hospitalized, and was diagnosed as having a mild case of diphtheria shortly after a series of games with Chicago. Dooin claimed that Brennan's diphtheria was caused by the Philly pitcher handling the same ball juiced up inning after inning by a Chicago spitball pitcher.[43]

In the opening game, Tesreau held the Red Sox hitless for five innings, but Speaker got to him in the sixth with a triple after a fielding mix-up. When McGraw pulled Tesreau after seven innings, he had given up five hits and four runs. In the bottom of the ninth, with the Red Sox ahead 4 to 2, Giants right fielder Murray lined out to Harry Hooper, Merkle singled to center, Herzog singled to right, and Chief Meyers doubled to right, scoring Merkle and sending Herzog to third. With two on and only one out and the score 4 to 3, Joe Wood then struck out his tenth and eleventh batters, Fletcher and Crandall, to claim the first-game victory.

Within an hour Rice had completed his detailing of the entire game, inning by inning, for the *Mail*. His twenty-five-hundred-word description appeared on page one of the early evening paper, and within only a couple of hours of the suspenseful ninth inning. Rube Goldberg, with considerably less game responsibility, watched from the press box too. But what caught his eye was Smoky Joe Wood's habit of hiking up his trousers. When Wood looked toward first base, he pulled up his trousers; when he spat on his glove, he pulled up his trousers; when he prepared to throw the ball, he pulled up his trousers. "In fact," mused Goldberg, "if the separate and distinct times he pulled up his trousers could be concentrated into one sweeping motion, he would have pulled his trousers up over his head and out into the middle of Long Island."[44]

Everyone connected with the series "specialed" over to Boston that evening, both teams on the same train, and accompanied by all the writers, bigwigs, and various and sundry freeloaders. Harry Schumacher spent his trip interviewing Buck Herzog while the other Giants in their midst played poker and horsed around. Herzog explained the team's lightheartedness was due to their collective realization that Wood wasn't as good as they'd heard he was and that if the series was a long one, they would eventually get to him. Rice spent most of the trip writing. In addition to the four thousand words he had already sent off on the pregame and the game, there was his postgame column to get out for the next day's paper. In it he analyzed game one, thoroughly, and concluded that neither club showed much mastery over the other. "When the gods go, the half-gods arrive slowly," Rice commented, as he seemed to wonder out loud why the youngster, Tesreau, got the start over the Old Master, Mathewson. All totaled, Rice wrote six thousand words on the first game of the series.[45]

Game two was played at Fenway Park in Boston. Like the rebuilt Polo Grounds, Fenway was concrete and steel, and it too was new, its inaugural game played early in the 1912 season. "Honey Fitz" Fitzgerald, Boston's mayor—and incidentally the grandfather of John F. Kennedy—threw the first pitch at the dedication ceremony. Adams wrote that the Bostonians knew Fitzgerald as the man "who put the cop in Copley Square."[46] Fenway had a single-decked grandstand (the Polo Grounds' was double-decked), but there were wooden bleachers in left, extreme right, and center. A wooden pavilion was in the right field corner. The playing field was larger than the Polo Grounds, and it was irregularly shaped due to the contours of the Fens, the marshy area of the city upon which it was built. The outfield even included a ten-foot, inclined embankment in front of the left field fence. This obstacle became known affectionately as "Duffy's Cliff," a tribute to Boston's left fielder, Duffy Lewis, who could race up and down the hill with uncanny speed and agility. A ball hit into the left field seats was a ground rule double. The left field line was 321 feet, center field 488 feet, and right field 313 and 1/2 feet. Fenway could hold nearly thirty-two thousand fans.[47]

The weather was gray, chilly, and misty for Wednesday's game two. "In a slashing, storming battle that tore the hearts out of 32,000 crazed fans and broke down even the players at work," Rice wrote after the game, "New York and Boston fought eleven rounds into the edge of dusk to-day." The score was 6 to 6, noted Rice, eventually. A tie. Game called due to darkness. "The game will be played over on the Boston field to-morrow." Rice covered the game in full detail for the *Mail* readers anyway, and inning by inning. For the duration of the eleven innings, his two fingers typed away, creating a full-blown, pitch-by-pitch written description of the game. Had he written his account in present rather than past tense, it could almost have passed for a live play-by-play description of the kind baseball radio broadcasters would verbally begin to produce about a decade later.

Rube Marquard went the distance for New York the next day, and with the help of a dazzling, game-saving, over-the-shoulder catch by right fielder Josh Devore in the ninth, the Giants beat the Red Sox 2 to 1.

Back in New York on Friday, Boston went with Wood, again up against Tesreau. Adams talked mostly about the weather: "The day is close and dark and muggy; it mists but the bugs are wild and buggy. They wonder whether the rain will fall, and whether they'll see a game of ball. And the day is close and muggy." Risking his reputation, Adams forecast the dope as follows: if Boston amasses more runs than New York, Boston will win; but if New York scores more than Boston, New York would win. Rice said much the same thing: "Joe Wood—or Joe Won't—but if Joe Doesn't, Frenzied Reader, these storming Red Sox are up against one pale green time of it—are in for a battle with their broad backs to the wall, leading a hope as dim as sunset sinking into dusk."[48]

Adams and Rice were on the ball; Joe Did. For even though the Giants picked up nine hits off Wood, strong defense saved the game for Smoky Joe. Boston won by putting three runs across home plate to New York's one. Boston was up two games to one. Pondering over the enthusiasm of the partisan crowd, and yet noting their general habit of nonpartisan applauding of good plays from *both* teams, Adams mused that "the suspicion comes over one that the American people is rather fond of baseball." The next day, mounted police had to restore order after the massive crowd at Fenway forced down the outfield fences at the beginning of game four (five with the tie). The young Red Sox pitcher, Hugh Bedient, went on to beat Mathewson by holding New York to four hits and one run; the Red Sox won 2 to 1. After the Sunday off, play resumed Monday at the Polo Grounds. New York's Marquard beat the Red Sox 5 to 2, relatively easily. By now, Adams was whining, good-naturedly, that had he known the series would last this long, he wouldn't have agreed to cover the games for a lump sum; instead, he would have held out for piecework. With piecework, if they played seven or eight games, Adams wouldn't have minded as much the week of ball. But without any increase in the pay, "this thing of going to a game in the morning, staying there until after 4, and then writing until 7 cuts into my afternoons frightfully."[49]

Meanwhile, competing with newspaper front-page stories about the World Series was news of the attempted assassination of Teddy Roosevelt. On the evening before the seventh game, the newspapers reported that John Schrank had plugged Roosevelt in the chest with a .38 caliber bullet. This was the famous Milwaukee incident in which Roosevelt, after having been shot outside his hotel, continued with his planned speech on behalf of his Progressive party candidacy for president. On stage at the auditorium, and with the bullet lodged in the soft tissue of his chest, Roosevelt told his shocked audience that it would take "more than that to kill a Bull Moose." He went on to talk for ninety minutes, reading from his prepared fifty-page speech that he had carried with him, folded in half and tucked into his breast pocket; he winged it whenever he came to the gaping bullet holes on each page. After his talk, and with a characteristic flash of his teeth, Col. Roosevelt exclaimed to the press, in fun, "Gosh! Shot again!"[50]

That might explain where Rice got the spirit in his description of the seventh game of the series at Fenway, played the day after the shooting. "In that first tearing assault they got seven hits and six runs before this fusillade of shrapnel and cannister left Boston stunned and crushed. The impossible had happened. The world was coming to an end. Gibraltar could be toppled over by human hands, for a ball club had faced Joe Wood at home in the best game and shot him to death within one round."[51]

Joe Wood's "death" helped bring true Rice's prediction that the series would go the distance. For the first time in World Series history, the championship battle went to an eighth game, as New York won game seven 11 to 4. The rest of Rice's prognosticating also was about to come true—that the 1912 World Series winner wouldn't be determined until the last inning of the last game, in this case, the tenth inning of game eight. A coin flip had given Boston the home field advantage. "There is glory enough for all in a fight like this—and the only pity is that one must lose where another must win," Rice wrote. "Both have fought with too much heart and courage," he continued, "to miss the laurel which only one can wear." But however much Rice elevated and celebrated a winning contest over the mere winner of it ("Where the war cups clink to the dregs we'll drink/—TO THE TEAM THAT LOSES A FIGHT LIKE THIS!"), in truth the typical fan's heart went only to the winner. Adams got this right in his last series piece with a rhyming sentence written just before the first pitch of the final game: "Win, and the world is with you, lose and you drink alone, for the baseball fan, since the world began, has a heart that is made of stone."[52]

Their memory is also long. The thirty-thousand-dollar Snodgrass muff! Seemingly never forgotten over the years and remembered as one of the biggest boners in baseball history. The last game of the series was tied 1 to 1 at the end of nine innings. In the top of the tenth, against Wood, who relieved Bedient in the eighth, the Giants scored the go-ahead run on back-to-back doubles by Jack Murray and Fred Merkle. In their turn, against Mathewson, Boston pinch-hit Clyde Engle for Wood. Engle hit a high, lazy fly ball to left center. Snodgrass waved off Red Murray, the left fielder, and moved under the ball easily. Out, or so everyone thought. But the ball hit Snodgrass's mitt—and bounced out! Engle took second on the error.

Harry Hooper was up next. In a bunting situation, the New York infield played in, trying to hold Engle close to second; Snodgrass was in and fairly close to second too. Hooper bunted a couple of balls foul before he took a full swing and drove the ball deep over Snodgrass's head. "I made one of the greatest plays of my life on it, catching the ball over my shoulder while on a dead run out in deep left center," recalled Snodgrass. "They always forget about that play when they write about that inning."53

Engle had rounded third by then. Snodgrass almost doubled him up in a close play at second. With one out now, Mathewson was pitching to Yerkes. Matty walked him. Two on. Tris Speaker up. He fouled an easy foul pop-up toward first base. Matty could have caught it himself. Merkle could have easily caught it. Chief Meyers, the Giant catcher, raced down the line for it. The ball fell between all three of them. It was Merkle's ball, but Chief Meyers later said that the Red Sox bench—situated on the first base side—created the confusion in Merkle's mind by coaching him off the ball as they first yelled for Matty to take it, then for Chief to take it. "Well, that's all right," said Meyers about the coaching help, "That's all part of the game."54

Reprieved, Speaker singled sharply to right, driving Engle across the plate and moving Yerkes over to third. The score was now tied. Manager McGraw then ordered Matty to walk Lewis, loading the bases. Larry Gardner was up next. He sacrificed to Josh Devore, scoring Yerkes with the winning run.

Like every other sportswriter, Rice didn't hesitate to immediately lay the blame for the Giant loss on the bad hands of Fred Snodgrass. "By muffing an easy fly ball in the tenth round, Fred Snodgrass to-day cost New York the championship of the world and Christy Mathewson one of his gamest, greatest games." Snodgrass's error was also said to have cost the Giants thirty thousand dollars; the difference between the winning and losing player shares was $4,029.89 to $2,800.50.55

But in a more extended analysis of the last game, Rice also included the Merkle/Mathewson/Meyers foul-up as perhaps as significant as the Snodgrass blunder. It was a real shame, thought Rice, that what stood in the way of the Giant victory were two plays "which you or I, weary reader, who possibly haven't handled a ball in years, could make with one hand while lighting a pipe with the other."56

Rice sympathized with both Snodgrass and Merkle (who already was famous for the "Merkle boner" in 1908). "They didn't do it on purpose, you know, just as you and I haven't done a lot of things on purpose which we wish we hadn't done at all." Rice went on, reminding his readers, "These things are all part of the game, and one has to take the muffs with the home runs—or let both go."[57]

While the stone-hearts were lambasting Snodgrass, in particular, for the Giant loss, Rice, characteristically, was analyzing the Giant loss in a more heartfelt way. Winning, not losing plays, he theorized, actually made the difference. From his vantage point, the Giants didn't lose the game in the tenth by way of an error; the Red Sox won the game in the fifth by breaking the Giant's spirit when Harry Hooper made a spectacular catch in right field: "When Hooper raced to the right field wall, launched himself into midair yesterday and hauled down Larry Doyle's almost sure home run, he not only made the greatest individual play of the series, but saved the game beyond all doubt. But for this super-miraculous catch—one of those things that couldn't possibly happen but sometimes does through a combination of nerve, speed, and luck—the game would have gone to New York 2 to 1 within nine rounds."[58]

Joe Wood agreed. He said that Hooper's catch took the heart out of the Giants. Wood recalled that Hooper ran back at full speed and dove over the railing and into the crowd, and "in some way, I'll never figure out how, he caught the ball—I think with his bare hand. It was almost impossible to believe even when you saw it." Hooper, himself, thought it was divine intervention. In fact, this one catch was so remarkable that more than a decade later, after having covered more than five thousand sporting events in twenty-two years, Rice still thought it was his greatest baseball thrill: "This was a thriller that saved a championship for Hooper's team, brought $30,000 to the Red Sox as the winner's end of the purse, and took its place as one of the greatest plays ever made."[59]

Even Manager McGraw agreed with the essential spirit of Rice's analysis. The loss wasn't Snodgrass's fault and McGraw never did point to this play as the reason for the Giant loss. "I can name twelve plays that were worse and that figured as much or more in losing us the championship," said McGraw right after the last game. He went on to say that this play "just happened to be more in the limelight and to come at the toughest spot of the fight." Reporters hounded McGraw for years after the incident to reveal what he did to Snodgrass after the series was over. At the end of McGraw's thirty years in baseball, he said he never gave Snodgrass one word of reproach; in fact, he raised his salary a thousand dollars for the next season.[60]

Ever the teacher and defender of fair treatment to one and all, Rice ended his 1912 World Series coverage by reminding his readers that to be human is to err, or error, whichever the case may be:

> We hold no brief for what he's done;
> Nor classic "bone" he may have spun;
> No booster for a man that's down
> Who helped to lose the great game's crown;
> But from the throng, with glaring glim,
> Who curse what happened there, let him
> Who's yet to make his first mistake
> Step up and pan him for the break.[61]

When all was finally written about the 1912 World Series, the eight games in nine days created enough excitement for Rice to give his New York readers more than fifty thousand words of informative, lively, and thoughtful copy. All in a week's work, for Rice.

Rice attended a one-room schoolhouse in his early years. This is the class photo from Spout Springs Country School, 18th District, Nashville, Tennessee, around 1888. Seated third from the left in the front row is Henry Grantland Rice. He would have been in the third or fourth grade. (Hearst Collection, *Los Angeles Examiner,* Special Collections, University of Southern California Libraries)

As a teenager, Rice played sports at both the Tennessee Military Institute and the Nashville Military Institute. He continued his sporting interests at Wallace University School, participating in football, baseball, and athletics (track and field). In this 1896 photograph of the Wallace School football team, Rice is standing in the back row, second from the left. (Special Collections, Vanderbilt University)

Rice was an all-around athlete at Vanderbilt University. He was
known for his pluck in football, sticking with it for three years in
spite of multiple arm, rib, back, and shoulder injuries. He also
competed in track and field, and in class basketball. But he was
especially known for his competent baseball skills. He was a
shortstop and a solid hitter. Rice is pictured here in 1901 as the
captain of the Vanderbilt varsity nine. (Special Collections,
Vanderbilt University)

Rice's Vanderbilt University graduation picture, 1901. He graduated with a B.A. in Greek and Latin. He was one of thirty-two graduating seniors in his academic class, and was Phi Beta Kappa. (Special Collections, Vanderbilt University)

Katherine Hollis, one of eight Hollis children, from Americus, Georgia. Rice met her while he worked for the *Atlanta Journal.* She is pictured here at about the time of their budding romance, when she was in her early twenties. They were married in 1906. (Special Collections, Vanderbilt University)

Rice covered the 1905 World Series between the New York Giants (managed by John McGraw) and the Philadelphia Athletics (managed by Connie Mack). New York won, four games to one. Christy Mathewson, who Rice thought was the greatest pitcher he'd ever seen, pitched from 1900 until 1916. He won 37 games in 1908 and 373 games over his career. In the 1905 series, he had three starts and threw three shutouts. Pictured here is John McGraw on the left, and Christy Mathewson on the right. (Acme, Special Collections, Vanderbilt University)

This classic photo of Ty Cobb stealing third base and hook sliding around Jimmy Austin's tag was taken in 1909 by Charles Conlon. Ty Cobb was Rice's first big scoop at the *Atlanta Journal*. (Acme, Special Collections, Vanderbilt University)

In 1911 Rice moved from the *Nashville Tennessean* to the *New York Mail*. Pictured here is Rice (far left) covering the 1911 New York Yankee spring training camp at Savannah, Georgia. With Rice, from left to right, are Ed Curley, an unidentified reporter, Bunk MacBeth, Bill Slocum, Fred Van Ness, Harry Schumacher, and Fred Lieb. (Foltz, Special Collections, Vanderbilt University)

Shortly after Jim Thorpe's two 1912 Olympic gold medals were taken away from him, he played both professional football and baseball. Pictured here is Chief Meyers (left) and Thorpe (right) circa 1913, both in uniform for John McGraw's New York Giants. The two players roomed together. Thorpe played in the major leagues for six years. Rice, along with most of the other sportswriters, believed that Jim Thorpe was the greatest all-around athlete in the first half of the twentieth century. Late in both of their lives, Rice tried to help get Thorpe's medals returned to him. He was unsuccessful. (Acme, Special Collections, Vanderbilt University)

Bobby Jones at age fourteen playing for the U.S. Amateur title in 1916 at Philadelphia's Merion Golf Club. Rice, by then with the *New York Tribune,* was an expert golf writer. With the exception of Jones's Boswell, sportswriter O. B. Keeler, no other writer watched Jones as carefully or as caringly as Rice did either through Bobby's so-called wilderness years, 1916–1923, or the fat ones from 1923 until his retirement in 1930. (International News Photos, Special Collections, Vanderbilt University)

At age thirty-seven, Rice was too old for conscription, but in his estimation not too old to be useful during World War I. He volunteered for duty late in 1917, not as a journalist, but as a soldier in the field artillery. Rice served in France as a first lieutenant. Besides artillery, Rice was also given brief duty with *Stars and Stripes,* the military daily newspaper. (Hearst Collection, *Los Angeles Examiner,* Special Collections, University of Southern California Libraries)

Rice covered the Jess Willard–Jack Dempsey fight in Toledo, Ohio, on July 4, 1919. Tex Rickard, the promoter, billed the boxers as "The World's Greatest Fighting Men." Rice thought otherwise, since neither man fought for their country in World War I. At age twenty-four, the 6'1", 185-pound Dempsey defeated the 6'7", 245-pound Willard in three rounds. Soon thereafter Dempsey was known as "Jack the Giant-Killer." (Special Collections, Vanderbilt University)

Rice had first met and covered "Big Bill" Tilden in 1919 at Forest Hills at the Nationals. "Little Bill" Johnston, who Rice said was no bigger than a sack of peanuts, whipped Tilden three sets to one by discovering Tilden's weak backhand. After Tilden corrected the weakness, he dominated tennis during the 1920s. Tilden was a colorful and theatrical player who was already twenty-seven when he won his first National Singles title in 1920. (Special Collections/Vanderbilt University)

Grantland Rice was a near-scratch golfer. He picked the game up while he was in Nashville and continued to play regularly. He found the game provided not only good copy for his stories but also an escape from the pace, noise, and crowds of the city. (Hearst Collections, *Los Angeles Examiner,* Special Collections, University of Southern California Libraries)

In April 1921 Rice played golf with newly inaugurated President Warren Harding. Pictured at the White House is the foursome: Harding, Rice, Ring Lardner, and Undersecretary of State Henry Fletcher. Rice reported that the president played a "good average game" that ranged between 95 and 100, and he praised as virtuous Harding's habit of brooking no alibis for bad shots. The Rice-Lardner team trounced Harding-Fletcher, five-up. (Special Collections, Vanderbilt University)

Rice was among the flock of reporters who traveled to Shelby, Montana, to see the 1923 Jack Dempsey–Tommy Gibbons fight. Rice is pictured here standing with some of his New York sportswriter friends at the Dempsey training camp in Great Falls, Montana. On the ropes are Edgar "Scoop" Glesson of the *Tribune*, Rice, Herbert "Hype" Igoe of the *World*, Lawrence Perry of the *Sun*, and Harry Newman of the *Daily News*. Gibbons stayed on his feet for fifteen rounds against the Manassa Mauler. Dempsey got the decision. Rice praised Gibbons's stout heart. (Special Collections, Vanderbilt University)

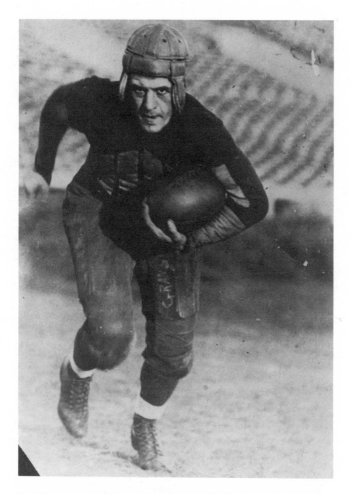

Red Grange, who Rice nicknamed the "Galloping Ghost of the
Gridiron," played for Robert Zuppke at the University of Illinois. But five days after his last collegiate game in 1925 he
turned professional, accepting an offer to play for the Chicago
Bears and electing not to finish his college studies. On Thanksgiving Day, 1925, at Wrigley Field in Chicago, Grange helped
draw what was then the largest crowd ever for a professional
football game. Ten days later at the Polo Grounds the Grange
name drew twice the Chicago gate and seventy thousand fans to
watch the Bears play the Giants. Grange is pictured here in 1924.
Grange's football jersey number was 77. When asked how he got
that number he reportedly said that he was right in line behind
the guy who got 76 and in front of the guy who got 78. (Acme,
Special Collections, Vanderbilt University)

Legendary Notre Dame football coach Knute Rockne (far left) puts his backfield through their motions during the 1924 season. At the time of Rockne's death in a plane crash seven years later, Rice was preparing to write the screenplay for a Hollywood movie of the coach's life. Rice would also figure in the immediate futures of the four players Rockne is seen coaching, for they would soon achieve their own legendary status by way of Rice's words. The players are Don Miller, Elmer Layden, Harry Stuhldreher (with ball in hand), and Jim Crowley. (University of Notre Dame Archives)

9

A Lousy Poet Emerged from the Argonne

Four days before the presidential elections of 1912, Rice summed up the race between Taft, Roosevelt, and Wilson in this way: "The Presidential Threesome is now approaching the Home Hole. Mr. Taft is already 9-down with 8 to play, but he is still slamming away at the white pill and calling upon his niblick with vast gusto. The Colonel is in a sand trap to the right of the green, stymied by Mr. Taft's caddie, who refuses to get out of the way. Mr. Wilson has a two foot putt for the match. And there you are."[1]

The *Mail* was vigorously endorsing Roosevelt. On the eve of the elections, Francis Albertanti, now Rice's sports editor, went so far as to write up an interview/endorsement with "Mike" Donovan, the veteran boxing instructor at the New York Athletic Club.

"Mr. Donovan, I know your time is precious, but I thought I would ask you to tell the *Evening Mail* readers what you think about Teddy?" asked Albertanti.

The sixty-three-year-old responded, "How can any sane man vote other than for this great man. Aren't the Democrats copying his stuff? And behold Wilson, a school teacher, trying to go to Washington. It's a joke. We want a man like the Colonel to look after our affairs. He treats us all alike, poor and rich. He plays no favorites. He won't stand to be bulldozed."

Donovan sparred with Teddy on a regular basis. "He's the best two-handed fighter in the world," Donovan said, speaking primarily of Teddy's spunk in the face of his political opponents. "I say again, Teddy is the greatest living statesman and it would have been a calamity if he died from that assassin's bullet. The people can't afford to lose him, I tell you, because he is the kind of man we want to better humanity. He's got red blood in his veins and courage."2

Taft was a golfer, the first of the golfing presidents. But Roosevelt thought golf was for dudes. Roosevelt even tried to warn Taft off golf by saying that a number of his western constituents protested Taft's golfing habit. "I myself play tennis," cautioned Roosevelt, "but that game is a little more familiar; besides, you never saw a photograph of me playing tennis, I am careful about that; photographs on horseback, yes; tennis, no. And golf is fatal." Taft lost the 1912 election. Of course, so did Roosevelt. The "school teacher" became president.3

Albertanti indulged Rice in his sizing up the last days of the presidential race in terms of a golf match. But he didn't much like it. In Albertanti's estimation, which was about the same as Roosevelt's estimation, golf was something that unemployed sheep herders played to pass the time. It certainly wasn't a sport, or barely even a game. As far as Albertanti was concerned, golf did not deserve any serious coverage on the *Mail*'s sports page.

When the *Mail*'s managing editor, Theophilus England Niles, called Albertanti into his office one day, no doubt at Rice's urging, to find out why Francis wasn't giving any space to golf, Albertanti asked Niles, "Golf? What's golf?"

"Why it's a game—an important game," replied Niles. "A lot of big businessmen are playing it."

"Then put it on the financial page," Albertanti retorted.4

Rice thought differently. First off, as an avid student of the popular histories of most sports, Rice's reading included American golf history. Thus, he knew the beginning of an American tradition was underway; it started in the summer of 1887 in New York's Central Park, when a native Scot and a linen merchant of Dunfermline and New York, Robert Lockhart, walked briskly into the pasture land, placed his gutta percha ball on the greensward, and, after a brief moment of Presbyterian prayer, swung mightily and whacked the ball far away into the daisies. The grazing sheep hardly took notice; but a roaming, blue-uniformed officer of the law did.

"Hey there! What you think you're doin'?"

"Hoots, mon!" protested the most important Scotchman at that moment in America.

"You're pinched!" responded the policeman.

"I dinn juist tak' yir meanin'."

"What th' hell are you drivin' at?"

"I'm drivin a wee ba'. Did ye no see it leave the club face? A braw skelp, was it no?"

"It sure was some soak," agreed the officer. "If it's soakin' you're interested in, come along to the arsenal and get yours. They'll soak you thirty days."

And off they went, arm and arm, to the Sixty-fourth Street station. Lockhart was arrested for the crime of committing golf in Central Park.

Lockhart was good friends with John Reid of Yonkers, a transplanted Scot and an iron works executive. By November of the year of Lockhart's adventures in Central Park, Reid had organized the first golf club in America, the St. Andrews Golf Club of Yonkers, named after the famed club in Scotland. Reid was the first president; Lockhart the first active member. There were fewer than ten members. It is said that the term "nut" was first coined to described these self-styled golfers of Yonkers.5

Their course consisted of six holes at North Broadway and Shonnard Place. Dues were five dollars a year. Each player had six golf clubs, many crafted from the hands of the grand old man of Scottish golf, Mr. Tom Morris. The members averaged one gutta ball apiece. When they broke a club, it was sent off to Scotland for repairs; when they lost a ball, a moratorium was called while the membership took up the hunt. Their seventh hole—the precursor to the nineteenth hole—was a couple of wide planks supported at each end by two empty barrels. Tubs of ice, water jugs, and various spirits were available to the players after their six-hole hike in the pastures. Since they often played the course three times in succession to accumulate an eighteen-hole score, they had the pleasure of quenching their thirst at the seventh hole three times as well.

Four years later the club purchased thirty-six acres of land at the foot of Palisade Avenue. The new clubhouse was a big apple tree. They hung their coats on its branches, along with the club demijohn and various straw sandwich baskets, which swung gently in the breezes. Club members were a constant source of amusement for jeering passersby on the nearby road. The peasantry, who saw this folly as just another passing fad of the idle rich, called the club players "The Apple Tree Gang."6

Of course, golf was not going to be a passing fancy. By 1894 there were about forty clubs in the United States. The Apple Tree Gang had laid out a 2,382-yard, nine-hole course at Grey Oaks and had doubled their membership and quadrupled their dues. A year later the famous Shinnecock Hills Club, at Southampton, Long Island, opened. The course was professionally designed;

William K. Vanderbilt brought Willie Dunn, the well-known golfer, over from Scotland to build the course in 1891. Stanford White, the famous architect, was commissioned to build a fashionable clubhouse.[7]

By then the country clubs had begun to include golf among their diversions. Even if modestly. The Country Club of Brookline, for instance, appointed a committee of three to lay out a golf course at an expense not to exceed fifty dollars! The course was such a smashing success that just two years later the club invested five thousand dollars in further improvements to the original course.[8]

Even the newspapers were astonished when, in 1896, the Ardsley Golf Club held its first tournament and unveiled a luxurious clubhouse costing $140,000. "Midas' Plaisance!" cried the press; newspapers nationwide ran stories about the "Millionaires' Club." Its members included John D. and William Rockefeller, John Pierpont Morgan, Chauncey Depew, Cornelius Vanderbilt, and Robert Ingersol. On 230 acres overlooking the Hudson River, Willie Dunn designed a nine-hole, thirty-seven-hundred-yard course. The Ardsley Casino, as it was called, opened its doors on the evening before the tournament with a Grand Ball; the strains of Strauss waltzes floated across the magnificent golf links to be played on the next day. The tournament itself was kicked off with a band concert courtesy of the Twelfth Regiment and a horseless carriage race from Washington Bridge to the site of the club, just north of Dobbs Ferry. *Cosmopolitan* put up a cash prize for the winner of the horseless carriage race; the "engineers" who drove the newfangled carriages, which broke down about every other mile, were met with gibes along the way of "get a horse!" The winner of the eighteen-hole golf tournament was Reverend Doctor Roderick Terry, who went around the course twice in an even 100; he was politely applauded for his victory by the congregation of wasp-waisted women and mutton-leg sleeved men.[9]

Soon the United States Golf Association was organized by the leading clubs. The first Open Championship was held in 1895, in October, at the Newport Country Club. Eleven golfers entered. Mustached Horace Rawlings won the event with a total stroke total of 173 for the thirty-six-hole tournament.

So it was with a good sense of this early history of golf that Grantland Rice began bugging Francis Albertanti about giving up some space on the sports page for golf. Rice rightly sensed that this sport was going to be big one day. After all, by the turn of the century the British golfers were already beginning to go on tour in the States, hence attracting the curious. Harry Vardon and J. H. Taylor took first and second respectively in the 1900 Open. Four years later, the American of Australian extraction, Walter Travis, who had never touched a golf club until he was thirty-five years old, returned the favor by winning the British Amateur. English-American exchanges became more common. Early women's golf in America, for instance, was given a considerable boost by the visit of Mrs. Dorothy Campbell Hurd, the British women's champion. It was clear to Rice that these exchanges could and would eventually get America's dander up and would lead to the further spread of the sport in America.

But besides knowing golf's history and sensing its future popularity, Rice's interest in golf was also personal. While still in Nashville, he had been eager to find some kind of outdoor competitive game that he could enjoy lifelong and that might be somewhat therapeutic for his bum shoulder (from his football days). While he was covering the Southern Amateur in Nashville in 1909, he became intrigued with the swing of the club and the flight of the ball.

Golf certainly wasn't unknown in the South when Rice was growing up, but it probably wasn't physical enough to get his attention then. It was even played while he was a student at Vanderbilt. One of his classmates, a fraternity brother, Tom Webb, pioneered what is thought to be the first game of golf played in the state of Tennessee. In 1896, Webb and five other Nashville locals played the game on about seventy-five acres of pastureland known as Thompson Commons, near the Vanderbilt campus. They dug holes and used tomato cans for the cups. Webb became the Tennessee state champion in 1913.[10]

Rice started taking lessons at the Nashville club from club pro Charlie Hall, who later taught for decades at the Birmingham Country Club. After the first lesson, Hall thought Rice was a natural. Rice felt natural, too. The sportswriter fell for the game hook, slice, and bunker. "I found a sport I could stick with—a sport destined to stick with me," said Rice.[11]

Besides its popularity and the therapeutic reasons Rice gave to explain his interest in golf, there were several other good reasons for following the game closely. One was purely practical: it provided good copy. Most sportswriters got their stories from the press box, the locker room, hotel lobbies, or train rides to and from sporting events. Rice could go these traditional locales one better because he was one of the few sportswriters who could link up with one notable or another for a leisurely round of golf and conversation. These rambling conversations often produced insights, dope, and interviews for his columns. "I never dreamed that golf would open as many doors of friendship, provide as much grist for my typewriter and engender as many kernels of philosophy, as has this game," said Rice.[12]

Another reason was moralistic. Rice was fascinated by golf, because it was like no other on the question of infractions. "You are attacking an inert ball. Also, you are on your own. You are the referee." In other words, Rice liked the moral test of golf. "Nine times out of ten you must call the penalty on yourself—if a penalty is to be called." He said golfers can either play the game by the rules, or they can cheat. "You are meant to play the ball as it lies," he reflected, "a fact that may help to toughen your own objective approach to life." There was something elemental about the connection between the nature of golf and that of being human. "A man's true colors will surface quicker in a five-dollar 'Nassau' than in any other form of peacetime diversion that I can name," Rice claimed.[13]

A final reason for Rice's interest in golf was less tangible: playing golf gave him a temporary escape from the pace, noise, and congestion of the city. Whereas someone like Damon Runyon was entirely at home in the big city and was held spellbound by its roar, Rice was forever in spirit seeking to be somewhere else.

Of the weary faces on the streets, the wrangling of buyers and sellers, and the din of the traffic, Rice was vaguely uneasy. Golf was a world apart. It indulged his nomadic habits and extended his Southern pastoral inclinations. The sport was played on acres of grass and in the midst of trees (Runyon told Gene Fowler that the "bravest thing in New York is a blade of grass"), and largely industrial-proof. On the golf course, the faces were ones he knew, and the only wrangling was over who should pay at the nineteenth hole; the entire experience, for Rice, was serene and poetic. "It is a game of pleasant exercise, of friendly intercourse, philosophical rather than physical, set out in the open, well apart from the grind and grip of the city."[14]

These bucolic sensitivities were regularly given poetic expression, too. Every so often in his columns—usually just put there, like huge punctuation marks between paragraphs—were romantic if not nostalgic poems that had nothing directly to do with sport. Instead, almost off-handedly, he was speaking aloud on behalf of others, perhaps, about a sense of despair and alienation often felt by modern city dwellers. One poem, "Somewhere Out," is typical. It was placed directly after some baseball commentary, and directly preceding a four-line ditty about golf:

> Somewhere out—from the toil and grind;
> Somewhere out—where the road is kind;
> Somewhere out—where the green trails wait
> For weary feet through the city's gate;
> From the snarl and tangle in marts of trade

To the peace of God in the open shade—
Through the purple dusk—through the silver dew—
Where the rose-sweet dreams of the years come true.

Somewhere out—and we who drive
The soul and heart through the city's hive,
Where life is bound in the city walls,
Have little care where the Red Road calls,
Or little choice where the Trail may wait
So that it leads from the city's gate
To the sea-girt east or the northern snows,
To the sunlit west or the southern rose.

Somewhere out—from the grip of greed;
Somewhere out—as the road may lead;
Or where the winds of the world may drift,
As the burdens fall and the shadows lift;
Wherever the peace of God may wait
And love shall come to the twilight gate;
Through the purple dusk—through the silver dew—
Where the rose-sweet dreams of the years come true.[15]

So Rice's interest in golf wasn't casual. It was vocationally useful, avocationally challenging, and (without getting too philosophical) metaphysically self-defining in a rough sort of way. He was first and always *being* a sportswriter, but he was *becoming* a golfer. A good one too, with a handicap in the single digits only a few years after making the sport's acquaintance, and with steady par-shooting performances in various informal and celebrity tournaments throughout the 1920s.

Back at the sporting desk, so long as Rice kept his golfing commentary restricted to his columns, Albertanti couldn't say too much. If Rice wanted to be prissy, that was his business, his *Evening Mail* sports editor must have thought. Rice's readers were growing in number all the time, but chiefly, Albertanti gathered, because Rice knew and stuck to his principal business: knowledgeable and lively sports reporting on the real and manly sports, such as baseball and football. His popularity certainly couldn't have been because of his idiosyncrasy of commenting on "mere golfing," for God's sake, rationalized Albertanti. The sports editor simply couldn't bring himself to see what all the fuss was about. Albertanti never got the point of Rice's occasional ditties about the joy of hitting a small, white ball with funny-looking sticks. An Albertanti-puzzler was the four-liner following "Somewhere Out":

When Homer smote his bloomin' lyre,
He heard men howl by land and sea.
In voices high and even higher,
"I sunk a ten-foot putt for three."

By 1913 Americans had been doing pretty well in the rivalry with England in such sports as tennis, yachting, boxing, and polo. Even Thorpe's 1912 Olympic victories gave America something to crow about. But the British and the Scots still had the bragging rights in the sport of golf. The Americans were improving, though. And an American (Coburn Haskell) had invented a rubber-cored golf ball that was much more responsive when walloped than the sometimes mulish gutta percha balls. The design of home courses was getting better too; they were getting longer and more difficult.

England's Harry Vardon, who had won six British Open titles, was usually given the nod as the world's greatest golfer at the start of the second decade of the twentieth century. When he and Edward "Ted" Ray, the reigning British Open title holder, made an exhibition tour in the United States in the summer of 1913, the competitive juices of American golfers began to flow. So did Rice's. Over Albertanti's objections, Rice was determined to give coverage to the British champions' tour and to the American golfers' response to it.

But Rice's golf reporting came out of his hide. Besides his usual coverage of the busy-as-ever baseball season, he was also doing his Sportlight column. In addition to his normal baseball coverage, he was asked to write up a second daily column, "Playing the Game," that extended the baseball coverage even further. Surely this would keep Rice busy enough, figured Albertanti, to discourage any golfing peripatetics. Between the two columns, Rice was putting out around fifteen hundred words on baseball dope alone, not counting his day-to-day baseball reporting. But this was a walk, for Rice, especially compared to the daily productivity of his Nashville days.

Golfing stories gradually began creeping into the Sportlight column. Not long before the golf professionals played in the Shawnee Open and the amateurs were to battle for the national amateur championship at the Garden City Golf Course, both in early September, Rice volunteered to add yet a third daily feature column under the byline of "Jigger," and right under the nose of Albertanti. A "jigger" was an early-twentieth-century golfing stick; the subject of the new column was strictly golf—information, analysis, swing and grip techniques, golfing psychology, personality studies, equipment improvements, and so on. This was not the typical newsy brand of eyewitness sports reporting; Albertanti still wouldn't send a real reporter to a golf match. So instead, Rice, the teacher, was giving his readers nothing short of an ambitious semester-long introductory course on golf.

The authority and accuracy of these features must have astonished Rice's sports editor. No one connected with the paper had known how much Rice really knew. Albertanti finally recognized that Rice was about 4 up with 3 to play in the ongoing contest over whether or not golf was going to be seriously reported in the *Evening Mail.* Albertanti grudgingly conceded the match play to Rice.

"Jigger" began writing up golf in earnest, both in the how-to-and-why-bother column and in featured sports stories, some of which even became front-page news. Johnny McDermott, the American champion among the pros, was paired with Vardon in the Shawnee Open, which Rice covered. Both Vardon and Ray were entered. Vardon had had trouble with the greens, Ray faded, and McDermott won the tournament easily. "Vardon would hit an iron approach 12 feet from the cup. You could see McDermott's chest expand as he hit one nine feet from the pin." After the tournament, and during the award ceremony, McDermott welcomed the two British golfers, but ended his welcome by saying " . . . but you are not going to take back our cup!" referring to the United States Open Tournament Cup.

Both British golfers were insulted by McDermott's outburst. The golf committee demanded that McDermott apologize to the pair. Which he did, saying that he was sorry if he had hurt their feelings. The apology over and accepted, McDermott then turned to Vardon and Ray, and said, "But you are not going to take back our cup!"

Even the largely unflappable Rice was taken aback by McDermott's lack of manners. But as Jigger, Rice explained that McDermott simply and honestly didn't much care for foreign golfers; Jigger called it a "rugged sort of antipathy." It was almost obsessive. Jigger explained that McDermott wasn't especially cultivated, and beyond his dislike of visiting golfers, "he couldn't write very many treatises upon other subjects." McDermott had no idea of offending anyone; the American simply blurted out what he felt to be true—which was to say forthrightly that he was going to beat them both at the United States Open later that month.[16]

The nineteenth Open Championship was held at the Country Club of Brookline, in Massachusetts, the same club that twenty years earlier had spent less than fifty dollars to lay out its course. This amount had been exceeded a bit by 1913; it was estimated that the ninth and tenth holes alone at Brookline cost at least fifty thousand dollars, due in part to the need to do excessive rock blasting from tee to green.[17]

The 170 professional and leading amateur golfers who entered the Open created such a large field that two days were set aside for qualifying. The best thirty-two scores for each day would qualify sixty-four players to play in the seventy-two-hole championship. Two rounds, thirty-six holes, would be played each day in the championship. Besides Vardon, Ray, and W. E. Reid from England, the American pros included such players as Alec Smith, McDermott, George Low, and Charles Blair MacDonald, a transplanted Scotsman. The amateurs—none of whom were expected to finish in the top ten—included Chick Evans, Jerry Travers, and Francis Ouimet. The field also included a young caddie from the Country Club of Rochester by the name of Walter Hagen.

This was Hagen's first-ever National Open. He'd heard about the flap over whether or not the Americans were good enough to keep the cup. When he arrived at Brookline, he went directly into the locker room where a number of American golfers—including McDermott, Travers, Evans, and Oiumet— were talking. The black-haired youngster stood tall and blithely said, "The name's Hagen. I've come down from Rochester to help you fellows stop Vardon and Ray."[18]

At the end of the first thirty-six holes in the championship round, Reid and Vardon tied at 147; Ray shot a 149. McDermott came in at 153, Jerry Travers, 156, and Hagen (misspelled by Rice, consistently, in the *Evening Mail* as W. Hagin) finished the two rounds comfortably in 151. Also shooting 151 was Francis Ouimet, a Bostonian and a former caddie at the Brookline course.

Ouimet was the Massachusetts amateur champion, tall, rangy, pleasant-faced, and just twenty years old. He had picked up the game at the early age of five. His older brother, Wilfred, and his friend, Richard Kimball, had marked out a 120-yard golf course on the dirt street in front of their Brookline home, using their heels to dig out the two cups at each end of the "course" underneath two distant lampposts. The three of them played the course every day after school. By the time he was thirteen his every waking, nonschool moment was given over to this challenging game, either as a caddie or a player.[19]

On the second day of the tournament, the weather turned ugly. At the end of the morning round, the third round, Vardon and Ray were both tied at 225. Ouimet was still out on the course, and holding his own. Rice was following the youngster. About two thousand other spectators, including "a fair sprinkling of women," noted Rice, braved the driving northeast rainstorm and trudged through the wet grass to follow Ouimet. They very nearly encircled the 18th green, and let out a cheer when Ouimet sank a putt for par for a 74 and a three-round total of 225, tying Vardon and Ray. "Hagin" was two strokes back; McDermott was down five.

In the afternoon round, Ray and then Vardon shot 79s, tying each other with total scores of 304 apiece. No surprises here, given the reputations of the two British golfers and their status as tournament favorites. Somehow, in the gray, dripping dusk, Ouimet had to display the stamina of a golfer twice his age and experience and play the last four holes one under par to tie. Rice saw the dramatic finish.

On the 17th, Ouimet hit his second shot to the green but left himself a twenty-foot, downhill, sidehill putt. Without a flutter, he stepped up and holed the putt for a 3. Then, on the 18th, he was on the edge of the green in two strokes. With his mashie, he pitched to within about seven feet of the cup. Now with three thousand spectators surrounding him and praying for his success, he calmly walked up to his ball, barely looked at the hole, and boldly stroked the ball into the middle of the cup for a 79, creating a three-way tie for the National Open title. Oiumet's *invictus*, according to Rice, was:

> Out of the tie that corners me,
> Black though it be from tee to pole,
> I thank what golfing gods there be
> I sunk my putt at that last hole.[20]

The next day, on the still wet and muddy course, five thousand spectators showed up to watch the playoff for the American title. Few in the crowd thought Oiumet could keep up with the two pros. At the turn for home, the three golfers were still even, each having taken thirty-eight strokes. Seven holes later, Ray was four down to Vardon, but Ouimet, unbelievably, was one up on Vardon. On the 17th, Ouimet drove down the middle of the fairway and hit his second shot fifteen feet from the hole. Both Vardon and Ray broke. Ouimet calmly sank his putt, and the two chaps took fives to Ouimet's three. At the end of eighteen holes, Francis Ouimet had completely beaten back the British challengers and turned the golfing world upside down with his five-stroke victory over Vardon (who took a six on the 18th) and six strokes to the good over Ray. This relatively unknown amateur was the 1913 United States Open champion. Overall, McDermott finished fifth, with Hagen right behind him—Hagen would win the 1914 Open, leading the tourney from wire to wire. McDermott's six-year career, however, was quite suddenly about over. He had been a complete wreck ever since his short "speech" to Vardon and Ray at Shawnee; his pride was wounded because of the heavy criticism his apparent incivility received from the press and the public. Combined with some personal problems, this criticism—which he thought was terribly undeserved—ended his golfing career. Within a year he faded into obscurity, was admitted to a sanitarium, and was largely forgotten.[21]

It was Ouimet who now garnered national acclaim. "His achievement is beyond all words," wrote Rice of Oiumet's miracle victory, "not to be measured in the countless printed lines of adulation. When one achieves what no one has achieved before in the 400 years' history of a sport, not so much in what was accomplished as in the manner of its accomplishment, there is nothing to be added." Rice added anyway: "The Hall of Sporting Fame has room for but one at the ultimate top and the name which belongs there is OUIMET."[22]

Ray received third-place prize money of $100; Vardon won $150; and Ouimet, an amateur, received the equivalent of $300 in a trophy plate. Vardon praised Ouimet at the award ceremony, speaking of the trouble he and Ray had with the youngster's nerve and steady play: "We were only trailing along to-day, looking for an opening that never came. He outplayed us all week." The London papers heaped just as much praise on Ouimet. Typical was the *Standard*, which wrote, "The garlands have withered on English brows in yachting, polo and tennis. Now comes a further reverse in golf, which Americans may be said only to have taken up seriously in the last twenty years." The *Chronicle* claimed that Ouimet's victory was brilliant: "Never was laurel more brilliantly won. The youthful American was pitted against two of the most expert golfers in the world and outplayed his formidable opponents fairly and squarely."[23]

Even though Rice, along with everyone else, lauded to the skies Ouimet's skill, nerve, and brilliance, he stopped short of massaging Ouimet's victory into a symbol of American golfing superiority over the English. He cautioned the many boasters to look at the facts. England sent only three golfers to the Open. Two of them finished in the top three of 170 golfers. Furthermore, America had sent four golfers to compete in the British Open earlier in the year; of the four, only one even qualified and the best he could do was finish fifth. So England had done considerably better with three entries in the American Open than America had done with four entries in the British Open.

Rice noted that England could have done even better at Brookline had there not been a bit of a tiff between two of their golfers. It was reported that the 225-pound Ray got so mad at the English trio's predicament on the last round of regulation play that he lost his temper and actually took a swing at W. E. Reid, decking the 130-pound third member of the English golfing contingent. At the time, Reid was in an even better position to win than Ray, but he broke up after the unprovoked attack. So in all fairness, Rice argued, the Britons were still the Americans' golfing superiors. "We had one twenty-year-old amateur with superhuman qualities that made up for general comparative deficiency," Rice wrote, "but through the recent tournament we most certainly failed to show that our golf was on a par with England's."[24]

Yet. Rice knew and welcomed the fact that front-page coverage of Oiumet's epic victory would inspire the American public to take up the game in greater numbers. Ouimet, the young Bostonian, wasn't of blue-blood stock; his father was French Canadian and his mother was Irish American. The former caddie, a kid who worked summers when he was in high school, was pleasantly unassuming. He made good hero copy.[25]

After 1913, golf grew remarkably. Within the next ten to fifteen years the number of serious golfers soared from around a couple hundred thousand to about a couple million; the number of clubs grew from thirteen hundred (up from forty in 1894) to about forty-five hundred. Albertanti and the myriad of other sporting editors like him couldn't ignore the sudden popularity of the game; Rice, especially, and a few other newspaper and magazine writers, such as John Kieran, Rex Beach, Ring Lardner, George Ade, Bud Kelland, and Rube Goldberg, would do their part to create American golf history by promoting the bejesus out of the game.[26]

This Rice did, in particular, with freelance articles in such magazines as *Collier's, American Magazine,* and *McClure's;* even by 1913 Rice had begun contributing regular magazine articles to these and other national weeklies and monthlies. His longest association was with *Collier's,* in which he published pieces for more than three decades, beginning in 1912. Golf was regular subject matter or a sporting reference point in many of these articles. Additionally, Rice promoted the sport with newspaper columns and features on playing the game well, interviews with champions, and copy on regular tournament play. He even took up golf as a book subject. A year or so after the Brookline tournament, Rice teamed with Jerome Travers—then the Open champion and a four-time American Amateur champion—to write *The Winning Shot* (1915). The popular book went beyond the techniques of golf; it was an excursion into golf psychology. The book included lively accounts of miraculous shots, tips to playing steadier golf, analysis of frames of mind to either cultivate or avoid, advice on the whys and wherefores of controlling nerves and tempers, and examples of golf's ever-present "fickle goddess" and her elastic humor. Of course, it was full of verse, such as the following "Duffer's Requiem" (with his apologies to Robert Louis Stevenson):

Under the wide and starry sky
Dig the grave and let me lie;
Gladly I've lived and gladly die
Away from the world of strife;
These be the lines you grave for me:
"Here he lies where he wants to be;
Lies at rest by the nineteenth tee,
Where he lied all through his life."[27]

Between 1887 and the mid-1920s, on average, a new convert to golf purchased a set of golf clubs every thirteen minutes; and every three days, on average, a new golf association was organized. Grantland Rice's steady personal and professional commitment to the game was instrumental to its remarkable growth in America, both in its recreational and competitive forms.[28]

By the end of 1914 Grantland Rice had clearly made quite a name for himself in New York and throughout the nation. He was also beginning to make real money. In spite of whatever doubts he may have had when he jumped from the South to New York, by 1914 he not only had paid his dues but also was beginning to be recognized in New York for the talents he had been known for in the South: he was an incredibly competent, knowledgeable, hard-working, and personable sportswriter. Even though the *Evening Mail* had upped Rice's salary to one hundred dollars a week and was syndicating his "Sportlight" column (along with O. O. McIntyre's and Rube Goldberg's columns), Rice didn't have to think long before accepting an offer from Ogden Reid to join the sporting staff of the *New York Tribune* in 1915. The *Tribune* offered him an unbelievable $280 a week. His freelance magazine and book writing was going wonderfully well, but a regular income nearly three times what he had been earning on the *Mail* was a financial windfall to Rice, Kate, and eight-year-old Floncy. Besides that, this was clearly a promotion to the New York newspaper elite.[29]

Rice moved his typewriter and stuff from Broadway and Fulton to the Tall Tower on the south end of the triangle made by Park Row, Nassau Street, and Spruce. His move to the *Tribune*—his last and longest formal tie to a single newspaper—positioned Rice to become the sportswriting giant on Park Row (not that this was in any sense an intention that Rice himself had). He would stay with the *Tribune* for the next fifteen years.

One can only imagine the feeling Rice must have had on his first day on the job within the walls of the historic *Tribune* building. He had stood the test in New York, to no one's surprise but his own, and had landed a job on a legendary American newspaper, a mere fourteen years after his start as a cub reporter on the *Nashville Daily News.*

The *Tribune*, started by Horace Greeley in 1841, was one of New York's first penny papers, following Benjamin Day's *Sun* and James Gordon Bennett's *Herald* by just a few years. By the time Greeley died in 1872, the newspaper was nothing short of remarkable. Whereas James Gordon Bennett's *Herald* was conducted more as an industrial art, often mocking its reader, as one journalism historian has explained, the *Tribune* was genuine folk art that maintained a certain reverence for its reader and the popular culture it created. Greeley is remembered for helping the average reader to understand the essential elements of nation-building by way of reasonable, kind, and fair reporting and commentary. In the Midwest, the "Try-bune," as the farmers called it, was "next to the Bible."[30]

After Greeley's death, the paper fell to Whitelaw Reid. It was bolstered by the financial fortune Reid acquired through his marriage to Elisabeth Mills, daughter of Darius Ogden Mills, a multimillionaire banker and businessman. But with the comfort of this guaranteed subsidy, the *Tribune* wasn't run as a profit-making business, and it became less and less competitive among the some twenty-five dailies in New York. So much so that the paper was practically moribund when it was taken over in 1912 by the Reids' son, Ogden Mills Reid, and his hard-driving, self-assured wife, Helen—who had been Elisabeth Mills's private secretary for seven years before she and Ogden married in 1911. The *Tribune* had been losing money at the rate of two or three thousand dollars per week for a number of years; it had lost $1.135 million in the five years before Ogden took over. In circulation it was the smallest of the major New York newspapers at twenty-five thousand a day; this was about the same circulation as when Ogden's father, Whitelaw, succeeded Greeley some forty years earlier, even though New York City's population had quadrupled during this time. By comparison, the *New York Times* grew in circulation from about twenty thousand to more than two hundred thousand in these years.[31]

But the *Tribune* was about to recover its former prominence. It wasn't so much Ogden Reid's creative leadership that brought the *Tribune* out of its gradual journalistic atrophy as his simple exercise of good judgment in hiring; he then exercised even better judgment by getting out of the way of those he hired. Franklin P. Adams had gone over from the *Mail* a year before Rice, and had started up his soon-to-be-famous "Conning Tower" feature column. Heywood Broun had left the *Telegraph* and was moved within the *Tribune* from general assignments to sports by George Herbert Daley, the sporting editor. Fred Hawthorne, also a general reporter on the *Tribune*, was reassigned to sports. With the addition of Rice, the *Tribune's* sports page was everyman's delight. It had humor, solid analysis, broad coverage, and exceptionally good writing. Other papers could claim single, big-name bylines (Runyon at the *American*, Fred Ness at the *Globe*, John Wheeler at the *World*, and Sam Crane at the *Journal*), but the *Tribune* had begun to muster a group of snappy writers who really knew their stuff.[32]

The oversize, perpetually rumpled Broun had won a regular byline owing to his slightly unorthodox, funning yet pointed sports coverage. He was an unabashed Giants fan/reporter—it is said that he would stand up and cheer any good fortune for the team from his seat in the press box. Broun once wrote about a Philadelphia Phillies trade whereby their starting shortstop would be replaced. Broun thought this was a therapeutic trade: "He does not look like a shortstop; he does not act like a shortstop; and only by grossly circumstantial evidence will he ever be convicted of shortstopping. Now he must drop his disguise and go back to the outfield."[33]

For a short time the likable Broun was asked to double as the sports editor. The job was short-lived. He was asked by Reid to go find another good columnist for the *Trib* sports page, but to try to hold the weekly salary to fifty dollars, or fifty-five if absolutely necessary. Broun went after W. O. McGeehan, the caustic stylist on Hearst's *Journal* who was writing under the pseudonym "Right Cross." McGeehan wanted to write under his own name. Broun agreed. Then Broun closed the deal by saying, "Mr. McGeehan, I am authorized to offer you a salary of fifty dollars or fifty-five—which would you prefer?" Shortly thereafter, Broun became the *Tribune's* drama critic.[34]

Rice, meanwhile, settled in on the *Trib*. He took his column with him from the *Mail*, and its title. Even though he'd been in New York for four years and had achieved considerable notoriety, his typical and genuine modesty still provoked him to introduce himself to the *Tribune* readers as though he were a newcomer. He admitted in his inaugural column that he was, like Rudyard Kipling's "tramp royal," a drifter from job to job, and that he too had felt the magic lure of a call to a newer road. He said he'd strive to please and be pleased to strive; that he would make many mistakes, but they'd be of brain and not of heart; and that he knew only one way to write sports: "To write each chapter as it seems to us." He pledged

> To dig beneath the Alibi
> And grapple with the Proper View;
> To come up with the How and Why
> And coyly slip it to you.[35]

The *Tribune* that day also ran some tributes to their newest columnist. American League President Ban Johnson congratulated the *Tribune* on their prize catch. Johnson said that he had always admired the happy vein in which Rice wrote, and that he was clever, keen, and versatile. His baseball writing, Johnson thought, was brilliant; but in the other sports, said Johnson, Rice was quite at home as well. Howard Mann, the sporting editor of the *Chicago Evening Post,* in verse, paid tribute to Rice's grace, having followed Rice from Atlanta to Cleveland and eventually to New York:

> And even in benighted Chi we love his Grandoldope,
> So in our woolly western way we voice this earnest hope
> That while the major magnates plot and crafty Feds intrigue,
> He bats a cool .500 in the *New York Tribune* League.[36]

To remove any possible confusion about his sports philosophy, Rice apparently felt it important to clue his readers in on his perspective from the very start, in his first column. As was his habit, he worked out his views in his trademark verse, in this instance with a new year's dedication "To Sport":

> In you I feel the Pulse of Life;
> In you I see Art and Romance;
> Born where red-flowing blood is rife
> Of Courage—and the Goddess Chance;
> The call on Nerve and Brain and Heart
> Where each in turn must do its part.
>
> You've shown the fickleness of Fame,
> How brief the laurel's fleeting day;
> The emptiness of all acclaim
> That greets the player—and the play;
> How one at Morning knows the height
> But passes, long forgot, by Night.
>
> You've shown the fickleness of Fame,
> But with it the eternal worth
> Of one who dares to Play the Game
> Beyond the scorers of the earth;
> Who sees, above the maudlin roar,
> Something beyond the final score.[37]

Something beyond the final score. Paradoxically, in his consistent repetition of this belief that there was some kind of transcendent significance to sport, Rice accepted the apparent internal contradiction that sporting life could be at the same time both not serious and serious. He never worked out this view in any heady sort of way; rather, it was an intuitive understanding or sense or feel, always indirectly implied but also and always left directly unsaid. It is arguable that Rice's indirect expression of the not serious/serious nature and significance of the sporting world went a long way toward accounting for his own growing popularity as a sportswriter. The increasing anonymity, rush, and boredom of the modern industrial city was compensated for somewhat by the familiarity, liveliness, color, and drama of the sporting world. Rice's ever-present light touch gave his readers the rational reassurance that he knew full well that sport was not to be taken literally as a life-and-death matter—it was only a game. Yet because so many people cared so deeply about sports and those who played it, Rice also took the sporting world, and his role within it, quite sincerely and earnestly, remaining faithful to what he considered sport's essential value: it was an active antidote to the nation's growing physical, intellectual, and moral passiveness, and to the trivializing tendencies of modern life. Since ordinary people cared so much about their sports, their teams, and their heroes, Rice knew that sport was inherently far more than mere diversion or entertainment.

On the one hand, Rice the realist clearly understood that the activity of sport was not serious when compared with activities associated with satisfying our *creature needs*. There's nothing really world-shaking about sport's role in this regard. That is, survival or subsistence needs are naturally the primary needs in his account—food, shelter, clothing, basic freedom, and other creature comforts. Good health would be among these creature needs as well; and even though sporting activities can contribute to the good health of a people, for Rice, at least, the therapeutic aspects of sport were quite incidental to its essential justification. With respect to these creature needs, sport, then, was not especially serious; it was largely gratuitous—just sport, after all.

On the other hand, Rice the romantic intuitively knew that sport was properly serious when it came to the question of *human needs*. Sport, he thought, was worthy of our serious pursuit because by way of such enthusiastic participating, and even informed spectating, "the pulse of life" was experienced, in principle at least. Trite, perhaps—nerve, brain, and heart, and something beyond the score. But in a rudimentary way, for Rice, the virtue of sport was its legitimacy as a serious and worldly pursuit of the freely chosen: opportunities for unforced learning and growing, creative self-assertion, pursuit of excellence, the joy of striving, self-reliance, and adventurous self-testing—all vital, human needs. Sport, then, was potentially a moral, character-defining undertaking. Hence, Rice downplayed what he thought was transitory in sport: the extrinsic outcomes, such as scores, acclaim, and fame—this even though his voluminous writing about what sporting heroes did actually served to spread their fame and create their acclaim. Against this extrinsic transitoriness, Rice was mindful instead of the eternal and intrinsic worth of just playing the game, and playing it justly.

In this spirit, Grantland Rice quietly introduced himself to his *Tribune* readers, and, with syndication, to his thousands of readers across the nation.

"Extra! Extra! War with Germany!" blared the *Tribune*'s bold headline. Against the force of this tremendous news, Rice must have felt almost foolish reporting seriously on the story of sportswriter and California short-story writer Charles E. Van Loan, who, at Rice's urging, took a swing at making the longest golfing drive in recorded history. Until that time, the longest drive had been around four hundred yards. Van Loan walloped a golf ball two thousand yards, including carry and roll, and one-handed to boot!

Perhaps to show the general relativity of records as such, Rice had pointed the playful Van Loan to a good tee-off spot for his record try: the edge of the Grand Canyon, at a spot just above the Black Gorge, where the canyon is fourteen miles across and the drop to the river below is six thousand feet. Van Loan, the spirited *Saturday Evening Post* writer, had *Collier's Weekly* photographer Henry James Forman witness and photograph the one-handed drive. Mr. Forman reported that he followed the flight of the ball for a mile and then lost interest, but that he was willing to testify that it reached the river below.[38]

Thus, in April 1917 when America joined in the war against the Kaiser, what was serious and what was not was patently obvious. By June a 175,000-strong American Expeditionary Force, under the command of General Pershing, was training in France. By July conscription was underway. And by November the A.E.F was nearly two million strong.

The *Tribune*, more than any other New York paper, had been kettledrumming practically since the outbreak of the war in 1914. The famed and dashing special correspondent for the *Tribune*, Richard Harding Davis, covered the early days of the fighting. By the time the German blockade of Allied shipping was imposed, the *Tribune* was calling for the United States to enter the war to stop the Kaiser's "attack upon civilization by barbarism." This editorial by the *Tribune*'s political reporter, published on the first anniversary of the sinking of the British passenger ship, the *Lusitania*, earned the paper the first-ever Pulitzer Prize given for editorial writing. The *Tribune*'s circulation grew in excess of one hundred thousand.[39]

In the summer and fall months after America entered the war, Rice dutifully did his job, following the sporting news wherever it took him—as he had been doing in his first two years with the *Tribune*. But now his columns were thick with coverage of and commentary on baseball, boxing, and golf—and war. The contrast between war and sport was painfully obvious. On May 1, for instance, the *Trib*'s front-page headlines reported on the tragic torpedoing by Germany of an oil tanker on its way to New York; the ship was sunk, killing twenty-one, including the captain. On the same day, Rice's eight-hundred-word column fretted over the likely candidates to replace Honus Wagner as the King of Shortstops; after discussing the strengths and weaknesses of the top ten most likely candidates, Rice argued that thus far, no other Wagner had come along. The discussion seemed forced and halfhearted.[40]

"Isn't it hard," one letter to Rice began, "to become interested in such minor things as baseball when so many greater things are popping all around?" Rice answered that, of course, war overshadows sport, just as the tree overshadows the tomato vine. "But for all that, as a side dish, the tomato is still esteemed here and there along the highway." Life, he went on, isn't wholly a matter of greater things; the details still hold their humble places in the scheme of things, he philosophized.[41]

By way of reconciling the two worlds, Rice's meaty but lean columns were peppered with war talk and salted with sport commentary. One frequent theme was the way in which a sport-loving country such as the United States could produce brave, athletic soldiers. A single, nonathletic Hun or Turk with a rifle might easily end the existence of a star athlete from America or England, Rice wrote. But a regiment or a division of athletes would prevail over nonathletes "eleven times out of ten." According to his reckoning, more than fifteen million Americans had shown an interest in sport in one form or another. Too many millions in America had been taught the worth of playing out the game, he thought, not to be ready for any shock that might strike, and with whatever force. The call of the outdoors couldn't be much better preparation for the drill, the march, and the physical stamina needed for combat. What's more, sport, like war, depended upon grit, team play, and "naked valor," in Emerson's words.[42]

Rice advised that for those men who were not drafted or who didn't volunteer, as a matter of duty, they must keep healthy at home via sport and exercise: "The better health a citizen keeps the better he is able to stand up against whatever fate may befall." The more war gets on any nation's nerves, Rice argued, the more it leaves its depressing effect. One of the best tonics for this depression, he thought, was sport: a physical builder and a mental preparer—an exercise and an active commitment.[43]

Occasionally Rice would also speculate on the impact the war would or should have on the professional sports picture and on collegiate sports, as more and more athletes went "Over There." Naturally, he mused, war would take many of America's able-bodied sportsmen and thereby deplete the sporting ranks, with collegiate sport suffering perhaps the most.

Or, he would help stump for the large variety of benefit contests that were played to raise money for the war effort. For example, Rice was a major figure in promoting the various holiday fund-raising golf tournaments. Through club tournaments and professional exhibition matches, Rice figured that in the summer of 1917 golf generated more than five hundred thousand dollars for the Red Cross and the other war relief funds.[44]

He also published letters from soldiers, one of which was from a member of the Canadian Expeditionary Force who had just returned from France. After giving a short tutorial on the proper arm action for throwing a grenade—throw it like a cricket player, he coached, not a baseball pitcher— he spoke of the role of sport on the front lines. At Zillebeke, the soldier recalled, the Canucks regularly played pick-up baseball games behind their billets only a mile and a half from the front. All around the ploughed field and stone-based diamond, the "heavies" were playing war; but "the gang kept on playing (baseball) as though they were on some back lot in Toronto." Rice noted that one reason such pick-up games were encouraged and developed was to provide psychological recuperation from the frayed nerves combat produced; they built morale and provided a temporary diversion from the horrors of the battlefield.[45]

But Rice was still on the sidelines. At age thirty-seven, he was too old to be conscripted—but not too old to be useful, he thought. On the evidence of the hawkish nature of his columns between April and November of 1917, it was apparent that he was actually writing himself into the war script. Cheerleading wasn't enough; it was inevitable that he was going to volunteer. In early November, he wrote:

> By all the ghosts of No Man's Land,
>   Through all its fury, flame and flood,
> On through the anguish each must stand
>   In wallow-drifts of mud and blood,
> On through whatever hells may wait
>   With marching feet and rolling drum,
> Beyond the final grip of Fate
>   The Great Adventure whispers "Come!"[46]

Three weeks later, the call came again:

> Through the deep night, or in the crowded places
> Watching the mighty tide of drifting faces,
> Whispering, pleading, I can hear the call
> Across far plains or in the city's wall—
> "Come to your post and take your fighting chance
> For Life, for Love, for Liberty—and France—
> On through the ghosts who wait amid the slain
> To see if you have let them die in vain—
> Before the last great valiant chance is gone,
> Come on—come on—come on!"[47]

It isn't difficult to figure out from his newspaper copy what Grantland Rice was thinking he should do. But as to whether volunteering for the Great Adventure made good sense to anybody but himself, well, it probably didn't. With a wife and a ten-year-old daughter, and limited physically by a quirky shoulder to boot, his enlistment was problematic to say the least. Kate couldn't have been thrilled with his intention to volunteer, his laudable patriotism notwithstanding; and Floncy, his dearest Floncy, was certainly old enough to understand the possibility of losing her father in the war. Rice had to be sensitive to all of this. But there was the call; and like mariners who threw themselves off their ships when they heard the Sirens' charming song, Rice was similarly destined to throw himself directly into the war.

Rice faced a choice as to what war duty he would volunteer for. If being most useful to the war effort was the criteria, one would think he would follow other reporter friends who went to the front strictly as journalists. But not Rice. He had already turned down *Collier's* when, about this time, they asked him to go the front lines as a war correspondent; they offered him a dollar a word!

> Perhaps the time is nearing when we'll all go to the front;
> But what of it?
> The married man, the single man, the brawny and the runt;
> But what of it?
> Some twenty millions now have gone—the bravest and the best—
> From every land beneath the sun to face the final test;
> Why should we hope to hang around within a downy nest?
> So what of it?
>
> Perhaps among the fallen brave we'll find the grave is deep;
> But what of it?

Perhaps in somber No Man's Land we'll know our final sleep;
But what of it?
Since each of us owes God a death—and each has got to pay—
Why not swing out with valiant stride along the open way
To where the Great Adventure waits this side of Judgment Day?
So what of it?[48]

So it was to be for Rice; and so what of it if he wanted to fight and not write? On December 5, 1917, Grantland Rice left New York and his downy nest, and with a valiant stride set out for Greenville, South Carolina, where he was joining the infantry as a private in the First Tennessee. His fatalistic sensitivities, combined with his habitual reading of Rudyard Kipling, who made foot soldiering sound so romantic and tough and adventuresome, couldn't have made for a more enthusiastic enlistee.

His readers didn't even know he had left New York, for he continued writing his column without interruption through December. In January, under "The Sportlight" column head, the *Tribune* editors boldly wrote about Rice that "the soul of the poet has risen to the poetic heights of patriotic action." This peculiar sentence wasn't an announcement of Rice being killed off in the war, however much it seemed to read that way. Instead, the editors were simply announcing that Rice was in the army and that he would continue his column while he could, but only three days a week (he could only keep up his column for about six weeks, owing chiefly to fourteen-hour days of military duties).[49]

Hearing the call of duty to country did not entirely compromise Rice's good and responsible family sense; before he left for South Carolina, he made complete financial arrangements for Kate and Floncy. They would be financially secure while he was away and, heaven forbid, they would be taken care of to the best of his ability should he not return. Rice's *Tribune* salary was now three hundred dollars a week, and his column was syndicated by a long string of newspapers. He was also receiving royalties from his book-writing ventures, such as profit from his popular book of verse, *Songs of the Stalwart,* that Appleton and Company had published only two months before his enlistment. While he was gone, Kate was to receive whatever his regular and freelance writing income generated. In addition, he managed to pull together seventy-five thousand dollars in securities, which he gave to a lawyer friend for safekeeping. "If I didn't come back," he said, "at least there remained a tidy chunk for my two girls."[50]

By his own recollection, when Private Rice arrived for training in sunny South Carolina, the old South wasn't exactly balmy. It was about five degrees above zero and snowing at his destination, Camp Sevier. His army-issue pup tent had a rent in it as big as a frying pan. When he woke up the morning after his first night camping out in the mud and snow, he had caught a roaring cold that didn't entirely leave him until the Armistice. In fact, since Rice had a history of frequent colds and sinus troubles from then on, this cold or pneumonia—or whatever upper respiratory difficulty it really was—may have indirectly nagged him throughout the rest of his life.

Shortly after Rice pitched his tent, his infantry dreams were dashed when his unit was redesignated the 115th Field Artillery and put under the command of Brigadier General Gus Gatley, known affectionately by his troops as "Good Old Gus." Later Gatley would command the artillery section of the famous Rainbow Division in France.

From the start, Private Rice stood out from the majority of Southern farm boys in his outfit. "The fact that I was older than most and knew my left foot from my right probably had a lot to do with my becoming a Sergeant drill instructor, and then a candidate for officer training." With some help on the mathematics section of the officer's training course from Colonel John Geary, a big Irishman with a desert-rat mustache who had been the athletic officer at the Presidio in California, Rice was quickly commissioned a second lieutenant.[51]

Soon after, Geary called for Rice. "Lieutenant," Geary said, "I've got two jobs for you."

"Colonel," Rice replied, "I am already mess officer, telephone sentry, athletic officer and liaison officer of this outfit. I need more sleep, not more jobs."

"In this Army, "replied Geary, "it's not how many jobs you have—it's what jobs!"

"We need a VD officer," he continued. "Also, that patch of trees over there must be cleared for a baseball field—for a game two weeks from today. It's got to be ready. Gatley ordered it."

The "patch" of trees was a solid green forest. Rice negotiated with the colonel to do the easiest of the two jobs, clearing the forest, on the basis that he knew nothing about VD and something about baseball.

"Commandeer whatever you need," Geary told Rice.

The next morning Rice put 280 men to work with picks, axes, and dynamite, rooting up stump after stump. The noise attracted General Gatley.

"You've got every goddam man in the unit!" he roared. "Who gave you the authority?"

"Colonel Geary, Sir," Rice replied.

Two weeks later, on schedule, the 115th played that baseball game against the 114th.[52]

Lieutenant Rice crossed Gatley's path on one other occasion in training camp. It was necessary and common for artillery soldiers to practice solving problems connected to shooting their cannons. One morning Rice's entire company was in the field trying to figure out a problem and compute such things as sighting, range, deflection, and corrections for such measurements as powder temperature, wind direction, and shell weight. To everyone but Rice the problem seemed quite valid. Following orders nonetheless, Rice and his NCO batterymate were attempting to point—they hadn't figured out how to aim—their "four inch howitzer," in actuality a sawed-off pine log, at the supposed enemy.

Gatley arrived on the field and moments later strode over to Rice's unit.

"Lieutenant," he said, "what command are you about to give?"

"Point blank, fire," Rice replied.

"Why?" Gatley asked.

"Sir, at point-blank range I can't miss the target."

Gatley appeared pleased enough with Rice's response. "But what about the problem?" he then asked Rice. "Do you know what you're doing?"

"Sir," Rice answered, "I haven't the slightest idea."[53]

Rice may have eventually learned how to point, and even aim, that pine log. But it is a sure bet that he never learned how to handle a single piece of actual artillery equipment. Artillery had moving parts. Rice had a healthy aversion to anything with moving parts. It was not that he was a closet Luddite, only that he was thoroughly inept with anything mechanical. Even in civilian life, it was common knowledge among the sportswriting fraternity that although he could hunt and peck on a typewriter well enough, he couldn't change a typewriter ribbon; some friends said he even had a fight on his hands when rolling a fresh sheet of paper into his typewriter. Nor did he ever learn to drive an automobile, ever; before the war he relied on other drivers or on trolleys, cabs, and trains to get around; and not too long after the war he employed Charles Goering as his driver; Goering remained the Rice family and friends' chauffeur for more than thirty years. Even quite late in life, when all the world had been buzzing right along (and Rice along with it) electrically for several generations, the publisher of his memoirs misjudged Rice's level of mechanical sophistication and gave him a tape recorder to make his job easier; he talked into the machine for forty-five minutes before someone discovered that it wasn't even switched on. Rice went back to his trusty typewriter to finish the job, bad ribbon, crooked paper, and all.[54]

The 115th was due to ship out from Patrick Henry, Virginia, for France aboard the *George Washington* in April 1918. Not long before the regiment departed, Rice was sitting around a campfire bull session with a number of soldiers, one of whom was a lieutenant just back from France. Naturally, all the recruits wanted to know what to expect. Someone mentioned "cooties," everyone having heard that lice in the French battlefields were pretty bad.

"They are bad," admitted the lieutenant, "but they have their uses."

"How so?" asked the men.

"Well," the battle veteran explained, "a soldier beset with cooties doesn't bother much about gas shells, shrapnel, or anything else. He's too busy scratching."[55]

Once in France, in Cherbourg, Rice's artillery unit continued their training, waiting for their call to join the fighting. Finally, in July, the 115th was sent to the front lines. Rice marched out with his company, but before the unit got very far, the lieutenant received new orders. It seems that the higher-ups agreed with enlistee Alexander Woollcott—who until the war had been a drama critic for the *New York Times*—that Rice would better serve his country as a journalist on the staff of *Stars and Stripes,* the AEF daily military newspaper that had just started up in February 1918. Rice headed for Paris and reluctantly joined Woollcott, Will Irwin, Franklin P. Adams, and Harold Ross (later of *New Yorker* fame) as a writer of sports and things-in-general for the paper. During the summer months, Rice toured the entire Allied Front with Woollcott. Rice's special responsibility was to see that plenty of poetry found its way into the highly popular, eight-page newspaper. Besides his own poetry—which he was sending to magazines back in the States on a regular basis—Rice even organized a poetry contest for military personnel in Europe. During these months his outside reading was composed of the thousands of war-produced verses contributed by soldiers in the AEF.[56]

Rice did do his *Stars and Stripes* duty. But, in all honesty, he didn't much like it. He couldn't shake his famed reputation as a journalist long enough to get permission to do much of anything else. Quietly, however, he was working on getting reassigned to the 115th even though the war was winding down. It took him a few months, but he finally wrangled a special-duty assignment that got him reattached to his old unit. They were near the Belgian border, somewhere in the forest at Avicourt, and were part of the Meuse-Argonne offensive. He wanted to go into action, not write about it.

On the day Rice left for the front, his journalist friend Will Irwin wrote Kate Rice to tell her of her husband's departure: "Dear Kit: I saw Granny off to war today. I never saw such a 'departure for the front.' He marched out of here with the biggest backpack I've seen on a mortal, let alone a mule. He was packing enough equipment to quartermaster half the boys at the front." And loaded he was: blankets, frying pan, burner, gas mask, extra shoes, rifle, socks, shelter half, ammunition.[57]

Rice's incompetence extended from mechanical devices to cartography. It took him three days and nights to locate his unit; it must have seemed to him at the time that the entire 115th somehow knew he was coming and was hiding from him—they all knew he couldn't even aim a cannon, after all, much less fire it.

Looking for his unit, he plodded toward Montfaucon, sleeping under hedges and in shattered farmhouses behind the lines. Along the way he was shedding some of his heavy backpack load. He met a Frenchman who said the war would never be over because the generals didn't want to go back to being waiters and taxi drivers. In the woods at Avicourt, the ditches were clogged with the dead and wounded; the Red Cross ambulances were having trouble getting to them through the deep mud. Late on the third night, Rice found the 115th howitzer brigade huddled in the drowned forest. When he arrived, he had nothing left from his equipment pack but his raincoat. He quickly joined in helping his unit move their two-thousand-pound artillery guns and equally heavy caissons up to the heights of Montfaucon.

Rice said of himself that as a soldier and an officer he was "no great shucks." The artillery, he said, had it easy, stationed as they were in back of the lines. They would throw the big shells from afar, and only occasionally get shelled in return; sometimes they would get machine-gunned from the air. And given the incredible amounts of rain, the mud in the forest often worked in their favor. A German shell hitting five yards away, for instance, would often just stick in the mud, splattering the soldiers instead of shattering them. Even though Rice downplayed his own role in the war, his unit was glad to see him back. One fellow who served in the 115th with Rice recalled that both in training camp and in France, "the flaming spirit of the company was Grantland Rice." The army buddy went on to say that Rice marched off to the war "with a zeal and an ardor that quickened the heartbeats of his comrades." The war, to Rice, was a holy cause, according to his friend.

After Montfaucon, in late October, Lieutenant Rice was transferred again, this time to the First Army Corps headquarters, G-2, under General Gatley. Rice became the press officer. Again, the writer had been chosen over the soldier. In one story, he reported on the bitterness of fifty-five elderly members of the Landwehr who were brought in as prisoners. They told Rice that they had been deceived by the Allied soldiers. After many days of fraternizing between trenches with the Americans, they had been promised, they said, a great feast and a pack of cigarettes apiece if they would surrender. They finally agreed. The day arrived, but they were given no feast and no smokes. Rice released the story—always sensitive to the fair play in anything, sport or not. General Gatley told Rice he should never have written that story because it made the Americans out to be double-crossers. Nonetheless, and privately, Gatley agreed with Rice that it made a great story.[58]

Three days before the Armistice, First Lieutenant Rice was transferred again, this time to General Pershing's staff in the Third Army. Colonel Willey Howell, Rice's immediate supervisor in the First Army, officially and personally thanked Rice for his service, and expressed regret that he had been ordered to other duties: "Such faithful and intelligent performance of duty, everywhere that it has occurred, has helped the United States to have a greater share in the winning of the war and has increased the prestige of our army and our country throughout the world."[59]

At the Third, on one darksome, raining night, Rice volunteered to guide General Pershing himself, by auto (naturally, Rice wasn't driving), to some sequestered place a good ways from headquarters. Probably surprising even himself, the guide got Pershing to where he was going. After Pershing did whatever generals do, and without even a thank you to Rice, he left in the auto, leaving Rice to find his way in the rain back to headquarters by foot. Rice never forgot Pershing's inconsiderateness and later in life confronted the general with this instance as an example of how inconsiderate most generals usually were. Pershing said he didn't remember the incident.[60]

On the whole, it wasn't Rice's soldiering but his typewriter that kept his name in front of the public during the war. As the Third Army moved on into Germany through a gray-white fog that seemed to go forward with its advance, Rice wrote of the ghosts of the Argonne. Here is the first stanza of a six-stanza poem, "To the Rhine":

> You thought it a fog through the marching hosts,
> A gray mist onward creeping;
> But the fog you saw was a line of ghosts
> From the mates that you left sleeping;
> From the mates you left in the drifts of France
> With only a dream to sever,
> Who rose again for the last advance
> To follow The Flag forever.[61]

Elsewhere, and again, the ghosts of the Argonne haunted him:

You can hear them at night when the moon is hidden;
    They sound like the rustle of winter leaves,
Or lone lost winds that arise, unbidden,
    Or rain that drips from the forest eaves,
As they glide again from their silent crosses
    To meet and talk of their final flight,
Where over the group some stark tree tosses
    Its eerie shadow across the night.

They talk of war and its crimson glory,
    And laugh at the trick which Fate has played;
And over and over they tell the story
    Of their final charge through the Argonne glade;
But gathering in by hill and hollow
    With their ghostly tramp on the rain-soaked loam,
There is one set rule which the clan must follow:
    They never speak of returning home.[62]

Fan mail followed Rice. A young admirer wrote from Pueblo, Colorado, about a week after the Armistice:

Dear Mr. Rice,

My ma and me has red yore poetry a lot and we hev decided that we lik it bettern H. Longfeller's. My ma says its sorta apeelin. And when she says that, it shore is goin some, fer my ma aint long on words. But being as I seed yore poem in a paper with yore address attacht, I thot as how you might like to know we likt it, so I tole ma Id rite an she sed I mite. Well it shore is nice that the wars over fer now you uns kin com home. I gess they aint none of you what ait sorter glad.

Theys a lot of folks over here what is waitin worse fer ther boys to come home then they was to hear the war had quit. I know my ma is fer weve got a boy in the A.E.F. what were waitin fer. Gosh I'll shore be tickled green when they I mean you all get back.

Well, any how, I hope you'll over look a pore, green girl who aint never had enough schoolin fer to rite strait aritin to sich as you, an you a lutendahnt but I shore do like to read yore poetry.

So now if you haint got nuthin else to do, you ken rite me sum. My ma says that may be to strong fer you but I trust not.

Hopin you'll kinder overlook the mistakes I may hev maid, I remane,

        Very Respectively,
        Miss E. M. Heath[63]

After the Armistice, Rice was again reassigned, this time to the Occupation Forces in Coblentz under the command of General Drum. "Among other arrivals here was an infuriate poet, to wit, Lieut. Grantland Rice," wrote Damon Runyon. Rice was infuriate because his during-the-war hapless itinerancy seemed to be following him after the war as well. After traveling on his own a long way to reach his billet, and going without lunch and dinner, Rice arrived at the address given him by the billeting officer. It was a vacant lot.[64]

It was now mid-December. Of his reassignment to Coblentz, Rice wrote his wife, "My dearest Kit: I'll be glad to reach the end of the trail and get established at one place. I think I can also get a better line on what my future fate will be—as to how long I will be kept over. We are all tugging at the bit to get away, but as I wrote before my main desire and only one is to be with you—New York or Paris—it doesn't matter so long as you are there." Kate had managed well enough while "Grannie" (as he often called himself in his letters to Kate) was gone, in spite of her heartfelt loneliness for her husband; she had plenty to do, with Floncy to take care of. Kate, in turn, was looked after by many of the Rices' New York friends. In addition, Kate's own large family and Grantland's kin provided moral support for the sportswriter's wife during his absence. Besides Kate and Floncy, Rice also missed good food. He wrote to Kit: "We are getting pretty well fed up on our diet here but it is enough to live on. It consists mostly of beef and potatoes with rarely a change. The comissary [*sic*] has no flour, butter, bacon and only brown sugar that seems to be partly sand." What Grantland Rice wanted were his favorite foods: corn sauté, lemon meringue pie, and watermelon; he was also looking forward to restarting his habit of putting maple syrup over his sliced oranges and using ketchup as a topping for his ice cream.[65]

The First Lieutenant's attachment with the Occupation Forces was short-lived, as all his duty seemed to be. He was diagnosed as having chronic sinus trouble and shortly after Christmas was ordered to proceed to St. Nazaire to wait with tens of thousands of other soldiers for a ship home.

On his way to the west coast of France, he passed through Bar Le Duc, where Damon Runyon was getting stories from the soldiers on their way back to the States. He saw Rice, and the playful Runyon led off his story about him this way: "A lousy poet emerged from the Argonne this afternoon." Gerald Morgan, one of the military's head censors, balked at Runyon's lead, feeling that the sentence was a misstatement of fact.

"That story was about a Mr. Grantland Rice," Runyon said. "Mr. Rice emerged from the Argonne this afternoon."

"True. Quite true," said Morgan, "there is no question as to his emerging. No question at all. He has already borrowed a pair of my best socks."

"Mr. Rice is a poet," Runyon continued. "If you don't believe it, I have a copy of his last volume of poems, and will read from same to you at random."

"No, no," Morgan said hastily. "That is not necessary. We concede that Mr. Rice is a poet."

"Well, then," said Runyon, "what is the dispute?"

"It's that word that precedes 'poet' in your story. If you intend it in the editorial sense, which is to say, as your reaction to Mr. Rice as a poet it may be all right. But if you intend it as a statement of fact, us boys in the front office consider it open to question, without authentication."

"Ah, yes," said Runyon. "I see what you mean. Kindly come with me."

Runyon took Morgan to the nearby mess hall and pointed out Rice in the act of ingesting about three times his just and equitable share of rations. Rice was hunched over the table eating with one hand and scratching himself all over the place with the other.

"I understand," said Morgan. "You are quite right. Congratulations on your reportorial accuracy. Your story shall go just as she lays."[66]

In the end, the story went out as Runyon wrote it. But by the time the story appeared in the American newspapers, a meticulous copy editor had fixed it up to read: "A poet, lousy, emerged from the Argonne this afternoon."

However he emerged, Rice was soon to be on his way home from the Argonne. As seemed to be his fate, even when he persistently tried to get into the action himself, his real talent seemed to be that of a close watcher and a hardworking writer. Even in his own memoirs, what he remembered most about World War I was what he saw, not what he did: "I saw and experienced enough of the filth, suffering and horror of war to realize it never can account for anything that a slice of good Christian faith can't outstrip every time. I saw youngsters hurtling through the skies over France in small fighter planes, and I watched more than a few of them come down in flames. I saw kids and old men slugging through the mud to the front, and the heart inside me twisted as I watched those lines of walking wounded threading their tortured way back again, leaving so many of their buddies dead where they had fallen."[67]

In the end, Rice said, he found war to be a "quick distillation of life's tribulations, all wrapped up in a red, raw bundle. In war, however, the good in a fellow surfaces—or sinks—much quicker than in civilian life." In many ways, he thought, the same lessons of war applied to the world of sport. In this, they were both training grounds for trouble in ordinary life; one night when he was thinking of such things, he wrote the following lines:

Wars may be on again, wars may be over,
So far as the guns are concerned,
But life is a fight—not a dream in the clover,
No matter what road you have turned.
Fate is a party who ducks from the fighter
That faces him squarely and grins,
But, oh, what a wallop he takes at the blighter
Who trembles when trouble begins!
For its Trouble that toughens that fiber all through,
The best little trainer the world ever knew.

Perhaps we are through with the lung-burning gasses,
On which I am betting no cent;
But even if shrapnel or bursting bomb passes,
There is still the bill for the rent;
There's poverty, bitterness, worry or sorrow
To lead a left hook for the glim,
And it may come today, or it may come tomorrow,
So you might as well keep in trim.
And it's Trouble that strengthens the jaw,
The best little trainer the world ever saw.[68]

Rice didn't know it at the time, but soon he himself would have a round with Trouble and a chance to live the truth of what he'd written.

10

Booming the Game

At the time of the signing of the Armistice, the American government had announced that 250,000 soldiers would be sent home each month; but in the next three months fewer than 300,000 were shipped out. Rice waited for transport home along with thousands of others. While at the embarkation camp, he ran into one of his journalism cronies, Jack Wheeler. Before the war broke out, Wheeler had been a baseball writer for the *New York Herald*. He had been Christy Mathewson's ghostwriter since 1911, both for the *Herald*—who syndicated the Mathewson pieces to other newspapers—and for the McClure Newspaper Syndicate. Wheeler, possibly the first ghost sportswriter in the business, quit the *Herald* in 1913 over a salary dispute and started his own long-successful syndicate, the Wheeler Syndicate.[1]

Wheeler, also a first lieutenant, was an adjutant to General Hearn in the field artillery. He was responsible mainly for requisitioning French horses for the artillery brigade. Along with Wheeler in the embarkation camp was Colonel Frank Knox, who was in command of the horse section of the ammunition supply train. Knox, also a newspaper man, was the owner-editor of the *Manchester* (New Hampshire) *Union Leader*. The three of them—Rice, Wheeler, and Knox—finally boarded the U.S.S. *Rijndam* on January 27, 1919, for the two-week trip home. Knox, the senior officer, was put in charge of the many Casual Companies on board. Rice and Wheeler were Knox's adjutants. Everyone at the camp just wanted to get back home. Rice spoke for them all:

To get back home again—and there to see
Old friends and faces of long vanished days,
To hear some friendly voice call out to me
From street or corner of remembered ways,
Where rain or shine or wind-blown winter snow
The lights of home hold us their golden shield,
With soft, warm arms from out the long ago
In waiting welcome from the silent field.[2]

Not long after the "boat"—this is what Rice called the ship, an indication of the limits of his sea-going knowledge—sailed, Knox, who ironically would become secretary of the navy under Franklin Roosevelt, got terribly seasick. Miraculously, Rice and Wheeler didn't, so they were put in charge of the troops on the voyage home. Only the aviators gave the two journalists trouble, mostly for romancing the nurses assigned to the ship. Rice and Wheeler issued—and enforced—an order for all flyboys to be in quarters (their own) by nine o'clock. That worked, more or less, but smuggled wine (French cognac) was quickly substituted for the women, that and much song. Two out of three would have to do for most of the trip home.

But three days out of St. Nazaire, a flu epidemic broke out on board. It was deadly. Rice recalled, "It was a heart-rending sight, watching those men and boys dying like flies—knowing they were sinking but struggling that much harder to get home." The possibility of surviving the war only to succumb to microbes on the way home quickly subdued the entire ship. Wheeler and Rice spent much of the two-week voyage making out final papers on the dead and burying some of the victims at sea.[3]

The killer flu epidemic was trouble, for sure. But Rice faced personal trouble when the *Rijndam* landed at Newport News, Virginia, on a drizzly February 9, 1919. Rice immediately and eagerly headed for New York City to reunite with Kit and Floncy. With Wheeler and his bride, Elizabeth, the Rices were to spend a few weeks in Lake Placid to recover from the misery the war had brought them all. But Kate had some bad news. She quickly informed her husband that the lawyer friend to whom Rice had entrusted seventy-five thousand dollars in 1917 had tried to reinvest the money and had lost it all. Rice's life savings were gone. Just before Rice disembarked from the *Rijndam*, the attorney took his own life by swallowing poison.

There are different ways to react to such a situation—anger and resentment being the most understandable. Less common, perhaps, would have been simple compassion for the unnecessary suicide of his business associate. But Rice's response to this trouble was uncommon. Thirty years after the tragedy Rice wrote: "I blame myself for that poor fellow's death; I shouldn't have put that much temptation in his way." Of all things, Rice felt guilty, and almost personally responsible for the suicide. So much so that as soon as Rice got back on his feet financially, he started up a monthly contribution to the lawyer's widow. Only some of Rice's closest friends knew about his monthly practice; he continued financial payments to her throughout his life. So true that life was a fight, not a dream in the clover. The money was gone. Rice would start over.[4]

Historian Frederick Lewis Allen, in attempting to capture the opening of the postwar decade in America, chose to introduce his readers to a day in the lives of a fictive, moderately well-to-do couple, Mr. and Mrs. Smith, living in any typical city—it really didn't matter where—Boston or Cleveland or Seattle or Baltimore. By May of 1919 the Smiths were slowly adjusting to peacetime. The newspapers were full of the Peace Conference at Paris, the arrival of more troop transports from overseas, labor union problems, the prospects of the passage of the Suffrage Amendment, and the debates over the coming of Prohibition.

The end of the war brought with it higher prices for everything: rent, food, clothing. And higher taxes. Insofar as food was concerned, for example, the Smiths' food bill just about doubled between 1914 and 1919; Mr. Smith's income didn't keep pace. People were said to have remarked "that even the man without a dollar is fifty cents better off than he once was." Even so, things seemed to be looking up: the servicemen were reabsorbed into the job market more quickly than anyone expected, and even though stock prices had fallen immediately after the war as government contracts were canceled, there were still good prospects for international trade and for such industries as American shipping.[5]

Major changes were taking place in the newspaper world too. Increases in paper, postal, and labor costs during the war had driven the price of the dailies up. The penny papers were soon two and more cents; Sunday papers became five, then seven, then ten cents. Competition between the papers stiffened, driving many in the business out altogether: between 1914 and 1919 the total number of weeklies and dailies nationwide dropped from more than nineteen thousand to around seventeen thousand.[6]

The biggest of the newspaper fish began swallowing up the smallest, as newspaper consolidations became the norm: in Chicago the *Inter Ocean* merged with the *Record-Herald* under the name *Herald* in 1914, and then the *Herald* with the *Examiner;* in New Orleans the *Times-Democrat* consolidated with the *Picayune;* in Cleveland the *Leader* was combined with the *Plain*

Dealer in 1917; and in New York the *Press* and the *Sun* were merged. This last consolidation (in 1916) was engineered by the so-called newspaper "executioner" Frank Munsey. Soon other famous chains grew: Booth Newspapers, Brush-Moore, Scripps-Howard, Hearst, the Lee Syndicate, and so on. In the 1920s the number of newspaper chains grew to sixty and included more than three hundred dailies.[7]

Besides the consolidations and chains, another long run of tabloid sensationalism began early in the 1920s. Smaller page sizes, lots of pictures, and tinier brain-appeal would prove a successful combination in these postwar years. Three newspapers in New York City alone—the *Daily News, Mirror,* and *Graphic*—would soon grab one and a half million readers.[8]

Entertainment and escape were their collective lowest common denominator: the new-style journalism emphasized sex, scandal, crime, glamour, greed, conflict, rags-to-riches stories, celebrities, and stars. Sport would be among the racier tabloid subjects, especially since all of these topics carried over to the playing fields in the roaring and memorable 1920s.

Rice's job was waiting for him back at the *Tribune.* After eighteen years in the business, he was starting from scratch; but only financially, for his professional reputation, his talent, and his work ethic were still intact. His financial comeback was inevitable.

In the few weeks before the delayed opening of the 1919 baseball spring training season, Grantland Rice and all the other sportswriters immediately began to speculate on the direction of sport in the postwar decade. They guessed that sport would remain popular, but few if any foresaw what was ahead, the extent to which American sport was to become a mass consumer product.

At his desk in early March of 1919, Rice indulged in some general speculation about the upcoming decade. He asked in print what his readers were asking him: "What will be the attitude of the returned soldier to sport?" Practically the same, he responded, as their attitude toward home cooking and a late-morning sleep-in. "The soldier, freed from the iron-bound regime of 5:30 reveilles, inspections, hikes, drills and the rest of it, has a yearning to play or watch others play." Rice went on: "He has known entangling alliances of the Great Outdoors too long now to be held in. The thrill of competitive sport will be his main outlet for the future."[9]

To those who predicted that participation would rise, but spectating would drop—too passive for the social and physical energy whipped up by the war—Rice repeated A. A. Milne's lines:

> When the war is over and the Kaiser's out of print
> I'm going to buy some tortoises and watch the beggars sprint.[10]

Rice believed that in sport, the spectator will always be there; so long, that is, as there is a show that is worth an afternoon off. Even at the front, Rice recalled, there were hundreds of army ball clubs scattered over France. For every game played by eighteen or twenty men, there were always from two hundred to a thousand soldiers there to root for one side or another. One doesn't have to be enmeshed in a sport as a player to get a thrill: "It may be that one gets his thrill from a knockout, another from a two-base hit, another from a mashie planted against the pin in a hard match, and still another from a nip-and-tuck lawn tennis affair. But there always has been and always will be a vast margin in favor of those who would rather watch experts play than to play themselves indifferently."[11]

The entire world wanted to play again, Rice said, "to emerge as quickly as possible from the red mists and the black shadows and frolic in the sunlight." But however accurate he was about the existence of this pent-up play element, Rice was no better than any other writers at forecasting the extent of the coming boom in American sport. Nor was he particularly aware at the time that he would become a major player, even a superstar, in booming the 1920s games; even when he soon became such a popular shine, he was not particularly aware that he had become so highly regarded. Rice simply went back to the work that he loved,

> Fame and wealth and greed and gain, leave them to the old;
> I would rather turn again and find the road to spring
> Where young Pan is piping in a glen of green and gold
> And young April's waiting with another song to sing.[12]

In late March, Rice, along with legions of baseball writers, trooped off to Florida and South Carolina for spring training. The baseball owners decided to delay spring training a few weeks while they waited for more players to be released by the War Department. They also agreed to shorten the season to 140 games.[13]

The sportswriters' collective intentions that spring were to study up on the 1919 pennant prospects, get some sunlight frolic of their own, and help revive the national pastime. Interest in baseball had been on the wane since 1917 and since then, in Rice's words, "no one gave a bally rap who finished first or who finished last." Much of the color was gone; Wagner, Lajoie, Evers, Waddell, and Mathewson—all characters of one kind or another—were ending their careers. Except for Ty Cobb, who was now thirty-three, there weren't too many big names for the fans to follow immediately after the war; of these, the more colorful ones were Rube Marquard, Hank Gowdy, maybe Ping Bodie, and of course the hero-to-come, Babe Ruth, who in March of 1919 was still known primarily as a pitcher who could hit too, and of whom Rice that spring understated, when speaking of colorful players, "Still another is Babe Ruth, who has an unusual personality outside of his ability to pitch and bat."[14]

What did color Rice's return to covering sports was his unmasked disappointment that so many professional athletes—baseball players in particular—had sidestepped a duty he thought especially appropriate for the physically gifted: military service at the front. "The ball players described as the 'paint and putty patriots,'" he wrote shortly after his return from France, "who rushed to the shipyards in order to duck from under the draft, will need the best years they have ever known to escape the stinging repartee of the bleachers. Unless the aforesaid P and P patriots have abnormally thick hide. Which they very likely have."[15]

Men could avoid the draft by claiming hardship because they were supporting a family, or by volunteering for the Home Guard (the reserve units that took the place of the federalized National Guard), or they could volunteer to work in the shipyards, steel mills, and other war-related industries. Babe Ruth, for instance, enlisted in the Massachusetts Home Guard, thereby doing double duty, one to the country and the other to the Boston Red Sox. In the shipyards and mills, most of the ballplayers could continue their ball playing on industrial league teams. For instance, players were actively recruited for their playing talent at Bethlehem Steel and for their so-called "Schwab League" (after Charles M. Schwab, the company owner).[16]

Not all, but most of Rice's knocking was pointed but vague, generic stuff that did not usually name names: "It may or may not interest those frenzied baseball patriots who ducked both service and the draft by jumping to some ship league that the forthcoming summer may not be entirely pleasant for them." As was typical of him, when speaking of any specific athlete he would rather boost the virtuous than give space to those he thought had less moral or social substance.[17]

For example, Hank Gowdy was the first major-league ballplayer to enlist; he played forty-nine games during the 1917 season before leaving for military duty. In time he became a sergeant in the 166th Infantry, Rainbow Division. Rice made it a point to refer to Gowdy's selflessness and patriotism. The

Boston Braves catcher, whom Rice called Lank Hank, had crossed Rice's path a couple of times during the war. In early March Rice related the conversations he had had with Gowdy about baseball and other topics when the two were in France. He recalled how eager Hank was to return to the fields of play, of April, opening day, the old crowd, and all the noisy welcome that the players take as their own, but which is really a tribute to the game itself. "I've missed two years," Hank remarked, "and I'm no longer a kid. I wonder if I can get going again—Oh, boy—to lay up against the old pill just once more for two bases into the crowd . . ."[18]

During spring training, Rice continued to boost Gowdy with stories of his service overseas. Rice wrote that once in July 1918, Gowdy's regiment went up against the Germans this side of Oureq. Rumor had it that Gowdy had lost a leg in the battle, but a few hours after the worst was over Rice saw Gowdy slogging along the road leading into the woods near Fere-en-Tardenois. Seeing Rice, who told him of the rumor, the always cheerful Gowdy said, "That rumor is practically unfounded. I think I've walked both my feet off, but my legs are still hanging on."[19]

Rice told him that he would get a great welcome back home after the war was over. "Yes," said Gowdy, "a great welcome—until I whiff some day with the winning run left stranded on third. I know the old game and the old crowd too well to kid myself about that part of it."[20]

Things were pretty slow in training camp that year in Jacksonville, where Rice first set up for his March/April spring baseball coverage. The Yankees and the Dodgers were there. From Jacksonville, in April, he would hook up with the Giants and the Red Sox in Gainesville. He stayed mainly with these clubs on their northern route up to Columbia and Spartanburg, South Carolina, as the two teams played their exhibition games for a number of Southern cities.

In Jacksonville there was an ostrich farm right across from the ballpark. Rice and W. O. McGeehan, a fellow writer from the *Tribune,* spent the good part of three hours the first day of spring training waiting around to see one of the ostriches, just one, bury his head in the Florida sand. No ostrich did so, or even looked like it might. Rice grew weary and wandered off to cover the baseball players' conditioning drills; McGeehan, on the other hand, by then in a contemplative mood, began wondering about ostrich things. Eventually he dreamed up a promotional idea that he took to the Jacksonville Chamber of Commerce.

It seems that the Jacksonville locals had advertised that one of their ostriches, Percy by name, was alleged to be "the world's greatest eater." Colonel T. L. Huston, one of the New York Yankee partners, when told of the ostrich's appetite, scoffed; nothing, he said, could compare to the food bills he was presently picking up for his slugger, Ping Bodie. When McGeehan goaded the Chamber of Commerce with the counterclaim, the match was on. At precisely two minutes after nine o'clock on the evening of April 5, 1919, the two contestants, with their seconds, faced off, Ping glaring at Percy and Percy sharpening his beak on the canvas while both hovered over their first platters of the mutually agreed-upon food: spaghetti. Both eaters had their fans; the locals were cheering for Percy, while the Yankees and the sportswriters put their money on Ping.

It was agreed that both eaters would break clean from their empty platters. This worked well enough, as platter after platter was set before each contestant. By the third platter, Ping and Percy were even, string for string, with Percy getting the edge after he also ate his second's watch and chain. But by the seventh round, even strong men began to edge back from the ring, fearing that Percy might explode. Ping, meanwhile, continued to inhale his spaghetti, flashing his golden smile between mouthfuls and even refusing a napkin from his solicitous second. Percy was visibly tiring by platter number nine, and by the tenth his beak was sagging. Ping grinned, sensing the championship was almost within his mouth, and ate on. When the bell rang for the eleventh round, Percy hesitantly waddled out of his corner and toed his platter; his eyes were bloodshot, his sides were heaving. Ping, without pause, ate mouthful after mouthful after mouthful. Witnesses said that Percy, after watching Ping's incredible performance, realized that he was a beaten bird. Down in the mouth, Percy slowly dropped to his knees and tried to bury his head in his plate of spaghetti. Ping ferociously finished his platter while the timekeeper started to count Percy out. Ping won the championship, eleven platters to ten.[21]

Now this spaghetti eating contest would be entirely forgettable were it not for the fact that, in a sport-imitating-circus way, there was a resemblance of sorts, in spirit at least, between this Percy and Ping thing and a real sports championship a short three months later. In Toledo. Boxing. On the Fourth of July. A match between two humans, Jess Willard and Jack Dempsey, each about as different from one another as Percy was from Ping, and the match about as contrived.

Rice spent the first couple of months of spring and early summer covering baseball, writing his Sportlight column, and, with encouragement from his *Tribune* editors, expanding his ruminations on the game of golf. Spring training had given him plenty of time to work on his own golf game, rusty after his tour in France. It was his custom to play a round of golf almost daily during spring training. With everybody. Athletes, club managers and owners, colleagues, or with the famous from wider circles. It might have been Kid Gleason, the Chicago White Sox manager, one day, or Gowdy or Babe Ruth the next, or next a thirty-six-hole four-ball tournament with writer friends such as George Ade, Clarence Budington Kelland, and Sewell Ford. Ade would often winter in Florida to get out of the snow and cold in Brook, Indiana. Ade and Rice would hook up with fiction writers Kelland and Ford, both of whom were situated on the west coast of Florida, near Clearwater. The writers would grind out two thousand or six thousand words a day, then hack around together at golf courses in Belleair, or Tarpon Springs, or St. Petersburg.

It was Ade and Ford who invented "The Willing Ears Company, Inc." The idea of the company was to relieve the annoyed friends of golfers who were subjected to the monotony of listening to a full account of each and every stroke played, the effect of the wind, the condition of the course, and the rotten luck of the bad shots, the deft skill of the good ones. So when a golfer rushed up to a friend about to be bored to death with a rehashing of the eighteen or thirty-six holes, all the friend had to do was call Willing Ears. The company would dispatch an eager and attentive listener, a fully trained willing ear who would never interrupt, always pay attention, and absorb the entire recital of missed putts and bad lies. This service, they figured, would be a turn-away business at a charge of two dollars per hour.[22]

Besides the opportunity to fine-tune his own nearly scratch game and widen his circle of friends, these spring training sojourns contributed directly to Rice's continued skill as a golf writer. Thus it was in the early summer of 1919 that he thought it was about time to regularly write up the game. After trying out a few titles, such as "Gossip of the Golfers," or "Around the Links," Rice settled on "Tales of a Wayside Tee" for his golfing dope column. Around his other writing, Rice continued "Tales" in the *Tribune* throughout the 1920s.

Even in these early versions, Rice wrote with obvious authority whether he was analyzing previous matches, covering and encouraging women's club tournaments, dissecting the expert golfers' swings, giving practice and playing tips, holding forth on golf psychology lectures, forecasting upcoming national and international matches, or just sympathizing in verse with his fellow golfers about the difficulty of mastering the game:

They've sought me and they've brought me
And they've taught me Perfect Form;
The Proper Stance—the Proper Grip—
The Proper Arc of Arm;
They've sought me and they've taught me
From springtime unto fall;
The only bet they overlooked
Was How to Hit the Ball.

They've taught me twenty dozen things
In forty dozen ways;
The Mashie Flip—the Niblick Grip—
And how H. Vardon plays!
They've slipped me every angle in
The golfolistic frame;
The only kink they overlooked
Was How to Play the Game.

Or,

The bloke who lifts his well known dome
Will let it hang when he starts home.

And he who finds missed putts are rife
Is no companion for a wife.

Or, the occasional "Limerick of the Links," in extreme:

There was a dub golfer named Babbitt,
Who sliced with each club as he'd grab it;
    Until he, half wild,
    Killed his wife and his child
By slicing their throats from sheer habit.[23]

Rice's reputation as a golf expert was spreading quickly. *American Golfer* soon invited Rice to become its editor, along with managing editor Innis Brown, who was with the *New York Sun*. Rice had contributed from time to time to the magazine before the war, but with his editorship he was now able to further diversify his talents and seed his income. *American Golfer* had been started up by Walter J. Travis in 1908, the "Grand Old Man" of golf. Travis, its editor for ten years, created the publication more to promote the game of golf than as a commercial venture. In its earliest form it was nothing but a pamphlet. Travis said that he never asked anybody to subscribe to it or advertise in it. Almost everything in it—articles and advertising alike—came in over the transom.

Under the Rice and Brown editorship, *American Golfer* would become *the* golf magazine in the 1920s for those pleasantly addicted to the game. Resembling in style the *New Yorker* or *American Mercury*, *American Golfer* was tasteful, crisp, well illustrated, and boasted strong writing. Besides Rice and Brown, there were regular contributions on golf and other matters from John Tunis (mostly on tennis), Ring Lardner, O. B. Keeler, George Ade, Rex Beach, John Kieran, Bud Kelland, and the British golfer and golf-writing expert Bernard Darwin. In time *American Golfer* would grow in circulation to seventy thousand by the late 1920s before it lost steam during the Depression. It lasted until January 1936.

So between "Tales" and his continued association with *American Golfer*, there was good reason for Rice to be covering the twenty-fourth Open golf championship at Brae Burn in West Newton, Massachusetts, in June 1919. After a three-year hiatus, the Open was on again. In the 1919 tournament, Mike Brady and Walter Hagen were tied at the end of the regulation seventy-two holes. Hagen had won the tournament in 1914; Brady had led the 1915 tournament at Baltusrol after fifty-four holes, but faded as Jerry Travers won. Chick Evans, who had finished second behind Hagen in 1914, won the tournament in 1916—the last time it had been held.

By then Rice had certainly learned to spell Hagen's name correctly. He praised this great golfer, calling his play bold and aggressive after Hagen withstood a strong finish by Brady and won the playoff. Yet, it was the mystery of game itself that Rice celebrated more than the particular winner. As it turned out, on the 18th hole of the playoff, with Brady down by one—he was down by four at the 10th hole—Hagen badly topped his tee shot. The ball headed directly toward a four-foot-deep and six-foot-wide brook a hundred yards away. Just as it looked like it was all over for Hagen, the ball, bounding along, miraculously hopped the brook and rolled out into the fairway. Hagen made par, beating Brady by a stroke. Rice's lead on this day: "When two men meet on even mould in this baffling game of golf the gods elect the victor in advance. For there are few who can overwhelm fate. . . . To-day the gods of chance picked Walter Hagen for the new open champion of America." Victory in sport, true sport, Rice thought, sometimes becomes a matter for the gods to decide. Hagen just happened to be declared the victor, but more importantly, the contest itself was a winning one.[24]

Fresh from the elevating competition at Brae Burn, Rice must have sensed the plunge that he was about to take as he boarded the Pullman the last week in June on his way to the Willard-Dempsey fight. Not sport, he thought, but the sport business. Even less, a circus. Ping and Percy revisited.

The philosophical side of Rice surfaced in his column, written along the rails on his way to Toledo, Ohio. He tried in verse to speak to the thousands, like him, rushing to the heartland to witness the battle. All of us, he thought, needed some perspective on this thing called sport:

> What's the use of worrying
>   Up and down the way?
> What's the use of hurrying
>   Through an endless day?
> Never mind the growing score,
>   Never mind the pace;
> Life to me means something more than a pop-eyed race.
>
> There's something more to life
>   Than a winning game;
> Something more than endless strife
>   For a splash of fame;
> Competition, envy, greed
>   Where the welkin rings,
> I had rather take my heed
>   Of the simpler things.
>
> Where one doesn't have to bow
>   To the lust for fame
> That may vanish anyhow
>   By to-morrow's game;
> Out beyond the winning score,
>   Heedless of the pace;
> Out where life is something more
>   Than a pop-eyed race.[25]

Tex Rickard, the Phineas T. Barnum of the twentieth century, as some called him, had signed the fighting principals, Willard and Dempsey, many months earlier. Rickard's reputation for promotion and other lively diversions had grown since his 1910 staging of the Johnson-Jeffries fight. In the meantime he had run a gambling house in Ely, Nevada, ranched in Paraguay, and promoted the Willard-Moran fight in 1916. Nothing was small-scale for Rickard. Take the ranching episode. He invested four hundred thousand dollars in part of the Gran Chaco in Paraguay; in return he took more than five million acres of land, and stocked fifty thousand head of cattle on 325,000 acres of it; still he was nervous about overcrowding, since in his youth in Texas it was customary to give ten acres of grazing land per head.[26]

While in South America, Rickard bought and toured a small circus, dropped ten thousand dollars on a custom-made British automobile that was more or less useless in the jungles, and otherwise thrashed about noisily in the coastal cities of Brazil and Argentina staging boxing, wrestling, and cattle-roping contests. He even befriended Teddy Roosevelt while the Bull Moose was on an explore in the South American jungles.[27]

But in time Rickard returned to the States. When he heard that Jess Willard had won the title from Jack Johnson in Havana, Cuba, he saw another opportunity. He quickly managed to outbid the other local promoters for the Willard-Moran fight, and staged it in March of 1916 in Madison Square Garden. It turned out to be a ten-round "no-decision" fight; since Moran failed to knock out Willard, the champion held onto his title. Owing in part to a William Randolph Hearst morality crusade in the *Journal*, where professional boxing was denounced as a social evil, boxing was declared illegal in New York the following year; the New York legislature didn't legalize boxing again until 1920.[28]

In 1919, when Rickard signed Willard and Dempsey, boxing was still illegal in most states. Even though the war had boosted the status of boxing—owing to the extent to which the military trained its enlistees in the manly art of pugilism—there was still a strong moral and political aversion to the sport. Nonetheless, and over the objections of ministers and many politicians, Tex Rickard managed to set the Willard-Dempsey fight for July 4, 1919, in Toledo, Ohio, one of the few states where boxing was legal. The town would grow from its normal 225,000 to about 400,000 for the fight.

Rice gamely threw himself into the prefight hype, adding his two cents to the endless speculating customary before any contest of such national popularity. He dutifully visited the two training camps, pronounced both the fighters fit, and wondered out loud about the money-grubbing when both camps were charging daily admission of twenty-five cents to see the boxers exercise and spar.

Of seemingly more interest to Rice than the boxers themselves was the nature of the crowds at the hot, humid, and mosquitoed camps: "Packed in steamy layers after the manner of the succulent sardine, they gaze stolidly at the two leading figures, displaying as much animation as one might show in observing a telegraph post in action." Even though in Rice's opinion there was absolutely nothing going on in either camp, day after day the curious crowded in for a look: "There are sedate old gentlemen with chilly side whiskers, young girls with round and wondering eyes, ponderous looking matrons in mauve or pale heliotrope, prime looking old maids, any number of kids around ten or twelve years old; bums, yeggmen, old sports—those who know nothing and those who know all of the seamy side of life—a cross section cut out of humanity and lured daily to the spot through the immense amount of publicity imparted to the carnival."[29]

What did catch Rice's attention insofar as the boxers themselves were concerned was their false billing as "The World's Greatest Fighting Men." While most of the fight fans, and most of the country as well, tried to put the war years behind them, Rice just couldn't leave one aspect of it alone: Neither Willard nor Dempsey fought in the war. Thus they could hardly be called "fighting men," argued Rice.

Willard, at age thirty-six in 1917, married and with five children, sat out the war on his Kansas farm, refusing even to box for war fund drives. After he became the world heavyweight champion in 1915 by beating Jack Johnson, he all but refused to fight. Before he met Johnson, he had been boxing for almost three years. From 1911 through 1914, he had fought twenty-eight times. But after beating Johnson, he had fought only once, in the Rickard-staged Moran fight. Willard was unpopular with everyone, press and public alike.[30]

Dempsey, on the other hand, had been busy. He had fought nine times since the Armistice; two of the fights were exhibitions, and the other seven he won by knockouts, all within two rounds. Clearly, by 1919 Dempsey's career was on the rise. During the war, Dempsey applied for and received an exemption from the draft, with the assistance of his manager, Jack "Doc" Kearns, on grounds of family hardship; that is, Dempsey's family depended upon him for their survival. So Dempsey beat the draft, but to his credit he did serve the war effort in a number of ways, including agreeing to box for charity in a number of war-related fund drives staged by the Salvation Army or the Knights of Columbus for donation to the Army and Navy War Activities Fund and the Red Cross. He also aided in recruiting several hundred young men for shipyard work.[31]

Rice was unimpressed. He simply stated that as a matter of fact, neither Willard nor the young Dempsey (twenty-four at the time of the 1919 bout) were among the some fifty million soldiers who actually fought in the war. As a matter of fact, neither of them cared to fight at all. As a matter of fact, there was no touch of glamour or heroism in either one of them. As a matter of fact, they were perhaps two great businessmen, but not the world's two greatest fighting men.[32]

From a boxing standpoint, Rice thought the match between Willard and Dempsey was interesting, if only for the contrasts. Mostly it boiled down to a contest between one man who was young, keen, fast, impetuous, small by heavyweight standards (180–185 pounds), but with an instinctive inner fury for fighting, and who yearned for adulation and the plaudits from the crowd; and another man who was middle-aged (thirty-eight), huge (6'7" and 245ish pounds), ponderous, stoical, peaceful by nature (although he once killed a man in the ring, Bull Young, which had heightened his natural aversion to hurting anyone else), and just plain sick of the spotlight. Willard wanted the cash; Dempsey, the coup.

From the business side, Rice also pointed out that the match was interesting because of the daring adventure on the part of Rickard. In addition to putting up his own money, Rickard had persuaded Frank Flournoy, a Memphis cotton broker, to invest in the fight. Flournoy bankrolled Rickard for $150,000. Before one dime had been taken in, Rickard and his copromoter had guaranteed Willard $100,000 and Dempsey $27,500; sensing that the fight could produce the first million-dollar gate in sports history, Rickard ordered up a hundred-thousand-dollar wood arena to be built near Maumee Bay, an inlet of Lake Erie. The arena was thirty-eight feet high and six hundred feet across, it could seat eighty thousand fans, and it was surrounded by wooden and barbed wire fencing to keep out freeloaders.[33]

In addition to the pugilistic and entrepreneurial curiosities of the fight, there was the plain matter of its sensationalism. Rice, in pointing out why this event was so pop-eyed, said this: "Another thing that has helped has been the world's craving for a new sensation—a new thrill—something in the way of a competitive carnival to feed appetites whetted to the excitement by four years of war. But all these things put together haven't made either a fighting man."[34]

"So," Rice wrote, "on with the dance where ribald joy may ramble unconfined." And unconfined it was, with more than four hundred correspondents dashing off more than six hundred thousand words to tell the story of a contest that would take at most thirty-six minutes (a twelve-rounder). This, Rice thought, was telling in itself, as the previous September, when the First Army, five hundred thousand strong, brought about the downfall of Mont Sec—a four-year barrier of gore and death—it was recorded by only twenty-two reporters, who filed fewer than fifty thousand words. Yes, he thought, this was a "queer, quaint and smashing existence," as both Willard and Dempsey would leave the ring about as they entered it, as compared to some thirty thousand who were killed in the Argonne Woods. Is this carnival, Rice wondered, what our fighting men at Argonne died for?[35]

> Here they come—nut and bum,
>   Banker, yeggman—all the nation,
> File by file of varied style
>   In one vast conglomeration;
> Picking Jess or backing Jack,
>   Doping out the bloke who'll win it
> Where the atmosphere is black
>   With a million words a minute.
>
> - - - - - - - - - - - - - - - - -
>
> If Tex promotes another bout
>   (Here boy—I'll take another rickey)
> I hope they call the army out
>   And treat him as a Bolsheviki;
> Though Willard fade and Dempsey fret—
>   Let us forget—let us forget.

He ended the lengthy "Songs of the Impending Conflict" with a final chorus indited to Tex Rickard: "You made me what I am today—I hope you're satisfied."[36]

The night before the fight, Rice and fellow reporter Bob Edgren, who wrote for the *New York Evening World,* visited Willard. The giant said he thought of Dempsey as a little boy, and believed that the fight was a joke. "[I] outweigh him by seventy pounds," Willard said. "He'll come tearing into me . . . I'll have my left out . . . and then I'll hit him with a right uppercut. That'll be the end."[37]

On the morning of the fight, it was already obvious that Rickard wasn't going to see his first million-dollar gate (in the 1920s he would promote five consecutive million-dollar paydays). There were problems. The heat, well over 100 degrees for days, was cutting into the concessions profit; at that temperature, who wanted peanuts, melted ice cream, or rotten ham and melted cheese sandwiches? To make matters worse, there was a problem with the one thirst-quencher on hand. Battling Nelson, the tough former lightweight champion who had once gone forty-two rounds with the black lightweight Joe Gans before losing when he hit Gans below the belt, had been assigned to cover the fight for the *Chicago Daily News.* Being short of funds, the "Durable Dane," as he was called, camped out in a pup tent near the arena. On the morning of the fight, looking for a place to take his monthly bath, he stumbled into a hog shed where a fight concessionaire was storing several barrels of lemonade. Nelson mistook them for water, hopped in one of them and proceeded to suds up. Word spread, and since no one knew which barrel he used, the lemonade sales soured.[38]

The prefight publicity had backfired as well: word went out that seats were going fast (this was not true), thus discouraging the prospective fan, and that Toledo hotels and restaurants were gouging the fight fans (this was true). And with the federalizing of the railroads still in effect, it was practically impossible for fans to count on any excursion trains to Toledo, even though all roads, it was said, presumably led there. Ticket prices had been anywhere from sixty dollars down to ten dollars. But as tickets became easy to get, speculators were forced to cut their prices; by noon on fight day Rickard realized that the arena would only be half full, if that. The day before the fight, the *Tribune* was still predicting at least seventy-five thousand fans; on fight day, the *Tribune* reported fifty thousand in attendance. This was considerably exaggerated.[39]

At approximately three-thirty in the afternoon, after a few hours of preliminary matches and festivities, Willard and Dempsey entered the ring amid the white-shirted, straw-hatted, and cheering crowd of men and a good number of hatted, parasol-toting women, including Ethel Barrymore (the women were all collected together in a "Jenny Wren" section arranged for by Rickard). All guns and knives were collected at the gate by lawman-turned-sportswriter Bat Masterson and his helper, the balding, sometime fight referee Wyatt Earp. The arena, which Tex Rickard kept telling people was made of enough boards to stretch from New York to Chicago, wasn't half full. Even so, it did give new meaning to the phrase, "You'll be glued to your seat." Without a cushion (sold as a concession), anyone actually sitting down on the newly cut pine boards was sure to stay seated throughout the battle (and probably then some) as the fight fans' bottoms stuck freely to the pitch and resin oozing from the seats.[40]

Rice set up his typewriter in the press area, a mere ten feet from the ropes. Only a few minutes later, he said, he put his bare hand on his typewriter and at first thought he had started to handle the end of a lighted cigar, the metal was so hot. He sat next to Edgren and McGeehan, and in the midst of sport reporters either already famous in their own right or soon to be, including Masterson, Otto Floto, Ring Lardner, Tad Jones, Rube Goldberg, Ned Brown, Hype Igoe, Bugs Baer, and Damon Runyon.

It had taken Corbett twenty-one rounds to knock out John L. Sullivan. It took fourteen rounds for Fitzsimmons to knock out Corbett. Jeffries needed eleven rounds to drop Fitzsimmons. Jack Johnson needed fifteen rounds to take Jeffries, and Willard took twenty-six rounds to knock out Johnson. But in Toledo, on this blistering and humid day—reported variously to be somewhere between 112 and 114 degrees—Dempsey officially finished his day's work in nine minutes, only three rounds, and all but won the match just one minute and fifty-eight seconds into the first round when he hooked a three-quarter left to Willard's right jaw, dropping the giant, who, said Rice, "went down heavily with a dazed and foolish look, a simple half-smile crowning a mouth that was twitching with pain and bewilderment."[41]

Rice and the other ringside reporters didn't exaggerate at all when they to a one reported that Willard took the most terrible beating ever dished out in a heavyweight fight to that time. Willard was dropped seven times in the first round alone. Even McGeehan, a boxing specialist, hadn't seen anything like it; Willard just kept getting up, with the aid of the ropes, and "it seemed that no human being could stand the punishment that Dempsey gave Willard in that round."[42]

After the first knockdown, Willard slowly rose to his feet at the count of six. Ten seconds later, Rice reported, "another of Dempsey's terrific hooks lifted the human mountain from his tottering base, and once again he crashed to the sun-baked canvas with a thud that rolled forth the echo of his doom." This Dempsey did four more times. On the seventh knockdown, Willard sat on the canvas, dazed, bewildered, and helpless, "his big, bleeding mouth wide open, his glassy, bloodshot eyes staring wearily and witlessly out into space, as a 114-degree sun beat down upon his head that was rank with perspiration and blood."[43]

He could only be saved by the bell. But like the inverse of the old philosophical conundrum about whether a falling tree makes a crashing noise in a forest when there's no one there to hear it, in this case the question was: would thousands of people who were there hear a round-ending bell ring after Willard fell like a crashing tree? The bell apparently rang. No one heard it. Ollie Pecord, the referee, counted Willard out and raised Dempsey's hand at Doc Kearns's urging. Kearns, who had his own timekeeper in his corner, in fact knew that the round had actually expired a few seconds before Pecord had counted Willard out. Dressed in a red-and-white-striped shirt and wearing white shoes, Kearns quickly jumped into the ring to lead Dempsey to his dressing room; this urgency was because Kearns personally stood to win a ten-to-one ten-thousand-dollar bet with a gambler, John "Get Rich Quick" Ryan, that Dempsey would knock Willard out in round one.

But the official timekeeper grabbed a whistle and blew the match back on, foiling Kearns's intended swindle. That brought the two Jacks hurriedly back to the ring. Oddly enough, Pecord allowed the fight to resume even though Dempsey had left the ring. But by then Willard was pitifully helpless, his right eye completely closed, the right side of his face not just swollen but distorted and disfigured: six teeth were gone, and his jaw was broken. The fight lasted for six minutes more, remarkably with no more knockdowns, and Willard stayed game to the last. Rice compared Willard to Kipling's celebrated first-class fighting man Fuzzy-Wuzzy who soaked up British fire and still kept a-coming. "It was unbelievable. . . . It looked as if every punch must tear away his head, but in place of this the fountain continued to gush, the features continued to swell, the raw meat continued to pop open in deep slits as the red surf rolled from his shaking pulp-smashed frontispiece." If Willard had not been in reasonably good shape, Rice was convinced that he would have been killed. Willard couldn't answer the whistle for round four, and his corner threw a blood-splattered towel into the ring to signal the defeat. Dempsey, Rice acknowledged, was a marvel in the ring, the greatest hitting machine ever: "And how this Dempsey can hit!"[44]

However, Rice's commentary included a few ending paragraphs that have since become rather famous. Both boxers certainly showed Rice something; Willard, in particular, demonstrated incredible courage and pluck to continue as long as he did where lesser men would have simply given up immediately. But Rice still wasn't about to proclaim either man a true fighter, or Dempsey anything more than a champion boxer: "For it would be an insult to every doughboy that took his heavy pack through the mules' train to front line trenches to go over the top at dawn to refer to Dempsey as a fighting man. If he had been a fighting man he would have been in khaki when at twenty-two he had no other responsibilities in the world except to protect his own hide." Rice went on and on, pointing out that Dempsey missed his biggest chance "to prove his own manhood before his own soul."[45]

This particular judgment, so self-righteously pronounced and so nationally placed, hurt Dempsey's feelings deeply. Years later, and after Rice and Dempsey had become good friends, Dempsey wrote that Rice hit him below the belt and that the blow hurt far more than any of Willard's punches. But, of course, Willard hardly threw any punches, as Dempsey left the ring unmarked. Nonetheless, Rice's indictment was indeed severe, although the comments shouldn't have been any surprise to Dempsey as Rice had been after both fighters in print since way back in March. The day before the fight, Rice had again asked his readers to think of both men as boxers, not Fighting Men. "He called me a slacker and it hurt like hell because I knew I wasn't," said Dempsey. "He didn't know how much I wanted to fight for my country," Dempsey went on. "All he saw was the neatly packaged Jack Dempsey that Kearns had sold so well."[46]

In the aftermath of the fight, Rice remained cynical. Besides the "fighting man" stuff, Rice, tongue in cheek, said that it surprised him very much to hear that Willard and Dempsey overcommercialized the affair. In his feigned defense of them, he wrote that after all, it never occurred to either boxer to charge spectators twenty-five cents to see them eat; nor did they charge the city of Toledo even a penny for walking on their city streets, and they steadfastly refused to charge any fees for acquaintances to speak to them; they even refused to send a bill to the City of Toledo for honoring the city with their six-week visit. So there.[47]

All in all, the fight in Toledo was, indeed, a circus. Rice knew it. All the reporters knew it. The fans, most of them, probably knew it. It was one of those events that everyone knows is an Event, and whose significance was more likely a result of being able to say you had been there, than of actually being there.

> O jab and upper cut and punch,
>   O Jess and Jack—O phrases dreary—
> I've had them now for breakfast, lunch
> And dinner till I'm overweary;
> I've heard them stand around and guess
>   Until my brain began to caper;
> Who knows where there's a game of chess
>   That I can cover for the paper?[48]

With understandable relief, Rice departed from Toledo. Between his arrival and his departure the Volstead Act had taken effect. Prohibition was underway and the drink went underground.

> Since the fight is over and the final blow is hit,
> I'm glad that I can put away my gas mask for a bit;
> Since the fight is over and the cuckoos homeward fly,
> It doesn't even matter that the world is going dry.[49]

11

Who'll Cop the Series?

As it turned out, Rice could put his Toledo gas mask away for only a short couple of months. If the Willard-Dempsey fight invited cynicism, the next Big Event that Rice was to cover demanded it. There was something about the 1919 World Series that stunk.

In the weeks before the Willard-Dempsey fight, when Rice was walking the golf links and covering the final round of the U.S. Open at Brae Burn, he had some company. William "Kid" Gleason, the new manager of the Chicago White Sox, had brought a few of the Sox players to the golf championship, and had joined Rice on the day of the playoff between Hagen and Brady. Gleason had been a solid baseball player himself in the earlier days of the game. He had pitched for Chris Von der Ahe, the powerful and colorful owner of the St. Louis Browns in the 1880s. But when Gleason's arm began to crumble, Von der Ahe unceremoniously let him go. Gleason quietly went away, but was undaunted. The next year he showed up in Philadelphia, where he began to star at second base and at the plate. When Philadelphia finally played in St. Louis that year, Von der Ahe was mortally offended at his old pitcher. "Vy is it?" he said, "you didn't tell me you vas a second baseman also? Vy did you hide it from me ven you could pitch no more?" But at the time Gleason didn't know himself that he could play second. It was his nature, however, never to quit when things were going badly; he just played that much harder.[1]

That's what he admired in Michael Brady on the day of the playoff with Hagen. Gleason hadn't followed much golf until then. He had played it a few times, including with Rice during spring training. He called the game "soft and spongy" and thought that it really wasn't much of a sport. But the head-to-head playoff had lured Gleason to Brae Burn. On the 10th hole, with Brady down by four, someone in the crowd said Brady was beaten. "Beaten?" said Gleason. "Why beaten? The match isn't over yet, is it? Watch him start." Well, Brady did start and won three of the next four holes. Gleason then watched Brady play Hagen down to the wire, losing only by the fortuitous bounce of Hagen's ball over that brook. "A good, game man is never beaten," Gleason said, "and it's a big handicap to any man out there trying when all his friends quit."[2]

As Rice and Gleason sauntered along the course, between shots they visited about the new spirit of the White Sox. After its 1917 World Series win, the team had dropped to sixth place in 1918. Rice had predicted back in April that the White Sox would struggle just to finish in the first division, and "will have a tidy time of it climbing above third place." But Rice also acknowledged that the mental bearings of the White Sox had improved owing to the upbeat attitude of their smart, aggressive new manager, Kid Gleason.[3]

Now in mid-June, Gleason happily compared his club to Brady's never-say-die spirit. Joe Jackson and Buck Weaver were among the leading hitters in the American League at the time, Eddie Cicotte had nine wins in his first ten starts, and the Sox were definitely in the running for the American League flag. This club, Gleason felt, might get beaten, but it would never, ever quit. On the 18th hole, while Gleason and Rice followed the battling golfers, Gleason told Rice, "There are some days when we can't hit much, and there are days when our pitch goes bad. There are days when the breaks are all against us, too, but there are no days when we are not out there hustling and fighting and giving the best we have." As Rice and the Kid followed Brady up the fairway to the green, the White Sox manager added for emphasis, "It will be just this way to the end of the race."[4]

Well, this may have been true. Up to the end of the pennant race, the White Sox players may have hustled and fought and played their best. But there were serious questions about the efforts of a third of the White Sox players as they took the American League flag into the 1919 World Series against the Cincinnati Reds.

Going into the World Series, Chicago was the odds-on favorite. This had as much to do with history as with talent comparisons. The American League clubs had been taking their National League counterparts to school year after year. Not since 1914 had a National League club won the series (the Boston Braves beat Philadelphia in four straight games that year). The American League had won not only the last four series but also eight of nine going back to 1910.[5]

Furthermore, in spite of Cincinnati's legendary baseball history, the team hadn't figured as a serious contender for any baseball-related title for some forty-five years. The undefeated 1869 club had been pretty much the starting point of professional baseball; since then, the Cincinnati teams had not lacked leadership or talent, just championships. They had been managed by a collection of well-known baseball men, including Tom Loftus, Charles Comiskey, Buck Ewing, Joe Kelly, Ned Hanlon, Clark Griffith, Hank O'Day, Joe Tinker, Buck Herzog, and Christy Mathewson. And they certainly had had their share of roster talent at different times, including the likes of Mike King Kelly, Arlie Latham, Ollie Beard, Charles Comiskey, Tip O'Neil, Jesse Tannehill, Bug Holliday, Buck Ewing, Noodles Hahn, Sam Crawford, Mike Donlin, Al Bridwell, Joe Tinker, and Buck Herzog. Yet for all this leadership and talent, the Reds had not fared well in league competition before or after the World Series began in 1903. Their highest previous finish in the National League had been third place, in 1904 and again in 1918.[6]

Yet in the best-of-nine-game 1919 series, Cincinnati won over the White Sox five games to three. At first, their victory appeared to be one of those wonderful, dramatic, and surprising instances where the underdog wins out against all odds. But there was something about the series that was just plain odd. There were ugly rumors about gamblers and ballplayers getting together before the 1919 World Series even began; there was uneven play by the White Sox during the entire series; there were skeptical sportswriters, Hugh Fullerton of the *New York World* in particular, who cried foul shortly after the last out; and in time there was the odor of a fix, which got stinkier and stinkier over the next year.

In early September of 1920 a grand jury was called in Cook County to look into the general question of gambling in baseball. The grand jury was not precipitated by the 1919 World Series, but by news that a late August 1920 game between the Chicago Cubs and Philadelphia had been fixed. But when it was discovered that Charles Comiskey had held up the 1919 World Series bonus checks of eight of his players, presumably to give him time to look into the rumors of a fix, the grand jury extended its investigation into the 1919 series too.[7]

It will never be known exactly what happened: there was too little hard evidence, too many unsavory and finger-pointing characters, silence from the implicated ballplayers themselves, and too much cover-up "for the good of the game." In broad outlines, it appeared that a number of White Sox players were involved somehow and in varying degrees with efforts to throw the series to Cincinnati: Charles Risberg, Chick Gandil, Claude Williams, Happy Felsch, Eddie Cicotte, Fred McMullin, Joe Jackson, and Buck Weaver were implicated. On September 27, 1920, sportswriter James Isaminger of the *Philadelphia North American* published an interview with the small-time gambler Billy Maharg, who claimed that the White Sox intentionally lost the first two games for one hundred thousand dollars. Maharg implicated gambler and former featherweight boxing champion Abe Attell and big-time gambler Arnold Rothstein. Other names in the plot cropped up, including the malcontent former ballplayer and notorious gambler Hal Chase, the former Washington, White Sox, and Philly southpaw Sleepy Bill Burns, and gamblers Sport Sullivan and Nat Evans.

Four of the White Sox players fessed up quickly after the Maharg interview, including Cicotte and Jackson. Cicotte admitted that he had thrown the first and the fourth games by fielding carelessly and pitching sloppily; this he did, he said, for ten thousand dollars—for his wife and kids. Shoeless Joe Jackson admitted to the crime of just plain casual fielding and throwing, for a promised twenty thousand dollars, of which he received only five thousand, because the gamblers thought the team had double-crossed them by winning the third game. Maharg and Burns reputedly lost everything they had previously won on this game. Cicotte and Jackson implicated the six others, and named Gandil the organizer on the inside.

When Jackson left the courthouse after his confession, it is reported that a crowd of small boys gathered around their hero. One of them pleaded, "Say it ain't so, Joe. Say it ain't so." Joe looked down at them, with tears welling up in his eyes, and said, "Yes, boys, I'm afraid it is." The young boys, without a word, opened their ranks and silently allowed Jackson to walk through them.[8]

In Boston, the Roosevelt Newsboys Club met between the morning and evening editions and went on record denouncing what they called the "Benedict Arnolds of baseball." They said that those who were corrupt in the 1919 series "struck a murderous blow at the kids' game." The report said that it was a serious discussion by the newsboys club, many of whom knew the players intimately, one having earned admission to a game by carrying Joe Jackson's bats when he played in Boston, another once having borrowed Eddie Cicotte's glove for fielding practice while the Chicago pitcher took his turn at bat. The boys were quick to commend the "manly stand" of the Clean Sox, especially pitcher Dick Kerr and catcher Ray Schalk, but they condemned the eight crooked White Sox players, their fallen idols, and asked that they be punished.[9]

The White Sox soon became known as the Black Sox, as more confessions and interviews followed, and as suspensions were handed out to the accused players. In late October, the grand jury indicted all eight players, plus the small-time gamblers. Rothstein, the main fixer of the series, was never indicted, although records found after his death indicated that he did indeed pay out eighty thousand dollars for the fix.[10]

Months passed. Finally, in February 1921 the accused players were arraigned in a court of law. But important evidence had since been removed somehow from the grand jury records, and the gamblers had taken off for parts unknown. District Attorney Robert Crowe requested a postponement. Denied. The players then filed affidavits repudiating their signed confessions. Crowe then filed a motion of *nolle prosequi,* which halted the progress of the case entirely until he could regroup and find corroboration of Maharg's testimony. It wasn't until midsummer of 1921 that the trial reopened, mostly due to the determination of American League President Ban Johnson. Judge Hugo Friend presided at the trial. All the Chicago players except McMullin were reindicted; McMullin, a utility player, had appeared in the Series only for two at-bats as a pinch hitter, and went one for two; there wasn't enough evidence to indict him. Hal Chase and ten gamblers were also indicted.

Testimony began in mid-July. Comiskey, Sleepy Bill Burns, Billy Maharg, Kid Gleason, and catcher Ray Schalk testified. Rothstein, Chase, Evans, and Attell all evaded the trial. But on the third day of the proceedings, it was discovered that among the missing documents from the grand jury hearings were the original confessions of the players and their waivers of immunity. It seems that the attorneys for Arnold Rothstein (William J. Fallon) and Charles Comiskey (Alfred Austrian) had engineered the theft of the documents. All parties naturally denied involvement.[11]

The prosecutor charged that "a swindle and a con game has been worked on the American people." He asked for five-year sentences and two-thousand-dollar fines for each of the accused. The judge instructed the jury that the state's case must not only show that the players intended to throw the series games, but that their purpose in doing so was to defraud the public. The case went to the jury late on August 2. After a few hours of thinking it over, the jury acquitted the players and gamblers alike.[12]

One way of looking at this sad and sordid mess is to compare it to a famous old clown turn. It is the shtick where the clown is a woman dressed as a man who is dressed as a woman. When the performer walks on the stage, the audience first sees what appears to be a woman. Slowly the clown does a little of this and takes off a little of that and suddenly what appears is a man under the initial appearance of the woman. "Ah," the audience says, it was a man cleverly disguised as a woman. But then, about the time the audience marvels at how easily they had been fooled, another transformation takes place on stage. This isn't a man after all, as the audience soon sees a woman underneath it all. What they thought was a woman, plain and simple, actually turns out to be a woman dressing as a man who was dressed as a woman. Two levels of appearance and one of reality.

It seems that the 1919 World Series also was layered three ways. At first glance, there was the appearance of a healthy sporting competition between the two best teams in baseball. Then, on closer scrutiny, there was the persistent layer of rumor, suspicion, and gossip—nothing certain, of course—of a possible fix, given credence by the odd plays in the series. Finally, looking ever-so-closely, there was the complicated reality of what actually happened, which to this day still invites speculation as to whether or not the White Sox players actually and intentionally threw the series. With the help of Grantland Rice's text, it is possible to see all three of these "clownish" levels.

First Level. "Who'll cop the Series?" Rice rhetorically asked his readers one week before the first pitch was thrown. After a five-day running analysis of the strengths and weaknesses of each club, whether by the dope, the statistics, or the form (overall balance), Rice said, "the White Sox have the call." But, he added, the Reds were stronger than many observers thought: the team batting average was a high .270, with Edd Roush leading the league at .321; and they had five strong pitchers (Harry Sallee, Dutch Ruether, Hod Eller, Jimmy Ring, and Ray Fisher); sturdy defense; and an experienced manager in Pat Moran, who had won a pennant before while managing the Philadelphia Phillies in 1915. "There will be no slaughter," Rice forecast. The only rub, Rice remarked, was that if history meant anything, it was the National League's turn to win since it was accustomed to winning a world championship every five years, having won in 1909 and 1914. "This should be one of the best series of many years," Rice wrote, "well fought and well played from start to finish. For it is a meeting of class":

> 'Twas the day before the series, and all through Cincinnati
> Every fan in town was nutty and the rest of them were batty;
> You could sniff the wild excitement with its blend of hope and fears,
> And I ask you, who could blame 'em, after waiting fifty years?[13]

Insofar as describing what America in 1919 should expect its sport to be—that is, more than mere commercial entertainment—it is interesting that Rice gave a column over to the writer and playwright Porter Emerson Browne early in the series. Browne wasn't a baseball fan at all, and had devoted most of his writing to national problems in politics and struggles between capital and labor. But since Browne elected to see his first World Series game in 1919, Rice asked him what he thought of the sport.

Browne said he was neutral regarding who was winning or losing, in fact was so disinterested that he compared his trip to Redland Park to the vicarious interest of the young boy who might go to a funeral for the ride. "The game was to me, as the defunct party to the boy, merely incidental." Yet, he also felt that there must be something to the game of baseball "since so many people could get all het up to such a remarkable degree." So, Browne asked himself whether or not, all in all, baseball was good or bad as a national influence. Was the good that it might do sufficient to counteract what he perceived as the loss of millions of minutes spent by thousands of people in ballparks and in front of bulletin boards?

As he pondered this hefty question, he said he thought that the interest in baseball comes from two impulses: the normal desire of the healthful mind for clean and spirited excitement, and an earnest and intense spirit of local pride. He went on to say that in his opinion, baseball was one of the greatest nationwide stabilizing influences of the day. And even though he said he personally couldn't get any more out of a baseball game than he could from sitting on the sidewalk and watching people eat in a restaurant, he thought that this was his misfortune.

The great value of baseball, he thought, was that it was a good antidote to the way in which the world and its cares can bear down hard on humanity in general—especially in the aftermath of the First World War. Baseball, he thought, could help people forget their troubles, it could give them a clean and potent thrill, it could get them out in the open air, and it could stimulate their better selves with a native pride. "So here's to it!" Browne wrote, "America for Americans, and baseball for us all! One and inseparable! United we stand, divided we fall!"[14]

Level Two. The question still was: "Who'll cop the Series?" Was the series going to be on the up-and-up? Privately, Rice knew beforehand that there could be something queer about to go off. Who among those close to the action didn't so suspect? After all, there were rumors about a potential fix as far back as August. Rice heard them for sure. And in Cincinnati just before the games were to be played, Rice was staying at the Sinton Hotel with many of his reporter colleagues, including Runyon, Jack Wheeler, and one of his closer friends—in time his closest—Ring Lardner, who had left the *Chicago Tribune* and was now writing for the Bell Syndicate in New York. The Sinton was the White Sox hotel, and as everyone could soon tell, the hub of the rumor wheel regarding a possible fix. Like a magnet attracting iron ore, the Sinton lobby drew in hordes of professional gamblers. According to Maharg's account, Abe Attell was quartered in the Sinton in a large suite and had a gang of about twenty-five gamblers with him. "Their work was very raw," said Maharg. "They button-holed everybody who came in. They accepted bets right and left and it was nothing unusual to see $1,000 bills wagered." The betting was not only rampant, but it also seemed to be going the wrong way; the odds shifted in favor of Cincinnati, down from 7–10, then 5–6, and finally even money.[15]

The night before the first game, another of Rice's friends, "Champ" Pickens, who sometime later was the organizer of the Blue and Gray football game at Montgomery, Alabama, walked into Rice's room and said, "I've just been offered five to four on Cincinnati by a professional gambler."

"How much of it did you take?" Rice asked him.

"Take, hell! This Series is fixed," Pickens answered him angrily as he tossed his ticket on Rice's bed. "You can have it—I'm going to the race track."[16]

Rice knew that there were always dark rumors circulating around Big Events, especially where the gambling was heavy. He rarely took such rumors seriously. But this time he almost seemed to forewarn his readers that something odd might happen in this World Series. As if preparing his readers for some possible surprises, Rice's column the next day reviewed some historical instances of the greatest players in the game falling below their normal ability in postseason play: Honus Wagner out of gear in the 1903 Series; Ty Cobb hitting at around .375 for eighteen hundred ball games, yet only batting .275 in seventeen games in three series appearances; and the failure of the great Cubs machine including Tinker, Evers, and Chance to do anything at all in the 1906 World Series against the White Sox—Tinker's series average was .157, and Evers was .150.[17]

The next day he took his seat in the press box along with Fullerton, Lardner, and the others. Fullerton, whose suspicions were perhaps the strongest, enlisted the aid of Christy Mathewson, who was working for the *New York Times* for the series, to help circle any suspicious plays on his scorecard. Mathewson was in failing health after having contracted a type of tuberculosis, presumably from poison gas during the war. Mathewson tutored Fullerton, Rice, and Lardner on the variety of subtle ways any position could be played down just enough to escape suspicion, but to successfully influence the outcome of a game.

In reading Rice's coverage of the 1919 series today, it is possible in hindsight to read into his reporting a cautious disbelief that this was an honest contest. But nowhere did he explicitly say anything to the effect that the White Sox might be in the tank, nor did he even imply that any of the players intentionally played as badly as they actually did play. He just matter of factly pointed out how badly some of the White Sox players really played some of the time.

In game one, while he praised the Reds pitcher Dutch Ruether to the heavens for throwing a six-hitter and for hitting two triples and a single in his three trips to the plate, he thought Cicotte did himself in in the fourth. The subhead for Rice's coverage was GRANTLAND RICE TELLS HOW EDDIE CICOTTE TOSSED HIS OWN GAME AWAY BY FAILURE TO FIELD BALL QUICKLY. In the fourth, with the game tied 1 to 1 and with one out, Kopf, the Reds shortstop, "tapped gently to Cicotte. Eddie, instead of jumping swiftly for the ball, took his time with all the leisure of a steel striker. He made no attempt to hurry the ball along to Risberg for a sure double play." The Reds scored five runs with two out, sending Cicotte out of the game. Rice called Cicotte's performance an "amazing failure." The Reds won 9 to 1.[18]

In game two, which the White Sox also lost, Rice noted that the Red tide had risen another notch and that the Sox were "immersed up to their seamy necks, gasping for air." This time, Rice pointed a finger at Sox pitcher Claude Williams, who was "brilliantly unsteady" and "wilder to-day than Tarzan of the Apes roaming the African jungle from limb to limb," having walked six Reds, three in the fourth. What puzzled Rice was that the Sox got ten solid hits to the Reds' four, and with this game, the Sox still hadn't scored a single earned run.[19]

Even in Chicago's 3 to 0 win over Cincinnati in game three in Chicago, and in spite of Rice's opening seven paragraphs of praise for the courage, brains, and skill of undersized White Sox pitcher Dick Kerr (a Clean Sox) in holding the Reds to three hits, he noted that Chicago's famed offensive attack had failed to materialize: they still had scored only one earned run in twenty-six innings. "You can credit this offensive slump to fine Red pitching or to a sudden weakness around Sox batting eyes, but the fact remains that one earned run through three long afternoons is a decided change from the attacking power that carried Chicago to the top."[20]

Game four, also played in Chicago, went to the Reds 2 to 0. Still one earned run, now in four games. The groaning of the White Sox fans mingled with the squeals of the vivisected pigs coming from the slaughterhouse across from the ballpark, Rice observed, in a "vast medley of woe." He blamed Cicotte, mostly. "Strangely enough, the ancient wing held up and it was the ancient bean that went awry," Rice wrote, pointing to Cicotte's three mistakes in one inning—two misplays and one error of judgment—as Cicotte "blew his own game."[21]

"Dazed and bewildered" fans watched the White Sox drop the fifth game, 5 to 0. Rice called Chicago's play puny, utterly helpless, and feeble. On a long fly ball hit to Happy Felsh, "He first misjudged the ball, then misplayed it, and finally, backing squarely under it, permitted the ball to strike his glove and bound away." This play was officially scored a three-base hit, when in fact, Rice said, it was a three-base error.[22]

In game six, the Sox came back from a 4 to 0 deficit and won 5 to 4. After the Reds took a 4 to 0 lead, "the Sox, breaking and cracking in every department, were reeling and floundering and detonating like a disorganized set of unkept bushers—the worst-looking ball club that ever batted for a title." After they came back in the fifth and sixth, Rice said that the Sox had re-formed, rallied, and counterattacked, proving conclusively that the old spirit had not been utterly crushed: "They had done everything possible to lose the game before they finally scampered out from beneath the deadly spell."[23]

After the White Sox won game seven behind Cicotte, they lost the Series in the eighth game, 10 to 5, after Williams was sent to the "cooling showers" in the first inning to become the first player in World Series history to lose three games (he had won twenty-three during the season). In his final three paragraphs, Rice simply said that the Reds deserved their triumph; they played their best ball and produced the most effective all-around machine. "But whereas the Sox drew a spotty record of few stars and many goats, the Red balance predominated. . . . It was a victorious finish that Pat Moran (the Reds manager) deserved as he takes his established place as one of the greatest leaders the game has known."[24]

In the few weeks after the series, Rice didn't say much about the contest. He briefly analyzed the Reds victory and attributed it mostly to outstanding pitching by Reuther, Eller, Ring, and Sallee. Against them, the White Sox "in place of a .287 ball club at bat they looked to be a .111 array." A week later, he suggested that some of the White Sox losses stemmed from overconfidence, counting on past performances to carry the present: "The only past performance chart that counts is where both sides were trying. And the only effective way it can be used in completing the future dope is for both sides to continue trying. The plastic dope can only show what they ought to do if they give 100 per cent of what they have."[25]

Still, to this point, there was only rumor and suspicion about a fix. That and the lingering voice of Ring Lardner, who throughout the series—in the press box, on the train, in the hotel lobbies—sung his own spirited lyrics to the tune of "I'm Forever Blowing Bubbles," the piece that the band regularly played in the pregame activities at Redland Park in Cincinnati:

> I'm forever blowing ball games,
> Pretty ball games in the air.
> I come from Chi
> I hardly try
> Just go bat and fade and die;
> Fortune's coming my way,
> That's why I don't care.
> I'm forever blowing ball games
> And the gamblers treat us fair.[26]

Whatever Rice may have privately believed—or not wanted to believe—about the series, he publicly held the line that this was a bona fide, explainable sporting upset, the Reds playing above themselves, the Sox below. After all, he rationalized, 1919 was a year of upsets: the Reds and the Sox surprised their respective leagues by winning pennants; Dempsey upset Willard; in amateur golf Dave Herron upset Chick Evans, young Bobby Jones, Francis Ouimet, and Robert Gardner. And so on. The upset, Rice concluded, is the maker of sport. "If every event ran true to expected form there would be no thrill left," Rice wrote, "and the color would fade from the sportive landscape." A week later: "Sudden turns may happen at any time to any man, until mankind becomes a perfect machine. And when it does sport will decay faster than a water soaked poplar."[27]

But all of this was forced. 1919 wasn't a year of upsets at all, and Rice knew it. As expected, Cobb won the batting title for the twelfth time; Edd Roush led the National League in hitting; Grover Cleveland Alexander led the National League pitchers, and Walter Johnson the pitchers in the American League; William Johnston ended up on top in tennis; the two best golfers, Hagen and Brady, proved it in the Open; the man picked to win the Professional Golfer's Championship, Jim Barnes, won; and who else but Babe Ruth was expected to lead both leagues in home runs? He did, with twenty-nine.

Level Three. Now the question was: "Who *did* cop the Series?" Rice was well into covering the 1919 college football season when he finally mentioned the word "fix" in print. On October 28, about three weeks after the series was over, Rice discussed what he called "the fixing process." It would be easy, he wrote, to fix wrestling, or boxing, or maybe horse racing—mainly because all it would take is a single crooked athlete or trainer. Baseball, he said, was the hardest sport to fix. Even buying off a couple of players wouldn't be enough to guarantee anything since the number of chances the players would get couldn't be known in advance. Even a pitcher throwing as though he were in batting practice would be yanked from the game too soon to influence the outcome. "In baseball there are too many men to be reached to make it sure. And a baseball crowd isn't very easy to fool."[28]

Would eight players, including two pitchers, be enough? What seemed improbable at the time didn't seem so a year later when the news of the fix broke. Rice said he felt like he'd been kicked in the stomach. During the grand jury probe, and before the indictments, Rice avoided commenting on the proceedings. For instance, all the while that Charles Weeghman, former owner and president of the Chicago Cubs, was testifying that he had heard of a potential fix as early as August of 1919, Rice, in a "Tales of a Wayside Tee" column adjacent to the grand jury story, was holding forth on what he thought was the best composite golfer of the day: the drive of Bob McDonald, the full iron of Chick Evans, out of trouble by Walter Hagen, and so on.[29]

Finally, on the day the public was informed that the grand jury had indicted all eight players, Rice unloaded. He first complained that the National Commission—the game's supposed authority, but in fact perpetually shaky and without leadership well before the 1919 series was even played—should have investigated the rumors to protect the interests of the game. Then he called for drastic punishment if the indictments proved to be true in court, using as he often did reference to natural disasters: "When a gambler touches a sporting enterprise the effect isn't very much worse than a combination of fire, tornado, and flood. The wreckage is always complete." Rice stated the obvious: if the public made up its mind that even a small part of baseball was crooked, "the entire game might as well be chucked into the sewer so far as continued patronage in any large numbers is concerned."[30]

Those dastardly players mixed up in the crookedness, he said, were worse than thieves and burglars. "They are the ultimate scum of the universe, and even the spotted civilization of the present time has no place for them outside of a penitentiary." He railed on: the only complaint then would come from the existing thieves and burglars who would have to associate with the ballplayers in prison. This crime, Rice said, was the dirtiest crime in sport.[31]

Rice finally admitted in print that before and during the series there was "entirely too much smoke adrift for even a simple-minded person not to know that a big blaze of crookedness had been started somewhere." But, he went on, the situation then and for the year since, had a peculiar status: something more than mere gossip, but not a matter of direct certainty. No one in the know was talking. Until now. Rice lamented that this news was a terrific blow to the game, delivered at a moment when baseball was at its peak of popularity, with wonderful pennant races lasting into the last week of the season (the White Sox were vying with Cleveland at the time for the 1920 American League flag), and an authentic home-run king, Babe Ruth, packing them in from Boston to St. Louis.

Indignant though he was, and as unthinkable as it was that anyone would or could try to tamper with America's national pastime, especially a championship as sacred to the American public as the World Series had become, Rice was well aware that baseball had crooked incidents in its past. He was probably amazed that there weren't more of them.

Wagering on baseball, for that matter betting on almost all athletic contests, was the norm, even when the owners inveighed against the practice, as they sometimes did. At the parks, the gambling was often out in the open; all you had to do was wander behind third base in many parks and there you could place your bet right in front of God, the owners, and everyone. Even the owners were sometimes involved in the betting. When the horse racetracks were shut down during World War I, the betting shifted in earnest to the ballparks. Many of the owners, some managers, and many players were accomplished bettors.

Outside the baseball parks, in cigar shops, saloons, and billiard halls, betting was commonplace. Even in less sleazy surroundings, such as work sites, fans could bet in highly organized betting pools. Here, and for as little as one thin dime, a fan could take a try on which team would score the most runs, or on who would win the most games, or on almost any other angle of the game. In 1920 the *Chicago Tribune* estimated that the locals bought more than four hundred thousand pool tickets a week, and for a cost of $150,000. One expert of gambling in America in this era explained that betting on baseball was perhaps more of a national pastime than was the national pastime: "The National pastime of betting on games was immune to the economic ups and downs, and it took the 1919 World Series scandal to break the public faith that major team sports were incorruptible and you could at least bet on them with no danger of being cheated."[32]

But even before this big scandal, there were some pretty blatant cases of dishonesty:[33]

- John Taylor, it was claimed, had been "bought" for five hundred dollars in the 1903 postseason championship of Chicago between the

Cubs and the White Sox. After he was later sold to St. Louis, he was accused of throwing a game between St. Louis and Pittsburgh in July 1904. Taylor denied the charges, saying, "I am not a saint, and at times may have dissipated, but that don't make me a baseball crook."[34]

• In 1905 there was the incident involving Rube Waddell, who was offered seventeen thousand dollars by gambler Little Tim Sullivan to stay out of the World Series. Horace Fogel, former president of the Philadelphia Athletics, claimed that Waddell was given only five hundred in a Boston hotel and was double-crossed out of the remainder of the bribe. Connie Mack, on the other hand, was skeptical that anything of the sort took place: "You can't prove anything by me," said Mack, "although I don't believe that anything like that was carried out or attempted."[35]

• There were stories about how the New York Giants bribed their way to the 1908 pennant. Toward the end of the season, and right after the famous tie game with Chicago and Merkle's failure to touch second base, the Giants were to close the season against Philadelphia and Boston. Stories vary: one was that McGraw tried to get Philadelphia pitchers to ease up against them; another was that Boston, who was managed by Joe Kelly, an old Baltimore teammate of McGraw's, "laid down" and lost all three games against the Giants to help New York tie with Chicago for a playoff; yet another, with even more credence attached to it, was that someone in the New York organization had tried to bribe umpires Bill Klem and Johnny Johnstone to give the Giants a victory in the playoff game itself.

• Then there was the famous batting award scandal involving Ty Cobb and Napoleon Lajoie in 1910. Cobb and Lajoie were in a close race late in the season for the league batting title. No small gift was at stake, as the prize was going to be a new automobile presented by the Chalmers Automobile Company. After Cobb thought he had the title safely won, he sat out the last two Detroit games to prevent his average from dropping. Meanwhile, Lajoie amazingly managed to go eight for eight against the "helpful" Browns in a final season doubleheader at St. Louis. One of the hits was a solid triple, but of the other seven, six were on bunts down the third-base line; the normally slow-footed Lajoie managed to beat every throw. And the eighth was an official scorer's decision to give Lajoie a hit when the Browns' shortstop threw wildly to first. Cobb was unpopular throughout the league, and for that matter, throughout organized baseball. It was obvious that the Browns had conspired to help Lajoie win the title from Cobb. In the end, the players involved were not penalized, although the Browns' manager, "Peach Pie" Jack O'Connor, was fired, as was Harry Howell, a Browns' scout who had repeatedly visited the press box and tried to influence the official scorer's point of view as well as improve his appearance by offering him a forty-dollar suit of clothes to boot. Even though the final results show Cobb the statistical winner of the title, both Cobb and Lajoie were each graciously presented cars by Chalmers. After this, and instead of the prize-winning batting title, a most valuable player trophy was established.

• Then there was the notorious career of player/villain Hal Chase, who tried to fix games throughout his career. Baseball historian Harold Seymour called Chase a "malignant genius," and the archetype of all crooked ballplayers. Although an outstanding first baseman—the caliber of George Sisler, Lou Gehrig, and Bill Terry—he was obnoxious as well as dishonest. His career consisted mostly of laying down for the right amount of money or getting others to do so. He started out with the New York Americans in 1905 and stayed with them until 1913. Having undermined the entire succession of Yankees managers, he became manager himself in 1911 and led the team to a second-place finish in 1910 and to sixth place in 1911. Back to first base as a player in 1912, he had a run-in with Frank Chance, his successor as manager. Chance accused him of throwing games. Chase was peddled to the White Sox, but eventually in 1916 he landed on the Reds, where Christy Mathewson, then managing, suspended him late in the 1918 season for "indifferent playing." He was later, about six months later, cleared of the charge in a mostly whitewashed hearing by the new National League president, John Heydler; Chase was not even reprimanded. Instead, he was signed for the 1919 season by McGraw of the Giants—who, by the way, had testified against Chase at the hearings, claiming that Chase had tried to get one of his Giants pitchers, Pol Perritt, to throw a game for money. But by September of the 1919 season McGraw himself had to quietly remove Chase and infielder Heinie Zimmerman from the Giants lineup; when questioned by reporters, he said only, "I cannot talk of the matter." Chase did not play in the majors again, even though he apparently continued to play *with* organized baseball, given his involvement in the 1919 attempted fix.

So, before 1919 there was an easy acceptance of gambling on baseball, and there were incidents of crookedness in its past. Rice knew all of this; he lived through it. In fact, Rice could go back even further than these more recent examples of dishonesty. As part of his continued thrashing about the 1919 crookedness in baseball, he reminded his *Trib* readers that in 1877, Louisville of the National League expelled four players for crookedness—William H. Craver, George Hall, James Devlin, and A. H. Nichols. He used this incident for the lesson it should have taught all modern ballplayers, but obviously didn't. As Eddie Cicotte warmed up for the 1919 series, Rice wondered how Cicotte would have felt if he could have seen a picture of Devlin just forty-two years ago, the picture of a man in abject misery, threadbare and seedy, groveling at the feet of National League President Hulbert as he pleaded for mercy: "If he could have seen Hulbert hand him a $50 bill with this remark: 'That's what I think of you for old friendship; but damn you, Devlin, you are dishonest; you have sold a game; I never want to look upon your face again.' "[36]

But most of these incidents—either the recent ones or the more distant— were not within the easy memory of the public. They hadn't been vigorously investigated or reported. There were no major public scandals associated with them. For the most part, the incidents were covered up or explained away "for the good of the game." So, from the public's point of view, it wasn't too far from the truth when Rice went on to say that until the rumors were verified and the players finally admitted to an attempted fix, millions of fans would continue to believe that baseball had proved its honesty to the world: "For they [the fans] knew the vast majority of the players were honest and they believed these players could detect any dishonesty and protect their own game." In a later column he did mention the whitewashing of Hal Chase after Mathewson had three sworn affidavits that he had been throwing games, but since Chase was declared innocent and taken back into organized baseball after his suspension, there was no scandal—even if the behavior of the league president was itself rather scandalous.[37]

So the 1919 scandal was special. This was the World Series. News of the scandal chased most other news, such as the growing Red Scare, off the front pages. Commentators, pundits, cartoonists, and even politicians were shocked and disillusioned that America's national pastime could actually have begun to resemble ordinary life.

Rice was just as vigorous as anyone else in calling for punishment for the star players who "had sold out the public, their own mates, their own game, and their own souls." Naturally, he also had a message for the gamblers: stay the hell out. And to those who owned clubs and administered organized baseball: get yourselves organized. "The new law of life," wrote Rice, "is not Make, but Take—and yet the world wonders at its growing troubles." He went on to say, "The bulk of all great growth starts in poverty, just as the bulk of all decay comes in the midst of too much gold." Isn't it sad, he said, that 236,938 fans paid out $722,414 at the gate "to see a flock of crooked mannequins worked by strings held by a group of crooked gamblers?"[38]

But even after the scandal broke, Rice, and all the sportswriters for that matter, knew that this big story was far more complicated than merely crooked gamblers pulling the strings of crooked mannequins. Who *did* cop the series? It still wasn't entirely clear what had actually happened during the games themselves. Did the White Sox purposely throw the series? Baseball historians seem to think it is debatable that they actually did. It is true that the ringleaders—Gandil and Cicotte in particular—met with gamblers. The players initiated the idea of the fix, it is believed. And it is likely that this effort wasn't spur-of-the-moment, but was thought out well in advance, perhaps as early as sometime in August. It is also the case that money was paid out to the players for the purpose of throwing the series. No one seems to know, however, who got what. Nonetheless, it is clear that a plot was hatched between some players and the gamblers before the first game of the series.

But was the plot actually carried out? And, did the entire responsibility for the scandal actually rest squarely and solely on the shoulders of the players and the gamblers themselves? There are baseball historians who believe this is not necessarily so:[39]

- The so-called plot was so badly conceived and the secret so poorly kept that it almost appeared in retrospect that the intention was to create the illusion that there was a fix going on. Everyone heard the rumors. But the players seemingly had no idea or plan in advance of the first pitch exactly as to how they were going to pull the fix off on the field of play.

- Some of the players, without doubt, tried to lose. But no one knows whether these efforts actually resulted in losing games; the White Sox might have actually won a few of the games they were purportedly trying to lose, or even lost games they were trying to win—if they were trying to win any games. Claude Williams, in his testimony, claimed that he didn't know if they were supposed to win or lose game three. Jackson claimed that they were trying to lose game three but that pitcher Dick Kerr won it on his own.

• The Reds weren't a bad club at all, as Rice regularly pointed out before and throughout the series. They did win the National League pennant, after all. It certainly wasn't the case that the White Sox were so superior that it was inevitable the Reds would lose. The Reds had a solid team, plus they had Pat Moran, a more experienced manager in postseason play than was Kid Gleason. The Reds, in other words, could have won the series without help from crooked White Sox players.

• Then there were the statistical curiosities of the series. Oddly enough, it appears that some of the so-called Clean Sox players did worse than the Black Sox players did. For instance, Jackson led all hitters in the series by batting .375 with twelve hits, and Buck Weaver hit .324 with eleven base hits. Eddie Collins, on the other hand, a star Clean Sox and the highest-paid player on the team, hit .226. Jackson and Weaver played errorless ball, while Collins had two errors. Jackson hit the only home run in the series. Gandil (seven hits) drove in two of Chicago's three runs in game three, and Risberg tripled in the third run in that game. Fred McMullin went one for two as a pinch hitter. Both clubs had the same number of errors, eleven, and almost identical fielding averages (Reds .966, White Sox .968). It is true that the team batting averages were suspect, with Chicago's powerful line-up hitting only .224 for the series against Cincinnati's .255; and it is true that the Reds scored thirty-five runs to only twenty for the White Sox. But all in all, the statistics alone offered little evidence with which to pin a fix on Chicago.[40]

• Yes, there were a number of player confessions: Cicotte, Jackson, Felsh, and Williams. But the circumstances were less than fair: no counsel, rights waived, and high pressure. Jackson couldn't read or write. Some have thought that the confessions were so easily obtained that the players may have admitted to laying down out of fear, in order to convince the gamblers that they actually did do what they said they would do—lose on purpose.

• It is believed that there were some Clean Sox who knew about the attempted fix but did nothing to prevent it—hence culpability extended beyond the dirty eight.

• Comiskey was tightfisted. Even though he entertained the sportswriters with food and drink in the clubhouse, he was notoriously stingy with player salaries. Except for Eddie Collins, whose salary was fifteen thousand dollars and who, when bought by Comiskey, insisted in his five-year contract that his salary be carried over from his earnings in the Federal League, the players were poorly compensated. Joe Jackson, a premier player, was paid a salary of six thousand dollars, only half as much as the Reds' star outfielder Edd Roush. After twelve seasons in the majors, Cicotte was earning only five thousand dollars a season, and Claude Williams made only three thousand. In 1917, to avoid paying Cicotte a ten-thousand-dollar bonus for winning thirty games, Comiskey had the pitcher benched after he won his twenty-ninth late in the season. So, to some extent, Comiskey's "thriftiness" certainly contributed to the players' interest in finding some other way to get what they thought they were worth.

• Without going into all the details, during and after the series it is clear that Comiskey was primarily interested in protecting his investment, not in trying to find out what had actually happened. After all, Comiskey knew early on that something was up; Kid Gleason had gone directly to him to tell him that something was wrong with their boys. Comiskey even knew that Jackson had been given five thousand dollars, since Jackson had gone into the office of Harry Grabiner, the White Sox secretary, right after the World Series to ask what he should do with the money. Grabiner told him to keep it; he also told Comiskey what he had told Jackson. But then as now, denial and cover-up was the order of the day. Comiskey even signed seven of the suspected players for the 1920 season, and with substantial raises, in some cases with salaries doubling. Rice commented that owners in general had "no vision beyond the box office." Instead of leading the investigation, Comiskey frustrated it.[41]

• The broader leadership of organized baseball also looked the other way, hoping that the whole thing would fade like the other darker moments had. Some owners were known to associate frequently with gamblers, especially with Arnold Rothstein. And when the sports-writers tried to follow up their own suspicions after the series, major league spokesmen simply clammed up. When Hugh Fullerton publicly hinted the day after the 1919 series ended that the contest might have been fixed, Comiskey claimed Fullerton was spinning a yarn. *Sporting News* and *Baseball Magazine* both went after Fullerton, not Comiskey, calling him a "peddler of scandal" and a "fool." Rice remarked, "Not only the two league presidents, but also a big majority of the club owners have shown an unbelievable indifference in protecting the game and building for the future." Even when Ban Johnson finally pressed for the trial in 1921, he apparently was trying more to get back at his longtime enemy Charles Comiskey than to uncover the truth; Johnson was also trying to one-up the new baseball commissioner, Judge Kenesaw Mountain Landis, who had been appointed the "czar" of baseball in the offseason late in 1920, under the authority of the new "National Agreement" that was to replace the dysfunctional National Commission.[42]

All in all, especially with the bizarre nature of the trial, culprits other than the eight players escaped entirely: the professional gamblers, other players in the know, Comiskey and his staff, and even the entire hierarchy of organized baseball with their acts of omission.

What actually happened in the 1919 World Series will apparently never be known. But whatever the true extent of their culpability was, the accused White Sox players paid dearly in the end. For in the end, although they escaped conviction in a court of law, the Chicago eight were banished from baseball forever by Commissioner Landis, who thereby symbolically cleansed baseball of its adulterated past. "The scandal was not an aberration brought about solely by a handful of villainous players," baseball historian Harold Seymour wrote. "It was a culmination of corruption and attempts at corruption that reached back nearly twenty years."[43]

Rice did his best to help the American public recover from the aftershocks of the 1919 scandal. The ever-upbeat sportswriter knew that the sport of baseball was and would continue to be populated by characterless characters, but he also knew that the great majority of players were good and honest people who cared deeply about the game. He shared with his readers a discussion he had had with Bob Gilkes, the New York Yankee scout, about the scandal.

Gilkes had been a player with Cleveland thirty-two years earlier. "If you think this baseball scandal hits many of the fans hard," Gilkes said, "how do you think it affects old ball players who have given their life to the game?" Gilkes remarked that he had been in baseball for more than thirty years as a player, manager, and scout. "I can hold my right hand up to heaven and swear that in all that time I never saw a ball game thrown until this Chicago bunch came along," he said. Gilkes added that in all that time he had never been approached by a gambler or by anyone else to turn a crooked trick. He went on: "Just because there are a few crooks it is hardly fair to forget the honesty of the big majority. Baseball, on the average, still has been the cleanest of all games played."44

Rice agreed. To protect what he thought was still a traditionally honest game, he encouraged the proposed administrative reform of baseball so long as such measures could guarantee a keener vision, and a greater alertness and aggressiveness. The changes were long overdue.

By 1921, Rice was looking forward, not back, although perhaps never again as innocently as he or the nation once had:

> Sometimes I wonder how the light can break
> Through all the fog and shadow out the way;
> Sometimes I wonder if at dawn I'll wake
> To find night's darkness lasting through the day,
> Until I think of all the friends I've known
> And all their kindness in days gone by,
> And when I look again the fogs have flown
> Beyond the hills that meet a clean, blue sky.
>
> Sometimes I wonder how the world can stand
> The constant trouble that besets each state;
> The vast unrest that sweeps across the land
> And leaves its trail of bitterness and hate,
> Until, as one who marks a flaming fire,
> I see long lines still ready for the blow,
> Facing the terror of the matted wire
> To hear the call ring out again: "Let's go!"45

12

Uncle Sam, John Bull, and the Frogs

In the summer of 1921, within the space of a few weeks Great Britain staged four international championships in three sports: golf, tennis, and polo. The United States was to be strongly represented in them all, with Bill Tilden and Molla Mallory in tennis; Walter Hagen, Alexa Stirling, Bobby Jones, Chick Evans, Francis Ouimet, Jock Hutchison, and Jim Barnes in golf; and Devereux Milburn and Tommy Hitchcock in polo. All three sports had been internationally popular since the turn of the century. This was about the first time, however, that the United States simultaneously organized a strong collective of amateur athletes in all these sports for international competition.

In spite of shipping strikes and a mild depression after the postwar boom, Rice convinced the *Tribune* editors that covering the friendly strife between the English, the French, and the United States would be a healthy antidote to the depressing story of the unraveling of baseball. Perhaps boosting national pride could help America's sports fans to overcome the problems with the national pastime.

With Kate and Floncy in tow, Rice left New York in early May aboard the Old North State of the United States Mail Line for the two-week "boat" trip to England. The *Tribune* sent him off with a fanfare, announcing the departure of Mr. Rice, whose name "is as well known to lovers of sport as Babe Ruth's." Rice would be reporting on the Amateur Golf Cup (at Hoylake), the Open Golf Cup (at St. Andrews), the Golf Cup for Women (at Turnberry), the Polo Cup (at Hurlingham), and the Tennis Cup (at Wimbledon). And Rice was forecasting a strong American showing in them all.[1]

It had been sixteen years since an American had won the British Amateur. Even in 1914, with perhaps the strongest U.S. team, led by Chick Evans, Walter Travis, and Francis Ouimet, the Americans were trounced. In 1921, America would again be represented by Evans and Ouimet, as well as by nineteen-year-old Bobby Jones. Even at this young age, Jones was not inexperienced: he had already competed in three U.S. Amateur championships and one U.S. Open; he just hadn't yet competed overseas. Bill Fownes, the captain of America's team, was among the second level of the American delegation, which included Jess Guilford, Fred Wright, Woodie Platt, and Paul Hunter.[2]

The Hoylake course, home of the Royal Liverpool Golf Club, helped start England's golf boom back in 1875 and had been the site of the first amateur international match between England and Scotland. The course, like many in Scotland and England, was designed around the natural "links land"—the unoccupied links of land that stretched into or bordered the sea. Hence the name golf links, which the predominantly inland American courses imitated by creating artificial bunkers and sand and water traps.[3] But in spite of its history, Hoylake wasn't especially aesthetically pleasing. A drab road loafed along between dull houses leading to the flat-looking, treeless course. The American delegation was also met by unusually dry weather conditions and heavy sea breezes.

The Amateur was match play rather than medal (stroke), and was set up as a two-match-a-day format after the first day's one eighteen-hole match. (In match play, the golfers compete by counting the number of holes won; in medal play, the total number of strokes after eighteen holes are counted.) Evans, Jones, Ouimet, Wright, and Hunter all played the first gray and windy day, and all won. Woodie Platt had fallen down some stairs at the boarding-house near Hoylake and gashed his knee badly enough to force his withdrawal. Fownes and Guilford drew a rest for the first day. Tommy Armour, the young British star, won 4 and 2 and shot a 70. Rice said he would bear watching.

The course and the greens, Rice reported, were burnt brown as wallpaper. So dry were the greens that the hosts had to throw buckets of water around the pins on many of the holes just to slow the balls down enough to have a fair chance at dropping in the hole. On the second day, the two most experienced American golfers—Ouimet and Evans—were beaten. Only half the American team remained in the competition; among those still in was Bobby Jones. Guilford lost, and so did England's Armour. "Golf still works quaint wonders sounding to uncanny depths of mystery," Rice wrote, realizing that his dope on the matches was not coming true.[4]

In Jones's first match on the second day, he was two down with five to go against E. A. Hamlet, who was an eight- to ten-handicap golfer by American standards. "I can't hit a shot with any club in my bag," complained Jones moodily after three-putting from eight feet on the fourteenth. Somehow Jones pulled himself together, winning on the final hole, but shooting a horrendous 86. Jones came back in his second eighteen holes of the day to easily win, 6 and 5 against English ace golfer Robert Harris.

But this was not going to be a year for an American victory at the Amateur. "Once again the sun stalked like a tyrant with flaming sword, baking the course to even a further hardness, wrecking the nerves and disposition of countless players," wrote Rice. Fred Wright of Boston was the only American who survived the next day's rounds. Jones was beaten 6 and 5 by Cyril Tolley, the British title holder. Wright beat the sentimental British favorite, veteran John Ball, who had played in the first championship tournament at Hoylake some forty-four years earlier.[5] The next day, Wright was defeated by Bernard Darwin, the golf-writing expert for the *London Times.* Wright was up three at the turn, but lost his putting confidence on the hard and slippery greens. Darwin pulled uphill to tie the match at the 18th. On the 19th, with a crowd of ten thousand watching on, Darwin, grandson of the famous scientist Charles Darwin, beat Wright, who three-putted from twenty feet. The British gave the slender, weary Wright a big cheer for his gameness as he walked off the green. But in odd contrast, only a few of Wright's own teammates were on hand to rally him on during the match. In Rice's view, the losing Americans had let Wright down, considering the heavy burden that was on his shoulders. Rice thought Wright played heroically considering that three days before the tournament he was playing the poorest of the entire delegation.

Darwin, emotionally exhausted, lost later in the day to Willie Hunter, a wiry, tawny-haired Scot who weighed only 140 pounds. Hunter, a thirty-two-year-old post office clerk, then won the championship the next day, demolishing Allan Graham 12 and 11.[6]

America's embarrassing defeat caught the attention of President Warren Harding, who also golfed. Just before the American golfers sailed for England, Harding had played a round of golf with Chick Evans, so he had a personal interest in the contest overseas. The day after Wright's defeat, Harding called together his "golf cabinet" for a quasi-serious discussion of the grave "international situation precipitated by the inglorious defeat of the American golfers by the British." The president demanded to know how such a thing could happen. His cabinet was unable to answer the question and seemed dazed by the catastrophe. So the chief executive put the question to the attending newspaper correspondents: "Can anyone tell me what happened," he asked. "How did it come about? Frankly, I'm puzzled." There were various and heavy explanations. Finally, one correspondent explained simply: "No Prohibition." And the president joined in the laughter.[7]

Unlike previous presidents, Harding was a Grantland Rice "Sportlight" reader. As was Rice's custom, he had wished the new president good luck in verse in his column that spring, in conjunction with Harding's inauguration:

> Give us the team play that we've needed
> To drive together for the goal.
> Give us the dream for which we've pleaded
> That does not fear the braver role.
>
> A chief who'll be an inspiration
> Well worthy of the world's acclaim,
> Wherein a pennant winning nation
> Can follow one who plays the game.[8]

Harding wrote to Rice, thanking him for his kind wishes. "I have seen your verses in the *Tribune*," he wrote, "and wanted to drop you a line so that you would know of my grateful appreciation. Probably it is not important, but it will make me feel better if I have you know about it." Rice wrote back and asked after Harding's golf game, wondering if he might write about it. One thing led to another, and Harding eagerly accepted a golf date with Rice. Harding claimed he tried "to make it a point to play at least three afternoons in a week." He told Rice he wanted to take him on and to show him "how an official can forget the problems which are his."[9]

So early in April, before he was headed off to England, Rice, with Ring Lardner as his partner, met President Harding at the White House for lunch. This was to be followed by the golf match. Upon seeing Lardner, Harding said, "Rice is here to get a story. Why did you come?"

"I had a good reason," Lardner said. "I want to be appointed Ambassador to Greece."

"Why?" asked Harding.

"My wife doesn't like Great Neck," Lardner replied.

"That's a better reason than most people have," Harding responded.

The party adjourned to the Burning Tree golf club at Chevy Chase, Maryland. Harding brought his undersecretary of state, Henry Fletcher, to complete the foursome. The jolly foursome then went at it, well fortified by lunch and a good many highballs.

Rice's reporting on the president's game wasn't unlike his reporting on any other athletic curiosity. Rice described Harding's general abilities—he had "a good average game" that ranged between 95 and 100. Rice described his stance—square on every shot—as being much like Chick Evans's stance. And Harding's best club was the short mashie niblick over trouble, a tough shot for the best of golfers and which requires nerve and complete muscular control. Besides pointing to the few technical high points of Harding's game, Rice praised his habit of brooking no alibis. All in all, he reported, Harding was a regular human being, a hard fighter and a good loser; dignity without aloofness and a friendliness that was unforced. The article flattered both the man and his game.

Rice also flattered Fletcher by writing in the last paragraph of the article that the president "will have to go quite a distance before he picks up a better sportsman to team with than Henry P. Fletcher, Under Secretary of State, who also happens to be a golfer of no inconsiderable merit." This flattery did not go unnoticed. Fletcher followed up the *Trib* article with a thank-you note to Rice. Lardner and Rice had won the match, and Fletcher told Rice that he was "fully convinced that it was your clubs that were responsible for the tremendous walloping." Fletcher said that only if Rice had been playing with a baseball bat would the president and he have won. Finally, Fletcher concluded that on the basis of the last paragraph of the *Trib* article, "you are one of the most polite and accomplished diplomats I have ever met."[10]

But it was Lardner, never mistaken for a diplomat, who provided most of the day's fun. Rice recalled later that the president had a careless habit of hitting his tee shot and then absentmindedly walking right off the tee, on ahead of the foursome. On one hole Lardner was up next on the tee after Harding hit. Lardner called "Fore" a number of times, but Harding had walked on and was about forty yards down the course under an apple tree. Lardner hit his drive anyway, slicing the not-so-high-ball to the right, and directly for the apple tree. The ball struck a thick branch of the tree just above Harding's head, breaking the branch, and felling it onto Harding's shoulder. Startled, he waited for Lardner to walk to his ball and make the appropriate apologies. All Lardner said as he approached the president was, "I did all I could to make Coolidge president." Harding roared with laughter.[11]

Lardner wasn't through with Harding either. In Lardner's own account of the match, the scores were toted up at the nine-hole turn. The scorekeeper, Mr. Jarvis according to Lardner's account, read off the scores: Harding had a

54, Fletcher a 50, and Rice a 44. "Well," Lardner claimed he said, "I would rather be Rice than be President."[12]

Even if Harding and his golf cabinet couldn't fathom America's poor showing in the Amateur, Rice tried. He said it was a matter of different cultural traditions. Rice claimed that it was the "artisan golfer" who beat the Americans. The fact is that most American boys preferred playing baseball to golf—which was not so in England and Scotland. As the American boys grew into men, baseball playing usually stopped, whereas the young British or Scottish golfer continued to play around their jobs as clerks or mechanics or office workers. The reason was because they *could* continue. Playing golf in England or Scotland was cheap and within the means of almost everyone. In America, where golf was dominated by private clubs, the game was usually prohibitively costly for the average wage-earning American. So until the game was brought within the reach of everyone, Rice pointed out, the pool from which America drew its future champions would continue to be exclusive and small.[13]

After the men's loss, hopes were high that the American women could muster together for an upset win over the English. The British women's championship was to be held at Turnberry, Scotland, thirty miles out of Glasgow. Rice hustled to Turnberry to cover the matches. He noted a curious cultural difference between Scots and the Americans: in the United States, there was Prohibition but a strong interest in Sunday sport, while in Scotland, hanging wasn't enough for a heathen who played golf or other Sunday games, but they must have their Scotch. A Scot could inhale a quart of Scotch at one sitting, said Rice, but even "whistling on the Sabbath" was a heinous sin. The Scots, a wonderful people in every way, Rice noted, think Americans are crazy.[14]

America's best hope at Turnberry was the redheaded Alexa Stirling, out of Atlanta. As a youngster she and Bobby Jones played at the same course, East Lake, where golf professional Stuart Maiden, a Scotsman from Carnoustie, played. Stirling was Scottish by birth, having come over America from Scotland when she was seven. Stirling was Maiden's young pupil and Maiden was Bobby Jones's early role model and, later, his informal coach. She was the first golfer out of Atlanta—the city that would later be called the Golfing Capital of the World—to win a national championship. She won the U.S. Women's Amateur in 1916; when the championship was resumed after the war, she won again in 1919 and 1920; three successive wins.[15]

In late-nineteenth-century America, women were mostly golf onlookers while the men hacked around the club courses. The women were usually dressed in long and flaring skirts reaching to the ground, with heavy linings and dust-ruffles; huge hats precariously perched on their heads and held in place by enough long push pins to be used in a voodoo ritual; high boned collars, long puffy sleeves, and the unrelenting grip of whalebone, all of which made the women pay dearly for anything that could be mistaken for actual physical movement.[16]

By the turn of the century, the costumes loosened up a bit along with the social prohibitions against physical activity for women. Women graduated from Victorian-era games such as battledore, shuttlecock, croquet, and archery to slightly more robust, athletic games of tennis and golf. The boundaries of what constituted proper physical freedom for women were pushed even further, both socially and competitively, when they mounted the bicycle right along with the men. The "wheel" riding craze at the turn of the century helped change clothing styles too: women began wearing less restrictive clothing, including shorter and more comfortable skirts. Among the upper social strata, the Gibson girl image took hold, at least until World War I—women as wholesome, sophisticated, witty, and physically capable, comfortable on the tennis courts, at ease on the golf course, in control whether on horseback or bicycle.[17]

In golf, the American women had been competing against the British for the championship since the early 1900s. In 1905, Molly Adams, Margaret and Harriet Curtis, and Georgianna Bishop, the 1904 women's champion, along with a few others, went over to England for the competition. As a group, they were outplayed handily, although Adams got to the sixth round and Curtis to the fourth. Although from that point on Americans played more or less regularly in the British Amateur, the American women could only say they were gaining experience. None seriously challenged for the cup.[18]

In 1921, besides the veteran Cecil Leitch, who had won the British Amateur crown the previous year, the British golfers included the reigning English national champion, Joyce Wethered, who had defeated Leitch for that title, Molly Griffiths, who took second to Leitch in both the British and French championships, and Janet Jackson, the Irish champion. The British would dominate again this time, as Alexa Stirling unfortunately drew Cecil Leitch in the first round at Turnberry. Stirling, in part because of her Scottish ancestry, was popular in Scotland: she had "made a lasting hit over here," reported Rice, "with a combination that embraces a charm of manner, a lack of pretense and a corking good golf style." Nonetheless, Leitch beat Stirling 3 and 2 on the first day of the tournament in a driving rain and whistling wind. Leitch, in Rice's estimation, was simply a better golfer—more powerful and athletic. At 5'8" and 143 pounds, Leitch had the easy stride of an athlete, Rice reported.[19]

The remaining members of the American contingency, while fighting hard to stay in play, fell shortly thereafter, and all were out of the competition by the end of the third round. Though the showing of the Americans was distinctly disappointing, Rice noted after the competition that the players offered no complaints: "They are frank to admit the standard of play is higher here." Leitch won the Open after having come back twice from being one down with two to play.[20]

The other international sporting confrontations in early summer were either simultaneously scheduled or seriously overlapping, making it impossible for Rice to see them all in spite of what the *Tribune* had claimed before he set sail. "A combination of Henry J. Centipede and J. H. Argus might be able to cover the entire program if he had an airplane at his disposal with a Lick telescope attached," Rice wrote. The third week in June included the British Open and the Wimbledon tennis play, both starting on the same day. Polo began a couple of days before and continued after the golf and tennis matches.[21]

By the time the polo matches were to begin, Suzanne Lenglen, the French tennis idol, had already taken the tennis championship easily. Molla Mallory, Rice noted, fought with fine courage, but was overwhelmed by Lenglen's amazing skill, speed, power, and accuracy. Lenglen was not at all representative of French women's tennis of the day; she was exceptionally good. Even among the French it was admitted that she wasn't a typical French player, but "one of those rare geniuses that happen along once every three or four generations." Lenglen, groomed by her father for championship play, was only fourteen when she won the French Hard Courts championship; she made her first appearance at Wimbledon in 1919, winning the championship. By this time she was already a muscular and uninhibited player. "I just throw dignity to the winds," she is said to have said, "and think of nothing but the game." Besides being an athletic phenomenon, Rice thought she was a standout in every way: she was a flashy dresser—usually wearing low-cut, one-piece short dresses worn just below the knees—and had a temperament that combined coolness and dash, chance-taking and craft. At play, he wrote, she was astonishingly fast, active on her feet, a great jumper, and had fast and powerful hands. At her best, Rice marveled, "she is capable of giving a first-class male player a harder game than any woman that ever played. Two of Tilden's main qualities for example, are speed and power. They have helped to make him.

Mlle. Lenglen has both, not to a Tildenic degree, but to an abnormal one for a woman. There is no puff powder work about her play, not even when you compare it to the masculine game." The French star, he said, radiated personality. She was vivid in every way, "as vivid at play as a flash of flame." In the first match Rice saw, she wore a brilliant orange headband, presenting a striking contrast to her raven hair; in her second, it was a crimson band. He predicted that her confident, whirling and darting tennis style and her overall vigor and dash would make her a sensation when she came to America.[22]

Meanwhile, the first bright spot for the American party in England came with Bill Tilden's win at Wimbledon. Finally, Rice remarked, an American had come through. But in truth, Tilden's victory was about as predictable as Lenglen's. He had won Wimbledon the previous year. Even with a debilitating attack of boils and abscesses on his feet one week before the 1921 championship, he had plenty of foot speed to easily win the cup.[23]

William Tatem Tilden II, who had learned the game at the Germantown Cricket Club outside Philadelphia, was slower to master the game than the youthful Lenglen had been. Partly this was due to his odd upbringing for a boy in those times: he had received no encouragement to play any sports by his immediate family. His father was a huge man—Rice called him a "robust swashbuckler"—who was a leader of the Republican machine in Philadelphia and the president of the city's Union League Club. His mother was beautiful, tall, refined, and artistic—she had a voice trained for opera. Bill Tilden was raised by his mother and aunt and spent most of his youth dressed in Buster Brown collars and velvet suits. His mother died when he was eighteen; he lost his father four years later. By the time Tilden won his first national singles title in 1920, he was already twenty-seven. Rice had first met and covered "Big Bill" Tilden—he was about 6'4"—in 1919 at Forest Hills in the Nationals. Tilden got to the finals and was to play the veteran "Little Bill" Johnston, who, Rice said, was no bigger than a sack of concessionaire Harry M. Stevens's peanuts— Johnston weighed 121 pounds. Small or not, Johnston whipped the physically intimidating Tilden three sets to one, after discovering Tilden had a weak backhand stroke. That was the first and last time Johnston beat Tilden in a title match, as Tilden spent the next winter improving his backhand. He became practically unbeatable, winning the Nationals in 1920 and 1921. Thereafter he dominated the sport, winning through 1925 and then again in 1929.[24]

"You know," one English tennis expert commented when he saw Tilden play, "your Big Bill has such an extraordinary variety of strokes that I can't understand how he can decide upon his selection without getting confused." His cannonball serve and his change-of-pace chops and spins were a marvel to watch, especially in comparison with the slower and steadier hitting customary then. He also brought to the sport what Lenglen brought: color, a quality sportswriter Red Smith said typified the entire group of sporting heroes of the era—"there never was another troupe like this riot squad of the roistering 20s." For Tilden, the tennis court was a stage and his game a performance; he was stand-offish and show-offish. He, as much as any of the sporting giants of the time—Babe Ruth, Walter Hagen, Tommy Hitchcock, Jack Dempsey, Helen Wills, Red Grange, Gertrude Ederle, Bobby Jones— would come to be, in time, a national symbol of 1920s flamboyance, drama and melodrama, combativeness, melancholia, swagger, skill, graciousness, and greed.[25]

But for now, and on the international level, it was enough of a story that Tilden had won Wimbledon, again. The Americans who had lost in men's and women's amateur golf and women's tennis could breathe a bit easier, for the delegation of athletes could now go home with at least one cup in hand.

The polo matches were held at Hurlingham, England. Rice was no stranger to polo. He was fascinated by the sport, and had covered the 1913 international polo match in America. He watched then as the Big Four—Devereux Milburn, Harry Payne Whitney, and Larry and Monty Waterbury—defended the cup they had won in 1912 in dramatic fashion. In 1921, Milburn was captain of the U.S. Polo Team. Rice hadn't met him in person until now. The remaining members of the team were Watson Webb, Louis Stoddard, and a youngster who would change the sport from conventional short-passing-and-finesse to long-wallop-and-ride-like-hell, Tommy Hitchcock, Jr.

Hitchcock's father had captained the first American team that had faced the British at Newport around 1887. The son had been around the sport all his life, and developed into a fine rider and star junior player before the war. By the time America was dragged into the war, Tommy Hitchcock, Jr., had already enlisted as an ambulance driver. He was only eighteen. He volunteered for the French air service, the Lafayette Escadrille, and was one of the youngest flyers in France; he had brought down a few German planes before he was shot down behind the German lines. Somehow he survived the crash, was captured, and was sent to a German prison camp. The prison didn't hold him long: he promptly escaped and walked two hundred miles to freedom, living on herbs he could find along the wayside. Just shy of twenty-one in 1921, the fearless young man played in his first big international polo match with all the dash and confidence of an old-timer. Rice thought Hitchcock's life to this point was remarkable, "something one rarely sees beneath a sun that shines upon few novelties."[26]

Unless the American Four played at its absolute best, Rice predicted, the English team would retain the cup—they were more experienced, had more craft, and were chuckkers-full of Lords, Majors, and Colonels. For his uninitiated reader—in polo this was most of his readers—Rice explained that the game was sort of like English football, or soccer; a silly description, of course, because few of his readers knew anything about soccer either. Anyway, Rice put it this way: in polo, as in soccer, there are forwards, halfbacks, backs, and even goalkeepers, but instead of eleven people there are only four very energetic gentlemen, into whose persons the functions of eleven are crammed; the sides of a polo ground are usually boarded, made rigid so as to be used much as the cushion of a billiard table is used for shots. And, of course, the players weren't on foot. There you had it: on each team, four expert horsemen riding expensive, well-trained ponies. Of the fifty ponies the Americans were selecting from to create their stable of twelve, thirty-four were American-bred, most having come from Texas or California, with names like Teddy, Lucky Strike, Naughty Girl, and Auntie Agg.[27]

The English effusively praised the American team before the matches (it was a best-of-three series). They felt that the Americans were excellent, full of ginger, and would take a great deal of stopping. They described the American approach to polo as "the whirlwind Indian game," which, they said, was very sensibly based on how polo ought to be played. The American Indians, they thought, had always been the best expression of polo.

At age thirty-nine, Devereux Milburn was the American team's backbone. Rice thought he was perhaps the best back in the game and provided the steadiness to compensate for Hitchcock's tendencies to take big gambles. What Rice liked especially about Milburn was his approach to the game, which was essentially Rice's approach to sport too. The loquacious Milburn explained that winning, as the only goal of competitive sport, was overrated. "That is a lot of nonsense," Milburn said. "It is the battle—the contest—that counts, not the score. If two meet, one must win and one must lose. But they can both have a great afternoon!"[28]

The United States had three great afternoons, and two winning ones, as the U.S. Polo Team surprised the English with a convincing victory. The Americans had another cup to take back home. Hitchcock rose to the occasion, "playing with the power and dash of youth plus all the finesse of a veteran who had known many polo wars," said Rice. Milburn gave much credit for the victory to Hitchcock, who he called one of the greatest polo players in the world. "With a bit more experience, I believe he will be the greatest polo player of all time. . . . A great rider, a mighty hitter, a world of courage and stamina and a knack for the game." Much to the frustration of the English, this new Big Four—Stoddard, Webb, Milburn, and Hitchcock—was even better than the strong American team that dominated international polo play between 1909 and 1914.[29]

The continuing rub against America, from the English side at least, was their good-natured criticism of the way in which they believed the typical American competitor took his or her game: with utmost seriousness, a grim determination, and an earnest desire to win that was sometimes so strong as to squeeze out the joy of the competition itself. This was becoming more and more evident to the English as the Americans began to win British championships: first there was Tilden's high-strung approach to tennis, and now the reckless and aggressive play of young Hitchcock in the polo cup victory.

Bobby Jones, who was even younger than Hitchcock, would give the British a glorious example of this American way in sport in the British Open at the famed St. Andrews in Scotland. In 1920 at Deal, the Open was resumed after a five-year hiatus due to the war. Two Englishmen and two Scots finished in the first four, with America's top finisher, English-born-and-raised Jim Barnes, in fifth, the highest any American had ever finished in the twenty championships of the previous twenty-five years.[30]

Rice had known Bobby Jones for almost all of his nineteen years. Jones was born the same year Rice began writing for the *Journal*. When Rice got to Atlanta in 1902 he immediately looked up one of his good friends, Bob Jones, Sr., by then a local Atlanta attorney. Jones Sr. had played baseball for Mercer and had competed against Rice's Vanderbilt teams. They became friends. The Jones family lived in East Lake and just off the 13th fairway of the country club. The youngster's regular playing partners were Alexa Stirling and Perry Adair. Adair was the son of Atlanta real estate investor George Adair, a friend of Bob Sr. The older Adair was a sportsman, a gentleman, and the man who did more for golf in Atlanta then than anyone had ever done.[31]

By age five, Bobby had already started swinging a cut-down golf club; at nine he won the junior championship at East Lake; at thirteen he shot his first 80 on the tough East Lake course (only two par threes) and could drive the ball 240 to 250 yards; at fourteen he battled Perry Adair, who was three years older, to win the first Georgia State Championship, shooting a 70 in the afternoon round; and halfway through his fourteenth year he was already competing for the U.S. Amateur title in 1916 at Philadelphia's Merion Golf Club. Rice was then thirty-six and writing his column for the *Tribune* syndicate. He covered the tournament.

Jones's main problem in these early years was his temperament. He was a perfectionist: if every shot wasn't played up to his expectations, he blew. He was a hothead, a fighting cock, a club thrower, said Rice. At Merion, Jones was a sensation because of his young age, his good looks, and the obvious skill packed into the stocky 5'4", and 165-pound body. He was dubbed the "Boy Wonder" and the "Kid From Dixie." Jones qualified with a tournament-leading 74 in the morning round. In the afternoon round the gallery discovered the new phenomenon; the crowd's presence didn't help the youngster, as at the end of the round his card showed an 89. His combined scores still qualified Jones for the championship match rounds.

His first match was against Eben Byers, a veteran and the 1906 Amateur Champion. Rice had breakfast with Jones, advising him that Byers had a temper and wasn't above wrapping his hickory shafts around the nearest tree. The group of golfers playing behind Byers and Jones that day said that from a distance, it looked like a juggling act as the two players would hit, thrash around in agony, and then hurl their club in the air. At the twelfth hole, Byers threw a club over a hedge and clear off the golf course; he forbade his caddie to retrieve it. Jones eventually won the match, but in his view only because Byers had run out of clubs first. Jones survived until the quarterfinals, where he lost 5 and 3 to Robert Gardner, the defending champion. Chick Evans eventually won the Amateur that year.[32]

A year later, with World War I well underway, the U.S. Golf Association sponsored War Relief charity matches in and around New York City. As up-and-coming young golfers, Adair and Jones were sent up from Georgia to play in these popular affairs. With the Rices in New York, Bob Sr. asked Grantland and Kate to look after the twosome. Kate insisted that they stay with the Rices in their apartment at 450 Riverside Drive. The five of them, Kit and Granny along with ten-year-old Floncy, Perry, and Bobby, had a wonderful time. Rice reflected years later, "While Floncy scampered about and Kit burst her buttons to entertain Bob and Perry, I'd bang away at the typewriter getting out my column. Our living room reminded me of a set from *You Can't Take It With You*."[33]

In reading Rice's recollections of those days, combined with his faithful coverage of Bobby Jones's career play until his last round of tournament golf, also at Merion, after winning the Big Four in 1930 (U.S. Open and Amateur, the British Open and Amateur), it is clear that Rice cared a great deal for Jones. Almost like father and son. On Jones's stay in New York that year, Rice remembered how much Kit and he enjoyed having the two partly grown-up "sons" about the place. "How Kit, Floncy, and I relished their stay. One evening I took the entire brood to Coney Island—a great trip. We didn't miss a ride! It was during their stay that Bob and I became acquainted in a way few persons with a gap of 20-odd years between them ever do." Except for Jones's Boswell, sportswriter O. B. Keeler, no other writer, or anyone else for that matter, watched Jones as carefully or as caringly as Rice did.

In 1921, Jones was playing in the British Open at St. Andrews. With fellow amateurs Travers, Evans, and Oiumet, Jones joined the American professionals Jock Hutchinson, "Long" Jim Barnes, and Walter Hagen, who the previous year hadn't shot one round under 80 and had not finished even in the top fifty—a performance Rice said was "too dismal for words." As a group the Americans aimed to win, but their confidence was down, as Rice observed: "American golfers may get somewhere at St. Andrews British Open, but after what happened at Hoylake and Turnberry dejected Americans can only see another debacle in historic Fyfe." Rice agreed that there was little hope to hold off the British in what was looking more and more like a clean golfing sweep for them.[34]

Rice did play St. Andrews just before the Open began and found the Old Course along the North Sea to be fairly easy—except for the ever-present wind and gale conditions—when compared to some American courses such as the National, Lido, or Pine Valley (in Scotland Rice thought that the newer Gleneagles course was the best of the lot). On this basis, he predicted that of the Americans, the course should suit Jock Hutchinson's drive and pitch game in particular. In addition, Hutchinson was actually born and reared at St. Andrews, giving him almost a home-course advantage over all the other Americans and many of the internationals. The big names for the American opposition were George Duncan, a Scot, and veterans Ted Ray and Abe Mitchell, both Englishmen. Rice mentioned that Bobby Jones wasn't thought of as a potential winner, but that as a youngster he was "capable of almost any surprise, as he will not be working under any strain."[35]

And what a surprise it was. In the qualifying rounds, the Americans did well. Charlie Hoffner came in lowest of all the golfers at 73. Jones shot a respectable 76, Hutchinson a 77, and Barnes a 78. Jones held his own in round two, but in the third round his play deteriorated. He took forty-six strokes to finish the front nine. Starting the backside, he took a ghastly 6 on 10 and on the short 11th he needed a good putt just to get another 6. Bobby Jones then did the unforgivable. Before his putt and while standing on the putting green, he stooped over, picked up his ball, walked off the course, and withdrew from the competition. He quit, in the middle of America's remarkably solid efforts to win the international cup.

Jones was blasted by everyone, especially the writers in the British press, who thought such an action was reprehensible and an attack against the old game itself. Such behavior, they claimed, typified the Americans' over-serious nature. Jones's temperament and irreverence was exhibited then and there within full view of the entire world. Keeler would later remark that he thought that failing to finish his first tournament at St. Andrews was to become Jones's only real lifelong regret. Jones admitted that it was a terrible mistake and that he was embarrassed then, and from then on.

At the time of Jones's regrettable decision to walk off the course, Rice couldn't bring himself to say much about the incident in print, although he must have had a few choice words to say in private to the youngster. One month later when Jones was to play in the U.S. Open at the Columbia Country Club in Washington, D.C, Rice, when doping out the front-runners, said that "when Bobby Jones can fall heir to greater serenity and can build up a philosophy that will not permit mistakes to warp his mental poise he has the game to get anywhere."[36]

In the end, this single moment at St. Andrews was the turning point in Jones's career. At age nineteen, he was forced to face himself, didn't like what he saw, and set about to change it. He would never do any such thing in tournament or championship golf again, and his future deportment would become the benchmark of what it meant to play the game fairly and with honor and respect. Within a couple of years—and while finishing one degree at Georgia Tech and another at Harvard, and following in his father's footsteps by preparing to become an attorney—Jones gradually became a bona fide national and international sporting hero/celebrity of the ticker-tape variety.[37]

As the play continued at St. Andrews, one American golfer in particular, Jock Hutchinson, was dead-set to win back the championship for the United States. The Open was a seventy-two-hole medal tournament. After two rounds, Hutchinson was in first place, having shot a combined 147. But in round three, the Scottish American faltered and shot a 79, dropping him to eighth place. Meanwhile, the Oxford amateur, Roger Wethered, who had been sitting six strokes behind Hutchinson after the first two rounds, played round three in a remarkable 72 and broke the amateur record for the course. Surprising everyone, including himself, the normally weak-finishing Wethered continued his charge in the fourth round by breaking the course record for all golfers, shooting a 71 and playing the last twelve holes five strokes better than even 4's. His two-round day took only 143 strokes.[38]

Wethered had finished the fourth round before Hutchinson started; Jock knew in advance that he had to shoot at least a 70—better than anyone had ever shot—just to tie Wethered. Which he did, shooting exactly 70 to tie. The determined Hutchinson then won the playoff the next day. It was Uncle Sam over John Bull.

After their weak start, the American delegation returned home with three cups: one in tennis, one in polo, and a surprising one in golf.

Even though the Rice family's seven-week jaunt through the British Isles and France came to an end the last week of June, Rice's reporting on international sporting competitions of the day wasn't over. Barely a week after he found his land legs again, Rice was in Jersey City at Boyle's Thirty Acres covering an event of worldwide significance that had been brewing for nearly two years, which would draw the largest crowd in the history of sport and would be billed, legitimately, as the Battle of the Century; it would bring in a gate of well over a million dollars, and would once again cause Rice to wonder what the word "golden" meant in this, the Golden Age of Sport.

Customarily, when Rice spoke of the golden age of sport, he used the phrase to compare contemporary sports to a golden age of literature or a golden age of art. He was referring to an age that would be remembered for producing extraordinary and collective human excellence, creativity, and performance. He was also referring to the extraordinary popularity of watching and playing sports: "Crowds have never been as great. . . . There has never been a time in all history when as many, young and old, were taking an active interest in so many outdoor competitions." This was a big age, he said, and the sports champions—Stirling, Leitch, Lenglen, Tilden, Johnston, Chick Evans, Paddock, and Babe Ruth—were the pacemakers of this age. "No wonder," he wrote, "the populace is stirred up as the palpitating multitude were never stirred before."39

Yet Rice also knew that when the word "golden" began to mean only making money ("kale" as it was commonly called) instead of achieving something of moral value, then the motivation for sport becomes extrinsic instead of intrinsic. "Money is a wonderful institution," Rice wrote, "it is the basis of more than a few things in life, and in more than a few things is a leading incentive, acting as a spur to far keener endeavor. But in sport, for several reasons, the influence is far from being 100 per cent good."40

What Rice meant by the word "keener" was the older and broader meaning of the word; besides the more modern definition of sharp, alert, intense, and responsive, being keen in the older sense meant being brave. And money, Rice thought, compromised the spirit of keenness in sport. He reminded his readers of a certain episode in the life of D'Artagnan, the fighting Gascon of Dumas's *The Three Musketeers*. When he had nothing but his sword, he was ready for any danger, any adventure that might turn up, and to be taken with all the thrill of sport. But later in his career he amassed a large fortune. Riding along one day quite alone, this thought struck him with stunning suddenness: "I am rich—but am I any longer brave?"[41]

For Rice such keenness—the very condition of any golden age—comes by way of testing one's own mettle, by way of *doing* something, by way of striving; in sport, keenness comes from the clash, the strain, and the stress of competition. "Strength in the main comes from the clash of battle, not the spoils of victory," lectured Rice at the front end of a decade in sport when there was every sign that commercial success was becoming an easy substitute for the more difficult to achieve nobility of purpose. When this keenness is "overshadowed by a cloud of kale the old keenness departs." For the lasting good of sport, Rice thought, this confusion over what should be its *summum bonum* shouldn't be allowed. And even though sportswriters in general, through their booming and hype, were responsible in part for this incredible modern popularity of sport, he also believed that as a group they were no less responsible for pointing out and thereby preserving what was keen in the midst of all the kale.[42]

This wasn't ever easy, since as the French sometimes said of the Americans, no American can speak a complete sentence without figures in it. While this may have been a slight exaggeration, it was on the money when speaking of American boxing managers and promoters. It was clear that both Jack Kearns and Tex Rickard could speak fluent "kale" when the two men, who still hated each other, got together again to promote another Jack Dempsey match, this time against the French idol, Georges Carpentier, at Boyles Thirty Acres, a fen just outside of Jersey City, on July 2, 1921.[43]

Carpentier, who the American press dubbed "The Orchid Man," was a legitimate French, even European, hero. During the war Carpentier, an aviator, had been decorated a time or two for heroism; he was wounded twice by shrapnel too, once in the head and once in the right foot. Before and in the early years of the war—his career dated back a dozen years—Carpentier boxed reasonably well, beating American boxers such as Gunboat Smith and Kid Jackson and winning the light heavyweight title from Battling Levinsky; but he had a tendency to avoid losing fairly. When he discerned that he was going to be beaten, he either faked being hit below the belt in an attempt to win on a technicality, or he dropped his opponent by smacking him in the same location in an effort to lose on a technicality. In either case, the outcome wasn't actual, merely technical.[44]

What made Carpentier especially attractive to the fans was that he was especially attractive. That is, he didn't look or behave one whit like what a boxer was supposed to look or behave like. He was unmarked—no facial cuts or cauliflowered ears—and clear-complexioned and light-skinned. He also smiled a lot. His bearing was aristocratic, although he was in fact born in a French coal-mining town. He had closets full of fancy clothes, played bridge and billiards, and loved opera, dancing, plays, and highbrow literature. He was slender of build but nearly perfectly proportioned, causing writers, especially the female columnists, to compare him to a Greek warrior. He was well mannered, and his movement was graceful and ethereal, like a dancer's might be. To everyone, even the French, he was exactly what it meant to be French in the best of senses: he was gallant, intelligent, courteous, debonair, and brave.

Carpentier had recently earned his worldwide recognition in boxing by taking on England's best, Joe Beckett. Although most of the experts had picked the muscular two-hundred-pound Beckett to win, Carpentier flattened the English champion after a short flurry of punches in the first round. That contest helped get him the fight with Dempsey.

A Dempsey-Carpentier bout appealed to Kearns and Rickard because it offered the spectacle of a hero versus a villain. A medieval morality play. Good versus bad. It didn't matter that Dempsey, Kearns's fighter, was to be the villain and the hero would be a foreigner. Besides the difference in the two fighters' overall comportment, their comparative war service was useful to whip up interest in the bout. On almost exactly the same day that Carpentier dispatched Beckett, Dempsey's former wife, Maxine, gave a letter to the *San Francisco Chronicle* claiming that Dempsey's status as 4-A was obtained on false grounds. Her charges eventually resulted in Dempsey's famous "slacker trial" even though by the time the grand jury indicted Dempsey and Kearns in early February 1920 Maxine had recanted her story. Dempsey was eventually exonerated of the charge in a court of law, but the stigma of being a draft-dodger lingered.

Whether or not the sports age was to be golden in the commercial sense was answered when it was revealed that Dempsey's guarantee was to be three hundred thousand dollars and Carpentier's two hundred thousand. Dempsey's purse was more than the president of the United States would make in four years in office. In addition, each fighter was to receive 25 percent of the motion picture rights. This, and the hero/villain portrayal, grabbed worldwide attention that was clearly out of proportion to the actual significance of the contest. "For here are two men of ordinary mold," Rice reflected, "outside of one accomplishment, who for months have known more printed space than the presidents, kings and premiers of a dozen nations—than wars and rumors of wars—than all the foreign relations of a badly tangled world."[45]

In the middle of his hectic coverage of the British championships, Rice relayed to his readers occasional international opinions on the Dempsey-Carpentier fight. Not surprisingly, the foreigners believed that Carpentier could take Dempsey in spite of Dempsey's size advantage. They had seen heavyweight Fred Fulton fight in Europe; he was 6'5" and 240 pounds. They were told that Willard was even bigger. And Dempsey knocked Willard down seven times . . . well, the imagination took over. The word across the Atlantic was that Carpentier would prevail.[46]

In France, Rice reported just weeks before the big match, Carpentier was their "man of destiny." Since France had never in its history had a heavyweight champion, the mere fact that Carpentier was even fighting for the title was monumental. Rice noted that the French generally regarded their pugilists differently than Americans did theirs. In France, to be a boxer is to not just be heroic, but to be a social lion. Perhaps because the Americans have had so many top-rated boxers, their public takes them more casually, Rice speculated. More accurately, though, the typical French boxer was simply a healthy cut above the American boxers when it came to social grace, substance, and conformation.

Carpentier's physical appearance exaggerated even further the pugilistic differences between the two cultures, for as English writer and boxing fan and critic Arnold Bennett observed of Carpentier, "He might have been a barrister, a poet, a musician, a Foreign Office attaché, a Fellow of All Souls; but not a boxer." So, direct from France, Rice relayed to his American readers why the French were so taken with Carpentier: "So after all these gray centuries have come and gone, just when sport is in its golden age, a Carpentier arrives, and who can blame France for its ecstasy? And who, if Carpentier should win, could withhold hearty congratulations for her first heavyweight championship in twenty centuries?"[47]

But back in the States, Dempsey was the odds-on favorite to win, even if he wasn't the good guy. When Rice discussed what it would take for Carpentier to win, he concluded that since Dempsey had a twenty-pound size advantage and since Carpentier hadn't ever proved he could absorb real punishment, the Frenchman's chance to win depended entirely on an early, quick, and lucky punch.

Thirty-one hours before the fight, Rice came to some conclusions of his own. First, he didn't overintellectualize the fight by talking of good and evil, virtue and vice, or even Old World versus New World. Even if heavily hyped, he pointed out that this was still just a boxing match between two capable fighters. Second, he wished the two boxers a good night's sleep: "In the *Art of Preserving Health* you will read, 'O, sleep before you fight. Tis not too late tomorrow to be brave.'" Third, he thought that neither boxer was rightly trained for the fight: Dempsey, sparring practically daily in Atlantic City, had trained too much in the "jarring whirl of the crowd"; Carpentier, sequestered by his manager François Descamps in a barbed-wire-enclosed farmhouse in Manhasset, Long Island, sparred little, seemingly did little, and made "no violent effort to toughen his fibre against the punishment he will be forced to weather." When Ring Lardner and Frank Graham found their way to Carpentier's camp, only to be turned away at the gate, Lardner was so irritated that the next day he wrote that maybe it was all right that they were refused entrance, since the Frenchman had probably been practicing his ten-second nap.[48]

Fourth, Rice thought that there was an unknown psychological factor that figured into the fight as well. Since Dempsey had been sold as the villain in the promotion, there was no telling how the fans would react when he stepped into the ring. It was uncommon in sports for an athlete to be on his own home ground yet not be the crowd's favorite. "If this disfavor is openly shown," Rice observed, "no prophet can foretell the result, since no prophet can read aright the many possibilities of the human mind." In other words, if the crowd openly jeered Dempsey, or if they simply cheered louder for Carpentier, then Rice figured Dempsey could either droop and lose his ambition, or he could "lash himself into a destructive fury that would add steam to his punches." Interestingly, throughout his coverage of this fight Rice avoided using the slacker stuff against Dempsey; this could have been for any number of reasons: that the slacker trial vindicated Dempsey, that Rice's view had softened in the two years since the Willard fight, or that Rice had learned since the Willard fight that Dempsey, although a mauler in the ring, was gentle, sensitive, even timid, and a lover of children and animals, outside of boxing.

And finally, Rice pointed out that Dempsey had the most to lose and least to gain. Carpentier, a forlorn hope, merely had to show well, be gallant; if he lost, his worldwide following would still praise his gameness to step into the ring against the larger and stronger brawler. If Dempsey won, he would merely retain his championship against a much smaller opponent who was also the underdog. If Carpentier won, Rice noted, "he moves to a height Dempsey as champion could never know."

After he got his ruminating out of the way, Rice predicted that the fight wouldn't be a long one. He picked Dempsey to win and named the round. "The odds are that the battle ends in the immediate vicinity of the fourth round, with Dempsey in spite of psychology, the one most likely to be upon his feet." He commented on the silliness of George Bernard Shaw's prediction over in Europe that Carpentier could not lose and that he ought to be a 50 to 1 favorite. As the fight approached, the actual odds were about 2 to 1 for Dempsey.[49]

To encourage the some seven hundred sportswriters covering the fight to do what he thought was their job, namely hype the fight, Doc Kearns pushed the booze in their direction. In his room he had stacked cases of bootleg liquor, Prohibition be damned. Dempsey said later in his life that Doc told Rickard what to do on this matter of publicity: "Rickard, you'll make a million bucks if you listen to me and do as I say. Put a case of booze—Scotch, bourbon, gin—whatever you want, in each newspaperman's room. This way not only will they write, but they'll write good—if they can write at all! I know those guys." The fight grossed over $1.7 million. Kearns's advice was right.[50]

Five hundred million people were waiting anxiously for The Story of Three O'Clock, Rice gushed in what he called "The Day of the Fist":

> Poets and sculptors and writers
> Fall out of line for a spell,
> Step to one side with the blighters
> Who have only genius to sell.
> Where the crowd surges, elated,
> Kindly, I pray you, desist.
>
> Brains are a bit overrated,
> This is the Day of the Fist!
> . . . .
> There is still room for a college,
> There is still place for the brain.
> Those who are plastered with knowledge
> Have not wholly labored in vain.
> But learning not labor yet bothers
> The ghosts where our forbears exist.
> There's a whiff from the Cave of our Fathers,
> So this is the Day of the Fist.[51]

Boyle's Thirty Acres was only twenty minutes from New York. As was common whenever it was convenient, Kate Rice joined her husband for the Event. Kate was good friends with the wife of Rice's *Tribune* colleague, W. O. McGeehan. Sophie Treadwell McGeehan, a reporter in her own right, had been commissioned by the *Tribune* to cover the fight from a woman's perspective. In the hour or so before the bout, Kit and Sophie mixed with the crowd; part of Sophie's story covered the surprisingly large New York magnates contingent in attendance—John D. Rockefeller, Henry Ford, some Astors, William H. Vanderbilt, Jay Gould, Harry Payne Whitney. "The names at ringside," wrote Irvin Cobb of the *New York Times,* "would sound like the reading of the first hundred pages of 'Who's Ballyhoo on America.' "[52]

It had been raining on and off that day, and when it began to sprinkle, Kit and Sophie ducked into a little exit to somewhere to get out of the rain. The two ladies found themselves in an unoccupied small room and sat down on a rubbing table to wait out the rain. Just then a policeman came in, saying, "Ladies, where do you think you are?" "We're just trying to get out of the rain," they answered. "You've got to leave. You're in the Frenchman's dressing room!" replied the officer.

As the officer was escorting the women out of the dressing room, at that moment Carpentier came down the corridor. What Kit and Sophie saw told them all they needed to know about the likely outcome of the match. Kit recalled Carpentier as he approached them: "Dressed, he was as white as a sheet . . . thin . . . and Oh Lord, but he looked frightened. And several steps behind, wearing trunks and a heavy red sweater, and unshaven, came Dempsey—big, tough and bristling. He dwarfed the cops guarding him. I looked at Sophie who, of course, was staring. Studying the contrast between the two men, she said, 'That poor French boy. Why he'll be murdered!' We returned to our seats and waited for the Angel of Doom to claim Carpentier."[53]

The rain stopped finally; the sun shone brightly and the perspiration flowed profusely in the stifling humidity. During the lengthy preliminary matches, Rice sat in the ringside press area along with McGeehan, Heywood Broun, and his friend Don Marquis. Marquis, who wasn't actually covering the event, tried to stay cool by pouring twenty-five-cent bottles of White Rock mineral water over his head. He pretended to believe that the same two men were fighting for the entire two hours of the preliminaries; he admitted that some were knocked down and dragged out but he claimed that they merely went under the ring and then came back again.

At five minutes to three, with the preliminaries ended, a tremendous roar shook the seven-acre arena as Georges Carpentier entered the ring. He was dressed in a dove-gray robe with wide black piping at the cuffs and the edges. Rice said he leaped lightly through the ropes and returned the applause of the ninety thousand fans with a friendly smile and a wave of two clasped hands. Rice said that unless Carpentier was a great actor, he didn't show the slightest sign of anxiety, even appearing carefree; but Treadwell, who had had that closer look in the corridor, knew better and wrote that the challenger was close-shaven, unusually pale, and showed a "strange, strained and crooked smile." She observed that he "looked exactly like a clever, elusive, but guilty young gentleman who knew at last that the jig was up and was going along to headquarters to face the music."[54]

At 2:58, another roar went up, this time for Dempsey's entrance; this roar answered Rice's question with regard to how the champion would be received by the crowd: apparently with at least as much enthusiasm as for the foreigner, if not slightly more. No one really booed; there were a few isolated cries about Dempsey being a slacker. Dempsey wore only long white trunks with an American flag stitched to the belt, some red, white, and blue ribbons around his waist, his red sweater, and a cap tilted back on his head. Somehow a hint of a smile broke through his frowning and scowling and unshaven face, answering the applause, but Rice said he looked pretty grim and tense as he went to his corner. Kate looked at Sophie, squeezed her arm, and said, "It's all over."[55]

For the world, the fight was now the thing. It was even to be the first boxing match broadcast on radio, with Major Andrew White and J. O. Smith calling the fight. Ironically, the story that should have been the biggest news of the day was barely noticed: news of President Warren Harding signing the peace agreement formally ending World War I was wedged into a few single column inches in the next day's papers, while the fight news covered the rest of the papers' front pages and many pages following. At the signing, when the president was informed who had won the other fight, the one in Boyle's Thirty Acres, he showed little interest and asked merely, "Was it a good fight?"[56]

It may not have been a good fight, but it wasn't really a bad one either. Rice's lead was, "Human flesh and bone are still softer than iron. At 3:16 Georges Carpentier stood in the center of the ring receiving one of the greatest ovations ever given a fighter. At 3:27 the Lily of France lay stretched out upon the resin, now only one of the Broken Blossoms of pugilism."[57]

For three rounds, Carpentier more or less stood upright against Dempsey's crushing blows. But in the fourth, the round Rice had predicted, the champion's edge in weight, power, and strength showed itself, as he knocked Carpentier down with successive right and left hooks to the jaw. At the count of nine the Frenchman struggled to his feet and actually sprang, like a cat, at the waiting Dempsey, only to be met with a short right hook above the heart followed by a right to the jaw that dropped him like he'd been shot through the head. There was a quiver of leg movement at "eight," but nothing more thereafter as Carpentier was counted out by referee Harry Ertle.

In the first round, Carpentier, who fought straight ahead, almost lunging and parrying like a fencer, attempted a few quick intended-knockout punches. They didn't phase Dempsey. The surprisingly patient American, ever moving from side to side, was content to fight inside, throwing and landing body punches at will. The few head shots Dempsey threw, landed; the challenger's nose was bleeding and he had a cut over his right eye. Dempsey was cautious, for sure, perhaps remembering Tex Rickard's last words in the dressing room just before the fight: "Listen, Jack, take it easy on Carpentier. Give the people out there a good run for their money, but be careful. Don't kill him. Don't kill everything." Everything, of course, referred to this gate and all the future gates.

Marquis, meanwhile, had by the first round already doused himself with $3.50 worth of White Rock, trying to cool off. Still quite heated up, he decided to switch to Ruppert's beer. When the fight started, Marquis stood up, spilling water and beer in all directions, and began shouting "Carpentier! Carpentier! Carpentier!" and reproducing every one of the Frenchman's leads on his fellow reporter's heads, writers who were otherwise busy working on their own leads. When he tired of his jutting and thrusting lefts and rights and rights and lefts and as his voice began to give out, Marquis sat down in the midst of the broken bottles and said to his seatmate, Heywood Broun, "Now, you do it." Which Broun did. After all, this was not the era when sportswriters were admonished before each event, "There shall be no cheering in the pressbox."

In the weeks before the fight Broun said he had been for Dempsey. But after Carpentier stepped into the ring, he just couldn't bring himself to root for the American. Broun thought he was too methodical, too efficient. He admitted to his sentimentality: "Romance is silly stuff, but that doesn't prevent it from getting to you." Cheering for Dempsey, he said, "would be like giving three long cheers for the guillotine as Sydney Carton went up to meet it where it waited."

In fact, Broun went so far as to report that the challenger was "within a punch of the championship" in the second round. Dempsey crowded Carpentier early in round two, pelting him with inside punches. In the middle of the round Carpentier went on the offense, hitting Dempsey with a right, a left, and two more rights. A surprised Dempsey became momentarily defensive, and then Carpentier landed his best punch of the fight, a solid right to Dempsey's jaw that crashed down with a thud. Dempsey was back on his heels, arms down, and Carpentier followed with a mighty uppercut that missed. Broun maintained that had that uppercut landed, the challenger would have been champion. Dempsey, he admitted, had the better blows, but all the "good gestures" were Carpentier's. "The tragedy of life," Broun philosophized, "is not that man loses but that he almost wins."[58]

But Carpentier's moment of destiny came and passed. The powerful right he had thrown to Dempsey's jaw had broken the Frenchman's thumb in two places and sprained his wrist. That was what Rice meant in his lead by the essential softness of bone and flesh when up against iron, the cast-iron jaw of Jack Dempsey. It was here that Carpentier lost his steam. "He had landed with all the fury and power at his command," Rice wrote, "and yet his opponent, after rocking for one brief moment upon shaking legs, was again boring in with left and heavy right working as if he had never been brushed by a hostile glove." And a Marne for France turned into a Waterloo two rounds later, as Dempsey finished the Frenchman off with the right hook that dropped him with such force that Carpentier's feet flew high into the air, quivering, and huddled as they fell back to the floor.

As the challenger fell, and the count reached ten, Dempsey was the first to reach the fallen French idol. He helped pick up the bleeding and groggy fighter and carry him to his corner. After Carpentier's brain had cleared a bit and he could stand on his feet, Dempsey went to Carpentier, who was trying to smile, and said, "I am only sorry I had to knock out such a good man."

In the minutes after the fight, the world was alerted to its outcome. From ringside, all French ships at sea received this cabled flash, an all-time-low in international diplomacy: "Your Frog flattened in the fourth." In Paris, it was previously arranged that six army airplanes would fly over the city displaying red lights if Carpentier won, white lights if Dempsey was the victor. To the consternation of the Parisians, the planes flew the white.

Typically, a variety of American ministers and other religious moralists condemned the fight. Reverend John Roach Straton of the Calvary Baptist Church in New York City told his congregation that he went to the fight to get a firsthand look at the depravity of the 1920s. At ringside, he reported, he witnessed collective sin in the form of materialism, lawlessness, militarism, and immorality. He was particularly offended that so many women and "little girls" were exposed to the "half naked" men. Broun reported that it was actually a comfort to have Mr. Straton so close at hand: "Often we have been terrified at his expressed belief in divine vengeance falling upon the activities of assembled crowds of whose activities Mr. Straton disapproved. We felt cheered at the thought that there was hardly room for a thunderbolt to come between us and Mr. Straton."[59]

Nonetheless, for all except the ministers and perhaps those who were cheering for Carpentier, the fight ended as it was supposed to have ended. It was merely the old, old story, wrote Rice, of the good big man and the good little man, in which, if form runs true, there is only one ending to be written. "He was a good, game guy," Rice wrote of Carpentier, "but he never had a chance."[60]

13

It's the Big Blooie That Makes All the Talk

In the same way that champion athletes become household names, Grantland Rice by the mid-1920s was no mere sportswriter any more than Babe Ruth was a mere baseball player. Rice's celebrity status came not by pursuing it but by demonstrating honest productivity and established authority. Even if there were some who didn't much like his perpetually cheery, "Gee Whiz!" angle to competitive sport, no one could deny his range of sports information and knowledge, general goodwill, friendly habits, sense of humor, or professional and personal commitment to the high road when it came to confronting moral dilemmas.

Of course none of this was taken too seriously by Rice himself. He was prouder to be a member in good standing of the Society of Silurians than he was to have played golf with the president of the United States. The Silurians, an organization of "old-time New York ink-poisoned wretches," got its name in the early 1920s when, in a routine saloon get-together of veteran New York reporters, David G. Baillie—a *New York Tribune* political reporter and scholar—suggested, tongue in cheek, that they call themselves Silurians after the fossils of the geological period that produced the first air-breathing land animals. And among these self-declared lowlifes, Grantland Rice was perhaps the lowest. Which meant that he was a most revered Silurian, even when compared to the likes of such talented writers as Ring Lardner, Heywood

Broun, Damon Runyon, Paul Gallico, Westbrook Pegler, W. O. McGeehan, and John Kieran. It was fellow Silurian Gene Fowler who was to eventually dub Grantland Rice the Dean of American Sportswriters.[1]

Achieving this honorific status was due, in part, to being a hustling Silurian by the mid-1920s. "Yet, as much as he loved fun," John Wheeler said of him, "he was also a disciplined craftsman who turned out a prodigious amount of work." Rice had fully recovered his financial base by now, and then some; this particular Silurian was becoming quite wealthy, from a number of sources.[2]

He was being paid in the neighborhood of fifty thousand dollars a year for his *Tribune* duties, which included his Sportlight columns for the *Tribune* syndicate and his at-least-weekly golf column, Tales of a Wayside Tee. Sportlight was syndicated in anywhere from eighty to one hundred papers nationally, depending on who was counting, and had a likely total circulation of around ten million. He also made royalties from the earlier books of verse, *Baseball Ballads* and *Songs of the Stalwart*, and, after 1924, from *Songs of the Open*, and from his other published books, *The Winning Shot* with Jerome Travers, *The Boys Book of Sports*, and a selection of Rice columns, *Sportlights of 1923* (published in 1924). And he made money from his almost weekly magazine articles for *Collier's*, which he had been writing since 1915, and his occasional articles for *American Magazine*, *McClure's*, *Outing*, *Literary Digest*, and *Country Life*.

Rice also earned a salary as editor, with Innis Brown, of *American Golfer*. His contract with Centurion, its publisher, was set at a base of seventy-five hundred dollars per year, plus dividends earned as a percentage of the magazine's profits. Rice's *American Golfer* income alone matched the wages of the average major-league baseball player.[3]

In 1925 Rice had even written a play, in collaboration with Frank Craven, called *The Kick Off*. Craven was an accomplished actor and a good friend of Rice's who knew sports and had a great sense of humor. Once, on a trip to London, Craven was stopped by a butler as he was trying to visit an English friend. "Step aside," Craven ordered. "I've played a thousand of you." The Craven/Rice duo wrote a comedy/farce about the down-and-up season of a college football team, and about football and life in general. The play opened at the Nixon Theatre in Pittsburgh to mostly University of Pittsburgh and Carnegie Tech students and a few A.A.U. delegates who were conventioning there at the time. Ring Lardner and W. O. McGeehan were members of the Rice cheering section: both played Old Grad extras in the performance. Craven played the lead and McGeehan—cheerleader and actor—tripled as drama critic, giving the play rave reviews in the *Herald Tribune*. He thought the play would score a touchdown on Broadway. But no amount of hype could save it; the play died in Pittsburgh.[4]

Rice made another very brief debut as well in radio, as a play-by-play broadcaster in 1922. Radio was the new craze. By 1922 radio sales were reported at an incredible $60 million; by the next year, sales were at $136 million. Rice's debut came when the *Tribune,* radio station WJZ in Newark, New Jersey, and the Western Union Telegraph Company arranged to broadcast the 1922 World Series between the Yankees and the Giants. The year before, with the same two teams in the series, WJZ had experimented with a relay broadcast; Sandy Hunt, the sports editor of the *Newark Sunday Call,* sat in a box seat and reported the games by telephone to the WJZ station shack, where Tommy Cowan repeated what he heard over the air. But now, for the first time, baseball was to be broadcast directly "through the ether" from the Polo Grounds, and Rice was chosen to be the voice.

Using a device called a radiophone, Rice was perched behind the field box next to the visiting player's dugout. With earphones in place under his fedora and using the hand-held "phone" like a microphone, Rice went on the air at 12:30 to describe the slow-motion antics of baseball comedian Nick Altrock, the entrance of the two teams, and introductions of notables—Judge Landis, General Pershing, Jack Dempsey, and Christy Mathewson. More than one million fans within a three-hundred-mile radius heard the broadcast: "The *Tribune*'s sport expert described every play in the great game. They heard, too, the frenzied cries of the crowd in the dramatic moments, . . . Out over the ether there came even the cries of the peanut vendors with a surprising clarity that added a touch of realism to the most remarkable project ever undertaken in the annals of communication." Loudspeakers were set up at every radio store; crowds jammed around to listen to the drama. One man in Hackensack called in to say that more than two thousand people were listening at one store. At Princeton University, students cut classes for the day to hear the broadcast. The realism of the broadcast created a bit of a problem for the listeners, as when something, anything, would happen, Rice would watch it entirely through in silence, and then after the fact he would describe to the fans what had happened. "I would hear the crowd let out a terrific roar," one fan said, "and it seemed ages before I knew whether it was a single or a three bagger." No one seemed to really mind the delay since it hyped the suspense of Rice's somewhat droning Southern voice. Rice said it was a thrill to do the broadcast, especially since he quickly discovered that no one could talk back to him; but he didn't really know what to say half the time. Rice would later be on radio programs regularly—as a guest, or interviewer, or prognosticator—but he would never do another play-by-play. He said that when the first game of the series was over, he didn't remember what it was about; he had a vague idea who had won, but the details of the game were blurred. Although radio was about to change the face of sports coverage, Rice's voluminous contributions to sports reporting were destined to remain typed, not spoken. Ironically, baseball owners and sportswriters were adamantly opposed to the new technology: the owners feared sudden drops in gate receipts, and the writers fretted about losing their jobs if radio succeeded in cutting into the newspaper sports audience.[5]

There was also Rice the film producer. Filmmaker Jack Eaton approached Rice in 1920 suggesting they produce one-reel, typically ten-minute-long sports films to be used in conjunction with feature films at the theaters. Eaton, Rice, and cameraman Jack Hawkinson produced the films on a weekly basis, on such topics as water sports, thoroughbreds, hunting, fishing, or other sports having to do with the great outdoors. The trio stayed together for more than a year, but the schedule proved exhausting to them all and they dropped the project. After a four-year hiatus, Hawkinson and Rice started the idea up again, hooking up with Pathe. Over the next twenty-five years, first with Hawkinson, then Eaton again, Rice produced more than two hundred one-reelers. These films were not newsreels. They were short films, almost studies. For example, in one of the films Rice presented a dramatic contrast between the urban sports of baseball and football and the faraway activities of the outdoor huntsman. The film alternates between the two vastly different sporting venues, with first a flash or two of a Yale-Army football game in front of eighty thousand fans, then glimpses of hunters stealthily and quietly hunting wild sheep over the remote Canadian hills. A famous angler is pictured coaxing a trout out of the silvery waters near Calgary, then the viewer is transported to the tumult and the shouting at the Polo Grounds as Babe Ruth hits one out. Rice introduced the contrast this way:

> The stands and the stadiums leap to the roar
> Of the long end-run and the winning score.
> But still the wanderers seek the gate,
> Where the rivers run and the great hills wait.[6]

Rice eventually covered 123 different kinds of sports, recreations, activities, and diversions, from marbles to moose hunting, canoeing to horseshoe pitching, Dartmouth Winter Carnival to alligator wrestling. The films played in some seven thousand to eight thousand American movie theaters, in more than one thousand theaters in the British Isles, and eventually to houses all over the world. Through these shorts Rice said that he made contact with "countless moviegoers who may not know an inning from a goal post." His intention was to give the average American "a keener appreciation of sport in general." Rice's gutsy determination to stick with the idea of spreading the gospel of sport through film eventually earned him six Academy Award nominations and two Oscars for best short subject.7

But incredibly, and in addition to these far-ranging projects, Grantland Rice remained entirely committed to the fountainhead of all his creative contributions: sports reporting. Yes, Rice had become an editor, a published poet, a film producer, a radio personality, a book writer, a quasi-playwright, a magazine freelancer, and always a columnist. But in all of this it is easy to forget that what he did best and loved most was witnessing competitive sports firsthand and interpreting what he saw for his millions of avid readers. By way of example, if Rice were tracked through an entire year—let's say 1923—it would be learned that he traveled more than sixteen thousand miles by train on the way to producing ninety thousand eyewitness words by wire and mail. He seemed to be everywhere.

In mid-January of 1923 Rice boarded the train for Florida, now an annual working vacation tradition. While waiting around for spring training to start, he warmed up by covering the preliminaries for the year's first big contest: the National Horseshoe Pitching Championship! "This may suggest to you the scenic effect of a few bewhiskered citizens, surrounded by 200 or 300 spectators, working for a prize of $50 or so," he wrote. Not true. It so happened that the championship was for a prize of ten thousand dollars, and nearly eighty thousand spectators swarmed into St. Petersburg to witness the competition. Rice revealed that many of the star tossers trained in secret to hide from their rivals their individual techniques. The equine footwear they tossed wasn't just any old shoe thrown first by a horse; no, the horseshoes were carefully crafted, some silver-plated, some filed in certain ways to improve the feel, and all carefully guarded. A competitor's horseshoe was as important to the tosser, Rice said, as a favorite bat used by Babe Ruth or a favorite golf club used by Gene Sarazen or Walter Hagen.

Writing about the championship as though he were doping out the World Series, Rice said that Ohio was without question the greatest horseshoe-pitching state. "The Ohio product is usually dead on the nail, interpolating ringers often enough to make the noncombatant dizzy." All in all, the contest wasn't to be taken lightly. Those who have seen ballplayers, golfers, fighters, or tennis players in action, Rice reported, may think the contestants take their sport seriously. "But even their championships are matters of hilarious levity compared to the grim and serious determination of a horseshoe championship."[8]

In February more than five hundred athletes were preparing to head for spring training with the sixteen major-league ball clubs—most going south, some southwest, and one or two west, to Los Angeles. Rice spent most of his pre–spring training time freelancing, column writing, and working on his golf game. His golf outings were as much about pals as they were about pars, as much about Clubs as clubs. John Golden, one of the great men of the theater, organized a golf/social club called "The Not Very Club." This was typical of Rice's social set, to periodically become a club of one sort or another. This particular one had only six members: John Wheeler, Golden, Ring Lardner, John Sidall, editor of the *American Magazine,* James J. Montague, the Mysterious—a fellow who could shoot par with hoes, rakes, and shovels—and Rice. The club got its name from Ring Lardner's habit of commenting on another's tee shot; when one of them would hit a drive, another would say cheerfully, "Nice shot, old boy." "Not very," Ring Lardner would respond, drolly. Besides this bit of nonsense, it isn't known what else might have held the club together. This and other ad hoc groups were the frequent justifications for Rice's golfing expeditions all over the South and Florida: after all, he mused, there had to be a club meeting every so often.[9]

This was the way a more enduring organization, the Artists and Writers, came to be, with Rice smack in the middle of the inaugural planning and by acclamation its first ever—and only—president; the "fun" association survived into the Second World War, holding an annual winter golf tournament in Palm Beach, Florida. Ray McCarthy, who had been a golf writer for the *Tribune* between 1920 and 1924, started up his own publicity business. One of his Florida accounts was the Florida East Coast Hotel and Railway Company. On an advertising promotional trip to St. Augustine, Florida, in the spring of 1924, McCarthy brought along writer George Ade and illustrator Charley Williams. The threesome had a great time, and Williams told McCarthy that there ought to be an association for writers and artists.

McCarthy followed up on the suggestion, and the next spring in New York he pulled together a large gang of writers and artists to discuss such an association. Those attending read like a who's who of the New York creative set: Besides Ade, Rice, and Lardner, the original group included artists Rube Goldberg, Clare Briggs, and John Montgomery Flagg, and writers Bud Kelland, John Golden, Rex Beach, Billy deBeck, Fontaine Fox, Arthur Somers Roche, George Abbott, Arthur William Brown, Ray and Clair Maxwell, and Frank Crowninshield.

Each winter droves of writers and artists—mostly from New York—would assemble in Palm Beach for golf, card playing, and socializing. The golf tournaments were usually multiple-day affairs, just like the pros. Rice and Rex Beach were the real golfers: Rice won the first tournament, Beach the second, and then they traded back and forth for years until Hal Simms, the syndicated bridge columnist, joined in with an even better golf game. Beach, at 6'2" and 220 pounds, was variously talented. Besides his famous books, most of them about Alaska and the frozen north *(The Spoilers, The Silver Horde, The Iron Trail),* he was athletic and an outdoorsman. He had swum in the 1900 Olympic Games at Paris, played professional football with the Chicago Cherry Circle (Chicago Athletic Club), and was a solid boxer, a good skier, and a hunter who went after Kodiak bears without a dog. He was also a scratch golfer and a few strokes better than Rice; but Rice's temperament was better suited to tournament golf than Beach's. "I don't know how I ever managed to beat him," said Rice. "However, I think what favored me most was that I seldom worried in any match, particularly against Beach, because I knew he was a better golfer." Beach fretted and seldom shot his game against the relaxed Rice.[10]

The Writers and Artists (called "The Arthritis and Neuritis" by Montgomery Flagg) gradually grew in numbers and notoriety. Rice and the others would often invite guests, including Babe Ruth, Gene Tunney, and Tex Rickard, to play in the tournament. Most in the association membership were hackers, in the golf sense. But Rice recalled that their overall attitude toward the game was natural, unpretentious, and priceless. Once Rice was playing in a tournament foursome with John Golden and Billy deBeck, the creator of Barney Google. Off the tee deBeck hit what he thought was a snap hook into the tall underbrush rough. He disappeared for a while, then Rice heard him yell to his caddie, "Never mind looking for the ball, find me!" Another caddie found his ball in the fairway, and shouted into the thicket: "Here it is Mr. deBeck, out on the fairway." "You're a liar," deBeck yelled back while hammering away at the brush. "I've never been on the fairway in my life." On another occasion, and following a very bad round, Rube Goldberg came over to Rice the all-knowing golf writer and asked him hopefully, "Is there any way you can play golf except right or left handed?" Rice gave this much thought.[11]

All in all, these winter trips to Palm Beach were spring tonic for Rice and provided years of sociable friendship, which he thought was "the richest reward known to man." He went on to say, "In our various meetings that wonderful bunch contributed a large share of whatever deep pleasure I've found along the endless, winding road."[12]

Once the 1923 spring training season began, Rice was on the move around the South. The teams were scattered all over: Augusta, Georgia; Tampa, Orlando, St. Pete, and Bradenton in Florida; Hot Springs, Arkansas; Montgomery and Mobile, Alabama; even Seguin, Texas. Along the baseball trails, he found some time to follow an interesting golf match between a Mrs. Caleb Fox and Glenna Collett, then the national women's champion and perhaps the greatest American female golfer to that date. The winter before, and yet again in this winter of 1923, Fox beat Collett. She broke 80 to do it. Maybe this feat didn't seem too remarkable, even though no one had really heard much about her; but what got Rice's attention was that Fox had ten grandchildren and was sixty-three years old! "But while the snow of winter may be on her head, there is an unbounded amount of spring still in her heart."[13]

Then there was Babe Ruth. Rice and Ruth hit it off from the first time they met during spring training in 1919, when the Babe was a left-handed pitcher with the Boston Red Sox, the World Series champions in 1912, 1915, 1916, and 1918. Rice's first written comment about Ruth, made before he met him, was in March of 1919 when he was discussing the relative success of left-handers. Regarding Ruth, Rice wrote, "The left-hander has been awarded more than his share of sarcasm, but facts are to all intents and purposes as much facts as 'pigs is pork.'" Rice pointed out that Ruth, who had won eighteen and twenty-three games in his first two full seasons with the Red Sox, "has been a mighty factor in Red Sox success ever since his arrival." In late March Rice still hadn't met Ruth, only knew "of" him, and said Ruth's "unusual personality" made him one of the few new postwar players who had "color."[14]

But Rice was still reserved about Ruth's future. When Ruth, who had been holding out, finally signed his 1919 contract (ten thousand dollars a year for three years), Rice was asked by a fan why Grover Cleveland Alexander was being paid more by the Cubs than Ruth was getting from Boston. Rice admitted that Ruth could easily outhit Alexander, but as a pitcher, Alexander still had the edge, even though Rice acknowledged that Ruth was a great one: Ruth still hadn't won thirty games in a single season, and Alexander had won ninety-four games in his last three seasons, not counting 1918, when he worked in only two games. "A man is rated by the amount he has delivered, not by a future output that may or may not develop," Rice said. Of course, he was emphasizing for comparison only one of Ruth's talents, since it was to be

Ruth's hitting and not his pitching that would draw Rice's and the world's attention. It took only about three weeks for the sportswriter. The world would take a little longer, about half a season.[15]

In Tampa, the day before Rice would meet Ruth in Gainesville in an exhibition game against the Giants, the "pitcher" blasted a home run somewhere between five hundred and six hundred feet; Barrow later said he measured it at 579 feet. The next day, in Gainesville, Rice was watching batting practice and saw the twenty-four-year-old whack about ten balls clear out into the parking lot beyond the outfield. "Early in the game itself," Rice said, "Babe Ruth soaked one a mile toward centre, which Benny Kauff finally ran down, after a long pursuit. When the Babe discovered there were no fences around the battlefield he lost all interest in subsequent proceedings, and struck out twice. Why waste valuable ammunition when there's no fence or barricade to carry?"[16]

When Barrow introduced Ruth to Rice, the Babe said, "You sound like you got a cold?" "I have, sort of," replied Rice. Ruth then pulled a huge red onion out of his hip pocket and put it in Rice's hand. "Here, gnaw on this," Ruth said. "Raw onions are cold-killers." Rice said his first interview with Ruth went like this: "While Ruth talked I gnawed, with tears streaming from my eyes." Rice liked Ruth immediately, especially for his simple, plain honesty: "Babe from first to last said exactly what he thought."[17]

The next day, however, Rice was still guarded in his judgment about Ruth's hitting ability. Sure he had a wallop, and there's no question he could murder right-handed pitching. "But the sharp breaking curves of a left hander tie his full, free swing into knots," Rice wrote. In fact, Rice seemed to be more taken with Jim Thorpe of the Giants, not for his baseball skills especially, but because of the chastising Manager McGraw kept giving him for wrestling any teammate he could catch—which with his speed was all of them. McGraw had had to institute an iron-clad rule that none of his players could wrestle or "play" with Jim Thorpe. On the train ride up to South Carolina from Florida with the Giants and Boston, Rice reported that "Jim Thorpe still finds difficulty in securing a sparring or wrestling partner on his way North." Jim was yearning for his daily grapple, but his teammates kept hiding to avoid him. McGraw released the Olympic medal winner, allegedly because he couldn't hit the curve ball; Rice said the main reason "was that Thorpe was turning his team inside out" in those friendly wrestling matches.[18]

On April 18, in an exhibition game in Baltimore, Ruth knocked out four home runs; he was intentionally walked on his other two trips to the plate. A week later, Rice predicted that Babe Ruth would be a tremendous draw at all the ballparks. "His ability to pitch with spectacular effect one day and then drive the ball out of the lot the next afternoon—maybe—combined with certain eccentricities, lifts the renowned Babe well to the top."[19]

And the next day, only three weeks after having made the Babe's acquaintance, after watching him play in person, and after having seen some and heard about other of Ruth's Herculean—no, Ruthian—blasts, Rice admitted that Ruth wasn't just a pitcher who could hit, but a genuine major-league slugger who could swing harder than anyone he had ever seen. Even when Ruth missed the ball entirely he was something to watch: his momentum, once it got going, kept going so that his follow-through wound him up tightly, his spindly legs almost braiding themselves together; he would often fall down from the force his own swing generated. You couldn't help but watch his misses and imagine, "What if?" "With Babe Ruth," Rice said, "a miss and a hit are both as good as a mile. He isn't content with mediocrity, whether it be in oscillating the ozone or in bombarding the barricades."[20]

Rice gave tribute to Ruth in verse, "Sons of Swat: No. 1. Babe Ruth":

> When you can lean upon the ball
>   And lay the seasoned ash against it,
> The bally park's a trifle small,
>   No matter how far they've fenced it;
> Past master of the four-base clout,
>   You stand and take your wallop proudly;
> A pretty handy bloke about—
>   I'll say you are—and say it loudly.
>
> I've seen a few I thought could hit,
>   Who fed the crowd on four-base rations;
> But you, Babe, are the Only It—
>   The rest are merely imitations;
> I've seen them swing with all they've got
>   And tear into it for a mop-up;
> But what they deem a lusty swat
>   To you is but a futile pop-up.
>
> Somewhere among another throng
>   Where Fate at times became unruly,
> I've heard Big Bertha sing her song
>   Without an encore from Yours Truly;
> Yes, she had something—so to speak—
>   A range you couldn't get away with;
> But when you nail one on the beak
>   They need another ball to play with.[21]

In the winter before the 1920 season, Babe Ruth was bought by Colonel Ruppert, owner of the New York Yankees, for practically a song ($125,000 and a $300,000 loan to the Boston club). Boston needed the money badly; it was the type of business deal that anticipated precisely what President Coolidge was to mean a few years later by his phrase: "the business of the United States is business."[22]

That fact—that this was good business—did not get by the Babe himself. Early in the 1920 season the new Yankee prize had disappointed no one; of his first thirty hits, eleven were home runs. After one particularly good day at the Polo Grounds swinging that mighty all-or-nothing swing, knocking another one out, and trotting around the base paths in his now characteristic mincing, pigeon-toed steps, Ruth came over to Rice, who was covering the game, and said, "As far as I'm concerned, give me forty home runs and they can have their .400 hitters." Ruth went on, "It's the Big Blooie that makes all the talk."[23]

That first year with the Yankees Ruth made them all talk; in 1919 with the Red Sox, his 29 Big Blooies had broken Ed Williamson's 1884 mark of 27 home runs, but in 1920 he blasted 54 balls out of the parks. The Big Blooie also brought in all the money—the Yankees doubled their attendance in 1920, outdrawing the Giants in their own park, the Polo Grounds, and setting a league season attendance record of 1,289,422 that stood until they broke it themselves in 1946. In 1921 Ruth did even better, hitting 59 home runs, driving in 170 runs, scoring 177 himself, and batting .378. By 1922 he was earning fifty-two thousand dollars a year. Ruth fizzled a bit that year, as Rogers Hornsby, playing for the St. Louis Cardinals, took the major-league home run title with 42; Ruth powered out 35 in only 110 games (which could have been 50 if he had played all 154 games). He also flopped badly in the 1922 series that Rice was broadcasting, hitting an embarrassing .118, the lowest series average of any of the regular players for either the Giants or the Yankees.[24]

In 1923, Rice had predicted that Ruth would come back strong from that .118: "Just keep your eye on the Wham/On the Sheik of Slug and Slam." It was Rice's guess that Ruth might just do some off-season training, in accordance with the self-evident truth of Hugh E. Keogh's proverb: "Train to-day or wait for to-morrow to be outclassed."[25]

During spring training in 1923, Rice played a good deal of golf with a now more determined Babe, that and bridge and hearts on the train between exhibition games. Rice was curious about Ruth's unique batting stance, so during one of their golf games Rice asked him, "Why is it that you've adopted such a peculiar stance at bat?" Ruth characteristically closed his stance; as a left-handed hitter, his right foot was much closer to the plate than his left, his back turned a little toward the pitcher. As they sauntered around the golf course, an unusually sober and analytical Ruth explained that it was somewhat copied from the notorious Joe Jackson. Jackson was the first long-ball hitter to put one out over the right-field stands at the Polo Grounds. To Ruth, Jackson looked to be about the freest, longest hitter he had seen anywhere. Jackson used the closed stance, and Ruth theorized that this had a good deal to do with his success at the plate. So Ruth imitated Jackson's swing. "It brought my body around in a half turn," said Ruth, "and as I stepped into the ball with my right foot I was turning in a natural way in the same direction my bat was traveling. I tried this idea out; it worked great—and I've stuck to it ever since."[26]

On opening day of the 1923 baseball season, Rice joined all the New York baseball reporters for the first game in the newly constructed Yankee Stadium, the biggest stadium in baseball, and dubbed "the House that Ruth built." Until 1913 the Yankees had played in Hilltop Park, near 168th Street. These somewhat squalid accommodations were cast aside when owner Frank Farrell rented the newly built Polo Grounds from the Giants. The two teams shared the same facilities until 1920, when the Giants informed the Yankees that they were no longer wanted there. Ruppert and the team's other principal owner, Tillinghast Huston, wrangled two more seasons out of the Giants while they were building the new home of the Yankees at 161st Street: the new stadium would be a huge three-decker with a seating capacity of about sixty-five thousand. The Yankee management made sure that their left-handed pull hitter would continue to wow Yankee fans with his Ruthian blasts by making the right field line only 296 feet and the fence only 43 inches high.[27]

On opening day, Ruth didn't disappoint: "A white streak left Babe Ruth's 52-ounce bludgeon in the third inning of yesterday's opening game at the Yankee Stadium," Rice wrote. "On a low line it sailed, like a silver flame, through the gray, bleak April shadows, and into the right field bleachers, while the great slugger started on his jog around the towpaths for his first home run of the year." It was Ruth's first home run in Yankee Stadium and 198th of his career. The blast was witnessed by seventy-four thousand fans somehow wedged into the stadium. That was an attendance record, of course, and exceeded the previous record at the fifth game of the 1916 World Series between Brooklyn and Boston by more than thirty thousand. Crowds at other sports had been bigger, but to see that many people in one place for a baseball game, many standing five and six deep, was a spectacle, Rice said, that eclipsed the action of the game.

With two on and two out, Ruth came to the bat; there was a feeling of impending drama close at hand, Rice said. And then the Babe let fly with a terrific belt that barely rose ten feet from the ground. The ball landed halfway up the packed right field bleachers "as the sky above began to rock and the ground below began to shiver from the racket that arose." When Ruth crossed the plate, and the triple-tiered container roared—both Yankee and Red Sox fans alike—Ruth "was forced to take as many bows as his neck could carry," Rice said, "full proof that the crowd can remember as quickly as it can forget." The Yankees won the game, too, by a score of 4 to 1. And seventy-four thousand fans could later say that they were there and saw the greatest hitter in the game hit the first ball out of Yankee Stadium.

Ruth's baseball feats and his undisciplined social excesses (language, food, drink, and women) were both legendary even by the early 1920s. Rice never publicly commented on Ruth's personal habits, and seemed to accept Ruth for what he was, a man/boy who swung as lustily off the field as on. Given Ruth's upbringing at St. Mary's Industrial Home for Boys—in and out five times—and his overall juvenile delinquency on the streets of Baltimore before that, "It was a small wonder," Rice wrote, "that life as a baseball hero was a case of Christmas every day."[28]

Ruth's own transition from pitching to hitting symbolized what was happening to the game itself in the 1920s, as baseball went from defense to offense. Baseball needed supercharging after the scandalous 1919 World Series revelations. So the pitcher's job was made tougher. Doctored-up baseballs were officially outlawed in 1920; this didn't entirely stop pitchers from throwing licorice balls, or emery balls, or dirt balls, or spitballs, but pitches that moved suspiciously were more difficult to get away with now (even though any existing Big League spitballer who depended on the pitch for his livelihood could apply for exemption; seventeen did so). Yet, on the other hand, longer-traveling balls were quietly brought into the field of play to help jack up the offensive aspects of the game. The A. J. Reach Company—they made the baseballs—created a livelier ball, fittingly referred to as the "jack-rabbit ball"; when the ball was juiced up even more in 1930—when the Great Depression began to affect the business—one baseball writer said that if you held the ball up real close to your ear you could actually hear the little heart of the jackrabbit beating. Finally, the umpires were instructed to use more balls per game so that when a ball became scuffed or soiled, it was replaced with a new one; this again reduced the pitcher's effectiveness by eliminating even naturally induced funny pitches.[29]

All these changes were needed to boost baseball's entertainment value and drama, as the game became less "scientific" and more Big Bang. Ty Cobb's era of hit-and-runs, stolen bases, squeeze plays, bunts, and tight pitching duels was slowly coming to an end; Cobb himself in 1920 was starting his sixteenth year in baseball and was in his mid-thirties. According to baseball historian Harold Seymour, the combined batting averages for major leaguers in 1920 were 30 points higher than they were in 1915; they were about 45 points higher by 1925, and the teams were scoring two and a half more runs per game. Home runs climbed from 384 in 1915 to 631 in 1920, and to 1,167 by 1925. The public wanted to see the ball smashed all over the park and seemingly cared less now for the finer nuances of the game.

These changes helped baseball resell itself to the masses, catering as they did to the new American Dream: power, instant success, fame, and fortune. Some historians have said that the soaring popularity of the sport in the 1920s was chiefly due to its compensatory usefulness: whereas ordinary life was becoming thoroughly rationalized, urbanized, industrial-bound, bureaucracy-controlled, and ambiguous as to what constituted success and happiness, baseball provided escape and freedom, naturalness and rusticity, simplicity and irrationality, and an unambiguous measure of achievement (runs and wins that could be counted up).[30]

And if at this time there was any single person in baseball who could be called Superman, who could restore America's faith in their besmirched national game, and who could attract fans and headlines like no one ever before him, it was George Herman Ruth. Rice said that the Babe was clearly "the greatest single magnet sport has ever known." And with that 1923 opening-game home run, the Babe helped baseball fans everywhere find their yea-saying voices again; for once Rice may not have been exaggerating when he wrote, "And as the crash sounded, and the white flash followed, 74,000 fans arose en masse, and 74,000 expanding throats, in the greatest vocal cataclysm baseball has ever known, paid Ruth a tribute he will never forget."[31]

The year 1923 was only about one-third gone when Rice playfully yet wistfully challenged Rudyard Kipling's lines: "Therefore from job to job I've moved along,/Pay couldn't 'old me when my time was done." Rice admitted that he, too, had shuffled from job to job and had felt the call to newer roads, but old Rudyard was an amateur and "us professionals must eat." So was Homer an amateur, Rice said, "When he smote his bloomin' lyre," for he just covered the leading wars "Where mighty heroes ruled the fray," and then he rested up for a year or so between them. But the modern sportswriter's plight, and Rice's job, he said, was a good deal less leisurely and not so terribly inspiring: "But we must chat of bums and stars/And give them headlines every day."[32]

However frustrated Rice could occasionally be about his never-ending schedule, or however cynical he sometimes was about boosting even the bums, he never lost his enthusiasm for sport's essential values and its potential to do good. Shortly after baseball's opening day, Rice got himself into a debate about the significance of the rising popularity of American sport.

"Sport," his opponent said, "is ruining the United States. It is the curse of the age."

"How come?" parried Rice.

"Because," the critic said, "its grip is now on the entire nation. It is killing interest in art, literature and music. It is destroying all culture. It is costing millions and is taking valuable time away from business. To-day in this country you can start no conversation that doesn't lead directly to sport."

"But," Rice countered, "business, art, literature and music are all supposed to be doing fairly well. Even better than usual. And if art, literature and music can't stand up before sport, why blame the stronger wave?"

"Millions," the critic said, "are either playing some game or watching others play. This is all waste. To my mind, it is criminal."

"It is criminal, " Rice admitted, "if health building, clean recreation and companionship are criminal. Millions, perhaps, might be doing more useful things. But would they—even if there were no sport?"

Rice's written account of the debate then concluded. But he added that it seemed to him that sport really wasn't the great desire of the human race at all. No, "The great desire of the human race is to regulate some other portion of the human race, as vast caravans sweep by, singing: 'If anybody likes it, it must be wrong.'"[33]

In May, Rice covered the first of several boxing matches and eliminations, the biggest of which were carded to find a decent challenger to fight Dempsey for the heavyweight title. There had been practically a two-year drought in heavyweight title bouts. Of the possible contenders—including Jess Willard, now age forty or forty-three, no one really knew for sure—Rice figured it would be the relatively unknown Argentine boxer, Luis Firpo, who would be the next challenger:

> If Firpo dents another chin
> The loud-mouthed tumult starts anew,
> As Dempsey sniffs the kale ag'in
> And chortles at the ballyhoo.
> No wonder, after two lean years,
> The scent of kale always brings cheer.[34]

Eight contending boxers—Willard, Floyd Johnson, Firpo, Jack McAuliff, Fred Fulton, Jack Renault, Joe McCann, and Harry Drake—weighed in at Yankee Stadium, all 1,679 pounds of them, to have a go at becoming the next challenger. Rice called it a Parade of Pachyderms; sixty-five thousand spectators attended. When it was all over, Willard, showing surprising stamina and determination, had knocked out Johnson, who was twenty years younger, in the eleventh round; Firpo, with great power and a bull-like rushing, had stopped McAuliffe in the third. Naturally, what was to happen next was a Willard-Firpo bout for the chance to challenge Dempsey; both "game, both stunning hitters, both of the cavemen type," said Rice. It's just that in the meantime, Doc Kearns had already signed Dempsey to fight someone else.[35]

In Montana in March of 1922, a rich crude oil field was found. When the Kevin-Sunburst field was discovered, the town nearby, Shelby, was unheard of; after the strike, Shelby was still unheard of. So the local businessmen, needing to draw attention to the town's investment possibilities, decided to throw a heavyweight boxing match to advertise their good fortune. With everybody exploiting everybody else, the contract was signed one week before the Yankee Stadium fights; Kearns had extracted a guarantee for Dempsey of three hundred thousand dollars plus ten thousand more for training expenses to fight Tom Gibbons, from St. Paul, who was really only a light-heavyweight. Gibbons was supposed to get half of the gate if it totaled between three hundred thousand and six hundred thousand dollars, and 25 percent of any revenues beyond that. The fight was scheduled for July 4 in a town that was a full five hundred miles from the nearest true city.[36] About which Rice said that if Tom Gibbons were to get all that Dempsey left after taking $310,000 from Shelby, Tom might escape with his shirt and one shoelace, nothing more. In the end, it would turn out to be nothing more. But the bout was still more than a month away. Rice lamented:

> The melancholy days have come,
> The saddest of the year;
> Where ninety sporting events hum
> By side and front and rear.[37]

In the meantime, and among all his other column and writing duties, Rice covered the featherweight fight in which Johnny Kilbane, who had held the crown for eleven years, lost to the Frenchman and war hero Eugene Criqui. Next, with his good friend Frank Craven and the man who was becoming his best friend, Ring Lardner, Rice played, reviewed, and critiqued the newly re-constructed North Hempstead Country Club golf course for the *Tribune*. Rice then covered play at the Westchester Amateur golf tournament in New York, where he witnessed the two-time champion, Ed Sturges, take thirteen strokes on the par-four 15th at the Siwanoy course; Rice sympathetically de-scribed each of the thirteen swings, saying that the average golfer knew far more of this tragic side of golf than of the par-breaking side anyway. Finally, Rice caught the flyweight bout at the Polo Grounds between the titleholder, Britisher Jimmy Wilde, and Pancho Villa of Panay, Philippines.[38]

As evidence that there was a public appetite for the sport of boxing (and gambling, naturally) in any weight division, the flyweight championship brought in forty thousand fans to the Polo Grounds. Babe Ruth and his wife were among the personalities present; the Bambino was given a tumultuous reception and doffed his straw lid repeatedly. In the fight itself, youth was served, as the youngster Villa pounded the veteran Wilde at will for seven rounds and then dropped the game champ with a right hook to the jaw. "There in the dust of the rosin," said Rice, "lay one of the greatest fighters for his weight and inches that ever lived. He lay completely unconscious, with both eyes closed from the rataplan of flashing brown fists, his face bloody and scarred, his battered body still quivering from the pain."

In his some twenty-column-inch story, Rice gave most of the space to the loser, Wilde. The fight was all but over in the second round, but Wilde hung on for five more. Villa, who Rice portrayed as the "raging Filipino" and a "lithe, bounding, brown leopard," was given credit for being a "great little fighter" who earned "every sprig of the laurel that now adorns his swarthy brow." Wilde was portrayed as a "white skinned" veteran boxer who could "move forward against immutable fate with the rarest of all courage, the courage that sees defeat ahead and still fights through blood and blindness until darkness closes in and there is nothing left with which to make war." Rice thought that in the end, Wilde went down as a fighting man should, "all through, only because there is nothing left to give," and that Wilde, who was now on the long, long trail that led back into Has-Been-Land, "in defeat de-serves as much credit as he ever earned in a conquering career."[39]

One week later, Rice packed up and left for Shelby, Montana, to cover the Dempsey and Gibbons fight. In the manner of Rudyard Kipling, Rice took off "On the Road That Leads Away":

> On the road that leads away
> Where the crashing sock holds sway,

Can't you hear the big gloves chunkin' from Great Falls to Baffin Bay?
On the road that leads away,
Though I have no yearn to stray,
Yet the Boss yells out like thunder—"Pack your bally grip to-day."

So I'm shippin' West for Shelby where the next volcano bursts,
But what in ballyel now is the good in raisin' thirsts?
Though it takes me eighty hours flyin' westward on the wing,
Will the show last twenty minutes when the bell begins to ring?[40]

In the columns produced during his eighty-hour train trip to the general vicinity of Shelby, Rice mostly seemed to be trying to think up good reasons, or even just one reason, why he and all the other tourists were going in person to Shelby. This seemed especially important to figure out since it was common knowledge that no heavyweight from the John L. Sullivan days on had ever lost the championship while under thirty years of age. Dempsey was twenty-eight. So the upset was unlikely and the dope was all for Jack. All Rice could think up was the lure of the old slogan: anything can happen in sport. But that, too often, Rice commented, is only a mirage in the desert sky.[41]

After seeing Dempsey at his training camp in Great Falls, Rice thought Dempsey had lost none of his wild animal grace, despite the champion's two-year break from boxing. Rice compared Dempsey's restless yet graceful and gliding motion to the king cobra, a particularly deadly reptile. Rice knew what he was talking about; he was good friends with the curator of the Bronx Zoo, Raymond Ditmars, who helped him from time to time in animal-related Sportlight films. Just before Rice left for Shelby, he visited Ditmars, who had operated on the eyes of one of the cobras just a few days earlier.

"He doesn't like me yet," Ditmars said. "I'll show you how he feels." Rice and Ditmars walked together in front of the big glass cage. The cobra saw the surgeon approaching and immediately rose up on his serpentine tail until he was standing eight feet in the air. Then he started forward, his head weaving from side to side, right to left and left to right, zigzagging, until he finally struck at the glass barrier.[42]

Foolishly, on another occasion with Ditmars, over a many-martini lunch at the Chatham Hotel in New York, Rice asked the curator how high a cobra can strike. Rice believed that it was no higher than the height of its arc.

"You might be right," Ditmars said. "Let's find out."

Shortly they were at the zoo and standing in front of the cobra enclosure. Ditmars, armed with nothing but a broom, and Rice, armed with four martinis sloshing around under his belt, entered. The three cobras were napping until Ditmars prodded them with his broom and started herding them into a corner. Rice had his back to the door when one of the cobras faked left, dove right, and started an end run directly at Rice.

"Ray," Rice wheezed. "You're a snake short!" Rice, reeling from his liquid lunch, managed to stumble backwards, fell, and luckily landed outside the door of the cage. He never did find out how high a cobra can strike. But he was convinced after seeing more and more of Dempsey that the boxer's movements were definitely cobralike. And he looked just about as intimidating in the ring as a cobra did in a cage; Dempsey, Rice reported, gave himself daily facials with bear grease to toughen up his face, giving it the texture of a boar's hide.[43]

Kearns had insisted that the $310,000 be paid in installments before the fight. Two of these had already been paid, but to make even the second installment, the town had to practically hock itself under Kearns's threats to cancel the fight. To make the third would be impossible. The town was stripped, and Rice cynically commented that thus far Kearns hadn't yet seized the oil wells or the post office—but he'd gotten practically everything else. "In the wide open spaces loud rings the fuss—/Germany's lucky compared with us," Rice wrote, sardonically comparing Kearns's hold over Shelby to the plight of Germany in making reparations after World War I. By fight time the Montana slogan was "Peace at any price," wrote Rice.[44]

The ranchers, the cowboys and cowgirls, the Blackfoot Indians, and the plainsmen all gathered for the fight, but the tourists from the excursion trains and automobiles hadn't. On the last day of June, the fight was off; by July 1 it was on; on July 2 it was off; on July 3 it was on. Kearns agreed to gamble that he could get his final one hundred thousand dollars from the gate receipts. Finally the Great Northern excursion specials began arriving, eight of them, with a total of sixteen hundred fans. The cars began arriving, and the town of two thousand increased its population tenfold overnight. All told, around ten thousand fans paid to see the fight, and fifteen thousand more crashed the gates, led by One-Eyed Connolly, a professional gate-crasher, who had boasted before the fight that he would lead in a flock for free. Even then the forty-thousand-seat arena never filled up. Not even the marching of the Montana State Elks band and the Scottish Highlanders from Calgary could drum up the business. The fight was about to be a financial flop.[45]

Rice picked Dempsey to knock out Gibbons in five or six rounds. But by the fifth and the sixth, Gibbons was not only still standing but also scoring. Dempsey had failed to drop the challenger with body punches and close-range fighting. When he changed his strategy and fought from a distance,

Gibbons outboxed the champion for three rounds. Dempsey, a puncher rather than a boxer, then went back to his crowding style, hammering Gibbons with punches to the heart, ribs, and kidneys. Dempsey, "his lip often curled back over his white teeth as a wolf sometimes looks," tried desperately to bring Gibbons down. In the seventh, Gibbons slugged Dempsey with a whistling right to the mouth, driving Dempsey's upper lip between his teeth; Dempsey then clinched and desperately spent the next ten seconds trying to work his lip free.

But the rest of the fight was his. It didn't matter what animal Rice compared Dempsey to—cobra, wolf, dog, tiger—the champ simply out-punched Gibbons. Yet the St. Paul fighter withstood Dempsey's body attacks: round ten, round eleven, round twelve. After the twelfth Gibbons received a great ovation from the crowd: he had lasted longer against the champion than anyone else ever had. By the fourteenth, Rice was comparing Dempsey to the "African buffalo," charging "with frenzy and fury." In the fifteenth, the last round, Rice had practically run clear through the animal kingdom in describing the fighters, so when he saw Gibbons trying to hang on, clutching and grabbing at Dempsey, he switched to the sea world to describe the challenger, holding on "with the grip of an octopus," as the scowling champ tried furiously to knock Gibbons out. The crowd was roaring for Gibbons, who had never been knocked down in all his life, to finish the fight on his feet: "And so, with stout heart but quivering legs and weary arms, he reached blindly forward to hold and grip through an interminable time, through centuries and ages, until at last, as the terrific jabbing of Dempsey was flailing away and the human system was about to bend and break, the bell rang and Gibbons was still on his feet." Dempsey got the decision, easily, and Gibbons won a lot of friends for his heroic stand. "While they are talking of my fight," Jack Dempsey said after the fifteen-rounder, "I hope they don't overlook Gibbons. He sure surprised me. He's a great boxer."[46]

Three Pullman cars had been provided as the headquarters for the newspapermen and telegraphers. Covering the fight were 160 reporters, including Rice's Great Northern train travel mates Heywood Broun, Damon Runyon, Bide Dudley, and Hugh Fullerton. For the first time in history, stories were sent out by automatic telegraphy to places all over the country. When the final bell had sounded, Rice and the other reporters rushed to the Pullmans to telegraph their stories. At the other end of the wires, the newspapers hit the streets with the results. In New York, the first editions with some of the fight news appeared by around eight o'clock the night of the fight.

The newspapers went to great lengths to scoop the others. When the *New*

York American's first edition was being bought up, the editors of the rival *New York Tribune*, Rice's paper, were flabbergasted to see what appeared to be an entire page of photos from the fight. Now this—same-day photos from thousands of miles away—was impossible since photographs couldn't be sent over the wires. Yet the *American* had seemingly done the impossible. They called this mysterious piece of technology "Damon Runyon's Telegraphoto." In one prominent picture, Tom Gibbons was leaning up against the ropes defending himself while Dempsey charged. The *American* apparently figured that the gullible public would believe that the new "automatic telegraph" could relay such pictures. The *Tribune* editors weren't as gullible. They thought it was remarkable how much the photo in question looked like an International Film Service photo they had seen before, of the Dempsey-Willard fight in 1919.

Frederick B. Edwards of the *Tribune* went to press immediately to expose the *American*'s fraud, calling the pictures "Telegraphakos." The *Tribune*'s art department created an exact duplicate of the *American*'s fraud and published it. Both fakes used the same photograph of Dempsey beating up on Jess Willard, Jack backing Jess into the ropes, and watched by the same straw-hatted crowd. By taking the Toledo picture, retouching it here and there with an air brush and whacking off Willard's head and replacing it with Gibbons's, a picture was produced of Jack Dempsey severely punishing a challenger against some ropes—somewhere, sometime. Edwards said that a comparison of the original Toledo photo and the *American*'s fake one was "an interesting study for telegraph operators, photographers, air brush artists and backers of Zip the Great What-Is-It." It is to be regretted, the *Tribune* said, that P. T. Barnum didn't live long enough to see the day of the Telegraphako. "Ain't science won-der-ful!" concluded the *Tribune* editor.[47]

While the *American* readers received no real same-day pictures of the fight, the game Tom Gibbons received no real money for the fight. The expected gate never materialized. Kearns and Dempsey picked up the last of what the fight generated from the gate, estimated to be anywhere from thirty thousand to eighty thousand dollars, and quietly left town. Rice said that it would be a long time before any town of two thousand tried to put on another five-hundred-thousand-dollar show. For Shelby and especially for a few of the key locals, the fight was a financial wallop. Mayor Jim Johnson lost well over one hundred thousand dollars, and in the aftermath of the fight, several local banks were forced to close down. "Jack Kearns and Jack Dempsey alone gathered in the kale," Rice wrote, and "the pall over the city on Thursday was like a black shadow over a deserted battlefield and the loud blare of many bands had given way to a silence broken only by the winds from the endless plains."[48]

For Rice, the silence didn't last; it never did. Eighty hours later, back in the East again, he joined the huge crowds for the medal-qualifying rounds of the U.S. Open at Inwood Golf Club, Long Island, about an hour by train or car from New York City. The winner would receive about twenty-five thousand dollars if he happened to be a pro.

> Hagen, Sarazen, Hutchinson, Barnes,
> Kirkwood, Smith and Jones—
> But one will slice to the reedy tarns,
> And fill the air with groans;
> And one will hook to sanded ruts
> And one will lose his spin,
> And one will blow the one-yard putts,
> So I don't know who'll win.[49]

But wedged between the preliminaries and the finals of the Open was yet another event Rice wanted to cover in person. It was easy to get to, just across the Hudson River. Jess Willard and Luis Angel Firpo had already earned the right to box each other for the chance to challenge Dempsey for the championship. Whereas the championship match in Montana had attracted twenty-five thousand fans, the Willard-Firpo bout attracted one hundred thousand to Jersey City and Boyle's Thirty Acres. This was the difference between a local promotion and a Tex Rickard promotion. Except for the famous horse race a hundred years earlier between Eclipse and Sir Henry, the fight may have drawn the largest crowd to ever witness a sporting event this side of the Atlantic. Willard received 30 percent of the gate, and Firpo 22 percent; that roughly translated into $120,000 for the Kansan and $80,000 for the Argentine.[50]

Willard, Rice said, was simply too old to go the route. The younger and faster Firpo knocked out the "Kansas mastodon" in the eighth round. The fight wasn't deft; in a way it was a battle between two one-armed men, said Rice. Firpo had nothing but a walloping, mauling, always-telegraphed right that reminded Rice of a club used as one might break rocks in a quarry; Willard had only a jabbing left that rocked but never dazed the Argentine boxer. The huge crowd, fortified with nonalcoholic beverages—this was still the Prohibition era—such as buttermilk, lemonade, and pineapple drink, booed the foreigner and rooted loudly for Willard throughout the bout. Once

Willard was down and out, the fans switched their loyalties and rooted instead for the winner with a loud, shrill "Lou—I—I." The unrestrained cheering for the South American was heard clearly by Doc Kearns and Tex Rickard, both at ringside. Smelling another windfall, Rickard announced after the fight that preparations were underway to match Dempsey with Firpo for the title—and soon, within a couple of months.[51]

Meanwhile, back at Inwood the next day, the field of 350 had been cut to the final 77 qualifiers. Two days of golf, two rounds each day, a seventy-two-hole showdown. The pros—Kirkwood, Smith, Hutchinson, Sarazen, Barnes, and Hagen—were the top favorites, with three of the nine competing amateurs—Chick Evans, Bobby Jones, and Francis Ouimet—popular long shots. Rice liked Hagen, who had finished one stroke back in the just-completed British Open. Since January, Hagen had played in nine big tournaments, winning five, including the PGA, and finishing second in the other four. Gene Sarazen, the defending U.S. Open champion, failed to qualify for the final rounds of the British Open at Troon, and hence Rice thought he was slightly off his otherwise solid game.

But Rice was wrong; it wouldn't be Hagen or, for that matter, Sarazen either. After the first two-round day, Jock Hutchinson was in the lead, and the two Bobbys—Cruickshank and Jones—were only a few strokes behind. Cruickshank was a Scot who had moved to the United States two years earlier. He had served in World War I as a member of the famed Black Watch; he came through the thickest fighting in the war, survived a prisoner-of-war incarceration, and had seen his own brother blown to bits right beside him in France. After the war, in Scotland, he became the amateur golf champion and a long-distance runner at Edinburgh University. When he came to the States, he settled in Schackamaxon, New Jersey, and had, as a professional, won the Missouri Open and the New York Open. He was a tough competitor through and through.

Now, Cruickshank was only three strokes back after the first thirty-six holes. Hagen, Sarazen, Smith, Barnes, and all the rest of the contenders were "far in the ruck," reported Rice. Bobby Jones, who had finished the 1922 Open only one stroke behind Sarazen, was paired with Hagen for the first thirty-six holes. Rice followed the pair, reporting that Jones's play was at a pace that rivaled the famous racehorse Man o' War. He was tearing along like an "unleashed Zev," shooting a 144 total for the two rounds.[52]

"It's only a game, after all," remarked some philosopher, Rice recalled, "and some one must win." True enough, but how the win was won was what made the story a story for Rice. And this *was* going to be a story.

After the first eighteen holes on the second day, Bobby Jones was in at 220, Cruickshank 223, Hutchinson 224, and Hagen 225. On the final eighteen, Jones appeared to have the championship in hand, his first major championship after seven years of trying, even though he had trouble in the last few holes, including a sloppy 6 on the tough 18th. He finished with a 76. Cruickshank was still on the course; standing on the 17th tee, the Scot would have to play the last two holes one under par just to tie. When Cruickshank hooked his tee shot into the heavy rough on the 17th, some in the gallery began wandering off, saying, "That's it, Bobby Jones is the Open champion." But Cruickshank's second shot got him to the edge of the green, and he rolled a sixty-foot putt close enough to the hole to putt out for his par 4.

Now he had to birdie the 425-yard 18th, a dangerous hole flanked by water and sand. The 5'6" golfer lustily crashed his drive down the middle. As he approached his second shot, the gallery hushed. With a heavy mashie, he started his high pitch well to the left, allowing for the strong wind blowing to the right. The silence gave way to roaring applause as the ball dropped out of the blue sky six feet from the pin. Cruickshank then lined up the putt and rapped the ball cleanly into the cup, getting his miracle 3, tying Jones, and forcing a playoff for the championship. Once again it looked like Jones was going to face the fates, and lose.[53]

Rice's lead the next day was, "The red badge of courage always belongs upon the breast of the fighter who can break and then come back with a stouter heart than he ever had before." In the playoff, Cruickshank was a 10 to 7 favorite since he had finished strong and Jones had stumbled late in regulation play. Jones didn't sleep the night before the playoff.

Of the playoff's first seventeen holes, only three were halved. On the other fourteen, one or the other golfer won outright. By the time they reached the 18th tee, Jones and Cruickshank had each taken seventy-two shots. Cruickshank hit first, hooking to the left rough. Jones outdrove Cruickshank, but when his ball stopped rolling he was in the rough to the right. The Scot played his second shot safely, laying up short of the green, having no real chance to carry the strip of water guarding the green. Then it was Jones's turn.

This moment, Rice said, was the turning point in Bobby Jones's career. The big tournaments had been getting away from him. They said he couldn't win. They said that he was a great golfer but that he "lacked the punch." When Rice saw him on his way out to Inwood at the beginning of the tournament, he said Jones was close to throwing in full-time with his dad's law practice. He entered the tournament with an "I'll give it one more try" frame of mind, said Rice. There was much more to life, the twenty-one-year-old Bobby said, than the Amateur pay-as-you-go golf. Rice, trying to bolster him up said, "You never looked better."[54]

Now, Jones faced the biggest decision in his career: gamble or play it safe. Cruickshank was safe down the middle with an easy 5 in sight, and maybe even a 4. To play the gamble, Jones needed a full long iron to get to the green, over the water, some two hundred yards away. Here's Rice's account of what happened: "His hesitation was slight. For just a moment he sized up the situation, took out his straight-faced driving iron and tore into the ball with everything he had. For just a half a breath there was deep silence in the crowd. And then the first roar began as the white ball, sailing clean and true against the gray, shadowed sky, picked out a straight line for the pin and finally dropped just eight feet beyond the cup."[55]

Rice was extremely proud of his young friend. Jones had matched, even exceeded, Cruickshank's courage and skill the previous day on the same hole: "It was a tribute to a heart stout enough to trample psychology and imagination into the dust and come through at the big moment." Rice called the shot one of the boldest and greatest iron shots ever played in golf, much tougher to hit than Cruickshank's close-in pitch shot the day before. Golfers Ouimet and Lee Deigel were among the gallery of eight thousand looking on. They both thought Jones was making a mistake by pulling out his long iron. The lie was terrible, the green was well guarded, and the pin was one hell of a long way away.

Luke Ross, Jones's caddie, described the shot. Jones used a two iron. The ball was lying on loose dirt rough. "Give me that iron," Jones told Luke, and he "took one second to play the greatest golf shot any man ever saw before." Luke said he wasn't quite sure what would happen until he saw the look on Jones's face, his jaws set and his eyes blazing. "Yes," Luke said, "I knew we were home when I saw that look. Honestly, I think he'd 'a' knocked Jack Dempsey out with a punch if he had been in the way of this championship just at that shot."[56]

Following Jones's brilliant shot, Cruickshank tried to hit his 150-yard approach shot stone dead, but caught a trap to the left, hole high. He took a 6 on the hole, while Jones, from eight feet out, carefully laid up close to the cup and tapped in for his 4 and his first U.S. Open championship cup—what Jones thereafter referred to as THE CUP. After Jones's putt dropped, Cruickshank walked over to the amateur and held out his hand. Later, to the press, Cruickshank, a great sportsman, said, "Bobby Jones is the greatest of them all. Man! It was a bonnie shot. There never was such a golfer, and I'm proud to have stepped so close to him. He is now what Harry Vardon was at his very best—the greatest golfer in the world."[57]

Jones had played in four previous Opens, and in them had taken fourteen fewer strokes than any golfer, amateur or pro. Yet he hadn't won, until now. Rice knew that the youngster had triumphed over himself, his own worst enemy; he had also triumphed over fate. Jones had finally arrived, and he had come through in a way that no one who saw him at Inwood would ever forget.

After Inwood, Rice briefly settled back into his column writing. But not for long. Boxing was still the late-summer news, and it found its way regularly into Rice's Sportlight. All the while the fuss was being made over the proposed Dempsey-Firpo fight, Rice had been pushing for Dempsey to fight Harry Wills before, or even instead of, Firpo. In late May, and again in June, Rice suggested that perhaps the most skilled boxer around was the 6'4", 220-pound Wills. Wills was black, so it is significant that Rice, although still undeniably prejudiced, was so eager to promote the match, especially since blacks were not permitted to fight for the heavyweight title in the 1920s, although they could fight whites in the lower weight divisions. This was partly due, of course, to the long memories of whites who never quite got over Jack Johnson's reign. The black heavyweights usually just boxed each other; one of the best black heavyweights, Sam Langford, fought Harry Wills twenty-three times.[58]

Rice seemed to be quite comfortable indirectly helping Nat Fleischer, the boxing reporter who started up the *Ring* boxing magazine in 1922, to erase the color line for the heavyweight division. Fleischer was a vocal advocate of cleaning up boxing, and crusaded in particular for the sport to stop its blatant discrimination against black fighters. Although the calls continued to grow for a Dempsey-Wills match, it was Doc Kearns and Tex Rickard who temporarily put an end to the discussions and the idea. They were against any interracial heavyweight title fights. They thought such a fight would upset the delicate balance of the country's race relations. Dempsey, who was quite willing to fight Wills, said later that "Doc and Tex didn't think it would draw." So, in late July, the Dempsey-Firpo fight was signed and announced. It was to take place on September 14 at the Polo Grounds. Dempsey and Kearns were to receive 37.5 percent of the gate; Firpo would get 12.5 percent.[59]

Around the same day the heavyweight fight was officially announced, Rice motored over to the Polo Grounds to cover the Johnny Dundee and Eugene Criqui featherweight championship bout. The fight went the distance in front of forty thousand patrons, with the American Dundee winning a fifteen-round decision after knocking the titleholding Frenchman down three times, but not out. Criqui, Rice said, was the incarnate emblem of Henley's masterpiece: his head was bloodied but unbowed.[60]

The day after this fight, one of Rice's readers took him to task for giving so many words to boxing. "I am surprised at you," said the reader, "that with so many clean, healthy sports to take up that you give so much space to the fight game, a mixture of rotten commercialism and raw entertainment where the skill, courage and brains shown don't even compare with the headliners in baseball, football, tennis, golf, and etc."

Rice's response was at least honest and realistic. He agreed with his critic, and then some. Boxing, he said, is probably 97 percent business and 3 percent sport. But, he went on, it was entertainment that untold millions were falling for at the moment. Fights promise action, give decisive results, and require a relatively unsophisticated spectator insofar as knowledge of technique is concerned. Boxing, Rice continued, was about as commercialized as every other professional sport was; for that matter, it was about as commercial as civilization as a whole was becoming, no matter the continent. Rice didn't defend the commercialism, but thought it was a prevalent evil, much like the ubiquitous human faults of jealousy or envy. Realistically, he said, there was nothing commendable about greed; but it was, after all, one of the strongest human traits, and no one should be surprised that greed could be the driving force behind any and all human endeavors, including even art, writing, motion pictures, and politics.

There is no law, Rice said, that compels someone to pay five dollars or twenty-five dollars for a seat at a boxing match. Until the public quit paying, the commercializers would continue to profit, out of all proportion to whether or not the sport was useful, socially satisfying, or civilizing. There wasn't much altruism around, Rice commented. The reason a bricklayer holds out for fourteen dollars a day is because he thinks or knows he can get it; if he thought he could get eighty-four dollars a day he would hold out for that. Rice asked, "Who is collecting the gold, old dear,/Who is collecting the gold?"[61]

Like baseball fans fascinated by Ruth's Big Blooies, heavyweight boxing fans slobbered over the big knockout, far and away preferring that to a thirty- or forty-round dance. Tex O'Rourke, a boxing expert and Willard's trainer when he fought Jack Johnson, explained that the new boxing art wasn't a matter of any particular skill. Instead, it was a matter of simply wading in to close quarters and then nailing your opponent with a big punch that hurt, stunned, or preferably knocked the bejesus out of him: Socko![62]

Socko it was to be, the Dempsey-Firpo fight. In front of eighty-five thousand screaming, howling, shrieking fight fans, Dempsey and Firpo went at it, both determined from the first-round bell to throw the biggest of the Big Blooies. The fight lasted a little more than four minutes; at ringside, Grantland Rice wrote more than four thousand words about it.

According to Demspey, just before the fight Rickard reminded him that they had another million-dollar gate and that it would be a good idea to carry Firpo for four or five rounds at least so the fans would get their money's worth. Dempsey said, "Go to hell." Dempsey judged Firpo to be too dangerous to toy with. Which he was. When the bell sounded, Dempsey charged Firpo and swung wildly. Firpo, in a move he was not known to have, smoothly sidestepped Dempsey's punch and hit him with a short left uppercut. Dempsey dropped to his knees. The crowd was on its feet, and remained there from then on.

In an interview with Dempsey a few days before the fight, Rice asked him about getting knocked down early. "You feel now," Rice asked him, "that if Firpo knocks you down the fight will only be started?" Dempsey replied, "Just that way." Then, Jack's older brother, Bernie, who had once been a fighter himself and who was a regular Dempsey cornerman, cut in saying that few people had ever seen Dempsey really fight. "And you never will," he continued, "until he has been knocked down. When that happens you'll see a wildcat just beginning to start. I know, for I've seen it happen."[63]

Bernie wasn't exaggerating. Before the referee even began his count, Dempsey was up and all over Firpo. In seconds, Dempsey threw a right hook to Firpo's jaw. Firpo was down. When he got up at the count of nine, Dempsey went at him again, and dropped the challenger a second time. Firpo got up again, and clinched until referee Johnny Gallagher separated them. When Firpo started to step back, he dropped his hands; Dempsey stepped forward and hit the Argentine with an uppercut off the break and dropped him for the third time. Dempsey's tactic was less than sportsmanlike, as Rice duly noted; had the boxing rules been enforced just then, Dempsey would have lost the match on a foul, Rice reported.

With Dempsey standing over him, Firpo slowly rose again, only to be knocked down a fourth time; while he was getting up again, Dempsey got around behind Firpo and dropped him again. But when Firpo finally found his feet after the fifth knockdown, he came up swinging to defend himself and knocked Dempsey to his knees. Like a cat, Dempsey was up immediately and floored Firpo twice more—seven times he had been knocked down, and Dempsey had fallen twice to his knees, and the first round wasn't even over.

What happened next has become one of the most famous incidents in ring history.

During the preliminary matches Rice's typewriter was next to *Tribune* sportswriter Jack Lawrence's. During the final prelim, Lawrence said to Rice, "They're two big guys. If somebody goes through the ropes I hope it's Dempsey. At least he's lighter than that truck Firpo." Just before the main bout started, Rice moved down four seats, next to Bob Edgren of the *New York Evening World*.

No one, least of all Dempsey, thought Firpo would get up after the seventh knockdown. Rice said Firpo fell with a crash, and was "apparently far away in poppyland, gone beyond all recall." But Firpo got up once again, rushed Dempsey like the wild bull he was often compared to, and managed to get the champion up against the ropes; Firpo started pounding Dempsey with that quarry-club punch. One of his punches, a push-swing right, shoved Dempsey clean through the loosely strung ropes. Jack Lawrence got his wish, as it was Dempsey who sailed backwards out of the ring, landing directly on the sportswriter's typewriter. Rice, only four feet away, said Dempsey "came through head first, with his feet elevated. He came through with his mouth wide open and his eyes half glazed and distended with the look of the startled and the doomed." Startled too were Lawrence and Perry Grogan, a Western Union telegraph operator; they protected themselves by throwing their hands up, thus breaking Dempsey's fall. After the fall, the champion's ankles were still more or less on the canvas, and the two who cushioned his fall pushed Dempsey off them, and back into the ring—all before the referee had reached the count of seven.

For what was left of the round, unbelievably still the first, Dempsey and Firpo exchanged blows. When the bell rang, both fighters were throwing haymakers. Firpo dropped his arms and turned toward his corner, naturally believing it was time for a short rest; he figured he'd earned it. The furious Dempsey, who either didn't hear the bell or was too dazed to know what it signified, kept swinging. He hit Firpo three more times, the blows coming at least a full two seconds after the bell sounded. What the referee was doing at the time, Rice said, was something of a mystery, for Dempsey was not stopped, warned, or disqualified for fouling.

When the second round opened, Dempsey and Firpo tore into each other, at close quarters, hitting and clinching, with Dempsey again hitting Firpo on a Gallagher-called break. A few seconds later, Dempsey floored Firpo again. As the Argentine rose, Dempsey hit him with a left; on his way to the floor once again, Dempsey hit him with a right for good measure while Firpo was on his way down. This time, after the ninth or the eleventh knockdown, depending on whose counting counted, Firpo made vain efforts to rise, but remained spread out on the blood-splattered canvas for the count.

Without question the fight was what Rice called a melodramatic thriller beyond all words. It was four minutes "of the most sensational fighting ever seen in any ring back through all the ages of the ancient game," Rice wrote. The fight "was brief," Rice continued, "but in those four minutes there was crowded more actual fighting than most ring battles ever knew, no matter what the span of time."[64]

Yet Rice was bothered by Dempsey's "seeming fouls" that weren't called. Of course, it didn't help Firpo much that he didn't speak any English, but nonetheless a code of honor, Rice thought, wasn't heeded or enforced. Dempsey, Rice said, could have proven a finer sportsman. "Yet who can ask for any sportsmanship in the modern ring game," Rice reflected, "that is controlled purely by the commercial end. Perhaps it is the last word in foolish idealism to expect any sportsmanship from the boxing game." Dempsey later told Rice that Firpo's first punch, the right on the chin that put him on his knees, left him dazed. He suggested that at the time he wasn't much aware of codes, rules, or sportsmanship: "At that time I wasn't fighting for any championship or any million dollars. I was fighting to keep from being killed. I would have hit him at any place I found him."[65]

Maybe Rice even agreed a bit with Dempsey, as a couple of days after the fight, Rice admitted that for sheer, savage fury of attack, for whirlwind action and for brain-numbing episodes, he had never seen anything like it. This was a fight that was "a primal product drawn from the dim ages of the race." Rice seemed to acknowledge that in this kind of contest, far more fight than boxing match, there may be a point where the question of ethics is irrelevant. In the end he said that Dempsey's willingness to hit Firpo outside of the ring rules, his refusal to go to a neutral corner after a knockdown, and the question of his being helped back into the ring after being knocked out of it, "might be put down as the crafty act of the instinctive ringman who was out to win at any cost within the extended limits of the rules." Dempsey still maintained that he was simply trying to stay alive.[66]

Perhaps as an antidote to the savagery of boxing, Rice once again returned to his golf reporting immediately after the Dempsey-Firpo fight. He was off to the Flossmoor Golf Club, in Chicago, to cover the Amateur championship. Instead of a raucous crowd of eighty-five thousand fight fans, the tournament offered five thousand ever-polite, leisurely, hushed, and respectful members of a "gallery." The week-long tournament wasn't especially remarkable. This in itself was worth remarking on, since the rest of 1923 had been so memorable. About the only real excitement was a controversy over whether or not Max Marston's approach shot on the 13th hole in match play against Francis Ouimet rebounded from the rough off the leg of a Boy Scout and onto the green. What a contrast between this, a fairly friendly discussion, and the competitive attitude suggested by Jack Dempsey's comments to Jack Lawrence while the champion was momentarily resting on the sportswriter's typewriter: "You big _____, get me back in there; get me back in there, I'll fix him."[67]

In Marston's case, after a lengthy discussion as to whether the ball struck the Boy Scout on the fly, bounded from his leg upon the roll, or failed to hit him at all, the U.S. Golf Association officials allowed the ball to remain where it finally stopped, forty-five feet from the cup. The only surprise in all of this is why they didn't just ask the youngster himself; after all, he *was* a Boy Scout. Marston sank the putt and went on to eliminate Ouimet 3 and 2; Marston had beaten Bobby Jones the day before 2 and 1. The next day he met Jess Sweetser for the match play final rounds. On the 38th hole Marston finally prevailed, beating Sweetser by a stymied putt (Marston's putt blocked Sweetser's line— which the rules allowed) and winning the amateur crown. The crowd, Rice said, was excited. "Just after Jess Sweetser played his chip shot to the thirty-eighth from the edge of the course he was knocked to his knees by the stampeding gallery bent upon getting close enough to see every muscle quiver."[68]

Before settling into his fall routine of covering football and World Series baseball, Rice stuck with the golfers a while longer. Rudyard Kipling, he said, must have just come from a women's golf championship when he wrote, "The female of the species is deadlier than the male." Rice was covering the Women's National championship, and noted that the slim and young ladies were capable of teaching the two-hundred-pound male a thing or two about driving the ball straight ahead 220 yards at a whack. Golfing isn't at all in the bulge of the biceps or the width of the forearm, he said, as he watched the ladies: "Slashing it over the hill tops, down through the bunkered aisle/Shooting for pars and birdies, socking the ball a mile."[69]

Edith Cummings won the 1923 championship. Coming back from 2 holes down in the afternoon round, Cummings was deadly, Rice said, in the grim way she went about beating her final opponent, Alexa Stirling. Cummings, he said, rallied beautifully in the afternoon round with her free, firm, and slashing game. Despite the cold weather and the long, testing course at Westchester-Biltmore in New York, Cummings made up the handicap of two holes and picked up three more, winning with two to play. When she took the victory on the 16th hole, one of the first to congratulate her was her brother, golfer Dexter Cummings, the intercollegiate titleholder from Yale. He dashed from the gallery on the hillside and embraced his sister with such a rush that she was nearly swept off her feet.[70]

Rice had learned his lesson in the 1922 World Series; he stayed away from any play-by-play duties. The job went to Major J. Andrew White. Instead, Rice was talked into broadcasting a short after-the-game summary of the action. "This is the golden age of sport, the age of the multitudes shelling out golden shekels beyond all past records," he reminded his readers the day before the series was to open between the Giants and the Yankees, the third straight year the two teams faced each other. The 1922 series was indeed golden: the "subway series" between the two New York teams produced the first million-dollar gate in the history of the World Series.

The dope before the matchup was that it was pretty much an even call between the two teams, even though the Giants had taken the previous two series. Game one went to the Giants on a home run in the ninth inning that Rice had some fun with. The clock moved just past forty years, Rice said. As mighty Casey went to the bat? Sure enough. "Mudville is avenged at last!" Rice wrote, after Casey Stengel, lifting his stocky body on two quivering toes, drove the ball deep into left field between Bob Meusel and Whitey Witt. While the ball rolled to the fence, Casey's short piston-like legs motored him around the diamond; he beat the throw to the plate by twelve inches. It was a game-winning inside-the-park home run in Yankee Stadium. "So Mudville's raising hell again since Casey socked the ball!" Except that, even though the Giant fans were thrilled at the feat, there were no resounding cheers that rolled from flat to flat to greet Casey at the bat. "Probably," Rice said, "most of the 60,000 present had forgotten Mudville."[71]

In game two, Babe Ruth avenged his poor World Series performance of the previous year. He blasted two home runs, and the Yankees won 4 to 2. Ruth's first home run, hit in the fourth inning, sounded to Rice like a barrel of crockery being pushed down the cellar stairs. The ball bounded off the top of the right field roof and left the confines of the Polo Grounds. "At its top height the white ball, outlined against the hazy gray-blue sky," almost disappeared from view before it cleared the rim of the roof and bounded from sight into the field beyond. To Rice this was a true comeback from Ruth's 1922 performance; after his second home run in the next inning, the "Babe strode the tow path with the dignity of an evicted monarch returning to his kingdom." The crowd rose to pay him a thundering tribute.[72]

Stengel gave Rice more Casey-copy in game three at Yankee Stadium, hitting another home run and giving the Giants a 1 to 0 win. Game four was at the Polo Grounds. But Rice was at Ebbets Field. His sporting preferences were showing, as well as his status as *Tribune* star sportswriter, for he preferred to skip the fourth game to cover a football game, Notre Dame vs. Army. His lead for the game was entirely forgettable: "Brazil can cheer about its coffee as Ceylon raves about its tea. Let Florida and California speak with passion about their orange groves as Kentucky points with the finger of pride to the thoroughbred. But out in Notre Dame, South Bend, Ind., football grows on trees and bushes."[73] When the two teams met again in 1924, Rice's lead would be far more memorable. Rice had managed only a sideline pass rather than a pressbox seat for the 1923 game. He later recalled that on one wild end run, all four Irish backfield men came over through the sidelines simultaneously, knocking Rice down; two of the men had to jump clear over the prostrate Rice, who was looking skywards as they hurtled over him. "It's worse than a cavalry charge," Rice said to his sideline companion, "Brink" Thorne, Yale's 1895 football captain. "They're like a wild horse stampede." According to Rice, this sideline experience planted the vision in his mind of four horsemen outlined against the sky. But the image would not be articulated until the following year.[74]

Meanwhile, the Yankees had won the fourth game of the World Series. The series had been pitched as a contest between Brain and Brawn, that is, between McGraw's more intellectual approach to baseball—the scientific, calculating inside game of an earlier era—and the Yankees' swinging, walloping, hammering style. When the Yankees won the fifth game 8 to 1 to take a three games to two lead in the series, Rice explained that "Socrates had the brain of the ages, but Xantippe with a rolling pin drove him scurrying into the streets to seek the soothing solace of the hemlock juice from his favorite bootlegger." In other words, matter was winning out over mind, as the Giants got three hits to the Yankees' fourteen in game five.[75]

The next day, the Yankees came from three runs down, rallying in the eighth inning. Ruth had boomed another one, in the first, giving the Yankees their only run before the eighth. With the Yankees down 4 to 1 to start the inning, Ward, the first batter, popped out. Schang singled, then Deacon Scott hit safely and the crowd, Rice said, picked up the scent of carnage in the air, "that indefinable something that tips off the approaching hurricane." Next, a walk to Hofmann, to fill the bases. Another walk forced in a run, making the score 4 to 2. Nehf, the Giants pitcher who until now had held the Yankees down, was pulled. Rosy Ryan came in and promptly walked Joe Dugan. Another run, 4 to 3 now.

Babe Ruth came to the bat with the bases loaded; he had already broken two World Series records, having hit three home runs in a series and four home runs for his postseason career. The drama grew in intensity. Ruth fouled the first pitch, missed the second with a vicious cut, took a ball on the third, and then swung mightily at the fourth pitch, a fast curveball. The home-run maker lashed with full power, Rice said, and struck the empty October air as the ball broke a full foot below his whistling bat. Like the mighty Casey of forty years ago, Ruth had struck out. "Oh, what a fall was that, my countrymen!" But with two out, Bob Meusel ripped the ball up through the box, scoring two runs and rescuing Ruth and the Yankees from imminent despair. The Yankees won the World Series, and Babe Ruth's yelp of triumph was the loudest, according to Rice.[76]

After the series, the president of the National League, John Heydler, declared the contests the best ever. The paid attendance was more than three hundred thousand, and there were the $1 million in gate receipts. Baseball's hold on the public was the strongest ever, Heydler said; the current wave of intense interest had carried the game to its zenith. In particular, Heydler thought John McGraw deserved special recognition for his sportsmanship. A game loser, McGraw went over to the winners' dressing room to congratulate the Yankees for their splendid victory. "To-day, the day after the close of the series," Heydler said, "finds baseball at its highest point in the esteem and affection of the nation. It rules supreme as the game of games, without a rival."[77]

But baseball men were supposed to say this. Rice took Heydler's particular comments to a more general plane. It wasn't just baseball that was attracting spectators. It had been predicted that the Army–Notre Dame game would suffer from being held in the same city and at the same time as the World Series, but the game had sold out Ebbets Field, and many more fans stood outside the field still trying to get in. Yes, Rice reiterated, it was a Golden Age for sport—whether the game was baseball, football, golf, boxing, tennis, or played by men or women.

Some experts suggested that this popularity was some kind of vicarious substitute for the excitement of the war, but Rice believed instead that there wasn't that much psychology involved. He thought the reason that the number of paying sports spectators in 1923 was greater than that of the entire population of the United States was simpler to explain. The average human being, he said, cared for one or another aspect of sport, for recreation, exercise, or sheer entertainment, *just because.* But he quickly admitted that the widespread publicity given to sport by writers had helped to carry forth sporting tidings; the grip sport now had on the masses was due in part to the growing sporting intelligence of the entire country.[78]

For the remaining month or so of the 1923 sporting calendar, Rice covered collegiate football. Each week he previewed the games, picked winners in the top ten or fifteen games among the some two hundred fairly well-known college teams, covered one of the games himself, and then, on the Monday after, rehashed the various results. And in between the games, for the most part, his columns were devoted to more dope on football; Rice gave attention to deserving athletes whenever he could.

As the year ended, and Rice figured up his travels and the volume of his writing, he probably surprised even himself when he reported having traveled those sixteen thousand miles and typed out those ninety thousand words. Closer scrutiny shows that Rice was woefully underestimating himself, even if his regular columns, tales, and magazine writing is ignored. During the football season alone, his typical game coverage ran anywhere from twenty-five hundred to four thousand words. His football previews and postmortems ran just as long. He wrote more than ten thousand words on the Shelby fight alone. A safe guess might put Rice's productivity at about three times his own estimate, or the equivalent length of a couple of wordy novels.

When Rice reviewed the 1923 sporting year with his readers, he reported that the year more than kept pace with the procession of years past, and that its steadily progressive output reached out to new followers "with an appeal that is now covering every zone between the two guarding oceans." The same could have been said of Rice himself. "What a year!" Rice said.[79]

14

Mr. Fix-It

Little is known about Rice's private life. For instance, except for public anecdotes and a few letters, details about his relationship with his wife, Kate, and his daughter, Floncy, are skimpy; but by all appearances the bond between the three was sincere and unconditional love. Whenever possible Kate and Floncy joined Grantland on his trips, including baseball spring training; but the family also was frequently separated by extended distance and time. For instance, during those hectic sporting calendar weeks in 1923, Rice was gone for seven of nine consecutive weeks. When he was gone, however, Rice saw to it that Kate and Floncy were taken care of. Since the family was not wanting financially, Rice had not only Charles Goering as his chauffeur but also help for Kate in other household duties. Helga Christenson would be the Rice's household director and maid for more than thirty years. These two, Charles and Helga, were of incredible help to Kate when her husband was on the road. And as for the bond between Mr. and Mrs. Rice, it was always intact, never in doubt, even when they were apart. "And Kit, from the moment I slipped that gold band on your finger," Rice wrote in his memoirs, "you've been my constant sidekick—at least in my thoughts—no matter how many the miles that have often separated us."[1]

About those memoirs. So self-effacing was Rice that even in his own memoirs he fairly well excluded himself. He simply didn't think that his own life was an especially interesting topic for direct conversation. The memoirs weren't his idea anyway: they were suggested by Lowell J. Pratt, the publisher of *The Tumult and the Shouting;* Rice wrote them because he was asked to. In them he essentially tells what and who he saw and what he thought about what and who he saw.

But indirectly, Rice's memoirs do tell us a little something about him. They tell that this man belonged to everybody; he was common property, a thoroughly public figure. Of course, Rice's community chest was mostly his own doing. That is, given his full calendar, in truth Rice didn't have much unoccupied time on his hands. And add to this Rice's habit of doing for others whenever he could. It is closer to the truth that the reason not much is known about Rice's private life is that he didn't have much of a private life to know about.

But it is going too far to say that Rice was entirely comfortable as the public figure he had become by the mid to late 1920s. Sportswriter Red Smith, one of Rice's good friends, recalled that Rice was a restless sleeper. Smith said that Rice would thrash about in his sleep, tossing and turning and sometimes muttering. Every so often he would cry out in the dark: " 'No!' he would shout. 'No, dammit, no! Frankie, help me! No, I say!' " To Smith, interpreting these fitful episodes didn't require a Freud. The cries issued from a man who while awake, everyday, Smith wrote, "was saying *yes, surely, glad to, of course, no trouble at all, certainly, don't mention it.* Not only to his friends, but to all the others who imposed on his limitless generosity. And so, when he slept . . ."[2]

Without question, Rice was by constitution social. He couldn't have been otherwise even if he had a mind to. Everywhere he went he either came with someone, knew someone, met someone, found someone, hailed someone, or left with someone. Usually someones. But Rice's glad-handing habits were never, ever calculated or cultivated; his friendships were never fashioned in order to get anyone anywhere as a result of them. Even though Rice was clearly a *someone,* his affinity for *everyone* came easily, without affectation or motive. His friends report that Rice himself epitomized what it meant to be a friend: unconditional, natural, sincere, honest, generous, dependable, and persistent. Where others had companions, Rice's manner and manners crossed into that realm of friendship that the writer C. S. Lewis once identified as being beyond duty, necessity, and claims; such friendship, Lewis wrote, "has no survival value; rather it is one of those things which give value to survival." Rice's friendship was gratuitous.[3]

Of Rice's many circles of friends—athletes, newspapermen, famous personalities, coaches, promoters, business people—his fellow writers formed the tightest circle. When he cast back over his fifty-plus years of being a sportswriter, he said that his athlete-champion-star friendships were enjoyable for sure. But these feelings, he said, don't reach "the deeper glow that has come from my more affectionate connections with the writers and friends I've made along this almost endless trail."[4]

To have Rice as a friend was to have a unique friendship. By way of example, take Don Marquis. Rice and Marquis had remained good friends since their days in Atlanta, although by the 1920s both were firmly entrenched in journalistic careers that rarely crossed. Tragedy struck the Marquis family not long before the Christmas of 1923. Reina, Don's wife and herself a writer, suddenly dropped dead of a heart attack, leaving behind her husband of thirteen years and a five-year-old daughter. Marquis pretty much dropped out of sight, becoming almost entirely housebound—especially avoiding his established habit of conversation and conviviality with his peers at such places as the Players Club. Rice didn't let Marquis remain a recluse for long. The sportswriter was determined to get Marquis back into the world, somehow. Rice's vehicle was golf. First, Rice dragged his reluctant friend into a sporting goods store to buy the right golfing paraphernalia: clubs, tweed hat, and a pair of outsized knickers. About the only fun Marquis, a large man, could see coming would be "to drape these roomy trouserlings over his ample rump just to see how much time would elapse before the first person inquired, 'When does the balloon go up?' " When people told Marquis that he looked as big as a house in his knickers, he sportively responded that that was precisely the effect he was striving for.[5]

But getting the good-natured Marquis dressed as a golfer was easier for the persistent Rice than actually getting the writer to play the game. Every time Rice would set up lessons for Marquis, his friend would think up some excuse to procrastinate further, telling Rice that golf must be a good game or so many people wouldn't play it. Rice would argue that since Marquis was part Scottish, it was only natural for him to swing a golf club; Marquis would counter that since he was also part Irish it was just as natural that he should swing a shillelagh.[6]

When Rice took the tutoring into his own hands, patiently explaining the name and function of each club, Marquis would playfully rename them to suit himself: his driver he called Patrick after his favorite taxicab driver; his putter he named after himself as he thought himself to be the world's champion putterer; his long irons he named after people he thought had metal in their souls, such as his number-two iron, which he called Munsey after the notorious newspaper baron Frank Munsey.[7]

But the more Marquis playfully stiff-armed Rice, the more determined

Rice became. Eventually, after about two years of banter and missed appointments, Rice got Marquis to a golf course, only to find that his friend had "forgotten" to bring his clubs. As the two sat in the club's dining room for lunch, and after Marquis had refused to allow Rice to borrow clubs for him (preferring his own, of course), Rice, finally exasperated, called him a big sissy who was afraid to play the game. All the while and all around him, Don was hearing fervent, near-religious 19th-hole golf chatter around him; he finally said, "You're right, Grant. I am scared. In fact, these guys take the game so seriously I'm downright terrified."[8]

Eventually Marquis gave in to Rice's indefatigable prodding and took up the game, probably as much to get Rice off his back as anything else; he knew Rice wasn't a quitter and would be game to the end. Surprisingly, Marquis even rather grew to like the leisurely strolls around the links, although he never took the game or himself too seriously. Once, after Rice had taught him the basics, Marquis was soloing with fellow Player member William Tachau. Two golfers behind them asked to play through. Marquis and Tachau waved them on, and then stood to watch them drive off the tee. The first golfer whacked his ball long and true, a professional-looking shot. Tachau, wanting to know who it was that had hit such a wonderful shot, asked Marquis if he knew. "Sure," answered Marquis, "God."[9]

But what Marquis eventually told Rice he really liked about golf wasn't so much the game itself but the copy it gave him for his columns. In fact, Marquis explained to Rice, because of this new twist on his writing career, he was forced to give up his amateur standing in golfing circles. Marquis made a big to-do over the fact that since he was now every so often writing on the subject of golf, and consequently gaining financially from his golf writing, he would have to leave the amateur ranks of his Player playmates and turn professional! Some years after Marquis died in 1937, Rice paid tribute to that writing by telling a couple of his journalism friends that, truthfully, Don Marquis had written two of the funniest golf stories he had ever read ("Rattlesnake Golf," and "The Rivercliff Golf Killings," both appearing in his short story collection, *Sun Dial Time).*[10]

The humor of the situation aside, Rice did play a part in helping Marquis through his grief. Rice was always finding some sunshine somewhere and pointing it out to those he hung out with if they couldn't see it for themselves.

Another of his friends, his best friend during the 1920s and early 1930s, maybe his best friend ever, was Ring Lardner. It was perhaps this relationship in particular that reinforces Red Smith's observations of a sleeping Rice as a

Rice whose inner needs weren't entirely satisfied through his public life. When Rice went to New York in 1911, Lardner was writing baseball in Chicago for the *Tribune*. Two years later Lardner took over the popular *Tribune* column "In the Wake of the News." Lardner, no longer on the road with the Chicago ball clubs, used the time he gained to broaden his sports coverage as well as to freelance magazine articles. His national reputation began to grow with his contributions to the *Saturday Evening Post*. He would make the "busher" Jack Keefe of *You Know Me Al* famous on those pages. Gilbert Seldes, writing in *Vanity Fair*, situated Lardner as a remarkably popular American humorist who also was to become an idol of the intellectuals.[11]

Before the war Rice and Lardner often found themselves covering the same sporting events. They became friends. When John Wheeler returned from the war to start the Bell Syndicate, Lardner began writing a syndicated column for Wheeler and moved east to Great Neck, Long Island. This naturally created even more opportunity for Rice-Lardner contact. They traveled together whenever they could.

But even more, Lardner's wife, Ellis, became good friends with Kate Rice. According to Lardner's son, Ring Jr., "it was Kate and Ellis who really forged the bond between the two couples." Ring Jr. said Kate Rice was an original Southern belle, as original as Zelda or Tallulah Bankhead, but that she was much easier to get along with. Kate's "wit produced as much laughter as that of any nonprofessional on the New York scene, but she was practically unique among comics in her ability to transform herself into the most sympathetic of listeners." Like Rice himself, Ring Jr. went on, she had the innate knack of getting along with a wide range of people, "but she had a special regard for Ellis's integrity and judgment, looking up to her as, relatively speaking, an intellectual."[12]

There was something of a free spirit in Kate Rice, who was as socially spontaneous as her husband was. Once, the Rices were invited to a New Year's Eve party at the home of one of their friends. The guests were mostly writers of one sort or another. Kate gradually got into the spirit of the occasion. At one point in the gathering Kate grabbed a small figure off the mantel of the fireplace, which she apparently thought was of soft composition, and cracked one of the guests on the head with it. This left a big, bleeding gash in the guest's forehead, which so surprised Kate that she hit herself on her own forehead with the same object, creating the same result. Both the guest and Kate were doctored up, but for the rest of the bloody evening Kate's slowly reddening bandage began to match the color of her face. The next day, one of the curious guests called Kate to ask her if she was recovering well enough, and asked her by the by, "What did Granny say to you last night when you got home, Kate? Did he bawl you out?"

"I'll say he did—the worst I ever had."
"Did he! What did he say?"
"He said, 'Kitty, how could you?' "[13]

The bond between Kate and Ellis was between more common types than the bond between their husbands. Between Grantland and Ring the relationship was about as curious as the bond that can sometimes occur between two widely different species of animals who do not ordinarily keep common company. Some of Lardner's biographers have tried to puzzle their relationship out, seemingly becoming almost defensive, wondering between the lines how someone of Lardner's obvious talent could be so close to a mere sportswriter, and such a gushing one at that. Yes, Lardner was good friends with Scott and Zelda Fitzgerald who lived nearby, and with Rube Goldberg, Percy Hammond, Frank Adams, and James Preston. But he was closest to Rice, a man of an entirely different temperament and talent.

Donald Elder, a Lardner biographer who commented on the Lardner-Rice friendship, said that there could hardly have ever been two close friends with such different personalities. Rice was everything Lardner was not: "gregarious, talkative, enthusiastic, full of universal good will, optimistic, and outgoing." Rice was the champion of sports, Elder said, while Ring was the skeptical critic of them.[14]

In Lardner biographer Jonathan Yardley's view, "Rice was as ebullient as Ring was reticent, as sentimental as Ring was skeptical, as corny and obvious as Ring was subdued and subtle." Yardley thought that Ring must have regularly gagged on Rice's hero-worshipping copy.[15]

Ring's son, Ring Jr., also emphasized the differences between the two men. "Ring was a debunker of sports heroes, Granny a glorifier of them. Ring was reserved and taciturn, Granny outgoing and loquacious. Ring's views tended to be pessimistic with a sardonic flavor, Granny's optimistic and tinged with sentiment." But Ring Jr. went on to say that there was a side of his father that few people saw, except for his family and a few close friends. Ring Sr. couldn't relax with all the others, while Granny, Ring Jr. said, "was at his ease everywhere and with everybody; he knew an astonishing number of people by name, but that was only a fraction of the number that knew and greeted him."[16]

But Lardner's son also wrote that despite the real differences between these two men, they had a deep affection and respect for one another. There was an essential honesty in their separate personalities, and neither one enjoyed the company of mean-spirited or phony people. Once, Gene Fowler pointed this out about Lardner in particular when, of all things, he was speaking about his favorite streets in the city of New York. Next to Park Row, Fowler liked old Sixth Avenue; he recalled that so did Lardner. Ring liked Sixth over Broadway. On Broadway, Lardner once told Fowler, almost everybody was on the make; but Sixth was more interesting, "a street with no pretense." In fact, Lardner even wrote a song about Sixth, of which the only lines Fowler could remember were: "Oh, old Sixth Avenue!/I'll be having you. . . ." Rice would have gone along with the Lardner street comparisons. Besides their essential honesty, on the practical side, both men enjoyed similar things: golf, card playing, travel, humor, conversation, drinking, and gambling. These were their shared experiences and somehow in these similarities of interest the obvious temperament differences between them were of small account.[17]

The relationship between Rice and Lardner suggests some mystery about the deeper natures of both of these men. In his memoirs Rice said that in the many years he had known Ring, up until his death in 1933 of tuberculosis laced with alcoholism and insomnia, "I never quite knew that I knew him." So Lardner, even to Rice, was still something of an enigma. But no less was Rice to Lardner. At times Rice could be an out-and-out pest and no one would have begrudged Lardner for beating a quick escape—he was expert at it. But he didn't. Lardner stayed the course with Rice and vice versa, even though neither of them might have known precisely why. What was entirely missed by the Lardner biographers was that Rice was more than a mere gushing sportswriter. Underneath the more public Rice was a private Rice searching after something; this is precisely what the more private Lardner appeared to be doing in public. To some extent, then, it is entirely possible that each admired in the other what they were unable to find in or by themselves: Rice was fascinated by Lardner's social mask, while Lardner was intrigued by Rice's social nakedness.

Lardner had a public reputation as a hater of mankind. Many of his critics pointed to the pretentiousness and foolishness of so many of his characters, and often described Lardner as contemptuous and nihilistic. But as one of his biographers pointed out, Lardner did not hate the human race, only its tendencies toward selfishness and stupidity; he even had compassion for those who were so affected. Rice (among a few others) knew that privately he was loving and magnanimous, and shy. On the other hand, Rice comes off publicly as a lover of humanity. Yet we find in his interviews and his memoirs an occasional stunner of a comment, such as this one: that after spending all but ten years in the maelstrom of sport, and the vital segment of his life in crowds of fifty thousand to one hundred thousand people, "As I look back, the picture is a vast canvas of tumult and shouting, where, on many occasions, I was seeking a 'solitude I could call peace.'" This search for solitude could have come from Rice's own frustration with the foibles and follies of the human race, as we find near escape in some of his near poetry:

> I'm going back again—
> Perhaps to find the wraith of something lost,
> To miss the contest and the strife of men
> And all the game's wild glory, with its cost.
> To certain vanished mornings, slashed with gold,
> To shadows blown at deep dusk from the hills,
> I'm going back again before I'm old,
> Beyond the field of fortune and its thrills.
>
> I'm going back some day.
> It may be when young April comes again,
> Or when June twilights hold their purple sway,
> Or when December's snow-drifts sweep the glen.
> Or it may be amid the golden flame
> Of some far autumn—out beyond the din,
> As one who leaves the tempest of the game
> To seek the shelter of an ancient inn.
>
> I'm going back some day,
> Through the ghosts and shadows of a losing fight
> Or cheering crowds that might hold one at bay—
> To find, beyond it all, the peaceful night
> Of quiet valleys, or some friendly lane
> Where one can hear forgotten songs resung
> As far, white roads re-echo the refrain
> Of April mornings when the world was young.[18]

By the mid-1920s Lardner was reaching a million Sunday readers in New York alone with his syndicated column, not to mention the large audience he found through a number of "pieces" he was publishing. He was also admired by the intellectuals, praised in the *Dial* (in America) and in T. S. Eliot's *Criterion* (in England). Some of the literary critics—for whom, Gilbert Seldes said, Lardner "has apparently never cared a snap of his fingers"—praised his fluent and finished technique; they admired his masterful ability to write the American vernacular and to draw characters; they acknowledged his skill as a satirist and ironist, and the artistry of his lunatic humor. Seldes said that Lardner's mad fun had "the unnerving quality of seeming to be a little more logical than you yourself are, as if Lardner made the unconscious in us speak while we were expecting mere superficial logic." Seldes thought Lardner's writings demonstrated a "humor of preposterousness, resulting, somehow, in a keen fidelity to life." Lardner, he said, was purely American, and as native as baseball or cornbread; he was also terribly funny.[19]

Rice would sometimes tease Lardner in print. Lardner was quick to return the favor. Rice was forever making fun of Lardner's golf game. Lardner, in turn, would josh at Rice's Southern roots, claiming for instance that it was Rice and none other who invented the expression, "See you right soon." But there was one instance where Lardner may have gone a bit too far; even if Lardner was exaggerating, as caricaturists do, his description of his close friends, the Rices, as "Mr. and Mrs. Fix-It" in a May 9, 1925, short story appearing in *Liberty* gives an inkling of the fine line the Rices walked between being wonderful friends and damned nuisances.

The Lardner piece was subtitled "A Short Story of the Pestiferous Pastime of Minding Other People's Business." In it the storyteller, having only recently arrived in Chicago, gets to talking about his wife's friends. Now his friends, he says, are arguably pretty rummy, and "they seem to be lost without a brass rail to rest their dogs on." But Ada, his wife, met these people, Tom and Belle Stevens (a tongue-in-cheek resemblance to the Rices), that are the cat's nightgown, he said, when it comes to busybodies. Ada met Belle on the elevated. Belle butted in when Ada, who was unfamiliar with the city, was asking the guard where to get off for a party she was going to on the north side of town. Belle offered to guide her to the address, since she lived nearby.

One thing led to another, and Belle invited herself and her husband, Tom, to Ada's home the next day. The Stevenses promptly took over almost every decision the newcomers were or weren't about to make: where they should live, what dresses Ada should buy and where she should buy them, what kind of razor Ada's husband should use, how to fix Ada's sore feet by using the Stevens's chiropodist, and what football game they all should see together. The couples saw each other constantly.

"Well, it was about two months ago that this cute little couple come into our life, but I'll bet we seen 'em twenty times at least. They was always invitin' us to their place or invitin' themselves to our place and Ada is one of these here kind of people that just can't say no. Which may be why I and her is married." Ada and her husband couldn't escape the Stevenses effusive, well-meaning but oppressive and practically intolerable Southern hospitality. It was impossible to insult them, and in time nothing that the couple talked about getting or doing was worth a damn unless it was suggested or recommended by the Stevenses.

"Anyway, it began to seem like us and the Stevenses was livin' together and all in one family, with them at the head of it. I never in my life seen anybody as crazy to run other people's business. Honest to heavens, it's a wonder they let us brush our own teeth!"

The story ends as the Chicago couple secretly plan to go to Miami for the winter, partly to ditch the meddling Stevenses. "But a secret," the narrator-husband says, "is just about as safe with Ada as a police dog tethered with dental floss." The Stevenses, on the other hand, were planning to go to California for the winter. They invited their new friends, but Ada regrettably declined, blurting out that they were already booked for the South. Sad but undaunted, Tom Stevens used his many connections to entirely rearrange Ada and her husband's Southern trip: different and better train, different and better hotel. Meanwhile, Belle was busy making Ada take back all the clothes she had bought for the trip, picking out instead the "right" clothing for her. Then on the night before the couple was to leave for Florida, the phone rang and it was Tom Stevens.

"I've got a surprise for you," he says. "I and Belle has give up the California idear. We're goin' to Miami instead, and on account of me knowin' the boys down at the C. & E. I., I've landed a drawin' room on the same train you're takin.' How is that for news?"[20]

Lardner biographer Elder believed that this story caused a brief estrangement between the Lardners and the Rices—for about a week. That is possible, but unlikely, for Kate and Grant both had roaring senses of humor, including the ability to laugh at themselves. Anyway, as Lardner pointed out, they weren't insultable.[21]

Ring and Grant traveled together regularly; the two families also took working vacations together practically every winter throughout the 1920s, to Florida, California, and Nassau. In the winter of 1926 the Rices and the Lardners traveled together for three months, leaving New York for Belleair, Florida, to New Orleans for the Mardi Gras, to California for golf, and back to Florida to cover spring training. During the middle of the trip Lardner wrote to Scott and Zelda Fitzgerald: "The Rice's have been with us right along and we are still all speaking."[22]

This is sort of surprising—that they were still speaking and all—because in New Orleans, Rice was clear up to his balding head in Lardner's business, getting Lardner up to his neck in unwanted attention. It seems that Rice was overly concerned that Ring's appearance in New Orleans would go unnoticed; Rice thought that Lardner deserved some special attention and busily set up this party and that to make his otherwise shy friend happy. Ring, who had heard that writer Sherwood Anderson was also in town, in desperation rang up the author. The two had never met, but they each admired the other's work. In a pleading voice, Ring said, "Please, Sherwood, you do not know me, you have never seen me, you do not even know that you have invited me to dinner tonight?" "Yes," Anderson said, "I know. I even know where." Down in the French Quarter, there was a little place just opened by a Frenchman who, until recently, had been the chef at Antoine's, Anderson said. "It is a little place and dark. . . . Good wine. Good food." Ring said, "O.K. I'll bring my wife and Mr. Fixit and his wife. I hope it is very dark and very dirty. If it isn't very dirty have them shovel a little dirt into the place. I'll be there."

Anderson's recollection of that evening was that it was special for everyone. Lardner's face, Anderson said, was long and solemn, and was wonderful. He believed it was a mask. "All the time, when you were with him, you kept wondering . . . 'what is going on back there?'" Which was much like Rice's observation about Lardner that he never really knew that he knew him. What Anderson recalled most vividly about that evening was the warm affection everyone there had for Lardner. The mask dropped away for that evening, said Anderson, and "there was something loose and free in the little room." It was Ring. "I had never known any one just like him in writing in America. He awoke a certain feeling. You wanted him not to be hurt, perhaps to have some freedom he did not have. There was a feeling . . . 'if anyone hurts this man I'd like to punch him on the jaw.'"

The warm affection was poured over him, Anderson remembered, "as we poured the wine down our throats. We loved him. I cannot help thinking it was a rare and a rich evening in his life. He laughed. He talked. He drank the wine. He told stories. It was a good evening for him. It was something more than that for the rest of us." There must have been some internal satisfaction for Lardner as well since he set the evening up all by himself, without Mr. Fix-It's help; but, knowing Rice's determination to have the last word when it came to being a self-appointed social secretary, Mr. Fix-It no doubt picked up the check.[23]

Whenever possible, Floncy Rice was included in these extended vacations with the Lardners too. She traveled from one coast to the other and back with her family. It was rather appropriate that Floncy was born on Valentine's Day, for she was especially remembered for her multiple overlapping relationships. The 5'4" bundle of indecision was a blond and blue-eyed beauty. She was soft-spoken, willowy, exceptionally graceful in her movements, poised, ready to see the humorous side of things, and was blessed with a pleasing personality. Her schooling had come by way of the Dwight School for Girls at Englewood, New Jersey. She attended Smith College for a year, but she didn't take much to academics. Instead, and partly as a result of her travels in the States and abroad, Floncy became interested in acting. At first her parents discouraged her acting inclinations; but when it was clear she wasn't going to remain in college, they set her up with lessons.[24]

Her early career was on the stage; she debuted at age twenty-two in Ring Lardner's and George S. Kaufman's "June Moon," playing the part of Goldie. In time, she would become a Hollywood contract actress for MGM, enjoying a relatively successful ten-year career making B movies, perhaps relying on her beauty, which was more natural than her talent.[25]

In an interview she gave in 1938, four years after she had landed in Hollywood, she was particularly sensitive to becoming more than "Grantland Rice's daughter." Even though Rice was certainly in a position to help her with the studio management—since by then he had been producing the Sportlight Films for many years and had movie contacts—she firmly asked him to let her make it on her own. She believed that her father had had something to do with Lardner writing a part for her in "June Moon"; she wasn't happy about it. But even if it had been discussed between them, Lardner seemed particularly enthusiastic about doing it anyway, for he was especially fond of Floncy. So, by 1938, on her own, she had landed major or leading roles in such not-so-memorable films as "Navy Blue and Gold," "Paradise for Three," "Double Wedding," "Married before Breakfast," and "Beg, Borrow, or Steal." Shortly thereafter she may have peaked when she appeared with Dennis O'Keefe in "The Kid from Texas."[26]

In the "Who's Who in the Cast" for the comedy "June Moon," Lardner, in jest, wrote of Floncy that she was the daughter of Grantland Rice, the taxidermist. "Miss Rice's parents," he continued, "have no idea she is on the stage and every time she leaves the house to go to the theatre she tells them she has to run down to the draper's to buy a stamp. On matinee days she writes two letters (that's what they think) . . ." Ring Lardner, Jr., recalled that the part written either especially for Floncy or at least with her in mind—a cynical song publisher's disillusioned secretary—was showy and had some good lines, but that given her inexperience it wasn't particularly demanding.[27]

In a letter to Kate Rice written shortly before the play was to open at the Adelphi in Asbury Park, New Jersey, Lardner said that Floncy was doing well in some rehearsal performances in Atlantic City, but that he was busy rewriting parts of the play, working especially hard on the second and third acts. Floncy, he said, was getting two or three laughs, but would soon have better lines. "June Moon" turned out to be quite successful, opening in New York in early October three weeks before the Wall Street crash. About Floncy's ability, shortly before the New York opening, Lardner was quoted as saying cryptically that she had taken to acting like a duck to golf. The play made it through the theater season in New York and went on the road for the next two years.[28]

Ring Lardner, Jr. believed that Ring and Ellis regretted not having a daughter. (They had three boys.) Floncy, who was five years older than the oldest Lardner boy, Jim, was about the only young female that either Ring or Ellis had had any contact with; both, he said, may have seen Floncy as the daughter they never had. When she was in her mid-teens, and an exquisite beauty as a sub-deb, plenty of suitors were already throwing themselves at her feet. During the 1926 winter trip with the Lardners, Ring, quite amused, heard firsthand from Floncy the dramatic explanations of how she simply wilted at the prospect of choosing between her many admirers. As Ring listened, and from the incredible stress of these frequent situations, Floncy would let loose with her favorite slang expression, "I can't breathe." Lardner borrowed this claustrophobic phrase as the title for one of his most famous short stories for *Cosmopolitan,* published later in the same year as the long winter trip. In it he captured Floncy's already notorious shilly-shallying.

Floncy's behave-alike in the story, in the space of one week, and according to her diary, managed to get engaged to three different men, all of whom she promised to marry in December (these were only her mid-July entries). Gordon, one of the three soon-to-be husbands, called long distance to speak with the then vacationing girl, having gotten her phone number from her family's maid, Helga. Gordon "asked me if I still loved him and I tried to tell him no, but I knew that would mean an explanation and the connection was so bad that I never could make him understand so I said yes, but I almost whispered it purposely, thinking he wouldn't hear me, but he heard me all right and he said that made everything all right with the world."[29]

It isn't exactly clear how many times Floncy actually was engaged or married (the fictional character claimed to have been engaged at least five times a year since she was fourteen). Floncy was to become something of an item in the Hollywood gossip circles, which may have led to exaggeration of her amorous activities. Even Ring Jr. was romantically tied to Floncy in the late

1930s. He admitted dating Floncy for a while when she was between husbands; another Lardner, Jim, and Floncy had a short relationship, growing close shortly after Ring Sr. died in 1933. But Ring Jr. said that "Floncy and I may have gone as far as to hold hands, but it seemed a bit farfetched, after we had been photographed together in the forecourt of Grauman's Chinese Theatre at a Selnick premier, for a wire service caption all over the country to report our engagement just because the name combination was newsworthy."[30]

Floncy was married three or perhaps five times, most of them sudden decisions. All, except the last in 1944, ended quickly, two or three of them in one year or less. Her parents weren't especially pleased with some of her decisions, or probably with any of the first few. In one early case, Granny and Kit refused to give their permission, fearing that Floncy and her intended were totally unsuited for each other, until Floncy threatened to elope. That marriage lasted about a year, ending in a Reno divorce. In her next-to-last wedding, to Robert Wilcox, her leading man in one of her 1939 films, a sheriff in Honolulu gave her away. That one lasted four months following a trial separation after only six or seven weeks. Even her last and only lasting marriage, to Fred Butler, a businessman from La Jolla, California, was so sudden that Grantland couldn't get a plane reservation out west in time to give her away. He commissioned a family friend to do it for him.

However exasperated Floncy's parents must have been with her from time to time, there is nothing to indicate anything but warm love between the three of them. Even as she tried to distance herself from her father in order to get out from under his giant shadow, and even when she seemed to pine for the day when he would be known as Florence Rice's father, their relationship was enduring and endearing. In a short verse Floncy wrote to her father on Father's Day later in both of their lives, she expressed her sentiments about him this way:

> If only every son and daughter
> Could know the joys and all the laughter
> That you have brought me, through the years—
> The courage and the wisdom
> And the drying of my tears—
> Your gentle understanding
> And the greatness of your heart—
> They'd know why Father's Day, to me-
> Is one to set apart.

It was signed, "much love, Floncy."[31]

When Floncy left for Smith College in September of 1924, Kate and Granny moved from Riverside Drive, their home for the past thirteen years, to 1158 Fifth Avenue. Their new home overlooked Central Park at Ninety-seventh Street. Clearly, the Rices were now firmly entrenched in New York. They would live there for the rest of their lives, with home visits to either Nashville or Americus, Georgia, arranged whenever possible or necessary.

In Rice's newspaper world, Frank Munsey was trying to buy up the *New York Tribune* from Ogden and Helen Rogers Reid. Munsey, by then publisher of the *New York Herald*, had gradually swallowed up smaller or weaker newspapers. He bought the *New York Press*—a pioneer in sports reporting—in 1912, then consolidated it with the *Sun*, which he purchased in 1916. Four years later Munsey bought the *Herald*, its Paris edition, and its associate paper, the *Evening Telegram*, after James Gordon Bennett's death in 1918. By 1920 in New York there were still fourteen established general-circulation newspapers in business, under ten owners. But Munsey's appetite for consolidations was insatiable. He bought the *Globe* in 1923 and merged it with the *Sun*. Then, the next year, he went after Rice's old paper, the *Mail*, merging it with the *Telegram*. Buying and then killing off the newspapers he bought was why Munsey was known as the "grand high executioner," or sometimes as "the butcher," and why Don Marquis so easily named his two-iron golf club after Munsey.[32]

Munsey's *Herald*, a morning paper like the *Tribune*, wasn't doing particularly well. Both papers were supporters of the Republican party. Since the *Tribune* wasn't showing a profit either, and since the Reids were shoring it up with their own funds, Munsey figured that the two papers should merge. But Munsey hadn't counted on how strongly the Reids felt about their family's newspaper tradition. The Reids refused to sell. Munsey faced what he called their "deep sentiment and duty" to the historic *Tribune*; in other words, he faced principles. So instead of buying, Munsey sold. For five million dollars. The *New York Tribune* became the *New York Herald Tribune*. With the circulation of the *Herald* and the *Tribune* now combined, the merger produced a much stronger circulation and advertising base for the Reids; the paper now had the momentum it needed to become one of the top-ranked papers in American journalism. Ogden Reid informed the *Tribune* readers of the merger by saying that the *New York Herald Tribune* would show "that a newspaper can serve the public not only with good writing, brevity and enterprise, but also with conscience and courage."[33]

When Frank Munsey died about a year later, leaving a long trail of newspaper graves behind him and a fortune of twenty million dollars to show for it, William Allen White, the famous editor of the *Emporia Gazette* in Kansas, published a terse obituary, saying: "Frank A. Munsey contributed to the journalism of his day the talent of a meatpacker, the morals of a money-changer and the manners of an undertaker. He and his kind have about succeeded in transforming a once-noble profession into an eight per cent security. May he rest in trust!"[34]

Ogden Reid quickly extended Rice's contract with the paper through the remaining years of the decade. Reid gave Rice a free hand to do what he thought best with and for the sporting section. He was made an associate editor, but in his contract it was clear that he still aimed to be, by definition, nomadic. That is, Rice didn't have to stay in the office. Although he was given the authority for and supervision of the Sporting Department, he would assume these responsibilities "provided that [he] shall not be required to render such services during fixed hours or at any particularly designated time." So Rice, the born reporter, reported still.[35]

There was a football game that year, in 1924, that over the years has become probably the most famous football game in American sports history, not because it was unforgettable—few people will remember both teams, or the final score (it was 13 to 7)—but because of this Grantland Rice lead:

> Outlined against a blue-gray October sky, the Four Horsemen rode again. In dramatic lore they are known as Famine, Pestilence, Destruction and Death. These are only aliases. Their real names are Stuhldreher, Miller, Crowley and Layden. They formed the crest of the South Bend cyclone before which another fighting Army football team was swept over the precipice at the Polo Grounds yesterday afternoon as 55,000 spectators peered down on the bewildering panorama spread on the green plain below.

Well, the lead won't be forgotten, but it has been misremembered from time to time over the years. Here's sportswriter Tim Cohane's version of Rice's lead cited from memory in 1963: "Out from a cold, gray October sky, Four Horsemen rode again. They are known in literature and dramatic lore as famine, fire, pestilence, and sudden death, but these are only aliases. Their right names are Stuhldreher, Crowley, Miller, and Layden."[36]

Knute Rockne, who had been the head coach at Notre Dame since 1918—and who had himself played football for the school—said that the epic of the Four Horsemen was the story of an accident. He was referring to the fact that four unremarkable freshmen football players had as seniors become one of the most memorable and capable football backfields of this era, perhaps of any era.

As freshmen, they were "Not so hot," Rockne recalled. One halfback was a sleepy-eyed youngster who, Rockne said, looked like he was built to be a tester in an alarm clock factory (Crowley); another halfback seemed half puzzled by everything going on (Miller); the quarterback's main strengths seemed to be his sharp, handsome face and his clear, commanding voice, for he made as many mistakes as he called signals (Stuhldreher); and the fullback, who could run like a streak, mostly just ran into the opposing tackles instead of slits in the line (Layden). Average players, Rockne figured. Just average.[37]

Stuhldreher had come from Massillon, Ohio. Miller, from Defiance, Ohio, followed his brothers to Notre Dame; one brother, Harry ("Red"), was third team All-American, and another, Walter, played with George Gipp on the 1919 Notre Dame team. Crowley came from Green Bay, Wisconsin, and had played for Curly Lambeau at Green Bay High; Lambeau had also played with the Gipper, but in 1918. Layden's home had been Davenport, Iowa, and he had at first matriculated to the University of Iowa, but a bad knee (from basketball) scared off the Iowa coach; Layden's high school coach was Walter Halas, older brother of George Halas of the Chicago Bears, and he contacted Rockne, who took a chance on the fullback. "The four did not play as backfield in their freshmen year," said Rockne. "I had seen them in practice and survived the experience."[38]

In 1922 Notre Dame had easy games early in the season, beating Kalamazoo, St. Louis, Purdue, and DePauw. Their first big game was against Georgia Tech. This was the school that under John Heisman in 1917 played Cumberland University and rolled up a score of 222 to 0. At some point in that game—Heisman recalled it was about the time Tech's Golden Tornado team had scored its first one hundred points—the Cumberland backfield began losing confidence, and interest. Every time a Cumberland ball carrier got the ball he was subject to a thorough thrashing. One Cumberland halfback found himself with the ball momentarily, but was quickly trashed, and fumbled. The ball rolled toward his teammate, the other halfback.

"Fall on it, Pete, fall on it."
Pete looked at the fellow with complete scorn.
"Fall on it yourself—I didn't fumble it."[39]

College football by then was considerably livelier than in years past. The forward pass gradually won broader acceptance. As the Western and Southern schools resorted to a passing game—some more than others—the more conservative and once powerful eastern schools became less dominating and less successful. Mass plays were being replaced by varied offensive formations, and many coaches were relying more on the pass. For instance, Captain Rodgers and his West Virginia team did practically nothing but pass the ball in a game against Princeton in 1917; Princeton was defeated soundly and saw the light. They had learned that the forward pass wasn't just another play. It was becoming football itself.

As the game began to change, the spectator needed some tutoring. Heisman and some of the other famous coaches such as Pop Warner and Knute Rockne were frequent and willing contributors to the public's knowledge. They were sought after by such weekly magazines as *Collier's*. Rice, as a dedicated and expert football writer, joined in when he could to help the growing number of football fans learn more about the newer wrinkles in the game.

Rice and John Heisman had remained friends since Rice's days in Atlanta, and they teamed up to write a monograph called *Understand Football*. Its purpose was entirely explanatory and was aimed at helping the uninitiated learn how to watch a football game. The concise, sixty-three-page, fifty-cent booklet included chapters and drawings on football offenses, defenses, generalship, special plays, positions, a glossary of football terms, referee functions, penalties (and referee signals for them), and outstanding records.

But in the Rice-Heisman handbook it was clear that the game in the 1920s was not radically pass-happy. Even though the forward pass was popular, it was restrictively used. By contemporary standards football was still run-and-punt conservative. Line bucks and end runs dominated the ground game. Even Heisman, clearly a football innovator, was surprisingly cautious. For instance, some of his basic strategies were:

• Never run two end runs in succession. Give the boys a chance to catch their wind.

• Never use an end run when you are within twenty yards of your own goal. Too dangerous.

• Don't try an end run on the near sideline. Too little room to run.

• Use line bucks for short yardage.

• If the ball is well in your own territory, punt instead of going for a first down. If it is inside your 10, punt on first down; inside the 20, punt on second, and so on.

- When in doubt, punt.

- Never pass behind your own 30 yard line.

- Never pass on first down. Your opponents might intercept and you have lost three chances to advance the ball.

- Don't pass if you are making first downs by rushing. Why risk it?

- Don't pass for a touchdown unless you have to, when, for instance, you are desperate and only have one down remaining. Persist in rushing the ball.[40]

When Georgia Tech took on Notre Dame in 1922, Rice had picked Tech by a touchdown or two. Instead, and with the help of the four sophomore backfield men, Notre Dame upset Tech 13 to 3. This was in spite of Stuhldreher making the biggest mistake of his career. He chose to pass on second down on the Tech 5 yard line. The pass was incomplete. The rules stated then that if a pass was thrown over the goal line and was incomplete, it was a touchback and the other team took possession of the ball on their own 20 yard line. Nonetheless, Rockne was encouraged by these four young men. Maybe they weren't so average after all, he thought.

But they were still small, weighing an average of only 160 pounds. And this was in their senior year. Individually they weren't especially impressive, but together they were, well, according to Rockne himself, absolutely the best—ever. Their records, according to their coach, made them unique as a continuing combination in the backfield. They lost only two games out of thirty—both to massive Nebraska teams in 1922 and 1923. By October of 1924, having beaten up on Lombard (40 to 0) and Wabash (34 to 0), Notre Dame took the field against Army. Rice's pick the day before was Notre Dame, mostly owing to the "speed, power and team play" of what he called the best backfield in the country. Even though two New York radio stations were broadcasting the game, the rivalry between Notre Dame and Army clearly justified playing the game at the Polo Grounds. By game time at 2:30, Rice was comfortably poised at his typewriter in the press box along with some of New York's best—Runyon, Gallico, Broun, Fowler.

To see Rice work a game such as this one was to realize just how much a reporter Rice was. And he was best under such pressure. "Every game and every play tells a story," Rice wrote when, with Heisman, he was instructing his readers how to watch a football game, "and the idea is to read the story as it is being written on the field." Rice was an uncanny reader.[41]

This was the story of a South Bend cyclone striking—couldn't be snared . . . could be surrounded . . . but breaks through . . . keeps on going . . . take to the storm cellars at top speed . . . rips and crashes through a strong Army defense with more speed and power than the warring cadets could muster. "Notre Dame won its ninth game in twelve Army starts through the driving power of one of the greatest backfields that ever churned up the turf of any gridiron in any football age. Brilliant backfields may come and go, but in Stuhldreher, Miller, Crowley, and Layden, covered by a fast and charging line, Notre Dame can take its place in front of the field."[42]

It took Rice around four hundred words just to introduce the story, for after the praise he heaped on the Four Horsemen and Notre Dame's quick if light front line—the Seven Mules as they were called—he described Coach McEwan's game Army stars as well.

It was all Army in the first quarter as Rockne had started his second string. The idea was to let the fresh, hard hitting get over with before the Horsemen and the Mules took the field. So, Rice said, the cyclone started like a zephyr. Army controlled the football for much of the first quarter, making three first downs (quite a feat then). Notre Dame held. Late in the quarter, "in the wake of a sudden cheer," out rushed the Four Horsemen.

Nothing happened immediately. And, said Rice, when Army's Wood kicked out of bounds on Notre Dame's 20 yard line early in the second quarter, "the cloud in the west was no larger than a football." But suddenly it started. Crowley peeled off fifteen yards. Signs of lightning and thunder. Layden got six. Then Miller picked up ten. Stuhldreher threw a forward pass to Crowley for twelve more. The winds were picking up. Miller ran for twenty around Army's right wing before Wilson threw Crowley out of bounds on the Army 10 yard line. "Crowley, Miller and Layden—Miller, Layden and Crowley—one or another, ripping and crashing through, as the Army defense threw everything it had in the way to stop this wild charge that had now come seventy yards." Throughout it all Stuhldreher led the blocking. Crowley and Layden added another five, and then Layden went straight up the middle and across the line for a touchdown "as if he had just been fired from the black mouth of a howitzer." Gale force winds. In that second period, Notre Dame had eight first downs to Army's none. The score at halftime was 6 to 0, Notre Dame.

In the third period, more trouble was in store for Army as Stuhldreher intercepted a pass at midfield. Crowley went fifteen yards; Miller and Layden combined for fifteen more. Notre Dame was stopped momentarily, the quiet before the storm, but then Crowley swung out wide around Army's left wing, cut back, and crashed over the line for Notre Dame's second touchdown. The cyclone had hit. Twice more in this period Notre Dame threatened to score, but Army held.

The Four Horsemen were kidders. Their occasional bantering wasn't anything like what has since come to be called "trash talking," but sometimes they did have fun with their opposite numbers. In this game, Ed Garbisch was Army's All-American center. He was exceptionally good and, when the Four Horsemen had been stopped at all that day, Garbisch was usually involved somehow. The four backs decided to tease Garbisch whenever a good gain was made at his expense. After such a play, one Horseman would politely inquire of another so that Garbisch, picking himself up off the ground, could hear:

"Is that the great Mr. Garbisch?"

To which another would solemnly reply:

"Yes, that's the great Mr. Garbisch."

Then, the next time Garbisch was flattened, Crowley would ask of Miller in amazement:

"You don't mean to say that's the great Mr. Garbisch?"

And Miller would respond: "If the number's correct it's none other than Mr. Garbisch in person."[43]

By late in the third quarter, Mr. Garbisch and company began playing football—maybe spurred on by the Horsemen's polite inquiries. Harry Wilson, Army's noted running back, finally broke through the Notre Dame defense for a thirty-four-yard gain. Even though Army was forced to punt, Wood, one of Army's quick punters, put the ball out of bounds at the Notre Dame 5 yard line. Layden was forced to kick from his own end zone. Army's punt receiver, Prentice Yeomans, called for a free kick (fair catch) on the 35 yard line. He was tackled, and Notre Dame was penalized fifteen yards. Three plays later, Army was on the 12. On fourth down, quarterback Neil Harding engineered a play fake up the middle to Bill Wood, drawing Notre Dame's entire defense into the line, and Harding, who kept the ball, sprinted for the last twelve around the right end and the only Army score of the day.

From then on, the game see-sawed. Neither team could do much of anything, and the game ended with Notre Dame winning 13 to 7. Rice wrapped up his fifteen-hundred-word story by praising the Four Horseman, again, giving credit to the Notre Dame interference, and giving Army some spirited words about their pluck.

So that's how Grantland Rice read this 1924 football story. It probably would have been just another football game if it hadn't been for that famous lead and, shortly thereafter, the famous picture of the Notre Dame backfield, with uniforms and balls, sitting astride those four horses. But Rice's words came first, and without them there would have been no point to the picture. Anyone reading Rice's story the day after the football game was reading the game as it was being written. His words, according to one commentator, made a million see in mind what only fifty-five thousand saw in flesh.

Over the years, Grantland Rice has taken some pretty good shots over the famous Four Horsemen lead. Some of these criticisms were mere funning, and fairly harmless. Red Smith, for instance, wondered out loud at what angle Rice had seen the Notre Dame backfield "outlined against a blue-gray sky" (he did not know that Rice had watched the previous year's game from the sidelines with Brink Thorne). Another popular criticism was the obvious overwriting. Wells Twombly said that Rice mixed his metaphors about twenty-four times in the opening lead of this 1924 game. Well, maybe not twenty-four times, but Rice was certainly guilty of mixing it up. Brawling metaphors and foaming hype. Yes, that was Rice. Vintage Rice. But according to sportswriter Robert Lipsyte, to his credit (Lipsyte had plenty of debits), Rice's creative writing was at least honest. "He was reporting a staged spectacle in a mock-heroic manner, extending the entertainment from the field to the page." Lipsyte went on to say that it is absurd to believe that ball games should be covered as hard news, like a fire, or as sociological indices. "If a game should be covered at all, beyond a box of statistics in a paper of record or a consumer-oriented evaluation, it might as well be in the spirit of the show, with crunching adjectives and smashing verbs."[44]

But there is one persistent claim that isn't so harmless. It has to do with the very idea of where Rice got this immortal lead in the first place. The claim is that Rice borrowed the idea from someone else and gave no credit either then or later. Since this was a lead that created not only the Four Horsemen, but in part, Rice's legend too, it is worth sorting out its probable origin. Outlined against more than three-quarters of a century of blue-gray October skies is a nasty and careless repetition of the claim that Grantland Rice was a plagiarist. The story first appeared in print in Jerome Holtzman's book *No Cheering in the Pressbox* (1973). Sportswriter Robert Lipsyte signed on to the story in his book *Sportsworld* (1975). Since then, and instead of checking the facts, some recent scholars have perpetuated the story. In his book on the creation of Notre Dame football, Murray Sperber has given the charge new legs with his repetition of it; even Charles Fountain, a Rice biographer, has repeated the story.[45]

The source of the plagiarism charge issued from the distant memory of a newspaper and publicity man one generation removed from Rice. "I dropped the idea for Granny Rice's lead on the Four Horsemen," said George Strickler, "and I don't remember that Granny ever thanked me." Strickler was Knute Rockne's publicity man, and at the time was a student at Notre Dame. He went on to become the NFL's publicity director for a while, and later was the assistant general manager and public relations man for the Green Bay Packers. Eventually he wrote about football for the *Chicago Tribune* and eventually becoming the paper's sports editor until his retirement in 1969.[46]

According to Strickler, he accompanied the Notre Dame team to New York for game. He inaccurately recollected, "I think the score was tied at 7–7 at the half. Notre Dame only won the game by one touchdown, 14–7." Strickler said he was standing in the aisle of the press box at halftime talking to Grantland Rice, Davis Walsh, Damon Runyon, and Jack Kofoed, although he wasn't sure in recollection if the fourth fellow was Kofoed. The four of them were discussing the Notre Dame backfield.

The night before Notre Dame had left by train for New York, Strickler said he saw (for about the seventh time, he said) the Rudolph Valentino movie, *The Four Horsemen of the Apocalypse.* It was showing at the recreational hall on the Notre Dame campus. "I don't remember too much about the story," Strickler noted, "but I can still see those ethereal figures charging through the clouds—Death, Pestilence, Famine, and War."

So, said Strickler, he joined the conversation of the four reporters, all agreeing that the Notre Dame backfield was doing a tremendous job, and how they were cutting Army down, and "I said, 'Yeah, just like the Four Horsemen.' That's all I said."

That night, when the evening editions were on the newsstands, Strickler said he picked up the *New York Sun* and saw Rice's lead about the Four Horsemen. In fact, though, Rice's lead first appeared Sunday morning in the *New York Herald Tribune* and ultimately that same day in some one hundred other papers that subscribed to Rice's syndicated work. But no matter when Strickler actually saw the lead, he believed that he was responsible for it, not Rice. As he recalled the incident fifty years later for sportswriter Jerome Holtzman, he mentioned that the last time he saw Granny was at a Notre Dame and Oklahoma game much later. They were in the bar at the Oliver Hotel. Strickler said, "Granny acknowledged that he heard it from me, but in his book he was confused on where he got the idea."[47]

Rice's memoirs didn't appear until after his death in 1954. In Rice's own recollections, it was chiefly the sideline incident during the Army–Notre

Dame game the previous year, in 1923, that provoked the idea of horses and cavalry. Granny, Strickler said, "tied it up to something he had written the year before. But, heck, he only saw Notre Dame once in '23, when they played Brooklyn, and they didn't do much. The Four Horsemen weren't even the regular backfield that year." But, of course, Notre Dame didn't play Brooklyn; they played in Brooklyn at Ebbets Field, exactly where Rice said he saw the 1923 game between Army and Notre Dame, October 13. And Rice also saw the Four Horsemen in the regular backfield: "The Army fought to the finish, but Army with all its power had nothing to match that spirally array of backfield talent made up of Cowley, Layden, Miller and Stuhldreher, all sweeping forward back of a fast aggressive line that continually got the charge."[48]

Strickler said that in the bar at the Oliver, he asked Rice what would have happened if all four writers had used the same idea for their lead, and Rice said, "Well, I don't know. Maybe it wouldn't have been so good if everybody had used it." Also years later, Strickler said he asked Davis Walsh the same question. Walsh said, "We'd have probably all been famous like Rice."[49]

There are a couple of reasons that Strickler's self-serving claim should be challenged. First, from everything known about Grantland Rice before and after 1924, such "borrowing" was clearly out of character for him. There has never been any other such incident reported where Rice is politely or otherwise accused of plagiarizing an idea from anyone. His leads, hackneyed, overblown, and otherwise, came from wherever it was that Rice's mind seemed at the time to take him. As he read the games on the field, court, or ring, the emotion, action, surprise, romance, beauty, rhythm, and poetry of sport—combined with his wide-ranging intellectual background—suggested metaphors, epitaphs, similes, images, and analogies. He was forever interpreting the text on the field by telling his own readers what the event "was like." My gentle readers, he was seemingly saying, let me tell you what I saw in terms of something else you are familiar with, like certain wild animals, natural phenomena and disasters, historic events, characters in great literature, heroic moments or people, or even in terms of some common everyday occurrences.

But there's another and more objective reason to challenge Strickler's version of the lead's origin. Rice had used the Four Horsemen lead before, more than once. In 1922, Rice, in a discussion of the coming 1922 World Series between the Giants and the Yankees, noted the changing seasons this way: "The Four Horsemen of Autumn are rounding the corner—the fragrant odor of burning leaves, twilight practicing quick starts for an early rush, a trifle more hop to the wind's fast one, and then—another world's series."[50]

Then, again, he used the Four Horsemen idea in September of 1924—only a few weeks before the Notre Dame and Army game. Rice covered the opening international polo match between the Americans and the British at Meadowbrook, Long Island, New York. With the society blue bloods from two continents looking on, including the Prince of Wales, the United States outrode and outplayed England in front of forty thousand fans. Rice set the scene after the Prince received a royal welcome from the hosts—whose polo team would soon be a royal pain to the Brits—as the match was about to start: "Within a few minutes he [the Prince] was to see the most amazing polo he had ever seen or dreamed about. There was a flare of extreme beauty to the scene as the vivid coloring from the big crowd finally blotted out the light blue seats and left the deep, green sod of Meadowbrook completely surrounded."[51]

The Prince, it was reported, wasn't at all pleased with the first chukker or two of English play (they played eight), and apparently so much so that when the score was 10 to 1 in favor of the United States, he left his seat, went to the players enclosure and spoke individually to each player, trying to rally them. It isn't known what he said, but the Brits played with more spirit after the Prince's chat, even though they still went on to lose 16 to 5.

Meanwhile, Rice was busy trying to keep track of the play-by-play and the record-setting number of goals scored as each chukker was played. In his story the next day, Rice marveled at the speed play and mallet work of the American team's top four players. Except for Captain Lacy's play for England, America's guests were outridden and outplayed in every department of the sport, and never had a gray wisp of a chance, reported Rice. These four polo players "stand silhouetted stark against the outline of sporting history as one of the greatest combinations that ever galloped over turf." About England's predicament, there was nothing to be done, wrote Rice, when "you are struck by a combination typhoon, earthquake, avalanche and tidal wave coming head on." But, he went on, "Lacy alone, as great as he was, was not enough to meet the Four Horsemen of Modern Polo, who were not only outriding and outhitting their invading rivals, but in addition, were working together with a blend of team that was remarkable to look upon."

For Rice's front-page story, the *Herald Tribune* carried the bold subhead: "Four Horsemen of Modern Polo Sweep Invaders Off Field in Individual and Brilliant Team Play." The headline on the continuation page read: "Four Horsemen of Polo Sweep Invading Britons From Field."

So, given Rice's honest character and his previous and even recent use of the Four Horsemen comparison, it seems unlikely that George Strickler "dropped the idea" to Rice for the Notre Dame lead. Grantland Rice was no plagiarizer.

But what George Strickler apparently did do that permanently ingrained the Four Horsemen in our collective imagination was to arrange for the picture a couple of days after the game itself. Strickler said that he got the idea as the team was leaving New York on Sunday morning. He wired his father, who was then working at Notre Dame as the school's butcher, to arrange for four saddled horses to be at the Monday afternoon practice. This he did. Strickler also arranged to have a commercial photographer show up at practice time as well. Strickler, the horses, and the photographer all converged on Rockne while practice was underway. The stunt was explained, Rockne stifled his immediate objections, the players were hoisted onto the nags and given footballs, and with the quick click of the shutter, the Four Horsemen were immortalized.

Within the week the picture of the Notre Dame backfield appeared from coast to coast, and everyone from then on referred to the group as the Four Horsemen. Strickler received royalties each time the shot was used; he claimed that he made about ten thousand dollars in 1924, with most of it coming from that picture.

If it is a question of who is in whose debt, it is more likely that George Strickler owed Grantland Rice for coming up with the marketable image of the Four Horsemen in the first place. In any case, between the two of them, Rice and Strickler, Rice's transient words were from then on fixed permanently to the legend of those four football players who rode again and again and forever then, "Outlined against a blue-gray October sky."

"Outlined against a blue-gray October sky, the Four Horsemen rode again." So wrote Rice on October 18, 1924, in the *New York Herald Tribune*. This, the most famous lead in sportswriting history, gave these four football players immortality: (left to right) Don Miller, right halfback; Elmer Layden, fullback; Jim Crowley, left halfback; and Harry Stuhldreher, quarterback. (University of Notre Dame Archives)

Rice covered both of the Dempsey-Tunney fights. In the first, in 1926 in Philadelphia, Tunney won a ten-round decision. In the second in Chicago in 1927, and pictured here, Tunney escaped a knockout in the seventh round when Dempsey failed to move to a neutral corner after knocking his opponent to the canvas. Several seconds elapsed before the referee was able to pick up the count, thus giving Tunney more counts than ten. Tunney recovered his feet and outboxed Dempsey in the remaining three rounds, winning the "long count" fight in a unanimous decision. (Sport Parade, Special Collections, Vanderbilt University)

Rice is seen here in January 1928 in Miami Beach playing golf. The foursome includes golfer Jim Brophy, boxer Gene Tunney, golfer Jock Hutchinson, and Rice. Tunney was the heavyweight champion, having beaten Dempsey for the second time three months earlier. Tunney fought once more, winning over Tom Heeney in a technical knockout. He then retired from the ring. (World Wide Photos, Special Collections, Vanderbilt University)

At the annual Artists and Writers golf tournament and outing, Rice is pictured in 1929 shaking hands with novelist Rex Beach at the Palm Beach Country Club. Rice defeated Beach two and one, defending his championship from the previous year. (P&A Photo, Special Collections, Vanderbilt University)

Having just boarded a ship bound for the Bahamas at the 1929 Artists and Writers outing, good friends Ring Lardner and Rice are seen working together to solve the problem of hitting golf balls off the deck's surface. Lardner's foot is serving as Rice's tee. (Pictorial Press Photos, Special Collections, Vanderbilt University)

On a small fishing boat in the late 1920s Rice has propped himself up against the wheel to take a much earned nap. He had just hooked a four-hundred-pound shark, but handed the fish over to someone else in the party. Rice had lost interest, he said, and as a fisherman he thought that these big ones looked much better in the water than on someone's line or on a wall. The shark was eventually cut loose. (The Granger Collection, New York)

Rice continued to cover Bobby Jones's career as both an amateur and a professional. Rice saw first-hand many of Jones's thirteen national title wins, including the last two wins in his remarkable Grand Slam in 1930. They remained friends after Jones's retirement and played golf together whenever they could. In 1936 Kate and Granny were accompanied by Bobby and his wife, Mary, on a working vacation trip to the Olympic Games in Berlin. (Special Collections, Vanderbilt University)

Rice covered the 1932 Olympic Games in Los Angeles as a syndicated columnist with Jack Wheeler's North American Newspaper Alliance. There he met Babe Didrikson. Didrikson had qualified for all five individual women's track and field events, but she was only allowed to compete in three. She won two (javelin and 80-meter hurdles) and placed second in the high jump. For the rest of Rice's life he boosted her athletic feats and called her the greatest all-around female athlete in the first fifty years of the twentieth century. (Sport Parade, Special Collections, Vanderbilt University)

Rice is seen here interviewing the California tennis player Helen Wills Moody for Rice's weekly thirty-minute NBC radio program sponsored by Coca-Cola. Shortly after this interview in April 1932, Wills sailed for England to compete for the Wightman Cup. Rice covered Wills's entire career (which included seven U.S. and eight English championships), starting when she was a serious-faced youngster of twelve or thirteen. She won her first Forest Hills title at the age of seventeen in 1923 and her last Wimbledon title in 1938. Her brand of competitive, not social, tennis earned her the title of "Little Miss Poker Face." (Hearst Collection, *Los Angeles Examiner*, Special Collections, University of Southern California Libraries)

Florence (Floncy) Rice, Grantland and Kate's daughter, was an aspiring actress. Here she is pictured on a Hollywood set in the 1930s putting makeup on her father, either for a gag or for a Rice cameo appearance. (MGM, Durward Graybill, Special Collections, Vanderbilt University)

In the 1930s Grantland and Kate Rice began spending part of their winters in southern California, generally in the Los Angeles area, where they stayed at the Beverly
Wilshire Hotel. Since by then Rice was no longer writing for a single newspaper, it
was possible for him to write his syndicated column and to meet his other writing,
reporting, and film-producing obligations from wherever he happened to be. Floncy
was now living in the Los Angeles area with her husband, Mr. Fred Butler, and this
regular sojourn provided an opportunity for Granny and Kate to enjoy an annual reunion with her. In this 1935 photograph Rice is standing with his two dashing
women, Floncy and Kate. (UPI/Corbis-Bettmann)

382

Babe Ruth gave Rice plenty of wonderful copy all through the 1920s and early 1930s. Rice genuinely liked the Babe and saw in Ruth's swing what sportswriter W. O. McGeehan saw: America's most magnificent national gesture. Babe retired in 1935, but even late in his career he could pull off remarkable heroics. Here he is seen in the first All-Star Game in 1933 at Comiskey Park in Chicago hitting a line-drive home run into the right field stands in the third inning. With Ruth's "big blooie" help, the Americans beat the Nationals 4 to 2. (Acme, Special Collections, Vanderbilt University)

Yet another colorful baseball player was "Dizzy" Dean, who pitched for St. Louis. In this foursome, Dean was attempting to prove that he could play golf with the best of them—but without clubs. Dean, clubless, is on one knee in the act of picking up his ball, preparing to send it on its way with only his pitching arm. Looking on are Rice; Billy deBeck, creator of the King Syndicate cartoon "Barney Google"; and P. Hal Sims, the noted bridge expert and golfer. A few months before this 1935 photo, in the 1934 World Series between St. Louis and Detroit, Dean was hit in the head by Billy Rogell's throw to first base as he tried to break up a double play. "They x-rayed my head," Dean said later, "and didn't find anything." (Hearst Collection, *Los Angeles Examiner,* Special Collections, University of Southern California)

Ring Lardner and Grant Rice were especially close friends, so much so that they even purchased adjacent beachfront properties in East Hampton, Long Island, in the late 1920s. Ring's wife, Ellis, and Kate Rice were likewise close. The two families traveled together almost every winter, sometimes to Florida, often to California. Pictured here are Lardner and Rice during one of their working vacation trips on a Hollywood movie set in the early 1930s, watching with pleasant curiosity as a character actor sets about to repair some kind of problem he is having with his thingamajig. (Special Collections, Vanderbilt University)

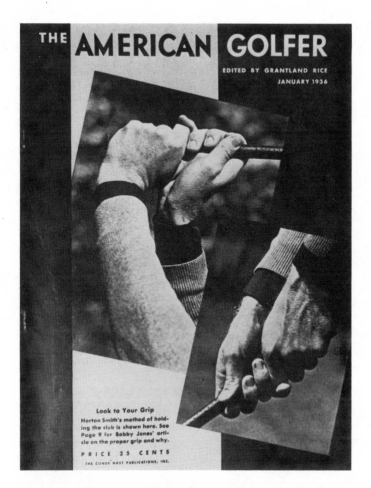

THE AMERICAN GOLFER

EDITED BY GRANTLAND RICE
JANUARY 1936

Look to Your Grip
Horton Smith's method of holding the club is shown here. See
Page 9 for Bobby Jones' article on the proper grip and why.

PRICE 25 CENTS
THE CONDÉ NAST PUBLICATIONS, INC.

American Golfer began publishing in November 1908 under the editorship of Walter J. Travis. Rice was asked to edit the magazine in 1919, along with managing editor Innis Brown. During the 1920s this magazine was quite successful with its crisp and tasteful format. Circulation had risen to seventy thousand before Conde Nast Publications, Inc. bought it in November 1928. It lasted until 1936. Pictured here is the last number of the *American Golfer,* January 1936. Shortly after the magazine folded, Rice was asked to be the editor of another magazine, *Golf.* Rice served as editor from the magazine's inception in 1938 until it folded in 1941. (Special Collections, Vanderbilt University)

Rice enjoyed the out-of-doors immensely. When he found the time, he hunted and fished all over the United States, and in Mexico and Canada. A favorite hunting grounds was the thirty-six-thousand-acre Ichauway Plantation of Robert W. Woodruff, the president of Coca-Cola. Woodruff and Rice were close friends for two decades. Taking a pause to refresh their horses from a hunt at Ichauway are Bob Woodruff (left) and his two guests, Rice and "Chip" Robert. (Special Collections, Vanderbilt University)

Rice was easy to like. Sportswriter Fred Russell said that Rice wouldn't have seemed out of place in the pulpit or standing in a daily double line at the racetrack. Another sportswriter, Tim Cohane, noted that in Rice there was an intriguing blend of quiet friendliness with the unmistakable quality of a lion. George M. Cohan called him a "virile saint." And too, there was that hat, the beaten-up Confederate gray fedora Rice wore almost everywhere he went. Everyone but Granny, Fowler said, knew there was a halo under it. (Special Collections, Vanderbilt University)

Rice was a member of all sorts of groups: formal men's clubs or perhaps country clubs, as well as informal ad hoc societies of one sort or another. In this 1949 picture, Rice is pictured with a watermelon in hand for a posed shot of the Village Green Reading Society, a group of sportswriters and friends who met to escape city life and discuss poetry and other subjects. Naturally, Rice was a charter member, his shirt indicating he is number one. Sitting on the ground is Joe Stevens. In the second row are Tim Cohane (left), Rice, and Red Smith. In the back row (left to right) are Willard Mullin, Herman Hickman, Frank Graham, and Charlie Loftus. They are sitting outside of Herman Hickman's getaway shack in Connecticut, which Hickman said he was "too poor to paint, too proud to whitewash." The watermelon was the Society's dessert and Rice's contribution to the good times. He would plug it, pour a bottle of bourbon into it, and let it ferment during the day's discussions. (Special Collections, Vanderbilt University)

As the hands-down dean of American sportswriters in the first half of the twentieth century, Grantland Rice worked lifelong at his craft. Besides writing his near-daily columns, he could be found variously on the radio, producing his one-reel films, his column The Sportlight, picking the football All-America teams, writing magazine articles, composing verse, fundraising, helping a young sportswriter learn the ropes, or otherwise spreading the gospel of sport and sportsmanship. Above all, however, Rice was most comfortable and most especially competent as a sports reporter, under a deadline, covering the derring-do of others. (Special Collections, Vanderbilt University)

Grantland Rice poses at his typewriter only a few weeks before his death on July 13, 1954. He was still a member of the working press on the day he died. And on that day he was still working. (Special Collections, Vanderbilt University)

> Born—live—and die—cradle along to grave.
> The march is on—by bugle and by drum—
> Where only those who beat life are the brave—
> Who laugh at fate and face what is to come,
> Knowing how swiftly all the years roll by,
> Where dawn and sunset blend in one brief sky.

15

Sport for the Fun of It?

At the end of the 1924 intercollegiate football season, the ever-evolving rules of the game were as usual under review. When Walter Camp—the father of American football—summarized the 1924 football season, he mentioned some of the more controversial changes in the sport. Football was just beginning to experiment with kickoffs from ground placement. It was well into October before the kickers picked up this knack, but since they were kicking off from the 50 yard line it didn't take them long to start blasting the ball over the end line. The rule was quickly revised, as the rule makers saw that the ball would have to be moved back to at least the 40 yard line for the kickoff.

Other issues were up for discussion at the winter meeting of the Intercollegiate Football Rules Committee. Coaches were making more use of free substitutions, not just of individual players but also of entire elevens. Camp noted, almost breathlessly, that in its game against Indiana, Coach Amos Alonzo Stagg's University of Chicago team used six guards, six halfbacks, three centers, three quarterbacks, five tackles, five ends, and five fullbacks—thirty-three men, or three complete elevens. On the other hand, Camp pointed out, Indiana played right through until the last few minutes of their game against Ohio before they made a single substitution. Another issue was the point-after-touchdown kick. There was not much drama to the almost automatic one-point kick, Camp noted: "Probably in the long run, the consensus of opinion will bring the elimination of this extra point, counting the touchdown as 7 points."[1]

Maybe the hottest topic was the growing use of the "huddle system." In the past, the quarterback had called the plays at the line of scrimmage (corresponding roughly to the modern "no-huddle offense"). The signals may have been spoken sentences with a word omitted here or there, or maybe a disguised and intricate numbering system. In any case, in the 1924 season, especially in the Midwest, it became common for the players to huddle to ensure that they got their signals straight. When Iowa beat Yale a couple of years earlier using the system, the eastern schools began experimenting with it. Coach William "Bill" Roper of Princeton used the system successfully for the first time that year.

Camp reported that he had studied the new system thoroughly. He said it had certain advantages, but that it wasn't necessarily a progressive change. He admitted that it didn't take any more time to run a play, contrary to what the critics guessed. He said it was even a bit quicker. He also agreed that it could neutralize the impact of noisy crowds in a big game—when the ball was positioned near the sideline, crowds were duty-bound to scream their heads off so that the signals couldn't be heard by the players. But clearly, Camp wasn't convinced that huddling was an improvement: ". . . following the operation closely, it certainly strikes one as taking in some way some of the life out of the team. They do not seem to strike into their plays with the same snap and abandon that characterized the older method. There is something exhilarating and driving in the voice of a good quarterback who brings out his signals with a snap, a vigor that seems to penetrate the team itself, and this silent method of giving signals seems to lack that driving quality." Camp seriously questioned whether the new silent system was all that useful and predicted that it was only a passing phase of the game.[2]

On March 14, 1925, the Intercollegiate Football Rules Committee reconvened at 9:30 in the morning in New York after a lengthy Friday night meeting that lasted until midnight. Walter Camp was its recording secretary. He had been directly involved in football rules since the 1880s, and was eager to debate the changes in the game under discussion at the meetings. When Camp hadn't arrived by ten o'clock or so, Bill Roper was sent to find him. Roper went to Camp's hotel, the Belmont. When Roper couldn't raise Camp by knocking on his room door, the hotel staff took the door off its hinges and found Camp in his bed, dead of an apparent heart attack at the age of sixty-six.[3]

Among the many contributions Walter Camp made to football was the marketing gimmick in 1889 of picking the mythical All-America football team. The idea was copied widely, but Camp's list—early on at least—was the tops. Over the years Camp had fairly exclusively picked the elevens himself, relying on his own preferences, like the way he preferred his quarterback to call the signals loudly, with authority, by himself, and without a huddle. Naturally, Camp received countless recommendations, but in the end the picks were his, and he tended to lean toward the East, given his geographical roots in New Haven. For ten years after 1889, for instance, only seven universities were represented on the All-America list: Princeton, Yale, Harvard, Pennsylvania, Cornell, Chicago, and Carlisle. By the time he made his final selection for the 1924 season, eleven universities were represented on the first eleven, five of whom could be considered "Western:" Michigan, California, Nebraska, Notre Dame, and Illinois.

Rice knew Camp, of course. They had a casual friendship prior to World War I, but since then they had taken in some games together and occasionally played some rounds of golf. They also were both contributors to *Collier's*, Rice in fact being something akin to a sporting editor for the magazine since he wrote regular weekly pieces. When Camp died, Rice paid tribute to Camp in a *Collier's* piece that explained how Camp had gone about picking the All-America team. Rice should have known better than to tell what he knew.

Rice noted that Camp had put together thirty-six teams and speculated that these great players represented the memory of the best of American football contests: "Battles in rain and snow, sun and shadow . . . the flying tackle and the savage line thrust . . . the forward wall braced for the shock . . . the graceful spiral careening against a sky of blue and gray . . . the long run down the field . . . the goal-line stand . . . the forward pass . . . the shrill of the kick-off . . . singing and the cheering of great crowds . . . young and old Americans gathered together on a golden autumn afternoon with bands playing and banners flying." Camp's quiet death, Rice suggested, may have been in the midst of such a dream, "that the Call to Quarters came and taps was sounded as the great knight came down the field."4

It didn't take Lee Maxwell, the president of Crowell-Collier publications, very long to tap Rice on the shoulder for the duty of picking up Camp's All-America selections. Who better than the most widely read sports authority in America? Rice said he could think of plenty of better people. "I squawked loudly," remembered Rice. He said he didn't want any part of the job. It was too big to be done right, Rice argued, since the game had long ago outgrown any single person's ability to pick a team. Maxwell insisted. The never-ending yea-saying Rice weakened, agreeing to do the job for a year. He would be affiliated with the *Collier's* selections for the next twenty-one football seasons.[5]

Rice had a bit of experience in picking mythical teams, since he and John Heisman had put together All-Southern teams from time to time. A couple of other things qualified him for the job, besides his encyclopedic knowledge of the game of football. His reputation for fairness was first-rate, and he knew all the right people to pull the job off with as much competence as was possible for such a controversial undertaking.

If Walter Camp liked the quarterback/signal approach to picking All-Americans, Rice preferred the huddle/discuss. After all, there was somewhere around eight million square miles to cover and a fair number of football fans to please from among the country's population of 110 million. Rice invited coaches, officials, and football writers to participate. Telegrams were sent to coaches between Berkeley and Hanover, and between Tulane and Minnesota. He assembled what he called the *Collier's* Board, including such writers as H. G. Salsinger of the *Detroit News,* Clyde McBride of the *Kansas City Star,* Braven Dyer of the *Los Angeles Times,* O. B. Keeler of the *Atlanta Journal,* and other writers representing various regions. In December, with Rice, who himself would see at least twelve teams play every fall, the *Collier's* board huddled, discussed, rated, and picked.[6]

So one-sided had the process been before, that Rice felt the need right from the opening snap to defend his approach to picking his 1925 All-America selections. In his lead he said he was trying to head off poison-dipped spears and regional war hoop battle cries by explaining his new protocol. This he did, giving the four tests he and his advisory body used to make the final selections, and making sure to drop as many names as he could to spread the blame/praise. From then on, and until 1947 when *Look* magazine put together some five hundred accredited football writers to make the All-America selections, Rice organized and supervised the *Collier's* national mythical team. For all of his squawking, it appears that Rice honestly enjoyed this annual responsibility.[7]

Grantland Rice received a letter in the spring of 1925: "So Babe Ruth ate his way into the hospital, did he?" queried the old-timer. "Well, the young fellers ain't up to the boys of my day. Now, I'll tell you what a good meal meant in the old days, and that's twenty years ago or more. I remember right here in Boston that Ed Killian and another feller sat down to lunch and ate $18 worth of food—and you could get more food for $18 in those days than four men could carry now. Did Ed Killian go to the hospital? I should say not. He shoved back the table, went out to the ball park and beat Cy Young 1 to 0 in a real ball game!"[8]

In early April, many weeks into the 1925 spring training season, Babe Ruth fell ill. En route to the North, having played exhibition games in Atlanta and Chattanooga, Ruth was taken off the Pullman in Asheville, North Carolina, presumably felled by a strong case of indigestion. Feverish and only semiconscious, he was transferred to St. Vincent's Hospital in New York for treatment. His physician, Dr. Edward King, explained that Ruth's diet was to blame. Reporters wrote that it was indigestion as much as anything else that caused Ruth to keel over and crumple up several times on the way from Asheville to New York.[9]

Ruth was known for his huge, hedonistic appetites, including his appetite for food. Harry Hooper, one of Ruth's teammates in Boston, recalled that as a rookie, Ruth once gulped six hot dogs and six bottles of soda before a game, belched loudly, and yelled "Let's go!" Now, in 1925, and before the Yankees had reached Asheville, Ruth allegedly had been told by a doctor that he was on his way to a good case of indigestion. The prognostication had little impact on Ruth, as he was reported to have eaten a large steak and plenty of fried potatoes the night before his attack, and the day of his attack he finished off a heavy breakfast with more fried potatoes. When he collapsed in the train while playing poker, he hit his head, causing further speculation that he had suffered a skull fracture.[10]

This was the famous "stomach ache heard around the world." The news spread quickly, if inaccurately. In England, for example, a good number of people thought Ruth had died. English correspondents frantically called their reporter brethren in New York to get the necessary obituary information. To W. O. McGeehan, Rice's colleague on the *Herald-Tribune,* there was no surprise that the Babe's stomachache gave vent to gargantuan moans as the world held its hands to its abdomen and groaned in sympathy. Ruth, McGeehan wrote, was America's national exaggeration.[11]

Ruth wasn't simply the highest paid athlete of the times or the most colorful (on and off the field). McGeehan explained that Ruth was America's demigod, and that his bat was to his age what the club of Hercules and the hammer of Thor were to other ages. McGeehan said that it was customary in sportswriting to assist in the making of a hero a week to keep the customers interested. Most of those heroes were artificial, he added. But not Ruth. He was a personality, maybe a crude one, but a personality and not to be belittled.

"There is nothing in the world that is more sincere," wrote McGeehan, "than the Babe when he swings at the baseball, whether he hits it or not." He thought the Babe's swing was our most magnificent national gesture.[12]

When the story first broke about Ruth's collapse and immediate hospitalization, Rice didn't say much of anything, except to comment about Ruth and food. Noting that the king had turned thirty-one that February, Rice said that under normal conditions he should be good for another six or seven years. But given his dietary habits, it was clear to Rice that unless Ruth changed the type and amount of food he stuffed down his alimentary canal, his abnormal physical capabilities—which had carried him nicely thus far—wouldn't be enough to carry him much further. Rice even predicted that unless Ruth's illness was an extended one, he would lead the Parade of Punch and hit more than forty home runs once again.[13]

McGeehan, on the other hand, found Ruth's stomachache story worth a couple of columns. McGeehan poked fun at *New York World* copy supposedly written by Ruth himself, noting how incredible it was that Babe Ruth covered his own stomachache, while it was happening, for the *World*. Remarkable, simply remarkable. With tongue in cheek, McGeehan wrote that Ruth had pulled off the greatest journalistic achievement of all time: though violently ill, he staggered to the wire and got his own story to his paper before he fell unconscious, thereby scooping Rice, Lardner, Irvin Cobb, and all the others. Just before he collapsed at the poker table, McGeehan theorized, Ruth must have sent for his typewriter, saying, "Unpack my typewriter. If anything is going to happen I want it to find me at my work. Before anything else I am a newspaper man. Accuracy. Terseness. Accuracy."[14]

Covering his own stomachache and hospitalization was indeed the act of a demigod. The wordy account that was published in the *New York World*, McGeehan quipped, was the model of "terseness and accuracy." At the hypothetical suggestion that perhaps Ruth didn't really write his own stuff, McGeehan said surely not. How could it be that a great metropolitan newspaper would countenance anything of the sort? "It is not nice to think of what the effect might be upon the earnest young men and women who are learning to become trained observers in the Pulitzer School of Journalism." He imagined that, the way things were going, it wouldn't be a surprise to see the horse race between Zev and Papyrus be covered similarly. He pictured the race's end, with Papyrus, after losing to Zev, would trot to his stall, sweating with his coat caked with mud, refusing the attention of his rubbers, and would squat down before the portable typewriter in his stall, "I must do my story for the *New York World*," said the gallant steed. "Nothing else matters."[15]

This—the practice of ghosting for famous personalities—was growing more and more common by the twenties. McGeehan called it "synthetic journalism." Those practicing it called it "making a living." According to Rice, who got the story from writer George Ade, sports ghostwriting had gotten its start about a generation earlier. Ade told Rice he had seen former boxing champion John L. Sullivan witnessing the Fitzsimmons-Maher fight in the 1890s. Ade said when he asked Sullivan what he was doing at the fight, Sullivan said a Boston paper had sent him down to write the fight up, adding, "I've got a young fella from Harvard with me who is doin' the writin'."[16]

The fight lasted only long enough to get the paper into the typewriter, about two punches. Maher knocked Fitzsimmons down with the first punch and then Fitzsimmons decked Maher with the second punch. The Boston paper's lead as written by Sullivan's Harvard ghost was: "E'en as the mantle of the dewey eve settled over the silvery Rio Grande tonight. . . ." It was signed by John L. Sullivan. Since then, ghostwriting had steadily become a popular way to sell papers.

In any case, Ruth's stomachache was front-page news. The public more or less bought the story that Ruth had had severe indigestion, especially since a story was put out that he was operated on for an intestinal abscess. The more cynical suspected that Ruth had contracted something sleazy that had little to do with overeating, more to do with over-brotheling. But the press said nothing. Stories that the entire affair was a mere publicity stunt to hype up the Yankees' opening-day game faded when Ruth did not return to the line-up until June. That was a good long time for recovery from mere indigestion. But the press still said nothing.

Ruth had already cost the Yankees a few hundred thousand dollars by not being in the line-up for the first six or so weeks of the season; one estimate put the loss at five hundred thousand dollars. Even so, apparently Ruth still figured he was something special. He apparently hadn't fallen low enough in his career by then, or learned anything in particular about his off-the-field behavior, for only a couple of months after his return, Miller Huggins, the Yankees manager, fined Ruth five thousand dollars and suspended him from the team indefinitely for "general misconduct." Huggins wouldn't specify what the infraction was, but when one reporter asked if the misconduct meant drinking, Huggins replied: "Of course it means drinking, and it means a lot of other things besides." Huggins went on to say, "There are various kinds of misconduct. Patience has ceased to be a virtue. I have tried to overlook Ruth's behavior for a while, but I have decided to take summary action to bring the big fellow to his senses."[17]

Ruth thought the fine and the suspension was a joke. Bootleggers and murderers get off for less, popped off Ruth. Figuring that he had more clout with Colonel Ruppert, a Yankees owner, than Huggins did, Ruth challenged Huggins's authority. Ruppert sided with Huggins, much to Ruth's surprise. Ruth apologized and promised personal reform. The suspension was good for several days and the fine was imposed. But in 1929, when Huggins died, general manager Ed Barrow returned the money to Ruth. Overall, the 1925 season was a washout for Ruth. He batted .290 and hit a mere twenty-five home runs—an excellent season for anybody else, but not for the Colossus of Clout.[18]

Ruth would do better in the seasons ahead—he would hit sixty home runs in 1927, and he led the Yankees to three consecutive pennants and two World Series victories (in 1927 and 1928). Off the field, his freewheeling spirit and his foolish but honest antics did nothing in the end to detract from his public image. They enhanced it. Who else would or could meet President Calvin Coolidge and say, "Hot as hell, ain't it 'Pres'?" Or who else, in explaining his intention to go on a hunting trip in the near future, would tell reporters that he was going to be shooting "peasants." When Ruth held out for more money in 1930, someone suggested that he should be more reasonable; after all, it was pointed out, this was the Depression and he was asking for more money than President Hoover was paid. Ruth reportedly said, "What the hell has President Hoover got to do with it? Besides, I had a better year than he did."[19]

Rice valued Ruth's friendship over the years, "pure, warm, unadulterated friendship with no holds barred, ever." Even during Ruth's chaotic 1925 season, Rice speculated for his *Collier's* readers that Babe Ruth had become without question one of the two most popular figures in the history of sport. The other was John L. Sullivan. Rice tried to put his finger on why it was that these two, over all others, had such an appeal to sporting fans worldwide. It wasn't necessarily skillful preeminence, since in Rice's opinion, Jim Jeffries was as great a fighter as Sullivan, and maybe better. In baseball, Ty Cobb, George Sisler, and Rogers Hornsby were arguably as brilliant—maybe more so—than Babe Ruth. Yet no other athletes had the drawing power of Sullivan and Ruth.[20]

Both, Rice pointed out, were roistering types, big, bluff, and boisterous. Neither was particularly religious about their training regimen. Both spoke directly, without compromise, diplomacy, or tact. Neither tried to conceal their rough edges; neither pretended to be polished or smooth. They both were wallopers and, said Rice, "the multitudes have always esteemed the roar or the thud of the wallop as the sweetest of music." In spite of their large physical sizes, both were graceful; both had enough speed, and neither was lumbering or ungainly.

Most of all, though, Rice believed, their personal magnetism came directly from their love of the game itself. Ruth had already made a fortune in baseball by then, yet the crowd could see in his every move that he was playing the game for fun above all else. Sullivan, who is said to have knocked out more than 150 opponents, loved to fight, and the crowd knew it. In spite of their less-than-professional jagged edges, both took pride in their craft. Sport was their soul's desire.

Neither hero—for they both were heroes, if by "hero" we mean the oldest of senses of having a noble purpose—was especially thrifty either. They spent what they earned—and more. As an example, Rice recalled later, Babe Ruth in the winter of his horrendous 1925 year visited Charles Stoneham's Oriental Park at Havana, Florida, to bet on the ponies. In less than two weeks Ruth blew somewhere between thirty thousand and fifty thousand dollars. To Rice, this was further evidence that having money wasn't particularly important to Babe Ruth. Living was.[21]

"Each gave to his game all that he had, at every start," Rice wrote, "with a deep appreciation of the great public that brought him fame and fortune." Both Sullivan and Ruth saw the great throngs as sponsors of their greatness and, as patrons, deserving of the finest work of the artist at every move. Rice continued: "Neither ever faked, neither ever shirked, and with all their crudities both, in addition to being skilled artisans at their trade, were dramatists of high degree with peculiar qualities of crowd attraction that no one else in the game has known." Rice thought they both were architects of their own personal destinies.[22]

When McGeehan referred to Babe Ruth as a demigod, he compared him to Pan, the Greek god of the woods, fields, and fertility, who has come down to us as part-goat and part-man, in all a rollicking and playful deity. On a trip down to Hot Springs, Arkansas, a few weeks before the 1925 spring training season—as was Ruth's annual habit in order to boil out all the nasty humors—he and McGeehan got to talking about the north woods. The drabminded, reported McGeehan, were in the same drawing room on the train and were bent on trying to make this playboy a commonplace and serious young businessman. But when the subject of the north woods came up, Ruth demanded eagerly of McGeehan, "When you were up there did you ever swing birches?"

McGeehan had never done that. Puzzled, he asked Ruth to explain. "Why it's easy and lots of fun," explained the Babe. He told McGeehan that you climb to the top of one of the birches when you discover a ridge with a big flock of them. At the top of one birch, you get the tree to sway until it bends way over. Then you let go of your first birch and grab ahold of a second. After that you just go on swinging from birch to birch. Ruth claimed he had gone miles through the woods without ever touching the ground.

From then on, said McGeehan, he knew he was speaking to a demigod, an eerie creature whose spirit was not of the common earth, but who belonged to the treetops, where he could play and look down upon the groundlings.[23]

Yes, Rice agreed, Ruth was really just a kid, a man-boy with a heart that seemed to arrest itself for life at about age fourteen or fifteen. He was a perpetual swinger of birches, who, to borrow words from Robert Frost, might have liked to "get away from earth for a while/And then come back to it and begin all over."

> May no fate willfully misunderstand me
> And half grant what I wish and snatch me away
> Not to return. Earth's the right place for love:
> I don't know where it's likely to go better.
> I'd like to go by climbing a birch tree,
> And climb black branches up a snow-white trunk
> *Toward* heaven, till the tree could bear no more,
> But dipped its top and set me down again.
> That would be good both going and coming back.
> One could do worse than be a swinger of birches.[24]

Grantland Rice predicted that the 1920s would be known as the commercial age of sport. It seemed to him that no matter which way he turned, the old dollar sign was the first sight in the landscape. He gave a couple of examples from his mailbag. A request came in, he said, for him to write up a certain country club golf course. The board of directors reasoned that if Rice were to give the club a boost, then the inevitable flock of new membership applications would create a waiting list. The two-thousand-dollar membership fee for the existing members would then become valued at three thousand.

Another letter came in after his 1925 All-America team was announced. The writer complained that Rice hadn't given player Whoosis and a certain Whatsits team enough public praise. "This team," wrote the indignant member of the town's chamber of commerce, "is a big boost for the town. It gets the town more advertising and brings more business here. It deserves more mention than it has received." Rice didn't comment directly, but he recalled that the Illinois–Ohio State game that year had brought in an estimated six hundred thousand dollars to Columbus; there were thirty thousand visitors to the city who had to be housed and fed and sold things. "So now added to the peevish alumni," Rice observed, "are the local haberdashers, innkeepers and restaurant owners."[25] But like a futile struggle in a tar pit, Rice's own energetic, enthusiastic, and prolific professional work was helping, despite his protests, to promote the growth of modern sports.

With his football brethren he was tabulating All-America picks either by telegraph or in person. During the football season Rice would throw open his Fifth Avenue home for a drop-in on Saturday nights. Any and all of the coaches in town for a game that day—Rockne, Robert ("Zup") Zuppke, Jock Sutherland, Bill Roper, Pop Warner, Dan McGugin—would show up at the Rice's for a spot of Tennessee "milk," a popular Prohibition-era drink. Kate and Grantland graciously hosted these gatherings as often as they could. Besides the socializing, Rice naturally bent the coaches' ears for their perspectives on potential All-Americans.

Also in the fall of 1925, Rice covered the World Series between Pittsburgh and Washington. The *New York Herald Tribune* bragged that their photographs of the opening game had been flown by airplane from Pittsburgh to their presses in New York. Walter "Big Train" Johnson was on the mound for the Senators in game one. Even after nineteen seasons, Johnson had enough gumption to strike out ten Pirates, and allowed only five hits as Washington won 4 to 1.

But only a few hours after the game, the baseball faithful were saddened to hear of the death of Christy Mathewson, "Big Six," who had died of the white plague, tubercular pneumonia. The forty-five-year-old Mathewson, who had fought in World War I, had never fully recovered from being "gassed" while in France. Matty had had a number of spells of lingering sickness since 1920, but he began failing seriously during the early part of the 1925 season.

Matty died with his wife at his bedside. His quiet courage held to the last, it was reported, as shortly before he passed he told his wife, Jane, "It is nearly all over. I know it and we must face it." After giving his wife his final instructions regarding burial, he sat up a bit, smiled, and said: "Now, Jane, I suppose that you will have to go out and have a good cry. Don't make it a long one. It cannot be helped." Jane left the room, had her cry, and returned to find her husband, still smiling and rousing himself for the last time; his final words to her were "Are you sure you are all right?" After that he closed his eyes and left her.[26]

"He walked upon clean ground from his first public appearance to the

Pennsylvania grave that will hold his dust," Rice eulogized. Mathewson's death rocked Rice. They were the same age, forty-five; they both had been in France—although not together; and it was Mathewson's unbelievable World Series record of three games and three shutouts that Rice had covered in his first trip to New York in 1905. They also had played golf together, often, before the war. In 1911, shortly after Rice got the job with the *Mail*, he and Matty had left the Schenley Hotel, while Rice was covering the Giants on a road trip in Pittsburgh, to play golf. That was the first time Matty broke 80 and "for the first time in his life knew a joy that meant more to him that morning than a pitching victory."

Now, back in Pittsburgh at the same hotel, Rice's thoughts reflected back to what Christy Mathewson's life had meant to the sporting world. "He was a great pitcher, a great competitor and a great soul," Rice wrote. But instead of dwelling on Mathewson's statistical accomplishments on the field, Rice told his readers of Christy's impact on the game of baseball itself. He was a rare sports personality who appealed to a hundred million people, Rice wrote, through a magnetic personality attached to clean honesty and undying loyalty to a cause. Rice said Mathewson lifted the game instead of dragging it down, that he was above the clamor of the crowds knowing as he did how fickle crowds could be; and yet that he held to a code of fair play, cleanness, service, and strength. "He was the only man I have ever known," Rice grieved, "who in spirit and in inspiration was greater than his game."[27]

The world remembers, perhaps, but it certainly marches on. The day after Mathewson's death, Rice continued his reporting on the remaining games of the World Series. Besides baseball, Rice also covered the late 1925 boxing matches—including the Tunney-Gibbons fight where Tunney did what no other boxer, including Dempsey, had done to Gibbons: knocked him out. Rice also reported on weekly football games, and he covered the national amateur golf tournament, won by Bobby Jones.

Rice seemingly missed nothing, even reporting on the Knights of Columbus track games at Yankee Stadium, where ten thousand fans saw various college and club stars run. Willie Ritola, the Finn, was there. So was Jackson Scholz, the Olympic 200-meter champion. DeHart Hubbard, the Michigan sprinter, beat Scholz and Chet Bowman, the intercollegiate champion, in three distances of 50, 75, and 100 yards. What Rice didn't cover in his own report of the K. of C. track meet was his own contribution to making the games entertaining. He was still producing the one-reel Sportlight films. Between events of the *Herald Tribune*–sponsored meet, the arc lights were dimmed and on a screen set up near the pitcher's mound in Yankee Stadium, footage from some of Rice's sports films was shown. Other film clips were shown as well, including a promotional film of the dedicated work of the Knights of Columbus. In addition, the results of each of the events were shown on the screen through "stereopticon slides"—maybe the first scoreboard videos ever.[28]

All in all, Rice's own sincere and indefatigable efforts to cover and promote the sporting world had side effects that were fast becoming main effects. As America's sporting intelligence increased, so did its shrewdness. For example, when Red Grange, the Illinois running back, turned professional at the end of the 1925 college football season—and without graduating—a new age in American sports began. The story started a year earlier when Robert Zuppke's strong Illinois team met Yost's Michigan squad. Michigan hadn't lost a football game since 1921; Illinois hadn't been beaten since 1922. Illinois was dedicating its new football stadium that day in late October 1924. Nearly seventy thousand fans came to see if Fielding Yost's claim that Harold "Red" Grange could be stopped was true. It wasn't. Grange took the opening kickoff and ran ninety-five yards for a touchdown, this in an era when kickoffs were rarely returned for touchdowns. Within the next ten minutes of the game Grange scored three more touchdowns, on runs of thirty, forty, and fifty yards.[29]

Rice didn't see Grange run that day. Grange's incredible display of openfield, breakthrough running came on the same day that Rice was watching the Notre Dame and Army game. Rice gave legendary status to the Four Horsemen, but Grange's exploits got Rice's attention too. The sportswriter must have been in a legend-creating mood that week, for only six days after the Four Horsemen were invented, Rice began referring to Red Grange as the "Galloping Ghost of the Gridiron."

> A streak of fire, a breath of flame,
> Eluding all who reach and clutch;
> A gray ghost thrown into the game.
> That rival hands may rarely touch;
> A rubber bounding, elastic soul
> Whose destination is the goal.[30]

Like Ruth and Sullivan, it was Grange's suddenness, his at-any-moment-he-could-do-it flare, that created a sense of anticipation. Football fans sat forward a bit in their seats every time Grange carried the ball. Playing in Zuppke's single-wing formation—designed for him in 1923—Grange scored thirty-one touchdowns in three seasons, nineteen games, at Illinois; including kickoff and punt returns, he gained 3,637 total yards. Toward the end of the 1925 season, his last at Illinois, the *New York Times* proclaimed that Grange was "the most famous, the most talked of, and written about, the most photographed and most picturesque player the game has ever produced."[31]

One promoter in particular saw that Grange's unique way of flitting and darting and slashing was a crowd pleaser—meaning a moneymaker. Just before his final season under Zuppke, Grange secretly accepted an offer from Charles C. "Cash and Carry" Pyle, a Champaign, Illinois, theater operator, to play professional football for the Chicago Bears in the struggling National Football League after his final Illinois game. This he did. Five days after his last college game he appeared in uniform for the Chicago Bears at Wrigley Field on Thanksgiving Day, 1925.

Rice covered Grange's last collegiate game. Illinois played Ohio State in Columbus in front of 85,200 football fans. "His Orange '77' flashed often enough in the golden sun to lift the crowd more than once to its feet, as he cut his way off tackle or circled an end for eight, twelve or fifteen yards while heading for Ohio's goal." That afternoon Grange carried the ball twenty-one times for 113 yards, ran back kicks for 28 more, and passed for 42 yards on nine attempts as Illinois beat Ohio State 14 to 9. And although Grange wasn't in his top form, said Rice, "These eighty-five thousand souls understood here, in the gathering shadows, that they were looking upon the last amateur run of a backfield star, whose ballyhoo had driven Dempsey and Wills from the sporting pages. They were looking upon the final sprint of the Galloping Ghost, including all the adjectives you can think of or find in the dictionary."[32]

Both Zuppke and Rice regretted Grange's decision to cash in before finishing his college education. The national debate over Grange's decision focused on the very meaning of amateur college athletics. On the one hand, there was a long-standing consensus that college football was properly secondary to a college education. It was to be not-for-profit, intrinsically self-justifying, and for the greater glory of the local university. On the other hand, it was just as clear to the sports promoters and the cynics that if the college game could draw huge crowds, there was no good reason to believe that its stars couldn't or shouldn't go on to do the same for the professional teams. Grange was both colorful and entertaining to watch. He had grace, rhythm, a solid work ethic, and a pleasing personality. Every time he touched the ball he was a threat to break into the open and score. This one player, Pyle argued as he sold Grange to George Halas and Ed Sternamen, the owners of the Bears, could instantly pump life (and money) into the National Football League.

But Rice sensed that this would be just the first commercial lure to be placed in front of the most competent college football players. Understandably, Rice said, one hundred thousand dollars was hard to turn down, not to mention the promise of endorsements and film ventures that soon would follow. Pyle, indeed, quickly saw to it that Grange's name was associated with a wide array of commercial products, including food and drink, shoes, caps, and sweaters. Rice felt that the easy money Grange was promised would dry up fairly quickly in professional football. He said that this lure was contagious. It isn't always bad fun, he said, so the typical college player turning pro continues playing for a year or two or three, and then, either through injury or competitive weakness, gives up the ghost. "And about four years later they are merely pro football players without a trade, profession or occupation." Rice continued his commentary by noting, "It might seem that if a college education was worth anything at all it was worth something more than a pro football career."[33]

In Grange's case, Rice argued, it was a matter of simple specialization. Grange appealed to the masses because what he did was specific, easy to see, and wildly unpredictable. "It takes no expert to thrill at the sight of a man running 50 yards in the open as vain hands are extended in his direction without impeding his progress," Rice wrote. Make no mistake about it, Rice admitted, Grange was as great a ball carrier as any who had ever played—once he got past the line of scrimmage.[34]

But, Rice also argued, Grange wasn't a George Gipp, a Jim Thorpe, a Willie Heston, or an Ernie Nevers. Where the latter four were all-rounders, Grange was a flaming specialist. Rice had seen Grange play in the opening game of his last season, against Nebraska at Urbana. The Nebraska defense stopped Grange cold; this they did by never letting him get started, hauling him down in the backfield for most of the afternoon. His longest gain was seven yards, as Illinois lost 14 to 0 to powerful Nebraska. Yet there was something about Grange and his spectacular possibilities, even if there were days when he wasn't especially spectacular. Somewhere in the neighborhood of 500,000 spectators saw Willie Heston play for Michigan through four years of football between 1901 and 1904; twenty-one years later, around 373,000 fans saw Grange play in his last season alone, and another 227,000 saw him play in his first five professional games that year: in all, more than 600,000 spectators in 1925 saw the Galloping Ghost gallop.[35]

After his Thanksgiving Day professional debut in Chicago, Grange and the Bears played seven games in ten days in such cities as Philadelphia, New York, St. Louis, and Boston, again breaking all local attendance records. A week later they had played ten games in seventeen days. Next up was a

Pyle-promoted exhibition covering seven thousand miles in thirty-five days, in which the Bears barnstormed in the South and the West, playing fourteen games. Grange was covered as Babe Ruth was covered; Damon Runyon, Westbrook Pegler, and Ford Frick were among the sportswriters trailing after the Ghost.[36]

But Grange's performance was disappointing. "From a near-superman," Rice commented in his column, "Grange turned into a second-class back before the first two weeks of his pro career were over." Rice further editorialized that Grange had let Pyle use him as a decoy to lure out crowds to come to see a star. But given the ridiculous schedule—this was not baseball, after all—all the eager fans saw was a bedraggled athlete trying to gain a yard now and then, or to keep from losing more than two or three. "No near superman ever flopped at greater speed."[37]

Grange's career as a running back never really developed. Before the 1926 season Pyle tried to buy into the Bears (for one-third ownership), but Sternamen and Halas refused. Pyle then tried to start up a second pro team in New York, but he was blocked by the owner of the New York Giants. Not finished yet, Pyle, with Grange in hand, started up an entire league, the American Football League. Pyle and Grange owned one of the teams, the New York Yankees. They did well enough in 1926, but the other teams didn't. The league failed, but Pyle talked the NFL into giving the Yankees a "road team status" for the 1927 season. In the third game of that season, Grange suffered a permanent knee injury, all but ending his potential to dazzle and flit and dart—which he wasn't actually doing much of anyway. Pyle and Grange went their separate ways, Pyle to other sports promotions and Grange back to Chicago, where he played for the Bears until 1935 as a good defensive back and a fairly good straight-ahead runner. Grange later went on to become a radio and television broadcaster.[38]

Grange's 1925 decision to make football a career prompted Rice to argue for deemphasizing college football. Things were beginning to be taken too seriously if the college player could be lured out of his primary obligation—getting his degree—and into a secondary one on the promise of money. "The game as it stands today," Rice said, "has become too much a vast entertainment." Rice proposed stronger grade eligibility standards; he wanted the schools to abolish scouting; he suggested that travel be reduced; and he felt that many of the fall schedules were set up simply to make money: "We asked a certain well known coach why his team attempted such a killing schedule. 'It is all a matter of economics. We still have a big stadium deficit that must be paid off.'"[39]

Yet when Rice worked his way through all of the excesses on his own, he concluded that there was one problem in particular that was at the root of what was wrong with college football. At bottom it wasn't economic pressure within the university. It wasn't pressure from excessive coaching salaries—most of them received comparatively small paychecks. It wasn't simply the size of the crowds either, as eighty thousand spectators have been known to watch a boat race without compromising the competition or the competitors. It wasn't really even the gate receipts themselves that were problematical, for even if Harvard and Yale each took in $600,000 for an entire football season—as they reportedly did in 1925—one week of World Series play brought in more than $1.1 million, and already by then two of Dempsey's prizefights had passed the million-dollar mark for one hour of action. Furthermore, most of the football money went toward funding the other nonrevenue sports on campus—track and field, rowing, basketball, hockey, golf, tennis, lacrosse, and the rest. On a typical campus of seven thousand students, Rice pointed out, nearly six thousand of them would play one recreational or competitive sport or another. That takes money.

No, it wasn't any of these singly or even taken together that was taking college football in the direction of professional entertainment. To Rice it was mostly the pressure being exerted by the Old Grad. It was the Old Grad whose emotional connection to his or her university was making frenzy replace reason in college football. It was the Old Grad who could and did scout other teams (the coaching staffs were too small then to allow for coach-scouts). It was the Old Grad who could extort certain changes in the program with the threat of withdrawing endowments, and who could demand the removal of a coach if there were one or two bad seasons in a row. It was the Old Grad who expected favorable press coverage of his team or its star players. It was the Old Grad who would give the fifty-dollar handshake to a player or who could "sponsor" a needy recruit, and who might have a heavy bet out on the results of the game. And it was the Old Grad, usually, who demanded a winning team and a noisy ballyhoo for the winner when it arrived. A winning team made for a winning Old Grad.[40]

But Old Grads read the sporting page, too. "Naming All-America teams causes most of this too rabid football interest," suggested one of Rice's readers. To which Rice replied that in specific cases this wasn't especially true. He noted that his 1925 All-Americans included few Harvard and Yale players, but they turned away thousands at the gates for their games; there was no All-American clamor for Army and Navy players, yet one hundred thousand applications for tickets were chucked into the wastebasket; Cornell and Penn drew a record crowd, but no athlete on either team made the selection list. Grange, Rice said, was an exceptional case and "will soon be a myth, a romantic ghost from forgotten years." If no college All-Americans were ever named, Rice claimed, interest in college football would be every bit as keen as it was.[41]

Still, Rice had to have been haunted that the incredible popularity of college football—including the excesses that came with its growth—in some way or another *was* connected to his own typewriter ballyhoo and his creations such as the Four Horsemen and the Galloping Ghost. And since his journalistic and reportorial contributions covered a wider sporting field than any other single sportswriter of the times, Rice also had to wonder if all of his writings and doings, taken together, were contributing heavily to the sporting fuzz buzz that would make the 1920s forever known as the Golden Age of Sport, in the commercial sense.

But even if the ostensible causes of the cashing in on sport were still fairly complicated, unspecified, and not self-incriminating, to Rice, the effects were still fairly plain, specific, and age-incriminating. As the 1925 sporting year came to a close, after he had personally traveled more than fourteen thousand miles and written nearly eight hundred thousand words and watched boxing, golf, tennis, and World Series and football championships where more than three million fans had watched along with him, Rice answered the rhetorical question, "What is sport?":

> Clink—clink—clink—you can hear it rattle,
> You can hear it rattle by land and sea;
> Not for the fun of it—not for the battle—
> But say, how much is there in it for me?
>
> Sport for the fun of it? Say, stop your kidding;
> What's my cut for the principal part?
> Hey, there, somebody, start up the bidding,
> Slip me enough and I'm ready to start.
>
> There is gold in the fame I'm winning;
> Gold in the headlines—gold in the cheers;
> Gold—gold—gold—that's the stuff I'm spinning,
> Play by play through the golden years.[42]

16

Somebody Will Paste Mr. Dempsey Some Day, but When—and Who?

"You can put it down," Rice predicted early in 1926, "that the first good man who meets Dempsey, if ever, will take him." And Dempsey, Rice continued, probably knew it better than anyone else.[1]

Dempsey hadn't fought a title bout since September 1923. In the three years since he had lived as a celebrity could, in a constant state of active loafing—traveling, playing vaudeville tours, film contracts, boxing exhibitions, touring Europe. He also had married Ida Estelle Taylor Pencock, a second-rate Hollywood actress, which had caused a rift between Dempsey and his manager Doc Kearns. Estelle disliked boxing and low-life boxing bums. Kearns hated Estelle and Estelle hated Kearns, and each saw the other as a potential threat to Dempsey's considerable assets, which they both liked to spend. After a few rounds between the two of them, Estelle won in a close decision awarded on points by referee Dempsey. The Kearns-Dempsey marriage was over, officially, in 1926. Four years later the marriage between Jack and Estelle was over too.

Meanwhile, all the world was getting itchier and itchier for Dempsey to fight, rather than just fight with, somebody. Estelle didn't want Jack to return to the ring—ever. Kearns claimed that Dempsey was too soft by then anyway, and wouldn't fight again—ever. He spent a good portion of 1926 filing one lawsuit after another trying to prevent Dempsey from fighting again. Kearns told Rice that he had another potential champion waiting in the wings, a twenty-one-year-old named Napoleon Dorval: "I honestly believe Dorval will be the next heavyweight champion of the world. At least he will be champion within two years." He wasn't.[2]

The only two heavyweights who seemed to legitimately have a shot at a Dempsey fight were the black boxer Harry Wills and the white former marine Gene Tunney (christened James Joseph Tunney). Boxing promoter Tex Rickard wasn't much interested in a Wills-Dempsey match, a "mixed match" as Rickard called it. Rickard told Rice that even though it would be a great fight, he was afraid of it. "I am in the business of providing public entertainment," Rickard went on. "I am not a promoter to decide championships, but to give the public entertainment that will make money for me and my associates." The promoter simply didn't want to take any risks that he didn't have to take.[3]

For a variety of political and social reasons—much of which centered on the vagaries of the New York State Athletic Commission and the politicians in New York—the Dempsey-Wills fight, promised as early as 1922, was never promoted and would never come off. The three-member commission and other assorted boxing-related jobs were patronage appointments of the governor. At first, the commission supported a Dempsey-Wills fight, mostly, it seems, to appease black voters in Harlem. But for an unknown reason—perhaps fear of the race riots that followed the 1910 Jack Johnson fight—the Athletic Commission soon backed away from ordering Dempsey to fight Wills.[4]

But the commission didn't have the final say. Dempsey's license to box in New York had been pulled by the license committee when he didn't respond to the original order to box Wills. This three-man committee, which did have the last word, announced in mid-August that it had granted Tunney a license to box in New York, but unless Dempsey fought Wills in the Empire State he would fight no one in New York.

Rice's first glimpse of Gene Tunney fighting was in early July 1921. Rickard had agreed to give Tunney a match against the Canadian fighter, Soldier Jones, in the preliminaries of the Dempsey-Carpentier fight. At the time, Rice recalled, Tunney was known only as a soldier-boxer who had won the light heavyweight title of the American Expeditionary Force in France. Tunney later said of his fight against Jones that it was a "sorry exhibition that I gave at Boyle's Thirty Acres that afternoon."[5]

Two years earlier, Tunney had broken the knuckle of his middle finger on his right hand when he knocked out an American Indian by the name of Lewis in France on his way toward the AEF championship. When Tunney returned to the States after his discharge late in the summer of 1919, he decided to become a professional boxer, having been in love with the sport since his earliest days in Greenwich Village, New York, where he was born on May 25, 1898. But the knuckle injury haunted him. For nearly a year, in an effort to heal his hand, he took a self-imposed exile from the ring. By way of lumberjacking through the winter in Algonquin Park, Ontario, and hiring on as a laborer through the spring in Poland Springs, Maine, Tunney worked. Although his hand healed, he gained fourteen pounds through the experience.[6]

When Rice saw Tunney box against Soldier Jones, only his second fight since the time off, the heavier Tunney was slow; so slow in fact that he himself said that he couldn't get out of his own way. Tunney did win, the referee stopping the match to save Jones, but the Canadian easily hit him on the chin time and again. "Had I not possessed a rather tough chin," Tunney later recalled, "I am convinced that my career would have ignominiously ended on that day."[7]

A few days after that fight Rice and Heywood Broun were in the Polo Grounds press box covering the Giants. Walter Trumbull, then the sports editor for the *New York Post,* brought Tunney in to introduce him around, making a big fuss over Tunney's future. Rice asked Tunney what his plans were. Tunney replied: "My plans are all Dempsey."

"Very interesting," Rice said. "But why not sharpen your artillery on Harry Greb, Carpentier or Tom Gibbons before you start hollering for Dempsey?"

"I suppose I'll have to beat them on the way up," Tunney said. "But Dempsey is the one I want."

After this meeting with Tunney, Rice thought to himself that the young and forthright fellow would make a wonderful insurance salesman, "but certainly had no business having his features and brains scrambled by Dempsey's steel fists."[8]

On the way up, Tunney did beat Greb (not in their first meeting—Tunney lost in fifteen rounds in the bloodiest fight Rice ever covered—but four times thereafter), and Carpentier, and Gibbons. In fact, on his way to the Dempsey fight, Tunney had fought about sixty bouts, winning convincingly against such fighters as Jack Renault, Jimmy Delaney, Martin Burke, Tommy Loughran, Johnny Risko, Jack Herman, and Bartley Madden.[9]

Until June 5, 1925, Grantland Rice still wasn't particularly impressed with Tunney. In fact, in a *Collier's* article that appeared on June 6, but which was written several weeks earlier, Rice speculated about which of the likely *twelve* contenders for Dempsey's title would eventually prevail. Behind Wills and Gibbons was Tunney, of course. But Rice was taken with Bostoner Jimmy Maloney as being "almost ready for the championship salvo." Rice gave Tunney only a few lines.[10]

On June 5, Gene Tunney met Tom Gibbons at the Polo Grounds. Rice was there. So were forty thousand spectators. Gibbons was picked by most experts to win, having recently knocked out the black boxer Kid Norfolk. Instead, the Polo Ground boxing fans saw Tunney do what no man had ever done to Tom Gibbons: knock him down, and then knock him out. One minute into the twelfth round, Tunney shot a right flush to Gibbon's jaw, and according to Rice's account, "Gibbons struck the floor as if he had been nailed with an axe." By the count of seven Gibbons struggled to his feet, but Tunney whirled in and hit him again with the same crashing right. Gibbons was on his back. Try as he might, Gibbons couldn't get upright and was counted out.

Rice was impressed, even though Gibbons, at age thirty-six, had clearly fought his last fight. Tunney was twenty-seven. After only two or three rounds, it was clear that Gibbons never had a chance. Tunney outboxed him, outsped him, and eventually outhit him. "Tunney fought a fight that will carry him far forward on the championship trail," Rice wrote, adding that Tunney was as "cool as a thin segment of cucumber on ice."[11]

A few months later Rice profiled Tunney for *Collier's*. "Watch That Leatherneck!" Rice exhorted his readers. "Gene Tunney, soldier, boxer, student, philosopher and sportsman, may never be heavyweight champion of the world. But if he ever arrives," Rice predicted, "the wide gap between the days of John L. Sullivan and the present time will be well bridged, for Tunney will be the most popular king of the heavyweights since John L.'s brilliant reign."

Rice based his prediction on Tunney's overall character—"a keen brain, a stout heart, clean living, and a lot of concentrated effort." In addition, it was clear to Rice and everyone else that Tunney was a different and better boxer in 1925 than he had been up to then. He was bigger, stronger, faster, and he had taught himself how to hit and hit hard. Rice believed that if Tunney were to be champion, it would be a storybook ascension. Tunney joined the military at the first call in World War I; he didn't drink, smoke, or sleaze around; he could actually read and write—more, he was a serious student of good literature; he was good-looking, pleasant-faced, and had an attractive smile and a good share of social magnetism. Rice told his readers that the boxer was something of a self-styled philosopher and that he could discourse at length on topics that are "supposed to call for a much higher brow than is required by the art or science of pugilism."[12]

Following the Gibbons fight, Tunney finished out the year with knockouts over Jack Herman and Bartley Madden, and won a decision over Johnny Risko in Cleveland. The night of the Risko fight, James J. Corbett was in the audience. Then nearly sixty years old, Corbett was playing the theater circuit and happened to be on the bill that night in Cleveland. Thirty-three years earlier, Gentleman Jim had knocked out heavyweight champion James L. Sullivan, America's first real national sports hero. That fight in 1892 was a night of firsts: indoor and under electric lights, gloved, the Marquis of Queensberry rules, and sponsored by an athletic club; the bout elevated boxing from the age of bare-fisted brawls to the era of commercial sports.[13]

Tunney had long ago studied Corbett's essentially defensive fighting style and had always admired the college-educated Irishman. Corbett, who until the night of the Risko fight had never seen Tunney box before, went to Tunney's dressing room after the fight. "If you had Dempsey in there tonight you would have knocked him out," Corbett told Tunney. According to Corbett, the only reason the fight went the distance was that Risko knew how to cover up when under attack. Dempsey didn't. "When you fight Dempsey," Corbett continued, "fight him exactly as you fought Risko tonight and you'll surely win." This was the first time Corbett and Tunney met, but thanks to Rice, the two would shortly meet again: in the ring.[14]

After the Risko fight, Rice, always a promoter of sorts in his own right, thought that Tunney clearly had a shot at a fight with Dempsey, who was still fighting perpetual exhibition matches, at the time in Germany. So Rice put together a match for Tunney, not for the record books, but for publicity. If Dempsey could put on boxing exhibitions, why not Tunney? Still producing his one-reel films, the Sportlight, Rice dreamed up an episode featuring a three-round exhibition match between Tunney and Corbett.

With his coproducer Frank Craven, Rice assembled the principles atop the Putnam Building in midtown Manhattan. Craven would later become one of Rice's regular traveling mates, along with writer friends Bud Kelland and Bruce Barton. So there they were up on the Putnam roof, Craven and Tunney, talking Shakespeare, Corbett fretting about his spindly legs when compared to Tunney's and asking if he could wear long white trousers (he did), and Rice introducing the two, a generation apart, both as great "scientific" boxers. Eventually they went at it, with Tunney politely taking the most defensive approach in the defensively fought rounds. "Corbett," Rice recollected, "was brilliant." Feinting with his left, then punching with the left, a left feint and a left hook; a right feint and a left jab, mixing up his punches beautifully. And he had bewildering speed, Rice reported. Tunney, even closer to the action, came away with just as much respect for the aging Corbett. "I honestly think he is better than Benny Leonard," said Tunney. (Leonard was the lightweight champion from 1917 to 1935). "It was the greatest thing I've seen in the ring. I learned plenty."[15]

It isn't certain that Gene Tunney really learned anything from Corbett that day. But by the winter months of 1925–1926, it was clear to Rice and Corbett and to almost everyone else that Tunney was a serious contender for the heavyweight championship, and that his next bout ought to be against Jack Dempsey. Tunney went to Florida to prepare "systematically and diligently," in his words, for just such a fight.[16]

Meanwhile, Grantland Rice was also in preparation—for a vacation. To his readers he admitted that the physical strain of his yearly reporting was limited to only two-finger fatigue and hauling a typewriter around; nonetheless, traveling thousands of miles by train every year and coming up with about twenty-five hundred words a day, seven days a week, did take its psychological toll. "By the time the human butterfly, seeking sporting nectar or sustenance, has fluttered back and forth around championship flower gardens of football, golf, tennis, baseball, boxing, track and field, hockey and what not," Rice pointed out, "the frayed wings might just as well be hung up in the closet for repairs." So Rice repaired to Florida, too.[17]

While there, he took Tunney out for a round of golf and polite conversation, along with golfer Tommy Armour. By then Tunney was obsessed with Dempsey, Rice recalled. Instead of a leisurely stroll on the lawns interrupted only by casual swings of the club, Gene would hit his drive, toss aside his club, and run down the fairway, throwing punches in the air, jabs and hooks, and muttering, "Dempsey . . . Dempsey . . . Dempsey." Armour told Rice that Tunney's brain knew nothing but Dempsey. "I believe Jack could hit him with an axe and Gene wouldn't feel it," Armour observed. Armour said he didn't really know if Dempsey had slipped or not since he'd been away from real boxing, but that he would sure put down a chunk of money on Tunney when they met.[18]

Even though Tex Rickard had more or less signed Tunney to fight Dempsey just about the same time Rice and Armour were watching Tunney box eighteen holes, it was well into August of 1926 before the site and date was finally set: September 23 at the new Sesquicentennial stadium in Philadelphia.

As Dempsey stepped into the ring in front of perhaps 130,000 people, Tunney, who was already sitting on his stool, got up and greeted Dempsey at the ropes.

"Hello, Champion," Tunney said.

"Hello, Gene," Dempsey answered.

"May the better man win," Tunney said.

"Yeh—Yeh," Dempsey muttered.

Dempsey's bodyguard, Mike Trent of the Chicago Police Department, didn't much care for Tunney. Trent had read in the newspapers that Tunney read books in his spare time, a weakness in general, thought Trent, and a fatal habit for a fighter. "Come on Jack," Trent shouted from the front row, "knock that big sissy into my lap." Trent was escorted out from the bout by an usher.[19]

Tunney wouldn't win the fight, Rice predicted, through any Dempsey weakness. He would have to win it through his own skill, speed, stamina, and punching power—through his ability to nail an early opening and make it count. Rice noted that Tunney, who early on seemed to have soft skin and vulnerable hands, had toughened up over the years. Rice claimed that Tunney was not a natural-born fighter, but a student of boxing—the movement, timing of punches, speed on impact, overall conditioning, and patience. Dempsey, on the other hand, as Rice continued doping out the fight, was a natural product, naturally fast and shifty, with great hitting power in both hands, long range and short.[20]

In spite of Tunney's fine character, diligent training, full measure of courage, boxing skill, and methodical planning, Rice still believed that natural skill would win out over Tunney's "artificial" (as Rice called it) skill; and "there is no schooling that can give the natural resiliency, speed and leverage which some men possess and others do not." Apparently Rice forgot his prediction six months earlier that the first good man who met Dempsey would take him. Rice picked Dempsey to win by doing what Dempsey had always done, whanging away at close quarters; Rice gave Tunney only a rickety chance to even be on his feet at the end of the fight, much less win it. Even though Dempsey, now thirty-one, might be slipping somewhat, the legendary scowling, brawling, murderous "killer"—a legend that Rice, of course, helped create—was still installed as the betting favorite by around 3 to 1. Among sportswriters, few gave Tunney a chance—W. O. McGeehan, Rice's fellow *Herald Tribune* writer, picked Tunney and was ridiculed for it.[21]

Even Gentleman Jim picked Dempsey. Corbett had been hired by Hearst's Universal Service to cover the training period and the fight. But the series of articles was actually written by a Corbett ghost, writer Gene Fowler. Fowler knew that Corbett had *never* doped out a fight correctly. Ever. Corbett was telling his friends at the Friar's Club and the Lambs that Dempsey would win by a knockout in about the sixth round. Fowler, who knew that Corbett never read his own stories in the paper, and who wanted to keep Corbett-the-false-prophet's string of misses unblemished, and who himself felt sure that Dempsey would win, switched Corbett's prediction in print. From the Dempsey camp in Atlantic City, on the eve of the bout, Fowler had Corbett say that Tunney would win the match by a decision, his left jabs and superior footwork outpointing Dempsey's crosses and hooks.[22]

The *Herald Tribune* sent their three heavyweights to cover the fight: W. O. McGeehan, Harry Cross, and Rice. In addition, three other reporters covered the crowd in what McGeehan called the "most extensively ballyhooed event in the history of sport." The *Herald Tribune* did its part. In the Sunday edition alone, just a few days before the bout, the sporting pages numbered ten. When Ogden Reid, the paper's owner-publisher, saw the coverage he exclaimed to the man mostly responsible for it, Rice, "Grant, you're making the *Tribune* more of a sports paper than anything else! At this rate, we're becoming ALL sports, and damn the rest of the world!" To which Rice said he said, while barely managing a straight face, "You could do worse."[23]

The Battle of the Century, as Rickard billed it, attracted fans from Hollywood, San Francisco, St. Louis, Chicago, Boston, and all points north and south of that line. The crowd was a marvelous and indiscriminate collection of the highbrow and the low. More than two thousand millionaires (including William Randolph Hearst, Harry Payne Whitney, Vincent Astor, Percy Rockefeller, and Joseph Pulitzer) were said to have been at ringside, in addition to state governors, cabinet members, mayors, bankers, judges, athletes (Gertrude Ederle, Babe Ruth), and actors (Tom Mix, Charlie Chaplin), all alongside the hijackers and the leather rollers, the Arnold Rothsteins and the Abe Attells.

Rice may have been having second thoughts about his prediction the night before the fight. His last words before the ten-round battle qualified his prediction that Dempsey would win: "There are those in competition who can lift themselves up beyond anything they have ever shown. For these there are no impossible odds. They have beaten better men by sheer flame of spirit in the crisis, rising to the heights that for them were believed impossible." Rice went on, saying that Tunney must in some way find this flame to overcome the obvious physical handicap of speed and power that he would face in ring against Dempsey.[24]

Rice's first words from ringside after the fight let the world know that Tunney had found the flame: "Gene Tunney, the fighting marine, is the new heavyweight champion of the world. In the presence of 135,000 persons, who sat through a driving rainstorm in Philadelphia's Sesquicentennial Stadium,

Gene Tunney gave Dempsey one of the worst beatings any champion ever took. He not only outpointed Dempsey in every one of the ten rounds, but the challenger hammered the champion's face almost out of shape. It was like nothing human when the tenth round ended."[25]

From the surprising first round on, Tunney, who McGeehan said looked more like a zealous young Irish priest than a fighter, shocked the crowd and bewildered Dempsey. It was a punch in the first round itself that Tunney would later claim won the fight, and had it not slightly missed Dempsey's jaw, might have produced a knockout. At the outset, Tunney *leaned* outside of Dempsey's repeated, charging left hooks. As Dempsey continued his rushing strategy, Tunney next *stepped* outside of the lefts, encouraging Dempsey in his thinking that Tunney was afraid of him. Finally, in the center of the ring, as Jack wound up with another left, Gene feinted and made Jack believe he was again going to step outside, which caused Jack to lengthen his punch. Then, according to plan, Tunney instead stepped *in,* instead of out, and plastered Jack high on the cheek with his right. The force of Dempsey coming into the punch and Tunney's throwing the punch from his heels, shook Dempsey to his shoes. Although Dempsey recovered, Tunney knew from then on that the fight was his.[26]

So convincing was Tunney's victory that Rice said even Tunney seemed bewildered by it. By Rice's count, Tunney must have landed at least a hundred clean punches to Dempsey's five or six. The new champion, Rice reported, after seven years of preparation had finally earned his title by courage, coolness, generalship, and skill.

So the predictors were wrong, except maybe "Corbett," or the Belgian Crown Prince Leopold, of all people. From Brussels, on the eve of the fight, Crown Prince Leopold, the heir to the Belgian throne, picked Tunney to beat Dempsey. Leopold, who had watched Tunney win the light-heavyweight AEF title back in 1919, admired Tunney's technique of "hit, stop, and get away." He thought that Tunney's scientific technique would get the better of Dempsey's notorious straightforward, no-nonsense brand of fighting.[27]

The other notable winning prediction came from "Corbett." The day after the bout Corbett began receiving congratulatory phone calls at his Philadelphia hotel for his correctly predicting the outcome of the fight, nearly to the letter. Knowing nothing about Fowler switching his prediction in print, Corbett thought the phone calls were good-natured ribbing for once again missing the bout. But when Corbett was shown Fowler's "Corbett" piece picking Tunney in ten, Corbett, instead of being riled, puffed up. After all, this was his first correct pick, ever. He rose to the occasion, and floated downstairs making all of the appropriate hotel lobby appearances; as Fowler later recalled, by the time Gentleman Jim returned to New York he convinced himself that he actually *had* picked Tunney to win.

At the conclusion of the fight, Dempsey asked his handlers to take him across the ring to Tunney. Dempsey, weak-kneed and partially blinded by the blood and ooze in his eyes, hugged Tunney and congratulated him. "All right, Gene," he said. "All right, good luck." As Dempsey was helped out of the ring, suddenly the fight fans started cheering, louder and louder. Not for Tunney, but for Dempsey. There was something classy about the way Dempsey had lost, and later, about the way he refused to alibi for his loss. He told the press that the better man won. He said that he couldn't get going and that he felt sluggish (later there were stories that Dempsey had been poisoned on the train from his training camp to the stadium, maybe accidentally, maybe intentionally). "Tunney was fighting a truly wonderful battle," Dempsey said after the fight. "My hat is off to him. He whipped me fairly and squarely. Gene fought a remarkable battle. He met me at my own game."[28]

Even if Dempsey refused to make excuses for his loss, there were plenty of red-faced dopers who did: it was simply that Dempsey had stayed away from the ring too long; it was that Doc Kearns's unrelenting lawsuits to block the fight distracted Dempsey; it was that Tunney was just a clever sports psychologist who kept tricking Dempsey during the fight; it was that Dempsey had been poisoned on the train to the stadium, or maybe in his training camp. In other words, so most of the excuses went, the fight came out the way it did because Dempsey wasn't quite right at the time, not because Tunney was a better boxer.

There was one other theory that went beyond Dempsey's temporary lapse. The 1919 White Sox scandal forever changed the way the American public and press looked at the Big Events; there was less wide-eyed trust, more collective squinting and skepticism. Boxing, of all of the commercial sports, especially wasn't any pink tea anyway: its history was full of disreputable mugs and pugs and thugs. So even a promotion as huge as this, the Battle of the Century, was still not beyond suspicion. And who was a leading suspicioner? A fellow by the name of "Grantland Rice," of all people.

Rice and fellow *Herald Tribune* sportswriter W. O. McGeehan arrived in Philadelphia by train on the night before the fight. Their strategy was to get plenty of sleep before Dempsey and Tunney met the next evening. After supper, heading back to their hotel, one of them (no doubt Rice) remembered that there was a roulette wheel in downtown Philadelphia only a couple of blocks from City Hall. They agreed to only stay for a few spins of the wheel.

This was about ten o'clock. By about two in the morning, Rice was ahead twelve hundred dollars, but McGeehan was eight hundred dollars down.

"Let's get out of here," Rice said, "and get some sleep."

"Like hell!" replied McGeehan, "I'm going to get even!"

When five o'clock rolled around, all they had left between them was taxi fare to the hotel. Naturally, during these whirls they both drank plenty of speakeasy whiskey. Rice covered the fight that night with a pretty fair hangover, in addition to a raging cold and sore throat—the chronic cold and sinus problems were almost constant companions in these, his later years. Sitting at ringside in the pouring rain didn't help matters either. His typewriter was useless during the fight. Instead, he dictated his description, round by round, to his wire man, who telegraphed it to the paper.

With Rice at ringside, besides McGeehan, were Ring Lardner and Benny Leonard, the former lightweight champion. When the fight was over Rice went back to his hotel with Lardner. Rice was in bad shape but still had another deadline to meet. It was customary to file an overnight story that would appear the day after the actual fight coverage. These pieces were generally more reflective, less hurried, and were intended to be more of a personal summing up, kind of a what-it-all-means story. In this case, with Dempsey having lost, it was Rice's intention to go easy on Dempsey. After all, Rice had helped build Dempsey up over the years; furthermore, Dempsey was taking his loss with surprising grace. Rice also intended to give Tunney a healthy tribute for his patient, sustained pursuit of the championship and for his heady approach during the fight itself. But as it turned out, Rice would do neither. Ring Lardner, good, good friend and regular travel companion, stepped in to rescue the ailing Rice.

"Take a slug of bourbon and lie down," said Lardner. "I'll file your overnight." Rice wasn't in a position to argue. He was simply too sick to meet his deadline. He accepted his friend's offer of help; later he would regret his decision.

Benny Leonard had told Lardner before the fight that he suspected that the fix was in for Tunney to win. Besides the fact that Lardner had bet fifty dollars on Dempsey, Lardner was more suspicious than most reporters anyway. Ever since the 1919 Sox scandal, Ring had great difficulty believing in sports, which in his earlier years he believed were among the most honest and natural of human enterprises. Lardner, however, being a Midwesterner, still had a soft spot in his heart for such Midwest and West symbols as Notre Dame and Dempsey. He didn't much care for Tunney, the Easterner. When Lardner and Rice went to Tunney's training camp in New York when the fight was a few weeks away (before Tunney had relocated to Stroudsburg, Pennsylvania), they ran into Tunney walking toward them over the brow of a hill. He was carrying a fat book under one arm.

Tunney greeted them enthusiastically. He told the reporters that he'd been out walking and reflecting on his communing with nature. Ring pointed to the book. "What's the title?" he asked Tunney.

"*The Rubaiyat* . . . ," Tunney replied casually.

Brimming with his love of nature, Tunney gushed that he simply couldn't take his eyes off the breathtaking scenery. Fixing his solemn, prominent eyes on Tunney like a heat-seeking missile fixes on its target, Lardner asked him, "Then why the book?" Being a prig, which Tunney clearly was, was one thing; but being inauthentic to boot was something else again. Lardner hated pretentiousness.[29]

It was with these combined prejudices that an angry Lardner launched himself into writing Rice's overnighter. "Rice's" question was: how could Dempsey have not only lost, but in the process have allowed his face to be hammered into a bloody parallelopipedon? One answer was that Gene Tunney was a much better fighter than he had ever been given credit for being. The other answer was that Dempsey fought a "queer" fight, for Dempsey. "Rice" listed the uncharacteristic signs of queerness: he was practically a stationary target; he never followed up on his bull-like rushes; he threw barely fifty punches in ten rounds; when he threw his punches many of them missed their intended target by two or three *feet;* from the seventh round on, when Dempsey knew he was behind on points, there was never any real effort to throw the haymaker. Summing up, "Rice" made no direct allegation that the fight was fixed; only that some people "in the know" thought so. He did acknowledge that Tunney was underrated, and that he was courageous and intelligent, skillful and crafty. But Dempsey, on the other hand, in this fight was "a flivver, a bust, a paluka, a mug, a third-rate boxer and a third-rate fighter." Generalizing to the sport of boxing in general, "Rice" lambasted the entire show for the amount of money at stake. The boxers "are getting, as a rule, about ten times as much as they deserve. The public and the press together are largely responsible for this. Both are building fake heroes who are heroes in no sense of the word."[30]

If Dempsey's fight was out of character for Dempsey, so was "Rice's" overnighter for Rice. Now it may be that Rice was actually sympathetic with "Rice"; but it was not a story the real Rice would ever have put in print. With nothing but rumor to substantiate the claims of a fix, Rice would be fair. Not surprisingly, he didn't write a word about the fight for more than a week; then he only speculated about the next likely challengers to the new heavyweight champion, maybe Jimmy Delaney or Jack Sharkey, or maybe Paul Berlenbach or Tommy Loughran. Instead of postfight banter, he threw himself into college football and the World Series between the Yankees and the Cardinals, and other timely news: one story was the predicament in South Dakota of Cavour High School's football team, which was so light and small that year that the coach decided to field two additional football teams of girls to play preliminary games before each of the six scheduled boys games; on the eve of their first start when the boys were to play Lake Preston, the coach admitted he expected the girls to draw the crowds, and he hoped that they would stay around for the boys' game.[31]

It was relatively easy for Rice to forget the "Rice" piece for, in St. Louis, he witnessed Babe Ruth's record-breaking three home runs in game four of the series. This was the stuff Rice was meant for:

> After the manner of a human avalanche hurtling on its downward way from blue Missouri heavens the giant form of Babe Ruth fell upon the beleaguered city of St. Louis to-day and flattened it into a pulp of anguish. If another mighty planet had slipped its ancient moorings to come crashing through unlimited space against the rim of the earth it could not have left one sector in its path more dismantled or forlorn . . . there has never been another one like this bounding Bambino of blast . . . wrecking an entire ball game with his fifty-two ounce bludgeon . . . a noise that sounded like a barrel of crockery being thrown down the cellar stairs and an egg-shaped baseball sailing over the right field stands into Grand Avenue . . . and another over the right field grandstand that bounded on for two or three blocks . . . the next a whirling missile was just gathering its full force as it crossed the high center field barrier and crashed into the crowd at least 450 feet from the plate . . . a stunned and startled crowd just wondering who let old Doc Thor or the bolt-heaving Jupiter into the show. . . .[32]

According to Rice's recollection a quarter of a century after the Tunney-Dempsey bout, neither boxer spoke to him for several months after the Lardner piece. Rice couldn't tell either of them that the words weren't his, that he had a ghost. Yet according to Tunney's recollection six years after the event, he spoke with Rice directly about the fix accusation. In a conference with Rice shortly after the Philadelphia fight, Tunney recalled that he tried to dispel the flying rumors of a fix.

"But Grant, do you think I wouldn't know whether Dempsey was trying?"

Tunney asked. "There is one fellow that a fighter can't deceive about the honesty of his efforts and that is his opponent." Tunney told Rice that in order to get the fight with Dempsey in the first place, Billy Gibson, Tunney's manager, had offered Dempsey the entire purse if Gene won. But Jack evidently didn't think Tunney had much chance of winning since he didn't bother with the offer. So money couldn't have bought the championship from Jack. Hence, no fix.[33]

Tunney went on to say that Rice wasn't convinced. At least he wasn't convinced, Tunney remarked, until the seventh round in the second Dempsey-Tunney fight nearly a year later. In any case, it was obvious even then that Dempsey wasn't through after the Philadelphia fight no matter what excuses were given for his loss to Tunney—or maybe especially because of the excuses given. Anyway, despite Rice's prediction, Gentleman Gene Tunney, the smarty-smarty who passed up his ties with everyman to hobnob with the literati and be a social swirler, wasn't a popular champion; Dempsey, the man who began the Golden Age of Sport and the man who would end it, was more popular after he lost than before, and Rickard saw even more millions ahead.

So did everybody else. A big fight, or even the recent World Series, Rice noted, was now considered a flop if it didn't pass the million mark. "Sport now swings along to the jingle of more gold than any one could have believed possible a few years ago." But, Rice warned, whether the golden flow is good for the welfare of sport is another matter. Money and larcenous maneuvers are close pals. Even the 1926 World Series created fix-suspicion merely because it was the third series in three years to go a full seven games. More games, more money. "It is all a matter of business," Rice claimed, "business in which there are no ethics of any sort." The way Rice figured it, probably more than 30 percent of all the boxing matches at the time were cooked. Rice called for a national regulatory body to supervise the gnarly sport of boxing.[34]

This fix preoccupation, appearing only a month after the first Dempsey-Tunney fight in a number of Rice columns and in the Tunney conversation, suggests that Rice privately believed what "Rice" publicly wrote. Either that or—less likely—he felt the need to be consistent and at least suggest to his faithful readers that Rice and "Rice" were one and the same reporter. But as the 1920s began coming to a close, it is clear that however much Rice was still foaming and bromiding at the mouth over the inherent beauty, drama, and heroics in sport, he was also sharing an ever more realistic and sophisticated view of sport with the public. Things are not always what they seem.

When you recall how many cheated
When cash was lighter than it is,
Among the winners, or defeated,
It makes no difference in this biz—

Now that the golden tide is breaking
With added cash and more for sale,
Why should you wonder if the faking
Grows in proportion to the kale?[35]

This verse, entitled "You Name the Game," appeared only two weeks before another big scandal broke: that Ty Cobb and Tris Speaker had been accused of conspiring with "Dutch" Leonard and "Smoky Joe" Wood to bet on an alleged fixed baseball game late in 1919 between Detroit and Cleveland. The charges, leveled by Kenesaw Mountain Landis and based on letters in the possession of Leonard—one written by Cobb and the other by Wood—explained to some extent the mystery of why both Cobb and Speaker had been released from their respective managerial posts (Detroit and Cleveland) at the end of the 1926 season. It was alleged that Cleveland, who had second place locked up, was going to help Detroit finish third by throwing a game on September 25, 1919. As the foursome met under the Navin Field grandstand the day before the game, they agreed to the fix, and then each was alleged to have put money down on the sure bet.[36]

Wood, when interviewed by Landis about the betting, fessed up that although he did not place any such bet on any such game, betting by players was common. He recalled one instance when the entire Washington club lost all the pocket cash they had with them when they bet on a game that Speaker had won from Walter Johnson. They won it all back the next day.

Before Landis did anything in particular about this scandal, other than encouraging Cobb and Speaker to resign (Leonard and Wood were no longer in baseball), other sensational allegations came up regarding other even earlier games. Swede Risberg and Chick Gandil of the notorious Black Sox team came forward with claims about games as early as 1917 being fixed between Detroit and Chicago and between St. Louis and Chicago; then again in the 1919 season it was Detroit and Chicago. And so the stories went on, until finally Landis invoked a five-year statute of limitations on baseball offenses.[37]

A month later, Landis decided that Cobb and Speaker and the others were not guilty of fixing the game in question, in spite of the evidence to the contrary. "Landis completely exonerated them and restored them to good standing," so the *Herald Tribune's* story reported. Hercules cleaning out the filth of the Aegean stables wasn't so bad a job, Rice commented, when compared to the effort that would be required to stop the cheating in professional sport.[38]

> "We ain't gonna steal no more, no more—
> We ain't gonna steal no more;
> But how in hell can the people tell
> You ain't gonna steal no more?"[39]

Nonetheless, and in spite of the growing skepticism and cynicism of the age, sport was without question central to American national life. Rice estimated that in 1926 alone, attendance at various competitions amounted to more than sixty million, and twenty million athletes, old and young, male and female, took part in some form of training or competitive sport.[40]

On the more playful, participatory side, Rice included some examples of the popularity of sports, estimating that there were somewhere around three million avid golfers, about one million tennis players, more than three hundred thousand school and college football players, more than five thousand competitors at the Penn Relays, a quarter of a million soccer players, and 780 school basketball teams in the state of Indiana alone. On the spectating side, Rice remembered 1926 by such memorable events as Gertrude Ederle's most vivid performance of swimming the English Channel (she was the first woman to do so, and in a time faster than any man); Bobby Jones losing one crown (the amateur) but winning two others (the British and U.S. Opens); Bill Tilden's domination of tennis being broken by the Frenchman Henri Cochet; Harry Greb losing the middleweight title to Tiger Flowers; and, of course, the Dempsey and Tunney fight, where the two boxers pocketed nine hundred thousand dollars, a pay rate of about thirty thousand dollars a minute.[41]

What was coming in 1927 was Ruth's astounding mark of sixty home runs, Tommy Armour winning the U.S. Open, Bobby Jones regaining the amateur title, the French winning the Davis Cup (it took ten years for the United States to win it back), Lindbergh flying to Paris, and, of course, Dempsey attracting yet another million-dollar gate, the fifth in the 1920s. "Dempsey," Rice wrote, "is the greatest drawing card sport has known."[42]

From a financial standpoint, the second Dempsey-Tunney fight was an even bigger success than the first. The wilder estimates before the fight were that it would pull in three million dollars; the $2,658,660 it actually couped certainly wasn't a disappointment. The fight was scheduled for Soldier Field in Chicago, one day shy of a year after their first battle. To pick the eventual challenger, and to add to the hype leading up to the fight, Rickard had promoted an elimination round of sorts; Sharkey, the Boston heavyweight, met and defeated Maloney; with that victory, Sharkey earned the right to face Dempsey, with the winner to then meet Tunney.

In the thirty months before the Dempsey-Sharkey fight, Dempsey, now thirty-two, had fought only once, against Tunney. Sharkey, twenty-four, had fought thirty-three bouts over the same span of time, and had beaten Godfrey, Wills, McTigue, and Maloney within the last five months. Nonetheless, forty-five seconds after the start of the seventh round at Yankee Stadium, Dempsey dropped Sharkey flat on his face with a left hook to the jaw after doubling him up with two questionably legal blows in the belt region. The knockout blow was delivered just as Sharkey was backing away, doubled up, his right dropped, and his head slightly turned toward referee Jack O'Sullivan as if to either complain or claim a foul. He hadn't gone to one knee to make the claim, as was the rule.[43]

Rice thought the two low punches were fouls; the first Rice said was a right that was at least eight inches below the belt, and the second right was even lower, at least ten inches low. In the aftermath of the fight, no consensus was reached as to the legality of the blows. Some thought that Sharkey had just hiked his trunks up high and that he had a history of crying foul. Depending on where the spectator sat, the blows were either clearly well below the belt or appeared somewhere near the belt. In a poll taken of thirty-four writers covering the bout, twenty of them were certain that Dempsey had fouled, while fourteen were certain no foul was struck. And given the camera angle, the fight films were inconclusive as well. But from Rice's side of the ring, there wasn't any doubt: Rice said it was one of the most palpable fouls any crowd ever looked upon. W. O. McGeehan, who like Rice was sitting at a right angle to the fighters, called the blows low and the fight "The Battle of the Strange Coincidences."[44]

Rice's overnighter sounded much like "Rice's" Dempsey v. Tunney overnighter. He claimed that the fight was queer, strange, bizarre, and ill-scented. When a sporting enterprise like boxing runs into the millions, he wrote, the idea is to keep the best entertainer, the thrill maker, on the bill as long as possible—and apparently, he said, by any means. It was crowd bait, not real and fair competition. Whatever the age had become, he went on, it certainly wasn't a sporting age.

And the real makers of the ballyhoo, Rice claimed, weren't the Rickards or

the papers. No, it was the public, Rice argued, who wanted these showy entertainments. He called it a Sap Age. "The public may charge its predicament to
the ballyhoo, but the public doesn't have to read the ballyhoo or heed its siren
call. The public can duck any time it wishes to." But however frowzy these
modern spectacles were becoming, Rice still chatted regularly and amiably
about them; he still hyped, doped, and covered them; and he clearly made his
handsome living and personal fame from them. And if, in the case of boxing,
he truly was biting the golden gloves that fed him, in truth his bite left no obvious teeth marks. And so it went:

> Money to the left of them, and money to the right;
> Get the check book ready, kid, and never mind the fight;
> Some one has to win or lose, but that's a minor hitch
> When they're splitting millions up and everyone is rich.[45]

Now, with Sharkey out, it was to be Dempsey and Tunney again, in a fight
with another famous seventh-round incident that would generate argument
for years to come. No beaten heavyweight champion had ever to this point
come back to win a lost title. But given the gossip surrounding the outcome of
Dempsey's first fight with Tunney, the oddsmakers certainly weren't counting
Dempsey out. A hot question was whether or not *this* fight would be on the
level, especially given that it was being held in the wide-open boomtown of
Chicago. An even hotter question seemed to be whether or not anyone who
would be attending the ten-round fight at huge Soldiers' Field would be able
to see the fight at all. The five-dollar seats were eight hundred feet from ringside—the equivalent of four city blocks; picture yourself, in New Yorker terms,
according to the *Herald Trib*, standing at Times Square looking at a traffic cop
at Forty-sixth Street and Broadway. The twenty-five-dollar seats were around
430 feet from ringside, and the pricy forty-dollar seats were at "ringside," forty
and more feet away. But the distance apparently did not matter, as the tickets
sold briskly; more important than seeing the fight anyway was for each of the
104,000 fans to be able to say "I was there when . . ."[46]

The semicynical side of Rice was amazed that the fight itself—as perhaps
symbolized by the distance of the seats from the ring—was mostly just a
sideshow. When Rice visited promoter and big-game collector George Getz a
couple of days before the fight in his suite at the Chicago Athletic Club, Getz
summarized for Rice what the fight meant to Chicago itself. "This has been
called a three-million-dollar show," Getz told Rice. But, Getz went on, "Three
million won't even touch it." Counting private cars, railroad transportation,

hotel bills, food, and other incidentals, fight fans would spend more than twenty million dollars in Chicago. The nearly three million for tickets was chicken feed, Getz said, and hardly worth mentioning. The profit to Chicago should be around eight million dollars, Getz predicted, with an additional $300,000 in taxes for the government and about $280,000 tax money for the buoyant and bounding state of Illinois.[47]

This was one of the astonishing turns in modern civilization, Rice reflected. The fight itself was the Big Event, but the big news was the big money being made by the big people. Instead of a fight being backed by the roughnecks of the fight game, it was being financed by the leading bankers, the socially elect, the governor, mayor, industrialists, and what you might call the leading citizens. Seven governors and eighteen mayors would attend the fight, as well as several senators and congressmen. The tickets were being sold not by the soily, but by the hoity-toity: Trust companies were selling four hundred thousand dollars' worth of tickets, and the railroads were handling at least two hundred thousand dollars' worth of tickets for the trip and fight combined. All of this just to find out if Dempsey had tanked his last fight with Tunney. In the hullabaloo, Rice pointed out, "one almost forgets about the fighters in the general swirl that surrounds them, most of it tinted with shining gold."[48]

By fight day, the odds had come from 9 to 5 that Tunney would win to even money to 6 to 5 for Dempsey to beat fate and come back. After hanging around Chicago and the training camps and social gatherings for ten days, Rice eventually gave Dempsey at least an even chance to win back the heavyweight crown. He based his guess on Dempsey's flaming ring spirit against all the logic of the ring. Tunney, he thought, was still not a natural, and was not particularly keen about his profession. Dempsey, on the other hand, belonged to the ring as naturally as Babe Ruth belonged to baseball.

Also naturally belonging to the ring were the sure-thing gamblers, racketeers, and crooked politicians. Chicago at the time wasn't short on any of these. Given the suspicions following the first fight in Philadelphia, Tunney wanted to let the world know that at least he was straight and insisted that the fight contract include the following convoluted clause: "The parties hereto in the performance of their obligations hereunder will use all reasonable efforts to have the contest conducted with utmost fairness and to discover and expose to the other any circumstances, facts or transactions involving any persons whatsoever which might interfere with the fairness of such contest and the management and decision thereof." In other words, "no fake fellas"; or in Tunney's affected words, "I would not ever feign a knockout."

The most persistent rumor flying around town was that Tunney was going to take a dive in the seventh round. The various commissioners and civic leaders were all "het up" by the possibility that the hoodlums were plotting to steal the fight and pull off the biggest coup in sporting history. Commissioner Kelly, chairman of the South Park Board of Commissioners, announced that he had it on good account that none other than Al Capone had bet fifty thousand dollars on Dempsey. Overall, the estimates were that some ten million dollars had been bet on the fight.[49]

Part of the prefight preparations included a rules conference held a day or so before the fight by the Illinois Boxing Commission. Both fighters were represented. It was there that a clarification of the knockdown rule was discussed. Accounts differ as to which fighter's representative brought up the point, but the rule was discussed at length. It was agreed by both parties that in the event of a knockdown the man scoring it should go to the farthest neutral corner, and, in the event he refused, the count would not be started until he complied. So a suspension of the count was the penalty for disobeying the rules.[50]

By seven o'clock in the evening, a couple of hours before the main fight, forty thousand fans had found their seats. Next, and from their seats, they tried to find the ring. One fan said he could see better from his home in Fort Wayne, Indiana. A family of four was armed with telescopes. A majority of the five-dollar-seat fans had field glasses slung around their necks. Visibility was further limited by the many photographic "bombs" lighting up the stadium. The smoke from these flashes sent heavy clouds of smoke into the eyes and faces of the ringside workers. Just breathing was a chore, as the sportswriters braved the smoke and were packed into seats around the ring; Rice mentioned that the seats were so close together that a thin man could sit in them only if he sat on one of his hips. In addition to the writers stuffed together at ringside, Graham McNamee was setting up to broadcast the fight to an estimated fifty million listeners; the broadcast was carried by seventy-three stations hooked up to the NBC radio network.[51]

The gray skies took on a duller leaden hue as the clouds gathered. Rain threatened. By nine o'clock in the evening at ringside an unbroken mass of mostly male fight fans extended several hundred feet. Fewer women attended this second fight than their first, although here and there you could catch the flash of a dress or a short skirt and bobbed hair, but the crowd was at least 90 percent, maybe 95 percent, male. Anticipation for the main event gathered force; there was a roar as Dempsey made his way into the ring wearing a white sweater covered by a long white coat that fell to his feet. While Dempsey waited for Tunney, Jack Sharkey and Jim Jeffries came over to shake

Dempsey's bandages. Another roar announced Tunney, who was wearing a long coat of red, blue, and gold. Jack greeted Gene as he entered the ring. "How are you, Gene?" asked Dempsey. "Quite well, Jack, and you?" Tunney responded. The announcer announced: "This is a fight for the world's heavyweight championship."[52]

Dempsey wore black trunks trimmed in red. Tunney wore pure white. As the two boxers stood under forty blazing arc lights in the center of the ring at Soldiers' Field minutes before the Fight of the Century, referee Dave Barry again quickly reviewed the rules. No kidney blows or rabbit punches (a punch thrown behind the opponent's head at the nerve center where the base of the skull and the cervical vertebra meet). Barry went on:

"Now I want to get this one point clear. In the event of a knockdown, the man scoring the knockdown will go to the farthest neutral corner. Is that clear, Jack? Is that clear Champ?"

Both boxers nodded "Yes."

"Now in the event of a knockdown, unless the boy scoring it goes to the farthest neutral corner I will not begin the count until he does."

After more nodding, and a few more details, Barry then paused impressively and said: "Shake hands now and come out fighting."

This they both did.

For the first six rounds the fight went pretty much as it did a year earlier. Tunney boxed; Dempsey fought. But by all accounts Dempsey did look considerably better than he had in Philadelphia, tanned and generally more agile and much better at defending himself. He was also successfully using the rabbit punch every time Tunney failed to tie him up. Nonetheless, Tunney still used his left successfully and at will. In the fourth round Tunney dazed Dempsey with a wild right; by the sixth Dempsey was bleeding from his right eye and his left ear; his left eye was swollen.

Although Dempsey had landed some solid blows at close quarters in the third round, Tunney was easily ahead on points as they came out for the seventh round. About fifty seconds after the controversial round started, Dempsey rushed Tunney. Tunney led with a straight left, but Dempsey crossed it with a long right. It hit high, but as Tunney danced backwards a couple of steps, Dempsey followed. Dempsey hit Tunney on the chin with a long left hook, and then another right put Tunney against the ropes. As Tunney rebounded off the ropes back toward Dempsey, the challenger threw another left hook, a terrific blow to the jaw that caught Tunney moving into the punch.

Tunney started to fall back and down, sliding against the ropes; on the way down, for good measure Dempsey hit him again with a left-right, left-right combination. Somewhere in the neighborhood of seven vicious punches in all (Tunney would later say he didn't even remember the last three) knocked Tunney down for the first time in his life. It looked like the fight was over. Tunney, slumped down and goofy-eyed, was sitting-laying-reclining with his left arm hanging on the ropes. Barry moved in to start the count, but stopped when he saw that Dempsey was still standing near and behind the fallen Tunney. Barry yelled at Dempsey to go to the other corner. Dempsey refused. Barry grabbed Dempsey around the waist and moved him to the farthest neutral corner. By this time four seconds had elapsed. The timekeeper, who was counting anyway, gave Barry the count at "Five!" when the referee returned from escorting Dempsey. Instead Barry shouted "One!" over the fallen Tunney.

When Tunney's eyes refocused, he noticed that the distance between his eyes and the canvas was awfully short. Only then did it dawn on him where he was. "I must have been knocked down," Tunney told himself rather foolishly. "Look here, Tunney, you must get up. Sure, sure, get up! But what shall I do when I do get up? I've never had to get up before." While the count inexorably continued, Tunney sat there and tried to figure out what to do next. Clinch? No, those Dempsey rabbit punches would be killers. Invite Dempsey in and try to land a lucky punch on the overconfident challenger? No, Dempsey's chin was always tucked on his chest and more exchanges were too dangerous. There was one other idea.

At the count of "Nine!" Tunney was up—and running. The champion decided that the best approach would be to make Dempsey chase him. Tunney's many years of running backward in his roadwork would be useful now. Dempsey came toward him, crouched low and wearing a savage scowl, his right up for defense, his left dragging low along the canvas. When Dempsey threw the left, Tunney picked it off and circled right. Dempsey followed but was swinging wildly, missing Tunney badly with his flurry of furious swings. Tunney could circle faster than Dempsey could chase; the old lion couldn't catch the retreating antelope. Weary of the hunt, Dempsey stopped for a brief second, according to Rice, and growled "Come on and fight." But Tunney let the crowd roar and rave and jeer as he danced away, a ghost that Dempsey couldn't reach.[53]

Toward the end of the dramatic round, Tunney was beginning to regain the offensive, at the bell actually landing a punch just below the heart that Dempsey later said was the hardest punch he ever took. By the eighth, Tunney had recovered. He went out to meet Dempsey, Rice observing that he looked like the Tunney of the earlier rounds and that there was no sign that he had been dropped in the previous round. Midway through the eighth Tunney threw a right hook to Dempsey's jaw, and down he went to both knees; but before Barry could get past the count of "One!" Dempsey bounced up and continued his desperate efforts to win a fight he already knew he had lost. This continued for another two rounds as Tunney fired away at will, cutting Dempsey badly; Tunney easily blocked or ducked Dempsey's flailing swings. At the bell in the tenth, Tunney was still throwing rights and lefts to Dempsey's blood-smeared face and the challenger was still gamely trying to break through the champion's defense; neither boxer heard the bell and the seconds had to separate them. The "long count" fight was over. It was Tunney in a unanimous ten-round decision.

There was talk of a third match. Dempsey's popularity after the second fight soared; after all, he fought bravely and he dropped Tunney. Dempsey, a good loser, gave Tunney credit for a smart fight. Tunney was willing to fight the old Manassa Mauler again, but stipulated the fight would be fifteen rounds, not ten. Discussion followed between Rickard and Tunney's representatives, who agreed to meet any reasonable demand Dempsey might make. Given Dempsey's seventh-round performance and the brouhaha over the "long count," there was every reason to believe a third fight would be even more profitable than the second. But Dempsey wasn't interested. In response to Rickard's pleadings, Dempsey telegrammed Rickard: "Count me out, Tex."[54]

Rickard had promoted seven Dempsey fights that collectively drew well over eight million dollars. Dempsey's no-nonsense approach to the sport, his rough-and-ready style, his murderous glare, his sheer will, heart, and determination, his ring spirit, and his single-minded thought—knockout—all made him a promoter's dream, the greatest individual drawing card in the history of sport. Tunney's highfalutin tastes, his priggish attitudes, his affected speech patterns, his bookishness, his clean living, his upper-class social calendar, and his scientific, unemotional, and premeditated boxing style were entirely incompatible with public popularity. For God's sake, he even had a reason-based philosophy of training and boxing, and he could articulate it all by himself; this wasn't sport, it was all business. The "high-hat" was too damned civilized.

With Dempsey out, the melodrama went with him. Everybody lost interest, even Tunney. Rickard had to meet a contract obligation with Tunney for a challenger in 1928. After a messy series of bouts to determine who would meet the defending champ, somehow Tom Heeney surfaced over Sharkey, Risko, and Delaney. Before the Heeney match Tunney became engaged to Polly Lauder, a socialite from a wealthy steel-industry family. Tunney had also decided to retire from the ring, but he did box Heeney first. Tunney won by a technical knockout in the eleventh round, and Rickard lost somewhere around four hundred thousand dollars, his first financial sock on the chin in twenty-one years of promoting boxing. Rice covered the fight. He called Tunney's boxing "masterful," and noted that the champion gave one of the finest exhibitions of scientific boxing that the ring had ever seen. But Rice also observed in passing that the Yankee Stadium crowd of around forty thousand looked on in silence with about as much visible excitement as might be found in a crowd watching a surgical operation. Tunney thought that the fight with Heeney was his most skillful performance of his entire career. "Everything clicked in unison," he said. Little clicked with the crowd. The Golden Age of American boxing was officially over.[55]

17

Shadows from the Night

In a Ring Lardner roast of Grantland Rice as the 1920s were coming to a close, Lardner claimed that "Horace Grantland Rice" had recently taken to beekeeping to fill up his time.

"You'll get stung!" warned his friends when he mentioned his new project.

"It won't be the first time," Rice retorted.

Lardner reported that Rice had reserved the hours between midnight and four o'clock in the morning to attend to his bees. He fed them, shaved them and gave them their baths, and then tucked them in for bed with their bottles. He then sang them to sleep with improvised lullabies such as "Bee-lieve me if all youse endearing young swarms," etc.

With these chores done, Lardner then explained, Rice would spend his late mornings ripping up his mail; then he would write a couple of columns for the *New York Herald Tribune* syndicate, do an article for *Collier's,* make the first draft of an evening's radio speech, turn out an editorial, two poems, and a few essays for the *American Golfer,* plot or title a sports Sportlight movie short, change the beds, empty the ashtrays, get lunch, and set out for New Haven or St. Louis or wherever they are playing that day. Lardner's description of Rice's days was a bit of a stretch, but not much. Rice was a busy bee.[1]

Lardner and Rice remained close friends throughout the twenties and into the early thirties; that mysterious bond between them remained strong until the end, that is, until Ring's death in 1933. In 1928 the two families jointly purchased a four-acre tract of beachfront property at East Hampton, Long Island. There they each built summer homes, side by side, and with no fence between their properties.

Although the Rices had been living in their flat at 1158 Fifth Avenue since 1924, they had been renting summer homes over the years in a number of places not far from New York. They had summered at Plandome and Port Washington, Long Island, and also a little farther south on the island of Bellport. Rice's so-called cottage at East Hampton was a huge four-bedroom Cape, complete with maid's quarters. Lardner's home had thirteen rooms, plus a two-room apartment over the garage. Rice recalled their first summer at East Hampton in 1929 in their own home: "perched on our porch on our dune, we could stare straight out and into the bull rings of Lisbon . . . or perhaps it was the clearness of the gin cocktails. At any rate, nothing but gulls, whales and water separated us from Portugal and Spain."[2]

Which, as it turned out later, was unfortunate. With nothing but gulls and whales and sand and water in front of them—since both the Rices' and Lardners' were on, and not behind, the dunes—within only two years both homes were heavily damaged by storms. While the Lardners and the Rices were in Florida in the winter of 1931, a northeasterner struck their beachfront properties, almost directly it seemed. With thirty-foot-high waves crashing onto the beachfront, the foundations of both homes were quickly undermined. Then, within days, a second storm struck, doing a million dollars' worth of damage from Fire Island to Montauk Point.

Between the two storms, bulkheads had been built. The bulkheads saved both the Rice and Lardner properties; but where there had once been a hundred feet of beach and another hundred feet of sea grass between the homes and the ocean, after the storms, both homes were hanging over the water, most of the foundation structures having been swept out. Within a few weeks both homes were blocked and moved back from water's edge, and this time set behind, not on, the remaining dunes. The damage to Rice's home was in the neighborhood of twenty-six thousand dollars.[3]

Much like the storms in 1931 that would force Rice to rebuild his beach home, the stock market crash of 1929 forced Rice to rebuild his financial foundations—for the second time in his life. The crash quickly ruined Rice's considerable stock investments. In the immediate aftermath of the crash Rice found himself once again scrambling to recover his losses. He would exit the crazy 1920s the same way he entered it: more or less broke, but clearly not broken. Rice lived his own copy: always an uphill heart.

The summer of 1929, Rice recalled as the family moved into the East

Hampton home, was "absolutely lovely." Although there were clear signs that an incredible sporting decade was coming to a close—there was the sorry state of boxing, for example—the athletic highlights were still significant: Bill Tilden had won his seventh amateur tennis championship (it would be his last); Bobby Jones was finishing his seventh straight year winning one or the other national golf championship; Walter Hagen, now thirty-seven, won the British Open golf championship; Glenna Collett won the U.S. Amateur golf title for the fourth time; Helen Wills held on to her supremacy in tennis; and in the most recent World Series (1928), Babe Ruth at thirty-five years of age had increased his World Series home run record to thirteen and had set eighteen other series records. It might not have been the bull market in sports that the country was accustomed to, but there was still solid enough evidence that the romance between the public and this sporting business wasn't over just yet.

But by November the country's economic prosperity was officially over. On September 3, the day the market peaked, Rice was in California, by then a favorite travel and vacation haunt of his, especially since daughter Floncy now lived in Los Angeles. Rice was up north on the Monterey Peninsula at Pebble Beach covering the National Amateur golf tournament; Jones was there, so was Ouimet (now thirty-six), the young Charley Seaver, George Von Elm, and Jess Sweetser. Rice colorfully described the twenty-five hundred fans following Bobby Jones this way: "There were greens and golds, crimson, yellow, purple and pink and from far away, standing on a nearby hillside, it was like a moving flower garden." Rice also described the sheer terror of playing Pebble Beach, flanked as it is by an interesting natural water hazard, the Pacific Ocean.[4]

But the problem with the National Amateur for Rice and everybody else that year wasn't the course; it was that Bobby Jones lost, and lost early, in his first match play round to Johnny Goodman, a former caddie and sophomore at Omaha University. Jones's quick exit was a disappointment for sure for the thousands of fans who had been following him daily. The considerable numbers of considerably skilled golf writers at Del Monte found themselves covering a finals match between Harrison R. (Jimmy) Johnston of St. Paul and Dr. O. F. Willing, a Portland dentist. Ring Lardner quipped that whereas the inn and boardinghouse keepers had trouble finding space for the hordes of spectators that descended on Monterey peninsula at the beginning of the tournament, after Jones was knocked out the mass exodus was so great that the chambermaids had to move from room to room, sleeping a little in each bed, just so they would have something to do the next day.[5]

Lardner also commented on Rice's coverage of the finals match. Ordinarily, Lardner wrote, Rice could make a finals match sound thrilling even when it wasn't. Well, Lardner said, for this finals match Rice was going along swimmingly for about the first six or seven hundred words, rippling along like Johnny Weismuller, the swimmer, headed downstream. Then, Lardner said of Rice, you could almost feel him approaching a row of half-submerged bridge pilings. So lost for copy was Rice at this point in his coverage, that he tossed in five or six paragraphs about the comeliness, the mental sufferings, the self-control, and the ultimate delight of Mrs. Harrison R. Johnston when her husband won up 4 with 3 to go. For once, Lardner wasn't exaggerating. Dressed in blue with a flowing scarf thrown loosely over her shoulders, "Mrs. Johnston's first smile came at the twentieth hole," Rice reported, "where her husband finally had a chance to take the lead. He touched her foot with his putter just before he walked to the ball, smiled at her, and she in turn smiled back." So far as Lardner could recall, Rice had never once resorted to writing about Bobby Jones's wife.[6]

Without Jones in the tournament, Rice indeed was at a loss, though not without occasional copy. He followed Lord Charles Hope for a bit, to the 18th, where after a good drive, the Lord hooked his second into the ocean rocks and seaweed. He dropped another ball without looking for the errant ball. He wound up and promptly hooked again, but directly into the Pacific this time. He then played another and that also sailed out into the ocean blue. Then another. Kerplunk. When he reached in his bag for yet another ball, the Lord discovered there was none. So he took off looking for the first wild shot and lo and behold he found it resting and playable in the seaweed and rocks. Between the ebbing and flowing tide he stepped up, his swing cutting through the weeds and missing the rocks, and he hit the ball directly onto the green and putted out for a birdie 4, avoiding a probable 12 or so.[7]

The next day, as the golf tournament continued and as the nation watched its stocks begin to plummet, the ever-optimistic Rice might have been thinking of Lord Hope's miraculous recovery from pending disaster. "This has happened before," the nervous forecasters reassured everyone; "a bad break," "an exaggerated but necessary market correction," "a readjustment to a more secure technical position." Lord, hope. After its initial drop, the market rallied somewhat during the next few weeks. But then the market began to decline once again.[8]

By the end of September Rice had returned to New York. He covered the Jack Sharkey and Tommy Loughran fight at Yankee Stadium. At the start of the second round, Sharkey tore into Loughran, nailing him with a stinging left followed by an overhand right that caught Loughran squarely on the bridge of his nose. "You could hear the punch whistle through the air, as Sharkey's glove landed with a thud you could hear fifty yards away," Rice wrote. It reminded Rice of the way Stanley Ketchel described such devastating punches: "It smelled like a hot brick." Loughran went down. At the count of five he rose, dazed and apparently temporarily blinded by the punch. He held onto the ropes and groped along. He had no idea where he was or what was going on; he was floundering and apparently out of his head. "His eyes were gone and his mind was a blank. He was merely a dummy walking along the ropes as Sharkey, with narrow eyes, watched him but made no move to put him away." To his credit, Jack Sharkey stayed away, apparently waiting for Loughran's head and eyes to clear, even though he could have rushed Loughran and pounded on him as soon as he found his feet. It was uncharacteristic but greatly appreciated sportsmanship for boxing, Rice noted. But Loughran couldn't find himself along the ropes or anywhere else in the ring; the referee carefully guided the dazed Loughran back to his corner and ended the fight.[9]

By now, hope wasn't enough to cope with the tumbling stocks. The market fell faster and faster. Something was terribly wrong. Like the bewildered Loughran, the country was reeling, dazed and temporarily blinded by a thudding economic punch. By late October the forced selling began, and the alarm was sounded. Rice had a fair number of securities, one of which was Goldman, Sachs and Company. This company had confidently reassured its investors late in September that things would be sunny soon; they had even sponsored the Blue Ridge Corporation, an investment trust that would exchange leading "blue chips" at their current prices. Rice was heavy into Goldman, Sachs. But like everyone else, he held out, thinking that the market would rebound and that the mass liquidation was temporary. By the time Rice realized what was happening and sold his stock, the price had dropped from 121 to 3! As historian Frederick Allen described it, "Billions of dollars' worth of profits—and paper profits—had disappeared. The grocer, the window-cleaner, and the seamstress had lost their capital. In every town there were families which had suddenly dropped from showy affluence into debt. Investors who had dreamed of retiring to live on their fortunes now found themselves back once more at the very beginning of the long road to riches. Day by day the newspapers reported the grim reports of suicides." And with these losses, Allen went on, came the realization that the giddy postwar American hopes, at least the materialistic ones, were shattered.[10]

In the middle of all the commotion, and while preparing to cover weekly college football games and the 1929 World Series between the Cubs and the Athletics, Rice opened one of his Sportlight columns with this reflective verse. He called it "Fear":

> I have no fear, I thought, of what might fall;
> Of pain that I might know from some deep thrust;
> Of life or death, down to the final breath,
> Where darkness closes in above the wall;
> I have no fear, I know of men or fate,
> Of being broken on the turning wheel,
> Of blows and blood that flows in some red flood
> From wounds made by the bitter hand of hate.
>
> Then why should I fear shadows from the night,
> Dim, silent shadows I can hardly see,
> Made up of ghosts that come in phantom hosts
> To shut both sun and star adrift from my sight?
> They will not touch me, for they have no form,
> No substance that could deal a direct blow,
> And yet they seem through every hopeful dream
> To whisper of the coming of the storm.[11]

In his memoirs, Rice wrote that for him, the crash and the shadows from the night that followed it had been a blessing of sorts. He said that had it not occurred he would have soon been a dead millionaire: "Without further incentive to earn money . . . something I've had to do since the age of twelve, I might have drunk myself to death."

It is unlikely that Rice would have suffered the fate he predicted for himself had the crash not occurred. Rice drank before—and after—the crash. He also worked hard before and after the crash. Whatever financial losses Rice may have experienced did not deter him from continuing his calling and recovering his losses. But changes were in order, for sure. For example, after the crash the *American Golfer* began to wobble. By 1929 when Conde Nast bought the magazine for his stable—which included *Vogue, Vanity Fair,* and *House and Garden*—the *American Golfer* was doing quite well. Its circulation had grown to some seventy thousand. Rice had put together a number of wonderful contributors, including Britisher Bernard Darwin—perhaps the finest golf writer ever—O. B. Keeler, John Kieran, Rex Beach, John Kieran, George Ade, and Bud Kelland. Other writers also contributed to the classy magazine, including John R. Tunis on tennis and Lardner on just about anything he chose to concoct. Rice had just finished lining up golf pros Tommy Armour, Walter

Hagen, and Mac Smith for further magazine promotion when twenty pages of automobile advertising suddenly dropped out of the magazine after the crash. Even though the *American Golfer* held on for seven more years, it was no longer a source of stable supplemental income for Rice.

For nearly thirty years, Rice had been directly employed by a single newspaper. He had been on the staff of six different newspapers, his longest affiliation having come with his present job on the *New York Herald Tribune.* As a *Herald Trib* writer he was by definition also syndicated by the Tribune Syndicate; somewhere in the neighborhood of one hundred papers subscribed to his Sportlight column. But early in 1930 Rice decided to throw his lot with Jack Wheeler's North American Newspaper Alliance—the same syndicate (Bell) that Lardner had been with since 1919—and give up his ties with the *Herald Tribune.* This decision would mean that his syndication could continue much as it had been, but that he would no longer be on the staff of any particular newspaper. The *New York Sun* picked up Rice's columns for the New York readers, while the non–New York papers continued to buy Rice, but now through Wheeler. According to Wheeler, Rice was soon appearing in ninety-five newspapers with a circulation of more than ten million.[12]

Without an official desk in any city room, Rice usually worked out of his flat; sometimes he would set up shop at the Sportlight Films office at the Graybar Building in New York, and in the summer he would carry his typewriter with him to the East Hampton "cottage." Of course, when he had had a desk in a city room he wasn't sitting at it much anyway. But what the move to Wheeler's group really meant was that Rice could pretty well do whatever he wanted to do and cover whatever events he wanted to cover.

In addition to continuing with his weekly *Collier's* articles and the Sportlight Films projects and assorted other invited writing projects—introductions for this, summaries for that, editing this—Rice also stepped up his radio presence. He wasn't any Graham McNamee, the premier radio personality of the day, and he knew it. He had limited his broadcasting for the most part to brief Friday night football forecasts sponsored by Cities Services, or perhaps to having his World Series summaries read on the air the night after a big game. But by March of 1930 Rice had linked up with the National Broadcasting Company for a weekly broadcast. The broadcast was sponsored by Coca-Cola, and was the beginning of a long and warm relationship between Grantland Rice and the president of Coca-Cola, Robert Woodruff. McNamee was the program's master of ceremonies. The half-hour program featured Rice interviewing a famous sporting personality or a celebrity of one kind or another bookended by live music from a thirty-one-piece all-string dance orchestra and occasional vocalists. The program was broadcast coast-to-coast to nearly fifty NBC network radio affiliates.

Rice was introduced to the audience as the leading authority in the world of American sports. His columns and articles were read by millions, the promotion went on, and he was said to be the final arbiter on sporting questions. Coca-Cola promoted their new program by distributing some three million theater-type tickets throughout the country; these pasteboard advertisements served to introduce the idea that the radio listeners could have a "front seat" via the radio each Wednesday evening. The company sent six hundred thousand radiograms announcing the new program to all their soda fountain dealers and their customers for plastering on windows and counters:

> RADIO LISTENERS　　　EVERYWHERE USA
> TUNE IN THIS WEDNESDAY NIGHT AND EVERY WEDNESDAY—
> NEAREST NBC STATION—WE ARE TAKING COCA-COLA OFF THE
> ICE PUTTING IT ON AIR—COAST TO COAST NETWORK—FROM
> NEW YORK—HEAR GRANTLAND RICE LEADING SPORTS AUTHOR-
> ITY INTERVIEWING CHAMPION ATHLETES—LISTEN TO NOVEL
> ORCHESTRA UNLIKE ANY EVER BROADCAST—LIQUID MUSIC—
> SPARKLING ENTERTAINMENT. EVERYBODY WELCOME.[13]

By the end of the 1920s, radio had established itself as an important industry: by 1929 radio sets and paraphernalia sold to the tune of $842,548,000, an increase over the 1922 figures of 1,400 percent. Radios were in one in three homes; popular programs included Roxy and His Gang, the Happiness Boys, the A & P Gypsies, and Rudy Vallee. They would hear McNamee, as he gaped at the mass of humanity gathering for the second Dempsey and Tunney fight, say, "All is darkness in the muttering mass of crown beyond the light. It's like the Roman Coliseum."[14]

As the decade closed, aggregate newspaper circulation figures were still on the upswing but advertising revenue was dropping sharply, by 15 percent in 1930, 24 percent in 1931, and 40 percent in 1932. Newspaper advertising losses were radio's gains, but there was a stubborn loyalty to newspaper reading: between 1914 and 1940, the aggregate circulation of daily newspapers nearly doubled, while the national population increased only 30 percent. There was room for both radio and newspapers. And Rice made time for both.

In his first six radio programs, Rice interviewed Ty Cobb, Stewart Maiden (Bobby Jones's teacher at East Lake Country Club in Atlanta), James J. Corbett, Horton Smith (the young golfer from Joplin, Missouri), Tris Speaker, and Martha Norelius (an Olympic swimmer and gold medalist in 1924 and

1928). As the show continued, Rice lined up other celebrities, such as Bobby Jones, Babe Ruth, Tommy Milton (two-time winner of the Indianapolis automobile race), James Montgomery Flagg (the artist, on the theme "Why I Hate Sports"), Rogers Hornsby, Walter Hagen, Sidney Franklin (bullfighter), John Golden (theater), Count Von Luckner (war hero and noted sportsman and lecturer), Irvin Cobb, Dr. Frank Chapman (from the American Museum of Natural History, who spoke on "Birds"), Ring Lardner, and a long parade of football coaches—the first round of which included Knute Rockne, Mal Stevens (Yale), Major Sasse (Army), and Bill Roper (Princeton).

Rice's broadcasts were live. Most of the interviews were conducted in the New York studio, although some were from one or another sporting site. Occasionally the program was aired live with Rice in one studio and his guest in another. For example, for the Tris Speaker interview, the NBC technicians experimented with the technique of "switching." The radio listener was able to hear the miracle of Rice in New York interviewing Speaker in Chicago, asking him about Connie Mack's Philadelphia pitching strength, or the greatest play he'd seen this season, or who was the best catcher ever. This feat of switching was tricky then. It required the utmost in precision; eighty separate movements were required in the ten times the program was switched from New York to Chicago and back. The radio engineers, the "heart beats" of this newest technology, would cue Rice from the control room; Rice—in trepidation, given his aversion to technology of any sort—would then push his button to switch; then there would be complete silence from the radio speaker for two seconds until Tris Speaker spoke. A slip of a finger would have left millions of listeners wondering what happened to their program. Although the Coca-Cola motto then was "The Pause That Refreshes," the pause between many switches was anything but refreshing for all concerned.[15]

Rice's Coca-Cola show was understandably stiff, but always interesting and entertaining. And although tightly scripted, there were occasional slips. Babe Ruth was once a Rice guest. Just once. The Babe rehearsed his portion of the script before the broadcast. He got most of it right. But just before air time, Ruth had somehow scrambled up his copy of the script. McNamee was frantic, the producer was frantic, the orchestra leader, Len Joy, was frantic. Before Rice could get Ruth under control, the Babe, well, the Babe was the Babe. At one point in the Rice-authored script, Ruth was supposed to refer to the Duke of Wellington's historic remark that the Battle of Waterloo had been won on the playing fields of Eton; what Ruth actually said was, "As Duke Ellington once said, the Battle of Waterloo was won on the playing fields of Elkton." When, after the show, Rice asked Ruth how he could have loused up such a short sentence so thoroughly, the Babe said, "About that Wellington guy I wouldn't know. Ellington, yes." Ruth went on, "As for that Eton business—well, I married my first wife in Elkton (Maryland), and I always hated the goddamn place. It musta stuck."[16]

Ring Lardner was a favorite radio guest. By then Lardner was a familiar New York celebrity. His short stories and articles appeared in leading national magazines. Collections of his stories began appearing as early as 1916 with the publication of *You Know Me, Al: A Busher's Letters.* The books *Treat 'Em Rough* (1918) and *The Big Town* (1921) followed. By the time of Rice's radio interviews, Lardner had written *How to Write Short Stories* (1924), *What of It?* (1925, the title suggested by Rice), *The Love Nest* (1926), *and The Round Up* (1929). His play with George S. Kaufman, *June Moon* (Floncy Rice's theater debut), had opened in 1928.

Of course, not everybody held Lardner in such high esteem. On the night Lardner was guesting on the NBC broadcast, one of the bright boys of the studio dropped into the control room with an expectant gleam in his eye.

"Where's the bullfighter?" he chirped hopefully.

"Why, he's not on until next week. Ring Lardner's scheduled for tonight," the engineer told him.

"Oh, only Ring Lardner," the fellow replied. And he turned on his heel and walked out.[17]

On the air, Lardner was nervous—he confided once to Rice that he'd been sick for three days thinking about Wednesday Night Live on NBC. His voice was a low, pleasant Midwest drawl with a bored tremolo rhythm, and a timing that never included a pause for laughter, refreshing or otherwise:

Rice:	Well, Mr. Lardner, I'll start off by introducing myself. I'm Grantland Rice.
Lardner:	You'll have to speak louder, Mr. Rice. I'm not a Southerner.
Rice:	You've had a great deal of experience in sports, both as a competitor and a reporter. The radio fans would like to hear some of your experiences and opinions.
Lardner:	All right, just as long as you don't make me talk about myself. I'm like Will Rogers that way.
Rice:	Well, Mr. Lardner, I'll begin by asking you what you think of Bobby Jones.
Lardner:	I don't know much about him. Whenever I need a lawyer, I usually hire one right here in New York. (Jones was a practicing attorney and only played in the big tournaments.)
Rice:	I refer to his golf playing. What makes him win so many championships?

Lardner: He's foxy. He won't play anything but golf. You put him on a tennis court and Bill Tilden would make a sucker out of him.

Rice: What was the greatest thrill you ever experienced in sport?

Lardner: I think it happened the other night. I was walking down Broadway and passed twenty-seven song-writers, and one of them nudged the other twenty-six and said, "There goes Kid Chocolate."

Rice: Speaking of fighters, what do you think of Jack Sharkey?

Lardner: I never saw him fight. I've only seen him when he was in the ring.

Rice: What was the largest amount of money you ever made in a fight?

Lardner: I can get just as personal as you, Mr. Rice. You've lost a lot of hair since the first time I met you.

Rice: Well, we'll talk about something else. How is it that the Notre Dame football team wins so many games every season?

Lardner: I think it's because they're all foreigners and they can't understand Rockne's instructions.

Rice: Did you ever play football yourself?

Lardner: I went out for football at Yale, but I got hurt the first day.

Rice: How did you get hurt?

Lardner: Tad Jones wouldn't give me a uniform.

Rice: Mr. Lardner, do you mind giving advice to young boys?

Lardner: No. I've got four of my own.

Rice: You've got four boys?

Lardner: Yes. The third one was fifteen years old yesterday. He is just beginning to put a few words together.

Rice: How old is your oldest?

Lardner: He's eighteen. He can talk as fast as Floyd Gibbons.

Rice: Is he interested in sports?

Lardner: Yes. He wants to be a pitcher in the big league. The only trouble is, he can't pitch.

Rice: What have you advised him to do?

Lardner: Join the Philadelphia Nationals.

Rice: You were quite a pitcher yourself, weren't you Mr. Lardner?

Lardner: Yes, Grantland. May I call you Grantland? I mean, just for tonight?

Rice: That's all right. I was going to ask you how you threw your fast ball.

Lardner: I usually threw it to third base.

Rice: To third base? What for?

Lardner: Oh, there was always a chance I'd catch the batter napping.

Rice: What do you think of Babe Ruth?

Lardner: He'd never get a home run off me.

Rice: What would you do, always give him a base on balls?

Lardner: No, I'd stay in some other league.

Rice: Did you ever see Carnera fight?

Lardner: No. We keep ours in separate cages. All they do is sing.

Rice:	I understand you like football arguments. Did you ever win one from Bob Zuppke?
Lardner:	Ich no spriche ze Deutsch.
Rice:	Do you ever talk to Yost?
Lardner:	No. My parents taught me never to interrupt.
Rice:	How did you happen to give up golf?
Lardner:	I kept getting anonymous letters from the greens committee.
Rice:	What did the letters say?
Lardner:	I couldn't read them. They were anonymous.
Rice:	When you *were* playing golf, Mr. Lardner, what was your favorite shot?
Lardner:	The explosion shot off the tee.
Rice:	Didn't you ever use a driver?
Lardner:	Oh, yes, we've got one now. He's a Danish fella named Paul Christoferson.
Rice:	Do you think Helen Wills will come back?
Lardner:	Has she been away?
Rice:	I'm disappointed in you, Mr. Lardner. You don't give me much information.
Lardner:	Let *me* ask the questions. Then everybody will learn more.
Rice:	Well, go ahead.
Lardner:	Why don't you get Gene Tunney on this program? You could ask him just one question and by the time he got through answering it, the time would be up.[18]

Radio critic Louis Reid, writing in the *New York American,* thought Lardner's gift for nonsense was just what the country needed in the Depression. To call Lardner's radio humor "wisecracking," as some critics had referred to it, was inept, Reid wrote. Most wisecrackers aren't wise. Lardner's bubble-bursting witty remarks, on the other hand, exhibited a keen insight into human nature and the same shrewd philosophy that characterized his short stories. Lardner's brand of nonsense echoed that evening through the parlors of America and momentarily took people's minds off the problem of how to pay the gas bill.[19]

After his separation from the *Herald Tribune,* Rice's life was even more nomadic than it had been. His year was largely determined by the regular cycles of the sporting calendar and by where his family happened to be located. Despite all of his travels, Rice's annual schedule was becoming fairly habitual and would continue to be so for his remaining twenty years.

Since Floncy was in Los Angeles, he and Kate would usually leave New

York for California sometime in mid-December to be with their daughter for Christmas. Rice's favorite hotel was the Beverly Wilshire. The Rices might remain in the Golden State for two or three months, where Granny would both attend to his many irons in the fire and play many irons on the local country club golf courses, such as Riviera and Lakeside.

Around about late February or early March, Granny and Kit would board the train for Florida. More golf for sure, but there was also spring training to cover. The Rices favored the Gulf side of Florida, especially the area around St. Petersburg and Sarasota. But he spent time in each of the baseball camps up and down the Florida coasts. For instance, during the spring of the high tides at East Hampton, the Rices and the Lardners made the Flamingo Hotel in Miami Beach their base camp for several weeks. Lardner had been hospitalized for a time due to failing health—mostly tuberculosis and a sort of morosis of the liver—but had been released in time to go south with the Rices in the spring. Like all hotels in Florida, the Flamingo had fallen on hard times, with the market crash dropping the bottom out of the tourist season. To promote the hotel as a favorite of the rich and famous, the Rices and the Lardners were each given a free stay. Ellis Lardner wrote to one of their sons, John, that "None of us wanted to come here anyway but with a cottage and meals free for three weeks we couldn't afford to refuse." It doesn't appear that either Lardner or Rice was expected to do any hotel promotion as compensation for their stay. It was apparently enough that they just stayed there, and gave their permission for a kind of "Kilroy was here" quid pro quo.[20]

When spring training closed down, the Rices would usually travel up and over to Kit's family's home in Americus, and then go up to Nashville where they would visit with Rice's family and his old friends. Although his father had died quietly about the time Rice went overseas during World War I, his mother and two brothers were still among the Nashville locals. His visits with his mother were special to Rice; at seventy she was spirited but in failing health.

In none of Rice's travels, even those to visit relatives, was he playing hooky, for he still wrote daily, answered his correspondence, and managed his diverse business interests. On his way back to New York, Rice always stopped off in Kentucky for the Derby at Churchill Downs. The Derby had been around since the days of the "little red hoss," Aristides, who won the first Kentucky Derby in 1875. Rice's own lifelong affair with the ponies stretched back to his days with the *Nashville Daily News,* when among his other duties he was expected also to cover the daily clockings at the local racetrack, Cumberland Park. The horses trained at dawn, so during the racing season Rice came out of the gate by at least 4 A.M. daily. At that time, Rice recalled, "The Cumberland Derby was much more important than the Kentucky Derby. And there was much more blue grass in Tennessee than there was in Kentucky."[21]

As a preview to the 1931 Kentucky Derby, Rice interviewed Irvin Shrewsbury Cobb from Louisville for his weekly NBC radio program. Cobb, born in Paducah, Kentucky, was a journalist and a humorist who spoke with a tobacco-chewing drawl. He came up about the same time as Rice; he started with the local Paducah paper, then went on to New York where he was editor of the humor section of the *New York Sun* and then the *World.* From newspapers he worked his way onto the staff of the *Saturday Evening Post,* and later became a regular contributor to *Cosmopolitan.* In time he was popular on the radio, and over the years he wrote some sixty books of fiction.

When Rice opened the interview by referring to the Derby as the "Darby" to get Cobb going, Cobb quickly corrected his Southern friend. "Just one moment, kind sir. What business has a country boy from Tennessee got calling the Derby a Darby? You might possibly get away with that Darby stuff—if you had spats and a monocle and an Oxford accent and a set of those large, limpid British adenoids such as only true Britons have. But you—why you are as Southern as chicken gravy on a presiding elder's vest." Cobb went on to say that he couldn't fool the radio audience either about where he was born, mentioning that George Ade once told him that he could have gotten his hats blocked in Paris and his pants pressed in Rome and his hair cut in Constantinople and his laundry done in London—and he'd still look like Paducah, Kentucky.

As the Cobb interview progressed, the humorist explained that fast horses in Tennessee and Kentucky came naturally. Why, Kentucky had more tombstones erected to horses than to statesmen, Cobb pointed out. From the pioneer days, he said, when his people and Granny's people were coming through the wilderness and settling what was then America's frontier—with a demijohn in one hand, a squirrel rifle in the other, and some potlicker spilt on the whiskers—they had to have fast horses. "Why my grand daddy couldn't have got there at all if he hadn't owned a faster horse than the sheriff did back where he'd come from. Who did your great grand daddy shoot, Mr. Rice?"

When he finally got serious for a few minutes, Cobb reflected a bit on why the Derby was so galvanizing. Yes, he said, the race is only about two minutes long, but for one fleeting period the spirit of the Old South is revived. It isn't horses that are running at Churchill Downs on this spring day every year. "Tradition, by-gone romance, dimmed echoing poetry, the ghosts of ancient glories and ancient ideals and ancient heroes—they're all there speaking down the home stretch and past the grandstand and on into the sunset's gilded afternoon of remembered days."

When Rice asked Cobb to paint a word picture on the air for the radio audience as to just what a Kentucky Derby looks like, Cobb tried. He spoke of the molten gold braceletlike track, the velvety emerald greensward, the brocaded terrace of beauty and color of the eighty thousand humans in the grandstand, and the satin coats, slim legs, and panting nostrils of the kings and queens and princes and princesses of the equine kingdom—each a vision of courage, heart, and speed. But as Cobb wound down, he admitted to Rice's listeners that it was useless to describe in words what it was like to experience the Derby. Until you go to Kentucky and behold the Derby in person, he said, "you ain't never been nowheres and you ain't never seen nothin'."[22]

Following his annual pilgrimage to the Derby, Rice usually returned to New York, his headquarters for the remaining part of the year. When he wasn't covering a fight at Madison Square Garden, a polo match at Meadow Brook, a big horse race at the Jamaica track, a tennis competition at Forest Hills, or a crew race on the Hudson River at Poughkeepsie, he could be found working at home on Fifth Avenue or more commonly at the East Hampton home, allegedly resting up or socializing—one and the same for Rice. For instance, after the hurricane-relocation of his beach home, Rice had an acre or so of turf to play with. He created what he called an "all-around sporting club." No membership fees. Just a friendly little club for friends and neighbors. He put in a nine-hole chip-and-putt course, a croquet layout, a horseshoe pitching area, an archery lane, and naturally, he adopted a convenient swimming hole—the Atlantic Ocean.

On many Sunday afternoons throughout the summer months the Rices entertained their "club membership," which averaged around forty players per week. The regulars included artists, writers, and sporting figures such as the Irvin Cobbs, the Percy Hammonds, the Tunneys, the James Prestons, the Harold Rosses, the Bobby Joneses, the John Goldens, the P. Hal Simses, the John (Jack) Wheelers, and the Frank Crowninshields. Wheeler, now Rice's boss of sorts, recalled those wonderful afternoons. He noted that however big Granny's heart was, big enough to embrace almost everyone, the two who still meant the most to him were "his pretty wife Kate and their daughter Florence." Rice's marriage, Wheeler said, was an enduring love affair. Once, at one of these summer club gatherings, Granny came in from playing chip-and-putt golf to find about ten or so guests sitting around talking. Kate happened to be out of the room. Granny looked at the group of friends and asked, "Where is everybody?" To him, Kate was "everybody."[23]

The Rice's next-door neighbors, the Lardners, were consistent guests, of course. Ironically, one of the major reasons the Lardners had bought the beach property in the first place was to be less accessible. Their primary home had been in Great Neck, too close to New York for Ring to escape frequent and now less-wanted social contacts; by the early 1930s he hadn't the time or the energy any more to be so available. He wanted solitude. Ring called his new home on the beach "Still Pond—no more moving." Although he hadn't abandoned all social life then, he was cutting back considerably. And there was the garrulous gadfly Rice, the indomitable Mr. Fix-It, building a raucous sporting club next door to Still Pond!

But Rice's sporting club was not without its own Ricean irony. The sport, he said, was very pleasant, but no match for the "conversation that crackled over the sea grass on those occasions." But in contrast to this hall-of-fame socializer, we still find lingering the other side of Rice and his occasionally revealed longing for the solitude he was flat incapable of deliberately realizing, ever. He was almost resigned to the gift of his public nature and to the inexplicable fact that others—his family, friends, and, well, everybody who met or knew him—just wouldn't or couldn't give him up to any kind of Still Pond:

> I have been in crowds all my life,
> And I possibly always will;
> I have been part of their strife;
> I have seen them droop and thrill;
> I can hear their rush and roar
> In the wake of the winning score.
>
> I have been in crowds all my days,
> And that's why I sit and dream
> Of the hills and their lonely haze,
> Or a rock by a mountain stream,
> Or a road through the woods again,
> Where there are more trees than men.[24]

In the late months of a typical year from the 1930s on, Rice regularly covered a Saturday college football game of his choice—for he was still doing the All-America selections—made occasional trips for his Sportlight Films productions, wrote furiously his columns, articles, and verse, lined up guests for the NBC radio broadcasts, and covered the World Series.

Two golf competitions that Rice covered annually were the U.S. Open and the National Amateur. In 1930 Bobby Jones, who had dominated the sport of golf throughout most of the 1920s, set sail for Europe and two months of competition. Rice didn't make the trip despite the fact that Jones told him he was seriously thinking of retiring from golf and wouldn't much longer be copy for his sportswriter friend and confidant.

Besides the British Open and the British Amateur, Jones was scheduled to compete in the Walker Cup matches. He won the Walker Cup. Then in late May he finally won his first British Amateur title at St. Andrews. Bobby Jones had accomplished what no other golfer had ever pulled off: he had won all four major titles at one time or another in his career.

"There are now no more golfing worlds for him to conquer," wrote Rice after Jones's St. Andrews win. Little did he know what would happen next, for Jones's feats within the next four months exceeded even Rice's fanciful imagination. After Jones won the British Open at Hoylake, Rice gushed that this was an incredible achievement—winning two of the four—and that it set up the possibility of Jones setting a record in golf "beyond the dream of any mere mortal." An American returning from the Hoylake match told Rice that he'd never seen anything like it in sport before. "Here were 20,000 Englishmen and Scotchmen apparently pulling for Bobby Jones to win. They have made him their great idol of sport," he went on. It was not his skill alone at golf that attracted such a following, not even just his competitive spirit, but his entire demeanor: "His personality got to them and gripped them."[25]

When Jones landed in New York, he was greeted by an all-day, all-night celebration, complete with a ticker tape parade down Broadway to City Hall, where Mayor Jimmy Walker gave him the keys to the city, and an evening dinner at the Vanderbilt Hotel with Rice as the master of ceremonies. The next day Jones and his entourage, including Rice, headed out to Minneapolis for the next step in Jones's quest: the U.S. Open at Interlachen, where some twelve hundred amateur and professional golfers were gathering for the show . . . and waiting for Bobby Jones.[26]

Rice accompanied Jones on a preliminary round a couple days before the Open. He reported that Jones's game was fairly solid, except that he was having a bit of trouble with his long irons and woods. When asked how he was handling the pressure, Jones said that he felt good, that he wanted to win, naturally, but that he wasn't wrought up over it: "If I don't win I certainly won't shoot myself or dive in one of Interlachen's lakes." Jones was as lighthearted about the match as he had been about any other that Rice had seen him play.

By the fourth round, Jones was up by five strokes. But in the last round, the second eighteen holes that Saturday, MacDonald Smith, the Scot Jones had just beat at Hoylake by only two strokes, came in with a two-under 70 with Jones still on the course. By the 16th hole, Jones was two over par, three up over Smith. But a topped tee shot on the long par-three 17th caromed off a tree, and ended up wherever lost balls mysteriously go, even those watched by eight thousand pairs of eyes. Double-bogey, his third double-bogey of the round. Needing a par on the treacherous, uphill 18th to hold on for the win, Jones drove well enough but left his approach shot forty feet short of the pin. Jones studied the putt for what seemed to be forever, stepped up, and calmly struck the ball smartly with his putter, "Calamity Jane," up one slope, up another, a slight break to the left, and into the hole for a birdie three. The third of the big four was his. And Rice was seemingly for once without words, as he blandly underwrote the results of the U.S. Open: "Bobby Jones broke all records in the history of golf this afternoon by winning his third major championship in succession and this is a matter of statistical data that goes back 500 years. This is a plain statement of fact that no adjective can adorn." Later Rice simply said that Jones's play that day—in trouble and out, repeatedly—was masterful. "He kept a light, firm grip on his club and a tight grip on his heart and head, and in this way put up an impregnable barrier that not even the best of the pros could beat down."[27]

Ten weeks later, Jones teed up for the Amateur at Merion, just outside Philadelphia, and the same course where his career began some fourteen years earlier as a fourteen-year-old boy wonder. Now, at twenty-eight, Jones was better known by all the world than anyone else in the world, except maybe Charles Lindbergh and the Prince of Wales. Of the three, even if Lindbergh accomplished the most outstanding achievement, Rice thought Jones was the most outstanding personality.

The Merion test was two rounds of qualifying medal play on two successive days to produce the top thirty-two amateurs. The third day in the morning match play began; by noon there were sixteen, by nightfall there were eight; on they played until there was but one.

In a practice round with Jones the day before the championship, Rice reported that Jones was in fine mental form, this in spite of a summer-long bout with some kind of stomach virus. As they walked together, Jones told Rice that in all his years of playing golf, he'd discovered that it is best played by "feel." Hard to describe, for sure, but as Jones explained, when you have it completely, you don't have to think of anything. You just meet the ball. Even though this seldom happened to Jones, much less in title golf, "Today," Jones went on, "everything's falling into one piece—perfect."[28]

After that round, and after watching Jones the next day effortlessly shoot a first round of 69, one under par, Rice wrote that "an old familiar shadow has once again fallen across the field at Merion. . . . A much thinner shadow fell across the same course fourteen years ago, but the shadow then was only fourteen years old. Shadows, after all, must have some age. That is what helps to make them shadows." Rice appeared to know in advance what was going to happen that week, as he recalled that someone else had once said, "Coming events cast their shadows before."[29]

With a 73 on the second qualifying round, Jones, according to Rice, was so relaxed he almost appeared to be loafing. That's what golf-by-feel does, and the feeling stuck around long enough for Jones to play through all his matches effortlessly. He beat Ross Sommerville, the Canadian champion, 5 up with 4 to play; then he put away Hoblitzel of Toronto by the same margin. With thousands of spectators escorting Jones around the course, Rice said that it was hard to get close enough to Jones to see his smooth swing: "You couldn't see Jones on Wednesday with a stepladder and a Lick telescope." In fact, U.S. Marines—fifty of them—had been called in by the Merion Cricket Club to cope with the fawning Jones gallery.[30]

The next day in the quarterfinals, Bobby breezed through Fay Coleman 6 and 5, and in the semis he bested Jess Sweetzer 9 and 8; in the Sweetzer match he was only one up at thirteen in the morning round, but Jones played the last sixteen holes in something like six under. Meanwhile, Gene Homans, son of Shep Homans (the famous Princeton fullback), beat eighteen-year-old Charley Seaver of Stanford—the all-around athlete and great kid who would later be the father of baseball pitcher Tom Seaver. Homans, a bespectacled golfer from Princeton, had come back from five down against Seaver, winning on the last hole to earn his place in the finals against Jones. The two— Seaver and Homans—had eaten dinner together the night before their match. After supper they took in a motion picture show together.[31]

As the huge gallery took off with Jones and Homans the next day, the world buzzed. Francis Powers of the *Chicago News* borrowed Rice's Notre Dame lead: "There goes another race by the Four Horsemen of the Apocalypse over the fairways of Merion, and this time their names are Jones, Jones, Jones and Jones." From a friend and an Atlanta restaurant owner, Johnny Boutsies, Jones received this telegram: "E TON E EPITAS." The Greek slogan used by the Spartan mothers when sending their sons off to battle, and as they buckled on their shields, meant roughly, return from battle "With it, or on it."[32]

Although the twenty-two-year-old Homans had tied Bobby for medalist honors a year earlier at the Pebble Beach course before Jones was knocked out in the first round of match play, he didn't have a chance against Jones this time. Jones didn't play all that well, but his sound and smooth swing, determination, concentration, and competitive self-control—the combination of which set him apart from all other tournament golfers that year, and any year since—gave him an 8 and 7 victory against Homans. It gave him what George Trevor had called the "Impregnable Quadrilateral of Golf," or more popularly what O. B. Keeler had been calling the Grand Slam of Golf. Keeler and the entire golf world thought the Grand Slam to be an absolutely impossible achievement.[33]

> All roads that lead to any place
> Well worth knowing,
>
> Lead uphill always in the face
> Of headwinds blowing.
>
> And only weary feet may find
> The goal that's waiting,
> Through care and struggle, strain and grind,
> Through hurt and hating.
>
> Vain hands reach out from those who stop,
> And start no rally;
> The olive grows upon the top,
> Not in the valley.[34]

Jones had made a promise to himself while he was playing in the Open tournament at Interlachen. He realized then that he was tired and that he simply didn't enjoy the pressure of competitive golf any more. Rice recalled that Jones had always been keen for the thrill of championship golf, but that he had also always hated the accompanying fanfare of the crowds, the parades and such, and of being public property on and off the course. In mid-November 1930 Bobby Jones made good on his promise and politely retired from golf competition, doing the right thing and at the right time. On top of the mountain. And with his shield.

In the few years immediately before the market crash and in the few years immediately after it, a number of thoughtful writers regularly questioned whether there was any necessary connection between progress of a technical sort and the progress of civilization as a whole—especially in the moral, artistic, or intellectual senses. Aldous Huxley, for example, argued that technological cleverness is only a single, if powerful, component of what constitutes a civilized life. Exaggerating this component helps to multiply the possibilities for increasing the amount of waste, improvidence, and destruction carried out in the name of progress. Furthermore, the tidy illusion is created that better technology will somehow or other make humans better as well—more expansive, cleverer, and more virtuous. "Because we use a hundred and ten times as much coal as our ancestors," Huxley wrote, "we believe ourselves a hundred and ten times better intellectually, morally, spiritually."[35]

On the other hand, Huxley and others believed that individual and collective happiness depended largely upon experiences that did not necessarily have anything to do with such wonderments as the invention of the internal combustion engine, the telephone, the radio, or moving pictures. It seemed clearly to be the case, Huxley said, that the life of a factory worker in the late 1920s and 1930s was less satisfactory, in spite of the luxuries and amusements provided by technology, than the life of the artisans of the earlier ages. This was the case, he thought, largely because the technical component of common life is aimed at incessant simplification: making things easy, quick, handy—in short, convenient. In days past, if we wanted to decorate the walls of our home, we had to paint or draw; if the urge to listen to music arose in us, we had to make our own; or if we wanted to enjoy a dramatic performance, we had to organize the show ourselves. Huxley wrote that motion pictures, the record player, and the radio were essentially distractions and that they did nothing in themselves to satisfy an individual's desire for self-assertion and self-expression. They provided none of the happiness that comes from something personally accomplished.[36]

Sport figured into this thinking in an ironic way. And Grantland Rice clearly understood the irony: that sport could be celebrated both for being a creative antidote to the cult of technical progress and as a successful example of the extent to which such technological progress could be measured and cultivated. Sport has always been one of the primary opportunities to personally *do* something of intrinsic social and individual worth. In fact, the rise of sport in the 1920s and 1930s was nothing if not a kind of romantic response to the passing of a more self-reliant age. Hero worship and sports consumption served as compensation for the alienation created by jobs and lifestyles produced by urbanization, industrialization, and bureaucratization. Sport was a familiar, ordered world that offered an escape from modern life.[37] Yet on the other hand, in these decades, science and technology were themselves being increasingly applied *to* sport. Such applications could reduce sport to little more than the obsessive pursuit of records, and its meaning to little more than a vindication of the theory of progress.

Grantland Rice's coverage of the 1932 Olympic Games in Los Angeles illustrated this paradox. His coverage revealed the conflict between a more modern quantitative/technical/progressive sense of sport and an older qualitative/

human/moralistic sense; it underscored the tension between preoccupation with the score and a sense that there was a greater significance to sport beyond the score.

The 1932 Summer Olympics were a record-breaking mother lode. Around fifteen hundred athletes from thirty-seven nations competed for two weeks in fourteen major sports and 135 different competitions. Nearly twenty world records were broken, and some forty Olympic records were set. In track and field, all Olympic records but the hammer throw and the long jump were beaten. Records toppled in other sports too, such as cycling, men's swimming, rowing, and almost every sport that women competed in. The 1932 athletes broke four times more records than in all the other Olympics combined. Many of their records were in the books until the 1960s.

The popular thinking at the time was that these outstanding performances were attributed to the wonderful facilities, and to the general levels of good feeling and beneficence that existed during the games. But there was more to it than that. The new age of athletic training and conditioning had arrived. "Thereafter, ambitious athletes took on a much heavier burden of self-discipline," wrote Richard Mandell, a cultural historian, as from this moment on, "conditioning became specialized, scientific, and methodically directed at the establishment of new records."[38]

Without question, Grantland Rice did his part in whipping up interest in the record-breaking possibilities at Los Angeles. As early as April, nearly four months before the Olympics, Rice was already promoting the potential of these Olympics, the first held in North America since 1904. In speculating on the American athletes' chances for success in the running events, he reminded his readers of the relatively recent troubles Americans had had in the Olympics: in 1924 in Paris, the United States won only one running event; in 1928 at Amsterdam the Americans again won only one race, Ray Barbuti's victory in the 400 meters. Rice opened the month of April claiming that the 1932 "Olympic urge will bring a much keener effort to hundreds who, in giving their best, should leave a trail of shattered marks behind." He closed the month predicting that maybe four Olympic records would be broken in track and field, and maybe even six "when you consider the talent now at work and the tremendous forward urge an Olympic year brings."[39]

In May and June Rice increased the frequency of his coverage of Olympic hopefuls and his speculations about the likely record-breaking outcomes. "One factor," he wrote, "which will help build up attendance at the Olympic Games, is the prospect of seeing new records being established." He went on to say that the average citizen gets a great kick out of watching a record cracked. It gives him something to talk about for the rest of his life, Rice explained.[40]

By the first week of July, Rice had left New York for California. The Olympics were still almost one month away. From the time his train pulled into Union Station in Los Angeles to the extinguishing of the flame at the games' end, Rice devoted every Sportlight column to one or another aspect of these Olympics.

Yes, he did shill for the event and for the record books. For a mere twenty-two dollars, Rice gushed, you could see twenty-six different shows, including the opening and closing ceremonies and the best athletes in the world— "flaming youth at its peak—roistering in the midst of split seconds and split inches—setting new targets for future generations to shoot at."[41]

But for all of Rice's emphasis on breaking records and specialized training regimens of this international competition, his reports were dominated by something else: the human side of the formal gathering and its edifying possibilities.

Despite the Depression, Rice told his readers, the 1932 Olympic Games were going to be the greatest sporting show ever with regard to quantity and quality, color and class, speed and stamina and skill. In his coverage before the Olympics, Rice tried to give his readers something of the flavor of the preparations for the competitions. He covered the training areas, toured the Olympic stadium and the 133-acre Olympic Village, and wandered on up to Palo Alto for the track and field qualifying trials. At the trials Rice acknowledged the tension and heavy strain on the competitors, but he also wrote about the almost fatherly way Lawson Robertson, the American Olympic coach, handled his athletes to get them to relax before their competitions: "They have all been allowed to do pretty much as they pleased, play golf and tennis, swim or loaf around. You can see the weight men smoking their pipes with no attempt at intensive training."[42]

During the week before the opening ceremonies, Rice discussed the general prospects for the Americans, interviewed many of the international athletes, boosted girl-wonder Babe Didrikson and swimmer Helene Madison, and interviewed any number of hopefuls, including Dr. Patrick O'Callaghan, the Irish hammer thrower and decathlon star who was also considering competing in his other strong suit, boxing; Lord Burghley, the keen, alert, gracious, and courteous captain of the British track team, who in a 400-meter-hurdles race had beaten the Italian Facelli in spite of going black at the last hurdle— he ran thirty yards beyond the finish line because he couldn't see the tape and was afraid he would fall too soon; Percy Williams, the popular Canadian sprinter who would be facing a stiff test from the likes of Americans Eddie Tolan and Ralph Metcalfe and the German Arthur Jonath; Santiago Lovel, the Argentine superheavyweight boxer, who boxed any and all sailors—one at a time—on the ship from Argentine to the Pacific coast, flattening them all within minutes; and Bill Carr and Norwood Hallowell, the American runners. "The last time I ran against John Cornes of Great Britain," Hallowell said, "he told a joke just as we started." "What was the joke?" Rice asked. "I've forgotten," Hallowell replied, "but it was good enough to make us all laugh, and we were still laughing when the gun was fired."[43]

As for the games themselves, the human drama was Rice's constant touchstone. In his coverage of the track and field competitions, Rice wove dramatic descriptions that included the context of the contest, the crowd's participation in it, and the come-from-behind excitement of the winning throw, jump, or run. Rice spoke warmly of Babe Didrikson's first gold medal at the games, in the javelin throw, where the lithe, slender-looking girl outpitched her much larger rival, the German Helen Braumuller. "And then Mildred Tex Babe Didrikson got a running start and sent the javelin on its way," Rice wrote. "The big crowd broke into a roar the moment it stuck and quivered in the green turf." He noted that it was the whiplash whirl of the Babe's powerful wrist and forearm that carried her to triumph, with a throw eleven feet beyond any previous Olympic throw.

There was the last hammer throw of Ireland's Dr. Pat O'Callaghan, the giant 240-pound Celt, who still needed three inches more to win the event. As he started his wind up, a boding hush fell upon the scene, and "he thewed like an Auroch's bull, with a chest as thick as a hillside, finished his final whirl and let nature take its course." Even before the big hammer hit the ground, the crowd was cheering, for the mighty doctor had thrown the spinning hammer five feet beyond his nearest competitor.

In the 800-meter run, English schoolteacher Tom Hampson had to run the legs off the greatest field ever in this Olympic event. "This was a race that caught and gripped you from the starter's gun to Hampson's final desperate drive through the last forty yards to overhaul the flying Canadian [Alex Wilson] and leave him behind," Rice wrote. Hampson had said it would be his final race, and during it, in the last forty yards, the lead changed hands three times, but at the last it was Hampson who came up on even terms with Wilson, "his feet thudding into the dirt, who opened up a streak of golden daylight and began to pull away."

Then there was the stunning 1,500-meter run of the little Italian, Luigi Beccali, who upset the world's best, including the American Glenn Cunningham and New Zealand's John Lovelock. From the back of the pack in the home-stretch, "A new Ben Hur had set his chariot in motion. Luigi Beccali was running for the glory of the past, for the ghosts that still haunt the seven hills." The killing drive to the tape, which Luigi grasped and tore in half, gave the 5'6" city employee from Milan a surprising triumph.

Rice was sitting next to Will Rogers when he watched Bill Carr from Pine Bluff, Arkansas, outrun Californian Ben Eastman in the 400 meters. Eastman led early, and the Far West crowd of sixty thousand broke into a wild thunder of cheering. After the final turn it was clear to Will Rogers that the Stanford runner would win, and he yelled out, "Eastman wins!" But then Carr came on. In a perfect rataplan of rhythm, Carr increased his speed. "It was the master painting a masterpiece," said Rice, as Carr finished close to five feet ahead of Eastman. Rice said that suddenly Eastman knew he didn't have a chance as Carr pulled alongside and then moved ahead, but, Rice said, Eastman never quit. He ran his race. It took a world of heart to keep driving as Carr inched ahead, running with the feet of another Mercury.[44]

Toward the end of the games, Rice told his readers that the 1932 Olympics had hardly been the flop that was generally predicted, given the Depression and the jealousies and feuds of international competition; instead, they were without question the greatest sporting pageant in world history. The best contribution of the Olympics, Rice reflected, was to the betterment of world understanding. This, he thought, was a far more important measure in the long run than the new records set.

As if to help his readers see the significance of collective human virtues over individual velocities, the day after the Olympics ended, Rice boosted some of those Olympians who had not won their events: Ralph Metcalf, the Marquette Express, who appeared to win the 100-meter race, but was later given second place by the cameras, not the judges; Ralph Hill, who made a game finish in the 5,000-meter run, coming within a foot of winning in spite of being fouled twice by another runner; Nishida, the Japanese pole vaulter, who had never before cleared 13'9", and who met the supreme test by clearing the bar at 14 feet, finishing second to Miller of the United States only by a final vault; Canadian Alex Wilson, whose out-of-nowhere run in the 800 meters broke the previous world record and forced Hampson to beat 1:50 to win by a narrow margin; Gon, the Korean runner for Japan, muttering to himself, obviously in a daze just fifty yards from the finish of the marathon, staggering, swaying, but dead game to the last as he flopped over the finishing line in a heap; Lenore Kight of Pennsylvania, the plucky seventeen-year-old schoolgirl who in the finals of the 400-meter swimming race was just out-touched by

Helene Madison, holder of twenty world records; the Italian eight-oared crew who surprised all the best teams—the United States, Canada, and Great Britain—and found themselves leading with only ten yards to go before the U.S. crew practically had to lift their shell from the water to win by the span of a hand; Evelyn Hall, who lost to Babe Didrikson in the 80-meter hurdles but almost caught the Texas whirlwind at the tape, and actually startled the confident Didrikson in a near-upset.

Rice concluded his tribute to the also-rans by reminding any of his readers who were among those who were asking again and again for the final score of the Olympics, that there was only one reasonable reply: "There is no official Olympic score."

After all, these were the Olympic *Games,* Rice implied. Yes, one measure of their success was the extent to which scientific and technical training could improve the boundaries of human performance. But though such records were to one extent or another enduring, what was far more important in athletics in the long run was what was endearing: the *experience* of competing in the first place, even if the result happened to be last place.

18

With Roving Heart and Restless Feet

She was often called "Grant's girl." From the moment he witnessed the feats and the braggadocio of Mildred Didrikson in the 1932 Olympics until his own death in 1954, Rice effusively boosted the "other" Babe. In his opinion, Babe Didrikson was the finest of all the women athletes he had ever covered.

Women's competitive sport didn't get much of a look from the sportswriters in Rice's day. It wasn't so much that women's athletic competition was flourishing and the male sportswriters chose to ignore it; it was mostly that for a variety of reasons women's opportunities were so limited—especially at the professional levels—that its development was at least half a century behind that of the men.

One outlet for women was college athletics, but even here the women were socialized into exercise or recreational sports skills instruction. When and if a sport did catch on that wasn't particularly consistent with ideas of what a proper woman should be, the rules were modified to ensure that the ladies playing it weren't especially challenged physically. For example, women began playing basketball in colleges at the same time men did—in the early 1890s. The game was wildly popular with the female students, enough so that the game grew beyond physical education classes, beyond intramural status, and into a varsity sport in a number of colleges. But it wasn't long before the rules were modified to limit the competitiveness of the sport: no talking during play,

459

no "snatching" of the ball away from the opponent, and no exertion since in-dividual players were limited to designated areas of the court to reduce the amount of running in the game. The natural contact and occasional roughness of basketball were erased; the more polite version for women inhibited the de-velopment of both skills and public interest.[1]

Besides the cold-water effect of stereotyping—that women should be, above all, women; graceful, dependent if not submissive, delicate, and non-physical—there was the additional fear that women's collegiate sports might actually begin to resemble the men's. By the 1920s the women educational leaders had effectively discouraged women's varsity competition in part be-cause of the growing evils in the men's "win at all cost version": exploitation, cheating, commercialism, specialization, and injuries.

From the 1920s into the 1950s, the industrial recreation leagues gave women their best opportunities to play competitive sports. Sometimes these local programs simply made certain recreational sports available for inter-ested female workers. In the 1920s the Western Electric Company in Chicago, for instance, offered bowling, horseback riding, and rifle shooting. Other companies, however, fielded competitive sports teams, sometimes made up of their own employees and sometimes including players recruited from out-side the company, to play against other industrial teams. The intention was to advertise the company name by sponsoring traveling women's teams in such sports as basketball or baseball.[2]

Eventual, if grudging, support from sports organizations such as the Ama-teur Athletic Union and the International Olympic Committee slowly in-creased women's opportunities at the national and international levels. But conservative views about how much women could or should do practically strangled the competitive instincts out of them. Women had only just gained permission to compete in track and field in the Olympics of the 1920s. As an experiment in the five-event women's track and field portion of the 1928 Olympics, the officials approved a "long distance" running event for women: 800 meters! Even so, several of the women collapsed after the race. The sight of the exhausted, grimacing ladies so upset the antifeminists that there was an immediate call for banning any running race longer than 200 meters for women in international competition. In fact, Comte de Baillet-Latour, the president of the International Olympic Committee, used this race to argue for eliminating *all* women's competition in the Olympics and returning to the ancient Greek version: all male. In the end, and with infinite stupidity, the In-ternational Amateur Athletic Federation decided that running with contorted faces and falling down in a heap after a race just wasn't something women should do; it also wasn't something anybody should watch. The upshot was that no running event longer than 200 meters was held for women in Olympic competition for the next thirty-two years.[3]

Grantland Rice covered more women's sport competition than most male sportswriters did. When he found an outstanding swimmer or diver, a golfer, tennis player, or Olympic athlete, he didn't hesitate to write her up. Whether it was Suzanne Lenglen or Helen Wills in tennis, Glenna Collett and Helen Hicks in golf, Gertrude Ederle, Aileen Riggin, and Eleanor Holm in swimming, or Elizabeth Robinson in track and field, he would profile a woman champion just as effusively as he did the men.

But Didrikson was his favorite. Rice had heard about this young clerk-typist with Employers' Casualty Company of Dallas when she ran (and jumped) off with the Women's National Track and Field championships in 1932. In these championships, as the only member of the Employers' Casualty team, she won six gold medals and broke four world records. For years Colonel Melvorne McCombs, the owner of Employers' Casualty, had been an example of an aggressive promoter in the industrial leagues. He recruited talented athletic women out of high school, gave them clerical jobs, and sent them hither and yon playing basketball or whatnot for the company store. Mildred "Babe" Didrikson was his most famous find.[4]

Rice didn't see Didrikson in person until her winning performances in 1932 in Los Angeles. Even by then, at age nineteen, Didrikson's all-around skills, her wiry strength and her unusual agility, impressed Rice: she was a one-woman track and field team, and a class competitor in tennis, swimming, baseball, boxing, golf, and basketball. Before the 1932 Olympics began, Rice predicted the obvious: "She will be one of the sensations before the Olympic curtain rings down." Babe apparently felt the same way; she was not boastful, Rice said, just confident in her ability to win at everything. "I like all sports," she said, "not especially for the honor of winning, but because I like running, jumping and throwing things. My future? Well, I guess I plan to keep on setting records."[5]

A week before the Olympic Games in Los Angeles were over, but after Didrikson had finished with records in all of her events—world records in the 80-yard hurdles, and the high jump, and an Olympic record in the javelin— Rice invited her out for a round of golf at the Brentwood Country Club. Wanting to share what he thought was a real find with a few of his sportswriter cronies, he put together a fivesome, Babe and Rice taking on the trio of Westbrook Pegler (*Chicago Tribune*), Paul Gallico (*New York Daily News*), and Braven Dyer (*Los Angeles Times*). The trio was willing enough to play the round, motivated in part by a healthy skepticism about Babe's own hotel-lobby claims that she had once shot an 82 and could drive the ball 250 yards. The Los Angeles press and even some of her female competitors hadn't taken kindly to this youngster who was so outspoken about her athletic powers.[6]

The round of golf, only her eleventh, proved to Rice and anybody else who cared to watch that Didrikson's ability to pick up practically anything physical came naturally. Standing on the first tee, she was dressed in an old pink dress (which she made herself), topped off with a white hat banded with a red, white, and blue ribbon perched crazily on her head. Here she was on a strange course, with borrowed clubs, six months after her last round, and playing with four male sportswriters she had just met. But she was confident as ever. As she wound up and whistled the clubhead through the ball the doubting Pegs, Pauls, and Bravens began their eighteen-hole conversion. They admitted later that even though her grip was messed up, she had one of the finest golf swings they had ever seen. On the 9th tee, now warmed up to the game, she finally and fully unloaded: 250 yards down the middle of the fairway. "It ain't braggin' if ya' can do it," that drive said.

After a somewhat erratic first nine, Babe came back in a 43 with several three-putt greens. She consistently drove the ball ten to fifteen yards farther than any female golfer Rice had seen; her untutored swing, he reported, was already as fine as either Glenna Collett (Vare) or Helen Hicks; her hands and wrists were strong, her arms steely, all perfectly suited for her free, lashing style of swinging. She was born to play anything, but in Rice's judgment she would quickly become a champion golfer in particular.[7]

By the short 17th hole, Rice and Didrikson were even with the Pegler-Dyer-Gallico trio. Gallico drove the green, but both Granny and Babe were in sand traps. "Babe," said Rice, "we've got to do something." One or the other of them—they each gave the other the credit—cooked up a solution. "Hey Paul," shouted Babe, "I'll race you to the green." Now Gallico was even more of a male chauvinist than most sportswriters typically were then. He had been a Columbia oarsman; he had gone a round with Dempsey to see what it would feel like to get knocked around a bit—he lasted one minute and thirty-seven seconds and got himself knocked goofy; and he had experienced a variety of other champions firsthand: he caught passes from Benny Friedman, caught baseballs thrown by Herb Pennock, rode with speedboat driver Gar Wood, and hitched a racecar ride with Cliff Berege at the Indianapolis Speedway and a plane ride with acrobatic flyer Al Williams. Rice knew that the thirty-five-year-old Gallico wouldn't back down from a challenge from any man, much less a woman. Off they went a-sprinting. Babe easily kept two feet ahead of Gallico all the way to the green. Watching Babe's steady lead over Gallico, Rice recalled, was like watching Rusty the electric rabbit at the dog track. When they reached the green, Gallico collapsed. Rice came out of the trap to save his par; Gallico was still wheezing when he finished out the hole in a trembling four-putt. Didrikson and Rice won the hole and the match.[8]

In an article for *Vanity Fair* appearing a couple of months after the golf match, Gallico profiled Didrikson. He talked about the Brentwood excursion, testifying to Babe's uncanny ability to hit the long ball and to sneak long, lazy irons up to the cup. After the petty bets were settled, he said, the four men didn't know whether to invite Babe into the men's locker room for a bath and a drink, or to say—"Well, good-bye, kid, see you later." Eventually Babe traipsed off with some of the women, but as the men sat around in their towels telling lies, he said that they all missed her in a way; he thought this "strange, nineteen-year-old girl-boy child would have probably been right at home there."

Gallico called her a Muscle Moll. This urge—to be a Muscle Moll—apparently smolders in many women, he said, but if one has to be one, then it is best to be the Muscle Moll to end all Muscle Molls. And Babe was just that, he wrote. She was a champion of champions, and in his opinion, she was unquestionably the greatest all-around athlete America had ever produced. No man could do half of the things she could do, or do them as competently.

"I went through the whole list of sports with her, trying to find something she couldn't do—fencing, bowling, skating, billiards, swimming, diving—she is adept at all of them. Finally I said—'Great Guns Babe, isn't there anything you don't play?' 'Sure,' she said—'Dolls.'"

As a paragon of Muscle Molls and a champion athlete, Gallico wrote, he still thought she wasn't very happy. She had told him that her two interests in life were to crack every existing track and field record for women and crack them so they would stay cracked, and to find a husband. But he thought that with regard to the second interest, she was wistfully jealous of the non–Muscle Molls, knowing she could compete fiercely in everything but "man-trapping." However much Gallico seemed to admire her feats—he even said to his readers about the incomparable Didrikson, "You can't have her. I like her."—Gallico's blind stereotyping of Didrikson as being somehow less woman, not more, and maybe more man than woman, all because of her feats and her physical appearance, was brutal.

At a garden party at the Chapman Park Hotel where the women were housed in Los Angeles for the Olympic Games, Gallico described the group of American female athletes—swimmers and divers mostly—clowning on the lawn with a group of male athletes. They were all good-looking, he said, and were joining hands and dancing in gay meaningless circles. The circles came together, the huge circle sweeping everybody up into the fun. In a shaded corner of the lawn stood Didrikson, dressed in her Olympic uniform with the shield of the United States on the chest.

Springboard diver Georgia Coleman broke the circle and ran over to Babe. "Come on, Babe," she coaxed. "Come on, get in here with us, we're having a Paul Jones." Babe said, "Shoot honey, ah can't! I'm competin' tomorrow. . . . Ah can't play tonight." Gallico went on: "The circle formed again and went spinning around the lawn, a rim of young, laughing faces. The greatest athlete in the world stood on the outside, looking on."9

In his lengthy boost-and-burst profile, incidentally, Gallico's recounting of the golf match against Didrikson made no mention of the footrace on the 17th hole. But for Rice, the "other Babe" was simply the greatest all-around female athlete of his age. And along with Ruth, these two immortals were the most colorful competitors he had the opportunity to cover. "They stand above the mobs and the multitudes," he wrote. "They will still be alone and above the others when you and I are dust."10

Besides Ring Lardner, Rice's regular traveling companions to various sporting events through the 1920s had been Westbrook Pegler and W. O. McGeehan. The three of them often covered the same events. McGeehan and Rice were both then writing for the *Herald Tribune;* when the sporting event was big, both were assigned to cover it. Before Pegler turned his professional attention to politics and politicians, he covered sports. To Pegler, the so-called Golden Age of Sport was the "Wonderful Era of Nonsense." Pegler was a notorious debunker; Rice thought that Pegler was the most fearless writer he had ever known. When Lardner was with them, this traveling group had to be an odd quartet, for three of the four men sang their songs of sport just a bit off-key; Lardner, McGeehan, and Pegler were all known for their sour notes. That the ever in-tune Rice was a praise-singer didn't bother these three at all.

But what apparently did annoy them, as well as Rice's later travel companions, was Rice's chronic habit of running late for the train. Besides the fact that he never wore a watch, he was inevitably waylaid going from here to there by acquaintances and strangers alike; not a rude fiber in his body, Rice would be cordial at his own and sometimes his travel companion's expense. His more punctual friends had usually boarded and were already settled in the drawing room with drinks and a deck of cards when, just as the train started to pull out of the station, Rice would come running, gray-suited, fedora-hatted, typewriter-swinging: outlined against a blue-gray train station wall, this One Journalist ran again. In dramatic lore he was known as the Dean of American Sportswriters. This was only an alias. His real name was Granny Rice. He ran frantically for the caboose of the South Bend Express before which another laughing conductor swept him up by the arm at Grand Central Station yesterday afternoon as fifty-five thousand spectators peered out at the bewildering scene from the platform below.

Rice's travel companions changed by necessity in the early 1930s. Pegler and Rice rarely covered the same events any more. Ring Lardner's combination of ailments worsened, taking him off the road entirely by the summer of 1933. That summer Lardner stayed home at East Hampton, confined almost completely to bed. Granny and Kate were about the only friends Ring would see by the end of the summer. Lardner was terribly thin and weakening daily. Kate and Granny came over to visit whenever they could, often passing the time by playing bridge with Ring and Ellis.

On September 25, 1933, Rice was in his New York home packing up for yet another Big Event of one sort or another. Kate was in East Hampton. It had been a busy month for Rice, in and out of New York all month long. He covered Miss Virginia Van Wie's win over Helen Hicks in the women's golf championship in Highland Park, Illinois; Englishman Fred Perry's win in the United States men's tennis championships over Aussie Jack Crawford at Forest Hills; and George Dunlop's victory over Max Marston in the men's amateur golf championships at Kenwood Country Club in Cincinnati.

Around midnight Kate called. "Granny," she said quietly, "Ring died a little while ago. Young Ring came over to tell me. I've been with Ellis and I've just this minute returned."[11]

The news didn't come as a shock, Rice said later, since Lardner's death had been expected. Rather, Rice recalled, it came as "a heavy wrench." Lardner was only forty-eight, five years younger than Rice.

Rice wrote his grief that night. As was his habit over the years when any of his friends or acquaintances died, he put his thoughts and feelings in verse. His Sportlight column on September 27 was simply titled "Ring Lardner":

> Charon—God guide your boat—
> On to the journey's end.
> Keep it safe and afloat—
> For it carries a friend.
> One who has given the world

Drama and wit and mirth—
One who has kept unfurled
    The flag of a cleaner earth.

Charon—the night is dark—
    Watch for a port ahead—
Stick to the wheel of your barque—
    Charon—a friend is dead;
The friend of a shattered age,
    Standing upon time's brink—
The friend of the printed page,
    For those who could read—and think.

Here is one you can say
    No one can fill his gap—
Left in a morbid day—
    Left on a yellow map—
One where the bright sword gleams,
    Set for the cutting blow—
One who has followed dreams
    Greater than men might know.

Charon—here is a mate
    Where mystic shadows lie—
Ready to face all fate,
    When fading dock lights die;
Drama—or wit—or sport—
    What we may have on earth—
Bring him safely to port—
    The gods should find his worth.

Charon—I speak for a friend—
    Wherever the reefs may form,
On to the journey's end,
    Keep him away from the storm;
Where the last candle's burned,
    Out where the dark is deep—
Give him the rest he has earned—
    Bring him a dreamless sleep.

I wish you could know his worth,
    Out in the realm of ghosts—
What he has meant to the earth,
    What he has meant to the hosts
Of those who can understand
    The message of brain and heart,

Flashed upon sea or land
    With only the master's art.

Clean as the west wind's sweep—
    Strong as the northern gale—
Charon—a friend's asleep—
    Give him your stoutest sail—
Out through the mystic gate,
    Over the ghostly foam,
Let all your half gods wait
    Till he is safe at home.

Out of this drab corral,
    Drama—or life—or sport—
What can you say when a pal
    Sails for an unknown port?
When the last candle's burned—
    When the last sunset gleams—
Here's all the luck you've earned—
    Luck—to the end of dreams.[12]

It is impossible to know the full extent to which Ring Lardner's death affected Rice, then or after. Rice was something of a fatalist, and more so than most, it seems, he was able to accept or at least reconcile the deaths of his many friends. Only a few days before Lardner's death, Rice published his famous poem "To the Last of All," working from Shakespeare's "Cowards die many times before their deaths:/The valiant never taste death but once." The opening two stanzas:

Whether it's heaven—or whether it's hell—
Or whether it's merely sleep;
Or whether it's something in between
Where ghosts of the half-gods creep—

Since it comes but once—and it comes to all—
On the one fixed, certain date—
Why drink of the dregs till the cup arrives
On the gray day set by fate?[13]

Rice and Lardner and Gene Fowler used to poke fun at death in regular meetings of what they called the Happy Morticians Club. The three of them would get together for lunch or dinner and share their gallows humor. Jack Dempsey recalled having been invited to join their threesome one day in New

York. He said he sat down to lunch and was confronted by a rambling Rice and a dour and intense Lardner. Lardner asked Dempsey for his thoughts on death. Dempsey, who did not realize that this "club" was a big, satirical jest, launched into a serious extrapolation of his views on death and dying. Lardner listened, and then turned to Fowler and said that Dempsey had ruined the entire afternoon for him and that his time was too precious to become that depressed. That was Dempsey's first and last invitation to the Happy Morticians. Fowler later explained to Jack that the trio was just having fun with the absurdity of the subject. As far as Rice was concerned, said Dempsey, it was "nothing short of laughing at different aspects of dying from a cut-rate point of view."[14]

But no matter Rice's sense of fatalism or humor about death in general, Lardner's passing had to have stung Rice pretty deeply. There was a flurry of death-related poetry just before and just after Lardner died. But in it, instead of giving in to the tragic sense of life, Rice consistently called for an uphill heart in the face of bad breaks, even the ultimate one:

> It's all in how the mind is set,
> And so it's well enough to know
> Most days are rainy, dark and wet,
> Or windswept with a hint of snow;
> And if by chance the sun breaks through
> To dance among the fading vines
> From just one narrow slit of blue,
> It's all the brighter when it shines.[15]

Within a day of Lardner's death, Mike Donlin died too. Donlin, also known as "Turkey Mike," was one of the most colorful baseball players ever, full of swagger; rough, tough, profane, and likable. Rice remembered him well—his cap worn at a belligerent angle over one ear, the prodigious plug of tobacco stuck away in the corner of his jaw—for he played with Christy Mathewson on the old New York Giants. Donlin and Mathewson were Manhattan's idols back in 1905 when Rice covered the World Series between the Giants and the Athletics. While Mathewson hurled his three shutouts, Turkey Mike swung the bat and created New York's offense for the series victory:

> Was that another life and age—was that another world?
> When Matty pitched and Donlin swung, as pennants were unfurled?
> And yet it was but yesterday when these two ruled the beat,
> When Turkey Mike and Matty kept the mob upon its feet.[16]

Donlin's death brought up in Rice memories of his old days, long ago, the days of the Lozier automobiles, the Gibson girls, Uneeda biscuits, the square bottles of Mount Vernon whiskey, velour wraps for women, Steinway pianos, Edith Wharton, John Drew, and John McGraw and the immortal New York Giants. In the age of evolution, Rice noted, we are all supposed to improve. But it wouldn't hurt baseball, he said, to have a few more Mike Donlins around—his dash, his color, a hitting fool and frustrated actor, the Babe Ruth of his day. Donlin died in Hollywood at the age of fifty-six of what was then called an "athletic heart."

> Sometimes I wonder if the years that slip beyond recall
> Are marked upon the book of time as week ends after all?
> We hit the line with unchecked youth—and as the vision gleams
> We find that we are gray and old along the road of dreams.[17]

Only a couple of months after Lardner's and Donlin's deaths, Bill McGee-han died of a heart attack. He, like Lardner, hadn't been especially healthy for a number of years, so his passing wasn't a complete surprise either. Rice recalled that in 1926 he was on location in New Brunswick, Canada, to shoot a Sportlight film on moose hunting with his crew. The one-reeler was titled *The Call of the Wild*. McGeehan was with Rice on the shoot, and Rice conned him into being the "heavy" in the episode. McGeehan was supposed to track this giant moose through the tundra, muskeg, and blueberry bushes. The moose wasn't much interested in being in the film, and it took off before the camera started rolling. Bill's heart was weak even then and it began acting up under the strain of trying to stay up with the camera-shy moose. He couldn't. So to finish the shoot they ended up "renting" a dead moose from a native guide. They propped him up in the wild with stilts, baling wire, and ropes. Then they propped Bill up much the same way and had him bang away with his muzzle loader at the already dead critter to get the footage.[18]

> Lonely the road now winding
> On where the last inn waits,
> With so many pals now finding
> Sleep through the twilight gates.[19]

In the years following Lardner's and McGeehan's deaths, Rice faithfully and indefatigably continued to follow his calling. But the road to his own last inn was certainly lonelier now that so many of his friends were crossing over.

Rice himself was aging; this series of significant deaths served to remind him that his own road was shortening too:

> Lonely and long the highway
> That leads to a sunset sky,
> As one by one from the byway
> They wave for a last good-bye.

Ever social, in the later 1930s and beyond, Rice latched on to other travel mates such as actor Frank Craven, sportswriter Henry McLemore, writer Clarence Budington Kelland, and writer/advertising man Bruce Barton—all productive men, all sports lovers, all entertaining, and all golfers. Kelland, a famous novelist and short-story writer, was Rice's most frequent traveling companion. Rice said Kelland required advance notice of a trip—from two hours to one week—and he didn't seem to care where they were going or what sport or event Rice was covering. Something interesting would always happen on these little adventures, Kelland seemed to reason. One weekend Rice and Kelland traveled to Columbus, Ohio, to cover the Ohio State game against Jock Sutherland's Pittsburgh Panthers. When Rice got to the press gate he presented his two tickets and started to walk in.

"No good," the man at the gate told Rice and Kelland.

"What's the matter with them?" Rice asked.

"Look," the gatekeeper said, handing the tickets back to Rice. The tickets weren't even for the same sport, much less for the Ohio State vs. Pitt game. They were for the International Polo Matches at Meadowbrook.

Kelland and Rice spotted Jock Sutherland entering the stadium with his team at another gate. The two of them ran for the team gate and crowded right in, as Rice told his good friend Sutherland, "Jock, today I'm your assistant coach and Mr. Kelland here is your new team doctor." Jock nodded, and that's the way Rice covered that particular game.[20]

Gene Fowler, who had given Rice the appellation of "Dean," suggested to Rice that they ought to be on the lookout for a "Junior Dean." After considerable discussion, the two of them thought that maybe Georgia-born Henry McLemore, who was covering sports for the United Press, might qualify for the title. The seemingly never-serious Fowler told McLemore of their little plan, but informed him that he would have to pass a series of tests before he could become Dean Junior. The Dean, McLemore was told, will be watching. Henry was game.

McLemore and Rice covered a golf tournament in San Francisco in the late

1930s. They were having dinner in the St. Francis Hotel with Tommy Laird, a veteran San Francisco reporter. Rice knew Laird from way back and knew how much he idolized the boxer Stanley Ketchel. Laird had covered all of Ketchel's middleweight bouts in 1908 and 1909 when Ketchel was at his peak. To Laird, there was nobody better than Ketchel, then or now.

The dinner was pleasant enough, but to Rice's mind awfully sedate. He decided to liven things up and test McLemore at the same time. Rice leaned over to Henry and whispered that to get some conversation going that he ought to talk boxing with Laird and that he could start off by telling Laird that Ketchel was no good. McLemore took the bait like a tiger shark, Rice said. The Junior-in-waiting leaned across the Dean and, facing Laird, told him that "Ketchel was a lousy bum."

Laird turned crimson and, sputtering, screamed, "What!" Then he flew across the table and grabbed the baffled McLemore by the shirt collar and proceeded to whack him a good one. As McLemore tried to escape the enraged sportswriter, a woman nearby, for whatever reason, joined in and throttled Henry with her loaded handbag. In Rice's estimation Henry failed this test, but, he reported later, McLemore did better as time went on and as he caught on.[21]

By all appearances, in these years Rice was as reliable and happy and influential and entertaining and lauded as ever. But there was also an unmistakable and understandable change in his writing: there was much less sparkle. What haunted Rice in the last couple of decades of his life, besides the loss of so many of his good friends, was what Arthur Brisbane, the Hearst columnist, called the enemy of all journalists: loss of enthusiasm. The reporter is like a lightbulb, Brisbane explained. If he stays too long and is not exceptionally fortunate, age and the current of news running through him will gradually burn out his enthusiasm and burn him out too. "Then, like the lightbulb," Brisbane said, "he goes to the scrap heap."[22] Rice was exceptionally fortunate, talented, and wildly successful; there would be no scrap heap for Grantland Rice since there was enough naturally juiced-up current running through him to power his light—though with less wattage—right up to the end. But his Sportlight was becoming unmistakably dimmer, and it continued so over the next fifteen years; his daily columns through the remainder of the 1930s and into the 1940s bear witness to his gradual loss of journalistic vitality.

What was remarkable in a way is that Rice stuck to it as long as he did; over fifty years. So many of his friends had either abandoned the sports "toy department" altogether and gone on to other enterprises, or they had died. One of them, Paul Gallico, said his farewells to sport in 1936 after a mere thirteen years in the press box for the *New York Daily News,* turning to writing fiction. Years after he left the sports pages, Gallico recalled that he was simply scared stiff of becoming an old sportswriter. What prompted his departure was an incident at Madison Square Garden in 1933.

It was fight night at the Garden and the occasion of a lightweight championship. The prelims started at 8:30. Gallico was in his ringside seat doing what his newspaper paid him to do: cover the preliminaries and the big bout. Just before the main card, in the few minutes of buzz and hum before the main fight, a sportswriter came in (Gallico didn't name him—it may have been Runyon): "I can still see him. He was wearing a coat with a fur astrakhan collar. He plunked his typewriter over everybody's head and climbed over us to his seat." Next, Gallico recalled, this pompous sportswriter stood up to full height and counted the house; he was making sure that everybody in the house had seen his arrival. From about the fourth row a voice shouted, "Sit down! You're only a sportswriter." From that moment on, Gallico said, he ceased being a sportswriter. It took him three years to get organized, and he got out.[23]

Rice, on the other hand, stayed on, even though to many sportswriting was still regarded as a fairly invisible and shaky, if not sometimes even shady, occupation. And he stayed on in spite of some forces that were actively working against him and his kind throughout the pre–World War II years.

First, there was the problem of the sports page reader's growing skepticism about the run-of-the-mill sportswriter's objectivity. Sportswriters had always had to walk a fine line between honest and dishonest personal points of view. Rice recalled that even in the earlier days it was amazing how many ordinary people accused the writers of being on Babe Ruth's payroll "because we happened to chuck a few rosebuds in his direction." But there was now a growing belief that all sportswriters were on the take. As always, promoters and professional team owners needed publicity to get their spectators and radio audiences, and the sportswriters needed the promoters and owners for their stories. It wasn't unusual at all for promoters to buy gifts for influential reporters, or to throw bashes for the mass of reporters covering a big event. When Rice was given a gift from a promoter, his usual practice was to buy the promoter an even more expensive gift in return. When promoter Tex Rickard one Christmas gave Rice a traveling case as a gift, Rice gave Rickard a golf bag and a set of matched clubs worth three times the baggage.[24]

When it came to accepting free hospitality, Rice was careful here too. For instance, in 1929 Tex Rickard was in the early stages of promoting the Jack

Sharkey–Young Stribling fight in Miami Beach when he was stricken with a ruptured appendix. He died. Bill Carey, one of the managers of Madison Square Garden, was asked to step in as the promoter, along with Jack Dempsey. Carey leased Fisher's mansion, right on the Miami beach, for all-day and all-night revels. Four hotels were used to house the journalists, with the Drake as the headquarters. All journalists covering the fight—some 435 strong—were admitted free. According to Rice, he personally saw Nat Fleischer, the accountant for the bash, sign a check for $32,100 for booze alone. And this was still during Prohibition. The entertaining went on for seven weeks prior to the fight. One week before the fight none other than Scarface, Al Capone, threw a big cocktail party for the sportswriters and scattered hundred-dollar bills throughout the huge crowd of freeloaders. Rice wanted to cover this entire situation with a clear conscience, he recalled in his memoirs, so he stayed away from the partying for the most part, paid for his own room at the Flamingo at straight rates, and did not attend Capone's party.[25]

Besides the promoters, another potential source of compromise was the generosity of the owners of professional clubs. The Depression had greatly reduced newspaper revenues; this created poorer papers and in many cases poorer reporters, or at least less secure reporters. Since, for example, the baseball clubs depended on baseball reporters assigned to their clubs for much of their publicity, the ball clubs began picking up the tabs for the writers traveling on the road with the club. It was considerably easier now for the baseball reporter to become the shill. This suspicion of the compromised reporter who wouldn't say anything that could hurt "the club" created a more skeptical sports page reader.

Another force that affected Rice in particular in these later years was the predicament he faced in syndicating his columns. The logistics of writing a syndicated column were becoming complicated. To cut expenses for their agencies, such as the North American Newspaper Alliance, columnists such as Rice were expected to batch their columns. Rice would have to write maybe a week's worth of columns at one sitting and mail the batch to the subscribing newspapers. The quicker telegraph transmission was reserved for big-event reporting. Naturally, there is an inevitable staleness to columns written so far in advance. If not stale, then often such columns could be irrelevant by the time they appeared or even flat wrong about who would or did do what, when and where and why and how. In addition, instead of running Rice's columns as written, the editors at the subscribing newspapers could cut and splice or even kill them at will or as necessary for either relevancy or space restrictions;

this created often incomplete or greatly shortened published columns, which added to the impression that there wasn't much to chew on in Rice's Sportlight. In some papers, such as the *Atlanta Constitution,* the Sportlight columns appeared irregularly, and were often whacked up. The *Constitution* may have bought Rice's column to keep other local papers from using his popular name rather than as a service to its own readers.[26]

But there was an even greater force at work in these years than either the questionable professionalism of sportswriting or the changing day-to-day needs and practices of the newspapers and syndicates. This was the growing *seriousness* of the age itself. Gallico touched on this change when he said his farewells to sport. He, like so many sportswriters then, was in the gee-whiz sportswriting camp. During the twenties, Gallico recalled, there was a giddiness and a devil-may-care attitude among the people as a whole, including sportswriters and others in the world of sport. "Everybody was happy. There was a big boom. There were no problems. You could let yourself go on sports." In the sports contests of the day there was always believed to be a passion play of sorts—our side versus theirs, the goodies versus the baddies; if the conflict wasn't natural or obvious, as a writer you could invent it quickly enough to satisfy the mobs. Yes, it was naive, Gallico remembered, but relatively honest and innocent. After the Depression and in the years building up to the Second World War, all of this changed.[27]

Naturally, newspapers reflected the change. Herbert Bayard Swope, a giant on Park Row and the executive editor of the *New York Morning World,* had put together a remarkable staff of writers in the twenties for the paper's op-ed page. Swope was a distinguished reporter, a war correspondent, an astute managing editor, and the winner of the first Pulitzer Prize awarded for journalism. On the "Page Opposite" he rounded up such writers as Heywood Broun, Franklin P. Adams, Alexander Woollcott, Deems Taylor, Walter Lippmann, Harry Hanson, humorist Frank Sullivan, editorial writer Frank Cobb, and many other notables.

Swope said later that all of these men could think. He said that they were free of the pettiness and bitterness of personality that he saw creeping into the newspaper business after the Depression. Their places were taken by less thoughtful critics; what became fashionable were "realistic critics" who took great delight in smothering wholesome sentiment and condemning the twenties from all sides. As far as Swope could see, the new breed of newspapermen were collectively hell-bent on stifling at the source "any love of life for life's once-sweet sake." He thought that in the newspaper business, the Depression was the twilight of good fellowship and mutual trust. "Laughter," Swope said, "went away."[28]

Historian Frederick Lewis Allen described these times as disquieting largely because the Depression and its aftermath wrecked so many of the basic assumptions by which the typical American had carved out his or her life: that a college education would guarantee getting a good job; that hard work and loyalty to the firm would bring success; that poverty was either simple and local misfortune or a result of ignorance or incompetence; that investing in "blue chip" stocks was smart; and that the American economic system was inevitably destined for great, inspiring, and perpetual growth.[29]

What was especially troubling was the lingering collective sense of not knowing exactly what had happened, what was happening, and what might logically happen next: nobody, it seemed, could figure any of it out. So it wasn't a surprise when editors commented, after seeing a *Fortune* survey, that the newer generation was understandably cautious: subdued, fearful, unadventurous, unwilling to storm heaven, afraid to look foolish, unable to dramatize its predicament. Security became the watchword. The sons and daughters of the pioneers didn't mind some small wagering on a sporting outcome or on bingo, but, Allen explained, they didn't want life as a whole to be a huge gamble.[30]

On the playing fields, courts, and courses, what was missing was "color." Rice was no longer covering the colorful athletes of the past: Christy Mathewson, Bobby Jones, Babe Ruth, Red Grange, Walter Hagen, Jack Dempsey, Devereaux Milburn, Suzanne Lenglen, Bill Tilden, Ty Cobb, Knute Rockne, or the Four Horsemen. Didrikson gave him some good copy, but Fred Perry (golf), Frank Shields (tennis), Virginia Van Wie (golf), George Dunlap (golf), Primo Carnera (boxing), and Cotton Warburton (football)? There were exceptions, of course: the Dean brothers—Dizzy and Daffy, Carl Hubble, Max Baer, Tommy Armour, Jesse Owens, and Joe Louis. But by and large, what was fading out in sport was what a colorful athlete could bring to the fore: drama, the sense of the unexpected, romance, the joy of life. Without doubt Rice and the many other sportswriters of his day created much of this color by the way they pitched their coverage of sport in the twenties; but the feats they wrote about weren't entirely exaggerated, and were inspired by playful athletes who by and large didn't take themselves or their times too seriously.

In the mid-thirties, Tommy Armour wrote a piece for *Vanity Fair* on this theme of fading color in sports. He shared some anecdotal examples of colorful athletes—Hagen, Sarazen, Cruickshank, Tilden, Grange, Walker, and Greb—and then suggested a reason for the impoverished sense of the gaudy

in sport. He thought that it was the substitution of athletic technique for inspired athletic personality—itself a sign of the growing seriousness with
which the athletes were taking themselves and their sports. He said that the
newer athletes clearly were masters of their nervous system: "They can do
marvelous tricks of co-ordination performed by trained seals or the beautiful
and cold feats of the curtain-raising acts of acrobatics and jugglers." But in his
opinion his fellow athletes' increase in smooth perfection was erasing the element of suspense. You don't expect them to miss. And they usually don't. To
the younger athletes, Armour wrote, there is one simple way of making four,
and that's by way of adding two and two. To the earlier athletes, there were an
infinite number of ways to make four. He concluded his thought-piece on the
direction this new mechanical age would inevitably go: "With the falling tide
of color in athletics, due to glorifying mechanics and the minimizing of the
personal element we may be headed for the time when a rousing athletic
event will be a competition between a couple of teams of tire-repairmen."[31]

Besides anticipating the invention of modern-day race-car pit-crew competitions, Armour also predicted something else. Whenever the field of competition loses its color, you can be certain that, if for no other reason than the
profit motive, the color will be provided from somewhere else. Armour noted
that already in the 1930s the brisk, big bands provided the color for otherwise
dreary college football games. Armour guessed that such entertainments
would be necessarily extended in the future as the crowds looked for the spectacular or the garish. Armour would not be surprised that the gap was gradually filled with perky marching bands and flag twirlers and leggy dancers,
cartoony mascots, exploding and instant-replay scoreboards, laser shows,
cheerleading organists, and "color" broadcast announcers.

This change to more seriousness, or even overseriousness, wasn't lost on
Rice. When he reflected back on his life, he noted that he thought he came
along in happier times. He marked the change with the disappearance of the
old verse writers: Franklin P. Adams, Bert Leston Taylor, Judd Mortimer
Lewis, Don Marquis, Hugh E. Keogh, and Frank Stanton. For twenty-five
years, beginning in 1905, Rice had been keeping a poetry scrapbook of some
of these versifiers. But he quit collecting pieces for his treasured little book in
1930. There wasn't much left to collect; good poets suddenly disappeared. The
seriousness of the age from then on seemed to squelch the poetic impulse in
the writers and the interest from the readers. Everybody lost enthusiasm.
Given the shadows cast by the Depression and then the war, Rice said, "most
of the true singers have had little heart with which to sing."[32]

Rice seems to have already recognized the growing seriousness with which sport regarded itself when he covered the 1932 Olympics. Four years later he, Kate, and Bobby and Mary Jones took a working vacation to cover the Berlin Games. Rice and Jones had remained close friends after Bobby's retirement from golf in 1930. Jones had given these in-between years largely to the designing and creating of the beautiful Augusta National Golf Course. The course had opened in 1932. Rice, one of the first men of national prominence to be invited to join the club, called it a "course of dogwood blooms and mockingbird songs." Jones had been unable to get the U.S.G.A. to let him host the U.S. Open there because the Augusta course dried out by midsummer, when the Open was held. Instead, and with Rice's counsel on the best date for the sportswriters coming back from spring training in the South, Jones decided to host a new tournament, the First Annual Invitation Tournament, in late March of 1934. Jones decided not only to host the tournament, but to play in it. He was going to try a comeback.[33]

For a week, Rice had Jones to write about again. But even Rice knew that the odds for a successful comeback weren't good. "It can be stated officially and openly in advance that this masters tournament at Augusta is not going to be any one-man show." And it wasn't. Jones struggled with his short game throughout the tournament—which quickly became known from then on as the Masters—and finished in a tie for thirteenth with none other than Walter Hagen, another old-timer. Between them, in their day, they had won twenty-three major titles. When a big international argument broke out after the tournament about whether Bob Jones should have tried a comeback at all, given his poor showing, Rice defended his friend's decision with a simple statement: "You'll find that to win is much—to compete is even more."[34]

But things were changing quickly. At the Berlin Olympics with Jones, Rice took in an international spectacle that appeared to announce to the world that winning was what counted the most. "I'll not forget the sight of those German storm troopers, in their severely cut black uniforms . . . looking every inch the super race." They were in the streets, Rice recalled, and out at the packed Reich Sportsfeld, at the Hofbraus. They didn't stroll. They marched. And they "gutteralized with the quiet, confident bearing that betokened their Cheshire cat scorn of 'less endowed' mortals."[35]

Max Schmeling, the German boxer, had only one month earlier thoroughly beaten Joe Louis in their first fight; Louis would win the rematch in a fight lasting a mere 124 seconds two years later. German nationalism and Nazi power was on the rise, and Hitler was attempting to showcase it in these Olympics. Germany then, Rice recalled, was without question a living, throbbing world poster. It was "painted in the garish hues of a nation well primed for war." Sport, for the blustering, humorless, and precise German organizers, was reduced to a mere political tool. Behind the festive opening ceremonies and procession of athletes there was little more than a choosing up of sides; the salutes each nation gave the dais in which Hitler and his cronies sat were about equally divided between the Nazis stiff arm and the "eyes right." Remarkable international athletic feats did occasionally shine through these shadows—in track and field, for example, there were the performances of Jesse Owens, Helen Stephens, Kitei Son, Jack Lovelock—but even the spectacle couldn't hide the propagandistic intentions and the advent of a more serious world, seriously divided.

In America there were still some positive outcomes, despite this grimmer turn. The changes in everyday American life in these years generally increased opportunities among the masses to play themselves instead of paying to watch others play. The five-day work week, which had become more necessary with the general shortage of work, introduced more weekend leisure time for many. So if the professional and college sporting events weren't especially magnetic and the athletes less classy, then there was always time-filling by way of recreational pursuits. In this sense, sports were becoming democratized. Public relief agencies employed millions of Americans who helped build public beaches and swimming pools, automobile parkways, playgrounds, softball fields, and golf courses. Although the private country clubs took a beating during the Depression (1,155 clubs belonged to the United States Golf Association in 1930; by 1936 there were only 763), the number of public golf courses increased dramatically (from 184 in 1925 to 576 in 1935). So even though some of the spectator sports revenues flattened out and the color seemed to be draining out of elite contests, more men and women than ever were throwing themselves into golf, softball, bridge, skiing, bicycle riding, roller skating, and swimming.[36]

In his columns even Rice began turning away somewhat from the Big Events and the Big People. As always, he was an all-sport reporter and writer, but more and more, besides the verse—always the verse—he found his copy in nature, interviews with the old sporting gang of players, coaches, and managers, recollections of days and feats gone by, golfing instruction, horse racing, and relating personal experiences and adventures.

From time to time in these later years, Rice would write up one of his hunting or fishing trips. An avid outdoorsman and friend of explorers and guides, Rice was often invited to take part in all kinds of excursions: deep sea fishing for bluefish, swordfish, or tarpon; freshwater fishing for salmon or trout; and duck or quail hunting. This he did all over the country, in Canada, and in

Mexico. In truth, Rice enjoyed being in the outdoors far more than bagging the game or harpooning the fish. He said he was quite willing to let all the game fish of creation go their finny way without any hook of his gaffing their jaws. As far as the hunt was concerned, he also admitted that even though hunting to him was second only to golf in his sporting hierarchy, most places he hunted he established as a sanctuary: he wanted more birds to be there after he hunted than before. Red Smith remembered that Granny was happy just being in the wilds, preferring often to be the chief cook for his hunter friends rather than the great white hunter. "Somewhere, still, adventure has its day," Rice wrote, and "Somewhere still, romance rides down the world."

> Somewhere there is a port that I must find
> On some calm sea beneath a stormless sky,
> To lift this restless fever from my mind
> And bring content some day before I die.[37]

A favorite hunting grounds for Rice was Ichauway Plantation, the thirty-six-thousand-acre site owned by Robert Woodruff, president of the Coca-Cola Company. Ichauway, in Georgia, was not a hunting preserve. It was an old-fashioned plantation—wooded, deep cover open country, river, creek, swamp, with at least six varieties of game to pick from.[38] Rice was a frequent member of Woodruff's hunting and fishing parties. Sometimes they would fish for big-mouth bass, or hunt quail, or go after doves. In Woodruff's famous "triple test" he would take his guests out to do all three—the same day. From dawn to breakfast they fished the rapids of the Ichauway-Nochauway Creek (Creek names meaning Land Where the Deer Sleep and Home of the Pigeon Roost). Next they would hunt quail from breakfast to lunch. After lunch the party would hunt dove until sunset. Rice described one of these exhausting "triples" for his readers. But what comes through in his account isn't so much the killing; it was the beauty of it all, the magnificent exhibitions of the champion hunting dogs, and the fellowship. Of course, Rice may have had more time than the others to commune with nature; the others in his hunting party rode well-groomed horses, while he was given Jasper, a mule. Rice wasn't especially good at riding horses. To get his transportation moving he would have to sing to it: "git along, little Jasper, git along." His singing annoyed his fellow hunters. Who knows what it did for the game. But it seemed to help Jasper move along, although Rice reported that the mule's only interest was in chewing anything from a dried bush to a burnt stump. He didn't even bother about food; he just wandered from here to there and sometimes back again; he "just didn't give three whoops in Gehenna about anything." Rice got to thinking that this mulish philosophy may end up ruling the world someday. Our master minds, he suggested, may soon find that Mr. Gray was right when he wrote, "The paths of glory lead but to the grave." So why bother about it? Jasper knew it all the time.[39]

Of all the game that Rice had hunted, it was the wild turkey that earned his lasting respect:

> I know Hubbell's screwball is loaded with guile;
> For broken field running Red Grange is still picked;
> The cunning of Tilden still leads by a mile.
> But the wary wild turkey has got 'em all licked.
>
> With more eyes than Argus to safeguard his luck,
> With more ears than leaves on a plantation oak,
> He can outrun a horse and can outfly a duck.
> And he's harder to find than a pal when you're broke.[40]

He had hunted wild turkey from time to time on the plantation and elsewhere. Roy Rogers, the Ichauway Plantation manager and expert hunter, had helped Rice learn how to hunt turkey. If you could find its feeding grounds and beat it to the table for breakfast, you had a chance to get close enough to get one shot off before it took off, Rice said, "like an air mail plane sixty yards away." If you missed, the bird was practically impossible to find again. Ranging from fifteen to twenty-five pounds and maybe three feet or so tall, the wild turkey gobbler is difficult to see due to his blended markings of gold, black, gray, red, and green. They are alert; they see well; and, as Rice said, they can hear you breaking a match four hundred yards away.

On one turkey hunt at Ichauway with a guide, Roy Carter, the two of them hid in a deep swamp in black darkness before the dawn and in the pouring rain. Rice waited and waited, breathing as quietly and as little as possible. After more than two hours, a number of turkeys glided in. One landed only twenty yards away from the hardly breathing hunters. Rice didn't hesitate. He blasted the bird neck-high with his shotgun. He missed. The bird "went up in the air like a rodeo bronc," Rice recalled later. But when he came down, with a great thrashing the bird disappeared into the swamp. Not about to lose his bird, Rice went right in after it, headlong and headstrong into the swamp. When Rice caught sight of the turkey's tail feathers behind a clump of reeds, Rice dove in. It was now a hand-to-wing mortal combat. Rice said it was like jumping directly into a threshing machine. The turkey practically beat Rice to death with his wings. So Rice, in self-defense, began swinging his shotgun stock like he was taking batting practice—but with all the pitchers throwing at you at the same time. The two of them went at it for a while, winging and swinging away. Eventually the turkey went down for the count and a wobbly Rice was seen slowly dragging his prize twenty-four-pounder out of the swamp. An exhausted, bleeding, and bruised Rice said he felt like Dempsey after he had finished off Firpo. The bird, with well-rung neck and all, wasn't a pretty sight either.[41]

As a monument to Rice's courage and perseverance—not to speak of honoring the same qualities in the bird—this particular turkey was stuffed, mounted, and placed alongside the fireplace in Woodruff's hunting lodge. No real effort was made to pretty up the bird, and it was mounted almost as it was finally subdued: not shot, but battered, bruised, torn, and practically defeathered. The bird-versus-man fight became legend over the years, and the story was told to every visitor to Ichauway from then on, about how that gentle and kind Southern gentleman, Grantland Rice—"You know, that sportswriter who writes about winning being less important in the long run than how you play the game"—had stood toe-to-spur with this plucky and noble wild turkey and beat the living stuffing out of it.

19

Sunshine Park

On the eve of the sixty-seventh running of the Kentucky Derby in 1941, Rice doped out the race for his faithful readers. Our Boots and Porter's Cap would be the favorites, but neither would be even money. Then there was Whirlaway, whose zigzag, up-and-down, in-and-out racing style would draw support too. From what Rice could discern from the trainers and owners, there were two schools of thought about this particular running. One claimed that this year's Derby would be a two-horse race—Porter's Cap and Our Boots; the other school believed the race was wide open with possible winners including Whirlaway, Blue Pair, Robert Morris, Dispose, and Market Wise.

Over the years Rice had covered thoroughbred horse racing regularly at all the great tracks: Pimlico, Santa Anita, Aqueduct, Belmont, Jamaica, Saratoga, Churchill Downs. He loved the sport, talking to the trainers and owners, and the chanciness of the whole show—meaning the wagering. He'd seen all the great horses run: Man O' War, Exterminator (Old Bones), Twenty Grand, Equipoise, Count Fleet, Sea Biscuit, Johnstown. Rice saw in these particular horses a furious desire to win and often compared them favorably to the famous two-legged competitors he had covered through the years: Ty Cobb, Jack Dempsey, Tommy Hitchcock, Babe Didrikson, or Ben Hogan.

Of all the horse races, there was no question which race was his favorite: the Derby at Churchill Downs. Besides its colorful history, every year when he arrived in Louisville, he felt that he was coming home again. Louisville wasn't Nashville, but:

> Whenever I see the blue grass waving, down in Kentucky or Tennessee—
> Whenever I hear the South wind calling over a road that used to be—
> Whenever I see the bourbon mingle with frosted ice where the juleps wait,
> The years drop off where a bluebird's singing,
> "Welcome Home," by the open gate.[1]

The betting for the 1941 Derby was festive and gay, Rice reported. Maybe a record, he thought. The high point of the betting at the Derby had been in the slaphappy and giddy days of 1926 when the betting crowd wagered almost $695,000. By 1929 the bets were still rolling in, in excess of $675,000. But that was the last year that the betting surpassed $600,000. By the 1940 race, the wagering had dropped to a mere $465,000.[2]

Rice's favorite in the 1941 Derby wasn't a long shot by any means, but the horse he liked wasn't picked by anyone to win going away either. It was the fast-flying three-year-old, Whirlaway, owned by Warren Wright and trained by Ben Jones. Rice had seen Whirlaway run five times. He didn't win once. One week before the Derby, there was a final tune-up at the Keeneland track in Lexington, Kentucky. Whirlaway had been racing on the Florida tracks for a few weeks, but his stock had taken a deep dive. He had been an early-season favorite, but he began losing his speed and drive in early March. He had been beaten ten or twelve times on seven different tracks. While almost everyone else had quit on Whirlaway by then, his trainer Ben Jones told Rice he was still sticking by his horse: "I haven't quit on him yet. All he needs is more racing."[3]

More racing he got. In the few weeks before the Derby Whirlaway began showing his stuff. He had won his last two starts before Keeneland, and seemed to be gaining in stamina and speed. Whirlaway wasn't a big horse, and he wasn't blessed with an early foot either, tending to lag back from the gate and getting more bumping than the fast starters did. What he was blessed with was finishing speed, and if he found his way into the running by the final furlong he was difficult to beat.

But in the Keeneland race, Whirlaway not only lost to Our Boots for the fourth time in five starts, but lost in the stretch, and by a whopping six lengths. The track was heavy, almost gluey, and as the horses came into the back stretch they were head-to-head. Whirlaway responded to the roar of the crowd and pulled ahead one full length. But Our Boots didn't give up. He challenged back, pulled up head to head again, and slowly began to widen the gap. Whirlaway fell back and the Derby hopes of his owner Warren Wright seemed to fall by the April wayside. Rice had watched the race and gave the only explanation he could think of for why a good stretch runner would fall back after taking the lead: Whirlaway must have thought he had already won the race because he usually wins at the wire.[4]

By Derby day the race was still wide open. There were so many factors to consider: the condition of the track, the weather, the size of the field, the starting positions, and—beyond that—the indefinable angle of how a horse might actually feel through the two minutes and a few extra seconds needed to write the story of the race.

Eddie Arcaro would ride Whirlaway in the Derby. Ben Jones told Rice that if anybody could ride Whirlaway the right way it was Arcaro. "Arcaro will save him for the run down the stretch," predicted Jones. Whirlaway was something of an unpredictable horse—a half-wit, Jones called him—because you never quite knew before a race where his head was; sometimes even during a race he might take a notion to zig-and-zag around horses on his own seemingly just for the sport of it all. Jockeys never quite knew when this spirit would come upon him. But, Jones went on, Arcaro, a strong jockey, was always prepared for the unexpected.

On race day, Churchill Downs was jammed with more than ninety thousand race fans. As they listened to "My Old Kentucky Home," the horses paraded to the post. Our Boots and Porter's Cap were still the favorites and offered the shorter prices at post time. Whirlaway was the last horse in the paddock and was given a walk-around to get accustomed to the huge crowd. Ben Jones had schooled Arcaro on precisely how to ride this "crazy" horse. He told Arcaro exactly what to do and how to do it. "Hold him back a bit. Keep him clear of interference. If there is an opening inside, take it. But most of all, save him for that one burst of speed at the head of the stretch and he'll give it to you." To help Whirlaway focus inside, Jones only blinkered one eye—his right; that way maybe he wouldn't be so prone to ziggity-zagging whenever he felt like it, Jones thought, since a horse doesn't usually like to run into darkness.[5]

The strategy worked perfectly. At the race's start, Our Boots stepped into a soft spot out of the gate and almost went to his knees. He couldn't recover and ran in the back. Dispose took the early lead and ran a blazing three-quarters and a fast mile. Blue Pair and Porter's Cap made the mistake of chasing Dispose and had little left for the stretch. Using his strong hands perfectly, Arcaro held Whirlaway back, held him back, held him back—no zig, no zag—until the stretch. "Then," Arcaro said after the race, "I turned him loose and let him go. We seemed to go by horses as a train slips by telephone poles." Whirlaway won by eight lengths in a time of 2:01.24.[6]

Arcaro said he never had to use the whip and that the biggest problem he had was keeping Whirlaway from running wild the whole race. Rice told Arcaro that from the press box it looked like the jockey was riding a "chestnut comet." Arcaro responded that he'd never ridden a horse that wanted to run more. Rice learned a bit later that the reason Whirlaway lost at Keeneland to Our Boots was that the jockey that day, Eads, wasn't strong enough in the hands to hold Whirlaway back long enough to produce the horse's famous stretch run.[7]

Arcaro, on the other hand, had big and strong hands. He believed that as a jockey he did his best riding in the last two hundred yards of a race and that when he was on a horse that really wanted to run, all he had to do was use the "hand ride." In hand riding, Arcaro explained, you tune yourself with the rhythm and motion of the horse; as he pushes off on his jump, you go with him with your hands so that you feel *one* with your horse. You're running together.[8]

Whirlaway went on one week later to win the Preakness too. Then it was the Belmont. It was shortly after this that Rice let his readers know his opinion of Whirlaway: "The most colorful champion we have in sport today," Rice wrote, "is Whirlaway, a horse." Not Don Budge in tennis, not Joe Louis in boxing, not Bob Feller or Joe DiMaggio in baseball. Whirlaway won and he lost. He might be a bit on the goofy side, Rice said, but he ran like the wind and captured the hearts of the crowd.[9]

When Rice talked more fully with trainer Ben Jones about Whirlaway's unique nature after the Belmont win, Jones said he had never spent as much time with a horse as he had with Whirlaway. "He intrigues me," Jones said. A horse as good as Whirlaway shouldn't have had so many losses. Whirlaway was fast and strong and game, for sure. In a workout before the Belmont, Whirlaway ran the mile and a quarter in just a trifle over 2:02. Any other horse running that kind of strong workout would have shown the aftereffects: lathered up, disinterested in food or even water. Not Whirlaway. After his run he didn't look any different than before it; before his saddle and bridle could be removed he pulled away from his handler and began cropping grass in the rain.[10]

Jones reminded Rice before the Derby that he had called Whirlaway a halfwit; or maybe "either he was or I was." But, Jones, said, "I was wrong, at least about Whirlaway." Whirlaway was just hard to figure out. If he could talk,

Jones said, he'd never lose a race—Whirlaway would say what jockey he wanted to ride him, how the jockey ought to ride him, and whether he even felt like running the full race that day, or maybe only part of it and which part you could count on him to run and which part you'd have to take your chances on. He'd probably even help figure the odds. It was Whirlaway's *mind*—his horse sense—that gave him his uniqueness, his personality, his carefree spirit, and his uncanny ability to run to win when and where it really counted, Jones said. That was the source of his color.[11]

When Rice rhetorically asked himself what color was, he answered that it was a certain classy ability combined with certain "other qualities" that causes talk, creates interest, and gets the human imagination to start screaming with possibilities. That's what Whirlaway had, he thought. And that's what Rice thought was on the decline in the 1930s, 1940s, and beyond, a "descent that almost equals Lucifer's skid from heaven to hell." The athletes of the day, he said, were simply too mechanical. And in this mechanical age, Rice lamented, a dreary efficiency was replacing the inherent color of human, that is, flawed, characters. The old romance of sport was gone. How in the world was it, he asked himself and his readers, that a horse could be a more exciting competitor than the entire stable of human competitors?[12]

Part of the answer to Rice's question was, of course, that the world was at it again: World War II. It was difficult for anyone to be angst-free under these circumstances. The question that nagged was whether or not Americans ought to be at play at all during such difficult times. Sport wasn't exactly "essential" to the war effort. After some lobbying by the baseball owners, President Roosevelt issued a near proclamation that baseball should go on in spite of the war. He reasoned that spectator sports were a healthy diversion and escape for the hard-working Americans who would be making uncomfortable sacrifices in other parts of their lives. Furthermore, the president thought that the millions serving in the armed forces might benefit from a small degree of normalcy provided by following the fortunes of their favorite teams in the pennant races. "Play ball" was heard throughout the war.[13]

But the long arm of conscription was reaching into the ranks of baseball and all the other popular sports. Roosevelt stopped short of declaring baseball an "essential industry," thus depriving the business of transportation allocations or draft deferments. So the players were not exempted from the draft. Neither were college students, at least the older ones, some of whom were athletes. In college football, Rice actually thought that the war might be somewhat therapeutic. He argued that since college ball had become by then such a big business, exaggerating the importance of winning as it did, a nation focused on war might allow the college administrators and trustees to clean up the sport without interference from busy or absent alumni and the money-grubbers.[14]

By August 1941 a new draft law took effect that helped baseball a bit. The law set a ceiling of age twenty-eight for selectees. Already enlisted or drafted soldiers who had reached their twenty-eighth year by July 1 could apply for discharge, although they didn't have to. For most ballplayers, though, the law wasn't a break. Cleveland pitcher Bob Feller wasn't exempt. Neither were other younger players such as Sam Chapman of Philadelphia, pitcher Mickey Harris of the Red Sox, or pitcher Gadis Swigart of the Pirates. More than a thousand major-league ballplayers would eventually serve in the armed forces.[15]

With older players available and with the president's edict that the games go on, baseball survived the war, barely. According to the *Sporting News*, on opening day in 1944 only 40 percent of the players who had been on the 1941 rosters were still in the starting lineups. Like every other business or industry, baseball contributed in its own way to the war effort. For instance, professional baseball helped sell war bonds. The baseball parks were also used as collection points for a variety of material contributions to the defense industry; for example, in 1943 the baseball fans brought with them a million pounds of scrap metal, twenty-three thousand pounds of rubber, and twelve thousand pounds of waste fat. Even baseballs hit into the bleachers were thrown back onto the field of play in order to be given to the various military camps for their recreational use.[16]

When, in 1943, Philip Wrigley, the gum-making owner of the Chicago Cubs, realized the beating that baseball was taking at the gate, he helped initiate the All-American Girl's Softball League (the word "Softball" was changed to "Baseball" two years later). This was a professional softball-baseball league that started with four franchises in the Midwest (South Bend, Indiana; Rockford, Illinois; and Kenosha and Racine, Wisconsin). In time, ball games were played before enthusiastic fans in Chicago and Peoria, Illinois; Kalamazoo and Muskegon, Michigan; and Fort Wayne, Indiana. Except for shorter basepaths, the game eventually looked much like men's baseball. But there were strict rules for guaranteeing that the eighteen- to twenty-five-year-old women remained ladylike on and off the field. Politeness, proper posture, general etiquette, and feminine dress and appearance were mandatory; there could be no jeans or slacks in public, no short hair, no T-shirts. And short dresses were to be worn on the field of play. In the first couple of years the league went so far as to require that the players attend Helen Rubenstein's charm school and beauty salon. The league was a successful substitute for the colorless wartime male version of the sport. It was still going strong in the later 1940s, bringing in nearly one million fans annually, but eventually the league died out from lack of spectator interest in the early 1950s, for reasons including the growth of men's minor-league baseball, the move to the suburbs by previous city dwellers, and the increasing popularity of television.[17]

After his personal observations of death and destruction in World War I, Rice was no hawk when it came to this war. But he did support the idea of athletes being drafted or volunteering. Rice believed that there was certainly the physical aspect to consider; that is, that most competitive athletes were in better fighting shape than the common young male citizen was. But Rice seemed to understand that the type of war now being fought wasn't going to be of the hand-to-hand variety, so he argued that there was a more important psychological imperative at stake insofar as the athlete-soldier was concerned. He thought that the arrival of a famous athlete on the front line earning twenty-one dollars per month like everybody else would be a morale booster for the troops and source of satisfaction for the people at home helping the war effort.[18]

If direct participation in the war effort wasn't a possibility for celebrity athletes, either because of infirmity or age, fund-raising was another way to participate. Even before Pearl Harbor, raising money for the United Service Organizations (USO) military recreation programs was common among athletes. These efforts met with varying success.

On the less successful side were contrived challenge contests between athletes in sports other than their own. For example, what would happen when 4,191 base hits collided with 714 home runs on a golf course? To raise funds for the USO, Ty Cobb went head-to-head with Babe Ruth, first at the Commonwealth Country Club near Boston, then again at the Fresh Meadow Country Club in Flushing, Long Island. Rice tried to help the fund-raiser by doping the match out—having played many, many rounds of golf with each baseball player over the years. Both could shoot in the 70s, Rice said, but Ruth was more consistently a sub-80 golfer. Both were lefties, both were long hitters, Cobb was in better shape (190 pounds) though older (fifty-four), Ruth younger (forty-eight) but now full-figured (230 pounds). Ruth lost the first round, 3 and 2 before a gallery of two thousand; they finished the full eighteen in response to popular demand, with Cobb shooting an 81 and Ruth an 83. Cobb said after the nerve-racking match that he was proud of his surprise victory over Ruth: "I finally have beaten the Babe at something."[19]

The gate at the first match wasn't bad, but it was disappointing. So the papers boosted the second match enthusiastically and generally predicted the Long Island attendance would be in excess of four thousand. This prophecy was not self-fulfilling. Since Cobb was a notorious dawdler on the course, in this second match Ruth brought along a cane rest seat so he could sit while Cobb ruminated over each of his shots. Ruth said in the first match that Cobb took so long to line up his putts that he could actually feel himself aging. Ruth also showed up at the first tee with a bobby pin holding his thick mop of hair in place. Cobb, whose china-blue eyes practically popped out, said: "What would his old pals of Murderers' Row say if they could see him now?" Ruth told the nearly bald Ty to pipe down, and that he was just jealous of Ruth's locks; "You belong in the bald-headed row, Cobb, with those other has-beens of the dead ball era." And so they played and bickered and whacked their tee shots all over the place, never once being on the same fairway for their approach shots. Eventually, after a terribly long day and nineteen holes, the Babe won out, as he evened up the match. A third and deciding match was discussed. But the anticipated four thousand at Fresh Meadow had turned out to be a mere two hundred, and the two never finished the series. The fund-raiser flopped.[20]

In a more successful USO effort, Bobby Jones and a team of select golfers took on Walter Hagen's U.S. Ryder Cup team in a two-day match a month later in Detroit. With the war on, the Ryder Cup team hadn't played against the British for a couple of years. The Ryder Cup was the golfing equivalent to the World Series for professional golf. To give the team some competition and to raise some charity money, these challenge matches were set up through the P.G.A. In 1940 Gene Sarazen challenged the cuppers with a group of all-star pros; this year Craig Wood issued a challenge and put up one thousand dollars of his own money to bet that his select team could beat the Ryder team. Hogan's team included Sam Snead and Byron Nelson. The challengers, besides Wood, included Jones, Lawson Little, Ben Hogan, Jimmy Demaret, and Gene Sarazen. Rice predicted the Jones team would beat the cuppers. They did, as the thirty-nine-year-old Jones won the deciding match over Henry Picard. The P.G.A. announced after the match that twenty-five thousand dollars was raised for the USO.[21]

In these war years Rice's life routines weren't altered in any significant way. He continued to hustle as many money-making projects as he could. Apparently his expenses were considerable; he was financially caring for his aging Nashville relatives. His mother was dying. This brought him home in late August 1941 for a while. Upon her passing, Fred Russell of the *Nashville Banner* wrote that he hoped she knew "that she gave to the world of sports a son who'll never be replaced as long as a baseball is knocked or a football is kicked or a golf ball is smacked and the typewriters and telegraph wires tick-tack from the press boxes to report it." Although Beulah Rice had lived eighty good years, her son felt a deep loss when she passed.[22]

For the duration of World War II, Rice gave whatever time he could find to helping the cause by lending his name to various charities, organizations, and committees. Whenever fund-raising ideas came up in the world of sport, Rice's name surfaced with them, for he was without doubt the most famous nonathlete sports figure in America. At war's end the War Finance Division of the Treasury Department awarded Rice a special Treasury No. 1 citation for distinguished services rendered in behalf of the war financing program. This citation was awarded in spite of Rice's withdrawal on ethical grounds from one of the biggest fund-raising fiascoes of the entire war.[23]

Rice was asked by Secretary of War Henry Stimson to serve as the president of the Army Emergency Fund in 1942. The fund was intended to provide a source of ready money for emergencies that could not be met quickly enough by the American Red Cross or by the army itself. The money would come in part from charity football games between enlisted army personnel and National Football League teams. But the largest part of the projected fund was to come from a charity heavyweight boxing match between Joe Louis and Billy Conn. Rice agreed to serve as president of the fund.

Both Conn and Louis were privates in the army. In 1941 and before either of them were in the service, Conn became the eighteenth challenger heavyweight champion Joe Louis would face. Even though Conn gave away twenty-five pounds to the hard-hitting Louis, Conn's youth (he was twenty-three) and speed were almost more than Louis could handle. In front of 54,487 fight fans at the Polo Grounds, Conn had outpointed Louis for eight rounds as they came out for the thirteenth. Conn had won the eighth and ninth rounds; he also won the eleventh and the twelfth, decidedly. Had Conn been content to box out the next nine minutes, he would have pulled off one of boxing's biggest upsets. But Conn gambled and went for the knockout instead. For most of the thirteenth the two boxers swung away at each other until Louis finally found an opening. A killing left hook to the jaw, followed by an even harder right, stunned Conn. Louis continued hammering Conn and then dropped him to the floor with a right uppercut. Conn was counted out with only two seconds remaining before the bell ended round thirteen. After the fight Conn said he blew his big chance by going for a knockout instead of being satisfied to win. "There's too much Irish in me," Conn said. Rice, who covered the fight, said Conn simply gambled away a million dollars in the belief that he could outslug a half-groggy Louis: "The bludgeon was too much for the saber."[24]

Mike Jacobs promoted Louis's fights and knew there would be great interest and good money in a rematch. The gate for their first fight was $451,743. Jacobs was projecting a gate for a second fight of around one million dollars. Jacobs was asked to make all the arrangements for the proposed match on behalf of the Emergency Fund. Things got a little fuzzy after this, but the long and the short of it was that both Louis and Conn owed Jacobs's Twentieth Century Sporting Club money—Louis owed $59,805 and Conn was in debt for $34,500. Louis also owed the IRS $117,000 and one of his own managers, John Roxborough, $41,146. Apparently trying to be helpful to Louis, an army officer wondered out loud to Jacobs whether it might not be appropriate for the boxers to skim their debts off the top of the profits? This was not an idea that either fighter was especially interested in, as they both reiterated later that they would have been glad to fight for free. Louis had already fought two charity bouts anyway. Jacobs, on the other hand, thought the idea was wonderful.

By the time Rice got wind of the plan, it was too late to do much about it since the War Department had already agreed to the idea. After all, it was reasoned, the fund would still profit by three-quarters of a million dollars. So what if Louis and Conn were able to settle their private debts in the process? Jacobs alone would receive $94,305. Rice's view, on the other hand, was that the fighters were now army privates, not private citizens. They were not entitled to profit in any way from a charity match. The fund, he argued, should receive the entire gate and nothing less. Rice followed his convictions and immediately sent a letter of resignation to the secretary of war. They would have to run the Army Emergency Fund without him.

The War Department tried to. They asked John Kieran, now a radio personality in addition to being a writer and Rice's vice-president, to take over the committee. Kieran, who later said he made a big mistake, bought the argument that at least the fund would benefit significantly if not fully. But it wasn't long before other sportswriters caught wind of the under-the-table deal. The scam turned public, and Congressman Donald O'Toole of New York called for a federal investigation. He said the entire affair was sordid and hypocritical and that the army was making a mockery of an otherwise good-hearted idea. "There can be no scolding of the civilian for lack of morale,"

O'Toole said, "when the Army itself fails to recognize the seriousness of the war." The newspapers and the public, when all the details were finally revealed, agreed with Rice's perception of the plan. An editorial in the *Philadelphia Record* opened with the line: "My country, 'tis of *me.*" Originally, the editorial continued, the idea was really swell. But it was unfortunate "for boxing that a committee of muddle-headed sport writers got the sport into this mess." The writer did note that Grantland Rice, one of the most highly respected men in his field, quit the committee. "He didn't say much—but it is quite apparent he couldn't stomach the change in plans by which the funds were taken away from the Army Relief and given to the fight promoters."[25]

Public pressure was turned up on the War Department to rethink the plan. Secretary of War Stimson called for an inquiry. He was forced to call off the fight entirely. It was never held.

Rice never did retire from his calling, although he did slow down. After the war, at age sixty-five in 1945, he was still gamely active in a sporting world that sought to accommodate newer technology, increased consumerism, suburbia, and faster-paced living. While the world changed around Rice, he pretty much stayed the same: he relied on trains and coast-to-coast travel; a typewriter and thousands of sentences, millions of words, though less verse; friends, family, and Southern congeniality; golf and the nineteenth holes; the ponies and gambling.

The sporting world, often a smaller version of the larger world, was changing around Rice as well. There was Branch Rickey's Jackie Robinson experiment, and eventually integrated sport. There was more night baseball (cautiously underway in the 1930s), which changed daily deadline habits, sleep and eating patterns, and even hotel lobby interview practices. There was baseball's gradual expansion away from the East, as ball clubs began moving west. There was airplane travel for teams and their entourages, which severely reduced a reporter's opportunity to get to know the players the way leisurely train travel did. There were more women's sporting events, although the bigger and splashier breakthroughs for women were still a couple of decades away. And, in maybe the most dramatic change for sportswriters in particular, there was the growing popularity of televised sport. What did the sportswriter now say to newspaper readers the day after they had seen a sporting event for themselves in the comfort of their own homes?

While television may have immediately helped the popularity of some sports, most notably professional football and later basketball, televised major-league baseball practically killed off minor-league baseball, and it over-exposed boxing, saturating the interest of fight fans. Rice thought that televised sport was not as beneficial as so many believed it was or would become. "Back in the middle 1940s," Rice wrote, "a cloud no larger than a small man's hand suddenly appeared above the fields of sport." He was referring to television. Within a few short years, he continued, this cloud became a raging storm.[26]

The immediate impact, Rice observed, was to wreck the minor leagues; he also thought television was responsible for an attendance drop of half a million in the big leagues themselves. Even college football, he recalled, wasn't helped much. In 1949, with television, Rice tracked attendance at Yale, Penn, Michigan, Southern California, and UCLA, and found that on average the attendance for football games at these schools was dropping by about ten thousand spectators a year. When the NCAA stepped in to restrict television to the big game of the week—Notre Dame vs. Anybody, Michigan vs. Ohio State, Oklahoma vs. Texas—the attendance for local nontelevised college games still fell, since everyone was watching the bigger game on television instead.

Rice also witnessed the havoc television brought to boxing. Televised fights practically killed the smaller boxing clubs where the sport was being taught. This development brought out Rice's sarcasm: "Here the International Boxing Club raised a new type of boxing fan—the TV savant." The average fighter, Rice went on, doesn't need to know the basic principles of the left hook, the feint, or the jab. Neither does the spectator. "So they make a perfect combination," Rice quipped. At Madison Square Garden, where fights had pulled in fifteen thousand to eighteen thousand fight fans, the fight cards were only drawing five thousand after the advent of televised boxing. "The medium has wrecked boxing as a science and an art," Rice claimed. As far as he was concerned, TV was reducing boxing to hillbilly entertainment, without the music.[27]

Given Rice's aversion to things mechanical and electronic, it's no wonder that television irritated him. It even stumped him, personally. There's the story about Rice and television that Frank Graham and Red Smith told. Graham, one of Rice's newest travel mates, was a gifted sportswriter and columnist and if not the inventor of the "conversation piece" in sportswriting, did it better than anyone before him. Graham was thirteen years younger than Rice. Smith, Rice's other traveling colleague in these years, was writing sports for the *Herald Tribune,* Rice's old paper, and was the most-syndicated sports columnist other than Rice himself; he would soon inherit Rice's mantel as "Dean." During the 1950 World Series between the Yankees and the Phillies, Rice, Smith, and Graham stayed in a suite together at Philadelphia's Bellevue-Stratford Hotel.

Rice, whose general health was gradually worsening, was dreadfully sick with a heavy cold. He barely managed to cover the first game of the series. The October weather in Philadelphia was chilly and Rice hadn't brought a topcoat; Smith and Graham had to commandeer one for him. But on the second day of the series, the weather was even trickier and Rice's health was even worse. Since Rice didn't really have any deadlines to meet as a syndicated columnist, Graham and Smith suggested that their sick colleague stay in the suite and cover the second game by watching it on television. Smith and Graham had the hotel manager, Jack Schaeffer, send a television up to the suite.

Rice wasn't one to be shut in when there was excitement going on at a ball field. He reluctantly agreed to stay in the suite, although he protested that he couldn't operate one of those "devil-boxes." (Smith recalled that Rice could swing a golf club and punch keys on a typewriter, but he couldn't change a tire on a car or even tune a radio.) Before Smith and Graham set off for the game, Rice reminded them that he wasn't happy about being left behind: "You know me with gadgets. I won't know how to get the game."

"I'll show you," Smith said. He turned on the set and turned the dial to channel 3 for the game. There was a cowboy western on at the time.

"See?" Red said. "When it's time for the ball game just turn the set on again." He was about to turn the set off when Rice said, "Leave it on, I might get mixed up."

So in the middle of a western shoot out, Smith and Graham went to the game leaving Rice propped up and staring blankly at the small, flickering screen.

About an hour or so after the game was over, Graham, accompanied by sportswriter Bill Corum, got back to the hotel. Smith had stayed to work in the press box; he was often the last to leave. As Graham and Corum came down the corridor, they heard voices coming from Rice's room.

"I guess Granny has company," Corum said.

"No," Graham said.

As they walked into the suite, there in the shadowed alcove they found Granny stoically watching some kid show, *Howdy Doody* or something.

"Damn!" Granny said. "They have some terrible programs on this thing."

The two sportswriters asked him why he hadn't turned the thing off and he said he'd forgotten how. When Graham pointed out that he didn't have to sit there and look at it, he didn't say anything.

Afterwards, Graham told Corum that it probably was true that Granny couldn't turn off the television set, but that in all likelihood Granny was also simply too polite to leave his seat while the television was talking.[28]

By this time Rice's column was no longer running in his New York flagship paper, the *Sun*. Nothing was appearing in the *Sun*. After nearly 120 years, the paper folded in January 1950. The Scripps-Howard group, which published the afternoon edition of the *World-Telegram*, bought up the *Sun*'s assets and created the *World-Telegram and Sun*. When Scripps-Howard didn't renew its one-year contract with the Wheeler syndicate for Rice's Sportlight in 1951, Wheeler looked elsewhere for a New York paper to feature the column. But he ran into trouble. No takers. General, national sports columns, at least like Rice's, were out of fashion. Newspapers big and small could usually afford their own sportswriting staff and didn't need to rely as much on national syndication or national reporting. Perhaps even more to the point, apparently in the opinion of newspaper editors in general, Rice himself was out of fashion. Even though Rice's column was still subscribed to by some eighty-odd papers, the editors who used it ran it only occasionally, when they were low on sports copy; his column was to them something of a sports-page hamburger helper. To them, the meat was gone out of his column.

Bruce Barton, Rice's old and faithful friend, realized that Wheeler wasn't doing well finding a New York outlet for Rice. Barton lobbied Dan Parker, sports editor for the Hearst-owned *New York Daily Mirror*, to pick up Rice's column. It didn't take much to convince Parker that the *Mirror* could and should pick up Rice; Parker revered Rice anyway and was also an occasional versifier. Parker convinced the higher-ups, and a contract was signed. After the signing, Barton wrote to Charles McCabe, managing editor of the *Mirror*: "Thank you so much for giving us Grantland Rice. I was beginning to think I'd have to subscribe to the *Philadelphia Bulletin* or the *Baltimore Sun*."[29]

On March 5, 1951, after a three-month absence, Rice appeared in the New York papers again, where he dutifully reported on the latest doings at spring training from his outpost in St. Petersburg, Florida. After nearly fifty years covering spring training he was still at it:

> I saw a redbird winging—I heard a bluebird call.
> I heard above the swinging the crash of bat and ball.
> I heard a duffer cursing out in the bunkered glen.
> Could I be getting goofy? Could it be spring again?[30]

The day before Rice's column appeared for the first time in the *Mirror*—under the name "Grantland Rice" rather than as the Sportlight—Parker reintroduced the Dean of American Sportswriters to his own readers. In reading Parker's welcome to Rice, it is clear that the choice to go with Rice was based on sentiment. New York owed Grantland Rice for his many years of faithful and high-class service. Parker recalled his own arrival in New York, a cold town for ambitious sportswriters, all of whom arrive friendless and unknown. When the young Parker met Rice for the first time, this fine Southern gentleman introduced him around and helped him make friends among the veteran reporters. Parker noticed from the beginning that Rice lacked "side"; to the British having "side" meant that a person had to throw his weight around either to impress others or to reassure himself that he was something rather special. Rice didn't have it and that, Parker said, was the most beautiful side of Rice: "All of us who have come from the hinterlands have experienced Granny's acceptance of the lowliest among us as his professional equals." There were untold reporters who had had the same experience with Rice "introducing them around."[31]

Parker told his readers that besides Rice's natural friendliness, his name stood for integrity, authority, and the highest type of sportsmanship. Parker called Rice's pen kindly and his sporting intelligence uncanny. In an age that was producing highly specialized sportswriters—men and a few women who could write on one, maybe two sports—Rice could write with incredible authority on them all. It was the *Mirror*'s privilege, Parker said, to add Granny Rice—a true sportsman, scholar, and gentleman—to its sports section.

That March, Rice was sure to be found not only at spring training but also at the racetracks, usually at one particular race track. With either Smith or Graham, or maybe Fred Russell of the *Nashville Banner*, or a half-dozen other regular friends, Rice trotted off for the track more often even than for the golf course. John McNulty was another friend Rice liked to go to the track with. McNulty was a sometimes sportswriter, mostly a rewrite man, but also a writer of memorable books and wonderful pieces in the *New Yorker*. McNulty once wrote about what it was like to go to the track with Granny.

If he was in New York, McNulty and whoever else was going to the track that day would meet Granny in front of his house at Ninety-seventh and Fifth, and Rice's chauffeur Charles Goering—Rice still didn't and couldn't drive a car—would pick them up. On the way out of his building the elevator man, and maybe the doorman, would stop Granny, give him a couple of crumpled bucks and a piece of paper with the name of a horse on it and ask him to buy them daily double tickets. Rice would gladly comply, stuffing the bills and scraps of paper in one or another pocket of his gray suit.

He'd get in the car and hand out badges to everybody, including Goering. Charles would pull up to the newsstand on the corner of Ninety-sixth and

Lexington and stop. Granny would jump out—he wouldn't let anybody else do it—and buy all the afternoon papers, the *Morning Telegraph,* and a handful of scratch sheets. He'd jump back in the car and pass everything around. Once at the track, he'd buy a bunch of programs for everybody and pass them out too. At lunch he'd say, "Anybody want daily doubles?" and he'd take off for the two-dollar window with everybody's numbers, including the wadded-up orders from the elevator man or doorman. When he came back he'd give everybody their tickets, and most of the time he'd refuse to take their two bucks. That's the way it went all day.

Once, when somehow or other Rice was delayed when they arrived at the track, McNulty beat Rice to the program man and bought the necessary programs for forty-five cents each. When Granny got there, and McNulty handed him his program, Rice glared at him, real serious-like. "You greedy bum," he said. "Do you want to pay for *everything?*"[32]

On one of Rice's annual California winter trips a young, enterprising native son was interviewing the sportswriter on a national radio broadcast, trackside, at Santa Anita. He asked Rice, "What's your favorite racetrack?" fully expecting the polite and courteous Rice to plug Santa Anita. But instead of naming Santa Anita, or even some other California tracks, such as Del Mar or Hollywood, or even other well-known tracks such as Pimlico, Hialeah, Jamaica, Churchill Downs, or Saratoga, Rice blurted out "Sunshine Park." The startled reporter had never heard of Sunshine Park and made the mistake of asking Rice where it was. Well, it was about as far from California as you could get; Rice described its location as about middle ways from three points of the triangle made by Tampa, St. Petersburg, and Clearwater, in Oldsmar, Florida.

"Well sir," the young man inquired, trying again to get a plug if not for Santa Anita, at least for Los Angeles, "What's your favorite city? For climate, I mean." It happened to be a ratchety, miserable winter of cold and smog in Los Angeles that year, so Granny said, "Quebec." He explained, "You go there for snow, and you get it." End of interview.[33]

Rice had a longtime affair with Sunshine Park. In its earlier years, it was the location of the midwinter sporting capital of the universe, according to Rice. No baseball, no boxing, no football. But in a grove of trees was a playground that attracted farmers and storekeepers from the Midwest and the East who craved competition in chess, horseshoes, checkers, dominoes, roque, and bowling on the green. Tournaments. Trophies. Spectators from two years old to eighty. Intense earnestness behind the bushy whiskers, bursting pride held up by old-fashioned suspenders. But there was serenity and a brooding calm too: "The water oaks, fringed with venerable moss, form a dark green canopy through which one observes blue patches of sky, and through which the yellow sun comes drifting." An Illinois farmer might go after a New England storekeeper in horseshoes; a proper Vermonter might checkmate a tobacco-spitting Iowan in chess. Intersectional and state pride was keen in these competitions, but the contests were always tempered by the friendliness of the competitors. As for Sunshine Park through the winter, "there is nothing else like it in the world," wrote Rice; "there never was before and there never will be again."[34]

In these later years, Rice absolutely loved Sunshine Park's racetrack. And his love for this peculiar, old-fashioned, falling-down track says much about Rice's personal tastes, as well as his lack of "side." Rice admitted that when "Sunshine Park" popped out as his answer to the interviewer's question about his favorite racetrack, it was a subconscious response. He hadn't thought it out, and it even surprised him to some extent. After all, he'd been to every major track in the country at one time or another, and most of them over and over again. The big ones, such as Santa Anita, might do from $2 million to $2.5 million at the windows on big days. They were all magnificent tracks, all beautiful, all well kept, and they all had the best horses. And they all could easily handle crowds of thirty thousand to forty thousand.

Not Sunshine Park. Their typical mutual job was around $100,000 a day; on a big day, maybe $130,000. The Park drew anywhere from two thousand to maybe forty-five hundred fans a day. No Citations, no Whirlaways, no Exterminators, no Derby choices ever ran at Sunshine. The track was not particularly easy to get to either. Fred Russell recalled that whether it was the first or the fifteenth trip to Sunshine, Rice never knew how to get there. When Russell would pick Granny up in front of the Vinoy Park Hotel in St. Petersburg, Russell would ask Granny, "What's the best way to go?" Rice would invariably answer, "I have no idea: but somewhere, you cross the Gandy Bridge." And when they finally found the Gandy Bridge, Rice would usually rhyme some new parody ("Give me a handy guy like Gandy, building a bridge . . .") of Damon Runyon's verse about Jockey Earle Sande ("Give me a handy guy like Sande, bootin' 'em babies home").[35]

There was a small lake adjacent to the track that was supposed to be surrounded by rattlesnakes. When Dan Parker, his *Mirror* colleague, went with Rice to Sunshine for the first time, Rice insisted that they go out and find out in person whether or not the rumors were true about the rattlesnake infestation. A reluctant Parker followed his snake-hunting columnist, closely. Much to Parker's relief, all they found were a bunch of protective king snakes.

In describing the setting for this racetrack, the word "beautiful" wouldn't have come to mind. It was nothing compared to the surrounding Sierra Madres of the Santa Anita track, for example. Red Smith, when he first saw it, called it the Shoeless Joe among racetracks, "a sort of slum-clearance project in a rattlesnake colony." The horse barns were sagging shanties of mostly scrap lumber; there was peeling paint on the clubhouse and the grandstand; the clubhouse dining room was bare, plain, and small. But, said Smith, shoeless though it was, there was still an unmistakable carpet-slipper informality about it. [36]

At Sunshine, Rice said, "they give the $2 bettors and the bums the same break they give the Wideners, Vanderbilts, the Whitneys and the Wrights. Only none of these ever come here." What Rice loved about Sunshine was that it stood for ordinary, plain horse racing, not for the things that so often compromised big-time horse racing: glamour, hype, greed, fixes, doping, arrogance. There was nothing fake about Sunshine. The food was good. There was an open-air bar. The mutual windows were maybe fifteen feet apart but not more than six paces removed from a good view of the track.[37]

There were horses, but hardly any people. At all the other tracks, when trying to place a bet, Rice was pushed, shoved, jostled, stepped on, rushed, and otherwise hassled. At Sunshine there was plenty of breathing space. He was completely won over by the parking lot attendant's warning as Russell and Rice pulled into the track one day: "Not so close to that other car, please. We've got all the room in the world." This was followed by the astounding statement of the tip-sheet salesman, Russell recalled: "The other gentleman just bought one. You're in his party, aren't you? One's enough." Sunshine Park was just plain honest-to-goodness. And Rice drank it in.[38]

Sitting there before a race, pouring over the tout sheet, Rice would lunch on martinis, maybe some tomato juice, a dill pickle, and some Camembert cheese. There were nine races and anywhere from eight to twelve horses per race. The atmosphere was so friendly, Rice observed, that no one, including the track owners, actually expected to make any money, but they didn't even bother about it. After placing his bets, usually buying a fistful of tickets, he would step over to the track to watch the horses walk to post. The horses, he said, were as intimate as his friends; and just as friendly it seems, as Rice noticed that the horses nodded to you as they slowly walked by the grandstand. For the races themselves, he said he could get so close to the track that as the horses ran by him their hair would settle over his coat. The charm and character of the track, in Rice's mind, erased what others might have called its seediness.[39]

By and large, everyone left Rice alone at Sunshine. It was welcomed solitude for a change. Rice thought they didn't know who he was; they all did, but it didn't seem to make a difference to anyone, including and maybe especially Rice himself. He was treated pretty much like everyone else. He was just a common, ordinary person at Sunshine, not a celebrity. Every so often, however, in a small gesture to their most famous guest, the Sunshine management would offer a race in his honor called the "Grantland Rice Purse." Rice was usually embarrassed when this happened. But he tolerated the attention, and always bet on the race. He was a daily-double bettor, and claimed in his memoirs that "I honestly think I'm ahead in daily double bets." Russell wasn't so sure of that. He recalled that on the first "Rice Purse" at Sunshine, Rice had to present a trophy to a jockey who had just beaten him by a head and out of a $517.20 double. "Which he did," Russell said, "smilingly."[40]

> How long the Summer days were then—
> How slow time moved upon its way,
> When I was just a lad of ten
> I thought each year had come to stay.
>
> But now the fast years hurry by
> At dizzy pace from sun to snow,
> Like meteors against the sky
> That flame and vanish as they go.[41]

One of Rice's seemingly thousands of sportswriter friends, Tim Cohane, described Rice at age seventy as "a distinguished figure, his face an arresting blend of quiet friendliness and that still unmistakable quality of the lion." The lion part, Cohane remembered vividly. Cohane's first contact with Rice was through letters. While in his teens, Cohane wrote to Rice about becoming a sportswriter, and even enclosed some of his own youthful writing. Rice, Cohane said, "must have been a very busy man, yet he somehow found time to write encouraging answers." Much later, and after Cohane was an established sportswriter and an admitted, unabashed Rice imitator for the *World-Telegram*, Rice helped Cohane get a job with *Look*. This was in 1944. Soon after Cohane joined *Look*, he secured Rice to do their annual football forecast. But in 1947, Charlie Johnson, sports editor of the *Minneapolis Star* and one of the founding members of the then fledgling Football Writers of America Association, talked *Look* into letting the FWAA do its own All-America team for the magazine. *Collier's*, meanwhile, was still going strong with the annual All-America idea, and with Grantland Rice still heading the selections up.

At the end of Rice's 1947 football forecast in *Look,* as a visual gimmick, Cohane ran eleven head pictures of probable All-Americans for the 1947 season. Rice had nothing to do with the picks. The *Collier's* publishers were upset that Rice's name appeared in apparent conjunction with something or other to do with some aspect of the All-America idea, which *Collier's* thought was their inalienable right to promote. Even though Rice had no control over the *Look* approach and wasn't in on the probable picks, and in spite of the fact that the probable All-America idea couldn't have hurt *Collier's* much, the managers at *Collier's* issued an ultimatum to Rice: choose between continuing to do *Collier's* historic and prestigious annual All-America selections or doing the *Look* annual football forecast. No one issued ultimatums like that to Rice. So after nearly thirty years of association with *Collier's,* Rice cooly and immediately terminated his relationship with the magazine. *Look* gladly accepted the Rice affiliation, and even if it was simply for the prestige of his name, the *Look* editors arranged for Rice to collaborate with the Football Writers group to continue his participation with picking the All-America team. It was *Collier's* loss.[42]

On a trip with Rice in 1950, Cohane recalled the reverence with which people of all walks of life treated Rice. Even people who didn't recognize him apparently felt they should have, for they would come up to Cohane and ask who he was. Rice was now practically bald, still tan but less healthy-looking, and slower moving. Cohane remembered that he needed a steadying hand when walking through a lurching Pullman. Rice had tried airplane travel, but didn't care much for it, and it hurt his ears. As early as 1946 Rice was on a plane with fellow sportswriters on their way to Lexington, Kentucky, to see the running of the Bluegrass Stakes at Keeneland. They were flying in a thunderstorm. Their landing was delayed and the plane was forced to circle for a while in the dark clouds. Then, suddenly, the plane swooped down for a pass at the landing strip.

"I don't think we'll make it," said Harry Grayson, the sports editor of the Newspaper Enterprise Association, while nervously chewing on his unlit half-cigar.

"Well, if we don't, there's one consolation," said Rice, who was sitting stiffly next to him.

"What's that?" Grayson asked.

"Won't have to write any column tomorrow," Rice explained, never changing his focused expression.[43]

Cohane's experience traveling with Rice emphasized for him what everybody in the sports field recognized: "The name and face of Grantland Rice was as well known to America and internationally as any of the half-century of heroes, heels and harlequins of which he wrote." Cohane saw firsthand that in his field Rice had no match. In watching the way people talked to Rice, and in seeing the way Rice so naturally talked with them, Cohane recognized the storybook life of a man who went everyplace, did everything, knew everybody, and was the most famous and respected man in his craft, living or dead. It was trite to say it, but already, Cohane recalled, he was without question a living legend: "He came to be a symbol, a rich piece of Americana." And he looked it. His personal attraction was compelling, Cohane said, because it was so obviously honest and it represented, in the finest sense, a true gentleman of the South.[44]

By then Rice had become something of a national treasure. During these last ten years he was honored over and over again for his wide-ranging contributions. It seemed that practically every sporting or writers' association held dinners and ceremonies for him: he collected watches, golf clubs, plaques, trophies, and other whatnots that served to say that his contributions and his person were greatly appreciated, even revered.

On a more public scale, Ralph Edwards devoted his second-ever "This Is Your Life" national NBC radio broadcast to Grantland Rice a few days after Christmas in 1948. Rice was wintering in California, as usual. In conspiracy with NBC, Kate Rice, a bunch of friends at Vanderbilt University, Catherine Mecca, Rice's longtime secretary, and who knows who else set Rice up for the surprise show by telling him Edwards wanted to interview him about the upcoming college football bowl games. But when Rice arrived at the radio studios at 4:30, a half hour before the program was to air, instead of being put inside a small radio booth, Rice was seated, alone, on a stage in a large studio—in front of an audience of friends invited to look on. Floncy and her husband, Fred Butler, were there too. Floncy was living in Venice, California. They had no children, although they had three Siberian Huskies, Czar, Ciota, and Gay, who Rice called his "grandchildren."[45]

Edwards came on stage. He began reviewing Rice's birth in Murfreesboro in 1880, and his childhood there and in Nashville. Rice squirmed. Edwards asked him if he remembered anything about a cherry tree. Rice looked puzzled, squirmed some more, and drawled, "No, I don't think so."

"You didn't cut one down?"

"No, that was somebody else."

"Well, how about falling out of one?" Something flashed in Rice's mind. Then, a voice from behind the curtain: "Mama! Grant's fell out of the cherry tree and I believe he's broken his arm!" Stepping out from behind the curtain was John, his brother, who he hadn't seen in seven years.[46]

As the show moved along, Rice aged. His school days, and then the subject of his beloved teacher at Wallace School, C. B. Wallace, came up. "Were you a good student?" asked Edwards. Rice said he worked pretty hard, but that football and baseball took up much of his time.

"I wonder what Mr. Wallace thought of your efforts?"

"Not much, I suppose, but he taught me the rudiments of Latin and everything I know." Rice reached back through over a half a century and began to recite: "*Arma virumque cano Troiae qui primus ab oris . . . .*" Just then, again from behind that curtain, none other than Mr. Wallace himself uttered in a gentle Southern accent: "I never had to excoriate his epidermis." Rice practically fell off his chair. At eighty-nine, the chipper schoolmaster Wallace had flown out to California to surprise his old and famous student. Wallace stole the show, too, ad-libbing at will. As for his own age, Wallace said that the only older objects he had noticed were a few eagles seen on the plane flight on his way out to California. When Rice referred to a letter he recalled having written to Wallace a few years back in which he said that "if I have gained any measure of success in writing, I owe it all to you," the jocular Professor Wallace remarked: "Now right there's the best piece of writing you ever did."

As the show continued, and as Rice's career was reviewed—Nashville, Atlanta (somebody dug up an old copy boy to appear on the show who had worked for Rice at the *Atlanta Journal*), Cleveland, Nashville again, and New York—a panorama of half a century of sports history was sung onto the radio waves, as selected notables Rice had helped create came parading out from behind that curtain. As Edwards finished reading the most famous lead of them all, the one about the blue-gray October sky, the Four Horsemen— Harry Stuhldreher, Jimmy Crowley, Don Miller, and Elmer Layden—stepped out from history to celebrate with Rice. Then there were any number of All-Americans Rice had named. And then Jim Thorpe, who Rice had called the greatest all-around athlete of all time. And then Amos Alonzo Stagg, who Rice called "Lonnie" and who had known Rice since the days when Rice played shortstop for Vanderbilt against Stagg's University of Chicago baseball team. Stagg took the opportunity to announce that Philip Morris, the sponsors of Edwards's show, had established a "Grantland Rice Trophy" at Vanderbilt, a permanent award in honor of the students who best combine scholarship and athletic ability.[47]

After the broadcast, there was a party for Rice at the Hollywood-Roosevelt

Hotel, with speeches, toasting, an elegant banquet, and a big crowd. Besides the Four Horsemen, Jim Thorpe's presence was especially gratifying to Rice. Thorpe had worked various odd jobs since his athletic career had ended in 1929—as an extra in Hollywood (usually as an Indian chief), a lecturer, a day laborer, a Merchant Marine, and at the time of the Rice life celebration as a bouncer in a bar. They, Rice and Thorpe, would have talked some about Jim's competitive past at the bash, and especially about his Olympic feats and tragedy, for this was precisely the time that Rice and other sportswriters were beginning to lobby to help Thorpe get his Olympic decathlon and pentathlon medals returned to him.

Rice wrote to Avery Brundage, the head of the United States Olympic Committee, asking Brundage to see what could be done about returning Thorpe's medals and trophies. "It would, of course, be wonderful for old Jim if he could get those trophies back that he lost at Stockholm," Rice wrote to Brundage. "I have talked with him," Rice continued, "and he seems to be more interested in that than in anything else." Brundage wrote a cold and arrogant letter to Rice claiming that there was nothing he could or would do. "Jim was one of the greatest athletes of all time, we were on the same Olympic team and I was subsequently American all-around champion, so that I naturally have a very friendly feeling toward him," Brundage's puffed-up letter began. Thorpe and Brundage were on the same Olympic team in 1912. Brundage competed in the decathlon and the pentathlon (held for the last time in 1924) with Thorpe. Thorpe won the pentathlon, handily. Brundage finished sixth. In the decathlon, Thorpe set a world record and won so convincingly that his 1912 performance would have given him a silver medal in the 1948 Olympics in London. Brundage failed to finish the event.

Brundage claimed that since the medals had been given by the Swedish Organizing Committee and not the A.A.U. or the I.O.C., "I am very doubtful that they would have any interest in the subject." It was clear from Brundage's response that he intended to do nothing about what sportswriters and the public realized was a grave injustice. He concluded his letter to Rice by saying, "I regret that nothing can be done, but it seems to be a closed issue." This was in the summer of 1949.[48]

A couple of years later, Rice tried to help the Thorpe cause again, this time by way of his column. Warner Brothers had released a film on Thorpe's life, starring Burt Lancaster. It was called "Jim Thorpe—All-American." Originally, Thorpe had given film rights to MGM in 1931 for fifteen hundred dollars. When Warner Brothers bought the rights from MGM, Thorpe naturally thought he would be paid again for the rights. Not so, read the small print on the original contract. Warner Brothers paid Thorpe nothing. When the film was released there was a flurry of publicity. In December of 1951 Rice opened his Sportlight column with the question: "Just what happened to Jim Thorpe's stolen, lost or confiscated medals and trophies? What is the real truth involving the Amateur Athletic Union and the Olympic Committee?"

Rice published a letter he'd received from Jim's wife, Patricia; it gave her account of the fiasco. She reviewed the way in which Thorpe was entered in the Olympics by his coach, Pop Warner. He was ignorant, his wife said, "Ignorant, that is in the ways of the so-called White man." Everyone, she said, knew that he had played semiprofessional baseball at Rocky Mount, North Carolina. He played under his own name and was utterly unaware of any wrongdoing. The money he received, she said, didn't even cover expenses. "Jim, the simple Indian boy, played to keep in condition and because he loved the game." Thorpe told Rice that he played with the heart of an amateur—for the pure hell of it." No matter. Gus Kirby, then president of the A.A.U., publicly vilified Thorpe and stripped him of his medals and trophies from the czar of Russia and the king of Sweden, helped remove his name from the record books, and issued an apology on behalf of the United States to the I.O.C.

Patricia said that her husband had been trying to get his medals, his trophies, and, more importantly, his honor back since 1913. The hypocrisy, she said, was unbelievable, since there were then and now so many other well-known instances of so-called amateur athletes receiving mysterious sources of income in full view of the A.A.U. She said her husband wanted more than anything to be vindicated in the eyes of the world as an honest athlete. At the conclusion of the published letter, Rice mentioned that he had asked Brundage to help Thorpe's cause a couple of years earlier. "I received only a vague and unsatisfactory answer. I expected this. The A.A.U. has offered no help of any sort." Rice ended his appeal by calling this a criminal act.[49]

Brundage saw Rice's column. He wrote to Gus Kirby, his longtime colleague. "You know Grantland Rice better than I do, I believe. How could he write such tripe?" Brundage told Kirby he was surprised that so many newspapermen had fallen for the publicity efforts of the promoters of the Hollywood film on Thorpe's life. Brundage suggested that Kirby write Rice and convince him that he shouldn't harbor such ideas. Kirby did. But tact wasn't Kirby's strong suit. Kirby's opening sentence to Rice: "The heading of your article, 'Jim Thorpe and His Stolen Trophies' is untrue, unfortunate, unbecoming, and entirely unfitting for one of your great name and fame." Kirby wasn't finished. He said that Rice's column was filled with unwise, uncalled for, unfortunate and otherwise untruthful statements and innuendo. He denied that Thorpe was given any personal gifts and that the two trophies were given by donors of importance, of that there was no question, but that these were not of any great value and that after Thorpe's disbarment, they belonged not to him, but to the International Olympic Committee.[50]

The ever-courteous Rice responded to Kirby's letter. In it he admitted that the Thorpe situation "seems to be beyond anybody's grasp." But Rice went on to say that he'd gotten more requests to help Thorpe get his medals and trophies back than from anything else in his career as a sportswriter. Rice reiterated that Thorpe got just about expenses for his baseball jaunt, "much less than many so-called amateurs get in track and field, tennis, college football, and basketball." Rice asked Kirby, "What will the Olympic Committee or the A.A.U. do this year about the college athletes who have received scholarships, I wonder?" Rice was referring to the U.S. preparations for the 1952 American Olympic team to compete in Helsinki, Finland. Rice ended his letter to Kirby by noting that "thousands, I could say millions, would like to see Thorpe get his medals or other prizes back. It's about all he has left."[51]

Avery Brundage went on to become president of the International Olympic Committee in 1952. Thorpe died of a heart attack in Lomita, California, in March of 1953. With all the power and privilege of the presidency of the I.O.C., Brundage did nothing to help Thorpe either before Thorpe died, or after. Brundage headed the I.O.C. for twenty years. It wasn't until October 13, 1982, that the I.O.C., then under the leadership of Juan Antonio Samaranch, lifted the ban on Thorpe and allowed his name to be returned to the record books. Three months later Thorpe's medals were presented to his children.[52]

In Rice's memoirs, written in the fall and winter of 1953 and the spring of 1954 with the considerable research assistance of Dave Camerer, a former Dartmouth football player, former newspaperman, and associate editor with A. S. Barnes Publishers, Rice paid effusive tribute to Thorpe. Rice acknowledged that in his career, he seldom went out on a limb for any particular cause, sport, or individual. His attitude toward public projects of that sort, he said, was with the "sink or swim" school. But in the case of Thorpe, he made an exception. "If ever an individual was pilloried by the shabby treatment he received from most of the press and public," Rice explained, "Jim Thorpe was that man." He reiterated that the A.A.U. "robbed the Indian in a cold-blooded fashion," and named Avery Brundage, the keystone of the American Olympic organization, as the main culprit and as one who was entirely indifferent to Thorpe's situation.

Rice noted that after Thorpe's death, his body was more in demand than it ever had been in the last twenty years of his life. Civic do-gooders and chamber of commerce leaders in both Oklahoma and in Pennsylvania fought over the right to have Thorpe's burial mound for a tourist attraction. "Looking down on it all," Rice said, "old Jim must be chuckling an ironic chuckle."[53]

20

A Sporting Epitaph

Write this above my dust—in some lost grave.
"Here lies no hero—listed with the brave.
He had no thought of glory or fame.
Beyond the score—he only loved the game.
And when the bell gave out its ringing call,
He had not much to give—but gave it all."[1]

Grantland Rice's last published newspaper column was on the sport of baseball and the subject of sporting posterity. In it he wondered out loud how it was that somehow or another the Big Show always goes on, and that great baseball players are consistently replaced by other great baseball players, and often from quite unexpected spots on the map. His original intention was to write a piece just on Willie Mays—the newest great ballplayer—but the larger question came up while he was looking up Mays's hometown.

As a youth, Rice said, he often wondered how the stars of a certain era were to ever be replaced. He recalled his earliest memories between 1901 and 1906 watching Honus Wagner, Ty Cobb, Christy Mathewson, Rube Waddell, Nap Lajoie, Chief Bender, Eddie Plank, and Tinker to Evers to Chance. Who could ever replace such stars? he wondered at the time. But arriving on the scene between 1910 and 1920 were Walter Johnson, Eddie Collins, Babe Ruth, Joe Jackson, Pete Alexander, Tris Speaker. Who could take their places? Frank Frisch, George Sisler, Lou Gehrig, Dizzy Dean, Jimmy Foxx, Hank Greenberg, Mickey Cochrane, Bill Dickey, Joe Gordon, Carl Hubbell, Mel Ott, Ted Williams, and Stan Musial. Around 1950 Rice said that someone wrote that the game had run out of stars. Well, besides Williams, Joe DiMaggio, and Musial, up came Duke Snider, Roy Campanella, Yogi Berra, Jackie Robinson, Mickey Mantle, Alvin Dark, Phil Rizzuto, Pee Wee Reese, and Red Schoendienst.

Rice thought it curious that a number of star players came from small-town America. Except for maybe Ruth, who came from an industrial school in Baltimore, most of those he immediately recalled came from places that "no alert discoverer could ever locate." Cobb came from Royston, Georgia. Mathewson was from Factoryville, Pennsylvania. Walter Johnson was from Humboldt, Kansas; Musial from Donora, Pennsylvania; Larry Lajoie from Woonsocket, Rhode Island; Pete Alexander from St. Paul, Nebraska; Country Enos Slaughter from Roxboro, North Carolina; Tris Speaker from Hubbard, Texas; Jackie Robinson from Cairo, Georgia; Mickey Mantle from Spavinaw, Oklahoma; Ed Mathews from Texarkana, Texas.

And Willie Mays, the original subject for this final column, came up from Westfield, Alabama, Rice continued. In Rice's opinion, Mays was the most exciting player of all the recent crop. He was just returning from a two-year hitch in the army and by the middle of July he was quickly demonstrating what he could do with his bat. "It may be that Mays, now only 23, will find his early pace too fast," Rice wrote as he marveled at the way Mays could hit. But Rice was just as impressed with Mays's basket catches, his rubber arm, his swift-moving legs, and his irrepressible and contagious zest for the game. No player in Rice's memory had ever reached such all-around heights at age twenty-three—not even Wagner, or Cobb, or Speaker. Rice said it was too early to compare him with Ruth, Cobb, or any other twenty-year veteran star, but since time was a big factor in building a baseball reputation, he thought that Willie had a golden start. "There's no reason why Willie shouldn't go on. He has youth, power, speed, and unbounded enthusiasm."[2]

By this time in mid-July 1954, Rice wasn't too peppy; besides a nearly chronic sinus/cold/pneumonia, he tired easily. Although he had managed to take his annual California and Florida trips with Kate, he skipped the Kentucky Derby in May, and he didn't cover the nearby U.S. Open golf tournament at Baltusrol in New Jersey. Since attending these two annual events in particular was practically part and parcel of his sportswriting soul, his absence was noteworthy and a clear signal that his health was fading fast.

Even though Rice reported on practically nothing firsthand, he still kept busy that summer. He was working on his memoirs, *The Tumult and the Shouting,* with Camerer. He was also still active on a day-to-day basis with Sportlight Films, headed up by producer Jack Eaton and released by Paramount Pictures. The company was still going strong. In fact, in fifteen years of Academy Award competition, the black-and-white films were cited every year as one of the best three One-Reel Shorts of the year, even going up against the color shorts. The company received two Oscars and many Poll Awards over that span of time.

In May of Rice's last summer, Rod Warren, for twenty-five years the associate producer of the Grantland Rice Sportlights, resigned from the film company in order to rejoin Rice in a new venture. This new partnership was intended to explore the possibilities of biweekly fourteen-minute Sport Shorts for, of all things, that "devil-box" Rice was so intimidated by, television. Warren and Rice could see where the future of sport filming was going to be and they began working on this televised sport idea well before anyone else did. Under the new name Sportlite, Inc., Warren and Rice imagined a television version of what the Sportlight Films had been doing for years, but in color, and covering the entire field of sports, athletics, recreations, and pastimes of people everywhere, in the United States and throughout the world. That summer the two of them were in the process of pitching the idea to Coca-Cola, who they were hoping would become the sole proprietor of the productions. In June, Warren made up a variety of Coca-Cola color titles with Rice's photograph, in motion, plus his signature. Two pilot Sportlites were produced for demonstration purposes, one of them on tarpon fishing.[3]

By midsummer, Rice had also completed an invited piece on golf for a new national sport magazine being published by Time, Inc. Rice had been a consulting editor for *Sport* magazine for the past five years, and was helpful in spirit at least to the publishers of this newest attempt in sports journalism. Since December of 1953 when its first dummy issue was put together for the insiders of the sports community to preview, there was much talk surrounding the appearance of *Sports Illustrated,* scheduled to appear in August 1954. This new glossy magazine would claim that America was entering a new *kind* of golden age in sport. Even though this new age couldn't yet compare to the sort of heroes produced in the 1920s and earlier, the magazine would claim that it soon would. In many ways, the editors would argue, this new golden age already outdazzled the earlier age when measured by worldwide interest and participation, huge crowds, smashed records, and outstanding performances.[4]

Rice's contribution to the inaugural issue of *Sports Illustrated* described one of the greatest moments he had ever known in sport. It was vintage Rice. On a late June afternoon in 1929, he recalled, some ten thousand golf spectators were crowded around the 18th green at the Winged Foot Club at Mamaroneck, in Westchester County, New York. As the fans came running to the green, the vast babble of excited human voices, Rice said, was spreading the news that Bob Jones was on the verge of the worst catastrophe any U.S. Open competitor had ever experienced. "As Jones broke through the crowd and came upon the green, the babble suddenly was stilled. This was the silence of suppressed nerves." Each person seemed to be gripping the shoulder or arm of a neighbor, Rice said. "Since the first Scottish shepherds in the reign of King James had addressed an early golf ball with a shepherd's crook, I doubt if any golfer had ever faced a moment so packed with tension."

Jones—who was still a year away from his Grand Slam—had been six up with six holes to play against Al Espinosa. Espinosa took an 8 on the 12th, but with the tension off completely, he relaxed and came home with four 4s and two 3s to shoot 75. Jones, meanwhile, lost two strokes at the 13th, and then took a seven on the 15th. Suddenly he had to have 4-4-4 on the last three holes just to tie Espinosa. He got his 4s on 16 and 17. On the 18th, Jones's drive was solid, but his second shot hit the hard green and ran down a grassy bank. He chipped back onto the green, but left himself a curling twelve- to fourteen-foot putt that he had to hole to even get a draw for a playoff.

"On the green, Bobby Jones crouched partly on one knee studying the slanting line of the treacherous putt," Rice wrote. There was a break of about a foot and a half in this fast green. The spellbound spectators, Rice said, were an intimate part of the show. They knew what the putt meant, and Rice thought most of the onlookers were suffering right along with Jones. Jones studied the putt carefully, longer than usual for him. As Jones stepped up to the ball, Rice, who was standing a few rows back in the crowd, dropped to his hands and knees, and peered out from between the many legs of the crushing crowd pressing in on the green. Jones stroked the ball with his putter. It seemed short. Rice lost sight of the ball en route, but picked it up again near the cup. "Suddenly the ball hesitated, stopped—and then turned over once more and disappeared" into the cup.

Rice said that he had heard many a sudden roar in his reporting career, the great crash of noise, but never in his life before or since had he heard "the vocal cataclysm that rocked the oaks of Westchester" that day. Jones and Espinosa went into a 36-hole playoff. Jones won by more than twenty strokes.

Rice recalled that O. B. Keeler told him later that had Jones not sunk that putt and had he lost the U.S. Open that year, he probably wouldn't have played abroad the next year and wouldn't have ever won the Grand Slam. That putt was history, and it also created history; and Rice was there to fix the moment forever in our minds and hearts, much like he would do for the remainder of his sportswriting career.[5]

So Rice's last summer went. He kept busy, but he knew the end was near. Kate hadn't been feeling well, and that worried him. He wrote from his summer home in East Hampton to Nashville's Fred Russell toward the end of the first week in July that "Kate and I are just sitting in the sun now. She is much better, and soon will be all right. Listening to your arteries harden isn't such bad sport after all."[6]

By then Rice had finished his memoirs. In spite of his intuitive sense that his times were unique in the history of modern sport, he still and perpetually claimed that all records were meant to be broken. He ended his memoirs with the upbeat and almost obligatory thought (as far as his reading audience was concerned, anyway) that the best didn't belong to the past. He said the best "is with us now." And even better athletes will be with us in the future, he said. "When we arrive at the top athlete, the Jim Thorpe of the Year 2,000, we should really have something," he wrote. But by that time, Rice matter-of-factly acknowledged, "I will have slight interest in what the field has to show."[7]

But more fittingly and in a much more Ricean vein, he concluded *Tumult* with an eight-stanza verse. The poem was called "The Long Road," and in it he qualified his position on record-breaking as a measure of progress—that what he meant by "better athletes" was not reduced to merely winning athletes. He wrote of his dusty and torn, frayed and worn traveler's cloak that for a half century had known the road. The end was very near, he said, beneath a heavy load, "But from the valley to the topmost hill,/The sky is blue, the birds are singing still." He wrote of the wonderful athletes he'd seen—Ruth, Thorpe, Tilden, Jones, Cobb, Dempsey, Matty, Owens, Didrikson, Hagen, the Four Horsemen, Grange, Louis. "The mighty thousands who have done the same,/To leave the epitaph—He Played the Game."

In the final three stanzas Rice clearly reminded his readers that there was a good deal more to the sporting proposition than its quantitative results and a winning outcome. True to his lifelong gospel, winning was an important goal but not the be-all-and-end-all of sport competition. More important was the mettle testing, what he called a winning will, the "gift of fortitude":

But there is more than winning to this game,
Where I've seen countless thousands give their best,
Give all they had to find the road to fame,
And barely fail against the closing test.
Their names are lost now with the swift and strong,
Yet in the final rating they belong.

For there are some who never reach the top,
Who in my rating hold a higher place
Than many wearing crowns against the drop
Of life's last curtain in the bitter race.
Who stand and fight amid a bitter brood,
Knowing the matchless gift of fortitude.

Far off I hear the rolling, roaring cheers.
They come to me from many yesterdays,
From record deeds that cross the fading years,
And light the landscape with their brilliant plays,
Great stars that knew their days in fame's bright sun.
I hear them tramping into oblivion.[8]

The end finally came and came swiftly for Henry Grantland Rice. On July 13, 1954, the day of the All-Star game in Cleveland, and not long after finishing his final, completed column on Mays, he left his home on Fifth Avenue for the Sportlight offices on West Forty-eighth Street to give his column to Catherine Mecca for submission to the syndicate. He wanted to get a little more work done at the office before he caught the All-Star game on his television. He owned one now and had learned how to turn it on and off all by himself. It was around noon. Suddenly, while still in his Sportlight offices, he suffered a massive stroke. He was taken to the nearby Roosevelt Hospital. He went into a coma and never regained consciousness. With Kate and Catherine Mecca at his side, and Floncy on her way from California, Rice quietly died a little after six o'clock that evening.[9]

On July 16, a beautiful, sunny day, cool and breezy, Grantland Rice was buried. The funeral that day was held at the Brick Presbyterian Church at Park Avenue and Ninety-first Street. The honorary pallbearers included Bobby Jones, who by then was walking only with the help of canes, a victim of a crippling spinal ailment; sports columnist Bill Corum; Dan Parker from the *Mirror;* Jack Dempsey and Gene Tunney; Red Smith; Robert Woodruff; Ford Frick; Tim Cohane; Toots Shor (the New York bar owner bar none); Rube Goldberg; Herbert Swope; John Wheeler; Frank Graham; Jack Eaton; John

Golden, Herman Hickman (former football coach and television personality); and practically everybody else in attendance. The four hundred friends of Rice came from his Nashville hometown, and from the many worlds of sport, newspapers, industry, business, publishing, radio, the stage, the screen, and television.

To this standing-room-only assembly, Bruce Barton gave the eulogy. In it he said that Grantland Rice arrived at precisely the right time in American social history, for after the settling of the frontier and the weakening of the religious opposition to play, Rice was able to point to an alternative to the gospel of only work, "hard work, long hours—the harder and longer the more commendable." Grant, he said, was the "evangelist of fun and the bringer of good news about games." He did this, Barton said, never by preaching or by propaganda, but "by the sheer contagion of his joy in living, he made us want to play." His greatest gift to this country, Barton said, was to help make us a people of better health and happiness, and a people of greater strength in adversity.

As a person and friend, Barton said that Rice was naturally courtly, gracious, well-mannered, for sure, but beyond that, this Southern gentleman had that far rarer virtue of *pure courtesy*. Always instinctively aware of the feelings of other people, he gave himself to others unconditionally and had that spontaneous knack of being able to do the right thing at the right time in supporting the needs of the many people who crossed his wide and welcoming path. His generosity was legendary.

Rice always managed to make people feel better while in his presence, Barton said. His gift to his friends was to make them feel that they could do more, that they could be more. This gift was grounded in what Rice thought the major virtue in life was: courage. Grant wrote and lived the truth, Barton said, that "all things work together for good to him who is unafraid."

"Grant," Barton eulogized, "is not lost to us." To believe that such an exemplary life is ended would be to say that life itself is without meaning and that the universe itself is a ghastly joke. No, Barton said, Grant lives in all who knew him. And in Heaven, Barton said, they've already learned to love him, "telling his stories, talking his wisdom, cracking his jokes, and, we may be sure, encouraging play."[10]

After the funeral, they took the long drive to Woodlawn Cemetery in the Bronx. They put him away with a last prayer in the bright sun of this fine July day. "But from the valley to the topmost hill,/the sky is blue, the birds are singing still." Ralph McGill of the *Atlanta Constitution*, an old, old friend of Granny's, remembered that at the grave site the wind was making soft music in the branches, and the birds flew about and sang, and the prayer rang out confidently with its challenge, "Oh, grave where is thy victory?"[11]

Most certainly Bruce Barton spoke and spoke sincerely for all at the funeral. But the sincere speaking about Grantland Rice wasn't through by any means as his friends simply refused to let this gentle man go quietly. He wouldn't have wanted all the fuss, and they knew that, but they still all wanted to say something, to tell something, to explain something, to give something about this man who, they all marveled, had not a single enemy in the world.

They talked amongst themselves. Many of those attending the funeral headed back to Toots Shor's for a quick one and exchanged many of the old, famous stories about Grantland Rice, about his ideology, his habits, his daily-double addiction, his zero mechanical IQ, his Mr. Fix-It tendencies, about everything that made Grantland Rice Grantland Rice, and about their love for him and how he stood in the world, so much higher it seemed than any of them did, or could, or would.

They also talked to the world about their fallen friend. The tributes included the stiff but sincere words of William Randolph Hearst, Jr., who admitted that he had never tried to write an obituary before, that he knew his on Rice was woefully inadequate, but that he simply felt like doing it because Granny was a friend. He said he never knew of a mean word or a knock that Granny ever wrote and that they simply don't "come any finer, kinder or gentler than Granny—never have and never will."[12]

Then there were the unsentimental but honest opening words of *Los Angeles Times* sportswriter Bill Henry: "Nobody is going to start me sobbing over old Granny Rice, for he lived a long and useful life, he lived it the way he wanted to, he loved every minute of it and when his time was up he went the way, I imagine, he'd want to go—quick-like." But Henry couldn't help gushing a bit anyway as he recalled his days with Rice, going way back to Shelby, Montana, and the Dempsey and Gibbons fight and the Pullman train car the reporters had to live in, and the Golden Era, and how he was the head of it, and how Granny had some great stuff to write about, and about all the other Dempsey fights, and about how everybody was always reading his stuff. What Henry was saying was that when you thought about Granny's presence throughout this Golden Age, maybe it was Golden because Rice was among those writing it up.[13]

Bob Cooke of the *Herald Tribune* remembered a time when he, Richards Vidmer (who succeeded Bill McGeehan at the *Herald Tribune*), and another were at the Hialeah racetrack. They were lunching in the clubhouse prior to the first race. Between courses the third member excused himself and headed for the daily-double windows. On his return he looked at Vidmer and said, "Say, I've just met the greatest guy you ever saw!"

"Who's that?" Vidmer idly inquired.

"Grantland Rice."

To which Vidmer promptly replied: "That's the most unoriginal remark I ever heard."[14]

Henry McLemore couldn't write anything at all, at least right away. So he reproduced what he'd written about Rice two years earlier, and even then he had a hard time finding the right words to describe his friend. If you get bogged down in sentiment, he said, then you wind up speaking of him, as Gene Buck once described him, as "a knight whose plumes have never brushed the ground." McLemore, himself bogged down with sentiment, thought of Rice as "an angel with a racing form tucked under his wings." What Rice did in his life was to "lift us sportswriters from the saloon to the drawing room."[15]

A while later, McLemore was sitting around with sportswriter Braven Dyer discussing just exactly what it was that Rice seemed to give everybody he touched. Suddenly, it hit McLemore. Rice gave everybody a goal. McLemore said he himself never came close to reaching it, but Rice taught him that the goal was there, if not explicitly what it was: "just walking with him, just being near him, I saw the goal." Rice had dreams for everyone he knew, and hopes, and his talent and character seemed to light the way for approaching the goal of being better, of always striving to be better. Rice was a truly good man, McLemore said, and as he and Dyer chatted about how to end this piece, he said: "Braven and I are now trying to think of a line to end this column. We just want to let it go with this—the best one is gone."[16]

Vincent X. Flaherty, another Rice colleague, stumbled and fumbled through his column the day after Rice died. Flaherty remembered when he was coming up, still in the sportswriting minor leagues, but actually sitting in the press box at Yankee Stadium with the stars, when Rice walked up and said, "You're Vinnie Flaherty, aren't you? My name is Grant Rice." Flaherty was astonished to hear Rice call him "Vinnie," because only relatives and very close friends ever called him that. Rice had a way of helping the young guys feel they were meeting him on even terms. Even then, Flaherty said, he felt like he'd met a legend, the man who named Walter Johnson "The Big Train," Christy Mathewson "Big Six," Red Grange "The Galloping Ghost," and, of course, the 1924 Notre Dame backfield "The Four Horsemen." Yet Rice was one of the sportswriting gang, Flaherty said, and he honestly had no idea who he was or what he'd become. Somehow or another, he'd become property, the property of Flaherty and all other sportswriter kin; so much so, Flaherty said, that he wasn't surprised at all to hear that shortly after Rice died two sportswriters got into a terrible argument, which led to a fistfight, over a dispute about which one loved Granny the most.[17]

Frank Graham also wrote about his cherished friend. He remembered once riding through Central Park in a cab on the way to the Polo Grounds with Rice one day just a couple of years before his death. Grant spoke wistfully of a mutual friend.

"I don't see much of him any more," he said, "and I miss him. I read about him in the papers, though. I guess he's becoming a celebrity: he always seems to be with celebrities."

Then, after a moment, Rice asked Graham, "Do you like to be with celebrities?"

"No."

"Neither do I. Anyway, the chances are I wouldn't know a celebrity if I saw one."

Graham said Rice was very serious about this. Yet Rice saw one in the mirror every morning when he shaved. It was the measure of the man, Graham said, that two of his friends who would miss him terribly were Charles, his chauffeur, and Bob, the elevator man at his apartment house.[18]

One night in 1946 during spring training, Dan Parker recalled, several New York Yankees players were standing together in front of the grandstand at the St. Petersburg, Florida, dog-racing track, studying the next race. Off to one side of the group, looking a bit seedy in a ready-made suit, stood a young player, obviously dejected.

"What do you like in this race?" asked a kindly, gray-haired gentleman.

"I don't like nothin'," replied the young man, dejectedly. "I just lost my last two bucks."

"Well, you and I each have a deuce on the number 8 dog," said the stranger, handing him, to his utter astonishment, a pari-mutuel ticket. And five minutes later, Parker recalled, this gloomy-go-sorry youngster was jumping for joy in his hand-me-down suit. Number 8 had just won, and was paying $108. And that was Yogi Berra's first introduction to Grantland Rice. Eight years later, when the news came over the wires at the conclusion of the All-Star game that Rice had died, Yogi wept.[19]

For one week, then two, the testimonials, stories, remembrances continued. Besides all the American papers, the *London Times* paid him tribute as well. So did the magazines *Newsweek* and *Time*. So did Congressman Stuyvesant Wainwright, Fifth District in New York and a neighbor of Rice's in East Hampton, by reading remarks on Grantland Rice into the *Congres-*

sional Record. Wainwright noted that the current vogue in newspapers was to create antagonisms, to pit one man against another in order to get a story. Rice, on the other hand, he said, minimized the petty, the small, or the foul conflicts on which lesser men breed. Rice instead "pointed out the good that was in a man." In spirit, these remarks echoed columnist Ned Cronin's tribute in which he said that Granny lived in a world of his own, only inhabited by wonderful people. "He lifted all who knew him into this realm of tranquillity, eliminating their faults and their frailties and importing only that which was kind and good." For that matter, Cronin went on, "he could see nothing else in anyone."[20]

Even men from a far different school of sports journalism, the "get tough" variety, as it was sometimes called, wrote with feeling about Rice. One of them, Jimmy Cannon, who once said that "sportswriting has survived because of the guys who don't cheer. They're the truth tellers. Lies die," got mushy upon the death of Rice. Even though he said that the massive imagery Rice used in his stories seemed slightly ludicrous in the 1950s, in the context of the 1920s it was the right stuff: "We were a different country then. We laughed more. We didn't ask our heroes to die." Cannon told his readers that Rice cherished decency, and took the time to search for it in the characters of those he knew, and didn't get discouraged when the search kept coming up empty. As realism became the fad in reporting, Cannon said, Granny held onto his old ideals, thankfully and appropriately. The reason that those who copied him failed so miserably in their imitations was because "they couldn't steal from him his unshakable belief in the integrity of the human race." While Rice kept on looking for the clean excitement in sports, "we, who owe him so much, turned crabbed and became proud of our suspicions. House detectives worked at a poet's chore." His fragile talent, Cannon said, was simply not meant for a turbulent age.

Cannon said he was not bragging when he described Rice as a friend, because even though sportswriting was a competitive profession, Granny didn't recognize any rivalries among sportswriters. He was a great sportswriter who had melodious compassion; he was a glorious man, Cannon went on, and "I suppose I envied him more than any one who came my way. My life was enriched because of the time I spent in his company." Cannon ended his tribute reminding all his sportswriting colleagues how much they had learned from this pioneer writer: "All of us in this generation of sports journalism are improved because we borrowed some of his techniques," but Cannon admitted, "few handle the language with as much grace. Many croak because we can't sing." Now it may be, Cannon said, that Rice made games more important than they should be, but by so doing he would achieve an "immortality denied some poets who were fascinated by greater themes."[21]

When a person of distinction dies, it is certainly typical that most remembrances are embellished. Faults are glossed over, and, as Ned Cronin wrote when Rice died, the eulogizers "dedicate a ton of high flung wordage to the proposition that a kindly gentleman is no longer among the quick." Now he might owe money to everyone in town, be a bad risk in a poker game, or become abusive and insulting when drinking, but, Cronin said, "so long as he was fairly personable and reasonably cordial, his heirs could count on some pretty flossy literature being concocted to mark his departure from this vale of tears." This is such a longstanding practice, Cronin wrote, that the reading public was more or less "immunized against pasteurized prose of a post mortem nature." But in Rice's case, no lying was necessary. All this stuff they said about him was true. All sincerely written. All heartfelt.[22]

How else could what happened just over three months after Rice's passing, on Halloween night, October 31, 1954, be explained? That night Toots Shor threw an invitation-only, black-tie birthday party for Rice on what would have been his seventy-fourth. More than 250 Rice friends showed up to celebrate the man they so much admired and loved. Toots had told Rice a couple of years back that he would give him an unforgettable seventy-fifth birthday party; Toots had to push the date up a year, and to do without the presence of the honoree.

Toots was another of Rice's longtime friends. He had been a doorman, a bouncer, and then manager of various mob-owned speakeasies in the 1920s: Billy LaHiff's Tavern, Leon and Eddie's. He got his own joint in the 1930s called simply the Tavern, on West Forty-eighth Street. A high-stakes player, and unfortunately a Giants fan at the time, he bet the bar on his favorite team; he lost it lock, stock, and barrel. He started all over again and hustled up enough money from friends and the like, including Grantland Rice, to open what has been called the greatest sporting restaurant ever, at 51 West Fifty-first Street, the brick house, known as Toots Shor's. Attendance at the place was practically compulsory, Red Smith recalled. If you wanted to see anybody, you went there first—Ernest Hemingway or Chief Justice Warren, Yogi Berra, Gene Fowler, Jackie Gleason, Billy Conn, Frank Sinatra, Abe Attell. And Toots, an extension of his own tavern, was "loud, loyal, laughing, sentimental, boisterous, generous, considerate, and dead on the level," wrote Smith. Everybody was equal at Toots, which was to say everybody was a likable crum-bum. One night Charlie Chaplin was told to wait in line for a table like everyone else, which he didn't much like. No matter to Toots. "It'll be about a half-hour, Charlie," Toots bawled. "Be funny for the folks."[23]

Rice's memoirs were scheduled to be released on November 1, his real birthday. On October 31, Ed Sullivan had given over part of his television show, "The Toast of the Town," to plugging the book. Douglas Fairbanks, Jr., gave a graceful reading of Rice's verse, "Ghosts of the Argonne." "You can hear them at night when the moon is hidden;/They sound like the rustle of winter leaves." The tribute to Rice wasn't mere duty to Sullivan, for, like everyone else who had crossed Rice's path, Sullivan had his Rice story too. In 1924, when Frank Munsey was killing off New York newspapers, he had just bought and then shipwrecked the *Evening Mail.* Sullivan wrote sports for the *Mail* and was in Florida at spring training when the news came that he'd lost his job. When Rice heard of this, he talked the owners of the Ormond Beach resort into hiring Sullivan to be the "golf secretary" for the golf club. Sullivan's job consisted of arranging for golf stars such as Walter Hagen, Joe Kirkwood, or Glenna Collett to play exhibition matches at Ormond. He also served as the Ormond correspondent for the various wire services and dailies. Sullivan figured out that part of the deal was that Rice agreed to come to Ormand himself from time to time. Which he did. Rice was a headliner even then, recalled Sullivan later, and he was regarded by the younger writers with the same awe that a rookie ballplayer might have had for Babe Ruth. When Rice came to Ormond for his first visit after Sullivan's hiring, Sullivan got wildly excited and bit so hard on one of his front teeth that it fell out. While showing Rice around, Sullivan was forced to whisper the introductions through clenched teeth—oddly enough a practice not too far removed from the speech patterns later audiences would see on Sullivan's weekly television show.[24]

On Halloween, the 250 friends gathered upstairs at Toots's for a party like no other. The reception was on the second floor, the banquet on the third. There were so many greats in attendance that everybody began exchanging autographs. "I'm not much on autograph collecting," commented Baseball Commissioner Ford Frick, "but I'm not going to miss a chance like this." Like kids hanging around the side gate at the Polo Grounds or Ebbets Field, they tapped each other up, "Please?" as they pushed the program or the flyleaf of Granny's new book in front of each other. Aggressive prosecuting attorney Frank Hogan said he was so ashamed of being in the company of so many wonderful heroes and celebrities that when the autograph collectors were making the rounds he signed the name Ben Hogan instead of Frank Hogan.

Friends stretching over Rice's fifty-year career sat together, ate and drank together, laughed together, and remembered together. Kate Rice was there, of course. At the dais sat, among others, Bruce Barton, Jack Dempsey, Gene Tunney, John (Jack) Wheeler, Bugs Baer, Johnny Weissmuller, Ed Sullivan, Earle Sande, Vinnie Richards, Herman Hickman, Frank Hogan, Rube Goldberg, Ford Frick, and Rice's publisher, J. L. Pratt. Yogi Berra was there, so was Mel Allen and Don Ameche, the Four Horsemen, Frankie Frisch and Bernard Gimbel, Willie Hoppe and William Randolph Hearst, and Willard Mullin, the cartoonist, McLemore and McNulty, Francis Ouimet and Walter Hagen, Earle Sande and Red Smith, Jackie Gleason and Gene Sarazen, Horace Stoneham and Herbert Swope, and on and on.[25]

Gene Fowler wrote a short piece called "The Hat," which appeared in the Friends of Rice program. That beaten-up hat, Rice's gray fedora that came from somewhere that nobody ever knew, but which Rube Goldberg believed had been rejected by the Salvation Army. Fowler said it would have made anyone other than Granny look like a Mulberry Bend bum. The hat was certainly weathered, since snow fell on it at the Yale Bowl, sleet at Soldier Field, rain at Pimlico, and lightning singed it at the Polo Grounds. It was beer-splotched at Toots, and Jack Dempsey sat on it, maybe deliberately, at Madison Square Garden. Everyone knew the man and that hat, said Fowler, and everyone except Granny knew there was a halo under it.[26]

Behind the head table hung a large Mullin-created portrait of Grantland Rice. In the reception room, there was another Mullin portrait. On the program were a few readings, Fowler's text, and a telegram about Granny's service on behalf of sportsmanship and integrity from President Dwight D. Eisenhower. Then a number of his friends spoke briefly. It was the kind of party Rice would have loved, said Goldberg: "We keep expecting him to come through the door." And had he been there, Goldberg continued, "he'd be talking." He'd have spotted the presence of General Rosie O'Donnell and his West Point sidekick, General Blondie Saunders, both sitting across the room at Toots, and it would have reminded him of the time he arrived home one morning after an all-nighter, and with traces of wear and tear, answered Kate's questions about where he was this time, reassuring her that "Everything's all right, honey, I've been out all night with Rosie and Blondie."[27]

The birthday party was upbeat, no maudlin sentiment, no flowery statements. John Kieran spoke of the poet who said that when someone dies, a little part of all who knew them dies too, "but it was no little part of me that went on with Granny," he said. "A big chunk of my heart went with him." The closest the gathering really came to tears was when the jockey Earle Sande went to the microphone and apologized, unexpectedly. He said he couldn't make a speech, but that he'd try to sing what he had to say about Grantland Rice. Then, this fiftyish, balding man let loose in an excellent baritone, singing "Absent," the song that goes, "Sometimes between the long shadows on the grass/The little truant waves of sunlight pass/My eyes grow dim with tenderness, the while/Thinking I see thee; thinking I see thee smile!" Fortunately, Sande stopped it right there and sat down. This was fortunate because the corked emotions were beginning to flow in the silent room. The chance to applaud broke the spell. They didn't sing Happy Birthday, but they could have sung it loudly, for, as Red Smith remembered, Rice really wasn't absent. The merry friends of Grantland Rice caught themselves more than once gazing around the merry room expecting to see Granny at the merriest table.[28]

They met again one year later. Still looking for Granny, perhaps, 330 of Rice's friends and admirers, including Kate, reassembled at Toots Shor's on November 1, 1955, in part to honor the seventy-fifth anniversary of Rice's birth. The primary reason for the gathering, though, was to announce the first winner of the newly created Grantland Rice Memorial Award for sports reporting in the Grantland Rice tradition. The award was created and presented by the Sportsmanship Brotherhood. In 1939 the Sportsmanship Brotherhood had presented Rice with its annual award for his influence on sports and his personal resolve to keep fair play alive in the genre of sportswriting. The Brotherhood had been around since 1925 and had honored before Rice a variety of well-known figures, both in and out of sport, who furthered the aim of fostering the spirit of sportsmanship throughout the world: past honorees had included Walter Johnson and Lou Gehrig in baseball, Bobby Jones in golf, Devereaux Milburn in polo, and Amos Alonzo Stagg in football.[29]

Much like the gathering the previous year, the attendees still had trouble believing that Rice was gone. At the 1954 dinner, Caswell Adams had wandered about through the groups of guests offering to bet 8 to 5 that before the night was out, Granny would show up. "I've had no takers," he reported. "Everybody else believes it too." Now, one year later, somebody asked Adams if he was still offering those odds. "Yes," Adams said, "and still no takers." In the judgment of the luncheon guests, the Memorial Award was a fitting tribute to Rice and to what he stood for. The first winner, Fred Russell of the *Nashville Banner,* was deeply honored to have received it.

But in the years since Rice's day, the tributes to him and to his sportswriting style have waned. Few moderns would be as honored as Fred Russell was to be called Rice-like. In fact, to some sportswriters in the generation just after Rice's, to be called Rice-like was practically a professional curse. Sportswriters began to believe that Rice's contribution to responsible sportswriting, although a probable necessary phase in the history of the craft, was a regrettable one.

Wells Twombly, writing for the *San Francisco Examiner* in the 1970s, for example, flatly denied that there was any Golden Age of sportswriting and thought that Rice, as the dean of this age, was writing for dolts. Randall Poe, in a piece for *Esquire* on the sport of writing sports, claimed that more than anybody else in the 1920s it was Grantland Rice who certified and sold what Poe called the Hero Sandwich. In citing Rice's Four Horsemen lead, Poe claimed that it "has caused decades of vocational damage." Poe went on to say that besides the "brawling metaphors and foaming hype," Rice hid the score and told his reader nothing of the players on the field. As far as Poe was concerned, Rice suffered from Oscar Wilde's dictum "that to be natural is to be obvious, and to be obvious is to be inarticulate." As a final example, Robert Lipsyte, who wrote for the *New York Times* from 1957 through 1971, found Rice both a liberator and a destructive propagandist. Lipsyte admitted that as a liberator, Rice's embellishments freed sports reporters from the mere humdrum of reciting statistics. From Rice on, sportswriters were free to engage in crashing and smashing wordplay, biblical allusion, odd bits of Greek mythology, and endless similes from warfare or natural phenomena. But, Lipsyte went on, Rice as a propagandist was in the end destructive. He painted the lily: "By layering sports with pseudo-myth and fakelore, by assigning brutish or supernatural identities to athletes, the Rice-ites dehumanized the contests and made objects of the athletes." And the flower dies.[30]

But if the flower dies it will not be because of sportswriters like Grantland Rice, for there was nothing fake in either the man or his copy. The cynics and debunkers miss their mark. Most of them didn't know Rice, only of him; when they troubled themselves to read what he wrote, they seemingly didn't get much beyond his opening high-drama leads, for as a reporter of the actual play-by-play contests themselves, Rice was among the best ever. As for the embellishments: myth, certainly; sentiment, of course; folklore, naturally; kitsch, yes, sometimes that too. But the Rice critics have sadly underestimated and undervalued his contribution to the causes of sport and sportswriting. For behind these so-called exaggerations and embellishments and platitudes was Rice's fundamental loyalty to the basic *idea* of sport. And herein lies his edifying legacy.

Grantland Rice was no fatuous, unthinking cheerleader for sport. He was a reflective, knowledgeable, and steady yea-sayer to the essential sensibility and civility of the idea of sporting contests, no matter how badly or frequently this cultural idea can sometimes run amuck. He consistently chose to be a sort of anti-knock additive to the various sporting engines of his day. Rice knew full well that there were two broad classes of writing schools on sport—the boosters and the knockers—going back at least twenty-four hundred years to Greece and the lyrical odes of the booster Pindar, contrasted with the more cynical and critical attitudes of the philosopher Xenophanes or the poet Euripedes.

Pindar would sing of Xenophon's victory in the Olympic pentathlon around 464 B.C.:

> For victor in the Contests Five is he
> And in the foot race; so hath he attained
> Such glory multiplied by victory
> As mortal never yet before hath gained.[31]

Euripedes, on the other hand, would brace the athletes for not learning how to live a good life, and for being slaves to their jaws and obedient to their bellies: "In their prime they make a brilliant spectacle as they go about and are the pride of the state; but when bitter old age comes upon them, they are like coarse cloaks which have lost their nap."[32]

However accurate the Euripedes school may be, then or now, regarding the folly of either the athletes themselves or the habit of watching them, "of honoring useless pleasures for the sake of a feast," Rice's own personal constitution called for carrying on Pindar's tradition. On the victory of Epharmostus of Opus in a wrestling contest, Pindar sang:

> He abode the grapple of strong men older
> Than he, for the silver cups to be won;
> And by ring craft that shifteth its balance fast
> Never failing, he threw them. As Tempest blast
> Rang the cheering, as down the arena he passed
> In his goodlihead, goodliest deeds who had done.[33]

Rice was clearly up to something bigger than even his own generation seemed to recognize. But he didn't go out of his way to explain himself then or to defend his stance ever; he was comfortable letting his written words speak for themselves. Once when Rice was playing a friendly game of cards with a couple of so-called sourdough sportswriter friends, Westbrook Pegler and Marshall Hunt, Pegler said to Rice, "What the hell! Why do you keep writing that pantywaist stuff all the time?" Rice just smiled and said, "Deal the cards."[34]

But as Red Smith said at about the same time the sourdoughs were trying to distance themselves from Rice, "Make no mistake about Granny: he was a giant." While it may be that some of his copy seems like immature gushing to the generations since his death, Smith said that Rice was exactly right for his time and had he lived in another time he would have been exactly right for that one too.

On the personal side, Rice would have adapted to the needs of any age not just because of his sociability, but also because of his own constitution and his sense of duty to his chosen craft. Smith told the story of Rice's coverage of the Rocky Marciano and Jersey Joe Walcott heavyweight championship fight in Philadelphia in 1952. Rice arrived in Philadelphia on the afternoon of the fight, having just rolled in from covering a golf tournament in Washington. He showed up at the hotel where many of the sportswriters had been staying for several days. Rice had a patch covering one eye. When he was asked what happened, the seventy-two-year-old explained that he had slipped on a loose rug in his Washington hotel and cracked his head open. But no matter, he said.

In Philadelphia Rice joined the customary prefight cocktail party; then he trotted off with the other and much younger sportswriters to cover the fight. When Marciano won by a knockout, his friends from Brockton, Massachusetts, who had practically bet their farms on him to win, all stormed the ring. Like lemmings marching to their own drummer, Marciano's friends and fans surged in waves over the ringside press tables, stepping on typewriters, microphones, and various sportswriter body parts. During the charge, Smith glanced over at Granny and saw the bandaged, one-eyed sportswriter hunched over his typewriter, pecking away at his story, apparently oblivious to the melee around him.

Back at the hotel around midnight, the sportswriters opened a jug or two and rehashed the fight until about four o'clock in the morning. By eight o'clock that morning, Granny had shaved, bathed, and breakfasted, and was off to New York. The rest of the sportswriters didn't make it downstairs at the hotel until around noon. There they continued to talk about the Marciano fight; about how Marciano was knocked flat in the first round, and blinded in the sixth and the seventh, and knocked from pillar to post through the twelfth, but who still had enough strength to take Walcott out with a single shot in the thirteenth. "You think Rocky is tough?" said Jimmy Cannon. "How about that old bastard with the hole in his head?"[35]

Rice was tough constitutionally, and smart too. He knew exactly what he was doing: he was helping a relatively young country find its national spirit by way of shaping its sporting philosophy. Among the nonsportswriters mourning Grantland Rice's death was syndicated newspaper columnist Robert C. Ruark. He went a step further than most in commenting on the meaning of Grantland Rice. In all honesty, he thought Rice's column was often unbearably dull—rarely containing anything deeper than salutes to such things as golf and sportsmanship and Southern football. "He was a man," Ruark wrote, "who gave 50 years of his life to nothing but the trivial." Rice, he said, wrote authoritatively on subjects that the long-hairs of the times "would breezily dismiss as unworthy of consideration."

But Ruark also admitted that in his opinion Rice may have bitten a deeper mark on those times than even Walter Lippmann, Joseph and Stewart Alsop, and all the other great political columnists. Ruark was roughly of the same generation as Rice, and Rice's passing gave Ruark pause to think back a few decades. It seemed to him that in those earlier days there weren't so many of the "How to" books: "We did not make such a dreadful chore of believing in God or being nice to kids or just enjoying ourselves." Ruark added, "We didn't seek a motive for everything we did, or search too deeply into why it was necessary to do it. We just did certain things or didn't do certain things."

When one got to thinking about it, said Ruark, Helen Wills's feuds, the Babe's bellyache, Primo Carnera's lack of ability, and the feats of the Ruths, Granges, Thorpes, Dempseys, and Didriksons were of more real importance than those of Oppenheimer or Chou. For better and for worse, sport was simply what it was: one certain, familiar thing to care about in a world that was becoming increasingly complicated, fast-paced, and impersonal. And it was Grantland Rice, he said, who chronicled indefatigably these cares practically every day for more than fifty years.[36]

In other words, Rice didn't take sport or himself too seriously. This he could do because he saw sport as part of a larger, more ordered whole. Rice's works and life—his voice—perpetuated a narrative that was as self-evidently true to him as the course of the sun is to us all.

Since Rice didn't ever say much about the source of this narrative, it is worth some brief speculation about its possible origins. The narrative is to be found in his own roots. Rice lived as a Northerner for more than the last half of his life, but he lived as a Southerner from the beginning. And even though he cut his teeth in the New South, it is in the values of the Old South that we find the central core of Grantland Rice.

If there is any intellectual tradition that might explain Rice's philosophy of life and sport it would be that of the so-called Agrarian tradition of the Old South. There is a remarkable similarity between Rice—who he was and what he stood for—and the beliefs of that small band of teachers and men of letters associated directly with Nashville and with Vanderbilt University not too very long after Rice left the South. They were called the Nashville Agrarians, or sometimes simply the Fugitives.

As a literary group, the Fugitives were active in the 1920s. Some say that this collection of writers and poets was one of the most important and influential literary groups to ever exist in American letters. Four poets in the group— Donald Davidson, John Crowe Ransom, Robert Penn Warren, and Allen Tate—gravitated toward one another in the 1920s when it was all too clear that American tastes were becoming particularly materialistic, even when as late as 1920 nearly half of the total population still made their living as farmers. The South, too, in their opinion, was beginning to become dazzled by things that glittered and sparkled, even though the South was more rural than the nation as a whole—three out of four lived outside the larger towns, according to the census.[37]

The Nashville Agrarians published a collection of essays in 1930 under the title *I'll Take My Stand*. A shared conviction was that in the frantic pursuit of progress and things material, in the efforts to win control over nature, in the invention of supposed labor-saving devices, and in their strenuous consumptive habits, Americans had forgotten their original ends. The pioneering spirit continued into the twentieth century, but since industry and technology never define their goals, it was only pioneering on principle or from force of habit. With undesignated goals, and consequently with no sense of what the pioneering was for, production accelerates, eventually outrunning natural consumption, and thereby "the producers, disguised as idealists of progress, coerce and wheedle the public into being loyal and steady consumers, in order to keep the machines running."[38]

On the other hand, there is the agrarian tradition: reconstructed, said John Crowe Ransom, but unregenerate. "A farm is not a place to grow wealthy, it is a place to grow corn," wrote the teacher, editor, and novelist Andrew Nelson Lytle, who, like Rice, was born in Murfreesboro, and attended a military academy and later Vanderbilt. Though in no way defending the inhuman institution of slavery, Lytle and the others believed that the Southerner was swapping his traditional culture for machine-made bric-a-brac; this traditional Southern culture was essentially nonacquisitive and pastoral. A good and happy life depended on certain simple and elemental life experiences that revolved around good manners and hospitality, the preservation of human dignity and humane values, good conversation, a cooperative self-reliance, the family, a sense of vocation, and a natural and active leisure. "Throw out the radio and take down the fiddle from the wall," wrote Lytle. The Agrarians argued that humankind would be much better off if, collectively, there was less interest in seeking power and control, and more interest in being the well-behaved guests of an inexplicable host. "I believe," wrote Ransom, "there is possible no deep sense of beauty, no heroism of conduct, and no sublimity of religion, which is not informed by the humble sense of man's precariousness in the universe." Otherwise, the Agrarians thought, most of the life we would make for ourselves would be inevitably self-aggrandizing and hollow.[39]

There is no actual evidence that Rice was especially familiar with any of the Fugitives, or that he had studied any of their prose writing. But there is no evidence that he couldn't have been familiar with some of their writings either; Rice was a heavy reader, and his traveling companions reported that he would often have two suitcases with him on the road: one for his clean and dirty laundry, and the other full of books. But even if he was unfamiliar with these thinkers as a group, his connections to their philosophy are compelling. His own family roots were found in the Alabama agricultural tradition, and then later, his more immediate family concerns were agriculture-related in both Murfreesboro and Nashville, Tennessee; his early years were spent for the most part in the same social, cultural, and educational environment as the Fugitives, in Nashville; and his personal comportment, working habits, and values were formed in these early sportswriting years in the South.[40]

When Ransom argued for the good sense of pursuing the arts of living and not of escape, what he lamented was that after its defeat by the Union, the South had ever since been unable to offer America an example of its philosophy in action. Ransom wished that the South would reappropriate the principles of the unreconstructed Southerners and "make them an ideal which the nation at large would have to reckon with." The Fugitives may not have noticed it, but all the while they were busy making their case, Grantland Rice, a mere sportswriter, and under their very noses, was at least one Southerner who was doing precisely what Ransom and the others were wishing for: starting up a counterrevolution to what the Fugitives called the noise, force, speed, contrivance, waste, and dehumanizing drift of unthinking industrialism and progress. We can never go back, wrote Stark Young, but "out of any epoch in civilization there may arise things worth while, that are the flowers of it. To abandon these, when another epoch arrives, is only stupid, so long as there is still in them the breath and flux of life."[41]

By way of sport, Grantland Rice found a spirited lifeforce and grafted it onto his own roots. He recovered that strong yet gentle and heroic code of behavior consistent with the Fugitives' call to action, and which is still occasionally identified with the South: Southern chivalry. An old ideal, for sure, well rooted before the rise of the South, and reminiscent of the days of Chevalier Pierre Bayard or Sir Philip Sidney or maybe the Black Prince; or perhaps more common to the culture of the Japanese *samurai,* or to the ethos of the American cowboy and the Indian at their best. But updated, for Rice and the few others like him in the profession of sportswriting, modern sport could and should also embody the idea of the chivalrous: the virtues of courage and the uphill heart; the possibility of living an adventure or at least witnessing a few; the giving of oneself to a cause or a project or a dream; doing good deeds and with noble purposes; gallant and courteous conduct; fair play at all costs; winning with modesty and losing with grace; and all the rest that makes up life at the level of the highest common denominator.

Old-fashioned, perhaps, but well fashioned. One of his journalism colleagues, Victor O. Jones, wrote at the time of Rice's death that Granny preferred the deeds of high courage over dark conspiracies, and that he cared more for the touchdown run than the gate receipts. Certainly true enough. But what Jones thought even more important than these sporting preferences was what Rice stood so tall for as a human being. Jones said Rice would be a loss in any era, but "he is a particularly great loss now when the world needs innocence instead of guile, enthusiasm instead of cynicism, hope instead of despair, confidence instead of fear, fair play instead of victory at any price." The need remains.[42]

So in one sense it may be true to say, as Robert Ruark did, that Grantland Rice gave himself to the trivial for more than fifty years. But sport becomes trivial only when it is taken so seriously that the idea of chivalry—as Rice understood it at least—is squeezed out of it. Then it becomes mere entertainment, mere boredom-chaser, and simply and completely irrelevant—then anything goes, whatever sells, and it becomes a mere product without a goal or a principle. Thus severed from its fundament, the flower most assuredly dies.

The reason Rice's life is a life to reckon with is because he thought that in principle the idea of the chivalrous could belong to any age, even if the social and cultural life might depend less on horses than automobiles, less on castles and farms than on condominiums and factories. When sport is taken less seriously, more playfully, and at the same time infused with the standards and duties of chivalrous conduct, it escapes triviality and becomes a significant and dignified culture-bearer. In pointing out this goal, not to mention living it, Grantland Rice gave us a sporting narrative that is perfectly honest, perfectly decent, perfectly real, and perfectly true. Although some moderns may believe that Rice's contributions were perfectly awful, what they miss is the Big Story he was covering. By finding this Big Story embedded in the thousands upon thousands of smaller sporting stories he and his colleagues faithfully covered during the first half of the twentieth century, Grantland Rice helped give positive shape to our national conscience and character. His telling of this Big Story was his most endearing and enduring scoop.

Notes

Abbreviations

AJ	*Atlanta Journal*
CN	*Cleveland News*
GR	Grantland Rice
NDN	*Nashville Daily News*
NT	*Nashville Tennessean*
NYDM	*New York Daily Mirror*
NYEM	*New York Evening Mail*
NYHT	*New York Herald Tribune*
NYS	*New York Sun*
NYT	*New York Tribune*
TS	*The Tumult and the Shouting,* Grantland Rice's memoirs, published posthumously (New York: A. S. Barnes, 1954)
VUL	Grantland Rice papers, Vanderbilt University Library, University Archives, Special Collections

Chapter 1. Where There's Strife, There's Dope

1. William Henry Nugent, "The Sports Section," *American Mercury* 16, no. 63 (March 1929): 331.

2. *The Guardian,* or *Youth's Religious Instructor* 1, no. 4 (April 1819): 123–29; 1, no. 5 (May 1819): 158–61.

3. An extended discussion of these early forms of play can be found in Benjamin G. Rader, *American Sports: From the Age of Folk Games to the Age of Television,* 2d ed., 1–16; John Lucas and Ronald Smith, *Saga of American Sport,* 3–69; Betty Spears and Richard Swanson, *History of Sport and Physical Activity in the United States,* 4th ed., 17–96; and Frederick L. Paxson, "The Rise of Sport," *Mississippi Valley Historical Review* 4 (1917): 143–68.

4. See Melvin Adelman, *A Sporting Time: New York City and the Rise of Modern Sport, 1820–1870,* 27–29, 31–38; *American Turf Register and Sporting Magazine* 1, no. 6 (February 1830): 269–73, 2, no. 1 (September 1830): 3–12, and 2, no. 2 (October 1830): 57–61; *Niles Weekly Register* 12, no. 13 (May 31, 1823): 193–94.

5. This discussion of the important social factors contributing to the growth of sport includes the most frequently mentioned factors found in the following: Adelman, *A Sporting Time,* 91–101, 134–38, 269–86; John R. Betts, *America's Sporting Heritage: 1850–1950,* 4–48; Rader, *American Sports,* 1st ed., 2–43; Lucas and Smith, *Saga of*

American Sport, 3–69; Spears and Swanson, *History of Sport,* 65–96; Paxson, "The Rise of Sport," 143–68; Peter Levine, "The Promise of Sport in Antebellum America," *Journal of American Culture* 2 (1980): 623–34; Allen Guttmann, "Capitalism, Protestantism, and the Rise of Modern Sport," in Steven A. Riess, ed., *Major Problems in American Sport History,* 5–15; Stephen Hardy, "Urbanization and the Rise of Sport," in Riess, ed., *Major Problems in American Sport History,* 15–19.

6. See Bil Gilbert, *Westering Man: The Life of Joseph Walker,* 13–15, 22–24.

7. For a discussion of the idea of Americans seeking self-justification by practical works, see Lewis Mumford, "Origins of the American Mind," *American Mercury* 8, no. 31 (July 1926): 345–54.

8. For the sporting press function, see Betts, *America's Sporting Heritage,* 52–69; Adelman, *A Sporting Time,* 265–86; Jack Berryman, "The Tenuous Attempts of Americans to 'Catch-up with John Bull': Specialty Magazines and Sporting Journalism, 1800–1835," *Canadian Journal of History of Sport and Physical Education* 10 (May 1979): 33–61; John R. Betts, "Sporting Journalism in Nineteenth Century America," *American Quarterly* 5 (1953): 39–64; John Stevens, "The Rise of the Sports Page," *Gannett Center for Media Studies* 1, no. 2 (fall 1987): 1–11. Skinner, a government agent during the War of 1812, was with Francis Scott Key during the night of September 13–14, 1814, pacing the decks of the American cartel ship, the *Minden,* when flashing British rockets and bursting bombs shelled Fort McHenry and incited Key to compose the "Star Spangled Banner." See Edith Merwin Bartow, *News and These United States* (New York: Funk and Wagnalls, 1952), 113. Skinner's rationale for his journal can be found in *American Turf Register* 1, no. 1 (September 1829): 3.

9. As an example of these new journalism markets, Skinner had previously started up the *American Farmer* without a single subscriber, yet it survived until 1897. See Bartow, *News,* 20; for additional examples, see Berryman, "Tenuous Attempts," 37–38.

10. Skinner's explanation of "journalizing" experiences, in *American Turf Register and Sporting Magazine* 1, no. 1 (September 1829): 3.

11. Regarding the first gatherers of sporting intelligence, see Berryman, "Tenuous Attempts," 36, 51–52.

12. See Betts, *America's Sporting Heritage,* 53–54; Berryman, "Tenuous Attempts," 54–57.

13. For Porter, baseball, and Henry William Herbert, see Betts, *American Sporting Heritage,* 54; also see Adelman, *A Sporting Time,* 126–38, 248–49.

14. The relative success of the sporting periodicals is discussed in Frank Luther Mott, *American Journalism, A History: 1690–1960,* 3d ed., 194–95, 216, 297–98, 443–44. Some of the more popular periodicals of the day included the *New York Clipper,* 1853; *California Spirit of the Times,* 1854; *Horse Journal,* 1855; *Philadelphia Police Gazette and Sporting Chronicle,* 1856; *Billiard Cue,* 1856; *Sportsman,* 1863; San Francisco's *Our Mazeppa,* 1864; *Turf, Field and Farm,* 1867; *New York Sportsman,* 1865; *Baseball Chronicle,* 1867; *Forest and Stream,* 1873; and *Outing,* 1882. For the ideology of modern sport, see the lengthy discussion in Adelman, *A Sporting Time,* 269–89, of the New York

newspapers and the ways in which that press tried to justify sport on the ground that it promoted health, morality, and positive character values.

15. Baseball as a middle-class diversion is discussed in Adelman, *A Sporting Time,* 125–26, 138–42.

16. Hugh Fullerton, "The Fellows Who Made the Game," *Saturday Evening Post* 200, no. 43 (April 21, 1928): 18.

17. Other sportswriters of note included, for instance, in Cincinnati, Harry Weldon, Ban Johnson (later president of the American League), and Rennie Deacon Mulford; in St. Louis, the Spink brothers, Al and Charlie (Charles went on to start up the *Sporting News*), Jack Sheridan, Eddie Wray, Dick Collins, and Joe Campbell (later of the *Washington Post*); in New York, besides Crane, John Foster, O. P. Caylor, Eddie Roth (the father of the Smith-whiffed, Jones-biffed, Brown-skied school of baseball literature), and Charlie Dryden; in Pittsburgh, Joe Gruber and Aleck Moore (also a former player and close student of the game); in Boston, along with Murnane, Walter Barnes and Jack Morse; in Philadelphia, Frank Huff and Frank Richter; and in Denver, Otto Floto. See Fullerton, "The Fellows Who Made the Game," *Saturday Evening Post,* 18.

18. For the Chicago sportswriters, see Fullerton, "The Fellows Who Made the Game," *Saturday Evening Post,* 18–19, and Elmer Ellis, *Mr. Dooley's America: A Life of Finley Peter Dunne,* 25–26; for the Seymour quote see Fullerton, 19; for Dunne's description of Capt. Anson, see Ellis, *Mr. Dooley,* 26.

19. Examples of sensational headlines can be found in Edwin Emery, *The Press and America: An Interpretive History of the Mass Media,* 3d ed., 317.

20. Hearst's sports coverage is summarized in Nugent, "The Sports Section," *American Mercury* 16, no. 63 (March 1929): 329–38; also in Emery, *The Press and America,* 349–54, 519–45.

21. All the examples of sensationalism and sport can be found in the *New York Journal,* August 24, 1897.

22. The growth of newspaper dailies between 1880 and 1900 can be found in Emery, *The Press and America,* 443.

23. For the description of the streetcar ride to Athletic Park and the typical male clothing of the times, see Jack Norman, Sr., *The Nashville I Knew,* 115–17, 148.

24. For the account of professional baseball in Nashville and the use of Athletic Park (Sulphur Springs Bottom), see Norman, *The Nashville I Knew,* 25–27, 190; William Waller, *Nashville in the 1890s,* 91; Michael Benson, *Ballparks of North America* (Jefferson, N.C.: McFarland, 1989), 245–46.

25. The process of putting out the first edition of the *Daily News (NDN)* was pieced together from the description of the press room of the *Daily News.* See *Nashville Daily News,* July 19, 1901.

26. All references to Grantland Rice's (GR) copy on his first sports report in *NDN,* July 19, 1901.

27. The estimates of Rice's productivity are his own. See GR, *The Tumult and the Shouting: My Life in Sport (TS),* xv. His estimates are modest.

28. Connie Mack quoted in Anthony J. Connor, *Baseball for the Love of It,* 118. Leonard Shecter put the same idea across nineteen years later, but more bluntly: "No press, no interest, no baseball, no twenty-two year old shit-kicker making 35 grand a year at an animal occupation which requires less talent in many ways than it takes for a girl to remove her clothes in a burlesque show." Leonard Shecter, *The Jocks* (New York: Warner, 1969), 66. For Frick's observation regarding the anonymity of sportswriters, see Ford Frick, *Games, Asterisks and People,* 71.

29. Tim Cohane, *Bypaths of Glory: A Sportswriter Looks Back,* 135; Fred Russell, *Bury Me in an Old Pressbox: Good Times and Life of a Sportswriter,* 195.

30. Rice's average of three hours sleep, *New York Sun,* June 22, 1934; George M. Cohan quoted in Henry McLemore, *One of Us Is Wrong,* 186; also, Gene Fowler, *Skyline,* 45; John McNulty's version of Rice as saint quoted in Red Smith, *To Absent Friends from Red Smith,* 45.

31. One reason memories are dim with regard to Rice's authorship of *Casey's Revenge* is because even scholars have misrepresented its authorship. Tristram Coffin, for instance, tells us that it was Ernest Thayer himself, the author of *Casey at the Bat* (1888), who also wrote *Revenge.* Coffin wrote that whereas *Casey at the Bat* was reality, *Casey's Revenge* was dreamy and the product of a "lesser bard." *Casey's Revenge* appeared on September 6, 1907, in the *Nashville Tennessean.* Its author was Grantland Rice. It was later published in Rice's *Base-Ball Ballads* (1910). Coffin apparently relied on Charles O'Brien Kennedy's *A Treasury of American Ballads* in which Kennedy claims Thayer had written and published *Casey's Revenge* in the *San Francisco Chronicle* one month after *Casey at the Bat.* See Tristram Coffin, *The Old Ball Game: Baseball in Folklore and Fiction* (New York: Herder and Herder, 1971), 155. Another collector of Casey-related poems, who includes Rice-authored Casey poems, is Martin Gardner, *The Annotated Casey at the Bat,* 38–64.

32. The spirit of "Gee Whiz" journalism was exhibited by the Hearst writers. Arthur McEwen, a Hearst journalist on the *San Francisco Examiner,* explained the sensational approach to journalism this way: "What we're after is the 'gee whiz' emotion. We run our paper so that when the reader opens it he says: 'Gee Whiz!' " Emery, *The Press and America,* 353. The "Aw Nuts!" variety chiefly refers to sportswriters who were more cynical about what they covered, and who thought that sports were more often than not corrupt and that the public was gullible. The style is known for irreverence, for needling. Westbrook Pegler, Ring Lardner, and W. O. McGeehan are usually pointed out as illustrative examples of this approach to writing sports.

33. The books on Rice and his times include Charles Fountain, *Sportswriter: The Life and Times of Grantland Rice* (New York: Oxford, 1993), and Mark Inabinett, *Grantland Rice and His Heroes: The Sportswriter as Mythmaker in the 1920s* (Knoxville: University of Tennessee Press, 1994).

34. GR, *TS,* xvi.

Chapter 2. Up from the South

1. Clinton's geography is described in Mrs. Franklin S. Moseley, ed., *Snedecor's Greene County Directory* (Eutaw, Alabama: private reprint of 1855–1856 Directory, 1981), 66–67; for Huntsville as social and intellectual capital of the Tennessee Valley, see Willis Brewer, *Alabama: Her History, Resources, War Record and Public Men, 1540–1872* (Spartanburg, S.C.: Reprint Co. Publishers, 1975), 347.

2. There are no family records in the GR papers at Vanderbilt University regarding the Grantlands from Hanover County, Virginia. Nor are there any living relatives especially familiar with the Grantland (or, for that matter, the Rice) family genealogy. To complicate the matter, most of the courthouse records for Hanover County were burned during the Civil War. What is known about them in Virginia has been pieced together from the following sources: *The Vestry Book of St. Paul's Parish* (Hanover County, Virginia, 1706–1786), 201, 426, 464, 482, 552, 572, 626; *Hanover County Taxpayers* (St. Paul's Parish, 1782–1815), 53; *First Census of the United States* (Virginia, 1790 [Heads of Families], 1810, 1820); *Marriages of Some Virginia Residents* (1607–1800); *Virginia Land Records* (1787), 101; *Deed Books for Louise County* (1742–1759), 60, 72, 88, 92; *Wills and Deeds* (Hanover, Virginia), microfilm reel no. 461, 85.

3. For Madison County cotton and population, see Thomas Abernathy, *Formative Period in Alabama, 1815–1828* (University of Alabama Press, 1965), 24, 35, 38, 67–68; Brewer, *Alabama*, 346. Anne Royall, the early American woman journalist, reformer, and traveler, described what these pioneer settlers would have seen upon first arriving in the Huntsville area, especially near the prime cotton planting region near the Tennessee River that attracted the Grantlands: "The cotton fields now begin to appear. These are astonishingly large; from four to five hundred acres in a field!—It is without parallel! Fancy is inadequate to conceive a prospect more grand!. . . Although the land is level, you cannot see the end of the fields either way. To a stranger, coming suddenly amongst these fields, it has the appearance of magic. He is lost in wonder, and nothing but the evidence of his senses can persuade him it is reality." See Anne Newport Royall, *Letters From Alabama, 1817–1822* (University, Ala.: University of Alabama Press, 1969), 114–15.

4. There is a Rice family cemetery in Alabama on Highway 14 near Caples between Clinton and Pleasant Ridge (see O. N. Wiese, *Cemetery Records of Greene Country, Alabama*) with markers for many of the Rices and some for the Marriotts who were close friends of the Rices from their days in North Carolina. From these cemetery markers it appears that the Rices were originally from Nash County, North Carolina. Nash County was formed in 1777 from Edgecomb County where the Rices seem to have lived since before the American Revolution. The family is referenced in the following: *Abstracts of Early Deeds of Nash County* (North Carolina); *Abstracts of Early Records of Nash County* (1777–1859); *1782 Tax List, Nash County*; *Abstracts of Will Book I of Nash County* (1778–1868); *Federal Census of North Carolina* (Nash County, 1800, 1810, 1820); *Early Marriages in North Carolina* (Nash County, n.d.). Not much is known about John Rice. Born in 1755 in Red Bud Creek in Bute County (now Franklin

County), North Carolina, John was pensioned in 1833 when he was almost seventy-eight years old, four years before he died. In the war he was a private in the light horse brigade under Colonel John Baker for the last fifteen months of its existence. After it was disbanded he was commissioned as a lieutenant in the local Nash County militia, serving on active duty for three months. It appears that his regiment mostly harassed the Tories and was in turn harassed by the Indians. On one occasion in 1779 his regiment lost sixteen regulars to an attack by an Indian company. John Rice is listed in the Daughters of the American Revolution *Patriot Index,* 566. His pension application is on file in the Military Service Branch of the National Archives and listed in the *Index of Revolutionary War Pensions* (59062).

5. Virginia Hamilton, *Alabama* (New York: W. W. Norton, 1977), 103.

6. The probable Rice route to Alabama can be found in Hamilton, *Alabama,* 104.

7. For the farming production in Greene County, see Moseley, *Snedecor's Directory,* 64–65.

8. The Rice farm size can be found in *Federal Census of Alabama* (Greene County, 1840 and 1850).

9. Hopkins Rice's persistence and success, by way of tabulating citizen's dates of settlement prior to 1824 from Moseley, *Snedecor's Directory;* John Rice's retirement at age forty-two and personal property value, from *Federal Census of Alabama* (Greene County, 1860); for the description of the planter elite see Joseph E. Menn, "The Large Slaveholders of the Deep South, 1860" (Ph.D. diss., University of Texas, 1964), 1–5, 230; Jonathan M. Wiener, *Social Origins of the New South: Alabama, 1860–1865* (Baton Rouge: Louisiana State University Press, 1978), 7–16; Hamilton, *Alabama,* 107; for Hopkins Rice's overall wealth, see Menn, "Large Slaveholders," 350–51.

10. Joseph Baldwin, *The Flush Times of Alabama and Mississippi* (New York: Hill and Wang, 1957), 167; Hamilton, *Alabama,* 104–5.

11. For the myth that only two classes of Southerners existed and the reality that a more numerous class existed in between the two, see Hamilton, *Alabama,* 6; Frank Owsley, *Plain Folk of the Old South* (Baton Rouge: Louisiana State University Press, 1949), 7–9, 185; Lucille Griffith, *History of Alabama, 1540–1900, as Recorded in Diaries, Letters, and Papers of the Times* (Northport, Ala.: Colonial Press, 1962), 141. Owsley, the Alabama-born sectional historian and teacher, recaptured the spirit of such down-to-earth farmers: "[They] lived a life of great toil and many privations, but they were eminently social, kindly, and friendly. They practiced the most cordial and unstinted hospitality; and in a case of sorrow or sickness, or need of any kind, there was no limit to the ready service rendered by neighbors and friends. In those days, people who lived miles apart, counted themselves as neighbors, and even strangers became friends. There was this great advantage: that, while none were very wealthy, few were poor enough to suffer actual want." Owsley quoting Davis, *Plain Folk,* 131–32.

12. For the history of the *Mobile Centinel* and the *Madison Gazette,* see Abernathy, *Formative Period,* 153; Emery, *The Press and America,* 140.

13. For Thomas Grantland's newspaper publishing business, see Rhoda Ellison, *History and Bibliography of Alabama Newspapers in the Nineteenth Century* (Univer-

sity, Ala.: University of Alabama Press, 1954), 4–5; Mott, *American Journalism*, 140; Robert Jones, *Journalism in the United States* (New York: Dutton and Co., 1947), 198; Emery, *The Press and America*, 137–38. For the *Gazette*'s content, see Abernathy, *Formative Period*, 152; Emery, *The Press and America*, 140. For Thomas Grantland's popular reputation, see Matthew William Clinton, *Tuscaloosa, Alabama: Its Early Days, 1816–1865* (Tuscaloosa, Ala.: Zonta Club, 1958), 42. For additional information on Thomas Grantland's doings, see Tuscaloosa Genealogical Society, *Pioneers of Tuscaloosa County, Alabama prior to 1830* (Tuscaloosa, Ala.: Herff Jones Division, 1981), 345; Silas Emmett Lucas, Jr., *Early Alabama Newspapers, 1819–1893* (Easley, S.C.: Southern Historical Press, 1981), 150, 306, 344; Pauline Jones Gandrud, *Alabama Records* (Easley, S.C.: Southern Historical Press, 1980), vols. 5, 6, 13, 173.

14. GR, *TS*, 4–8.

15. A number of sources were used to put together this profile of Henry W. Grantland: genealogy records were provided by Mrs. R. K. Clifford Sharpe Coffee, ancestor to William Grantland (b. 1812), including citations to Virginia wills and census facts, marriage certificates, death certificates, land, and census information from Madison and Morgan Counties, Alabama; also, Gandrud, *Alabama Records*, vols. 3–7, 54, 64, 80, 85, 97, 115, 119, 127, 129, 137–38, 148, 161, 163, 189, including all wills, deeds, mortgage records, tracts, marriage records, superior court notes, estates, chancery records, and newspapers referring to Henry W. Grantland, his relatives, and his business dealings. Also useful was the *Nashville City Directory*, 1878, 1885, 1887, and 1902; William Waller, *Nashville in the 1890s;* Andrew Morrison, *American Cities* (St. Louis: Engelhardt Series, 1892); John T. Benson, Jr., *Historic East Nashville and Old Tulip Street Methodist Church* (Nashville: Trevecca Press, 1980).

16. Henry Grantland's probable wartime activities were reconstructed on some anecdotes Grantland Rice recalled about his grandfather and some evidence from two of Henry's daughters. Henry and Lizzie had three children: Beulah (Grantland's mother), Harry, and Elizabeth; Henry and his third wife, Mary—who was his sister-in-law—had a daughter, Orleen May or "Mary." The Tennessee State Library and Archives has United Daughters of the Confederacy applications from May Grantland (Orleen May) and from Elizabeth Grantland Atchinson, Chapter #1064, in *UDC Applications*, vol. 9 (1906–1907). It is customary in these applications to explain the type of military service their father completed, including specification of rank, regiment, immediate superiors, and so on. Also, see references to H. W. Grantland in *Confederate Veteran Magazine* 1 (January 1893): 30 and 2 (January 1894): 29.

17. GR, *TS*, 4.

18. For the Federals in the Tennessee Valley, see Peter J. Parish, *The American Civil War* (New York: Holmes and Meier, 1975), 161, 166. For the design and fall of Fort Henry, see Thomas Connelly, *Civil War Tennessee: Battles and Leaders* (Knoxville: University of Tennessee Press, 1979), 18, 23–24; Stanley Horn, *The Army of Tennessee* (Norman: University of Oklahoma Press, 1952), 80–83.

19. Horn, *The Army of Tennessee*, 73ff.; Walter Fleming, *Civil War and Reconstruction in Alabama* (New York: P. Smith, 1949), 62–63.

20. For Henry's volunteering for the cause and starting up his own company, see his daughters' *UDC Applications*. For Rice's comment on his grandfather's personality, see *TS*, 4.

21. For Henry Grantland's health problem, see *UDC Applications*. For the location and function of Blue Mountain, see Ethel Armes, *The Story of Coal and Iron in Alabama* (Birmingham: Chamber of Commerce, 1910), 178–83, 206–7. Ordinary and even contraband trading for war supplies was especially difficult for Alabama. The blockade of southern ports, especially the tight Federal control of Alabama's only port, Mobile, made latching onto necessary materials of war from outside the state practically impossible. Without railroads connecting northern and southern Alabama, contraband trading from the Federally occupied north with southern Alabama was no serious option. Instead, Alabama was forced to produce its own resources. In April of 1862, about the time Henry was transferred out of the field, the Congress of the Confederate States organized a corps of officers to organize a Niter and Mining Bureau. Within a year the outfit was released from the department's direct control and given independent status as a bureau of the War Department. The bureau's chief was Major (later promoted to lieutenant colonel) Isaac St. John. He was headquartered in Richmond. Blue Mountain was directly under the supervision of Captain William Gabbett. It was one of the chief producers of the niter or saltpeter used in the production of gunpowder. Before May 1, 1862, the entire home production of niter from all sources within the confederacy had not reached an average of five hundred pounds per diem, but within a few months production had risen to more than two thousand pounds per diem. Blue Mountain was especially productive throughout the war, and by the end of September 1864 this district alone had dug 222,665 pounds of niter, an average of well over several hundred pounds per day. For the activities of the Niter and Mining Bureau, see *The War of the Rebellion: A Compilation of the Official Records of the Union and Confederate Armies* (Washington, D.C.: Government Printing Office, 1880–1901), vol. 4 (3), 493; (2), 594. For the productivity of Blue Mountain, see *War of the Rebellion*, vol. 4 (2), 27, 29, 222; (3), 698. Additional information on the limestone caves in Blue Mountain and how niter was mined can be found in Fleming, *Civil War*, 101–2, 152–53; *War of the Rebellion*, vol. 4 (2), 26–28.

22. William D. Grantland's service in the niter caves is confirmed in the 1907 *Confederate Veteran Census*, Morgan County, Alabama. He entered service as a private in February 1862 at Somerville, Alabama. For Henry's probable rank, see *War of the Rebellion*, vol. 4 (2), 594–95; (3), 492–93.

23. For the indispensability of the niter and mining service, see *War of the Rebellion*, vol. 4 (2), 990–1018, letter from James Seddon, Secretary of War to Jefferson Davis, November 26, 1863. The quote from Seddon's letter is found on page 1007. Regarding the image of the niter and mining service, according to the historian Walter Fleming, after the enrollment laws were passed, "strange and terrible diseases were developed, and in all sections of the state, health began to break down." Fleming, *Civil War*, 99. Certificates were issued for such maladies as old age, rheumatism, fits, blindness, and assorted physical disabilities.

24. For the interruptions of work by the Federals, see *War of the Rebellion*, vol. 4 (2), 29. For work as their leading aim, see *War of the Rebellion*, vol. 4 (3), 94–95. For Major St. John's comments, see *War of the Rebellion*, vol. 4 (3), 697.

25. For John Rice as a likely Constitutional Unionist, see James L. Roark, *Masters without Slaves: Southern Planters in the Civil War and Reconstruction* (New York: Norton, 1977), chapter 1. The tombstone inscription was copied December 18, 1961, by Reverend Franklin S. Moseley; H. Herd, Tombstone Maker.

26. Roark, *Masters without Slaves*, 31.

27. For slave owner military exemptions, see Hamilton, *Alabama*, 25; Fleming, *Civil War*, 101, 107; James G. Randall and David H. Donald, *The Civil War and Reconstruction* (Boston: Heath, 1961), 251; Wiener, *Social Origins*, 18–19. For the number of large slaveholders, see Menn, "Large Slaveholders," 2.

28. For Grantland Rice's reference to his grandfather's opinion of General Braxton Bragg and preference for Nathan Bedford Forrest, see GR, *TS*, 5. Forrest, a cavalry officer, earned a reputation for pulling off wildly successful raids, skirmishes, and battles. Usually outnumbered, his raiders concentrated on destroying and harassing enemy outposts, depots, supply and communication lines, and railroads. No one seems to know exactly what Forrest actually accomplished, but like the proverbial beaver, he was busy throughout the war. General Sherman respected the Confederate cavalry to such an extent that he wrote to "Old Brains" Henry Halleck: "War suits them, and the rascals are brave, fine riders, bold to rashness, and dangerous subjects in every sense." Sherman named Forrest (along with John Hunt Morgan and William Jackson) as the type of leader of this class: "These men must all be killed or employed by us before we can hope for peace." Samuel Carter, *Siege of Atlanta, 1864* (New York: St. Martin's Press, 1973), 104.

29. The primary but scant information on John P. Rice's military service was pieced together from records provided by the Alabama Department of Archives and History in Montgomery and the manuscripts section of the Birmingham Public Library. No useful information was available from the National Archives records entitled "Compiled Service Records of Confederate General and Staff Officers and Nonregimental Enlisted Men." For the Nineteenth under General Bragg, see Brewer, *Alabama*, 620; Parish, *American Civil War*, 296–97; Connelly, *Civil War Tennessee*, 76. More detail is available in *War of the Rebellion*, series I, vol. 5 (4), 416; (6), 772, 819; (10), 383, 534, 552–53, 558–61, 738, 839, 853; (16), 764; (17), 633; (20), most of volume on Stones River; (23), 743, 958; (30), 15, 333; (31), 659 pt. 3, 617, 805, 816; (37), 346, 640, 656, 663; (39), 851; (52), 149. For the four days of fighting at Murfreesboro and the losses, see Horn, *Army of Tennessee*, 208–9; Brewer, *Alabama*, 620; *War of the Rebellion*, series I, vol. 5 (20), 658.

30. Roark, *Masters without Slaves*, 77, 120.

31. GR, *TS*, 4–5. With the profit from the sale of those leadlike cotton bales, combined with his prewar sawmill partnership and his interest in his second father-in-law's farm and mercantile business, Henry devoted his energies to making money. Historian James C. Cobb noted that even before the war, those Southerners connected

somehow or other to industrial ventures often profited even more from them than the planters did from their single-staple plantation production system. Cobb, *Industrialization and Southern Society, 1877–1984* (Lexington: University Press of Kentucky, 1984), 8–10. Henry reaped the benefits of the accelerated interest in an industrial progress mainly composed of the processing of agricultural products and raw materials. These were Henry's elements.

32. Cobb, *Industrialization and Southern Society*, 20–21.

Chapter 3. When Morning Ruled the Heart

1. For the description of the function of Southern general stores and the complicated financial network in textiles, see Roger L. Ransom and Richard Sutch, *One Kind of Freedom: The Economic Consequences of Emancipation* (New York: Cambridge University Press, 1977), 106–48. Henry Grantland's businesses were traced through the *Nashville City Directory*, 1870s, 1880s, and 1890s. Also see Waller, *Nashville in the 1890s*, 43, 59; Morrison, *American Cities*, 87–88.

2. GR, *TS*, 3.

3. For Bolling's job as the "office man," see Morrison, *American Cities*, 88. The First National Bank is discussed in Waller, *Nashville in the 1890s*, 43, 99.

4. For the description of East Nashville, Edgefield, see Don H. Doyle, *Nashville in the New South: 1880–1930*, 87–88.

5. For Henry's "promotion," see Waller, *Nashville in the 1890s*, 181.

6. GR, *TS*, 5.

7. For the Rice verse, see GR, *New York Tribune (NYT)*, December 25, 1923; for the "sounding instruments," see GR, *TS*, 5; for "One-Eyed Cat," see Waller, *Nashville in the 1890s*, 228.

8. The variety of seasonal boredom-chasers engaged in by Rice and his cohorts was described in 1949 by Rice's playmates of fifty-five years earlier in Nashville and can be found in the *Nashville Tennessean (NT)*, February 6, 1949.

9. For Rice's bird egg collecting, see Webb's recollections in Waller, *Nashville in the 1890s*, 226–33.

10. For the typical country school in Nashville, see Waller, *Nashville in the 1890s*, 211–12.

11. GR, *TS*, 6–7.

12. For the depression of 1893, see Doyle, *Nashville*, 52; also, for the cotton market drop, see Monroe Lee Billington, *The American South, A Brief History* (New York: Scribner, 1971), 215. For the larger context of the Panic of 1893, see Ransom and Sutch, *One Kind of Freedom*; Gavin Wright, *The Political Economy of the Cotton South: Households, Markets and Wealth in the Nineteenth Century* (New York: W. W. Norton, 1978). Regarding Henry Grantland's death, Grantland Rice has his grandfather dying at the age of ninety-five in 1915. *TS*, 4. But Henry Grantland actually died at ninety-four on February 17, 1926. *Nashville Banner*, February 18, 1926.

13. The post-depression Rice family life is discussed by GR, *TS*, 6.

14. Rice's reputation as the local recreation director was noted by his childhood friends in the *Nashville Tennessean,* February 6, 1949.

15. Waller, quoting Adams's recollections in *Nashville in the 1890s,* 218.

16. The Wallace University School mission can be found in Waller, *Nashville in the 1890s,* 30–31.

17. Calling these English schools public is a misnomer as they were in truth the private schools for the sons of the English leisure class. For the manly conduct idea, see Thomas Hughes, *Tom Brown's School Days* (New York: Macmillan Company, 1910), introduction by Hughes, xvi; for the idea of doing right, see Bruce Haley, *The Healthy Body and Victorian Culture* (Cambridge: Harvard University Press, 1978), 142. For Hughes's appeal for a more muscular pedagogy to help avoid intellectual priggishness, see Hughes, 29.

18. Hughes, *Tom Brown's School Days,* author's preface to the sixth edition, xxviii.

19. For Wallace's view on studying Latin and Greek, see Waller, *Nashville in the 1890s,* 31. The letter is quoted in Fred Russell's column, *Nashville Banner,* December 19, 1948; also see *Vanderbilt Alumnus* 34, no. 3 (January–February 1949): 11.

20. Doyle, *Nashville,* 3, 146, 235, Appendix A.

21. William C. Harvard and Walter Sullivan, eds., *A Band of Prophets: The Vanderbilt Agrarians after Fifty Years* (Baton Rouge: Louisiana State University Press, 1982), 22; Doyle, *Nashville,* 53–59.

22. For the description of the intent and attractions of the Nashville Exposition, see Doyle, *Nashville,* 144–56; Waller, *Nashville in the 1890s,* 103–16.

23. Waller, *Nashville in the 1890s,* 112, 215–16, 262–64.

24. Ibid., 103–16, 263; Doyle, *Nashville,* 144–56.

25. Doyle, *Nashville,* 51; *Vanderbilt University Catalog,* 1897.

26. *Vanderbilt University Catalog,* 1897–1901. Of the 838 students at Vanderbilt in the fall of 1897, 238 were in the Academic Department, a liberal arts program, and the remaining 600 were scattered across engineering, biblical studies, law, medicine, pharmacy, and dentistry.

27. GR, *TS,* 352; Jones's recollection in *Vanderbilt Alumnus* 16, no. 6 (April 1931): 161.

28. William Waller, *Nashville, 1900–1910,* 185; Waller, *Nashville in the 1890s,* 32.

29. For the virtues of school sport, see for example such turn-of-the-century physical education journals as *Mind and Body, American Physical Education Review,* and *Physical Training.*

30. "Our Physical Improvement," *Mind and Body* 6, no. 66 (August 1899): 134–35, published as excerpt from the *Milwaukee Medical Journal* (n.d.).

31. F. Marion, *Wonderful Balloon Ascents: Or, the Conquest of the Skies, A History of Balloons and Balloon Voyages* (New York: Charles Scribner and Co., 1871), 70–73. "It is reported that Franklin, more illustrious in his humility than the most brilliant among the lords of the court, when consulted respecting the possible use of balloons, answered simply, 'C'est l'enfant qui vient de naître?'"

32. The background for both the spirited play forms of the Western frontier pioneers and the American Indians can be found in Gilbert, *Westering Man;* Joseph B. Oxendine, *American Indian Sports Heritage;* Lucas and Smith, *Saga of American Sport,* 76–79; Rader, *American Sports,* 3d ed., 14; Peter Levine, ed., *American Sport: A Documentary History,* 17–34; Riess, ed., *Major Problems in Sport History,* 27–30; John R. Tunis, *The American Way in Sport,* 11–32.

33. The description of the gymnasium at Vanderbilt came from the *Vanderbilt University Catalog,* 1897–1901.

34. For the sport of basketball, see Waller, *Nashville, 1900–1910,* 190. The ups and downs of Rice's athletic career can be found in the *Comet,* Vanderbilt University yearbook, 1897–1901; also in the Vanderbilt University *Hustler,* the student newspaper.

35. *Atlanta Journal (AJ),* December 26, 1904.

36. GR, *TS,* 8.

37. *Comet,* Vanderbilt University, 1901.

Chapter 4. Pyrotechnic Displays

1. Lawrence S. Ritter, *The Glory of Their Times: The Story of the Early Days of Baseball Told by the Men Who Played It,* 34, 38; Rader, *American Sports,* 1st ed., 112; Ted Vincent, *Mudville's Revenge: The Rise and Fall of American Sport,* 41.

2. Steven Riess, *Touching Base: Professional Baseball and American Culture in the Progressive Era,* 174–77.

3. GR, *TS,* 8; Fred Russell, *Nashville Banner,* August 21, 1941.

4. Ritter, *The Glory of Their Times,* 1–2.

5. GR, *TS,* 8; Waller, *Nashville, 1900–1910,* 111, 133–34.

6. Fred Russell, *Nashville Banner,* August 21, 1941.

7. Gene Fowler, *Skyline,* 16.

8. GR, *TS,* 8. For the general estimation of sportswriting as a mere trifling, see Richard D. Mandell, *Sport: A Cultural History,* 179–95.

9. Vincent, *Mudville's Revenge,* 30–57, 59.

10. Peter Nye, *Hearts of Lions: The History of American Bicycle Racing,* 49–64.

11. Mandell, *Sport,* 186.

12. Nye, *Hearts of Lions,* 69–71.

13. The description of bicycle racing at the Garden was pieced together from numerous newspaper articles on bicycle racing in the *Atlanta Journal* between the years 1902 and 1904. Grantland Rice was in Atlanta during those years and saw to it that his readers were kept informed about bicycle racing in both the North and the South.

14. There are suggestions that football games were played in North America before the colleges became involved. Among the variety of eastern Indian tribes, the game had been popular as far back as whites had been witnessing Indian customs—and no doubt long before that. William Wood, in 1634, described a soccerlike version of football played among the Massachusetts Indians; he was not impressed with their skill, as

they "have no cunning at all in that kind, one English being able to beat ten Indians at football." A decade later Roger Williams found that the Narragansets in Rhode Island "have great meetings of foot-ball playing, only in summer, town against town, upon some sandy shore . . . but seldom quarrel." Joseph B. Oxendine, *American Indian Sports Heritage,* 61. One Southern old-timer recalled reading about an early football game played between the Creeks and the Ewitches somewhere around 1831 at Fort Mitchell, Georgia. His information about the contest came from a book, *Men and Manners in America,* published in 1833 by a touring Englishman identified on the book jacket only as "T. H." Along with the officers of the garrison and large numbers of Indian spectators, T. H. witnessed this great game. The "object of either party was to throw the ball as far as possible into their adversary's grounds and then make it pass between two poles, erected for the purpose of demarcation." The game, he said, was accompanied by some danger, since "the whole body of players sweep on like a hurricane." It was even risky to be a spectator, as he suggested that a "godly . . . gentleman could be safe only when perched in the boughs of a tree." In the end, the Creeks won out. The Ewitches, crestfallen, alibied, however, that none but their worst players had taken part in the game. T. H. said he had never seen a finer display of agile movement. *Nashville Tennessean,* October 10, 1910. The old-timer was referring to the book by Thomas Hamilton (1789–1842), *Men and Manners in America* (Edinburgh: W. Blackwood, 1833). In it Hamilton said this, in part, about the game: "The object of either party was to send the ball as far as possible into their adversaries ground, and then to make it pass between two poles, erected for the purpose of demarcation" (266–67). Even though Hamilton didn't mention the use of sticks, it is possible that Hamilton was witnessing the game of lacrosse and not a version of football.

15. Although the prevailing assumption was that the publicity that would derive from winning football teams would translate into larger student bodies, it is interesting that, for example, enrollments at Columbia between 1903 and 1909 flourished, although football was banished at the time; and Harvard and Yale both had winning programs in the same years when Harvard's enrollments slightly decreased and Yale's steadily decreased. See John Hammond Moore, "Football's Ugly Decades, 1893–1913" (reprinted from *Smithsonian Journal of History* 11 [fall 1967]: 49–68) in Steven Riess, *The American Sporting Experience: A Historical Anthology of Sport in America,* 168–89.

16. Rader, *American Sports,* 3d ed., 91–92; Amos Alonzo Stagg and Wesley Winans Stout, *Touchdown!* (New York: Longmans, Green and Co., 1927), 203.

17. John Heisman, "The Thundering Herd," *Collier's* 82, no. 15 (October 13, 1928): 12–13, 59–60; Moore, "Football's Ugly Decades," 172.

18. Waller, *Nashville in the 1890s,* 28–30; *Nashville American,* November 25, 1896.

19. Theodore Roosevelt, *The Strenuous Life: Essays and Addresses,* 155, 164.

20. For these early years of baseball, see Harold Seymour, *Baseball, The Early Years;* David Q. Voigt, *American Baseball,* vol. 1; Adelman, *A Sporting Time,* 91–183.

21. According to baseball historians, in 1889, at the famous Delmonico's in New York, a group of about three hundred baseball supporters, including Mark Twain, gathered to honor a group of professional ball players who had just returned from a

world tour. Albert G. Spalding, the president of the Chicago club and by then also the head of his own successful sporting goods business, thought it was about time that America have a National Game. One of the speakers, Albert G. Mills, claimed as much when he announced that "patriotism and research" had established the fact that baseball was, indeed, of American origin. For the next fourteen years, as baseball attracted increasing press coverage and spectator worship, the issue of origins festered. When Henry Chadwick in 1903 persisted in his claim that at least the basic features of the game of baseball originated from rounders, Spalding decided once and for all to call for settling the issue. With Mills as its chairman, a blue-ribbon committee was appointed, including a couple of senators and some prominent members, at one time or another, of organized baseball. After three years of "research," the committee claimed that baseball originated in America and that it was founded at Cooperstown, New York, in 1839 by Abner Doubleday. The conclusion was based solely on the testimony of one Abner Graves, who remembered having played ball with Doubleday sixty-eight years earlier in a game of town ball between Otsego Academy and Green's Select School; Graves claimed Doubleday spruced up the game and called it Base Ball; but, as it turns out, Doubleday went to school at Auburn, and at the time he was supposed to be playing ball with Graves, he was actually at West Point; and since Mills had known Doubleday from their days of soldiering during the Civil War, it was odd that Mills did not cite Doubleday as the probable inventor of the game back in 1889 in his speech at Delmonico's. In the end, the Doubleday story turned out to be mostly fanciful, even though as late as 1939 the myth of the American origins of the game was further perpetuated when the major leagues, with much fanfare, used the Mills report to justify baseball's "centennial" at Cooperstown and the dedication of the Hall of Fame.

22. For the growth of baseball after the Civil War, see Adelman, *A Sporting Time,* 137, 156–57. When Mark Twain learned that Spalding's touring baseball club had played an exhibition game in the Hawaiian Islands, he couldn't help but point out the contrast in cultures: "I have visited the Sandwich Islands . . . where life is one long, slumberless Sabbath, the climate one long, delicious summer day. . . . And these boys have played baseball there!—baseball, which is the very symbol, the outward and visible expression of the drive and push and rush and struggle of the raging, tearing, booming nineteenth century! One cannot realize it; the place and the fact are so incongruous; it's like interrupting a funeral with a circus." See Allen Guttmann, *From Ritual to Record: The Nature of Modern Sports,* 15. The baseball business was growing phenomenally by then, and was beginning to spread to such countries as the Philippines, Mexico, Manila, South Africa, and Cuba. In America, even though the baseball enterprise did not compare to the gigantic trusts of that age, it certainly wasn't a mere mom-and-pop grocery business either. By 1890 baseball was already big: the 100 National Agreement clubs (the Tripartite Pact of 1883 intended to bring harmony to organized baseball by regulating competition between the various leagues for players and territories) employed fifteen hundred players at an average season salary of $1,000 for a total payroll of $1.5 million; eight million Americans were paying about $2.75

million to watch these young men play ball. By around 1900 there were seventeen high class leagues (besides the American and National), including the Western, California, Eastern, New York State, Cotton States, Connecticut, Virginia-Carolina, and the American Association. One hundred thirty-six teams and more than two thousand players took to the playing fields each spring. Shortly after the turn of the century, the major and minor leagues from Cape Cod to the Rio Grande employed no less than thirty-seven hundred professional athletes with a monthly payroll of $740,000; club owners were to pay something in the range of $4.4 million in baseball salaries for one season. See Seymour, *Baseball, The Early Years,* 348; GR in *Atlanta Journal,* January 24, 1903, and April 23, 1905.

23. Seymour, *Baseball, The Early Years,* 356.

24. Wiener, *Social Origins,* 209–15; Cobb, *Industrialization and Southern Society,* 12–13; C. Vann Woodward, *Origins of the New South: 1877–1913,* 145–47.

25. This quote and all the preceding and following factual information regarding the fight between Baxter and the L&N can be found in Doyle, *Nashville,* 19–32.

26. Ibid., 31–32.

27. GR, *NDN,* July 7, 1901; *Vanderbilt Alumnus* 16, no. 6 (April 1931): 161.

28. GR, *TS,* 9–10.

29. Waller, *Nashville, 1900–1910,* 200–201, 214–15.

30. Ibid., 199.

31. GR, *NDN,* September 12 and October 10, 1901.

32. GR, "Short History of the Southern League," *AJ,* January 21–25, 1904; GR, *NDN,* July 20, 27, and 30, 1901.

33. GR, "Short History."

34. GR, *NDN,* July 24, September 24 and 25, 1901; also GR in "Short History."

35. GR, *NDN,* July 22, 1901. GR was quoting from the *Shreveport Times.*

36. The Southern League played Sunday ball in spite of the fact that blue laws were sometimes still enforced. For example, on August 6 the mayor of Chattanooga, Joseph Wassman, was arrested on the charge of violating the Sabbath when he and a party of Hebrew picnickers engaged in a game of baseball six miles from the city. *NDN,* August 6, 1901.

37. GR, *NDN,* August 7, 1901. It was common practice in these days, insofar as either newspaper or detailing of Southern League baseball was concerned, that only the surname of the ball player was used, or sometimes his nickname. It was rare to find regular use of first names, even in the box scores.

38. Ibid., August 1, 2, and 7, 1901.

39. Ibid., August 11, 12, and 13, 1901.

40. Ibid., August 14, 1901.

41. Ibid., September 8, 1901.

42. Ibid., August 29, 1901.

43. This was Grantland Rice's first-ever sporting verse, ibid., August 12, 1901.

44. The series between Nashville and Little Rock is described by GR in *NDN,* September 17, 18, and 19, 1901.

45. The aftermath of Nashville versus Little Rock is described by GR in *NDN*, September 23–28 and October 7, 1901.

46. Rice's comments and opinions regarding the handling of the Southern League pennant decision can be found in *NDN*, October 21, 1901.

Chapter 5. Friends, Scoops, and Sputtering Death Boxes

1. GR, *NDN*, November 17, 1901.

2. GR, *TS*, 10.

3. *AJ*, February 9, 1903.

4. GR, in John Kieran, ed., *The Final Answer*, 102.

5. Edward Anthony, *O Rare Don Marquis, A Biography*, 80–86, 89–90.

6. Ibid., 84.

7. GR, *TS*, 11.

8. Anthony, *O Rare Don Marquis*, 39.

9. Ibid., 84–85.

10. GR, *TS*, 11.

11. Anthony, *O Rare Don Marquis*, 85–86, 336.

12. Ibid., 81, 494.

13. Ibid., 114–17; Mott, *American Journalism*, 583.

14. Anthony, *O Rare Don Marquis*, 81–82, 89.

15. GR, *AJ*, January 31, 1903.

16. Ibid., March 27 and 29, 1903.

17. Ibid., April 5 and 10, 1903. The photo of Hale is incorrectly captioned "Happy Henry Hale." Although Rice, a.k.a. "Henry," was certainly one happy Henry about Hale.

18. The refurbishing of Piedmont Park is described in *AJ*, March 25, 1903. The grandstands and the press box are pictured in *AJ*, March 15, 1903.

19. Ibid., April 16, 1903.

20. Ibid., April 19, 1903.

21. Rice's meeting up for the first time with Raymond is told in GR, *TS*, 13.

22. Raymond's spitter was described by fellow New York teammate Rube Marquard in Ritter, *The Glory of Their Times*, 15; also, Raymond's career was further discussed by another teammate, Fred Snodgrass, in Ritter, 87–90.

23. The Ty Cobb scoop is told by GR, *TS*, 18–19. It is also described by one of Cobb's biographers, John McCallum, *The Tiger Wore Spikes: An Informal Biography of Ty Cobb*, 30–31.

24. GR, *NT*, June 5, 1910.

25. GR, *TS*, 30.

26. For the popularity of cycling, see Hammond in Riess, *The American Sporting Experience*, 194; for the easing of the legendary jolts and jars from city riding, see GR, *AJ*, February 1, 1903.

27. For the facts regarding the annual bicycle road race and for the prizes, see GR, *AJ*, June 25, 1902.

28. For a description of the second annual road race, including the outcome, see GR, *AJ*, July 5, 1902.

29. The account of the racing up to the big crash evening appears in *AJ*, April 6, 1903. For the evening of the crash and the fighting, see GR, *AJ*, April 7, 1903.

30. Ibid., April 9, 1903.

31. For Tom Eck's entrepreneuring, see GR, *AJ*, February 3, 1903, and January 1, 1904.

32. For Tom Eck's reputation among the racers, see GR, *AJ*, February 20, 1903.

33. GR, *AJ*, February 24, 1903.

34. For Walthour's reputation and his comparison to Babe Ruth in baseball, see Nye, *Hearts of Lions*, 70.

35. For Walthour's record breaking, see GR, *AJ*, July 8 and 9, 1903.

36. Ibid., March 21, 1904.

37. Ibid., April 10, 1903.

38. For the training techniques of these riders, see GR, *AJ*, January 25 and November 16, 1903; January 29 and February 27, 1904.

39. For Will Stinson's drug use, see GR, *AJ*, March 22 and 24 and July 4, 1902.

40. For Walthour's daughter's concern, see *AJ*, March 22, 1902.

41. Ibid., July 22 and 25, 1902.

42. GR quoting Walthour, ibid., May 14, 1902.

43. Ibid., June 1 and 9, 1903.

44. GR quoting Walthour, ibid., June 13 and 9, 1902.

45. Ibid., April 18, 1903.

46. The incidents regarding Walthour being asked to throw races and Walthour's attitude toward such requests is described by GR in *AJ*, July 19, 1903.

47. For Jack Prince's coliseum in Atlanta, see Ibid., March 1, 1904.

48. For Leander's desire to finish ahead of "that rebel," see GR, *AJ*, December 7, 1903. For Leander's description of the horn serenade, see Ibid., April 24, 1904.

49. GR's account of Walthour's ride against Lawson, including the prose and poetry quotes, can be found in *AJ*, March 17 and 18, 1903. Walthour won sixteen of seventeen starts in 1904 and won the world championship, a 62.5-mile event, in London that year, and again in 1905. He continued to race bicycles in the United States and Europe for the next decade. During World War I he served as the secretary to the Young Men's Christian Association division in France. After the war he raced mainly in Europe, eventually giving up competition after a bad track accident in the late 1920s. All told, Bobby had broken his collar bone twenty-nine times, and many other bones in his body at least once. He returned to the United States in the 1930s and worked for a New York sporting goods manufacturer, and later for an automobile magazine publisher. He contracted cancer in 1949 and died of pneumonia later that year at the age of seventy-one. In 1932 he was named one of Georgia's greatest athletes, along with baseball star Ty Cobb and golfer Bobby Jones (Rice was central to the life

stories of all three). In 1989 Walthour was inducted into the United States Bicycling Hall of Fame. For Walthour's obituary, see *New York Times*, September 3, 1949.

Chapter 6. Mudville Hearts Are Happy Now

1. When Rice was named in 1905 as the official scorer for the Atlanta Firemen (the ball club), his paper bellowed: "Mr. Rice, as all lovers of sport in this section know, is the foremost baseball writer of the day. He is an acknowledged authority on all branches of sport and since he became connected with *The Journal* some three years ago, he has made himself the most popular sports writer in the country." *AJ*, April 13, 1905.

2. Ibid., April 13, 1905.

3. Ibid., April 17, 1905.

4. Ibid.

5. Ibid., October 7, 1905; Henry Chadwick, ed., *Spalding's Official Base Ball Guide* (New York: American Sports Publishing Company, 1906), 59.

6. For baseball's status as the preeminent national commercial spectator amusement by 1905, see Seymour, *Baseball, The Early Years*, 345–47.

7. *Washington Post*, October 1, 1905; Chadwick, ed., *Spalding's Official Base Ball Guide*, 5, 61.

8. For baseball as business as usual, see Voigt, *American Baseball*, vol. 2, xiii; for the nonsentimentality of the baseball business, see Seymour, *Baseball, The Early Years*, 13.

9. For McGraw's reference to Brush's rationale, see John J. McGraw, *My Thirty Years in Baseball*, 156; for the Brush rules and the series, see Seymour, *Baseball, The Early Years*, 14–15.

10. GR, *AJ*, October 8, 1905.

11. For the number of clubs going to the South for spring training, see Ibid., April 9, 1905.

12. GR, *NDN*, July 30, 1901.

13. Regarding the marriage status of the World Series players, see GR, *AJ*, October 12, 1905.

14. For McGraw's regard for the 1905 Giants, and his comments on Mathewson, see McGraw, *My Thirty Years*, 159, 139–43.

15. GR, *AJ*, March 31, 1903. Waddell played for thirteen years (1897–1910), pitched in 421 games and won 203 of those. He was elected to the Baseball Hall of Fame, as was Christy Mathewson.

16. Waddell's circuitous route to the major leagues is described by Rice in *NT*, August 4, 1907.

17. *Philadelphia North American*, September 28, 1905.

18. Ibid., September 21, 1905.

19. For the theory that Waddell was bought off, see Dryden and Fogel, *Philadelphia*

North American, September 21, 1905; GR, *AJ,* October 1, 1905. For Criger's claim of an attempted bribe, see Seymour, *Baseball, The Early Years,* 379.

20. GR, *AJ,* October 9, 1905; *New York Times,* October 10, 1905.

21. GR, *AJ,* October 2 and 7, 1905.

22. *Washington Post,* October 7, 1905; *Philadelphia North American,* October 7 and 8, 1905.

23. Gardner, *Annotated Casey,* 3; *New York Times,* October 9, 1905; *Washington Post,* October 9, 1905; GR, *AJ,* October 9, 1905.

24. *New York Times,* October 10, 1905. For the features of Columbia Park, see Lowell Reidenbaugh, *Take Me Out to the Ball Park,* 2d ed. (St. Louis: Sporting News, 1987), 209; *New York Times,* October 14, 1905.

25. *New York Times,* October 10, 1905.

26. *Philadelphia North American,* October 10, 1905; GR, *AJ,* October 14, 1905.

27. *New York Times,* October 10, 1905; Voigt, *American Baseball,* vol. 2, 8–9; GR, *AJ,* October 13, 1905; *Chicago Tribune,* October 10, 1905; *Philadelphia North American,* October 10, 1905.

28. GR, *AJ,* October 10, 1905.

29. Ibid., October 10 and 11, 1905.

30. Frick, *Games, Asterisks, and People,* 81; GR, *AJ,* October 11, 1905.

31. GR, *AJ,* October 13, 1905. Rice's reference to Mount Pelee was to a volcano on the island of Martinique, French West Indies, which erupted on May 8, 1902, killing about thirty thousand people.

32. Ibid., October 14, 1905. In comparison to the length of Rice's wordy stories, United Press International, in March 1997, recommended that its writers not exceed three hundred words per story. *Harper's Magazine* 295, no. 1769 (October 1997): 11.

33. GR, *AJ,* October 14, 1905.

34. Ibid., October 15, 1905.

35. Ibid., October 16, 1905.

36. Regarding Rice's possible trip to Cleveland after the series, in an undated clipping from GR's papers in Special Collections at Vanderbilt University Library (VUL), there is reference to his visit in a Cleveland newspaper.

37. GR, *NT,* July 20, 1907.

38. GR recounted his conversation with Bates in *AJ,* March 18, 1905.

39. Ibid., March 31 and April 7, 1905.

40. For Rice's diet of corn whiskey and tin cans, see Anthony, *O Rare Don Marquis,* 208. For Rice's announcement of impending marriage, see GR, *TS,* 32.

41. Kate Rice described her introduction to GR in *TS,* 33. Rice by then was twenty-five. It isn't known how much dating Rice had done prior to meeting Kate. At Vanderbilt, surely, as a fraternity man he would have dated and socialized somewhat. But after college, with his sportswriting schedule and the demands made of him by his male cronies, it is unlikely that Rice did much serious dating until he met Kate.

42. Anthony, *O Rare Don Marquis,* 89–90.

43. Undated clipping in VUL.

44. GR, *TS*, 321–22; Hugh Fullerton, "The Fellows Who Made the Game," 185.

45. Kate described the wedding ceremony in *TS*, 34.

46. Although Lajoie was originally credited with the remarkable batting average of .422 in 1901, later statisticians corrected an apparent mathematical error, making his average .405 (543 times at bat, 220 hits). *Spalding's Official Base Ball Guide* in 1906 shows him repeating the champion batting feats in 1905, with an average of .329. But Major League Baseball's *The Little Red Book* shows Lajoie's teammate, Elmer Flick, as leading the League that year with a .306 average. *The Little Red Book of Major League Baseball*, 29th ed. (New York: Al Munro Elias Baseball Bureau, Inc., 1954), 9.

47. GR, *AJ*, March 12, 1905.

48. Grantland Rice wrote more sequels and parodies of Casey than any other writer, somewhere in the neighborhood of thirty. Many of these verses have been either printed as anonymous or mistakenly credited to other persons. For example, "Casey's Revenge" is attributed to a James Wilson in a 1907 quarterly magazine, *The Speaker*. The quoted stanzas of "Casey's Revenge" are from GR, *Base-Ball Ballads*, 15–16. Rice tinkered with "Revenge" over the years, but didn't seem to improve it much. For comparison, see "Revenge" in GR, *Only the Brave*.

49. GR quoted in "A Poet Despite the City," *Vanderbilt Alumnus* 19, no. 3 (December 1933): 9; GR, *NT*, February 6, 1949.

50. GR, "Casey's Revenge," in *Base-Ball Ballads*, 13.

Chapter 7. Back Home

1. For Luke Lea's background, see Doyle, *Nashville*, 98, 163.

2. GR, *TS*, 35.

3. For the subsidizing of the *Nashville American*, see *NT*, September 9, 1908.

4. Ibid., May 12, 1907.

5. Ibid., May 14 and 12, 1907.

6. GR, *AJ*, May 16, 1903.

7. For the description of the noise outside Rice's office, see Waller, *Nashville, 1900–1910*, 190–91. For Rice's poetic comment, see GR, *NT*, May 15, 1907.

8. For Rice's typical working day, see GR, *TS*, 35; beyond this account in his memoirs, further detail was found by way of autobiographical comments scattered throughout various interviews he gave over the years. But mostly, Rice's incredible level of work by way of his bylines, editorships, and columns is self-evident to anyone who reads his record firsthand in the *Nashville Tennessean* itself from 1907 through 1910.

9. Verner M. Jones's recollection, *Vanderbilt Alumnus* 19, no. 5 (March 1934): 3.

10. *NT*, February 6, 1949.

11. GR, *NT*, October 8, 1907.

12. Ibid., October 1, 1907.

13. Ibid., October 5, 1907.

14. Ibid., October 29, 1907.

15. Ibid., January 29, 1908.

16. Ibid., October 9, 1907.

17. Ibid., October 3, 1907.

18. Ibid., November 15, 1908.

19. Ibid., May 12, 1907, and August 27, 1908.

20. Ibid., January 1 and March 6, 1908.

21. Ibid., January 29, 1908.

22. *Comet,* Vanderbilt University, 1909, 380–81.

23. For the statistics on the Nashville Vols, see *NT,* November 22, 1908. For Rice's success in renaming the ballpark, see Waller, *Nashville, 1900–1910,* 216–17.

24. GR, *NT,* September 20, 1908.

25. Ibid.; GR, *American Magazine* 72 (September 1911): 590–99.

26. For Carmack's vacillating position on prohibition, see Doyle, *Nashville,* 162–63.

27. Waller, *Nashville, 1900–1910,* 93.

28. *NT,* September 1 and August 30, 1908.

29. The general details of the Carmack shooting can be found in Waller, *Nashville, 1900–1910,* 90–104.

30. *NT,* November 10, 1908.

31. GR, *NT,* November 12, 1908.

32. Doyle, *Nashville,* 164–65.

33. *NT,* April 14, 1910. For the full Kipling poem, see *Rudyard Kipling's Verse* (New York: Doubleday, 1940), 226–29.

34. GR, *NT,* January 21, 1909.

35. For the fate of whiskey drinking in Nashville, see Waller, *Nashville, 1900–1910,* 103; Doyle, *Nashville,* 167. For Rice's need for an alcoholic lift, see *NT,* January 21, 1909.

36. GR, *NT,* November 6 and 10, 1908.

37. Ibid., November 25, 1907.

38. Ibid., November 3, 1907.

39. Ibid., November 16, 1907.

40. Ibid., November 4 and 12, and December 3, 1908; September 21, 1909.

41. Ibid., November 25, 1908.

42. John Heisman, "The Thundering Herd," *Collier's Illustrated Weekly* 82, no. 15 (October 13, 1928): 12–13 and ff.

43. *Nation* 81 (November 30, 1905): 437, quoted in Lucas and Smith, *Saga of American Sport,* 242; also see Moore, "Football's Ugly Decades," 178–79.

44. For the kicking distances, see Heisman, "The Thundering Herd"; for Rice's description of the Vanderbilt and Ohio State game in 1908, see GR, *NT,* November 15, 1908.

45. GR, *NT,* December 19, 1909.

46. Ibid., November 7, 1909.

47. For the Vanderbilt loss to Michigan in 1907, see GR, *NT*, October 30, 1907. For the Allerdice rave, see GR, *NT*, October 28, 1908.

48. GR, *NT*, October 31, 1908.

49. Ibid., November 1, 1908.

50. *NT*, November 1, 1908.

51. GR, *NT*, June 16, 1908.

52. For the general idea of Dixon's play, see Woodward, *Origins*, 352. For the local Nashville pitch for the play, see *NT*, March 6, 1909.

53. GR, *NT*, March 9, 1909.

54. Doyle, *Nashville*, 87–107.

55. Ibid., 107–14.

56. Ibid., 113–20.

57. Jack Orr, *The Black Athlete: His Story in American History*, 25–32; Jeffrey T. Sammons, *Beyond the Ring: The Role of Boxing in American Society*, 30–34.

58. Randy Roberts, *Papa Jack: Jack Johnson and the Era of White Hopes*, 20; Sammons, *Beyond the Ring*, 14. According to Arthur Ashe, Sullivan actually did fight a black man. Apparently during one of Sullivan's tours in 1884 in the Southwest, a "near-giant" black stepped into the ring to take up John L.'s customary challenge to all comers to survive two rounds against him. Sullivan was offering five hundred dollars to anyone who could do it. This was in Tombstone, Arizona. Although the challenger did well enough for the first few seconds, actually knocking Sullivan off-balance with a looping right to the head, Sullivan crisply eliminated the challenger, "who was carried out feet first like a ton of coal." Arthur Ashe, *A Hard Road to Glory: A History of the African-American Athlete*, vol. 1, 26.

59. Sammons, *Beyond the Ring*, 35.

60. GR, *NT*, December 4, 1908.

61. Ibid., December 19, 1908.

62. Ibid., January 6 and 18, 1909.

63. Ibid., January 20 and 23, 1909.

64. Ibid., May 18, 1910.

65. Orr, *The Black Athlete*, 30–31; GR, *NT*, August 12, 1910.

66. GR, *NT*, May 18, 1910, and January 31, 1909.

67. Ibid., June 27 and July 3, 1910.

68. See Sammons, *Beyond the Ring*, 34–47; Charles Samuels, *The Magnificent Rube: The Life and Gaudy Times of Tex Rickard*, Appendix IV.

69. Jack Johnson, *In the Ring and Out: The Classic Autobiography by the First Black Champion* (1927; reprint, London: Proteus, 1977), 144–45; Samuels, *The Magnificent Rube*, 170–71 and Appendix IV.

70. GR, *NT*, July 5, 1910; Sammons, *Beyond the Ring*, 39; Roberts, *Papa Jack*, 23; Samuels, *The Magnificent Rube*, 171–72.

71. Rader, *American Sports*, 3d ed., 142–44; Roberts, *Papa Jack*, 140–47. For the interview by Muldoon, see GR, *NT*, July 6, 1910. The implication was that Jeffries had been doped. According to Johnson, however, if it was true that Jeffries had been

doped up, then the members of Jeffries's party—Corbett, Sharkey, Edgren, and Choynski—should have stepped in and prevented Jeffries from fighting. Since they didn't, it is unlikely that he was doped up. "About the only dope which Jeffries suffered from was that administered by myself in the form of jabs and uppercuts to the jaw," said Johnson. Johnson, *In the Ring*, 145–46.

72. GR, *NT*, July 6, 1910.

73. Ibid., July 10, 1910.

74. Ibid., July 14, 1910.

75. Ibid., July 6, 15, and 20, 1910.

Chapter 8. The Big Show

1. GR, *NT*, December 11, 1910.

2. GR, *TS*, 37, 40.

3. Ralph McGill, "Too Many Vacant Chairs," *Atlanta Constitution*, July 15, 1954.

4. GR, *Base-Ball Ballads*, 116–18.

5. Spick Hall, *NT*, January 29, 1911.

6. GR, *NT*, December 11, 1910.

7. Irvin S. Cobb, "Introduction," in GR, *Songs of the Stalwart*, viii.

8. GR, *TS*, 38.

9. Allen Churchill, *Park Row*, 216, 290; Emery, *The Press and America*, 452.

10. Mott, *American Journalism*, 446–48.

11. Churchill, *Park Row*, 10.

12. Mott, *American Journalism*, 497; Richard Kluger and Phyllis Kluger, *The Paper: The Life and Death of the New York Herald Tribune*, 135, 205. In 1886 the first line of type for a newspaper was cast in the *New York Tribune* plant. After years of experimentation, the German immigrant Ottmar Mergenthaler invented the Linotype machine. It largely replaced setting type by hand. But not surprisingly, it was quite noisy. There were many other inventive efforts to replace by-hand typesetting, one of which was a patent filed for the Paige typesetter and subsidized by Mark Twain in the amount of $190,000. Twain said it could do just about everything except drink, swear, and go on strike. The machine turned out to be a failure. The Linotype succeeded. Mott, *American Journalism*, 499–501; Emery, *The Press and America*, 337–39.

13. Fowler, *Skyline*, 59–60.

14. The faster pace naturally included the newspaper business. According to journalism historian Frank Luther Mott, the first Hoe octuple press could produce 48,000 sixteen-page papers per hour; within ten years, some presses could deliver up to 144,000 such papers per hour.

15. Mott, *American Journalism*, 593; Simon Michael Bessie, *Jazz Journalism: The Story of the Tabloid Newspapers*, 76–77.

16. GR, *TS*, 38.

17. Anthony, *O Rare Don Marquis*, 116.

18. Fowler, *Skyline*, 49; GR, *TS*, 40

19. Anthony, *O Rare Don Marquis*, 142.

20. GR, *NT*, July 3, 1910.

21. GR, *TS*, 38–39.

22. For the circulation numbers, exaggerated and real, see *New York Evening Mail* (*NYEM*), August 3, 1912; Kluger and Kluger, *The Paper*, 182–86.

23. C. E. Van Loan in *NT*, May 22, 1910.

24. Ritter, *The Glory of Their Times*, 144–45. Of course, as professional baseball matured, it also began to lose some of its charm. Even the umpires were wising up. Going, going, gone were the days when managers and players could successfully fool the umpires. Hugh Fullerton told the true story of how a dead man was forced to pitch a game. This happened in 1885 in Kansas City. Ted Sullivan was managing. His pitcher was getting hit hard. Sullivan was trying to figure out how to get him out of the game (this was before the days when you could just trot out and pull your pitcher). The rules stated that unless a pitcher was injured, he had to pitch the game. Sullivan wasn't exactly wishing his pitcher any harm, but it would have been a relief if one of the liners whistling through the infield would hit and maim his pitcher, and maybe even break his arm or something like that. Suddenly, Sullivan got a brainstorm. He hastily hunted up a friendly doctor, and when the inning was finally over he instructed his pitcher to simply drop dead as quickly as possible in the next inning. On the second pitch the pitcher did just that; he threw up his hands and sank to the ground. Amid the tremendous excitement, the emergency doctor ran out onto the field, felt his heart, and pronounced the pitcher dead. More excitement. The sorrowing teammates carried the pitcher off the field. Ted ordered his crack twirler to warm up and finish the game. But the umpire stopped him, and told Sullivan, "You can't put in another pitcher." Stunned, Ted argued back: "Why not? The man is dead!" The umpire, not even blinking, said, "Well, I'm sorry for that, but the rules say he must be injured. This man is not injured. He died of a heart attack. Therefore he'll have to stay in or you'll forfeit the game." And so, the "dead man," who by then was sitting in the visiting club's dressing room smoking a cigarette while waiting for the undertaker's wagon, had to come out on the field and finish the game. Hugh Fullerton, from the Hearst News Service, *NT*, January 9, 1908.

25. Van Loan, *NT*, May 22, 1910.

26. *NYEM*, October 6, 1913.

27. For the pennant races in August, see *NYEM*, August 3, 5, and 7, 1912. For baseball players and unionization, see Harold Seymour, *Baseball, The Golden Age*, 169–95.

28. Seymour, *Baseball, The Golden Age*, 194; *New York Mail*, August 7, 1912. For the makeup of the National Commission, see Seymour, *Baseball, The Golden Age*, 9–11. The National Commission in 1912 included both Johnson and Herrmann, but Pulliam had a breakdown in 1909 and killed himself on July 29. Pulliam's suicide was perhaps triggered in part by the stress and strain of his job. By 1912 the third man on the Commission was Thomas J. Lynch, a former National League umpire. See *Little Red Book* (1954), 2; Seymour, *Baseball, The Golden Age*, 19–30.

29. GR, *NYEM*, August 14 and November 7, 1912.

30. Ibid., August 13, 1912.

31. Ibid., August 21 and September 12, 1912.

32. GR, *TS*, 229.

33. GR, *NYEM*, September 5 and 26, 1912.

34. *NYEM*, September 30, 1912.

35. GR, *NYEM*, October 7, 1912.

36. Ibid., September 30, 1912.

37. Ibid., October 3, 1912.

38. Seymour, *Baseball, The Golden Age*, 148.

39. Adams's observations appear in *NYEM*, October 8 and 9, 1912.

40. For descriptions of the press box in the new Polo Grounds, see Benson, *Ballparks*, 257–60; Reidenbaugh, *Take Me Out to the Ball Park*, 166–76; *NYEM*, August 12, 1911.

41. Writer Gene Fowler, in his memoirs, reminisced about these press boxes. The early ones, like the type Rice was accustomed to, were little more than two built-in benches set one behind the other. They were sometimes enclosed with wire. The fans used to enjoy looking over the shoulders of the writers and, from time to time, they didn't hesitate to make constructive criticisms. Fowler recalled an incident at Sportsman's Park in St. Louis when sportswriter W. O. McGeehan was writing about an outraged St. Louis fan who had cracked a pop bottle over the skull of center fielder Whitey Witt of the Yankees. When another St. Louis fan read McGeehan's working copy over McGeehan's shoulder, the partisan pushed a hot dog into McGeehan's face and shouted, "Send *that* to New York!" Compare these working conditions, Fowler said, to the plush boxes of today (this was in 1961) where sportswriters sit "like members of the board." At the Los Angeles Coliseum, Fowler pointed out, the reporters have a private elevator, cushioned swivel chairs, elbow room, and eagle's nest privacy well above the playing field. They also enjoy free refreshments and instant statistical information at their fingertips. Fowler, *Skyline*, 46–47. For further descriptions of typical press box atmosphere, see Kluger and Kluger, *The Paper*, 196; also, *NYEM*, October 12, 1912.

42. GR, *NYEM*, October 9, 1912.

43. Ibid., October 7, 1912.

44. Rube Goldberg, *NYEM*, October 8, 1912.

45. GR, *NYEM*, October 8, 1912.

46. Adams, *NYEM*, October 9, 1912.

47. For descriptions of Boston's Fenway Park, see Benson, *Ballparks*, 41–42; Reidenbaugh, *Take Me Out to the Ball Park*, 50.

48. Adams, *NYEM*, October 11, 1912; GR, *NYEM*, October 11, 1912.

49. Adams, *NYEM*, October 11 and 14, 1912.

50. *NYEM*, October 15, 1912.

51. GR, *NYEM*, October 15, 1912.

52. Ibid., October 15, 1912; Adams, *NYEM*, October 16, 1912.

53. Ritter, *The Glory of Their Times*, 102.

54. Ibid., 175.

55. GR, *NYEM*, October 16, 1912. Matty pitched three games, allowing only two earned runs, but lost all three on bad defensive play on the part of his teammates; when Yerkes crossed the plate with the winning run, the Giant players rushed to the mound and carried Matty on their shoulders off the field in tribute to his gamely played series. The players received 60 percent of the first four games, including the tie game, with the winning team receiving 60 percent of the $147,571.70.

56. GR, *NYEM*, October 17, 1912.

57. Ibid., October 18, 1912. The "Merkle boner," as it has come to be called over the years occurred on September 23, 1908. The Cubs and the Giants were battling for the pennant. In the last of the ninth inning, the two teams were tied, 1 to 1. With the Giants at bat, and with two out, Harry (Moose) McCormick was on first. Merkle singled to right. Moose went to third. With runners on first and third, Giant shortstop Al Bridwell then lined to right center field. McCormick scored. Merkle, who had started running for second base, saw both the ball rolling in the outfield and McCormick easily cross the plate for the winning score. He pulled up short of second base and ran gleefully toward the clubhouse. He never touched second base. Meanwhile, the Giant fans poured onto the field since everyone thought the game was over. But Johnny Evers of the Cubs had seen Merkle fail to touch second. Evers called to the center fielder, Artie Hofman, to go and get the ball. But Joe McGinnity, who was coaching third base for the Giants, realized what was going on. He ran onto the field and intercepted Hofman's throw to Evers, and threw the ball into the stands. From somewhere else, Evers found a ball anyway and stepped on second base for a putout on Merkle. The rule then was that to technically complete the play, and since Bridwell was on first, Merkle had to touch second to formally end the game. Failing that, Merkle was therefore out, and the Cubs protested that clearly the game should have continued since it was still a 1 to 1 tie. The Giants argued that since Merkle wasn't called out, he wasn't out. The protests went to Harry Pulliam, the league president. The game was ruled a tie. Since the two teams were tied after the regular season ended in early October, they had to play the tie game over for the pennant. The Cubs won the playoff, 4 to 2. Ritter, *The Glory of Their Times*, 97–100.

58. GR, *NYEM*, October 17, 1912.

59. Ritter, *The Glory of Their Times*, 157. For Rice's statement that Hooper's catch was his greatest baseball thrill, see GR, *American Magazine* 97, no. 41 (May 1924): 216–22.

60. McGraw, *NYEM*, October 19, 1912. For McGraw's actions toward Snodgrass, see McGraw, *My Thirty Years*, 16.

61. GR, *NYEM*, October 19, 1912.

Chapter 9. A Lousy Poet Emerged from the Argonne

1. GR, *NYEM,* November 12, 1912.

2. *NYEM,* November 4, 1912.

3. Seymour, *Baseball, The Golden Age,* 45–46.

4. GR, *TS,* 61.

5. Rader, *American Sports,* 3d ed., 194; GR, *Fore! . . . with a Glance Aft,* 8–9.

6. This account of the quaint origins of the American golfing tradition is essentially Rice's studied account appearing in his book, *Fore!* 7–9.

7. Rader, *American Sports,* 3d ed., 194.

8. GR, *Fore!* 12.

9. Ibid., 18–19.

10. Fred Russell, *PGA Tournament Program,* Shoal Creek, n.d., 2, VUL.

11. GR, *TS,* 37.

12. Ibid., 53.

13. Ibid., 53–54.

14. For Runyon's comment about the bravery of a New York blade of grass, see Fowler, *Skyline,* 50. For Rice's description of the pleasantness of golf, see *New York Tribune (NYT),* December 1, 1917.

15. GR, *NYEM,* August 27, 1912.

16. GR, *TS,* 55–56; *NYEM,* September 10, 1913.

17. GR and Jerome Travers, *The Winning Shot,* 195–96.

18. GR, *TS,* 62.

19. GR, *The Boys' Book of Sports,* 204–11.

20. For Ouimet's play to tie, see GR, *NYEM,* September 18, 1913; GR and Travers, *Winning Shot,* 60. For the poetic tribute, see GR, *NYEM,* September 20, 1913.

21. GR, *NYEM,* February 9, 1915.

22. Ibid., September 22, 1913.

23. *NYEM,* September 20, 1913. The comments from the *Standard* and the *Chronicle* were quoted in *NYEM,* September 22, 1913.

24. GR, *NYEM,* September 22, 1913.

25. Rader, *American Sports,* 3d ed., 196.

26. GR, *Fore!* 23; Travers and GR, *Winning Shot,* 192.

27. GR, *Winning Shot,* 83; also see GR, *NYT,* February 26, 1915.

28. GR, *Fore!* 23.

29. GR, *TS,* 77.

30. Kluger, *The Paper,* 130; Emery, *The Press and America,* 174–80. Bennett's contribution to American journalism is summarized in Mott, *American Journalism,* 229–38. Mott emphasized Bennett's self-advertising style and journalistic recklessness. He credits Bennett with evolving a philosophy of journalism that was "half sheer opportunism and half humanitarian idealism." When Bennett's paper was attacked in print for its amorality, the competing editors claimed Bennett was a disgrace to journalism, and threw some fairly creative epithets at him; they called him a "polluted wretch," a

"turkey buzzard," an "obscene vagabond," a "common bandit," and an "unprincipled adventurer." A more balanced view of Bennett is found in James L. Crouthamel, *Bennett's* New York Herald *and the Price of the Popular Press* (New York: Syracuse University Press, 1989).

31. Kluger, *The Paper*, 8, 167, 175, 178, 181–82; Emery, *The Press and America*, 415.

32. Dale Kramer, *Heywood Broun: A Biographical Portrait* (New York: Current Books, Inc., 1949), 42–43; Kluger, *The Paper*, 187; *NYT*, January 1, 1915.

33. Kluger, *The Paper*, 196.

34. Ibid.

35. GR, *NYT*, January 1, 1915.

36. Howard Mann, *NYT*, January 1, 1915.

37. GR, *NYT*, January 1, 1915. The distinction that follows between creature needs and human needs can be found in the *Purdue Alumnus* 69 (summer 1982): 2–9.

38. Ibid., April 27, 1917.

39. Kluger, *The Paper*, 192–93.

40. GR, *NYT*, May 1, 1917.

41. Ibid., April 11, 1917.

42. Ibid., September 1, November 6, and December 25, 1917.

43. Ibid., May 1 and November 13, 1917.

44. Ibid., December 1, 1917.

45. Ibid., May 4 and November 13, 1917.

46. Ibid., November 1, 1917.

47. Ibid., November 17, 1917.

48. Ibid., August 1, 1917; also published in *Songs of the Stalwart*, 166–68.

49. GR, *NYT*, January 1, 1918.

50. GR, *TS*, 89.

51. Ibid., 90.

52. Ibid., 90–91.

53. Ibid., 91–92.

54. Goering and Rice met when Goering was a gunner with the Eighteenth Machine Gun Battalion of the Sixth Division during the war. Goering was also a mechanic who was especially handy with automobiles and such. GR, *TS*, 337–38; see also Red Smith, "They Call Him Granny," *The Sign* 34, no. 5 (December 1954): 57–59.

55. GR, *NYT*, January 5, 1918.

56. Mott, *American Journalism*, 628; Virginia Tracy, *St. Louis Globe-Democrat*, interview with Rice, October 2, 1942.

57. GR, *NYT*, 93.

58. For Rice's artillery experience and his press officer story, see typed biographical profile, unsigned, n.d., 15, VUL. For the observations of the comrade in arms with Rice, see Edwin Alger's radio broadcast script on Grantland Rice, "Who's Behind the Name?" December 29, 1930, VUL.

59. Howell to GR, November 16, 1918, VUL.

60. Damon Runyon, "The Brighter Side," *New York Daily Mirror,* September 17, 1937.

61. GR, "To the Rhine," six-stanza poem, typed, n.d., VUL.

62. GR, "Ghosts of the Argonne," *Songs of the Open,* 180–81.

63. E. M. Heath to GR, November 18, 1918.

64. J. G. Wharton, quoting Damon Runyon, Universal Service Staff Correspondent, dateline: "With the American Army of Occupation, Coblenz, Germany, December 17, 1918." Appearing in Wharton, "Grantland Rice: Biographical Facts, Quotes, and Odds and Ends," typewritten list, December 15, 1948, VUL.

65. GR to "My dearest Kit," December 14, 1918, VUL. For Rice's food preferences, see Alger, "Who's Behind the Name," 7; John Lardner, on the eve of the 1940 National Open Golf Championship, banquet comments on GR, 2, VUL.

66. Runyon, "Brighter Side," *New York Daily Mirror,* September 17, 1937.

67. GR, *TS,* 93.

68. Ibid., 94–95.

Chapter 10. Booming the Game

1. For the troop shipments home, see *NYT,* March 8, 1919. For Wheeler's background, see John Wheeler, *I've Got News for You,* 11–14.

2. GR, *NYT,* January 8, 1919. For the Rice-Wheeler-Knox trio, see GR, *TS,* 96–97; Wheeler, *I've Got News,* 82–85; John Wheeler, "My Most Unforgettable Character," *Reader's Digest* 87, no. 524 (December 1965): 99–103.

3. GR, *TS,* 96–97.

4. Ibid., 97.

5. Frederick Lewis Allen, *Only Yesterday: An Informal History of the 1920s,* 1–12.

6. Mott, *American Journalism,* 634.

7. Ibid., 636, 648.

8. Emery, *The Press and America,* 553.

9. GR, *NYT,* March 2, 1919.

10. Ibid., March 12, 1919.

11. Ibid., March 12 and 16, 1919.

12. GR, "A Song to April," in Kieran, ed., *The Final Answer,* 84–85.

13. Seymour, *Baseball, The Golden Age,* 255. According to Seymour, the baseball officials had been pressuring the War Department to release their ballplayers for the 1919 season. The previous season had not been a good one, and the owners were nervous about the upcoming one. To ensure profits, they secretly agreed to limit club payrolls; this would mean lower salaries for the players. The owners also cut the roster size from twenty-five to twenty-one players. According to Colonel Huston, a Yankees partner, the New York club was going to be strictly a business proposition. But the owners guessed wrong about what was going to happen after the war. It turned out

that there was no need to shorten the season, for even with only 140 games they drew more than six and one-half million fans; had they played the additional fourteen games they could have sold more than seven million tickets, numbers that matched the best seasons before the war.

14. GR, *NYT*, March 21 and 29, 1919.

15. Ibid., March 6, 1919.

16. Seymour, *Baseball, The Golden Age*, 248–51.

17. GR, *NYT*, March 9, 1919.

18. Ibid., March 2, 1919. According to Seymour, 124 American and 103 National Leaguers enlisted in the armed forces. Seymour, *Baseball, The Golden Age*, 250.

19. GR, *NYT*, April 3, 1919.

20. Ibid., March 2, 1919.

21. Ibid., March 25 and April 6, 1919.

22. Ibid., January 26, 1921.

23. For an example of Rice-encouraged women's club tournaments, see ibid., May 28, 1917. Rice was an early supporter of women's golf and tennis competition. For the three sets of verse, see ibid., May 25, April 18, and May 17, 1919.

24. Ibid., June 13, 1919.

25. Ibid., June 26, 1919.

26. Samuels, *The Magnificent Rube*, 176–77.

27. The former president described Rickard: "With me on the gunboat was an old Western friend, Tex Rickard, of the Panhandle and Alaska and various places in between. He now has a large tract of land and some thirty-five thousand head of cattle in the Chaco, opposite Concepcion, at which city he was to stop. He told me that horses did not do well in the Chaco but that cattle throve, and while ticks swarmed on the east bank of the great river, they would not live in the west bank. Again and again he had crossed herds of cattle which were covered with the loathsome bloodsuckers; and in a couple of months every tick would be dead." Roosevelt also reported that the wild Paraguay Indians thoroughly trusted Rickard and worked eagerly and faithfully for him. Theodore Roosevelt, *Through the Brazilian Wilderness* (New York: Charles Scribner's and Sons, 1914), 40, 45.

28. Samuels, *The Magnificent Rube*, 182–87; Rader, *American Sports*, 3d ed., 146.

29. GR, *NYT*, June 28, 1919.

30. Ibid., May 18, 1919.

31. Randy Roberts, *Jack Dempsey: The Manassa Mauler*, 42–44, 48–49; Jack Dempsey, with Barbara Piattelli Dempsey, *Dempsey*, 114–15.

32. GR, *NYT*, June 29, 1919. As a matter of fact, during the war Rice had already come to this opinion about Dempsey and other fighters who stayed stateside. When Rice was reassigned to *Stars and Stripes*, he had originally been assigned duty on the sports section. But within two months, mostly due to Rice's urgings, the sports section was suspended. Rice argued that when fighters such as Dempsey and Fred Fulton were reported to be fighting over the size of their purse (which they did), this was demoralizing to the doughboys overseas fighting for their country. "The glorified, the

commercialized, the spectatorial sport of the past has been burnt out by gun fire." *Stars and Stripes,* July 26, 1918.

33. Regarding the arena's dimensions and seating capacity, see Samuels, *The Magnificent Rube,* 209. With Samuels, Rice said the arena could hold eighty thousand; Roberts (*Manassa Mauler,* 59) claimed a capacity of ninety-seven thousand.

34. GR, *NYT,* June 29, 1919.

35. Ibid., July 1, 1919.

36. Ibid., July 3, 1919.

37. GR, *TS,* 117.

38. Dempsey, with Dempsey, *Dempsey,* 102, 106; Roberts, *Manassa Mauler,* 57–58. Roberts cites John Lardner's version of Nelson's lemonade dip, viz., that Nelson borrowed a bathing suit from Jack Kearns with the intention of bathing in Lake Erie, but came upon the six barrels of lemon syrup before he got to the lake; after his bath his underwear had to be torn off him in strips, and an angry Kearns burned his suit.

39. According to Rickard's biographer, the promoters' gross receipts were $452,522 on a paid attendance of less than twenty thousand. After their expenses, including a forty-thousand-dollar government tax, and 7 percent donated by previous agreement to the Toledo Charity Fund, and various political payoffs, and even after selling off the arena for twenty-five thousand dollars, Rickard and his copromoter actually lost some money. Samuels, *The Magnificent Rube,* 212–13.

40. Dempsey, with Dempsey, *Dempsey,* 106.

41. GR, *NYT,* July 5, 1919.

42. W. O. McGeehan, *NYT,* July 5, 1919.

43. GR, *NYT,* July 5, 1919.

44. Ibid. For the Kipling reference, see "Fuzzy-Wuzzy," in *Rudyard Kipling's Verse,* 398. Fuzzy-Wuzzy fought in the early campaigns of the Soudan Expeditionary Force, and was a "first-class fightin' man."

45. GR, *NYT,* July 5, 1919.

46. Dempsey, with Dempsey, *Dempsey,* 115; GR, *NYT,* July 4, 1919.

47. GR, *NYT,* July 6, 1919.

48. Ibid., July 5, 1919.

49. Ibid.

Chapter 11. Who'll Cop the Series?

1. GR, *NYT,* June 17, 1919.

2. Ibid.

3. Ibid., April 19, 1919.

4. Ibid., June 7 and 17, 1919.

5. Ibid., August 26, 1919; *Little Red Book,* 5–6.

6. GR, *NYT,* August 8, 1919.

7. Seymour, *Baseball, The Golden Age,* 298.

8. There are different versions of this famous episode. Folklore has it as quoted in the text, "Say it ain't so, Joe." Perhaps more precise was a newspaper quote at the time, in which a youngster asked Joe Jackson, "It isn't true, is it Joe?" *NYT*, September 30, 1919. Another version is given by James T. Farrell, who as a nineteen-year-old at the time recalled that the exchange occurred after a baseball game on September 26. As Jackson and Happy Felsch left the park, about two hundred or so men and boys followed the players. A fan cried out, "It ain't true, Joe." The players did not turn back. The call was taken up by the trailing crowd and uttered many, many times as the players walked to their parked roadsters, "It ain't true, Joe!" Eliot Asinof, *Eight Men Out: The Black Sox and the 1919 World Series*, 163–64.

9. *NYT*, October 1, 1920.

10. Arnold Rothstein was later shot and killed during a poker game. When the F.B.I. dug into his files, they found reference to four affidavits implicating Rothstein in the 1919 fix, including specific mention of payments of eighty thousand dollars to the ballplayers. Asinof, *Eight Men Out*, 286.

11. Four years later, when Joe Jackson was suing for back pay, these confessions mysteriously turned up in the hands of Comiskey's attorney. It is reported that Comiskey couldn't explain how they got there. Seymour, *Baseball, The Golden Age*, 324–39.

12. Seymour, *Baseball, The Golden Age*, 329.

13. GR, *NYT*, September 23, 27, 28, and 30, 1919.

14. Porter Emerson Browne, *NYT*, October 8, 1919.

15. *NYT*, September 28, 1919.

16. GR, *TS*, 105.

17. GR, *NYT*, October 2, 1919.

18. Ibid.

19. Ibid., October 3, 1919.

20. Ibid., October 4, 1919.

21. Ibid., October 5, 1919.

22. Ibid., October 7, 1919.

23. Ibid., October 8, 1919.

24. Ibid., October 10, 1919.

25. Ibid., October 11 and 16, 1919.

26. Asinof, *Eight Men Out*, 94.

27. GR, *NYT*, October 18 and 25, 1919.

28. Ibid., October 28, 1919.

29. For Rice feeling like he'd been kicked, see GR, *TS*, 106.

30. GR, *NYT*, September 29, 1920.

31. Ibid., September 30, 1919.

32. Harry Chafetz, quoted in Seymour, *Baseball, The Golden Age*, 280–81.

33. For a discussion of the honesty of baseball, see Seymour, *Baseball, The Golden Age*, chapter 14, 272–93.

34. Ibid., 282.

35. GR, *NYT*, September 30, 1920.
36. Ibid., October 3, 1920.
37. Ibid., October 14, 1920.
38. Ibid., October 3, 1920.
39. Seymour, *Baseball, The Golden Age*, 331–39.
40. GR, *NYT*, October 10, 1919.
41. Ibid., October 14, 1920.
42. Seymour, *Baseball, The Golden Age*, 295–96; GR, *NYT*, October 14, 1920.
43. Seymour, *Baseball, The Golden Age*, 293.
44. GR, *NYT*, October 20, 1920.
45. Ibid., October 23, 1920.

Chapter 12. Uncle Sam, John Bull, and the Frogs

1. *NYT*, May 3, 1921.
2. GR, *NYT*, May 18 and 21, 1921.
3. Rader, *American Sports*, 3d ed., 195; GR, ed., *The Bobby Jones Story*, 52.
4. GR, *NYT*, May 25, 1921.
5. Ibid., May 26, 1921.
6. Ibid., May 28, 1921.
7. *NYT*, May 28, 1921.
8. GR, *NYT*, March 3, 1921.
9. Warren Harding, letters to GR, March 9 and 17, 1921, VUL. For the Lardner and Harding exchange, see *TS*, 327.
10. Henry P. Fletcher to GR, April 15, 1921, VUL. For the account of the presidential golf game, see GR, *NYT*, April 15, 1921.
11. GR, *TS*, 327.
12. Ring W. Lardner, "The Presidential Golf Might Be Better," Bell Syndicate release, May 1921, copy at VUL.
13. GR, *NYT*, June 5, 1921.
14. Ibid., June 2, 1921.
15. Ibid., May 22, 1921; GR, ed., *The Bobby Jones Story*, 3–5, 117–21.
16. GR, *Fore!* 15.
17. Rader, *American Sports*, 3d ed., 126–28.
18. GR, *NYT*, May 29, 1921.
19. Ibid., May 25, June 22, and September 7, 1921.
20. Ibid., June 2 and September 7, 1921.
21. Ibid., May 26, 1921.
22. Ibid., June 24, 17, and 22, 1921; Rader, *American Sports*, 3d ed., 192.
23. GR, *NYT*, June 21, 1921.
24. GR, *TS*, 156–68.
25. GR, *NYT*, May 27, 1921; Red Smith, *To Absent Friends*, 362.

26. GR, *NYT*, June 12, 1921.

27. Ibid., June 15, May 28, June 10, 1921.

28. Ibid., June 15 and 16, 1921; GR, *TS*, 170.

29. GR, *NYT*, June 26, 1921.

30. Ibid., June 12, 1921.

31. GR, ed., *The Bobby Jones Story*, 5–6.

32. Ibid., 10–14; GR, *TS*, 78.

33. GR, *TS*, 79.

34. GR, *NYT*, June 12 and 7, 1921.

35. Ibid., June 19, 9, and 12, 1921.

36. Ibid., July 17, 1921.

37. GR, *TS*, 79.

38. GR, *NYT*, July 3, 1921; GR, ed., *The Bobby Jones Story*, 55.

39. GR, *NYT*, April 5, 1921.

40. Ibid., January 27, 1920.

41. Ibid., December 29, 1920.

42. Ibid., December 29 and January 27, 1920.

43. For the French comment on Americans' inability to speak without figures, see Tunis, *The American Way in Sport*, 108.

44. Roberts, *Manassa Mauler*, 110.

45. For the comparison of Dempsey's purse with the president's salary, see Roberts, *Manassa Mauler*, 106. For Rice's comment, see GR, *NYT*, July 1, 1921.

46. GR, *NYT*, May 24, 1921.

47. Arnold Bennett quoted in Roberts, *Manassa Mauler*, 102. For Rice's estimation of the French esteem for Carpentier, see GR, *NYT*, June 8, 1921.

48. Rice's prefight analysis appears in *NYT*, July 1, 1921. Lardner's irritation is found in Dempsey, with Dempsey, *Dempsey*, 130–31.

49. Rice's prediction for the fight is found in *NYT*, July 1, 1921.

50. Kearns's advice appears in Dempsey, with Dempsey, *Dempsey*, 132.

51. GR, *NYT*, July 2, 1921.

52. Dempsey, with Dempsey, *Dempsey*, 135; Roberts, *Manassa Mauler*, 120.

53. For Kate Rice's story of seeing Carpentier before the fight, see GR, *TS*, 119–20.

54. *NYT*, July 3, 1921.

55. Roberts, *Manassa Mauler*, 123.

56. *NYT*, July 3, 1921.

57. GR, *NYT*, July 3, 1921.

58. Heywood Broun, *NYT*, July 3, 1921.

59. Roberts, *Manassa Mauler*, 127–29; Broun, *NYT*, July 3, 1921.

60. GR, *NYT*, July 3, 1921.

Chapter 13. It's the Big Blooie That Makes All the Talk

1. Gene Fowler recalled that the Society of Silurians was an illustrious group that didn't take itself too seriously. These "waggish founders used to dine informally at the old Brevoort, the Lafayette, or at chophouses where the ale and the conversation hit the spot." When they gathered at Toots Shor's round bar, they found themselves feeling older than a fossil of *any* prehistoric age since Toots didn't have any clocks in the joint, not even a calendar. Fowler himself dealt with such passes of time philosophically. As if speaking for the group, Fowler's own sustaining precept was: "Keep the spirit unbroken, win or lose; and never tarry too long in the lotus land of the might-have-been." Fowler, *Skyline*, 154–56.

2. Wheeler, "My Most Unforgettable Character," 99–103.

3. For comparison's sake, the major-league baseball player median salary was about seven thousand dollars. In 1924 the Cincinnati Reds averaged about eight thousand dollars per player. Ruth's salary of more than fifty thousand was extraordinary; but so was Rice's by any standard, in or out of sports. Outside of sports, even by the end of the decade, before the market crash, two thousand dollars was considered the minimum family income requirement for basic necessities, and 60 percent of American families were below that figure. Seymour, *Baseball, The Golden Age*, 346–47. Contract letter to Rice from Morgan Shuster, President of Centurion Publishers, Inc., February 1, 1921, VUL.

4. GR, *TS*, 330. W. O. McGeehan, *New York Herald Tribune* (*NYHT*), November 17, 1925.

5. For the 1921 relay broadcast, see Seymour, *Baseball, The Golden Age*, 346. For the statistics on the popularity of radio, see Allen, *Only Yesterday*, 11, 64, 137. For the *Tribune* account and Rice's own observations, see *NYT*, October 5, 1922.

6. GR, cited in Percy Hammond, "Oddments and Remainders," newspaper column, n.d., VUL.

7. GR, *TS*, 257–60.

8. GR, *NYT*, February 8, 1923.

9. Wheeler, *I've Got News*, 280–81.

10. GR, *TS*, 309–11.

11. Ibid., 311–12.

12. Ibid., 311.

13. GR, *NYT*, February 10, 1923.

14. Ibid., March 23 and 29, 1919.

15. Ibid., April 18 and March 30, 1919.

16. Ibid., April 18, 1919.

17. GR, *TS*, 102.

18. GR, *NYT*, April 9 and 10, 1919; GR, *TS*, 103.

19. GR, *NYT*, April 19 and 25, 1919.

20. Seymour, *Baseball, The Golden Age*, 430. For Ruth's bombarding, see GR, *NYT*, April 19, 1923.

21. GR, *NYT,* April 26, 1919.

22. Seymour, *Baseball, The Golden Age,* 436, 353.

23. GR, *NYT,* June 5, 1920.

24. Ruth's numbers and salary appear in Seymour, *Baseball, The Golden Age,* 423–33; also, see GR, *NYT,* February 23, 1923.

25. GR, *NYT,* February 16 and 17, 1923. According to Rice, Hugh E. Keogh of the *Chicago Tribune* was one of the finest columnists Rice had ever read. Known in print as HEK, Keogh could write, verse included, with the best of them. He authored many one-liners, including, "The race is not to the swift—but that is where to look," and "The art of self-defense—100 yards in 10 seconds." Keogh shared Rice's views with regard to sportsmanship: "The rules of sport are all founded on fair play." Keogh's career was a short one. He started up his column in 1905 and died in 1911.

26. GR, *NYT,* March 15, 1923.

27. Seymour, *Baseball, The Golden Age,* 55, 428–29, 438; also see Reidenbaugh, *Take Me Out to the Ball Park,* 190–94.

28. GR, *TS,* 107.

29. Seymour, *Baseball, The Golden Age,* 423–25.

30. Rader, *American Sports,* 3d ed., 133–34.

31. GR, *TS,* 114; GR, *NYT,* April 19, 1923.

32. GR, *NYT,* April 28, 1923.

33. Ibid., May 1, 1923.

34. Ibid., May 5, 1923.

35. Ibid., May 13, 1923.

36. Roberts, *Manassa Mauler,* 152.

37. GR, *NYT,* May 31, 1923.

38. Ibid., June 1, 2, 3, and 7, 1923.

39. Ibid., June 19, 1923.

40. Ibid., June 26, 1923.

41. Ibid., June 28, 1923.

42. Ibid., June 30, 1923.

43. GR, *TS,* 262.

44. GR, *NYT,* June 29, 1923.

45. Ibid., July 4, 1923.

46. Ibid., July 5, 1923.

47. Frederick B. Edwards, *NYT,* July 6, 1923.

48. GR, *NYT,* July 6, 1923.

49. Ibid., July 8, 1923.

50. Ibid., July 13, 1923.

51. Ibid., July 8, 1923.

52. Ibid., July 14, 1923; GR, *TS,* 81.

53. Ibid., July 15, 1923.

54. GR, *TS,* 80–81; GR, ed., *The Bobby Jones Story,* 79.

55. GR, *NYT,* July 16, 1923.

56. Ibid.

57. GR, ed., *The Bobby Jones Story,* 87.

58. Roberts, *Manassa Mauler,* 141–45.

59. Ibid., 142–43; Dempsey, with Dempsey, *Dempsey,* 140–41.

60. GR, *NYT,* July 27, 1923.

61. Ibid., July 28, 1923.

62. Ibid., August 25, 1923.

63. Ibid., September 11, 1923.

64. Ibid., September 15 and 16, 1923.

65. GR, *TS,* 1923.

66. GR, *NYT,* September 16, 1923.

67. Roberts, *Manassa Mauler,* 187.

68. GR, *NYT,* September 27, 1923.

69. Ibid., October 6, 1923.

70. Ibid., October 7, 1923.

71. Ibid., October 11, 1923.

72. Ibid., October 12, 1923.

73. Ibid., October 14, 1923.

74. GR, *TS,* 178; GR, *NYT,* October 14, 1923.

75. GR, *NYT,* October 15, 1923.

76. Ibid., October 16, 1923.

77. John Heydler, *NYT,* October 17, 1923.

78. GR, *NYT,* October 19, 1923.

79. Ibid., December 30, 1923.

Chapter 14. Mr. Fix-It

1. GR, *TS,* 337–38, 34.

2. Smith, *To Absent Friends,* 42.

3. For Rice's poetry, see GR, *TS,* 313; GR, in Kieran, ed., *Final Answer,* 102. For Lewis's quote about friendship, see C. S. Lewis, *The Four Loves,* 103.

4. GR, *TS,* 319.

5. Anthony, *O Rare Don Marquis,* 288; the limerick is on p. 303.

6. Ibid., 334.

7. Munsey was a rags-to-riches businessman who had made his money from grocery chains, real estate, hotels, and banking; he habitually bought up newspapers, fiddled with them, and often sold them at a loss or flat killed them off entirely. He was ruthless, often firing employees on whims. His ideas weren't all that bad, but his management was. Mott, *American Journalism,* 554–57, 637–40.

8. Anthony, *O Rare Don Marquis,* 290.

9. Ibid., 336.

10. Ibid., 605.

11. Gilbert Seldes, "The Singular—Although Dual—Eminence of Ring Lardner," *Vanity Fair* 24, no. 5 (July 1925): 45, 94.

12. Ring Lardner, Jr., *The Lardners: My Family Remembered*, 168–72.

13. Wheeler, *I've Got News*, 270–71.

14. Donald Elder, *Ring Lardner: A Biography*, 229.

15. Jonathan Yardley, *Ring: A Biography of Ring Lardner*, 200.

16. Lardner, Jr., *The Lardners*, 168.

17. Fowler, *Skyline*, 156–60.

18. GR, *TS*, 349; GR, "To a Dream I Left Behind Me," in *Songs of the Open*, 58–59.

19. Seldes, "The Singular . . . Ring Lardner," 45, 94.

20. Ring Lardner, "Mr. and Mrs. Fix-It, A Short Story of the Pestiferous Pastime of Minding Other People's Business," *Liberty* 2, no. 1 (May 9, 1925): 5–8.

21. Elder, *Ring Lardner*, 239.

22. Lardner, Jr., *The Lardners*, 169–70.

23. Sherwood Anderson, "Meeting Ring Lardner," *No Swank*, 1–7.

24. H. H. Niemeyer, "No Help From Famous Father," *St. Louis Post-Dispatch*, May 15, 1938, miscellaneous clippings, Florence Rice file, VUL.

25. Lardner, Jr., *The Lardners*, 236–37.

26. Niemeyer, "No Help."

27. Elder, *Ring Lardner*, 281; Lardner, Jr., *The Lardners*, 181, 185.

28. Letter from Ring Lardner to Kate Rice, n.d., VUL; Ring Lardner quoted in *New York Daily News*, October 6, 1929.

29. Ring Lardner, "I Can't Breathe, Unedited Confessions of a Very Popular Girl," *Cosmopolitan* 81, no. 4 (September 1926): 40–43, 201.

30. Lardner, Jr., *The Lardners*, 254.

31. Holograph poem from Floncy Rice to her father on Father's Day, n.d., VUL.

32. Emery, *The Press and America*, 449–53.

33. Mott, *American Journalism*, 450–53, 639; *New York Herald Tribune* (*NYHT*), March 18, 1924.

34. Emery, *The Press and America*, 453.

35. Contract from *NYHT* in GR archives, VUL.

36. Cohane, *Bypaths of Glory*, 63.

37. Knute K. Rockne, "The Four Horsemen," *Collier's* 86, no. 18 (November 1, 1930): 14–15, 39, 42.

38. GR, *TS*, 179–80; Rockne, "The Four Horsemen," 14.

39. John W. Heisman, "Rough Humor," *Collier's* 84, no. 19 (November 9, 1929): 21, 47–48.

40. GR and John W. Heisman, *Understand Football*. Also see John W. Heisman, "Fast and Loose," *Collier's* 82, no. 16 (October 20, 1928): 14–15, 54–55.

41. GR and Heisman, *Understand Football*, 6.

42. GR, *NYHT*, October 19, 1924.

43. Rockne, "The Four Horsemen," 39.

44. Wells Twombly interviewed in Randall Poe, "The Writing of Sports," *Esquire*

82, no. 4 (October 1974): 173–76, 373–79; Robert Lipsyte, *SportsWorld: An American Dreamland,* 172.

45. Jerome Holtzman, *No Cheering in the Press Box,* 146–49; Lipsyte, *SportsWorld,* 173–74; Murray Sperber, *Shake Down the Thunder: The Creation of Notre Dame Football,* 175–79; Fountain, *Sportswriter,* 29–30.

46. Holtzman, interview with George Strickler, *No Cheering,* 145–48.

47. There are two ways to read Strickler's quote regarding Rice acknowledging his alleged debt. One way is that some time later Rice acknowledged to Strickler the debt, but that when Rice eventually put his memoirs together, he got confused. But another way to read his quote is that Rice acknowledged his indebtedness to Strickler and that he admitted that he got it wrong in his book. If it were the second version, and since Rice's book, *The Tumult and the Shouting,* was published posthumously, this conversation would have required Rice to come back from the Other Side to fess up to Strickler about it. The benefit of the doubt is given to Strickler that he meant it in the first sense.

48. GR, *NYT,* October 14, 1923.

49. Strickler, in Holtzman, *No Cheering,* 148.

50. GR, *NYT,* October 1, 1922.

51. GR, *NYHT,* September 14, 1924.

Chapter 15. Sport for the Fun of It?

1. Walter Camp, "Walter Camp's All-America Team," *Collier's* 75, no. 1 (January 3, 1925): 12–13, 42–43.

2. Camp, "All-America Team," 43.

3. *NYHT,* March 15, 1925.

4. GR, "An All-Time All-American," *Collier's* 75, no. 19 (May 9, 1925): 10, 46.

5. GR, *TS,* 207.

6. Until the 1925 picks, the All-America Football Team had been called "Walter Camp's All-America Team." Then, in 1925, under Rice's direction, the selections were called "*Collier's* All-America Football Team." But by 1926 and beyond they were presented simply as "The All-America Football Team."

7. The four tests were simply that: 1) the first-team running back selections were drawn from the starting backs, not the second-half backs (as they were called), even though in some cases the second-half backs were the best backs on certain teams; 2) majority opinion ruled, as polled from recommendations from leading coaches, officials, and football writers; 3) season-long contributions held sway over mere end-of-season heroics; 4) when all else was equal, the veteran player was given the nod over the less experienced player. See *Collier's* 76, no. 25 (December 19, 1925): 6–8.

8. GR, *NYHT,* May 31, 1925.

9. See, for example, John Kieran, *NYHT,* April 11, 1925.

10. Harry Hooper quoted in Ritter, *The Glory of Their Times,* 136–38.

11. W. O. McGeehan, *NYHT,* April 11, 1925.

12. Ibid.

13. GR, *NYHT,* April 11 and 16, 1925.

14. W. O. McGeehan, *NYHT,* April 9, 1925.

15. Ibid., May 10, 1925.

16. GR, *TS,* 150–51. Instead of opposing sports celebrity writing, the sportswriters were quite comfortable with it. The celebrities weren't doing the writing; the sportswriters were. Even though they received no recognition, the sportswriters earned income at the practice. Therefore it is no surprise, for example, that when Judge Landis tried to limit major-league players from "writing" on their sports—a common practice during the World Series—the New York chapter of the Baseball Writer's Association of America went on record against such limitations: "The New York Chapter feels that it is futile and presumptuous to attempt to place any limitations whatsoever upon the writing of sports or the purchasing of sport articles from any sources considered desirable by the editors." *NYHT,* November 11, 1925.

17. Voigt, *American Baseball,* vol. 2, 156; *NYHT,* August 30, 1925.

18. Seymour, *Baseball, The Golden Age,* 431–33.

19. Voigt, *American Baseball,* vol. 2, 157–58; Seymour, *Baseball, The Golden Age,* 428.

20. GR, *TS,* 114; *Collier's* 75, no. 25 (June 20, 1925): 10, 44.

21. GR, *TS,* 107–8.

22. GR, *Collier's* 75, no. 25 (June 20, 1925): 10, 44.

23. W. O. McGeehan, *NYHT,* April 11, 1925.

24. Robert Frost, *The Poetry of Robert Frost* (New York: Holt, Rinehart and Winston, 1969), 121–22.

25. GR, *NYHT,* December 2, 1925.

26. *NYHT,* October 10, 1925.

27. GR, *NYHT,* October 9, 1925.

28. Ibid., September 15, 1925.

29. Rader, *American Sports,* 3d ed., 139; GR, "Is Red Grange the Greatest?" *Collier's* 74, no. 25 (December 20, 1924): 14, 38.

30. GR, *NYHT,* October 24, 1925.

31. Rader, *American Sports,* 2d ed., 139; *New York Times,* November 22, 1925.

32. GR, *NYHT,* November 22, 1925.

33. Rader, *American Sports,* 3d ed., 141; GR, *NYHT,* November 27, 1925.

34. GR, *NYHT,* November 27, 1925.

35. Ibid., October 4, November 23, and December 13, 1925.

36. Rader, *American Sports,* 3d ed., 141–42.

37. GR, *NYHT,* December 18, 1925.

38. Rader, *American Sports,* 3d ed., 140–42.

39. GR, *NYHT,* December 6, 1925.

40. Ibid., December 15, 1925.

41. Ibid., December 17, 1925.

42. Ibid., December 30, 1925.

Chapter 16. Somebody Will Paste Mr. Dempsey Some Day, but When—and Who?

1. GR, *NYHT,* January 15, 1926.

2. Ibid., March 17 and May 19, 1926.

3. Ibid., May 17, 1926.

4. Rader, *American Sports,* 3d ed., 148–49; Roberts, *Manassa Mauler,* 216–19.

5. Gene Tunney, "A Man Must Fight," *Collier's* 89, no. 9 (February 27, 1932): 24–26, 56.

6. Ibid., *Collier's* 89, no. 8 (February 20, 1932): 14–15, 36.

7. Ibid., *Collier's* 89, no. 9 (February 27, 1932): 56.

8. GR, *TS,* 139–40.

9. GR, *NYHT,* September 18, 1927.

10. GR, "Who Gets the Next Million?" *Collier's* 75, no. 23 (June 6, 1925): 10, 28.

11. GR, *NYHT,* June 6, 1925.

12. GR, "Watch That Leatherneck!" *Collier's* 76, no. 13 (September 26, 1925): 23.

13. Rader, *American Sports,* 3d ed., 44–46.

14. Tunney, "A Man Must Fight," *Collier's* 89, no. 12 (March 19, 1932): 12–13, 36–37.

15. GR, *TS,* 142–43.

16. Tunney, "A Man Must Fight," *Collier's* 89, no. 12 (March 19, 1932): 13.

17. GR, *NYHT,* January 30, 1926.

18. GR, *TS,* 143.

19. For these prefight activities, see Tunney, "A Man Must Fight," *Collier's* 89, no. 13 (March 26, 1932): 16–17, 55–58.

20. GR, *NYHT,* September 9 and 16, 1926.

21. Ibid., September 19, 1926; Roberts, *Manassa Mauler,* 226.

22. Fowler, *Skyline,* 280–81.

23. GR, *TS,* 147.

24. GR, *NYHT,* September 23, 1926.

25. Ibid., September 24, 1926.

26. Tunney, "A Man Must Fight," *Collier's* 89, no. 13 (March 26, 1932): 55.

27. *NYHT,* September 24, 1926.

28. Ibid.

29. GR, *TS,* 147–50.

30. Ring Lardner ghosting for Rice's overnighter, *NYHT,* September 25, 1926.

31. GR, *NYHT,* October 1, 3, and 7, 1926.

32. Ibid., October 7, 1926.

33. Tunney, "A Man Must Fight," *Collier's* 89, no. 13 (March 26, 1932): 56–57.

34. GR, *NYHT,* October 13, 17, 19, 20, 28, 31, and November 2, 1926.

35. Ibid., December 7, 1926.

36. Seymour, *Baseball, The Golden Age,* 382–84.

37. Ibid., 385.

38. *NYHT,* January 28, 1927.

39. GR, *NYHT,* December 22, 1926.

40. Ibid., December 26, 1926.

41. Ibid., January 8, 1927.

42. Ibid., September 22, 1927. The four Dempsey fights prior to the second Tunney fight produced these gates: Carpentier, $1.6 million; Firpo, $1.2 million; Tunney, $2 million; and Sharkey, $1 million.

43. Ibid., July 19 and 20, 1927.

44. Ibid., July 22 and 29, 1927. W. O. McGeehan, *NYHT,* August 22, 1927.

45. GR, *NYHT,* September 22, August 5 and 10, 1927.

46. Ibid., September 13, 18, and 21, 1927.

47. Ibid., September 19, 1927.

48. Ibid., September 19, 1927.

49. This prefight discussion of a possible fix, including the wording of the fight contract, appears in Tunney, "A Man Must Fight," *Collier's* 89, no. 13 (March 26, 1932): 57–58.

50. GR, *TS,* 152; Tunney, "A Man Must Fight," *Collier's* 89, no. 14 (April 2, 1932): 12–13, 51–52.

51. GR, *NYHT,* September 23, 1927; Rader, *American Sports,* 3d ed., 149.

52. GR, *NYHT,* September 23, 1927; Tunney, "A Man Must Fight," *Collier's* 89, no. 14 (April 2, 1932): 12.

53. This account of the drama of round seven relies on the following: Roberts, *Manassa Mauler,* 258–59; Tunney, "A Man Must Fight," *Collier's* 89, no. 14 (April 2, 1932): 51; GR, *NYHT,* September 23, 1927; and Dempsey, with Dempsey, *Dempsey,* 191–205.

54. Tunney, "A Man Must Fight," *Collier's* 89, no. 14 (April 2, 1932): 52; Dempsey, with Dempsey, *Dempsey,* 206.

55. GR, *NYHT,* September 30, 1927, and July 27, 1928; W. O. McGeehan, *NYHT,* July 27, 1928; Tunney, "A Man Must Fight," *Collier's* 89, no. 14 (April 2, 1932): 52.

Chapter 17. Shadows from the Night

1. Ring Lardner, "The Keeper of the Bees," *Collier's* 83, no. 19 (May 11, 1929): 28, 56.

2. Lardner, Jr., *The Lardners,* 198; GR, *TS,* 336.

3. GR, *TS,* 337; Lardner, Jr., *The Lardners,* 204.

4. GR, *NYHT,* September 3, 1929.

5. Ring Lardner, "Bobby or Bust," *Collier's,* 84, no. 24 (December 21, 1929): 19, 51.

6. Ibid., 19; GR, *NYHT,* September 8, 1929.

7. GR, *NYHT,* September 3, 1929.

8. Allen, *Only Yesterday,* 266–81.

9. GR, *NYHT,* September 27, 1929.

10. GR, *TS,* 309; Allen, *Only Yesterday,* 280.

11. GR, *NYHT,* September 20, 1929.

12. John Wheeler, "My Most Unforgettable Character," 99–103.

13. Coca-Cola Company, *The Red Barrel,* April 15, 1930, 6.

14. Allen, *Only Yesterday,* 137–38; Roberts, *Manassa Mauler,* 256.

15. Coca-Cola Company, *The Red Barrel,* August 1931, 4–6.

16. GR, *TS,* 112–13.

17. *New York Telegram,* December 3, 1930.

18. Typed radio script of Rice interviewing Lardner, n.d., VUL.

19. Louis Reid, "The Loudspeaker," *New York American,* December 15, 1931.

20. Lardner, Jr., *The Lardners,* 202.

21. GR, *TS,* 267; GR, *New York Sun (NYS),* May 16 and 17, 1930.

22. Irvin Cobb interviewed by Rice, full text in Coca-Cola Company, *The Red Barrel,* June 1931, 19–21. Twenty Grand, the winning horse, was not the only record-setter that year: Coca-Cola reported that they dispensed nearly forty-seven thousand bottles of Coca-Cola from their many stands at Churchill Downs, also a record.

23. John Wheeler, "My Most Unforgettable Character," 99–103.

24. Lardner, Jr., *The Lardners,* 306; GR, *TS,* 338; GR, "How Will They Handle 'Em All?" *Collier's* 76, no. 14 (October 3, 1925): 19.

25. GR, *NYS,* June 2 and 21, July 2, 1930.

26. Ibid., July 3, 1930.

27. Ibid., July 13 and 14, 1930.

28. GR, *TS,* 84.

29. GR, *NYS,* September 23, 1930.

30. Ibid., September 25, 1930.

31. Ibid., September 27, 1930.

32. GR, ed., *The Bobby Jones Story,* 293, 295.

33. Ibid., 292.

34. GR, *NYS,* October 28, 1930.

35. Aldous Huxley, "Whither Are We Civilizing," *Vanity Fair* 30, no. 2 (April 1928): 64, 124; Huxley, "Progress," *Vanity Fair* 29, no. 5 (January 1928): 69, 105.

36. Aldous Huxley, "On Making Things Too Easy," *Vanity Fair,* 25, no. 5 (January 1926): 66.

37. Rader, *American Sports,* 3d ed., 116–50.

38. Mandell, *Sport,* 217.

39. GR, *NYS,* April 1, 16, and 30, 1932.

40. Ibid., June 7, 1932.

41. Ibid., July 7, 1932.

42. Ibid., July 15, 1932.

43. Ibid., July 26, 1932.

44. Ibid., August 1, 2, 3, 5, and 6, 1930. These five descriptive snippets do not do Rice or his reporting justice. It is better to read his entire and lengthy accounts of these and other Olympic events. When so focused and concentrated, as he was during these games, Rice was awfully good at what he did. Rice may have described Carr's run as a master painting a masterpiece, but in all truth, Rice's reporting for these sixteen days was itself masterful. For lengthier discussions of Rice's reporting see William Harper, "So Let's Keep Room for a Song," *World University Games Proceedings* (summer 1993): 99–114; Harper, "Just Sport," *Quest* 45, no. 4 (November 1993): 448–59.

Chapter 18. With Roving Heart and Restless Feet

1. Lucas and Smith, *Saga of American Sport,* 342–63; Rader, *American Sports,* 3d ed., 207–12.

2. Rader, *American Sports,* 3d ed., 215.

3. David Wallechinsky, *The Complete Book of the Summer Olympics* (Boston: Little Brown, 1996), 200–201.

4. Rader, *American Sports,* 3d ed., 215–16.

5. GR, *NYS,* July 23 and August 5, 1932.

6. In Babe's high jump performance in Los Angeles, after clearing the bar for a new world record (along with Jean Shiley), the judges declared her "western roll" illegal because her head preceded the rest of her body over the bar. She was still given a share of the world record, but deprived of her third gold medal. A bit later her style was legalized. Wallechinsky, *Complete Book of the Summer Olympics,* 219.

7. GR, *NYT,* August 9, 1932.

8. Holtzman, *No Cheering,* 62–66; Paul Gallico, *Farewell to Sport,* 290–91; GR, *TS,* 239–40.

9. Paul Gallico, "The Texas Babe," *Vanity Fair* 39, no. 2 (October 1932): 36, 71.

10. GR, *TS,* 238.

11. Ibid., 340.

12. GR, "Ring Lardner," *NYS,* September 27, 1933.

13. GR, "To the Last of All," *NYS,* September 22, 1933.

14. Dempsey, with Dempsey, *Dempsey,* 172–73.

15. GR, "Facing the Breaks," *NYS,* September 26, 1933.

16. GR, "Mike Donlin," *NYS,* September 28, 1933.

17. GR, *NYS,* September 28, 1933.

18. GR, *TS,* 260–61.

19. GR, "To W. O. M.," *NYS,* December 6, 1933.

20. GR, *TS,* 329.

21. Ibid., 333.

22. Fowler, *Skyline,* 160–61.

23. Gallico interviewed in Holtzman, *No Cheering,* 70–71.

24. GR, *NYS*, August 13, 1933; Fowler, *Skyline*, 46.

25. GR, *TS*, 134–36.

26. For Rice's syndication numbers, see *Vanity Fair* 39, no. 2 (October 1932): 40.

27. Gallico in Holtzman, *No Cheering*, 71–72.

28. Swope quoted in Fowler, *Skyline*, 180–81.

29. Frederick Lewis Allen, *Since Yesterday: The 1930s and America*, 124–27.

30. Ibid., 129.

31. Tommy Armour, "The Falling Tide of Color in Sport," *Vanity Fair* 42, no. 5 (July 1934): 30–31, 64, 68.

32. GR, *TS*, 314–17.

33. GR, *NYS*, March 21, 1934.

34. Ibid., March 19 and 31, 1934.

35. GR, *TS*, 251.

36. Allen, *Since Yesterday*, 119–24.

37. GR, *NYS*, February 2, 1934. For Rice's hunting interests, see *TS*, 342–47.

38. Robert Woodruff and Rice were quite good friends for more than twenty years, so much so that on May 1, 1951, Woodruff gave a dinner at the Links in New York in Rice's honor. The occasion was to make the announcement that an anonymous donor (one individual and one corporation) had given the Columbia University Graduate School of Journalism fifty thousand dollars to establish a Grantland Rice Fellowship Fund for up-and-coming journalists. The award was set up to commemorate Rice's fifty years of distinguished and notable work in the newspaper business. It was administered by the New York Community Trust. According to Joseph W. Jones, the retired senior vice-president of Coca-Cola and Woodruff's assistant for forty years, it was Woodruff who was the anonymous individual donor and Coca-Cola who was the corporate donor. Each party gave twenty-five thousand dollars to the Fellowship. This information is contained in personal correspondence from Mr. Jones, February 17, 1987, wherein the two parties are identified and permission given to so identify in this book. These scholarships are still being awarded in journalism at Columbia University.

39. GR, *NYS*, December 20, 1933.

40. Ibid., December 19, 1933.

41. GR, *TS*, 344–46. A good deal of background information regarding the Ichauway Plantation, the hunts, and the eventual last resting place of that glorious wild turkey was kindly provided in an interview with Mr. Joseph W. Jones. Before the turkey landed at Ichauway, Rice had the mounted bird sent to his New York apartment. When it arrived, and when the startled Kate saw this gobbler at the door—standing three feet high and sporting an eight-inch beard—she instructed her husband, the hunter, to send it back to where it belonged. That's how it came home to roost. According to Jones, to this day the turkey rests where it was first placed alongside the fireplace in Woodruff's dining room at Ichauway—a lasting monument to the Grantland Rice hunting style. See also Charles Elliott, *"Mr. Anonymous," Robert W. Woodruff of Coca-Cola* (Atlanta: Cherokee Publishing Company, 1982), 193–94.

Chapter 19. Sunshine Park

1. GR, *NYS*, April 24, 1941.

2. Ibid., May 2, 1941.

3. Ibid., April 24, 1941.

4. Ibid., April 25, 1941.

5. Ibid., May 5, 1941.

6. Ibid., May 5 and 9, 1941.

7. Ibid., May 5 and 7, 1941.

8. Robert Riger, *The Athlete* (New York: Simon and Schuster, 1980), 18–19.

9. GR, *NYS*, May 27, 1941.

10. Ibid., July 7, 1941.

11. Ibid., August 12, 1941.

12. Ibid., May 27, 1941. Rice's viewpoint is reminiscent of a chance comment by William Carlos Williams: "They've got it down to a science, where there's nothing to it any more." William Carlos Williams, *The Embodiment of Knowledge* (New York: New Directions, 1974), 51.

13. Voigt, *American Baseball*, vol. 2, 255–57.

14. Ibid., 256; GR, *NYS*, August 7, 1941.

15. *NYS*, August 19, 1941; Voigt, *American Baseball*, vol. 2, 257.

16. Rader, *American Sports*, 3d ed., 169; Voigt, *American Baseball*, vol. 2, 256–57.

17. Rader, *American Sports*, 3d ed., 220–21.

18. GR, *NYS*, March 24 and 30, 1941.

19. *NYS*, June 26, 1941.

20. Ibid., June 30, 1941.

21. GR, *NYS*, June 21, 1941; *NYS*, August 23 and 25, 1941.

22. Fred Russell, *Nashville Banner*, August 21, 1941. Rice had been a member in good standing of a number of clubs, including Coffee House, Dutch Treat, and The Players. In a letter dated May 13, 1942, Rice tendered his resignation from The Players due primarily to his financial predicament. He specifically mentioned in that letter the double burden of increased taxes and the expenses related to old relatives. Letter from Rice to Whitney Darrow, May 13, 1942; the letter is in the Hampden-Booth Theatre Library in New York.

23. Letter from S. George Little to Grantland Rice, December 16, 1944, VUL.

24. GR, *NYS*, June 19 and 20, 1941.

25. *Philadelphia Record*, September 25, 1942.

26. GR, *TS*, 263.

27. Ibid., 263–65.

28. Frank Graham, *New York Journal-American*, July 14, 1954; Red Smith, *The Sign* (December 1954): 58, 61; Red Smith, "My Press-Box Memoirs," *Esquire* 84, no. 4 (October 1975): 202–3, 250.

29. Bruce Barton, *New York Daily Mirror* (*NYDM*), March 12, 1951.

30. GR, *NYDM*, March 5, 1951.

31. Dan Parker, *NYDM*, March 4, 1951.

32. McNulty, in a letter to Red Smith published as a column, "A Letter About Granny," in Red Smith, *To Absent Friends*, 45–46.

33. Red Smith, *The Best of Red Smith*, 27.

34. GR, *NYT*, January 28 and 30, 1920.

35. Russell, *Bury Me in an Old Pressbox*, 195–96.

36. Red Smith, *The Best of Red Smith*, 27; also see Smith, "Granny's Horse Park," *To Absent Friends*, 49–51.

37. GR, *NYDM*, March 7, 1950, and March 13, 1951.

38. Russell, *Bury Me in an Old Pressbox*, 196.

39. GR, *NYDM*, March 7, 1950, and March 14, 1951.

40. GR, *TS*, 277; Russell, *Bury Me in an Old Pressbox*, 196. After Granny's death, Sunshine Park established journalism scholarships in his name at the University of Florida and Florida State. Sunshine also established an annual race in his honor, the Grantland Rice Handicap. See Red Smith, *NYHT*, March 18, 1958.

41. GR, "Of Late Years," in Kieran, ed., *Final Answer*, 33.

42. Cohane, *Bypaths of Glory*, 135, 145–46.

43. Fred Russell, retired sportswriter and editor of *Nashville Banner*, interview.

44. Cohane, *Bypaths of Glory*, 135.

45. GR, *TS*, 271.

46. Bolling Rice, the youngest of the three Rice brothers, was too ill to travel to California. He was suffering from an enlarged heart and a thyroid condition. He would die in 1950. John died in 1953. Grantland, the oldest of the three, would outlive both of his brothers. Letter from Bolling to Grantland, April 4, 1950, VUL.

47. "The Grantland Rice Trophy," *Vanderbilt Alumnus* 34, no. 3 (January–February 1949): 11; Fred Russell, "Professor Wallace Stole the Show," *Nashville Banner*, December 29, 1948.

48. Letter from GR to Avery Brundage, June 21, 1949; letter from Avery Brundage to GR, June 25, 1949, VUL. Also see Allen Guttmann, *The Games Must Go On: Avery Brundage and the Olympic Movement*, 26–27, 30.

49. GR, *NYDM*, December 13, 1951.

50. Letter from Avery Brundage to Gustavus Kirby, dated December 28, 1951; letter from Gustavus T. Kirby to Grantland Rice, dated January 24, 1952, VUL.

51. Letter from GR to Gus Kirby, n.d., VUL.

52. Wallechinsky, *Complete Book of the Summer Olympics*, 165, 186.

53. GR, *TS*, 235–36.

Chapter 20. A Sporting Epitaph

1. GR, "A Sporting Epitaph," in Kieran, ed., *The Final Answer*, 66.

2. GR, *NYDM*, July 18, 1954.

3. Letter from Rod Warren to Paul Lewis of the D'Arcy Advertising Co., September

9, 1954; letter from Warren to Robert Woodruff, president of Coca-Cola, October 11, 1954; memorandum from E. D. Sledge, Coca-Cola advertising executive, to Woodruff, October 13, 1954; letter from Woodruff to Warren, October 19, 1954; letter from Warren to Woodruff, October 25, 1954, Robert W. Woodruff papers at Emory University, Special Collections.

4. Gerald Holland, "The Golden Age Is Now," *Sports Illustrated* 1, no. 1 (August 16, 1954): 46.

5. GR, "Golf's Greatest Putt," *Sports Illustrated* 1, no. 1 (August 16, 1954): 80–81. Rice's original coverage of the tournament in the *NYHT* began on June 28, 1929, and concluded on July 1, 1929. Rice had picked Jones to win.

6. Fred Russell, *Nashville Banner,* July 14, 1954.

7. GR, *TS,* 355.

8. GR, *TS,* 355–56.

9. There are differing accounts of those last few hours of Rice's life. In many he was described as working at his typewriter on his next Sportlight column and keeling over on the spot. This is the way it should have been—dying while hunkered down over his typewriter, working "until at last a bony hand," as one of his verses went. This is a wonderfully romantic ending, but apparently it is not accurate. Sportswriters Bob Considine and Dave Camerer had Rice finishing a column and going to his offices, having remembered something he had forgotten to do. They said he collapsed while dictating to his secretary. Bob Considine, "Grantland Rice Memorial Lecture," Graduate School of Journalism, Columbia University, February 21, 1958, Woodruff papers, Emery University. This account reinforces Charles Fountain's version in his book on Rice. Fountain was able to interview Catherine Mecca, Rice's secretary for his last ten or so years. Rice had apparently begun another column at his home, but he was having difficulty typing; about four hundred words into a piece on which sports are hazardous to an athlete's health, he quit in midsentence. Charles Goering drove him to the Sportlight offices sometime after eleven o'clock. He gave his Willie Mays column to Mecca for the syndicate, and then began going over his mail with her. In conversing with her, his speech began to slur. She asked after him, and he said he was all right. He excused himself and went to the men's room. Mecca, concerned, found Jack Eaton and asked him to check on Rice. Eaton found Rice in the men's room dazed and incoherent. He was suffering a stroke. Fountain, *Sportswriter,* 286–87. Regarding Rice's intention to watch the All-Star game that day on television, his ownership of a television is inferred from the existence of a television repair bill for about this time and for his home address on Fifth Avenue. This is found in his papers at VUL.

10. Bruce Barton, "Grantland Rice," eulogy delivered July 16, 1954. Copy in R. W. Woodruff papers, Emory University. Also in *TS,* xi–xiii.

11. Ralph McGill, *Atlanta Constitution,* July 16, 1954.

12. William Randolph Hearst, Jr., *New York Journal-American,* July 18, 1954.

13. Bill Henry, *Los Angeles Times,* July 19, 1954.

14. Bob Cooke, *NYHT,* July 15, 1954.

15. Henry McLemore, *Los Angeles Times,* July 15, 1954.

16. Ibid., July 20, 1954.

17. Vincent X. Flaherty, *New York Journal-American,* July 14 and 19, 1954.

18. Frank Graham, *New York Journal-American,* July 14, 1954.

19. Dan Parker, *NYDM,* July 15, 1954.

20. Stuyvesant Wainwright, "The Late Grantland Rice," Congress of the United States, *Congressional Record,* 1954: 11483–84; Ned Cronin, *Los Angeles Daily News,* July 15, 1954.

21. Jimmy Cannon, *New York Journal-American,* July 16, 1954.

22. Cronin, *Los Angeles Daily News,* July 15, 1954.

23. Jimmy Cannon, *Nobody Asked Me, But . . .: The World of Jimmy Cannon,* 296; Red Smith, "World's Greatest Saloonkeeper," *To Absent Friends,* 5–7.

24. Smith, *To Absent Friends,* 48; Ed Sullivan, "Little Old New York," *New York Daily News,* n.d., VUL.

25. Guest List for Grantland Rice Dinner, Sunday, October 31, 1954. R. W. Woodruff papers, Emery University.

26. Gene Fowler, "The Hat," in the program for the Grantland Rice Dinner, at Toots Shor's, October 31, 1954. R. W. Woodruff papers, Emery University.

27. Bill Cunningham, "Dinner for Granny Unique in Sports," *Boston Herald,* November 2, 1954; Dick Young, "Granny's Party Greatest of All," *The Sporting News,* November 10, 1954; Smith, *To Absent Friends,* 47–48.

28. Cunningham, *Boston Herald,* November 2, 1954.

29. Kate, like a trooper, attended all of these ceremonies; in the various pictures of her at these affairs she appears to be quite sad in spite of the merriment going on around her. In a letter to Robert Woodruff shortly after the Toots Shor birthday party in November 1954, Kate wrote that she was still under a doctor's care (she lost her own mother that month) and that she hoped time would heal her horrible aching and loneliness at the loss of her dear Granny. Kate Rice was instrumental in seeing to it that her husband's memory wouldn't be forgotten when she donated his collected papers and personal library to Vanderbilt University. She died in 1966. Floncy died in 1973 in Honolulu. The Sportsmanship Brotherhood information comes from the general information handed out at the First Annual Grantland Rice Memorial Award Luncheon booklet and seating list. Robert W. Woodruff papers, Emery University.

30. Wells Twombly interviewed in Poe, "The Writing of Sports," 378; Ibid., 174; Lipsyte, *SportsWorld,* 172–73.

31. GR, "An Old Greek Custom," *Collier's* 89, no. 11 (March 12, 1932): 26.

32. Rachael Sargent Robinson, *Sources for the History of Greek Athletics* (published by the author, 1927), 116–17.

33. GR, "An Old Greek Custom," 26.

34. Marshall Hunt, interviewed in Holtzman, *No Cheering,* 30. Randall Poe has referred to the knocking school as the "Sourdough school," in "The Writing of Sports," 175.

35. Smith, "My Press-Box," 203.

36. Robert C. Ruark, "Wonderful Nonsense," *Boston Traveler,* August 2, 1954.

37. William C. Harvard and Walter Sullivan, eds., *A Band of Prophets: The Vanderbilt Agrarians after Fifty Years* (Baton Rouge: Louisiana State University Press, 1982), 24.

38. *I'll Take My Stand,* John Crowe Ransom, 15; Lanier, 123; Introduction, xiv–xvi.

39. *I'll Take My Stand,* Lytle, 205, 244; Ransom, 10. Regarding the idea of being a guest in sport, it is indicative of the times that in most gymnasiums around the country, scoreboards have been changed to *Home* and *Visitors* from the earlier designations, *Home* and *Guests.*

40. In the Grantland Rice papers at VUL, there is a collection of what remains of Rice's own personal library. There is no evidence from this collection that he read any of the work of the twelve Southerners who produced *I'll Take My Stand.*

41. *I'll Take My Stand,* Ransom, 1, 21; Stark Young, 328.

42. Victor O. Jones, "Grantland Rice," *Boston Daily Globe,* August 16, 1954.

Select Bibliography

Adelman, Melvin L. *A Sporting Time: New York City and the Rise of Modern Athletics, 1820–1870.* Urbana: University of Illinois Press, 1990.

Alexander, Charles. *Ty Cobb.* New York: Oxford University Press, 1984.

Allen, Frederick Lewis. *Only Yesterday: An Informal History of the 1920s.* New York: Harper and Row, 1931; reprint, New York: Harper and Row, 1964.

———. *Since Yesterday: The 1930s in America.* New York: Harper and Row, 1939; reprint, New York: Harper and Row, 1972.

Anderson, Sherwood. *No Swank.* Philadelphia: Centaur Press, 1934.

———. *Poor White.* New York: Viking, 1920.

Anthony, Edward. *O Rare Don Marquis: A Biography.* Garden City, N.Y.: Doubleday, 1962.

Ashe, Arthur R., Jr. *A Hard Road to Glory: A History of the African American Athlete.* 3 vols. New York: Warner Books, 1988.

Asinof, Eliot. *Eight Men Out: The Black Sox and the 1919 World Series.* New York: Holt, Rinehart and Winston, 1963; reprint, New York: Henry Holt and Co., 1987.

Bartow, Edith M. *News and These United States.* New York: Funk and Wagnalls, 1952.

Berkow, Ira. *Red: A Biography of Red Smith.* New York: Times Books, 1986.

Bessie, Simon Michael. *Jazz Journalism: The Story of the Tabloid Newspapers.* New York: E. P. Dutton and Co., 1938.

Betts, John R. *America's Sporting Heritage: 1850–1950.* Reading, Mass.: Addison-Wesley, 1974.

Cannon, Jimmy. *Nobody Asked Me, But . . .: The World of Jimmy Cannon.* Edited by Jack Cannon and Tom Cannon. New York: Holt, Rinehart and Winston, 1978.

Cash, Wilbur J. *Mind of the South.* New York: Alfred A. Knopf, 1941.

Churchill, Allen. *Park Row.* New York: Rinehart, 1958.

Cobb, Irvin. *Exit Laughing.* Indianapolis: Bobbs-Merrill, 1941.

Coffin, Tristram. *The Old Ball Game: Baseball in Folklore and Fiction.* New York: Herder and Herder, 1971.

Cohane, Tim. *Bypaths of Glory: A Sportswriter Looks Back.* New York: Harper and Row, 1963.

Connor, Anthony J. *Baseball for the Love of It.* New York: Macmillan, 1982.

Creamer, Robert W. *Babe: The Legend Comes to Life.* New York: Simon and Schuster, 1974.

Dempsey, Jack, with Barbara Piattelli Dempsey. *Dempsey.* Harper and Row, 1977.

Doyle. Don H. *Nashville in the New South: 1880–1930.* Knoxville: University of Tennessee Press, 1985.

Elder, Donald. *Ring Lardner: A Biography.* Garden City, N.Y.: Doubleday, 1956.

Ellis, Elmer. *Mr. Dooley's America: A Life of Finley Peter Dunne.* New York: Alfred A. Knopf, 1941.

Emery, Edwin. *The Press and America: An Interpretative History of the Mass Media.* 3d ed. Englewood Cliffs, N.J.: Prentice Hall, 1972.

Fountain, Charles. *Sportswriter: The Life and Times of Grantland Rice.* New York: Oxford, 1993.

Fowler, Gene. *Skyline.* New York: Viking Press, 1961.

Frick, Ford. *Games, Asterisks and People.* New York: Crown Publishers, 1973.

Gallico, Paul. *Farewell to Sport.* New York: Alfred A. Knopf, 1944.

Gardner, Martin. *The Annotated Casey at the Bat.* Chicago: University of Chicago Press, 1967.

Gilbert, Bil. *Westering Man: The Life of Joseph Walker.* Norman: University of Oklahoma Press, 1985.

Guttmann, Allen. *From Ritual to Record: The Nature of Modern Sports.* New York: Columbia University Press, 1978.

———. *The Games Must Go On: Avery Brundage and the Olympic Movement.* New York: Columbia University Press, 1984.

Holtzman, Jerome. *No Cheering in the Press Box.* New York: Holt, Rinehart and Winston, 1973.

I'll Take My Stand: The South and the Agrarian Tradition, by Twelve Southerners. New York: Harper and Bros., 1930; reprint, Baton Rouge: Louisiana State University Press, 1980.

Inabinett, Mark. *Grantland Rice and His Heroes: The Sportswriter as Mythmaker in the 1920s.* Knoxville: University of Tennessee Press, 1994.

Jaspers, Karl. *Man in the Modern Age.* London: Routledge and Kegan Paul, 1951; reprint, Garden City, N.Y.: Doubleday, 1957. (Original German edition first published in 1931.)

Jones, Robert W. *Journalism in the United States.* New York: E. P. Dutton and Co., 1947.

Kieran, John. *Not Under Oath.* Boston: Houghton Mifflin, 1964.

Kluger, Richard, and Phyllis Kluger. *The Paper: The Life and Death of the* New York Herald Tribune. New York: Alfred A. Knopf, 1986.

Koppett, Leonard. *Sports Illusion, Sports Reality.* Boston: Houghton Mifflin, 1981.

Lardner, Ring, Jr. *The Lardners: My Family Remembered.* New York: Harper and Row, 1976.

Levine, Peter, ed. *American Sport: A Documentary History.* Englewood Cliffs, N.J.: Prentice Hall, 1989.

Lewis, C. S. *The Four Loves.* New York: Harcourt, Brace and World, 1960.

Lipsyte, Robert. *SportsWorld: An American Dreamland.* New York: Quadrangle, 1975.

Lucas, John, and Ronald Smith. *Saga of American Sport.* Philadelphia: Lea and Febiger, 1978.

McCallum, John. *The Tiger Wore Spikes: An Informal Biography of Ty Cobb.* New York: A. S. Barnes, 1956.

McGraw, John J. *My Thirty Years in Baseball.* New York: Arno Press, 1974 (1923).

McLemore, Henry. *One of Us Is Wrong.* New York: Henry Holt and Co., 1953.

Mandell, Richard D. *Sport: A Cultural History.* New York: Columbia University Press, 1984.

Mott, Frank Luther. *American Journalism, A History: 1690–1960.* 3d ed. New York: Macmillan, 1962.

Norman, Jack, Sr. *The Nashville I Knew.* Nashville, Tenn.: Rutledge Hills Press, 1984.

Nye, Peter. *Hearts of Lions: The History of American Bicycle Racing.* New York: Norton, 1988.

Orr, Jack. *The Black Athlete: His Story in American History.* New York: Lion Press, 1969.

Oxendine, Joseph B. *American Indian Sports Heritage.* Champaign, Ill.: Human Kinetics Books, 1988.

Phillips, Ulrich B. *Life and Labor in the Old South.* Boston: Little, Brown and Co., 1929.

Rader, Benjamin G. *American Sports: From the Age of Folk Games to the Age of Television.* 1st, 2d, and 3d eds. Englewood Cliffs, N.J.: Prentice Hall, 1983, 1990, 1996.

Rice, Grantland. *Base-Ball Ballads.* Nashville: Tennessean Company, 1910.

———. *The Bobby Jones Story* (from the writings of O. B. Keeler). Atlanta: Tupper and Love, 1953.

———. *The Final Answer and Other Poems.* Selected by John Kieran. New York: A. S. Barnes, 1955.

———. *Fore! . . . with a Glance Aft.* New York: Conde Nast Publications, 1929.

———. "Golf Lessons and Comment." In *How to Play Golf,* edited by Innis Brown, 105–17. New York: American Sports Publishing Co., 1933.

———. *Only the Brave.* New York: A. S. Barnes, 1941.

———. *Songs of the Open.* New York: Century, 1924.

———. *Songs of the Stalwart.* New York: Appleton and Co., 1917.

———. *Sportlights of 1923.* New York: Putnam, 1924.

———. *The Tumult and the Shouting: My Life in Sport.* New York: A. S. Barnes, 1954.

———, ed. *The Boys' Book of Sports.* New York: Century, 1917.

———, ed., with Hanford Powell. *The Omnibus of Sport.* New York: Harper and Brothers, 1932.

———, with John W. Heisman. *Understand Football.* New York: Mac-Hill, 1929.

———, and Jerome Travers. *The Winning Shot.* New York: Doubleday, Page and Co., 1915.

Riess, Steven A. *The American Sporting Experience: A Historical Anthology of Sport in America.* New York: Leisure Press, 1984.

———. *Touching Base: Professional Baseball and American Culture in the Progressive Era.* Westport, Conn.: Greenwood Press, 1980.

————, ed. *Major Problems in American Sport History.* Boston: Houghton Mifflin, 1997.

Ritter, Lawrence S. *The Glory of Their Times: The Story of the Early Days of Baseball Told by the Men Who Played It.* New York: Collier Books, 1966.

Roberts, Randy. *Jack Dempsey: The Manassa Mauler.* Baton Rouge: Louisiana State University Press.

————. *Papa Jack: Jack Johnson and the Era of White Hopes.* New York: Free Press, 1983.

Roosevelt, Theodore. *The Strenuous Life: Essays and Addresses.* New York: Century, 1901.

Rubin, Louis D., ed. *The American South: Portrait of a Culture.* Baton Rouge: Louisiana State University Press, 1980.

Russell, Fred. *Bury Me in an Old Press Box: Good Times and Life of a Sportswriter.* New York: A. S. Barnes, 1957.

Sammons, Jeffrey T. *Beyond the Ring: The Role of Boxing in American Society.* Urbana: University of Illinois Press, 1988.

Samuels, Charles. *The Magnificent Rube: The Life and Gaudy Times of Tex Rickard.* New York: McGraw-Hill, 1957.

Seymour, Harold. *Baseball: The Early Years.* New York: Oxford University Press, 1960.

————. *Baseball: The Golden Age.* New York: Oxford University Press, 1971.

Shecter, Leonard. *The Jocks.* New York: Warner, 1969.

Smith, H. Allen. *The Life and Legend of Gene Fowler.* New York: William Morrow and Co., 1977.

Smith, Red. *The Best of Red Smith.* New York: Franklin Watts, 1963.

————. *The Red Smith Reader.* New York: Random House, 1982.

————. *To Absent Friends from Red Smith.* New York: New American Library, 1982.

Spears, Betty, and Richard Swanson. *History of Sport and Physical Activity in the United States.* 4th ed. Dubuque, Iowa: Wm. C. Brown, 1995.

Sperber, Murray. *Shake Down the Thunder: The Creation of Notre Dame Football.* New York: Henry Holt and Co., 1993.

Stagg, Amos Alonzo, with Wesley Winans Stout. *Touchdown!* New York: Longmans, Green and Co., 1927.

Tunis, John R. *The American Way in Sport.* New York: Duell, Sloan and Pearce, 1958.

Vincent, Ted. *Mudville's Revenge: The Rise and Fall of American Sport.* New York: Seaview Books, 1981.

Voigt, David Q. *American Baseball.* Vols. 1 and 2. Norman: University of Oklahoma Press, 1966, 1970.

Waller, William. *Nashville, 1900–1910.* Nashville, Tenn.: Vanderbilt University Press, 1972.

————. *Nashville in the 1890s.* Nashville, Tenn.: Vanderbilt University Press, 1970.

Wheeler, John. *I've Got News for You.* New York: E. P. Dutton and Co., 1961.

Woodward, C. Vann. *Origins of the New South: 1877–1913.* 2d ed. Baton Rouge: Louisiana State University Press, 1971.

Woodward, Stanley. *Paper Tiger.* New York: Atheneum, 1964.

Yardley, Jonathan. *Ring: A Biography of Ring Lardner.* New York: Random House, 1977.

Zaharias, Babe Didrikson. *This Life I've Led: My Autobiography.* New York: A. S. Barnes, 1955.

Index